H — WORDINESS

1	2	3	4	5	6	7	8	9
Counting Words	Is and Was	Of and Which	The Use of	There Is, It Is	Jargon	Distinctions, Definitions	Passive Voice	Noun Habit
177–78	181–83	183–84	186	183	515	190–91	179–81	186–88

I — EVIDENCE

1	2	3	4	5	6	7	8
Facts, and Degrees of Belief	Assumptions	Definitions	Proof	Fallacies	Citing Authority	Induction	Deduction
105–08	109–10	99–103	115–20	124–25	111–12	115–17	118–23

J — GRAMMAR

1	2	3	4	5	6	7	8	9
Parts of Speech	The Simple Sentence: Three Forms	Compound, Complex Sentences	Shifts in Structure	Agreement: Subject-Verb	Tense	Mood	Lie and Lay	Irregular Verbs
345–48	348–49	350–51	351–53	353–55	356–63	359–60	360–61	362–63

10	11	12	13	14	15	16	17
Pronouns: Subject and Object	Possessive Pronouns with Gerunds	Pronouns and Antecedents	Adjectives vs. Adverbs	Squinting Modifiers	Comparisons	Dangling Constructions	Restrictives, Nonrestrictives
364–68	368–69	370–72	373–74	374–75	375–76	377–78	384–86

K — PUNCTUATION / MECHANICS

1	2	3	4	5	6	7	8	9
Comma: The Introducer	Comma: The Coordinator	Comma: The Inserter	Comma: The Linker	Fragment	Comma Splice	Run-on	Semicolon	Colon
380–82	382–84	384–87	388–89	389–90	390–93	390–91	395–97	398–400

10	11	12	13	14	15
Parenthesis	Dash	Brackets	Quotation Marks	Italics	Ellipsis
403–04	403–04	405	406–09	407–09	409–11

L — SPELLING

1	2	3	4	5	6	7	8	9
Some Principles	Troublesome Words	Apostrophe	Hyphen	Virgule (Slash)	Diacritical Marks	Numbers	Abbreviations	Capitalization
413–15	416–19	421–23	424–26	426	426–28	428–29	429–30	431–33

*The letter-and-number coding can serve as pointers to weaknesses in your papers; for example, your instructor's marking of "H8" in a page margin would send you to 179–81 in the text to review the excesses of the passive voice.

†The page numbers in the boxes refer to the main text discussions; additional references appear in the Index.

The Complete Stylist and Handbook

The Complete Stylist and Handbook

THIRD EDITION

SHERIDAN BAKER
The University of Michigan

HARPER & ROW, PUBLISHERS, New York
Cambridge, Philadelphia, San Francisco,
London, Mexico City, São Paulo, Sydney

Sponsoring Editor: Phillip Leininger
Editorial Consultant: Walter D. Brownfield
Project Editor: Rita Williams
Designer: Leon Bolognese
Production: Marion Palen/Delia Tedoff
Compositor: ComCom Division of Haddon Craftsmen, Inc.
Printer and Binder: The Murray Printing Company
Art Studio: Vantage Art, Inc.
Cover Design: Chris Kristiansen

The Complete Stylist and Handbook, Third Edition

Library of Congress Cataloging in Publication Data

Baker, Sheridan Warner, 1918–
    The complete stylist and handbook.

    Includes index.
    1. English language—Rhetoric.   2. English language—
Grammar—1950–   . I. Title.
PE1408.B283   1984   808′.042   83-18530
ISBN 0-06-040442-6

Contents

Preface

The process makes the product—the essay, the poem, the speech, the painting, the home, the garden, the achievement awarded, the effort satisfied. For almost a decade, teachers and students in thousands of classrooms have tested *The Complete Stylist and Handbook* in achieving the essentials of composition and the graces of good prose through a basic *Rhetoric* and a supplemental *Handbook*. But teachers have recently asked for more help with the process. Hence this new edition.

In the *Rhetoric,* I have refocussed Chapters 1, 2, and 3 on the problem of getting started and finding something to write about, retaining the significance of discovering a thesis with an argumentative edge and of swinging a dialectical argument *pro* and *con,* which are the rudiments of thought and persuasion. Chapter 4 retains the structures of paragraphing and the form of the whole essay. Chapter 5 moves on to the rhetoric of description, narration, exposition, and definition.

At the request of many users, I have restored, though simplified, the syllogism in Chapter 6, and I have restored, though amplified, the aids to outlining in Chapter 7. Chapters on sentences and words, which seem the most durable parts of the book, remain as before, with some refining, some added detail, especially on parallelism, and some new examples and exercises. Indeed, there are new examples and exercises throughout the book.

But the basic approach, as in my short rhetoric, *The Practical Stylist,* remains the same, since, in more than two decades, it has proven itself fundamental. It stresses rhetoric as the art of communication and persuasion. It emphasizes argument as the quickest and clearest teacher of rhetorical principles. It begins with the two primal elements, inner idea and outer form, thesis and structure.

It proceeds step by step with the progressively smaller and more powerful units—paragraphs, sentences, words. Then the rhetorical process culminates in "Writing About Literature," with some new examples and aids, and in the research paper. Here, for the first time in any text, I explain and illustrate the Modern Language Association's new and simplified system for documentation, already standard in *PMLA* and other journals, and soon to be published in a new edition of the *MLA Handbook.* Consequently, for instance, I have dropped the "p." from my own references to pages and parenthetical cross-references. I have followed the new style throughout.

The *Handbook,* as before, begins with a short section on "The English Language," and covers grammar, spelling, punctuation, and usage, all newly considered. I have added a "Glossary of Grammatical Terms" and a considerable section on how to handle written examinations and how to write letters of application and personal résumés for the jobs to come. I have restored, as many have asked, a section on classical rhetorical devices, as they strengthen one's grasp of sentences and figures of speech. The *Handbook* thus reinforces chapters in the *Rhetoric,* offering material the teacher may integrate with assignments or assign separately, and the student may use for constant and ready reference.

I have revised the *Instructor's Manual* to match the new edition of the text, again adding possibilities for other angles and alternate uses and solutions for exercises. New diagnostic and achievement tests are available to help set priorities for assignments.

The Complete Stylist and Handbook again strives to show the student how important writing is in coming to grips with our ideas and ourselves, to demonstrate that writing is really our only steady means of getting our thinking straight and clear. Throughout, I urge students to see that style is both personal and public, a matter of finding one's self in language—as always, one's own personality written into reason and looking its best.

SHERIDAN BAKER

The Complete Stylist and Handbook

THE RHETORIC

CHAPTER 1

The Point of It All: Why We Write

WRITE FOR YOUR SHARE

Writing is one of the most important things we do. It helps us catch our ideas, realize our thoughts, and stand out as fluent persuasive people both on paper and on our feet in front of the meeting or the boss. Reading and writing have already enlarged your education and your speech. Even television, in its news and advertising, and in most of its shows, pours into our thoughts the words and habits that literacy—and written scripts—has built into our speech and thinking.

This language we share is Standard English—sometimes called "edited Standard American English," unfortunately making it seem like some unnatural necessity for the business we would rather not do. But it is our living language, in speech as well as print. Actually, even our most local and private dialects partake of its forms and vocabulary, as do our silent thoughts, however fragmentary, our "inner speech," as several psychologists and linguists have recently called it.* In fact, we automatically "edit" all our fragmentary thoughts for even our most spontaneous expressions, intuitively selecting from our store of possibilities, filling in the grammar, expanding, rephrasing, just as if we were writing and rewriting: ". . . er . . . I mean . . . but really. . . ." So writing is an extension of the way we naturally handle language. Writing simply straightens out and clarifies our intuitive editing, and in turn makes the

---

*Lev Vygotsky, *Thought and Language* (Cambridge, Mass.: MIT Press, 1962), with "Comments" by Jean Piaget; James Moffett, "Writing, Inner Speech, and Meditation," *College English* 44 (1982): 231–46.

editing itself more fluent. Writing perfects thought and speech. Indeed, over the millions of years from our first emotive screams and gurgles of pleasure to the bright dawn of literacy, writing—thinking in full dress—seems to be where speech has been going all the time.

So your writing in college continues a very long evolution from the cradle upward—your own and civilization's too. All of your studies, and even a good many of your pastimes, involve some writing. You take notes, assemble them, get back into your head what you have written from it. Composing your thoughts in notebooks pulls your knowledge into a meaningful flow, pulls new thoughts into the stream, and helps keep them there. Your lab courses require writing to augment that other language of mathematics. Computers demand a lively dialogue, with special languages to compose, translate, and command. Courses in history, philosophy, languages, economics, the social sciences, literature—all require some papers, short or long, and some examinations in spontaneous essays.

Your composition course prepares you for the challenge, not only of college but of the business of life ahead, whether in the executive suite or the courtroom, the hospital or the consulate, the legislature or the press room. You must write for admission to postgraduate studies. You must write proposals for grants and programs. You must write to persuade people of your worth—demonstrated in your literacy—and of the worth of your ideas. You must write to develop and advance them—and yourself. You must write for your share of life. Thinking and persuasion are your business, and the business of your course in composition. All communication is largely persuasion. Even your most factual survey as engineer or educator must persuade its audience to approval by its perception and clarity and organization—in short, by its writing.

ATTITUDE

Writing well is a matter of conviction. You learn in school by exercises, of course; and exercises are best when taken as such, as body-builders, flexions and extensions for the real contests ahead. But when you are convinced that what you write has meaning, that it has meaning for you—and not in a lukewarm, hypothetical way, but truly—then your writing will stretch its wings and have the whole wide world in range. For writing is simply a graceful and articulate extension of the best that is in you. Writing well is not easy. As it extends the natural way we express ourselves, it nevertheless takes unending practice, each essay a polished exercise for the next to come, each new trial, as T. S. Eliot says, a new "raid on the inarticulate."

In writing, you clarify your own thoughts, and strengthen your conviction. Indeed, you probably grasp your thoughts for the first time. Writing is a way of thinking. The process of writing not merely transcribes but actually creates thought, and generates your ability to think. Through writing, you discover thoughts you hardly knew you had; through writing, you come to know what you know. All kinds of forgotten impressions, lost facts, and surprising updrafts of words and knowledge support your flight. As you test your thoughts against their opposites, as you answer the questions rising in your mind and in the minds of your imagined audience, your conviction grows. You learn as you write. In the end, after you have rewritten and rearranged for your best rhetorical effectiveness, your words will carry your readers with you to see as you see, to believe as you believe, to understand your subject as you now understand it.

Don't Take Yourself Too Seriously

Take your subject seriously—if it is a serious subject—but take yourself with a grain of salt. Your attitude is the very center of your prose. If you take yourself too importantly, your tone will go hollow, your sentences will go moldy, your page will go fuzzy with *of's* and *which's* and nouns clustered densely in passive constructions. In your academic career, the worst dangers lie immediately ahead. Freshmen usually learn to write tolerably well, but from the sophomore to the senior year the academic damp frequently sets in, and by graduate school you can often cut the gray mold with a cheese knife.

You must constantly guard against acquiring the heavy, sober-sided attitude that makes for wordiness and its attendant vices of obscurity, dullness, and anonymity. Do not lose your personality and your voice in the monotone of official prose. You should work like a scholar and scientist, but you should write like a writer, one who cares about the economy and beauty of language, and has some individual personality. Your attitude, then, should form somewhere between a confidence in your own convictions and a humorous distrust of your own rhetoric, which can so easily carry you away. You should bear yourself as a member of humankind, knowing that we are all sinners, all redundant, and all too fond of big words. Here is an example from—I blush to admit—the pen of a professor:

> **The general problem is perhaps correctly stated as inadequacy of nursing personnel to meet demands for nursing care and services. Inadequacy, it should be noted, is both a quantitative and qualitative term and thus it can be assumed that the problem as stated could indicate insufficient numbers of nursing personnel to meet existing demands for their services; deficiencies in the competencies of those who engage in the various fields of nursing; or both.**

Too few good nurses, and a badly swollen author—that is the problem. "Nursing personnel" may mean nurses, but it also may mean "the nursing of employees," so that the author seems to say, for a wildly illogical moment, that someone is not properly pampering or suckling people for the necessary services. Notice the misfiring *it* (fourth line of quotation), which seems to refer to *term* but actually refers to nothing. And the ponderous jingle of "deficiencies in the competencies" would do for a musical comedy. The author has taken the wrong model, is taking herself too seriously, and taking her readers almost nowhere.

Consider Your Readers

If you are to take your subject with all the seriousness it deserves and yourself with as much skeptical humor as you can bear, how are you to take your readers? Who are they, anyway? Some teachers suggest using your classmates as your audience to solve the puzzle as to those invisible readers you hope to please and persuade. This is a good beginning. But the problem remains with all those other classes, with those papers in history or social science, with the reports, the applications for jobs and grants, the letters to the editor. At some point, you must become a writer facing the invisible public.

To some extent, your audiences will vary. You imagine yourself addressing slightly different personalities when you write about snorkeling and when you write about nuclear reactors. Hypothetically, your vocabulary and your tone would vary all the way from Skid Row to Oxford as you turn from social work to Rhodes scholarship; and certainly the difference of audience would reflect itself somewhat in your language. Furthermore, you must indeed sense your audience's capacity, its susceptibilities and prejudices, if you are to win even a hearing. No doubt our language skids a bit when down on the Row, and we certainly speak different tongues with our friends, and with the friends of our parents.

But the notion of adjusting your writing to a whole scale of audiences, though attractive in theory, hardly works out in practice. You are *writing,* and the written word presupposes a literate norm that immediately eliminates all the lower ranges of mere talk. Even when you speak, you do not so lose your identity as to pass for a total illiterate. You stand on your own linguistic feet, in your own linguistic personality, and the only adjustment you should assiduously practice in your writing, and in your speaking as well, is the upward one toward verbal adulthood, a slight grammatical tightening and rhetorical heightening to make your thoughts clear, emphatic, and attractive.

Consider your audience a mixed group of intelligent and reasonable adults. You want them to think of you as well informed and well educated. You wish to explain what you know and what you believe. You wish to persuade them pleasantly that what you know is important and what you believe is right.

Try to imagine what they might ask you, what they might object to, what they might know already, what they might find interesting. Be simple and clear, amusing and profound, using plenty of illustration to show what you mean. *But do not talk down to them.* That is the great flaw in the slumming theory of communication. Bowing to your readers' supposed level, you insult them by assuming their inferiority. Thinking yourself humble, you are actually haughty. The best solution is simply to assume that your readers are as intelligent as you. Even if they are not, they will be flattered by the assumption. Your written language, in short, will be respectful toward your subject, considerate toward your readers, and somehow amiable toward human failings.

THE WRITTEN VOICE

Make Your Writing Talk

That the silent page should seem to speak with the writer's voice is remarkable. With all gestures gone, no eyes to twinkle, no notation at all for the rise and fall of utterance, and only a handful of punctuation marks, the level line of type can yet convey the writer's voice, the tone of his personality.

To achieve this tone, to find your own voice and style, simply try to write in the language of intelligent conversation, cleared of all the stumbles and weavings of talk. Indeed, our speech, like thought, is amazingly circular. We can hardly think in a straight line if we try. We think by questions and answers, repetitions and failures; and our speech, full of *you know's* and *I mean's,* follows the erratic ways of the mind, circling around and around as we stitch the simplest of logical sequences. Your writing will carry the stitches, not those editorial loopings and pauses and rethreadings. It should be literate. It should be broad enough of vocabulary and rich enough of sentence to show that you have read a book. It should not be altogether unworthy to place you in the company of those who have written well in your native tongue. But it should nevertheless retain the tone of intelligent and agreeable conversation. It should be alive with a human personality—yours—which is probably the most persuasive rhetorical force on earth. Good writing should have a voice, and the voice should be unmistakably your own.

Suppose your spoken voice sounded something like this (I reconstruct an actual response in one of my classes):

> **Well, I don't know, I like Shakespeare really, I guess—I mean, well, like when Lear divides up his kingdom like a fairy tale or something, I thought that was kind of silly, dividing his kingdom. Anyone could see that was silly if you wanted to keep**

> **your kingdom, why divide it? But then like, something begins
> to happen, like a real family, I mean. Cordelia really gets griped
> at her older sisters, I mean, like all older sisters, if you've ever
> had any. There's a kind of sibling rivalry, you know. Then she's
> kind of griped at her father, who she really loves, but she
> thinks, I mean, like saying it right out spoils it. You can't really
> speak right out, I mean, about love, well, except sometimes, I
> guess, without sounding corny.**

Your written voice might then emerge from this with something of the
same tone, but with everything straightened out, filled in, and polished up:

> **The play begins like a fairy tale. It even seems at first a lit-
> tle abstract and silly. A king has three daughters. The two elder
> ones are bad; the youngest is good. The king wishes to keep his
> kingdom in peace, and keep his title as king, by dividing his
> kingdom in a senseless and almost empty ceremonial way. But
> very soon the play seems like real life. The family seems real,
> complete with sibling rivalry. The king, not the play, now seems
> foolish and senile. The older daughters are hypocrites. Cor-
> delia, the youngest, is irritated at them, and at her father's fool-
> ishness. As a result, she remains silent, not only because she is
> irritated at the flattering words of her sisters, but because any-
> thing she could say about her real love for her father would
> now sound false.**

You might wish to polish that some more. You might indeed have said
it another way, one more truly your own. The point, however, is to write in
a tidy, economical way that wipes up the lapses of talk and fills in the gaps of
thought, and yet keeps the tone and movement of good conversation, in your
own voice.

Don't Apologize

"In my opinion," the beginner will write repeatedly, until he seems to be saying "It is only *my* opinion, after all, so it can't be worth much." He has failed
to realize that his whole essay represents his opinion—of what the truth of the
matter is. Don't make your essay a personal letter to Diary, or to Mother, or
to Teacher, a confidential report of what happened to you last night as you
agonized upon a certain question. *"To me,* Robert Frost is a great poet"—this
is really writing about yourself. You are only confessing private convictions.

To find the public reasons often requires no more than a trick of grammar: a shift from *"To me,* Robert Frost is . . . " to "Robert Frost is . . . ," from *"I thought* the book was good" to "The book is good," from you and your room last night to your subject and what it *is.* The grammatical shift represents a whole change of viewpoint, a shift from self to subject. You become the informed adult, showing the reader around firmly, politely, and persuasively.

Once you have effaced yourself from your assertions, once you have erased *to me* and *in my opinion* and all such signs of amateur terror, you may later let yourself back into the essay for emphasis or graciousness: "Mr. Watson errs, I think, precisely at this point." You can thus ease your most tentative or violent assertions, and show that you are polite and sensible, reasonably sure of your position but aware of the possibility of error. Again: the reasonable adult.

You go easy on the *I,* in short, to keep your reader focused on your subject. But you can use the *I* as much as you like to *illustrate* your point, once established, using a personal experience among several other pieces of evidence, or even all by itself. Suppose you were writing about the limitations and dangers of conformity. You remember a wild ride that had almost killed you and your friends. Someone had wondered if your dad's new car would do 100 mph, and no one had dared to object. After you had set up your proposition—something like "The thrilling high-speed ride, if survived, will probably open the teen-ager's eyes to the dangers of conformity," let us say—you could then write all the rest of your essay illustrating your point with your personal anecdote, beginning your second paragraph with "Once three friends and I borrowed my dad's new car to go to a drive-in." This is the point: use the *I* to *illustrate,* or for rhetorical politeness, but not to apologize or to limit your subject to yourself alone. *Generalize* your opinions and emotions. Change "I cried" to "The book is very moving." But your personal happenings can nicely illustrate your thesis with an immediate and specific example.

Of course, your instructors will sometimes ask for a wholly autobiographical theme. Indeed, some courses focus altogether on the *I* of personal experience. And your autobiographical résumés in applying for medical and law school, for grants and jobs, will of course require the *I.* But for the usual essay, I repeat, use the personal anecdote and the *I* to illustrate a point, or to interject a tactful remark.

Consider Your Pronouns

Effacing the *I,* then letting it back in on occasion, fixes your point of view. But what about the other pronouns, *we, you, one? One* objectifies the personal *I,* properly generalizing the private into the public. But it can seem too formal, and get too thick:

> **FAULTY:** *One* **finds** *one*'s **opinion changing as** *one* **grows older.**
> **REVISED: Opinions change with age.**
> **REVISED:** *Our* **opinions change as** *we* **grow older.**

That *we* is sometimes a useful generalizer, a convenient haven between the isolating *I* and the impersonal *one*. *We* can seem pompous, but not if it honestly handles those experiences we know we share, or can share. Suppose we wrote:

> **As I watched program after program, I got bored and began to wonder what values, if any, they represented.**

We can easily transpose this to:

> **As** *we* **watch program after program,** *we* **are progressively bored, and** *we* **begin to wonder what values, if any, they represent.**

(Notice that shifting to the present tense is also part of the generalizing process.) Thus, *we* can generalize without going all the way to *one,* or to the fully objective:

> **Program after program, TV bores its audiences and leaves its sense of values questionable.**

We also quite naturally refers to earlier parts of your demonstration, through which you have led your reader: *as we have already seen.* But you will have noticed from the preceding examples that *we* tends slightly toward wordiness. Used sparingly, then, *we* can ease your formality and draw your reader in. Overused, it can seem too presumptuous or chummy. Try it out. See how it feels, and use it where it seems comfortable and right.

    You raises two different problems. The first is the one we have been discussing: how to generalize that *I* effectively into something else, either *one* or *we* or full objectivity. The indefinite *you,* like the indefinite *they,* is usually too vague, and too adolescent.

> **FAULTY: You have your own opinion.**
> **FAULTY: They have their own opinion.**
> **REVISED: Everyone has his own opinion.**
> **REVISED: We all have our own opinions.**

You as direct address to the reader poses a different problem. I have consistently addressed this book to *you,* the reader. But this is a special case, the relationship of tutor to student projected onto the page. None of my essays, I think, contains any *you* at all. Our stance in an essay is a little more formal, a little more public. We are better holding our pronouns to *one* or *we,* an occasional *I,* or none at all, as we find a comfortable stance between our subject and audience, and find our written voice.

THE POINT: ARGUMENTATION

The point is persuasion. Your written voice, your personal style, remember, is a part of your persuasiveness. But having a point to make is the real center of persuasion, the likely goal of most of your writing and speaking in college and in contemporary life. Hence the center of your composition course is indeed argumentation. Even explaining the Battle of Lexington or the Oedipus complex invites an argumentative thrust as you persuade your readers of the most significant causes and crucial events. Argumentation thus ranges through the coolest explanation, or exposition, up to the burning issues you support. Argument, as we will see as we move along, absorbs for its ends every kind of writing you can think of. Narration, dialogue, anecdotes, exposition, description, newspaper headlines, statistical tables, and chemical formulas may all illustrate the point you are making in that written personality of yours that gives it life.

Plan to Rewrite

As you write your weekly assignments and find your voice, you will also be learning to groom your thoughts, to present them clearly and fully, to make sure you have said what you thought you said. This is the process of composition, of putting your thoughts together, beginning with jotted questions and tentative ideas, all to be mulled over, selected, rejected, expanded as you discover your ideas and write them into full expression. Ultimately, good writing comes only from *re*writing. Even your happy thoughts will need resetting, as you join them to the frequently happier ones that a second look seems to call up. Even the letter-perfect paper will improve almost of itself if you simply sit down to type it through again. You will find, almost unbidden, sharper words, better phrases, new figures of speech, and new illustrations and ideas to replace the weedy patches not noticed before. Indeed, this process of rewriting is what strengthens that instinctive editing you do as you speak extemporaneously or write impromptu essays and exams when revision is out of the question. Rewriting improves your fluency, making each rewrite easier and less demanding.

So allow yourself time for revision. After you have settled on something to write about, have turned your ideas over on paper for a while, have found a central idea, and feel ready to write the whole thing out, plan for at least three drafts—and try to manage four. Thinking of things to say is the hardest part at first. Even a short assignment of 500 words seems to stretch ahead like a Sahara. You have asserted your central idea in a sentence, and that leaves 490 words to go. But if you step off boldly, one foot after the other, you will make progress, find an oasis or two, and perhaps end at a run in green pastures. With longer papers, you will want some kind of outline to keep you from straying, and probably some jotted notes even for short ones, but the principle is the same: step ahead and keep moving until you've arrived. That is the first draft.

The second draft is a penciled correction of the first. Of course, if the first has been really haphazard, you will probably want to type it again, rearranging, dropping a few things, adding others, before you can do much detailed work with a pencil. But the second, or penciled, draft is where you refine and polish, checking your dubious spellings in the dictionary, sharpening your punctuation, clarifying your meaning, pruning away the deadwood, adding a thought here, extending an illustration there—running in a whole new paragraph on an inserted page. You will also be tuning your sentences, carefully adjusting your tone until it is clearly that of an intelligent, reasonable person at ease with his knowledge and his audience.

Here is my penciled draft of the paragraph above, as it appeared on my first typescript:

The second is a penciling of the first. If the first has been really haphazard, you will probably want to type it again, rearranging, dropping filling out, before you can do much detailed work with a pencil. But the second, or pencil, draft is where you refine and polish, checking your spelling, sharpening your punctuation, clearing up your meaning, clearing out the deadwood, adding a thought here, extending an explanation there—you may need arrows leading you to the back of the page to write a whole new paragraph. You will also be tuning your sentences, so-

carefully adjusting ~~phisticating~~ your tone ~~into~~ *until it is clearly* that of the intelligent, rea-

sonable person ~~perfectly~~ at ease with his knowledge and

his audience.

Your third draft is a smoothing of all this for public appearance. Still other illustrations and better phrases will suggest themselves as you get your penciled corrections into order. My penciled paragraph, above, stood up unusually well. I chose it as an example of revision, in fact, because most of my other paragraphs are so crisscrossed and scarred, draft after draft, that their evolution would be too complicated to represent in any practical way. For a classroom paper, three drafts, with several rereadings of the first and the second, are usually adequate. But, if you have time, a fourth draft will do no harm. Reading aloud will frequently pick up errors, lapses in punctuation, and infelicities of phrase. You may have to retype a page of your most polished draft, as a brilliant idea hits you at last, or a terrible sentence finally rears its fuzzy head.

Here is a passage from a student's paper that has gone the full course. First you see the student's initial draft, with his own corrections on it. Next you see the passage after a second typing (and some further changes), as it was returned by the instructor with his marks on it. Then you see the final revision, handed in again, as this particular assignment required:

FIRST DRAFT

In a college education, students should be allowed to

choose ~~make~~ their own course. *All the* ~~Too many~~ requirements *they must take* ~~are discour-~~

discourage ~~aging to~~ people's creativity, and they cannot learn any-

thing *they are* ~~which is~~ not motivated ~~for him~~ to learn. ~~With~~ re- *R*

quirements *restrict* their freedom to choose ~~what he is interested~~ *and their eagerness to learn.*

They are only discouraged ~~in is taken away~~ by having to study dull subjects like Ger-

in which they can see no relevance to their interests. man, ~~which he is not interested in.~~

THE PAPER, WITH INSTRUCTOR'S MARKINGS

In a college education, students <u>should be allowed to</u>

choose their own curricula and select their own courses.   *can you get rid of the passive?*

redundant

relevant?

All the requirements they must take stifle their
creativity. Moreover, they cannot learn anything they   *true?*
are not motivated to learn. Requirements restrict their
freedom to choose and their eagerness to explore the subjects they are interested in. They are only discouraged   *activate*
by having to study dull subjects like German, in which
they can see no relevance.

REVISED PAPER

Students should choose their own education, their own
curricula, their own courses. Their education is really
theirs alone. Every college requirement threatens to
stifle the very enthusiasms upon which true education depends. Students learn best when motivated by their own
interests, but, in the midst of a dozen complicated requirements, they can hardly find time for the courses they
long to take. Requirements therefore not only restrict
their freedom to choose but destroy their eagerness to explore. Dull subjects like German, in which they can see no
relevance anyway, take all their time and discourage them
completely.

AIMING FOR A STYLE OF YOUR OWN

By writing frequently, you will create a style of your own—and with it, a good
bit of your future. But what is style? At its best, it is much like style in a car,
a gown, a Greek temple—the ordinary materials of this world so poised and

perfected as to stand out from the landscape and compel a second look, something that hangs in the reader's mind, like a vision. It is a writer's own voice, with the hems and haws chipped out, speaking the common language uncommonly well. It comes from a craftsman who has discovered the knots and potentials in his material, one who has learned to enjoy phrasing and syntax, and the very punctuation that keeps them straight. It is the labor of love, and like love it can bring pleasure and satisfaction.

But style is not for the gifted only. Quite the contrary. Indeed, as I have been suggesting, everyone already has a style, and a personality, and can develop both. The stylistic side of writing is, in fact, the only side that can be analyzed and learned. The stylistic approach is the practical approach: you learn some things to do and not to do, as you would learn strokes in tennis. Your ultimate game is up to you, but you can at least begin in good form. Naturally, it takes practice. You have to keep at it. Like the doctor and the lawyer and the golfer and the tennis player, you just keep practicing—even to write a nearly perfect letter. But if you like the game, you can probably learn to play it well. You will at least be able to write a respectable sentence, and to express your thoughts clearly, without puffing and flailing.

In the essay, as in business, trying to get started and getting off on the wrong foot account for most of our lost motion. So we will next consider how to find a thesis, which will virtually organize your essay for you. Then we will study the relatively simple structure of the essay, and the structure of the paragraph—the architecture of spatial styling. Then we will experiment with various styles of sentence, playing with length and complexity to help you find the right mix to convey your personal rhythm. And finally we will get down to words themselves. Here again you will experiment to find those personal ranges of vocabulary, those blends of the breezy and the formal, that will empower your personal style. Here, in the word, is where writing tells; and here, as in ancient times, you will be in touch with the mystery. But again, there are things to do and things not to do, and these can be learned. So, to begin.

EXERCISES

1. *To get a sense of how we expand and edit our inner speech, try sitting calmly, emptying your mind as much as possible, then gaze at some object and put down the first five or six words that drift along. I first tried a rhododendron bush outside the window, then a little Japanese vase. My rhododendron produced this:* green—sun—shimmer—pink—cream—evergreen—fertilize. *Then this:*

> The green rhododendron shimmers in the sun. Its creamy pink blossoms were beautiful last spring. It is an evergreen, and hardy, but should have fertilizer after blooming.

My vase produced this: red—orange—white—Imari—clipper—broken. *Then this:*

This little vase, with stylized chrysanthemums on a white background surrounded by a solid bright orange-red, is an imitation of Japanese Imari ware, some of which came to America by clipper ship. My mother had a huge Imari platter, which I broke when I was very small by slamming the dining-room door too hard. She was awfully good about it.

Try a few of these for fun.

2. *To find your own modern voice, translate the following passage from Walton's* The Compleat Angler* *(1653) into modern English and your own idiom. Try to say as economically and accurately as possible what he is saying, as if you were talking to, or writing to, one of your own contemporaries.*

The Chub, though he eat well thus dressed, yet as he is usually dressed he does not: he is objected against, not only for being full of small forked bones, dispersed through all his body, but that he eats waterish, and that the flesh of him is not firm; but short and tasteless. The French esteem him so mean, as to call him *un Vilain;* nevertheless he may be so dressed as to make him very good meat: as, namely, if he be a large Chub, then dress him thus:—

First scale him, and then wash him clean, and then take out his guts; and to that end make the hole as little and near to his gills as you may conveniently, and especially make clean his throat from the grass and weeds that are usually in it, for if that be not very clean, it will make him to taste very sour. Having so done, put some sweet herbs into his belly; and then tie him with two or three splinters to a spit, and roast him, basted often with vinegar, or rather verjuice and butter, with good store of salt mixed with it.

Being thus dressed, you will find him a much better dish of meat than you, or most folk, even than Anglers themselves, do imagine; for this dries up the fluid watery humor with which all Chubs do abound.

But take this rule with you, that a Chub newly taken and newly dressed is so much better than a Chub of a day's keeping after he is dead, that I can compare him to nothing so fitly as to cherries newly gathered from a tree, and others that have been bruised and lain a day or two in water. But the Chub being thus used and dressed presently, and not washed after he is gutted,—for note, that, lying long in water, and washing the blood out of any fish after they be gutted, abates much of their sweetness,—you will find the Chub, being dressed in the blood and quickly, to be such meat as will recompense your labor and disabuse your opinion.

3. *Try the same kind of translation with the following passage from Herman Melville's* Typee *(1846, Chapter 17), rewriting it in clear contemporary English and your own idiom. Melville (1819–1891) was a young New Yorker, who, after trying schoolteaching, shipped out as a sailor before the mast at nineteen. With a companion, he jumped ship at Nuku Hiva, Marquesas Islands, in 1842. They crossed the mountainous island,*

---

*Izaak Walton and Charles Cotton, *The Compleat Angler, or The Contemplative Man's Recreation,* ed. James Russell Lowell (Boston: Little, Brown, and Company, 1889): 66–67.

and dropped into the steeply enclosed valley, opening seaward, that was the territory of the Typees, a tribe of cannibals. The chiefs and warrior-elite ate enemies slain in battle, at ritualized feasts from which all commoners were excluded, but Melville had no way of knowing how far their dietary habits might extend. His friend escaped in two weeks, and he, eventually, in four. He had caught a fever, accompanied by a painfully swollen leg, in crossing the mountains. Kory-Kory was the man assigned to serve and guard him. The "Happy Valley" is the blissfully utopian mountain-valley in Samuel Johnson's Rasselas *(1759), from which no one who enters can escape.*

After making your translation, you might list ten of Melville's words (or short phrases) that sound odd in modern English, and beside each, your modern synonym. What can you say about the differences in vocabulary between Melville's American English of the 1840s and yours of the 1980s? What other differences can you see between his passage and yours? What things have remained fairly stable?

Day after day wore on, and still there was no perceptible change in the conduct of the islanders towards me. Gradually I lost all knowledge of the regular occurrence of the days of the week, and sunk insensibly into that kind of apathy which ensues after some violent outbreak of despair. My limb suddenly healed, the swelling went down, the pain subsided, and I had every reason to suppose I should soon completely recover from the affliction that had so long tormented me.

As soon as I was enabled to ramble about the valley in company with the natives, troops of whom followed me whenever I sallied out of the house, I began to experience an elasticity of mind which placed me beyond the reach of those dismal forebodings to which I had so lately been a prey. Received wherever I went with the most deferential kindness; regaled perpetually with the most delightful fruits; ministered to by dark-eyed nymphs; and enjoying besides all the services of the devoted Kory-Kory, I thought that for a sojourn among cannibals, no man could have well made a more agreeable one.

To be sure there were limits set to my wanderings. Toward the sea my progress was barred by an express prohibition of the savages; and after having made two or three ineffectual attempts to reach it, as much to gratify my curiosity as anything else, I gave up the idea. It was in vain to think of reaching it by stealth, since the natives escorted me in numbers wherever I went, and not for one single moment that I can recall to mind was I ever permitted to be alone.

The green and precipitous elevations that stood ranged around the head of the vale where Marheyo's habitation was situated effectually precluded all hope of escape in that quarter, even if I could have stolen away from the thousand eyes of the savages.

But these reflections now seldom obtruded upon me; I gave myself up to the passing hour, and if ever disagreeable thoughts arose in my mind, I drove them away. When I looked around the verdant recess in which I was buried, and gazed up to the summits of the lofty eminence that hemmed me in, I was well disposed to think that I was in the "Happy Valley," and that beyond those heights there was nought but a world of care and anxiety.

As I extended my wanderings in the valley and grew more familiar with the habits of its inmates, I was fain to confess that, despite the disadvantages of his condition, the Polynesian savage, surrounded by all the luxurious provisions of nature, enjoyed an infinitely happier, though certainly a less intellectual existence, than the self-complacent European.

4. *Now try out your own contemporary written voice against that of Arthur Schlesinger, Jr., translating the following passage into your own idiom. You will need to keep some of the author's words and phrases, of course, but make the transformation as thorough as possible. Would Schlesinger's article be more effective, or less, if it moved some of the way toward your version? All the way?*

What more astonishing adventure could there have been than that of the settlement of America? Anonymous men and women, renouncing a familiar and traditional existence, abandoning places where their families had lived for centuries, embarked on frail ships, crossed perilous seas and put down roots in an unknown and alien continent. It requires a violent thrust of the contemporary imagination to comprehend the courage—the courage and the despair and the hope—that lay behind countless individual decisions in quiet European villages. And so they came, laid their lives on the line, endured hardship and vicissitude. Many gave up or starved or were killed by disease or Indians. The survivors gradually came to terms with the new land.

Roanoke Island, 1585: the lost colony, the settlers mysteriously vanished, only the word CROATOAN carved on a post to mark the fact that Englishmen had tried to live there, the enigma of their disappearance unsolved to this day. Jamestown, 1607: two-thirds of the first settlers dying from famine and sickness. "There were never Englishmen left in a forreigne Country in such miseries as we," wrote one of them. "So lamentable was our scarcity," wrote another, "that we were constrained to eat dogs, cats, rats, snakes, toadstools, horsehides and what not; one man out of the misery that he endured, killing his wife, powdered her up to eat her, for which he was burned." Plymouth, 1620: half the colonists dying in the first year.

But the survivors hung on. "It is not with us as with other men," the Pilgrims said, "whom small things can discourage, or small discontentments cause to wish themselves at home again." They built their dwellings, organized their governments, enacted their laws, cleared their forests, discovered new crops and new ways to farm, heard the call of the dark and silent wilderness beyond. Nor was the invasion of America an English monopoly. The Dutch settled on Manhattan Island, Swedes along the Delaware, Scotch-Irish and Germans in Pennsylvania, French and Spanish in Florida. Whether sustained by relish of adventure or by the search for gold or by the desire to worship God as they saw fit, they were men and women beyond the reach of small discontentments.*

---

*From Arthur Schlesinger, Jr., "The Birth of a Nation—A Journey into America's Past," *Travel & Leisure* (American Express Publishing Corp.), July 1974. Copyright © 1974 American Express Publishing Corporation.

CHAPTER 2

Making a Beginning: From Subject to Thesis

GETTING SET

Get set! Writing an essay isn't exactly a fifty-yard dash, but you do need to get ready and get set before you can go to it. Writing requires a time and place, an habitual environment to coax and support those inspired moments that tap our deeper pools of experience and thought and then flow into language like a mountain spring. Though the water will often come only in muddy trickles, your best scheme is a schedule, one that will give you two or three sittings for each assignment. Your place should be fixed. It should be comfortable and convenient. Your times should be regular, varied in length from short to long, and set to fit your schedule and your personal rhythm, as morning person or night owl, sprinter or long-distance runner. Arrange your first period for a time as soon as possible after assignments, perhaps only half an hour for jotting, scribbling, free-writing, thinking on paper. Your next two sessions should be longer, the last with expandable time to get the job done.

WHAT SHALL I WRITE?

First you need a subject, and then you need a thesis. Yes, but *what shall I write?* That is the question, persisting from the first birthday thank-you letter down to this very moment. Here you are, an assignment before you and the paper

19

as blank as your mind, especially if your instructor has left the choice of your subject up to you. Look for something that interests you, something you know about, some hobby—something that shook you up, left you perplexed, started you thinking.

Writing will help you discover that something. Don't stare at that blank page. Set yourself the task of writing for ten minutes, no matter what. Start your pencil moving and keep it going, even beginning with *Good grief, what shall I write? Write on anything, the big oaf said. OK, but what what what what what? Fishing? Baby-sitting? Skipping rope? Crime? Nuclear power? Oh no. Crime? Rape? How about the time I ripped off a candy bar and got caught? The shock of recognition. Everyone's done it at some time or other. Everyone's guilty. Everyone's tempted. Something for nothing. The universal temptation of crime. . . .* Keep it going until your watch tells you to stop. That's a good start. Take a break and let your thoughts sink in and accumulate.

Probe your own experiences and feelings for answers as to why people behave as they do, especially in times of crisis. Prestige? The admiration of peers? Fear of not going with the gang? Why is fishing (let us say) so appealing to you? Why more so than water skiing or swimming or sailing or tennis or painting? Why don't some people like it? What might they object to? Now have another bout on paper, perhaps just writing the questions down, perhaps discovering some answers as you go. You have found your subject—and indeed have already moved a good way toward a thesis. The more your subject matters to you, the more you can make it matter to your readers. It might be skiing. It might be dress. It might be roommates, the Peloponnesian War, a political protest, a personal discovery of racial tensions, an experience as a nurse's aide. But do not tackle a big philosophical abstraction, like Freedom, or a big subject, like the Supreme Court. They are too vast, your time and space and knowledge all too small. You would probably manage no more than a collection of platitudes. Start rather with something specific, like running, and let the ideas of freedom and justice and responsibility arise from there. An abstract idea is a poor beginning. To be sure, as you move ahead through your course in writing, you will work more directly with ideas, with problems posed by literature, with questions in the great civilizing debate about what we are doing in this strange world and universe. But again, look for something within your concern. The best subjects lie nearest at hand, and nearest the heart.

You can personalize almost any subject and cut it down to size, getting a manageable angle on it. On an assigned subject, particularly in courses like political science or anthropology or sociology, look for something that connects you with it. Suppose your instructor assigns a paper on Social Security. Think of a grandparent, a parent, a neighbor, a friend—or perhaps yourself as a student receiving benefits, and how reductions would or would not affect your life. You will have a vivid illustration as well as one corner of the huge problem to illuminate. Nuclear energy? Perhaps you have seen on television the appalling space suits and mechanical arms required to handle the radioactive stuff along with something of its astounding problems. Perhaps you remember an article, or a sentence, that started you thinking. With subjects to find, keep an eye and an ear open as you read the newspaper or *Time,* or watch TV, and talk with your friends. Your classes and textbooks will inevitably turn up subjects for your composition course, if you watch for them, which you can bring into your personal range. Deregulating petroleum? You have probably seen the price of gas soar, your pocketbook shrink, and have taken to the bus, or your bike, or your heels. You need to find a personal interest in your subject to have something to say and to interest others.

FROM SUBJECT TO THESIS

Suppose, for the present, we start simply with "Drugs." Certainly, most of us have been tempted, or had to resist, or to go along, have experimented, or gotten hooked, or have known someone who has—especially if we include cigarettes and alcohol. "Drugs" is a subject easily personalized. Taking a subject like this will also show how to generalize from your own experience, and how to cut your subject down to manageable size. Your first impulse will probably be to write in the first person, but your experience may remain merely personal and may not point your subject into a thesis. As we have already seen, a personal anecdote makes a lively *illustration,* but first you need to generate your thesis and establish it for your reader. You need to move out of that bright, self-centered spotlight of consciousness in which we live before we really grow up, in which the child assumes that all his or her experiences are unique. If you shift from "me" to "the beginner" or "the young adult," however, you will be stepping into maturity: acknowledging that others have gone through exactly the same thing, that your experiences have illustrated once again the general dynamics of the individual and the group. So instead of writing "I was afraid to refuse," you write:

> The *beginner* is afraid to refuse, and soon discovers the tremendous pressure of the group.

By generalizing your private feelings, you change your subject into a thesis—your argumentative proposition. You simply assume you are normal and fairly representative, and you then generalize with confidence, transposing your particular experiences, your particular thoughts and reactions, into statements about the general ways of the world. Put your proposition, your thesis, into one sentence. This will get you focused. And now you are ready to begin.

WHERE ESSAYS FAIL

You can usually blame a bad essay on a bad beginning. If your essay falls apart, it probably has no primary idea to hold it together. "What's the big idea?" we used to ask. The phrase will serve as a reminder that you must find the "big idea" behind your several smaller thoughts and musings and drafts before you can start to shape your final essay. In the beginning was the *logos,* says the Bible—the idea, the plan, caught in a flash as if in a single word. Find your *logos,* and you are ready to round out your essay and set it spinning.

Suppose you had decided to write about that high-speed ride we considered in the first chapter—another case of group dynamics. The big idea behind that ride in the speeding car was that in adolescence, especially, the group can have a very deadly influence on the individual. If you had not focused your big idea in a thesis, you might have begun by picking up thoughts at random, something like this:

> **Everyone thinks he is a good driver. There are more accidents caused by young drivers than any other group. Driver education is a good beginning, but further practice is very necessary. People who object to driver education do not realize that modern society, with its suburban pattern of growth, is built around the automobile. The car becomes a way of life and a status symbol. When teen-agers go too fast they are probably only copying their own parents.**

A little reconsideration, aimed at a good thesis-sentence, could turn this into a reasonably good opening paragraph, with your thesis, your big idea, asserted at the end to focus your reader's attention:

> **Modern society is built on the automobile. Children play with tiny cars; teen-agers long to take out the car alone. Soon they are testing their skills at higher and higher speeds, especially with a group of friends along. One final test at extreme speeds usually suffices. It is usually a sobering experience, if survived, and can open one's eyes to the deadly dynamics of the group.**

Thus the central idea, or thesis, is your essay's life and spirit. If your thesis is sufficiently firm and clear, it may tell you immediately how to organize your supporting material. But if you do not find a thesis, your essay will be a tour through the miscellaneous. An essay replete with scaffolds and catwalks—"We have just seen this; now let us turn to this"—is an essay in which the inherent idea is weak or nonexistent. A purely expository and descriptive essay, one simply about "Cats," for instance, will have to rely on outer scaffolding alone (some orderly progression from Persia to Siam), since it really has no idea at all. It is all subject, all cats, instead of being based on an idea *about* cats, with a thesis *about* cats.

THE ARGUMENTATIVE EDGE

Find Your Thesis

The *about*-ness puts an argumentative edge on the subject. When you have something to say *about* cats, you have found your underlying idea. You have something to defend, something to fight about: not just "Cats," but "The cat is really a person's best friend." Now the hackles on all dog people are rising, and you have an argument on your hands. You have something to prove. You have a thesis.

"What's the big idea, Mac?" Let the impudence in that time-honored demand remind you that the most dynamic thesis is a kind of affront to somebody. No one will be very much interested in listening to you deplete the thesis "The dog is a person's best friend." Everyone knows that already. Even the dog lovers will be uninterested, convinced they know better than you. But the cat. . . .

So it is with any unpopular idea. The more unpopular the viewpoint and the stronger the push against convention, the stronger the thesis and the more energetic the essay. Compare the energy in "Democracy is good" with that in "Communism is good," for instance. The first is filled with platitudes, the second with plutonium. By the same token, if you can find the real energy in "Democracy is good," if you can get down through the sand to where the roots and water are, you will have a real essay, because the opposition against which you generate your energy is the heaviest in the world: boredom. Probably the most energetic thesis of all, the greatest inner organizer, is some tired old truth that you cause to spurt with new life, making the old ground green again.

To find a thesis and to put it into one sentence is to narrow and define your subject to a workable size. Under "Cats" you must deal with all felinity from the jungle up, carefully partitioning the eons and areas, the tigers and tabbies, the sizes and shapes. The minute you proclaim the cat the friend of humanity, you have pared away whole categories and chapters, and need only think up the arguments sufficient to overwhelm the opposition. So, put an argumentative edge on your subject—and you will have found your thesis.

That argumentative edge is *rhetoric,* putting an edge on our convictions. Rhetoric is the art of persuasion. It has earned a bad name from its artfulness—mere persuasive froth. But true rhetoric is persuasion alive with conviction. Persuade! And from where you are—with an amiable, reasonable prose that shows you *know* where you are.

Neutral exposition, to be sure, has its uses. You may want to tell someone how to build a doghouse, how to can asparagus, how to follow the outlines of relativity, or even how to write an essay. Performing a few exercises in simple exposition will no doubt sharpen your insight into the problems of finding orderly sequences, of considering how best to lead your readers through the hoops of writing clearly and accurately. It will also illustrate how much finer and surer an argument is.

You will see that picking an argument immediately simplifies the problems so troublesome in straight exposition: the defining, the partitioning, the narrowing of the subject. Not that you must be constantly pugnacious or aggressive. I have overstated my point to make it stick. Actually, you can put an argumentative edge on the flattest of expository subjects. "How to build a doghouse" might become "Building a doghouse is a thorough introduction to the building trades, including architecture and mechanical engineering." "Canning asparagus" might become "An asparagus patch is a course in economics." "Relativity" might become "Relativity is not so inscrutable as many suppose." Literary subjects take an argumentative edge almost by nature. You simply assert what the essential point of a poem or play seems to be: *"Hamlet* is essentially about a world that has lost its values." You assume that your readers are in search of clarity, that you have a loyal opposition consisting of the interested but uninformed. You have given your subject its edge; you have limited and organized it at a single stroke. Pick an *argument,* then, and you will automatically be defining and narrowing your subject, and all the partitions you don't need will fold up. Instead of dealing with things, subjects, and pieces of subjects, you will be dealing with an idea and its consequences.

Sharpen Your Thesis

Come out with your subject pointed. You have chosen something that interests you, something you have thought about, read about, something preferably of which you have also had some experience—perhaps, let us say, seeing a friend loafing while cashing welfare checks. So take a stand. Make a judgment of value, make a *thesis.* Be reasonable, but don't be timid. It is helpful to think of your thesis, your main idea, as a debating question—"Resolved: Welfare payments must go"—taking out the "Resolved" when you actually write your thesis down. But your resolution will be even stronger, your essay clearer and tighter, if you can sharpen your thesis even further—"Resolved: Welfare payments must go because _____." Fill in that blank, and your worries are practically over. The main idea is to put your whole argument into one sentence.

Try, for instance: "Welfare payments must go because they are making people irresponsible." I don't know at all if that is true, and neither will you until you write your way into it, considering probabilities and alternatives and objections, and especially the underlying assumptions. In fact, no one, no master sociologist or future historian, can tell absolutely if it is true, so multiplex are the causes in human affairs, so endless and tangled the consequences. The basic assumption—that irresponsibility is growing—may be entirely false. No one, I repeat, can tell absolutely. But likewise, your guess may be as good as another's. At any rate, you are now ready to write. You have found your *logos*.

Now you can put your well-pointed thesis-sentence on a card on the wall in front of you to keep from drifting off target. But you will now want to dress it for the public, to burnish it and make it comely. Suppose you try:

> **Welfare payments, perhaps more than anything else, are eroding personal initiative.**

But is this fully true? Perhaps you had better try something like:

> **Despite their immediate benefits, welfare payments may actually be eroding personal initiative and depriving society of needed workers.**

This is your full thesis, and you can write that down on a scrap of paper too.

Use Your Title

After your thesis, think of a title. A good title focuses your thinking even more sharply and catches your reader's thoughts on your finished paper. Your title is your opening opportunity. It is an integral part of your paper. Don't forget it.

Work up something from your thesis. It will be tentative, of course. Your thinking and your paper may change in the writing, and you will want to change your title to match. But a good title, like a good thesis, has a double advantage: (1) it helps you keep on track as you write; (2) it attracts and helps keep your reader on track as he reads. It is the first step in your persuasion. So try something attractive:

> **Welfare Not Warfare**
> **Farewell to Welfare**
> **Whom Does Welfare Benefit?**

You can probably do better. You will do better when you finish your paper. But don't make it sound like a newspaper headline, and don't make it a complete sentence. Don't forget your title as a starter, both for your writing and for your written paper. Capitalize all significant words (see 431–433 for details). Titles do not take periods, but do take question and exclamation marks if you need them. Your title and your opening sentence should be independent of each other. With a title like "Polluted Streams," for instance, don't begin with *"This* is a serious problem."

EXERCISES

1. *Below I have listed a series of subjects about which you might write. Transform each into an assertion, a thesis. Start by trying to transform some of the subjects into debating propositions. For example, "Welfare payments" becomes, "Resolved: Welfare payments must go." Having done that, you might take it a step farther by supplying a reason. For example, "Resolved: Welfare payments must go because they are sapping people's initiative." Now you have a clear thesis, although it may be a bit mechanical in form. All that remains is to dress it up for public appearance. "Welfare payments, perhaps more than anything else, are eroding personal initiative and destroying the work-instinct." Supply a thesis statement and a title for each of the following subjects:*

   1. Nuclear armament
   2. The appearance of our campus
   3. Student housing
   4. Jogging
   5. Computers
   6. Modern aristocracy
   7. A novel you have read. For example, *Huckleberry Finn*
   8. Unequal distribution of blacks and whites in occupational groups
   9. Gun control
   10. Careers for women

2. *The following sentences are all thesis-statements taken from actual students' papers. As you can see, the authors did not spot the built-in weaknesses. Explain what, if anything, you think wrong with each of these as thesis-statements. Then revise them as best you can.*

   1. I think we should all insist on unilateral nuclear disarmament.
   2. The campus of_____University (College) is unique in many ways.
   3. With the increasing enrollment at this university (and with the larger number of married students) steps need to be taken to increase student housing.
   4. From experience, I would believe that jogging can be helpful in more ways than one.
   5. Computers are the wave of the future.
   6. No matter how it used to be in this country, we have an aristocracy of money now.
   7. I believe that *Huckleberry Finn* is the result of Twain's contempt for the black race.
   8. I believe, and will try to show, that the unequal distribution of blacks and whites in occupational groups revealed in the last Census is the result of two problems: inferior education for blacks and discriminatory hiring by white employers.

9. How can anyone deny the constitutional right to bear arms?
10. Every modern girl is interested in a career.

BELIEVING IN YOUR THESIS

Notice how your assertion about welfare mellowed as you revised. And not because you have resorted to cheap tactics, though tactics may get you to the same place, but rather because you brought it under critical inspection, asking what is true in it: what can (and cannot) be assumed true, what can (and cannot) be proved true. And you have asked yourself where you stand. You do the same with any assigned subject, finding within it some kernel of personal interest, personalizing it—through writing getting *interested,* as we say.

You should, indeed, in any topic, look for a thesis you believe in, something you can even get enthusiastic about. Arguing on both sides of a question, as debaters do, is no doubt good exercise, if one can stand it. It breaks up old ground and uncovers what you can and do believe, at least for the moment. But the argument without the belief will be hollow. You can hardly persuade anyone if you can't persuade yourself. So begin with what you believe, and explore its validities.

Conversely, you must test your belief with all the objections you can think of, just as you have already tested your first proposition about welfare payments. First, you have acknowledged the most evident objection—that the opposition's view must have some merit—by starting your final version with "Despite their immediate benefits. . . ." Second, you have gone a little deeper by seeing that in your bold previous version you had, with the words *are eroding,* begged the question of whether responsibility is in fact undergoing erosion; that is, you had silently assumed that responsibility *is* being eroded. This is one of the oldest fallacies and tricks of logic. To "beg the question," by error or intent, is to take for granted that which the opposition has not granted, to assume as already proved that which is yet to be proved. But you have saved yourself. You have changed *are eroding* to *may be eroding.* You have gone farther in deleting the *perhaps more than anything else.* You have come closer to the truth.

You may wonder if it is not astoundingly presumptuous to go around stating theses before you have studied your subject from all angles, made several house-to-house surveys, and read everything ever written. A natural uncertainty and feeling of ignorance, and a misunderstanding of what truth is, can well inhibit you from finding a thesis. But no one knows everything. No one would write anything if he waited until he did. To a great extent, the writing of a thing is the learning of it—the discovery of truth.

So, first, make a desperate thesis and get into the arena. This is probably solution enough. If it becomes increasingly clear that your thesis is untrue, no matter how hard you push it, turn it around and use the other end. If your convictions have begun to falter with:

> **Despite their immediate benefits, welfare payments undermine initiative. . . .**

try it the other way around, with something like:

> **Although welfare payments may offend the rugged individualist, they relieve much want and anxiety, and they enable many a family to maintain its integrity.**

You will now have a beautiful command of the major objections to your new position. And you will have learned something about human fallibility and the nature of truth.

Once you believe in your proposition, you will discover that proving it is really a venture in persuasion. *Rhetoric* is, again, the art of persuasion, of moving the reader to your belief. You have made a thesis, a hypothesis really—an opinion as to what the truth seems to be from where you stand, with the information you have. Belief has an unfolding energy. Write what you believe. You may be wrong, of course, but you will probably discover this as you probe for reasons, and can then reverse your thesis, pointed with your new conviction. The truth remains true, and you must at least glimpse it before you can begin to persuade others to see it. So follow your convictions, and think up reasons to convince your reader. Give him enough evidence to persuade him that what you say is probably true; find arguments that will stand up in the marketplace and survive the public haggle. You must find public reasons for your private convictions.

EXERCISES

3. *To strengthen your witchcraft in discovering theses, put down quickly the first four or five subjects that come to mind—golf, cars, architecture, lipstick, tomatoes. These must have interested you sometime, somewhere. Now make each into an established one-sentence argumentative thesis on the pattern* Although _____ , golf accomplishes more because _____ .

ON FINDING YOURSELF AND YOUR THESIS

Well. Here is the secret. Toss any subject on the page: surfboards, schools, pickles, bicycles, blind dates, apples, underwear. Assert something *about* it.

You have a thesis, and an essay in the offing. You start with a subject that interests you, an experience, a shock, a hope, something you've read. With assigned topics, as we have seen, you look for some personal connection, if at all possible. You generalize your personal thrill or terror: not *I did,* but *people do.* You turn it into a thesis by affirming something about it: not "I like stamps," but "Stamps open the world." You evolve your written voice as you think up points and illustrations, discovering that revision is not only necessary and inevitable but positively creative as it brings your thoughts fully alive and makes them persuasive.

Now with the concepts and the style in hand, we need a framework, a structure, to put them in. This we will look at in the next chapter. But let us close with a student's paper to illustrate the points of this chapter as it looks ahead to the structural points of the next. In it, you can see the mechanics of typing, spacing, quoting, and so forth. The author has made a few small last-minute corrections in pencil, which are perfectly acceptable. Her writing is a little wordy and awkward. She is a little uncertain of her language. Her *one*'s, for instance, seem far too stiff and insistent. This is her first paper, and she has not yet fully discovered her own written voice. But it is an excellent beginning. It shows well how a personal experience produces a publicly valid thesis, then turns around to give that thesis its most lively and specific illustration. The assignment had asked for a paper of about five hundred words on some book (or movie, or TV program) that had proved personally meaningful. Even a memorable experience would do—fixing a car, or building a boat, or being arrested. The aim of the assignment was to generalize from a personally valuable experience and to explain to others how such an experience can be valuable to them.

Emily Maddox
English 123
Paper No. 1
September 15, 1984

On Finding Oneself in New Guinea

Reading for pleasure is not considered to be popular.   Opposing View

Young adults prefer the "boob tube," the television set

with which they have spent so many childhood hours. Too

many attractions beckon them away from the books ~~which~~ *that* the

teacher recommended to the class for summer reading.

One's friends come by in their automobiles to drive down

for a coke. The kids go to the moving pictures, or to the

beach, and the book one had intended to read remains on the

shelf, or probably ∧*in* the library, where one has not yet been

Thesis able to find the time to go. Nevertheless, <u>a book can fur-

nish real enjoyment.</u>

Generalized Support   <u>The reader enjoys the experience of being in another

world.</u> While one reads, one forgets that one is in one's

own room. The book has served as a magic carpet to ~~take~~ *Transport* one

to India, or Africa, or Sweden, or even to the cities and

areas of one's own country where one has never been. It

has also transported one into the lives of people with

different experiences and problems, from which one can

learn to solve one's own problems of the future. The young

person, in particular, can learn by the experience of

reading what it is like to be a complete adult.

A book is able to help the young person to mature even

further, and change one's whole point of view. <u>Growing ∪p

in New Guinea</u> by Margaret Mead is a valuable experience

Personal Experience for this reason. <u>I found the book on our shelf,</u> after hav-

ing seen Margaret Mead on TV. I was interested in her be-

cause the teacher had referred to her book entitled <u>Coming

of Age in Samoa.</u> I was surprised to find this one about New

Guinea. I thought it was a mistake. I opened it and read

the first sentence:

> The way in which each human infant is trans-
> formed into the finished adult, into the compli-
> cated individual version of his city and his cen-
> tury, is one of the most fascinating studies open
> to the curious minded.

The idea that the individual is a version of his city and his century was fascinating. I started reading and was surprised when I was called to dinner to learn that two hours had passed. I could hardly eat my dinner fast enough so that I could get back to New Guinea.

From this book I learned that different cultures have very different conceptions about what is right and wrong, in particular about the sex relations and the marriage ceremony, but that people have the same problems all over the world, namely the problem of finding one's place in society. <u>I also learned that books can be more enjoyable than any other form of pleasure.</u> Books fascinate the reader because while one is learning about other people and their problems, particularly about the problem of becoming a full member of society, one is also learning about one's own problems.

Thesis Restated

EXERCISES

4. *Now expand one of your thesis-statements from the preceding exercises into a paper about the length of the preceding example. First, introduce your thesis with a few remarks to get your reader acquainted with your subject, then write your paper straight through to illustrate your thesis as fully as you can. Then go back over this draft and make it publicly presentable, revising until you know you have done your best.*

5. *Making a thesis can also help your reading, and in all your courses. Therefore, at the end of each chapter, or other reading, try to put down* in one sentence *(and right in your textbook) that chapter's point: not* This chapter discusses racial discrimination, *but* Racial discrimination arises from powerful biological drives to seek one's own kind and to shun aliens. *This practice strengthens your knowledge, aids your analysis—has your author said it anywhere as well as you have?—and develops your ability to generate theses for your own thoughts. It works equally well for poems, stories, and plays.*

CHAPTER 3

Giving Your Writing Direction: Basic Structure

BEGINNING, MIDDLE, END

As Aristotle long ago pointed out, works that spin their way through time need a beginning, a middle, and an end to give them the stability of spatial things like paintings and statues. You need a clear beginning to give your essay character and direction so the reader can tell where he is going and can look forward with expectation. Your beginning, of course, will set forth your thesis. You need a middle to amplify and fulfill. This will be the body of your argument, the bulk of your essay. You need an end to let readers know that they have arrived and where. This will be your final paragraph, a summation and reassertion of your theme.

Give your essay the three-part *feel* of beginning, middle, and end—the mind likes this triple order. Many a freshman's essay has no structure and leaves no impression. It is all chaotic middle. It has no beginning, it just starts; it has no end, it just stops, fagged out at two in the morning.

The beginning must feel like a beginning, not just like an accident. It should be at least a full paragraph that lets your reader gently into the subject and culminates with your thesis. The end, likewise, should be a full paragraph, one that drives the point home, pushes the implications wide, and brings the reader to rest, back on the fundamental thesis to give a sense of completion. When we consider paragraphing in the next chapter, we will look more closely at beginning paragraphs and end paragraphs. The "middle" of your essay, which constitutes its bulk, needs further structural consideration now.

MIDDLE TACTICS

Arrange Your Points in Order of Increasing Interest

Once your thesis has sounded the challenge, your reader's interest is probably at its highest pitch. He wants to see how you can prove so outrageous a thing, or to see what the arguments are for this thing he has always believed but never tested. Each step of the way into your demonstration, he is learning more of what you have to say. But, unfortunately, his interest may be relaxing as it becomes satisfied: the reader's normal line of attention is a progressive decline, arching down like a wintry graph. Against this decline you must oppose your forces, making each successive point more interesting. And save your best till last. It is as simple as that.

Here, for example, is the middle of a short, three-paragraph essay developing the thesis that "Working your way through college is valuable." The student has arranged his three points in an ascending order of interest:

> **The student who works finds that the experience is worth more than the money. First, he learns to budget his time. He now supports himself by using time he would otherwise waste, and he studies harder in the time he has left because he knows it is limited. Second, he makes real and lasting friends on the job, as compared to the other casual acquaintances around the campus. He has shared rush hours, and nighttime cleanups with the dishes piled high, and conversation and jokes when business is slow. Finally, he gains confidence in his ability to get along with all kinds of people, and to make his own way. He sees how businesses operate, and how waitresses, for instance, can work cheerfully at a really tiring job without much hope for the future. He gains an insight into the real world, which is a good contrast to the more intellectual and idealistic world of the college student.**

Again, each successive item of your presentation should be more interesting than the last, or you will suddenly seem anticlimactic. Actually, minor regressions of interest make no difference so long as the whole tendency is uphill and your last item clearly the best. Suppose, for example, you were to try a thesis about cats. You decide that four points would make up the case, and that you might arrange them in the following order of increasing interest: (1) cats are affectionate but make few demands; (2) cats actually look out for themselves; (3) cats have, in fact, proved extremely useful to society throughout history in controlling mice and other plaguy rodents; (4) cats satisfy some human need for a touch of the jungle, savagery in repose, ferocity in silk, and have been worshiped for the exotic power they still seem to represent. It may be, as you write, that you will find Number 1 developing attractive or amusing instances, and perhaps even virtually usurping the whole essay. Numbers 2, 3, and 4 should then be moved ahead as interesting but brief preliminaries.

Interests vary, of course. This is the point. And various subjects will suggest different kinds of importance: from small physical details to large, from incidental thoughts to basic principles. Sometimes chronology will supply a naturally ascending order of interest: as a tennis match or hockey game reaches its climax; or as in any contests against natural hazards and time itself, like crossing a glacier with supplies and endurance dwindling. Space, too, may offer natural progressions of interest, as you move from portico to inner shrine, since architects also know the dramatics of arrangement. But usually interest ascends in ideas, and these quite naturally ascend from your own interest in your subject, in which, with a little thought, you can tell which points to handle first and which to arrange for more and more importance, saving best till last. In short, your middle structure should range from least important to most important, from simple to complex, from narrow to broad, from pleasant to hilarious, from mundane to metaphysical—whatever "leasts" and "mosts" your subject suggests.

EXERCISES

1. *In the following exercise, you will find groups of information and ideas haphazardly arranged. Rewrite the statements with the information arranged in an ascending order of interest and importance. Then, in a sentence or two, explain your reasons for using that order.*

   1. We are now being made to realize the negative aspects of the technological "progress" of the twentieth century: 50,000 highway deaths per year, air and water pollution, the population explosion, nuclear warfare, loss of privacy.
   2. Four different levels of government are investigating the effectiveness of the methadone treatment for heroin addiction. State, national, county, and city governments have all instituted research programs within the last year.
   3. Marijuana should be legalized because people are going to use it whether it is legalized or not. Legalizing it would make a sensible distinction between hard and soft drugs, would allow authorities to control the quality of the drugs available for sale, would eliminate criminal profiteering, and would prevent numbers of people from becoming cynical violators of the law.
   4. If you have gotten along without a credit card until now, applying for one is really a mistake. If you have one, you might lose it or have it stolen, and then you might be liable for the expenses run up by someone else using your card. Then there are the interest charges. Few people realize that the interest on most credit cards is 18 percent a year. And obviously, if you have a credit card, you are going to spend more than if you were using cash.
   5. Talking about scientific knowledge today, she identified three of its characteristics. First, this knowledge is not within the reach of most of us. Second, this knowledge is mostly new. And, finally, this knowledge has become almost the exclusive property of a very small group of scientists and engineers.

ACKNOWLEDGING AND DISPOSING OF THE OPPOSITION

Your cat essay, because it is moderately playful, can proceed rather directly, throwing only an occasional bone of concession to the dogs, and perhaps most of your essays, as you discuss the Constitutional Convention or explain a poem, will have no opposition to worry about. But a serious controversial argument demands one organizational consideration beyond the simple structure of ascending interest. Although you have taken your stand firmly as a *pro,* you will have to allow scope to the *cons,* or you will seem not to have thought much about your subject. The more opposition you can manage as you carry your point, the more triumphant you will seem, like a high-wire artist daring the impossible.

This balancing of *pros* against *cons* is one of the most fundamental orders of thought: the dialectic order, which is the order of argument, one side pitted against the other. Our minds naturally swing from side to side as we think. In dialectics, we simply give one side an argumentative edge, producing a thesis that cuts a clear line through any subject: "This is better than that." The basic organizing principle here is to get rid of the opposition first, and to end on your own side. Probably you will have already organized your thesis-sentence in a perfect pattern for your *con-pro* argument:

Despite their many advantages, welfare payments. . . . Although dogs are fine pets, cats. . . .

The subordinate clause (see 154) states the subordinate part of your argument, which is your concession to the *con* viewpoint; your main clause states your main argument. As the subordinate clause comes first in your thesis sentence, so does the subordinate argument in your essay. Sentence and essay both reflect a natural psychological principle. You want, and the reader wants, to get the opposition out of the way. And you want to end on your best foot. (You might try putting the opposition last, just to see how peculiarly the last word insists on seeming best, and how, when stated last by you, the opposition's case seems to be your own.)

Your opposition, of course, will vary. Some of your audience will agree with you but for different reasons. Others may disagree hotly. You need, then, to imagine what these varying objections might be, as if you were before a meeting in open discussion, giving the hottest as fair a hearing as possible. You probably would not persuade them, but you would ease the pressure and probably persuade the undecided by your reasonable stance. Asking what objections might arise will give you the opposing points your essay must meet—and overcome.

GET RID OF THE OPPOSITION FIRST.   This is the essential tactic of argumentation. You have introduced and stated your thesis in your beginning paragraph. Now start the middle with a paragraph of concession to the *cons:*

> **Dog-lovers, of course, have tradition on their side. Dogs are indeed affectionate and faithful. . . .**

And with that paragraph out of the way, go to bat for the cats, showing their superiority to dogs in every point. In a very brief essay, you can use the opposition itself to introduce your thesis in the first paragraph, and dispose of your opponents at the same time:

> **Shakespeare begins *Romeo and Juliet* with ominous warnings about fate. His lovers are "star-crossed," he says: they are doomed from the first by their contrary stars, by the universe itself. They have sprung from "fatal loins." Fate has already determined their tragic end. The play then unfolds a succession of unlucky and presumably fated accidents. Nevertheless, we soon discover that Shakespeare really blames the tragedy not on fate but on human stupidity and error.**

But usually your beginning paragraph will lead down to your thesis somewhat neutrally, and you will attack your opposition head-on in paragraph two, as you launch into the middle.

If the opposing arguments seem relatively slight and brief, you can get rid of them neatly all together in one paragraph before you get down to your case. Immediately after your beginning, which has stated your thesis, you write a paragraph of concession: "Of course, security is a good thing. No one wants people begging." And so on to the end of the paragraph, deflating every conceivable objection. Then back to the main line: "But the price in moral decay is too great." The structure of the essay, paragraph by paragraph, might be diagrammed something like the scheme shown in Diagram I:

Diagram I

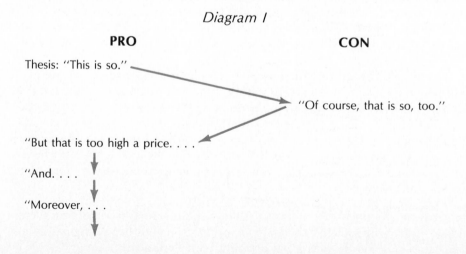

PRO   CON

Thesis: "This is so."

"Of course, that is so, too."

"But that is too high a price. . . ."

"And. . . ."

"Moreover, . . ."

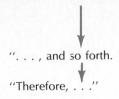

". . . , and so forth.

"Therefore, . . ."

If the opposition is more considerable, demolish it point by point, using a series of *cons* and *pros,* in two or three paragraphs, before you steady down to your own side. Each paragraph can be a small argument that presents the opposition, then knocks it flat—a kind of Punch-and-Judy show: "We must admit that. . . . But. . . . " And down goes the poor old opposition again. Or you could swing your argument through a number of alternating paragraphs: first your beginning, the thesis, then a paragraph to the opposition *(con),* then one for your side *(pro),* then another paragraph of *con,* and so on. The main point, again, is this: *get rid of the opposition first.* One paragraph of concession right after your thesis will probably handle most of your adversaries, and the more complicated argumentative swingers, like the ones shown in Diagram II, will develop naturally as you need them.

You will notice that *but* and *however* are always guides for the *pros,* serving as switches back to the main line. Indeed, *but, however,* and *nevertheless* are the basic *pros. But* always heads its turning sentence (not followed by a comma); *nevertheless* usually does (followed by a comma). I am sure, however, that *however* is always better buried in the sentence between commas. "However, . . . " at a sentence's beginning is the habit of heavy prose. *But* is for the quick turn; the inlaid *however* for the more elegant sweep.

The structural line of your arguments, then, might look like Diagram II, and an actual *pro-con* argument like Diagram III (38).

Diagram II

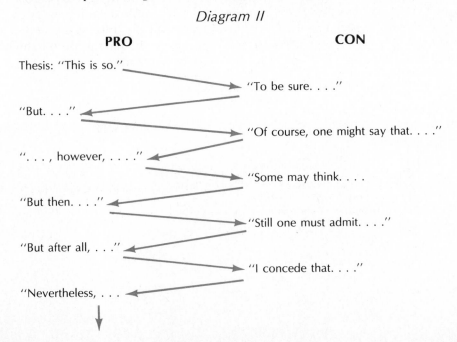

"Indeed, . . .

"Besides, . . .

"Therefore, . . ."

Diagram III
Controlling Handguns—Pro and Con

PRO   **CON**

Thesis: Possession of handguns should
be controlled.

To be sure, self-protection is a
natural right. . . .

But pistols in homes kill many more
relatives than intruders. . . .

Of course, ownership by sportsmen
and collectors is justified. . . .

Large numbers of weapons in homes,
however, give easy access to
theft. . . .

I concede that any restrictions
invade privacy and freedom. . . .

Nevertheless, the intrusion is no more
restrictive than registering an
automobile. . . .

Indeed, all arguments about individual
rights pale before the crime rate and
the annual slaughter of individuals. . . .

Besides, handguns kill thousands more
in the United States than in any
other country.

Therefore, controlling handguns is
reasonable and necessary.

Here is a short *pro-con* essay that gets rid of the opposition early and in one paragraph.

WOMAN AND HUMAN SUPERIORITY

Woman has kept the home fire burning for eons, probably since the discovery of fire. Her place has been in the home, and men have been all too happy to keep her in her place. Men are usually taller, stronger, and more aggressive, as war paths through forest and battlefield and stock market have demonstrated. Women themselves tend to give men the edge of superiority, if the men haven't already grabbed it for themselves. But although the weaker sex has been outshone and outshown in many ways, women are actually superior in the most fundamental qualities.

Of course, men are more muscular, but both the actuarial statistics and accounts of extended hardship, like that of the Donner Party in the last century, show that women have more physical endurance. Pictures of women runners at the end of marathons like the annual Boston run show them still in good shape while the men are collapsing, though both have given their best. The men have run faster, but the women have outlasted just as they will in the race of life. Women are also immune to a number of sex-linked diseases, which, like hemophilia, they carry while the men succumb. Women have achieved less in the arts and sciences, but actually their brains are bigger in proportion to their weight. Clearly, they have had less time and motivation to compete.

Their achievement and motivation lie where their true superiority is: in the compassion that nurtures and holds together the human race that men seem bent on tearing apart. Compassion distinguishes humanity from inhumanity. Jane Goodall, who, *In the Shadow of Man* (1971), found chimpanzees so very human in many ways, saw their indifference toward their suffering fellows as the crucial distinction. Woman has nurtured the young and the aged from long before that first fire put her in her place. If, as some anthropologists believe, man learned to walk by carrying food back to the wife and kids, he learned this consideration from the mother who cared for him during the human infant's extended dependency. Woman's superiority lies in her instinctive sympathy, her caring, her loving. As Ashley Montagu says, *"It is the function of woman to teach men how to be human."** Women may well catch up in the arts and sciences, in business and government, but if we ever achieve a peace on earth in which humanity can fulfill itself, we will do so because men have at last caught up to woman's true superiority.

EXERCISES

2. *To strengthen your feeling for the argumentative opposition, from which you develop your middle pro-con tactics, write three con-and-pro thesis-sentences, beginning "Although. . . . "*

3. *In the exercise that follows, you will find a series of general assertions. Supply one argument against and one argument for each proposition. Then combine the statements into one thesis-sentence that includes not only the assertion, but also the reasons against and for it.*

   EXAMPLE   Assertion: Movies should not be censored.

Con: Children should not be exposed to obscene and explicitly sexual images on the screen.

Pro: Obscenity is far too subjective a thing for any person to define for anyone else.

Thesis-Statement: Although young people probably should not be exposed to explicit sex in films, movies still should not be censored because obscenity is so subjective that no one can legitimately serve as censor for the rest of us.

1. Assertion: Discussion classes are superior to lectures.
2. Assertion: Rapid and convenient transit systems must be built in our cities.
3. Assertion: The federal government should subsidize large companies forced near bankruptcy.
4. Assertion: Medical schools should reduce the time required for a degree in general medicine from four years to two.
5. Assertion: States should prohibit the sale of beverages in nonreturnable containers.
6. Assertion: A guaranteed annual income would not wipe out poverty for all Americans.
7. Assertion: As exercise, golf is a waste of time.
8. Assertion: The law should require that all drivers and passengers in cars use seat belts.
9. Assertion: College students should study a foreign language.

*"The Natural Superiority of Women," *Saturday Review* (1 March, 1952): 35—to which I am indebted for the main point and several details.

RUNNING CONTRASTS POINT BY POINT

As you contrast your *pros* and *cons,* your natural dialectic habit of mind has probably instinctively pitted point against point, raising the opposition and answering it. You may do this almost sentence for sentence, as in our paragraph of dialectics about women's superiority, or you may do it more extensively in longer essays. But here lies the danger. You can easily dwell on one point too long, getting carried away with explanation and detail, and in any and all kinds of comparison.

Whether in a dialectical argument or a benign contrast, the point-for-point principle will keep you from losing your reader. Don't write all about sheep for three pages, for instance, then all about goats. Every time you say something about a sheep, say something comparable about a goat, pelt for pelt, horn for horn, beard for beard. Otherwise your essay will fall in two, your reader will be surprised when the goats come along, and you will need to repeat all your sheep points when you at last begin the comparison. The tendency to organize comparisons by halves is so strong that you will probably find you have fallen into it unawares, and in rewriting you will have to reorganize everything point for point—still arranging your pairs of points from least important to most. Finally, the most interesting comparison aims to demonstrate a superiority—"Resolved: Sheep are more useful than goats."

Of course, comparing and contrasting two poems, two stories, two ballplayers, is an essential process of thought too, an essential way to understanding. You may wish simply to set two similars, or dissimilars, side by side to illustrate some larger point—that excellence may come in very different packages, for instance. Comparing and contrasting can illuminate the unfamiliar with the familiar, or it can help you discover and convey to your readers new perspectives on things well known—two popular singers, two of Shakespeare's sonnets, two nursery rhymes. But, whether or not you are presenting one side as superior to the other, the structural tactics are the same: illuminate by comparing point for point, as long as the comparison illuminates.

EXERCISES

4. *In the exercise that follows, you will find a dialectical argument in which the author advances his thesis point by point. First, state the thesis, then number and identify the arguments both for and against the thesis. Also identify as* con *or* pro *the words or phrases the author uses to mark the switch from one side of the argument to the other. List the arguments for and against the assertion, and make another double list, headed* Pro *and* Con, *of the writer's transitional devices.*

The Hon. Mike Mansfield
United States Senator, Montana, Democrat
Senate Majority Leader
Testimony before the Senate Constitutional Amendments Subcommittee
October 28, 1971.

I welcome the chance to express my views pertaining to the proposed Constitutional Amendment that would limit the Presidency to a single term of six years.
I am particularly proud and pleased to join with the distinguished Senator George
D. Aiken from Vermont in this endeavor which I personally regard as one of the
most important reforms that our system of government could undergo.

In recent years there have been a number of significant amendments to the
Constitution of the United States. Correcting the matter of Presidential succession
and particularly extending the franchise of the ballot to young adults 18, 19 and
20 years of age represent enormous steps forward: steps that protect and enhance
immensely the Democratic processes of this Nation. In my judgment there is still
another step that must be taken in this area of Constitutional evolution. It is only
in providing a single Presidential term of six years, I believe, that this Nation will
preserve for its highest office a sufficient degree of freedom and independence
to function properly and adequately today and in the years ahead; years that will
produce enormous trials and tensions on the national and global scale, some of
which have yet to emerge.

By no means do I intend to imply that with this proposed amendment new
ground is being broken or that a topic of first impression is here being raised. Indeed, the suggestion of a single six-year term has been with us ever since the dele-
gates to the Constitutional Convention of 1787 thrashed over the question of a
President's term and his eligibility for re-election. It is interesting to note that popular election was not considered with any great favor at all during the proceedings
of that convention. But proposals limiting the tenure of the President were put
forth and discussed. Ultimately none were approved and the question then became moot when the suggestion for an electoral college system gained the widest
support.

Since the Constitution was ratified hundreds of amendments have been intro-
duced in the Senate and House of Representatives proposing a change in Presidential tenure. More than 130 of these recommended a single term of six years.
Twice, the House reported legislation providing for the six-year term. And in
1913, the Senate passed S.J. Res. 78 calling for a term of six years, but no action
was taken by the other body. Presidents themselves have been most active in
their support for the concept. Nearly 150 years ago Andrew Jackson recommended that the electoral college be abolished—also a good suggestion—that the
President be elected by direct vote, and that he be limited to a single term of either
four or six years. Presidents Hayes and Cleveland and William Howard Taft also
offered the proposal. In more recent years on this issue I have followed the lead
of the able and distinguished Senator from Vermont, the dean of the Republicans
and a wise and prudent judge on all matters and particularly on those affecting
the needs of democratic institutions in a rapidly changing world. That brings us
up to today, and I must say that the merits of the proposal dictate its need now
as never before.

It is just intolerable that a President of the United States—any President, whatever his party—is compelled to devote his time, energy and talents to what can be termed only as purely political tasks. I do not refer solely to a President's own re-election campaign. To be sure a re-election effort and all it entails are burdens enough. But a President facing re-election faces as well a host of demands that range from attending to the needs of political office holders, office seekers, financial backers and all the rest, to riding herd on the day-to-day developments within the pedestrian partisan arena. Surely this amendment does not represent a panacea for these ills which have grown up with our system of democracy. But it would go far, I think, in unsaddling the Presidency from many of these unnecessary political burdens that an incumbent bears.

Clearly such a change to a very great extent would free the President to devote a far greater measure of his time to the enormous task of serving all of the people of this Nation as Chief Executive. More time would thus be provided for policy-making and policy-implementing, for program initiating and for shaping and directing the kind of Administration a President chooses. More time would be provided for the kind of experimentation that a successful Presidency requires; such experimentation has come too infrequently in recent years, and as a Nation we suffer from that inadequacy. . . .

To sum it up, what this amendment seeks is to place the office of the Presidency in a position that transcends as much as possible partisan political considerations of whatever nature and source. That it cannot do the job completely, I would agree. The man who achieves the office carries with him his full political heritage. But its adoption would do much, I think, to streamline the Presidency in a manner that ultimately will make the position more fully responsive to the concerns of all Americans.*

THE INDUCTIVE STRUCTURE

The natural dialectical swing of the way we think has given us the basic *pro-con* structure. Similarly, our two essential directions of thinking—induction and deduction—provide structures for organizing an essay. In fact, we have been talking about deductive structure all along: setting out your Big Idea, your proposition, your thesis, then demonstrating, illustrating, and arguing its validity in detail, showing the parts that support the whole. This is the essay's usual and most useful structure.

But the inductive structure, though more infrequent, has its uses and can give your essays variety. Inductive reasoning starts with details and, considering *pros* and *cons,* works up to their ultimate significance. An inductive essay simply follows this same pattern, although the writer knows where he is going, probably having discovered it through writing and rewriting. He leads the

The Congressional Digest (March 1972): 80–84.

reader from detail to more significant detail upward to his thesis, simulating an inductive search and taking the reader along. Both inductive and deductive structures thus follow an ascending order of interest, and consider some *pros* and *cons* along the way. The inductive saves the opening thesis, however, for the end. You simply lead your reader in—by successive questions and their dismissal, or partial answers—to your main and conclusive point. "Is it this? Well, no." "Then may it be this? No, not exactly this either." "Then how about this? Ah, yes, this seems to be it." The deductive order, beginning with your thesis and then explaining it, is clearer. But the inductive order has suspense, a kind of intellectual excitement, if you can keep your answer from slipping out.

Inductive order probably works best for short essays, since you must keep the cat in the bag, and you can't keep him in too long. You simply use a question for your thesis-sentence and then simulate for your reader the train of thought by which you arrived at your conclusion. To illustrate the procedure, here is an inductive paragraph from an interview with George Harris, a man reminiscing about the Depression:

Topical Question Answer 1	**What was the worst thing about the Depression? Well, I don't know. I guess for some folks it was losing their savings. For us that wasn't so bad.** I only had about $400 in the McLain County Bank when it closed and I got some of that back later, about ten cents on the dollar. Then too, **being out of work was rough for a lot of people.** But even that wasn't so bad for me. I
Answer 2	lost my job with the coal company in 1931, but we lived on a farm. And with that and some odd jobs I picked up, I managed to keep pretty busy until I got a steady job again. Of course, I
Answer 3	**know a lot of people didn't have enough to eat or enough to wear during the Depression. For us that wasn't too bad.** We grew most of our own food, and my wife is pretty handy at sewing, so we got by. Nothing very fancy, you understand, but we
Main Answer (Thesis)	managed. No, I guess for us **the worst thing about the Depression was we got to feeling after a while that times just weren't ever going to get better.** It just went on too long. For us, things got a little rough in 1931 and they stayed pretty rough until I got a job with the Highway Commission in 1938. Seven years is a long time to keep hoping. It just went on so long.

This will give you an idea of inductive order. You may well use a short inductive section in a longer essay, especially for dismissing the opposition's arguments by putting them as questions ("Do we want unlimited freedom?") and then reducing them to absurdities. But, as I say, a wholly inductive essay is usually short, and you won't even find many of these, because your answer, your thesis, tends to keep slipping out of the bag and spoiling your surprise.

THE DEDUCTIVE STRUCTURE

Hang Your Essay from Your Big Idea

The deductive structure is the basic arrangement. It is much more widely used, and useful, than the inductive one, because it can sustain itself page after page, even through chapters in a whole book. You set down your thesis, your general proposition, then *explain* it in detail and at length, presenting *pros* and *cons* as needed. The mode of induction is question and partial answer; the mode of deduction is assertion and explanation. As we have seen, however, the usual deductive order does not simply begin with your Big Idea and then dwindle down to nothing. You match some of the inductive's suspense by saving your best for last. You can even include a short inductive paragraph or two for more suspense and variety. You start with your thesis, then jump down to your smallest small and work progressively uphill until you again reach your thesis, which is now restated as your conclusion and rounded off in a concluding paragraph. Again, the deductive order of presentation is the normal one we have been talking about all along.

To change Mr. Harris's inductive rumination about the Depression into a deductive structure, we simply make his opening question a thesis to be demonstrated: not "What was the worst thing about the Depression?" but "The worst thing about the Depression was its hopeless duration." In the following example, notice how deduction expands the inductive structure as it fills in detail and fills out thoughts and explanations for the reader. Notice how it uses the first-person statement, which happened to fall into an inductive pattern, as a piece of evidence in the more ample deductive structure, still giving the facts as Mr. Harris stated them.

> **For most Americans, the stock market crash was not the worst thing about the Depression. True, it carried away billions of dollars of investors' money, but relatively few of us felt directly affected. Few of us owned stock, and for most of us the market collapse was something that happened to other people, not to us. Of course, as we found out, the stock-market collapse was only the trigger, and soon more and more Americans found their lives directly affected. By 1932, twenty-five percent**

Topic

of the workers had no jobs. Yet, for many Americans, the worst thing about the Depression was not the bank closures, or being out of work, or even shortages of food and clothing. For many of us, the worst thing about the Depression was that it lasted so *long we almost gave up hoping that times would ever get better.* George Harris of Wellsburg, West Virginia, is a good example of how the Depression hit most of us.

In 1931, Mr. Harris had a job with the Green Coal Company as a tender on a boat that pushed coal barges up and down the Ohio River. His income was generally good, and Mr. Harris had managed to buy a small farm just outside town. But cutbacks in industrial production, particularly in the production of steel, soon forced cutbacks in coal mining as well. And in August of 1931, Mr. Harris was laid off. The next year, in 1932, the McLain County Bank closed, and with it went the only savings the Harrises had, $400, although later he did manage to collect ten percent of his lost savings. And so for the next seven years, Mr. Harris bounced from job to job, whatever he could get: a few days here, a few days there. He was thus able to hold onto his small farm, and on it he raised most of the food for the Harris family for the next seven years. Mrs. Harris, too, helped to cut corners by making most of the family's clothes, and by repairing things when they wore out. In this way, taking it one day at a time, and living as simply and as frugally as possible, the Harrises managed to get by until, in 1938, Mr. Harris once again got a secure and well-paying job with the County Road Commission.

So the Harrises are a good example of how the Depression hit many Americans. They lost some savings, they lost their jobs, they had to tighten their belts, but they managed to get by. For them, the worst thing about the Depression was not the deprivation; it was simply that the Depression went on year after year. As Mr. Harris says, "Seven years is a long time to keep hoping. It just went on so long."

Thesis

Demonstration

Restatement

EXERCISES

5. *Write an inductive paragraph like Mr. Harris's account of the Depression, beginning with a question like one of these:*

Should handguns be banned?
What makes a great baseball pitcher?
Should nuclear power be abolished?
Why is education necessary?

Then turn it around into a three- or four-paragraph essay in the deductive structure.

THE HYBRID STRUCTURE

Try Trimming Your Thesis

Actually, many an essayist operates about halfway between the inductive and deductive modes. The basic framework is deductive, but the thesis is trimmed, more open-ended, implied by a leading question, or suggested indirectly in the first paragraph or so, as in the opening of E. B. White's "Farewell, My Lovely":

> I see by the new Sears Roebuck catalogue that it is still possible to buy an axle for a 1909 Model T Ford, but I am not deceived. The great days have faded, the end is in sight. Only one page in the current catalogue is devoted to parts and accessories for the Model T; yet everyone remembers springtimes when the Ford gadget section was larger than men's clothing, almost as large as household furnishings. The last Model T was built in 1927, and the car is fading from what scholars call the American scene—which is an understatement, because to a few million people who grew up with it, the old Ford practically *was* the American scene.
>
> It was a miracle God had wrought. And it was patently the sort of thing that could only happen once. Mechanically uncanny, it was like nothing that had ever come to the world before. Flourishing industries rose and fell with it. As a vehicle, it was hard-working, commonplace, heroic; and it often seemed to transmit those qualities to the persons who rode in it. My own generation identifies it with Youth, with its gaudy, irretrievable excitements; before it fades into the mist, I would like to pay it the tribute of the sigh that is not a sob, and set down random

**entries in a shape somewhat less cumbersome than a Sears Roe-
buck catalogue.***

A fully inductive essay might have posed the question "Why did the Model
T dominate the American scene?" A deductive thesis might have been "The
Model T caught the American heart and mind because it was unique, exciting,
and heroically serviceable." We get White's point indirectly, but it is clearly
there, by the end of the second paragraph, setting the deductive frame for his
not-so-random entries.

Since the general movement from lesser to larger in any essay is a kind
of inductive progression, all hybrid structures have an inductive air, with a
fairly large number of questions replacing the assertions that would otherwise
guide the progress. You may easily set up a good hybrid by putting your thesis
as a broadly general question: "Why is Social Security necessary?"

The more direct the question, the more purely inductive the essay. You
launch a completely inductive essay when your questioning thesis asks for one
specific answer among several possibilities you will entertain and reject, *pro*
and *con,* before letting your reader know your answer: "Is the Model T me-
chanically reliable?" (Hardly); "Is Whitman an egotist?" (Not really); "Should
we make welfare payments?" (Yes). The more your question suggests your answer, the more deductive and direct you become: "Does the Model T's charm
lie in its quirky durability?"; "Is Whitman something more universal than a
mere egotist?"; "Are welfare payments really a socialistic and bureaucratic
evil?"

Virginia Woolf's famous essay "How Should One Read a Book?"[†] is an
almost perfect example of the deductive-inductive hybrid, as both her title and
her thesis suggest. Even her questioning title implies an unstated deductive
assertion: "One should read a book, and read it the right way." Her thesis,
also a question, likewise implies an unstated deductive assertion, which her
essay proceeds to illustrate: "How are we to bring order into this multitudinous chaos and so get the deepest and widest pleasure from what we read?"
Her thesis-question does not say exactly *how*—her essay proceeds to fill in the
answer somewhat inductively—but the question clearly suggests that we must
bring order from chaos to achieve the deep and wide pleasure she sees as the
purpose of reading. A thesis-question similar to Woolf's may get you a very
nice hybrid essay:

---

*© 1936, 1964, The New Yorker Magazine, Inc. From *Essays of E. B. White* (New York: Harper
& Row, 1977): 162, originally published in *The New Yorker* in 1936 over the pseudonym "Lee Strout
White." Richard L. Strout had submitted a manuscript on the Ford, and White, with his collabora-
tion, rewrote it.

†From *The Second Common Reader* (New York: Harcourt Brace Jovanovich, 1932).

How should one plan a vacation?
What is the greatest reward in sports?
What makes an effective teacher?

You may also set up the deductive-inductive hybrid by trimming a fully explicit thesis to get something of the open-endedness of a question. You simply trim the full-blown thesis at both ends, cutting away from the beginning the concessive "Although . . . " and from the end the explanatory "because. . . . " Your most completely stated thesis might be:

Although welfare payments may offend the rugged individualist,
we should nevertheless have a system of welfare payments be-
cause they relieve much want and anxiety, and they enable
many a fatherless family to maintain its integrity.

To remake this a thesis for a partially inductive essay, you simply trim it to something like: "All in all, we need some system to help those in need." You then proceed with a series of questions, or open-ended assertions, supplying the answers—the *cons* and *becauses*—as you go:

1. **But what about the threat to our ideal of self-sufficiency?**
2. **Private organizations already provide a number of charitable services.**
3. **But what about the actual needs of fatherless, poor families?**
4. **Surely our affluent society can care for its less fortunate members.**

And so on, until you have reached and dealt with the want, anxiety, and frustration that are the center of your submerged but emerging thesis.

EXERCISES

6. *Here is an excerpt, an essay in small, from Niccolo Machiavelli's famous, or infamous, The Prince (1513). Its thesis is open-ended. Its inner movement is essentially inductive, as it swings pro and con. Read it, considering, as always, what Machiavelli's true thesis is, what his pros and cons are, and whether his points follow the best order of ascending interest. Then answer the questions at the end and rewrite it in a fully deductive structure, rearranging his order of presentation if necessary.*

HOW CITIES OR STATES PREVIOUSLY INDEPENDENT MUST BE GOVERNED AFTER OCCUPATION

When those states which have been accustomed to live in freedom under their own laws are acquired, there are three ways of trying to keep them. The first is to destroy them, the second to go and live therein, and the third to allow them to continue to live under their own laws, taking a tribute from them and creating within them a new government of a few which will keep the state friendly to you. For since such a government is the creature of the prince it will know that it cannot exist without his friendship and authority and is thus certain to do its best to support him, and a city accustomed to freedom can be more easily held through its citizens than in any other way if it is desired to preserve it. Here we have the examples of the Spartans and the Romans. The Spartans held Athens and Thebes and created in both a government of a few; nonetheless they lost them. The Romans, in order to hold Capua, Carthage, and Numantia, razed them and did not lose them. They tried to keep Greece in the same way the Spartans had, permitting the country to be free under its own laws, but in this they were not successful inasmuch as they were compelled to destroy many cities of that province in order to hold it, for in truth there is no sure way of holding them other than by their ruin. And whoever becomes master of a city accustomed to living in freedom and does not destroy it may expect to be destroyed by it himself, for it has always as an incentive to rebellion the name of liberty and its own ancient laws which neither time nor favors received can cause the citizens to forget. And whatever action be taken or provision be made, as long as the inhabitants are not separated or dispersed, that name and those laws are never forgotten but provide a rallying point in every emergency, as is shown by the case of Pisa after many years of subjection to the Florentines. Cities or provinces used to living under a prince are accustomed to obedience, and when the ruling house becomes extinct they are unable to agree on a successor and, having no experience of self-government, they are slow in taking up arms and so with greater ease a prince may overcome them and feel secure in his possession of them. In republics there is greater life, greater hatred, more desire of vengeance, and the memory of their ancient liberty gives them no rest; so the safest way is either to extinguish them or go and live in them.*

1. *What is Machiavelli's true thesis? State it for him.*
2. *To which kind of government does he give least consideration? Is his placement effective?*
3. *For which of his alternatives does he give no examples? What are some possible cons to this alternative? Include them as you round out his dialectics for him.*

---

*Niccolo Machiavelli, *The Prince,* translated and edited by Thomas G. Bergin (Arlington Heights, Ill.: Harlan Davidson, Inc., 1947): 12–13. Copyright © 1947 by Harlan Davidson, Inc. Reprinted by permission of Harlan Davidson, Inc.

CHAPTER 4

Paragraphs: Beginning, Middle, End

THE STANDARD PARAGRAPH

A paragraph is a structural convenience—a building block to get firmly in mind. I mean the standard, central paragraph, setting aside for the moment the peculiarly shaped beginning paragraph and ending paragraph. You build the bulk of your essay with standard paragraphs, with blocks of concrete ideas, and they must fit smoothly. But they must also remain as perceptible parts, to rest your reader's eye and mind. Indeed, the paragraph originated, among the Greeks, as a resting place and place-finder, being first a mere mark *(graphos)* in the margin alongside *(para)* an unbroken sheet of handwriting—the proof-reader's familiar ¶. You have heard that a paragraph is a single idea, and this is true. But so is a word, usually; and so is a sentence, sometimes. It seems best, after all, to think of a paragraph as something you use for your reader's convenience, rather than as some granitic form laid down by molten logic.

The medium determines the size of the paragraph. Your average long-hand paragraph may look the same size to you as a typewritten one, and both may seem the same size as a paragraph in a book. But the printed page might show your handwritten paragraph so short as to be embarrassing, and your typewritten paragraph barely long enough for decency. Handwriting plus type-writing plus insecurity equals inadequate paragraphs. Your first impulse may be to write little paragraphs, often only a sentence to each. If so, you are not yet writing in any medium at all.

Journalists, of course, are habitually one-sentence paragraphers. The narrowness of the newspaper column makes a sentence look like a paragraph, and narrow columns and short paragraphs serve the rapid transit for which newspapers are designed. A paragraph from a book might fill a whole newspaper column with solid lead. It would have to be broken—paragraphed—for the reader's convenience. On the other hand, a news story on the page of a book would look like a gap-toothed comb, and would have to be consolidated for the reader's comfort. So make your paragraphs ample.

Plan for the Big Paragraph

Imagine yourself writing for print, but in a book, not a newspaper. Force yourself to four or five sentences at least, visualizing your paragraphs as about all of a size. Think of them as identical rectangular frames to be filled. This will allow you to build with orderly blocks, to strengthen your feel for structure. Since the beginner's problem is usually one of thinking of things to say rather than of trimming the overgrowth, you can do your filling out a unit at a time, always thinking up one or two sentences more to fill the customary space. You will probably be repetitive and wordy at first—this is our universal failing—but you will soon learn to fill your paragraph with clean and interesting details. You will get to feel a kind of constructional rhythm as you find yourself coming to a resting place at the end of your customary paragraphic frame.

Once accustomed to a five-sentence frame, say, you can then begin to vary the length for emphasis, letting a good idea swell out beyond the norm, or bringing a particular point home in a paragraph short and sharp—even in one sentence, like this.

The paragraph's structure, then, has its own rhetorical message. It tells the reader visually whether or not you are in charge of your subject, and are leading him confidently to see what you already know. Tiny, ragged paragraphs display your hidden uncertainty, unless clearly placed among big ones for emphasis. Brief opening and closing paragraphs sometimes can emphasize your thesis effectively, but usually they make your beginning seem hasty and your ending perfunctory. So aim for the big paragraph all the way, and vary it only occasionally and knowingly, for rhetorical emphasis.

Find a Topic Sentence

Looked at as a convenient structural frame, the paragraph reveals a further advantage. Like the essay itself, it has a beginning, a middle, and an end. The beginning and the end are usually each one sentence long, and the middle gets you smoothly from one to the other. Since, like the essay, the paragraph flows through time, its last sentence is the most emphatic. This is your home punch. The first sentence holds the next most emphatic place. It will normally be your *topic sentence,* stating the paragraph's point, like a small thesis of a miniature essay, something like this:

Jefferson believed in democracy because he firmly believed in reason. He knew that reason was far from perfect, but he also knew that it was the best faculty we have. He knew that it was better than all the frightened and angry intolerances with which we fence off our own back yards at the cost of injustice. Thought must be free. Discussion must be free. Reason must be free to range among the widest possibilities. Even the opinion we hate, and have reasons for believing wrong, we must leave free so that reason can operate on it, so that we advertise our belief in reason and demonstrate a faith unafraid of the consequences—because we know that the consequences will be right. Freedom is really not the aim and end of Jeffersonian democracy: freedom is the means by which democracy can rationally choose justice for all.

If your topic sentence covers everything within your paragraph, your paragraph is coherent, and you are using your paragraphs with maximum effect, leading your reader into your community block by block. If your end sentences bring him briefly to rest, he will know where he is and appreciate it.

This is the basic frame. As you write, you will discover your own variations, a paragraph that illustrates its topic sentence with parallel items and no home punch at the end at all, or one beginning with a hint and ending with its topical idea in the most emphatic place, like the best beginning paragraphs.

BEGINNING PARAGRAPHS: THE FUNNEL

State Your Thesis at the END of Your Beginning Paragraph

Your beginning paragraph should contain your main idea, and present it to best advantage. Its topic sentence is also the *thesis sentence* of your entire essay. The clearest and most emphatic place for your thesis sentence is at the *end*— not at the beginning—of the beginning paragraph. Of course, many an essay begins with a subject-statement, a kind of open topic sentence for the whole essay, and unfolds amiably from there. But these are usually the more personal meditations of seasoned writers and established authorities. Bacon, for instance, usually steps off from a topical first sentence: "Studies serve for delight, for ornament, and for ability." Similarly, A. A. Milne begins with "Of the fruits of the earth, I give my vote to the orange"—and just keeps going.

But for the less assured and the more structurally minded, the funnel is the reliable form, as the thesis sentence brings the reader to rest for a moment at the end of the opening paragraph, with his bearings established. If you put your thesis sentence first, you may have to repeat some version of it as you bring your beginning paragraph to a close. If you put it in the middle, the reader will very likely take something else as your main point, probably whatever the last sentence contains. The inevitable psychology of interest, as you move your reader through your first paragraph and into your essay, urges you to put your thesis last—in the last sentence of your beginning paragraph.

Think of your beginning paragraph, then, not as the middle paragraph's frame to be filled, but as a funnel. Start wide and end narrow:

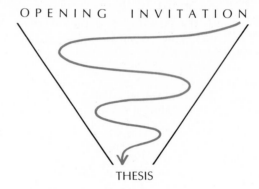

OPENING   INVITATION

THESIS

If, for instance, you wished to show that "Learning to play the guitar pays off in friendship"—your thesis—you would start somewhere back from that thesis-idea with something more general—about music, about learning, about the pleasures of achievement, about guitars: "Playing the guitar looks easy," "Music can speak more directly than words," "Learning anything is a course in frustration." You can even open with something quite specific, *as long as it is more general than your thesis:* "Pick up a guitar, and you bump into people." A handy way to find an opener is to take one word from your thesis—*learning, play,* or *guitar,* for instance—and make a sentence out of it. Say something about it, and you are well on your way to your thesis, three or four sentences later.* Your opening line, in other words, should look forward to your thesis, should be something to engage interest easily, something to which most readers would assent without a rise in blood pressure. (Antagonize and startle if you wish, but beware of having the door slammed before you have a chance and of making your thesis an anticlimax.) Therefore: broad and genial. From your opening geniality, you move progressively down to smaller particulars. You narrow down: from learning the guitar, to its musical and social complica-

---

*I am grateful to James C. Raymond, of the University of Alabama, for this helpful idea.

tions, to its rewards in friendship (your thesis). Your paragraph might run, from broad to narrow, like this:

> **Learning anything has unexpected rocks in its path, but the guitar seems particularly rocky. Playing it looks so simple. A few chords, you think, and you are on your way. Then you discover not only the musical and technical difficulties, but a whole unexpected crowd of human complications. Your friends think you are showing off; the people you meet think you are a fake. Then the frustrations drive you to achievement. You learn to face the music and the people honestly. You finally learn to play a little, but you also discover something better. You have learned to make and keep some real friends, because you have discovered a kind of ultimate friendship with yourself.**

Now, that paragraph turned out a little different from what I anticipated. I used the informal *you,* and it seemed to suit the subject. I also overshot my original thesis, discovering, as I wrote, a thesis one step farther—an underlying cause—about coming to friendly terms with oneself. But it illustrates the funnel, from the broad and general to the one particular point that will be your essay's main idea, your thesis. Here is another example:

> **The environment is the world around us, and everyone agrees it needs a cleaning. Big corporations gobble up the countryside and disgorge what's left into the breeze and streams. Big trucks rumble by, trailing their fumes. A jet roars into the air, and its soot drifts over the trees. Everyone calls for massive action, and then tosses away his cigarette butt or gum wrapper. The world around us is also a sidewalk, a lawn, a lounge, a hallway, a room right here. Cleaning the environment can begin by reaching for the scrap of paper at your feet.**

In a more argumentative paper, you can sometimes set up your thesis effectively by opening with the opposition, as we have already noted (36):

> **Science is the twentieth century's answer to everything. We want the facts. We conduct statistical polls to measure the President's monthly popularity. We send space ships to bring back pieces of the moon and send back data from the planets. We make babies in test tubes. We believe that eventually we will discover the chemical formula for life itself, creating a human being from the basic elements. Nevertheless, one basic element,**

**what has been called the soul, or spirit, may be beyond science
and all human planning, as Gore Vidal's recent novel *Kalki* suggests.**

EXERCISES

1. *Below is a list of thesis-sentences. Choose one (or its opposite), or make one of your
own on the same pattern. Then back off from it at least four or five sentences, and
write a funnel-like beginning paragraph leading your reader down to it: your thesis,
the last sentence of your beginning funnel.*

> **EXAMPLE** *with thesis italicized follows:*
>
> The coal operators will tell you that stripping is cheaper and more efficient
> than conventional mining. Their 250-cubic-yard drag-lines, their 200-cubic-yard
> shovels, their 50-ton trucks, can rip the top off a mountain and expose a whole
> seam of coal in a fraction of the time it takes to sink a shaft. "It is cheaper," they
> will say, "to bring the surface to the coal than to bring the coal to the surface."
> And of course they are right; in a sense it is cheaper. But visit Eastern Kentucky
> and look at the real price we pay for stripped coal. Visit a stripped area and you
> will see that, no matter how low the price for a truckload of stripped coal, *the
> real price for strip-mining has to be reckoned in terms of blighted land, poisoned
> streams, and stunted human lives.*

   1. Although motivated by proper concern for the public welfare, the FCC's ban of
      cigarette advertising on television is ineffective and discriminatory.
   2. Although currently exempt, camper buses and vans should face the same federal
      safety requirements as automobiles.
   3. Despite the evident advantages of artificial turf in football stadiums, it is dangerous
      and should, therefore, be banned.
   4. Even though durable and convenient, tape cassettes reproduce sound with only
      mediocre fidelity.
   5. Legalizing off-track betting may annoy some citizens, but, because it would
      weaken the underworld, we should support it.

MIDDLE PARAGRAPHS

Make Your Middle Paragraphs Full, with Transitions

The middle paragraph is the standard paragraph, the little essay in itself, with
its own little beginning and little end. But it must also declare its allegiance
to the paragraphs immediately before and after it. Each topic sentence must
somehow hook onto the paragraph above it, must include some word or phrase
to ease the reader's path: a transition. (1) You may simply repeat a word from

the sentence that ended the paragraph just above. (2) You may bring down a thought generally developed or left slightly hanging in air: "Smith's idea is different" might be a tremendously economical topic sentence with automatic transition. (3) Or you may get from one paragraph to the next by the usual steppingstones, like *But, however, Nevertheless, Therefore, Indeed, Of course.* One brief transitional touch in your topic sentence, or opening sentence, is usually sufficient.

The topic sentences in each of the following three paragraphs by James Baldwin contain neat transitions. I have just used an old standby myself: repeating the words *topic sentence* from the close of my preceding paragraph. Baldwin has just described the young people of Harlem who have given up, escaping into day-long TV, or the local bar, or drugs. He now begins his next paragraph with *And the others,* a strong and natural transition, referring back, reinforced with the further transitional reference *all of these deaths.* In the next paragraph, *them* does the trick; in the last, *other* again makes the transition and sets the contrast. The paragraphs are nearly the same length, all cogent, clear, and full. No one-sentence paragraphing here, no gaps, but all a vivid, orderly progression:

> **And the others, who have avoided all of these deaths, get up in the morning and go downtown to meet "the man." They work in the white man's world all day and come home in the evening to this fetid block. They struggle to instill in their children some private sense of honor or dignity which will help the child to survive. This means, of course, that they must struggle, stolidly, incessantly, to keep this sense alive in themselves, in spite of the insults, the indifference, and the cruelty they are certain to encounter in their working day. They patiently browbeat the landlord into fixing the heat, the plaster, the plumbing; this demands prodigious patience; nor is patience usually enough. In trying to make their hovels habitable, they are perpetually throwing good money after bad. Such frustration, so long endured, is driving many strong, admirable men and women whose only crime is color to the very gates of paranoia.**

Topic Sentence with Transition

End Sentence: The Point

> **One remembers them from another time—playing handball in the playground, going to church, wondering if they were going to be promoted at school. One remembers them going off to war—gladly, to escape this block. One remembers their return. Perhaps one remembers their wedding day. And one sees where the girl is now—vainly looking for salvation from some other embittered, trussed, and struggling boy—and sees the all-but-abandoned children in the streets.**

Topic Sentence with Transition

End Sentence: The Point

Topic Sentence with
Transition

Now I am perfectly aware that there are other slums in which white men are fighting for their lives, and mainly losing. I know that blood is also flowing through those streets and that the human damage there is incalculable. People are continually pointing out to me the wretchedness of white people in order to console me for the wretchedness of blacks. But an itemized account of the American failure does not console me and it should not console anyone else. That hundreds of thousands of white people are living, in effect, no better than the "niggers" is not a fact to be regarded with complacency. **The social and moral bankruptcy suggested by this fact is of the bitterest, most terrifying kind.***

End Sentence:
The Point

Check Your Paragraphs for Clarity and Coherence

Baldwin's paragraphs run smoothly from first sentence to last. They are coherent. The *topic sentence* is the key. It assures that the subsequent sentences will fall into line, and it is the first point to check when you look back to see if they really do. Many a jumbled and misty paragraph can be unifed and cleared by writing a broader topic sentence. Consider this disjointed specimen:

Swimming is healthful. The first dive into the pool is always cold. Tennis takes a great deal of energy, especially under a hot sun. Team sports, like basketball, baseball, and volleyball, always make the awkward player miserable. Character and health go hand in hand.

What is all that about? From the last sentence, we can surmise something of what the writer intended. But the first sentence about swimming in no way covers the paragraph, which treats several sports not in the least like swimming, and seems to be driving at something other than health. The primary remedy, as always, is to find the paragraph's thesis and to devise a topic sentence that will state it, thus covering everything in the paragraph. Think of your topic sentence as a roof—covering your paragraph and pulling its lines and contents together.

---

*From "Fifth Avenue Uptown: A Letter from Harlem," from *Nobody Knows My Name* by James Baldwin. Copyright © 1960 by James Baldwin. A Dial Press Publication. Reprinted by permission of Doubleday & Company, Inc.

POOR COVERAGE   GOOD COVERAGE

Swimming is healthful.

The first dive. Tennis. Basketball, baseball, volleyball. Character and health.

Sports build health and character.

Swimming. The first dive. Tennis. Basketball, baseball, volleyball. Character and health.

Suppose we leave the paragraph unchanged for the moment, adding only a topic sentence suggested by our right-hand diagram. It will indeed pull things together:

> **Sports demand an effort of will and muscle that is healthful for the soul as well as the body. Swimming is healthful. The first dive into the pool is always cold. Tennis takes a great deal of energy, especially under a hot sun. Team sports, like basketball, baseball, and volleyball, always make the awkward player miserable. Character and health go hand in hand.**

Topic Sentence

But the paragraph is still far from an agreeable coherence. The islands of thought still need some bridges. Gaining coherence is primarily a filling in, or a spelling out, of submerged connections. You may fill in with (1) thought and (2) specific illustrative detail; you may spell out by tying your sentences together with (3) transitional tags and (4) repeated words or syntactical patterns. Let us see what we can do with our sample paragraph.

From the first, you probably noticed that the writer was thinking in pairs: the pleasure of sports is balanced off against their difficulty; the difficulty is physical as well as moral; character and health go hand in hand. We have already indicated this doubleness of idea in our topic sentence. Now to fill out the thought, we need merely expand each sentence so as to give each half of the double idea its due expression. We need also to qualify the thought here and there with *perhaps, often, some, sometimes, frequently, all in all,* and the like. As we work through the possibilities, more specific detail will come to mind. We have already made the general ideas of *character* and *health* more specific with *will, muscle, soul,* and *body* in our topic sentence, and we shall add a touch or two more of illustration, almost automatically, as our imagination becomes more stimulated by the subject. We shall add a number of transitional ties like *but, and, of course, nevertheless,* and *similarly.* We shall look for chances to repeat key words, like *will,* if we can do so gracefully; and to repeat syntactical patterns, if we can emphasize similar thoughts by doing so, as with *no matter how patient his teammates . . . no matter how heavy his heart,* toward the end of our revision below (the original phrases are in italics):

Sports demand an effort of will and muscle that is healthful for the soul as well as the body. *Swimming is* physically *healthful,* of course, although it may seem undemanding and highly conducive to lying for hours inert on a deck chair in the sun. But *the first dive into the pool is always cold:* taking the plunge always requires some effort of will. And the swimmer soon summons his will to compete, against himself or others, for greater distances and greater speed, doing twenty laps where he used to do one. Similarly, *tennis takes* quantities *of energy,* physical and moral, *especially* when the competition stiffens *under a hot sun. Team sports, like basketball, baseball, and volleyball,* perhaps demand even more of the amateur. *The awkward player* is *miserable* when he strikes out, or misses an easy fly, or an easy basket, no matter how patient his teammates. He must drive himself to keep on trying, no matter how heavy his heart. Whatever the sport, a little determination can eventually conquer one's awkwardness and timidity, and the reward will be more than physical. *Character and health* frequently *go hand in hand.*

Here we can see the essence of coherence: REPETITION, (1) repeating parallel examples, like *swimming, tennis, team sports,* as if stacking them up to support your topic sentence; or (2) stringing them along by idea and word, sentence by sentence, as in *sports, swimming, dive.* Similarly *tennis, team sports,* and so forth, as one thought suggests the next.

Accustom Yourself to the Transitional Tags

We have already looked at some of the transitional bridges, first those that take you from the *pro* side of your argument to the *con* and back, and then those that, paragraph by paragraph, connect the paths of your thought from start to finish. Now let us simply summarize, in the table on 61–62, the common transitional possibilities, since beginners usually do not think of transitions, and since any and all transitions contribute importantly to the inner coherence of your paragraphs.

You should use such tags economically, of course. Make sure that your *however* means "however," that your *for example* supplies an example. You should vary them, and avoid switching your argument back and forth so frequently that you spoil your paragraph's coherence. The more various the transitional tags at your command, the more flexible your resources. Keep an eye open for unusual ones. A rare *contrariwise, mind you, egad,* or *alas* may give you just the right turn of humor or irony. But remember, these tags may easily become wordy. Make them work, or retire them with your revising pencil.

TRANSITIONS		USES

1. and
  or, nor
  also
  moreover
	furthermore
	indeed
	in fact
	first, second . . .
		You are adding something. *And* can be a good sentence-opener, when used with care.

2. for instance
  for example
  for one thing
	similarly
	likewise
		Again you are adding, and illustrating or expanding your point.

3. therefore
  thus
  so
  and so
  hence
  consequently
	finally
	on the whole
	all in all
	in other words
	in short
		You are adding up consequences, summarizing minor points to emphasize a major point.

4. frequently
  occasionally
  in particular
  in general
	specifically
	especially
	usually
		You are adding a qualifying point or illustration.

5. of course
  no doubt
  doubtless
	to be sure
	granted (that)
	certainly
		You are conceding a point to the opposition, or recognizing a point just off your main line.

6. but
  however
  yet
  on the contrary
	not at all
	surely
	no
		You are reversing or deflecting the line of thought, usually back to your own side.

7. still
  nevertheless
  notwithstanding
		You return the thought to your own side after a concession.

8. although
  though
  whereas
		You are attaching a concession to one of your points. Do not use *while* for *whereas; while* means, basically, "during the time that," and is thus ambiguous unless restricted to time. (See *Whereas, While,* in the "Glossary of Usage.")

9. because
  since
  for
		You are connecting a *reason* to an assertion.

10. if
  provided
  in case
	unless
	lest
	when
		You are qualifying and restricting a more general idea.

TRANSITIONS		USES
11. as if as though even if		You are glancing at tentative or hypothetical conditions that strengthen and clarify your point.
12. this that these those who whom he she	it they all of them few many most several	These relative and demonstrative words (adjectives and pronouns) tie things together, pointing back as they carry the reference ahead. But be sure there can be no mistaking the specific word to which each refers.

Lead Your Reader with Specific Details

Transitional tags help the reader around the turns, but specific details give him solid footing. He needs to step from detail to detail, or his progress will not be coherent. Your topic sentences are generalizations. Your reader now needs to feel the support of facts, the specific items, numbers, quotations, men, and women, that illustrate your general points. Mr. George Ramsey of Sacramento, California, likes to give his classes his Ramsey Test of Specifics. "Look at your paragraph, class," he says, "and score one point for each capital letter on a name of a person or place; score one point for each direct quotation; score one point for any numbers; and score one point for each example or illustration." Scores are frequently zero. All generalization. No specific details whatsoever. The reader has nothing under his feet at all.

The following paragraph by Loren Eiseley would score about ten. He has been writing of Alfred Russel Wallace's and Charles Darwin's conflicting views as to the evolution of man's brain, and has just referred to the small-brained humanoid apes:

> **These apes are not all similar in type or appearance. They are men and yet not men. Some are frailer-bodied, some have great, bone-cracking jaws and massive gorilloid crests atop their skulls. This fact leads us to another of Wallace's remarkable perceptions of long ago. With the rise of the truly human brain, Wallace saw that man had transferred to his machines and tools many of the alterations of parts that in animals take place**

**through evolution of the body. Unwittingly, man had assigned
to his machines the selective evolution which in the animal
changes the nature of its bodily structure through the ages.
Man of today, the atomic manipulator, the aeronaut who flies
faster than sound, has precisely the same brain and body as his
ancestors of twenty thousand years ago who painted the last Ice
Age mammoths on the walls of caves in France.***

To illustrate his opening generalization that "these apes are not similar," Eiseley adds the specific details of *frailer-bodied, great bone-cracking jaws,* and *massive gorilloid crests atop their skulls.* Rather than merely stating his general point about man and machines, he goes on to illustrate specifically with *the atomic manipulator* and *the aeronaut who flies faster than sound.* Notice that he does not say *manipulators* or *aeronauts,* plural, but takes *the* single and specific *aeronaut* and lets him illustrate the whole range of what man can do with machines. Notice especially how he extends his closing general idea into specific detail: not merely "ancestors," but ancestors of specifically *twenty thousand years ago;* not merely "lived," let us say, but *who painted,* and not merely "pictures," but *the last Ice Age mammoths,* and specifically on *walls* in specific *caves* in one specific country, *France.* The point is to try to extend each of your generalizations by adding some specific detail to illustrate it. Don't stop with *awkward player:* go on to *when he strikes out, or misses an easy fly, or an easy basket.*

Here are the five points to remember about middle paragraphs. First, think of the middle paragraph as a miniature essay, with a beginning, a middle, and an end. Its beginning will normally be its topic sentence, the thesis of this miniature essay. Its middle will develop, explain, and illustrate your topic sentence. Its last sentence will drive home the idea. Second, remember that this kind of paragraph is the norm, which you may instinctively vary when your topic sentence requires only a series of parallel illustrations *(swimming, tennis, golf, basketball, hockey),* or when you open your paragraph with some hint to be fulfilled in a topical conclusive sentence *(Sports build body and soul).* Third, see that your paragraph is coherent, not only flowing smoothly but with nothing in it not covered by the topic sentence. Fourth, make your paragraphs full and well developed, with plenty of details, examples, and full explanations, or you will end up with a skeletal paper with very little meat on its bones. Fifth, remember transitions. Though each paragraph is a kind of miniature essay, it is also a part of a larger essay. Therefore, hook each paragraph smoothly to the paragraph preceding it, with some transitional touch in each opening sentence.

---

*"The Real Secret of Piltdown," in *The Immense Journey* (New York: Random House, Inc., 1955).
© Copyright 1955 by Loren C. Eiseley.

EXERCISES

2. *Read the following paragraph from W. E. B. DuBois's* The Souls of Black Folk, *in which he describes Georgia's "Black Belt" (a name referring to the soil, not the people) as he saw it in 1903, and then answer the following questions:*

> It is a land of rapid contrasts and of curiously mingled hope and pain. Here sits a pretty blue-eyed quadroon hiding her bare feet; she was married only last week, and yonder in the field is her dark young husband, hoeing to support her, at thirty cents a day without board. Across the way is Gatesby, brown and tall, lord of two thousand acres shrewdly won and held. There is a store conducted by his black son, a blacksmith shop, and a ginnery. Five miles below here is a town owned and controlled by one white New Englander. He owns almost a Rhode Island county, with thousands of acres and hundreds of black laborers. Their cabins look better than most, and the farm, with machinery and fertilizers, is much more business-like than any in the county, although the manager drives hard bargains in wages. When now we turn and look five miles above, there on the edge of town are five houses of prostitutes,—two of blacks and three of whites; and in one of the houses of the whites a worthless black boy was harbored too openly two years ago; so he was hanged for rape. And here, too, is the high whitewashed fence of the "stockade," as the county prison is called; the white folks say it is ever full of black criminals,—the black folks say that only colored boys are sent to jail, and they not because they are guilty, but because the State needs criminals to eke out its income by their forced labor.*

1. What is most interesting about this paragraph?
2. What is the topic sentence of the paragraph?
3. How does DuBois use detail to support his topic sentence? Be specific.
4. Is there a consistent order of the details in the paragraph? Give examples to support your answer.
5. What transitional tags are there?
6. Does DuBois repeat key terms? If so, which and where?
7. Is the point of view consistent? If so, describe it.
8. Does the author interrupt his paragraph with parenthetical comments?
9. What do you think are the clearest evidences of coherence within this paragraph?

3. **(a)** *Pick a topic sentence from those following the example, or make a similar one and develop from it a full middle paragraph like a miniature essay, with beginning, middle, and end, making it coherent and full, with good transitions. Your paragraph should seem to be taken from the middle of a longer paper. You will have to imagine what comes before and after, supplying a transitional* But, Another aspect of, also, *and the like.*

   EXAMPLE, *with transitional touches italicized:*

---

*W. E. B. DuBois, *The Souls of Black Folk, Essays and Sketches* (Chicago: A. C. McClurg & Co., 1903): 125–26.

TOPIC SENTENCE: The streams tell the story as drearily as the eroded land.

The streams tell the story *as drearily as* the *eroded land.* In winter, *they* are red with running silt, and sometimes black with *coal* dust. *In summer, many* are no *streams* at all, merely gullies through which the *winter* rains have rushed. Before *the drag-lines stripped* the earth of its skin, the massed roots of grasses, shrubs, and trees held the soil in place and soaked up the *water,* easing it into the *streams* for a full year's run. Fish fed in pools below *grassy* banks and among the weeds that slowed the *water* to a leisurely pace. Now the *water* is soon gone, if not *poisoned* with *industrial waste,* and the *land* is *gone* with it.

1. No matter what the advertisements promise, the X-rated movie usually turns out to be dull and wearisome; it turns out to be two hours of heavy breathing.
2. The computer has contributed to the modern sense of alienation.
3. If the filibuster is supposed to guarantee respect for minority opinion, it usually turns out to be a flagrant waste of time.
4. The new sense of black pride is our increasing awareness of black accomplishments in the past.
5. If women are discriminated against in schools and in industry, they are far more discriminated against in politics.

(b) *Now check the coherence of your paragraph by answering the following questions:*

1. What is most interesting about this paragraph?
2. What is the topic sentence of the paragraph?
3. How do you use details to support your topic sentence?
4. Is there a consistent order of the details in the paragraph?
5. What transitional tags are there?
6. Do you repeat key terms?
7. Is the point of view consistent?
8. Do you interrupt your paragraph with parenthetical comments.
9. What do you think are the clearest evidences of coherence within this paragraph?

END PARAGRAPHS: THE INVERTED FUNNEL

Reassert Your Thesis

If the beginning paragraph is a funnel, the end paragraph is a funnel upside down: the thought starts moderately narrow—it is more or less the thesis you have had all the time—and then pours out broader and broader implications and finer emphases. The end paragraph reiterates, summarizes, and emphasizes with decorous fervor. This is your last chance. This is what your reader will carry away—and if you can carry *him* away, so much the better. All within decent intellectual bounds, of course. You are the person of reason still, but the person of reason supercharged with conviction, sure of your idea and sure of its importance.

If your essay is anecdotal, however, largely narrative and descriptive, your ending may be no more than a sentence, or it may be a ruminative paragraph generalizing upward and outward from the particulars to mirror your beginning paragraph, as in a more argumentative essay. The dramatic curve of your illustrative incident will tell you what to do. An essay illustrating how folly may lead to catastrophe—a friend dead from an overdose, or drowned by daring too far on thin ice—might end when the story has told itself out and made its point starkly: "The three of us walked numbly up the street toward home."

But the usual final paragraph conveys a sense of assurance and repose, of business completed. Its topic sentence is usually some version of the original thesis sentence, since the end paragraph is the exact structural opposite and complement of the beginning one. Its transitional word or phrase is often one of finality or summary—*then, finally, thus,* and *so:*

> **So the guitar is a means to a finer end.**
> **The environment, then, is in our lungs and at our fingertips.**

The paragraph would then proceed to expand and elaborate this revived thesis. We would get a confident assertion that both the music and the friendships are really by-products of an inner alliance; we would get an urgent plea to clean up our personal environs and strengthen our convictions. One rule of thumb: the longer the paper, the more specific the summary of the points you have made. A short paper will need no specific summary of your points at all; the renewed thesis and its widening of implications are sufficient.

Here is an end paragraph by Sir James Jeans. His transitional phrase is *for a similar reason.* His thesis was that previous concepts of physical reality had mistaken surfaces for depths:

> **The purely mechanical picture of visible nature fails for a similar reason. It proclaims that the ripples themselves direct the workings of the universe instead of being mere symptoms of occurrences below; in brief, it makes the mistake of thinking that the weather-vane determines the direction from which the wind shall blow, or that the thermometer keeps the room hot.***

Here is an end paragraph by Charles Wyzanski, Jr. His transitional phrase is *Each generation,* since he has been talking about the perpetual gap. His thesis

---

**The New Background of Science* (Cambridge: Cambridge University Press, 1933): 261.

was that differences, including those between generations, have stimulated life
to higher modes:

> **Each generation is faced with a challenge of making some
> kind of sense out of its existence. In advance, it knows from the
> Book of Job and the Book of Ecclesiastes and the Greek drama
> that there will be no right answer. But there will be forms of
> answer. There will be a style. As ancient Greece had the vision
> of *arete* (the noble warrior), as Dante and the Medievalists had
> the vision of the great and universal Catholic Church, even as
> the founding fathers of the American Republic had the vision
> of the new order which they began, so for the young the ques-
> tion is to devise a style—not one that will be good *semper et
> ubique* ["always and everywhere"], but one for our place and
> our time, one that will be a challenge to the very best that is
> within our power of reach, and one that will make us realize, in
> Whitehead's immortal terms, that for us the only reality is the
> process.***

Here is an end paragraph of Professor Richard Hofstadter's. His transitional word is *intellectuals,* carried over from the preceding paragraphs. His thesis was that intellectuals should not abandon their defense of intellectual and
spiritual freedom, as they have tended to do, under pressure to conform:

> **This world will never be governed by intellectuals—it may
> rest assured. But *we* must be assured, too, that intellectuals will
> not be altogether governed by this world, that they maintain
> their piety, their longstanding allegiance to the world of spiri-
> tual values to which they should belong. Otherwise there will be
> no intellectuals, at least not above ground. And societies in
> which the intellectuals have been driven underground, as we
> have had occasion to see in our own time, are societies in
> which even the anti-intellectuals are unhappy.†**

Remember a conclusion when you have used up all your points and had
your say. You and your argument are both exhausted. You will be tempted
to stop, but don't stop. You need an end, or the whole thing will unravel in
your reader's mind. You need to buttonhole him in a final paragraph, to imply

---

*"A Federal Judge Digs the Young," *Saturday Review* (20 July 1968): 62.
†"Democracy and Anti-intellectualism in America," *Michigan Alumnus Quarterly Review,* 59 (1953):
295.

"I told you so" without saying it, to hint at the whole round experience he has just had, and to leave him convinced, satisfied, and admiring. One more paragraph will do it: beginning, middle, *and* end.

EXERCISES

4. *Now try the inverted funnel, in which your topic sentence is some version of the thesis with which you began and your final paragraph broadens its implications outward to leave the reader fully convinced and satisfied. Using the thesis-sentences in Exercise 1, write two ending paragraphs for imaginary papers.*

   EXAMPLE *with the rephrased thesis (its topic sentence) italicized, and some of the evidence from the paper's middle summarized for emphasis:*

   > *So, at last, we should add up the real costs of strip-mining; we should admit that the ultimate price of coal is far too high if we must rape the land, poison the streams, and wreck human lives to mine it.* For after the drag-lines have gone, even after the coal itself has been burned, the bills for strip-mining will keep coming in. So far, following the expedient path, we have laid bare more than 2,600 square miles of our land, and we show no signs of stopping. Every year we strip an additional 50,000 acres. Just as we cut down our forests in the nineteenth century and fouled our air in the twentieth, we still blunder along toward ecological and social disaster. Isn't it time to stop?

THE WHOLE ESSAY

You have now discovered the main ingredients of a good essay. You have learned to find and to sharpen your thesis in one sentence, to give your essay that all-important argumentative edge. You have learned to arrange your points in order of increasing interest, and you have practiced disposing of the opposition in a *pro-con* structure. You have seen that your beginning paragraph should seem like a funnel, working from broad generalization to thesis. You have tried your hand at middle paragraphs, which are almost like little essays with their own beginnings and ends. And finally, you have learned that your last paragraph should work like an inverted funnel, broadening and embellishing your thesis.

Some students have pictured the essay as a Greek column, with a narrowing beginning paragraph as its top, or capital, and a broadening end paragraph as its base. Others have seen it as a keyhole* (see the keyhole diagram). Pictur-

---

*Mrs. Fran Measley of Santa Barbara, California, has devised for her students a mimeographed sheet to accompany my discussion of structure and paragraphing—to help them to visualize my points, through a keyhole, as it were. I am grateful to Mrs. Measley to be able to include it here.

ing your structure like this is very handy. This is the basic pattern. Keeping it in mind helps as you write. Checking your drafts against it will show you where you might amplify, or rearrange, helpfully. As you write more and more, you will discover new variations as each new subject pushes its way to fulfillment, like a tree growing toward full light. But every tree is a tree. Each follows the general pattern, as if fulfilling some heavenly arboreal keyhole. Similarly, this essayistic one works out in convenient detail the inevitability of Aristotle's Beginning, Middle, and End.

The student's essay that follows illustrates this basic structure fairly well. He has clearly thought about, and talked about, his subject, picking up facts from the daily news, and evidently, as he sat down to put his thoughts on paper, has looked to see what *The Encyclopaedia Britannica* had to say about "Conscription."

We Need a Democratic Draft

Armies make wars. The bigger the army, the greater the threat, as we saw twice in 1982, when Argentinian generals with a large army of conscripts thought invading the Falkland Islands would establish their regime, and when Israel's tanks rumbled into southern Lebanon and just kept going to Beirut. Now, America faces the question of expanding its army by conscription, and against considerable resistance both from a distrust of militarism and from a championship of democratic rights. Nevertheless, this country needs conscription, including, for effectiveness and fairness, the conscription of women.

Of course, the draft creates military and philosophical problems. Militarily, it forces men into a trade, or an apprenticeship, they do not choose, and forces them to fight and die. Ideally, a volunteer army is the best army,

Broad Subject

Opposition

Thesis

Topic Sentence, Opposition 1

THE KEYHOLE

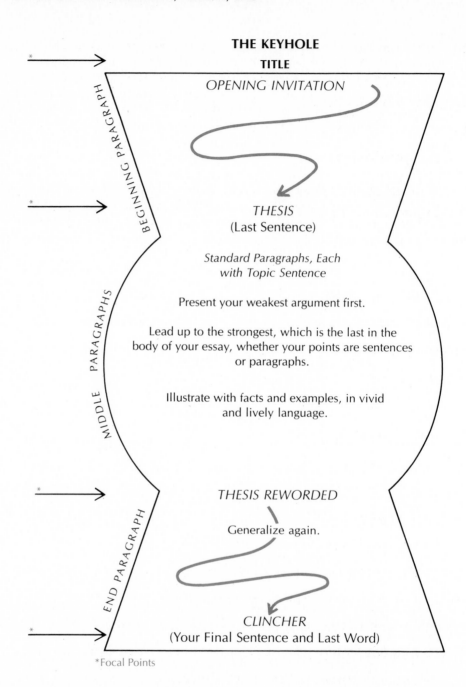

TITLE

OPENING INVITATION

THESIS
(Last Sentence)

*Standard Paragraphs, Each
with Topic Sentence*

Present your weakest argument first.

Lead up to the strongest, which is the last in the
body of your essay, whether your points are sentences
or paragraphs.

Illustrate with facts and examples, in vivid
and lively language.

THESIS REWORDED

Generalize again.

CLINCHER
(Your Final Sentence and Last Word)

BEGINNING PARAGRAPH

MIDDLE PARAGRAPHS

END PARAGRAPH

*Focal Points

fired by patriotism, resentment, or even despair, to defend home and country, like the Athenians at Marathon or
the Spartans at Thermopylae. In times of war, when patriotism rises, a drafted army approaches the spirit of a voluntary one, as farm boys, like Henry Fleming in Stephen
Crane's The Red Badge of Courage, rush off to enlist in the
Civil War, or a fraternity class, at Princeton, I believe,
volunteers as a group in World War I. Even draftees are
fired up for sacrifice to save the world for democracy, or
at least for freedom from Hitler. But a draft in peacetime
requires the military's severest indoctrination and punishment to keep it going and to prevent desertion. An individual's freedom is out of the question.

Middle: Specific
Evidence

The philosophical problem of the draft concerns that
freedom, which is at the heart of democracy. Does one's
elected government have the right to take him out of college or off his chosen job and force him into an endurance
contest designed for killing his fellow man? Those who resist the draft say an emphatic "No." They also argue on the
grounds of sexual discrimination, picking only men from
their careers and leaving women free.

Topic Sentence,
Opposition 2

But harsh necessity sets aside most of the military and
philosophical objections. The volunteer system, set up
after the Vietnamese War, has not worked. The army has
tried it and failed. Only the poorest and marginally educated have volunteered, and not in sufficient numbers,

Topic Sentence, *Pro*

Middle:
Authoritative
Evidence

according to a recent report in Time. The army's call for a draft, and the registration enacted for it by Congress under President Carter, prove that the volunteer army is inadequate in a world blazing with wars from Cambodia to

Specific Allusions

the Falkland Islands.

Topic Sentence

The idea of a peacetime draft, which the protesters resist, is unreal. The world is not at peace, and has not been for a single day since Hitler invaded Poland in 1939. Almost every nation maintains an army through conscrip-

Middle:
Authoritative
Evidence

tion, according to The Encyclopaedia Britannica, with required training and service varying from several months

Contemporary
Examples

to several years. Both Israel and China require service of both men and women, on the old democratic principle of everyone's sharing responsibility, and this evidently contributes to reducing resentment and increasing willingness to serve. Japan is a notable exception, with no army at all. But we are pledged to defend her, as we are our NATO allies, confronted by Russia's tremendous conscripted army. We must wake up to the war-like realities and generate some spirit of necessity to counteract the draft's built-in defect: the lack of professionalism and patriotism that makes a good voluntary army.

Thesis Restated

In short, America needs a draft of both men and women to face the necessities of an armed world around us, and with a system democratically fair and effective, as Israel has shown. No one would think of a draft if volunteers, with squirrel rifles from the cabin, could bring our army up to strength in numbers and intelligence. But the volunteer system has failed. A draft, or at least a registration of both sexes to be ready for a draft when dire reality hits us, is necessary now.

The Clincher

CHAPTER 5

Shoring Argument: Descriptive, Narrative, and Expository Paragraphs

As we have seen, the deductive order of presentation is the most usual and natural one, however casually or crisply it may be implied at beginning and end: first, the thesis, then a "leading away from" it *(de-ducere),* as you take your reader through an explanation of it, point by point. This is indeed the basic structure of argument: beginning assertion, middle demonstration, ending re-assertion. In this structure, we have looked at the simple and complex *cons* and *pros* of middle tactics, and the one psychological principle that underlies all possible arrangements of your middle points—the order of ascending interest, the saving of best for last. We shall now look more closely at the possibilities in arranging those middle points, the descriptive, narrative, and expository orders that illustrate your argument and carry your ideas.

DESCRIPTIVE PARAGRAPHS

Description is essentially *spatial.* Arranging details in some kind of tour through space is as natural as walking. When your subject dwells in and upon physical space—the layout of a campus, for instance—you literally take your reader with you. You organize your paragraphs virtually as units of space, one for the gate, one for the first building, conducting your reader in an orderly progress down the mall or around the quadrangle. Or you show him a rooming house floor by floor, from the apartment by the entry to the garret four flights up, where the graduate student lives on books and cheese. Within the paragraph, you similarly take your reader from one detail to the next in spatial order. Your topic sentence summarizes the total effect: "The Whistler Building was once elegant, three classic stories of brick with carved stone pediments." Then your paragraph proceeds with noteworthy details in any convenient spatial order: first the sagging front door, then the windows to the left, then those to the right, then second-floor windows, with their suggestion of dingy apartments, then those of the third, which suggest only emptiness.

Francine du Plessix Gray beautifully illustrates this process in picturing for us a small and boring ancestral castle on the flat coastal plains of western France. Notice how brilliantly her *platitude* speaks both its literal and figurative meanings, and how well *nobly* conveys the castle's deterioration:

> **The landscape out of Aunt Charlotte's window was as flat**
> **as any in my memory; there was not a hillock, not a rock, to**
> **disturb the monotonous platitude of its horizon. A serene,**
> **dead-straight alley of luxuriant chestnut trees stretched from**
> **the little castle to the country road. To the left, stood some di-**
> **lapidated buildings that had once served as stables and ser-**
> **vants' quarters. The old greenhouse to the right of the entrance**
> **had also been abandoned since the war, when the family for-**
> **tune declined sharply. In the flower beds circling about the cas-**
> **tle's entrance, only the simplest and most tenacious of flow-**
> **ers—hydrangeas, geraniums—fought their way nobly through**
> **tall clumps of weeds.***

A city's slum or its crowded parking, a river's pollution, a mountain's trees from valley to timberline—any spatial subject will offer a convenient route, from bottom to top, or top to bottom, left to right, east to west, center to periphery. You will instinctively use a series of spatial signals: *on the right, above, next, across, down the slope.* Your concern is to keep your progress orderly, to help your reader see what you are talking about. This is exactly the way Oliver Statler, in his *Japanese Inn,* takes us to the place he loves:

> **On this day, I have already progressed along the old**
> **Tokaido Road to the village of Yui. A new highway has been**
> **built a few hundred yards inland to avoid the congested main**
> **street of the village, but leaving Yui it swings back to the shore**
> **and runs between the sea wall on my left and the sheer face of**
> **Satta Mountain on my right.**
> **It is here, as I drive almost into the sea, that my spirits al-**

---

*From *Lovers and Tyrants* (New York: Simon & Schuster, 1976): 165. Copyright © 1976 by Francine du Plessix Gray. Reprinted by permission of Simon & Schuster, a Division of Gulf + Western Corporation.

ways quicken, for only Satta Mountain divides Yui from Okitsu, the next village, where my inn lies. . . . I notice men and women diving around the off-shore rocks, sharp knives in hand, hunting for abalone. Beyond them, fishing boats dot Suruga Bay. . . .

At the highest point of the pass, where the path breaks out of the pines and into the open, there is a breath-taking view, and anyone who finds himself there must turn to drink it in. He faces the great sweep of Suruga Bay and the open Pacific beyond, while waves break into flowers on the rocks far beneath his feet. Yui lies on the shore to his left and Okitsu at his right. Beyond Yui, bathed in mist far off on the left, looms the mountainous coast of Izu. Beyond Okitsu, on the right, is one of the loveliest sights in Japan, for the harbor that lies there is protected by a long arm of curving black sand, covered with ancient and twisted pines. This is the fabled beach of Miho. . . .*

As you can *see,* literally, from Gray and Statler, the best spatial description follows the perceptions of a person looking at or entering the space described, reporting the impressions, the colors, textures, sights, or sounds as they come, as again with the imaginary visitor in this description by R. Prawer Jhabvala of a modern house in India:

Our foreign visitor stands agape at the wonderful residence his second host has built for himself. No expense has been spared here, no decoration suggested by a vivid taste omitted. There are little Moorish balconies and Indian domes and squiggly lattice work and an air-conditioner in every window. Inside, all is marble flooring, and in the entrance hall there is a fountain lit up with green, yellow, and red bulbs. The curtains on the windows and in the doorways are of silk, the vast sofa-suites are upholstered in velvet, the telephone is red, and huge vases are filled with plastic flowers.†

This procedure may be seen in some novels, in the elaborate extension, paragraph after paragraph, at the beginning of Thomas Hardy's *The Return of the Native,* for instance, in which we are moved into the setting from a great distance, as if, years before moving pictures, we are riding a cameraman's dolly.

---

*Oliver Statler, *Japanese Inn* (New York: Pyramid Books, Random House, 1962): 14–16. Copyright © 1961, Oliver Statler.

†*Encounter* 22 (1964): 42–43.

Such descriptions take time. Description frequently blends space and time, with the observer's perceptions unifying the two as he moves through them, and takes his readers with him. You pick out the striking features, showing the reader what would strike him first, as it did you, then proceeding to more minute but no less significant details. This is the usual way of describing people, as in this paragraph (by the anonymous reporter for the *New Yorker's* "Talk of the Town") about an actual Englishman, whose odd occupation is mending the broken eggs brought to him by bird's-egg collectors:

> **Colonel Prynne, who is sixty-seven, lives and carries on his singular pursuit in a rambling, thatch-roofed, five-hundred-year-old cottage in the tiny village of Spaxton, Somerset, and there, on a recent sunny afternoon, he received us. A man of medium build who retains a military carriage, he was sprucely turned out in a brown suit, a tan jersey vest, a green shirt and tie, and tan oxfords. He has a bald, distinctly egg-shaped head, wears a close-cropped mustache and black shell-rimmed glasses, and seems always to have his nose tilted slightly upward and the nostrils faintly distended, as if he were sniffing the air. After taking us on a rather cursory tour of his garden, which is as neat and well tended as its owner, he remarked crisply that it was time to get cracking, and we followed him indoors, past an enormous fireplace, which burns five-foot logs, and up a flight of stairs to a room that he calls his studio.***

EXERCISES

1. *Write a paragraph describing a unit of space, taking your reader from the outside to the inside of your own home, for instance, or dealing with some interesting spatial unit as in the following paragraph from a student's paper.*

> The courtyard of the hotel at Uxmal was a wonderfully cool and welcome surprise after the sweaty bus trip out from Mérida. Surrounding the whole yard was a large *galería,* its ceiling blocking out the few rays of the sun that managed to filter through the heavy plantings that filled the yard. Overhead, along the *galería,* ceiling fans quietly turned, and underfoot the glazed tile floors felt smooth and delightfully cool even though the temperature on the road had pushed up past 100 degrees. Airy wicker chairs lined the railing, and just a few feet away, flowering jungle plants rose almost to the top of the stone arches on the second floor. Under the branches of a tall tree in the middle of the courtyard, out beyond

---

*The New Yorker (23 May 1964): 37. © Copyright 1964, The New Yorker Magazine, Inc.

the rail and the thick plantings, raised tile walkways crisscrossed the yard, bordered all along by neatly cultivated jungle flowers. And right in the middle of the yard, at the base of the big tree, a small waterfall splashed down over mossy rocks into a tiny bathing pool. The splashing water, the shade, the cool tile, all made the road outside seem very far off indeed.

NARRATIVE PARAGRAPHS

Narration is essentially *temporal.* Like space, time is a natural organizer, ancient and simple. Hour follows hour, day follows day, year follows year, life follows life. Again, you simply take your reader along the natural sequence of what happens—to us, or to nations, or to any items in experience or experiment. We understand processes most clearly by tracking the way they move through time, even processes complicated by other, simultaneous events:

> **And when this wheel turns, that lever tips the food into the trough.**
>
> **While this conveyor moves into the oven, the other one is bringing the chassis to point B.**
>
> **And all the time he talked, his hands were moving the shells and flicking the invisible pea.**

Any event, whether a football game or the inauguration of a president, can be best perceived as you have perceived it—through time—and you can bring your reader to perceive it by following the sequence of things as they happened, stepping aside as necessary to explain background and simultaneous events, guiding your reader along with temporal signposts: *at the same time, now, when, while, then, before, after, next, all the time.*

As Audubon, the nineteenth-century naturalist, describes in his *Ornithological Biography* the passenger pigeon and its astounding flights in masses a mile wide and 180 long, he naturally gives us his observations through the order of time. I have underlined the temporal words in one of his paragraphs:

> **As soon as the pigeons discover a sufficiency of food to entice them to alight, they fly round in circles, reviewing the country below. During their evolutions, on such occasions, the dense mass which they form exhibits a beautiful appearance, as it changes direction, now displaying a glistening sheet of azure, when the backs of the birds come simultaneously into view, and**

anon, suddenly presenting a mass of rich deep purple. They then pass lower, over the woods, and for a moment are lost among the foliage, but again emerge, and are seen gliding aloft. They now alight, but the next moment, as if suddenly alarmed, they take to wing, producing by the flappings of their wings a noise like the roar of distant thunder, and sweep through the forests to see if danger is near. Hunger, however, soon brings them to the ground. When alighted, they are seen industriously throwing up the withered leaves. . . .

You can most clearly explain any kind of development or decline—the civil rights movement, the decay of a neighborhood—by taking your reader up or down the path of time. Following the natural order of events, from past to present, is most usual and probably best. You can sometimes gain dramatic effect, however, by beginning with the present and moving back to former insignificance or splendor, as in describing a battered tenement that was once the mayor's mansion. But you will do your reader a favor by keeping to your order, whether forward or backward, and not reversing it inadvertently somewhere along the way.

Narration naturally includes a rich infusion of description. Time and space, as the physicists tell us, are functions of one another. You need space to represent time; you need time to cover space. You may stop your local history to show your reader a building floor by floor, for example, or to consider the impassive face of a news-vendor, framed in his stall by girlie magazines. Remember visual details in both narration and description. Reach for imaginative pictorial metaphors to convey your visual impressions to the reader. Details of sound and feeling will also convey your impressions. Frank A. Worsley does this surpassingly well as he describes his sailing journey, with Sir Ernest Shackleton and four others, in a small boat through grotesquely melting Antarctic icebergs:

They rose and fell on the heaving sea, drawing deceptively apart, then closing with a thud that would have smashed our boat like a gas-mantle between thumb and finger. Castles, towers, and churches swayed unsteadily around us. Small pieces gathered and rattled against the boat. Swans of weird shape pecked at our planks; a gondola steered by a giraffe ran foul of us, which much amused a duck sitting on a crocodile's head. Just then a bear, leaning over the top of a mosque, nearly clawed our sail. An elephant, about to spring from a Swiss chalet on to a battleship's deck, took no notice at all; but a hyena, pulling a lion's teeth, laughed so much that he fell into the sea,

> **whereupon a sea-boot and three real penguins sailed lazily through a lovely archway to see what was to do, by the shores of a floe littered with the ruins of a beautiful white city and surrounded by huge mushrooms with thick stalks. All the strange, fantastic shapes rose and fell in stately cadence, with a rustling, whispering sound and hollow echoes to the thudding seas, clear green at the water-line, shading to a deep blue far below, all snowy purity and cool blue shadows above.***

Narrative is the primary business of accounts like this, and of fiction, of course, but occasionally, as we noted in Chapter 1, an expository essay will give over its entire middle to a narrative of some event that illustrates its thesis. Of this kind is George Orwell's great essay "Shooting an Elephant." Orwell's thesis is that imperialism tyrannizes over the rulers as well as the ruled. To illustrate it, he tells of an incident during his career as a young police officer in Burma, when he was compelled, by the expectations of the watching crowd, to shoot a renegade elephant. Here is a narrative paragraph in which Orwell reports a crucial moment; notice how he mixes external events and snippets of conversation with his inner thoughts, pegging all perfectly with a topic sentence:

> **But I did not want to shoot the elephant. I watched him beating his bunch of grass against his knees, with that preoccupied grandmotherly air that elephants have. It seemed to me that it would be murder to shoot him. At that age I was not squeamish about killing animals, but I had never shot an elephant and never wanted to. (Somehow it always seems worse to kill a *large* animal.) Besides, there was the beast's owner to be considered. Alive, the elephant was worth at least a hundred pounds; dead, he would only be worth the value of his tusks, five pounds, possibly. But I had got to act quickly. I turned to some experienced-looking Burmans who had been there when we arrived, and asked them how the elephant had been behaving. They all said the same thing: he took no notice of you if you left him alone, but he might charge if you went too close to him.†**

---

*Commander F. A. Worsley, *Shackleton's Boat Journey*, Introduction and Notes by Duncan Carse (London: The Folio Society, 1974): 66–67.

†From "Shooting an Elephant," in *Shooting an Elephant and Other Essays* by George Orwell. Copyright © 1950 by the estate of the late Sonia Brownell Orwell; renewed 1978 by Sonia Pitt-Rivers. Reprinted by permission of Harcourt Brace Jovanovich, Inc., and S. M. Heath & Company Ltd. Published in Great Britain by Martin Secker & Warburg Ltd.

Orwell is simply recounting events, and his thoughts, as they happened, one after the other. Almost any kind of essay could use a similar paragraph of narrative to illustrate a point.

DESCRIPTIVE AND NARRATIVE PITFALLS

To select details and get them in order is not so simple as it may seem. Here are four of the most common flaws in descriptive and narrative paragraphs, against which you may check your own first drafts:

1. INSUFFICIENT DETAIL.   A few words, of course, can tell what happened: "I saw an accident." But if the reader is to feel the whole sequence of the experience, he needs details, and many of them. He also needs in the first sentence or two some orientation to the general scene—a topic sentence of setting and mood. The following is the opening of a paragraph from an essay that has already logically discussed its thesis that "haste makes waste." It is not a bad beginning, but a few more details, as we shall see in a moment, would help us know where we are, and at what time of day or night:

> **The sky was very dark. People were walking quickly in all directions. . . .**

2. DETAILS OUT OF ORDER.   The writer of the dark-sky paragraph went on in her next two sentences with additional detail:

> **The sky was very dark. People were walking quickly in all directions. The trees were tossing and swaying about. The air felt heavy, and lightning flickered here and there behind the gray sky.**

But, clearly, the further details are out of order. Although she has said the trees were moving, the air seems to have remained still. She eventually rearranged these details, but not before committing another error.

3. COMMENTS BREAKING INTO THE NARRATIVE-DESCRIPTIVE FLOW.   Our dark-sky student went on to intrude an editorializing comment, and a clever one at that. But she would have been better off letting her details *imply* the moral of the

story. Here is her paragraph, revised after conference, with the opening details of setting filled and rearranged, but with the intruding comment, which she actually deleted, left in italics to illustrate the fault:

> **One day, going home from school, I came to understand for the first time how costly haste can be. The sky was very dark, and people were walking quickly across the streets through the afternoon traffic. The air was heavy, and lightning flickered here and there behind the overcast. Suddenly, a soft wind moved through the trees, setting them tossing and swaying; and then came a great gust, sending leaves and papers scurrying, and rattling shop signs. Wet splotches the size of quarters began to dapple the sidewalk; and then it started to pour. Everyone began to run in a frenzied scramble for shelter.** *People should not lose their heads at the very time they need them most.* **At the street corner ahead of me, two girls, running from different directions, crashed together. A boy riding a bicycle slammed on his brakes to avoid them, and he went skidding, out of control, into the middle of the street. A car caught him squarely. Next day, still stunned, I read in the paper that he had died on the way to the hospital.**

4. SHIFTING VIEWPOINT.   The effect of a shift of viewpoint is about the same as that of the intruding comment. The narrative-descriptive flow is broken. The author seems to have jumped out of his original assumptions, from one location to another, as the italicized sentence shows:

> **My boys of Tent Five were suddenly all piling on top of me on the shaky bunk. I didn't feel much like a counselor, but at least I was keeping them amused. The giggling heap on top of me seemed happy enough. It was organized recreation time, and they seemed pretty well organized.** *The Chief hurried across the camp ground, wondering what was going on over there, and issuing a silent death warrant for the counselor of Five.* **I looked out through a wiggly chink in the heap and saw the Chief in the doorway, with his face growing redder and redder.**

The writer of this paragraph has let his imagination shift from his recollected location on the bunk, beneath the heap of boys, to his reconstruction of what must have been going on in the Chief's head, out on the campground. Similar unwarranted shifts occur when you have been writing *he,* and suddenly shift to *they,* or when you unwittingly shift your tenses from present to past, or past to present.

EXERCISES

2. *Write a paragraph in which you blend the incidents and thoughts of a crucial moment, as in Orwell's paragraph on 80.*

3. *Write two paragraphs that would be part of a longer essay, using the following excerpt from Alfred Kazin's* Starting Out in the Thirties *as a model (notice the effective topic sentence in both paragraphs).*

> The dinner was not a success. I kept trying to see everything through Ferguson's eyes, and I felt that everything looked very strange to him. For the first time, I had brought into our home someone from "outside," from the great literary world, and as Ferguson patiently smiled away, interrupted only by my mother's bringing in more and more platters and pleading with him to *eat something,* I tried to imagine his reactions. We all sat around him at the old round table in the dining room—my father, my little sister, and myself—and there poor Ferguson, his eyes bulging with the strain and the harsh bright lights from the overhead lamp, his cheeks red with effort, kept getting shoveled into him cabbage and meatballs, chicken, meat loaf, endless helpings of seltzer and cherry soda; and all the while I desperately kept up a line of chatter to show him that he was not completely isolated, our cousin Sophie sat at the table silently staring at him, taking him in. In our boxlike rooms, where you could hear every creak, every cough, every whisper, while the Brooklyn street boiled outside, there was a strangled human emotion that seemed to me unworthy of Ferguson's sophistication, his jazz, his sardonic perch on Union Square. But as Sophie sat at the table in her withdrawn silence, my sister stared wide-eyed at the visitor, my mother bustlingly brought in more platters, and my father explained that he had always followed and admired the *New Republic*—oh, ever since the days of Walter Lippmann and Herbert Croly!—I felt, through Ferguson's razor-sharp eyes, how dreary everything was. My father kept slurping the soup and reaching out for the meat with his own fork; since I had warned him that Ferguson would expect a drink, he self-consciously left the bottle of whiskey on the table and kept urging our visitor all through the meal to take another drink. My mother, who did not have even her personal appreciation of the *New Republic* to regale Ferguson with, had nothing to do but bring food in, and after a while Sophie took to her room and barricaded herself in.
> So the meal which I had so much advertised in advance—which I had allowed Ferguson to believe would be exotic, mysterious, vaguely Levantine—passed at last, and after he had charmingly said good-by to my parents and

I walked him back to the subway at Rockaway Avenue, he studied me quietly for a moment and said, "What the hell was so exotic about that?". . . .*

EXPOSITORY PARAGRAPHS

Develop Most Paragraphs by Examples

We naturally illustrate our general ideas with specific examples—through *exposition,* a setting forth, an explaining. To explain beauty, we hold up a rose. Most expository paragraphs follow this natural pattern. But exposition also includes the three more complex modes of illustration and development: (1) comparison and contrast, (2) cause and effect, and (3) classification, which we shall consider in a moment. With simple illustration, however, you begin with your topical assertion. You follow with three or four sentences to show what you mean. You round off with some concluding sentence or phrase. After your topic sentence, you may well fill your whole paragraph with a single narrative illustration, as does Albert Schweitzer in this paragraph from his "The Evolution of Ethics":

> **For the primitive man the circle of solidarity is limited to those whom he can look upon as his blood relatives—that is to say, the members of his tribe, who are to him his family. I am speaking from experience. In my hospital I have primitives. When I happen to ask a hospitalized tribesman, who is not himself bedridden, to render little services to a bedridden patient, he will consent only if the latter belongs to his tribe. If not, he will answer me candidly: "This, no brother for me," and neither attempts to persuade him nor threats will make him do this favor for a stranger.†**

Or you may illustrate your topical assertion with several parallel examples:

> **The undercurrent of admiration in hatred manifests itself in the inclination to imitate those we hate. Thus every mass movement shapes itself after its specific devil. Christianity at its height realized the image of the antichrist. The Jacobins practiced all the evils of the tyranny they had risen against. Soviet**

---

*Boston: Little, Brown and Company, 1965: 45–57. Copyright © 1962, 1965 by Alfred Kazin.

†*The Atlantic Monthly* (November 1958): 69. Copyright © 1958 by The Atlantic Monthly Company, Boston, Mass. Reprinted with permission.

Russia is realizing the purest and most colossal example of monopolistic capitalism. Hitler took the Protocols of the Wise Men of Zion for his guide and textbook; he followed them "down to the veriest detail."*

Your illustration may also be hypothetical, as it frequently is in scientific explanation. "Suppose you are riding along in a car," the scientist will say, as he tries to convey the idea of relative motion. "You drop a baseball straight down from your hand to the floor between your feet." And he continues by explaining that this vertical drop describes a long line slanting downward in relation to the line of the rapidly receding highway beneath the car. After this paragraph, he might have an additional one for each new aspect of relativity, illustrating each by the same dropped ball in its relation to curves in the road, the earth itself, the sun, and to whatever hypothetical platforms he may wish to put into orbit.

EXERCISES

4. *Write two illustrative paragraphs, using the same topic sentence for both. In the first paragraph, illustrate by one extended example, as in the paragraph from a student's paper below. In the second paragraph, illustrate the same point by several different examples. This student would have shortened his illustration from Marlowe, then added similar examples from Shakespeare, Jonson, Kyd, and so forth.*

But if the Elizabethan playwright had to be anything, he had to be a showman who could entertain and delight his audiences with the kinds of spectacle they loved so well. Witness, for example, Christopher Marlowe, whose play *The Tragical History of Doctor Faustus* was one of the most popular plays ever presented upon the Elizabethan stage. The play begins with the protagonist, Dr. Faustus, acquiring supernatural powers by signing a pact with the devil, Mephistopheles, who first appears before the audience "in the shape of a dragon." From that point on, as Faustus exercises his magical power, the stage is filled with showy and miraculous scenes, one after the other. Elaborately costumed angels, clowns, and devils appear. A Pope, Helen of Troy, an Emperor, and The Seven Deadly Sins, all troop across Marlowe's stage. The ghost of Alexander the Great shows up. There are pantomimes, dances, and songs in quick succession. And the sound effects must be exciting too, for fireworks are exploded on stage several times during the play. But, best of all, from the Elizabethan point of view, there is a good lot of violence and vulgar sexual humor sprinkled throughout. Oh, of course, the play ends piously enough: Faustus loses his soul for having bargained with

Topic Sentence

Illustration

---

*Eric Hoffer, *The True Believer* (New York: Harper & Row, Publishers, 1951): 94–95.

the devil. But for two hours, at least, Marlowe gave Faustus—and his Elizabethan audience—a heady excursion through all the pleasures of this world. The fact that the play was enormously popular and frequently revived on the Elizabethan stage is good evidence that Marlowe knew what his audiences wanted and gave it to them.

Comparison and Contrast: Run Similarities Side by Side

Comparison and contrast is another basic order of thought, another natural means of organizing a paragraph—or an entire essay. The process is indeed recurrent. It may be the very basis of thought itself, or at least one of the primary elements. All knowledge involves comparing things for their similarities and noticing their contrasting differences. We group all people together as People, and then tell them apart as individuals.

We instinctively know our friends in this way, for instance. Two of them drift side by side in our thoughts. We are comparing them. They are both boys; they are the same age and stature; we like them both. But one bubbles up like a mountain spring, and the other runs deep. Their appearances, mannerisms, and tastes match their contrasting personalities. One's room is messy; the other's is neat. One races his car; the other collects stamps. We compare the similar categories—looks, habits, hobbies, goals—and contrast the differences. In the process, we have come to know both friends more completely.

Your topic sentence sets the comparison and starts the contrast:

Topic Sentence
Contrast

Opposites seem to attract. My father is tall, blond, and outgoing. My mother is small, and even her dark brown hair, which is naturally wavy, has a certain quiet repose about it. My dad does everything at a cheerful run, whether he is off to a sales conference or off to the golf course with his foursome on Saturday mornings. My mother never seems to hurry. She hums at her work, and the house seems to slip into order without effort. She plays bridge with a few friends, and belongs to a number of organizations, but she is just as happy with a book. When dad bursts in at the end of the day, her face lights up. They grin at each other. They obviously still find each other attractive.

Comparison and Contrast: Illustrate by Analogy

An analogy points up similarities between things otherwise dissimilar. With an analogy, you help your reader grasp your subject by showing how it is like something familiar. Your topic sentence asserts the comparison, and then your paragraph unfolds the comparison in detail:

> **School spirit is like patriotism. Students take their school's fortunes as their own, defending and promoting them against those of another school, as citizens champion their country, right or wrong. Their school is not only their alma mater but their fatherland as well. Like soldiers, they will give their utmost strength in field games and intellectual contests for both personal glory and the greater glory of the domain they represent. And, in defeat, they will mourn as if dragged in chains through the streets of Rome.**

Here is E. B. White describing Thoreau's *Walden.* His comparison shows that analogy is really a form of extended metaphor:

> **Thoreau's assault on the Concord society of the mid-nineteenth century has the quality of a modern Western: he rides into the subject at top speed, shooting in all directions. Many of his shots ricochet and nick him on the rebound, and throughout the melee there is a horrendous cloud of inconsistencies and contradictions, and when the shooting dies down and the air clears, one is impressed chiefly by the courage of the rider and by how splendid it was that somebody should have ridden in there and raised all that ruckus.***

Topic Sentence with Analogy

Analogy Extended

Analogy Extended

That is probably as long as an analogy can effectively run. One paragraph is about the limit. Beyond that, the reader may tire of it.

EXERCISES

5. *Write a paragraph comparing two people—like the one on* 86.

6. *Develop a paragraph by some humorous but apt comparison like E. B. White's above. You might find a helpful model in Mark Twain's two extended analogies—comparisons that clarify the unfamiliar by bringing the familiar alongside:*

---

*From "A Slight Sound at Evening," from *Essays of E. B. White* (New York: Harper & Row, 1977): 235–36. Copyright © 1954 by E. B. White.

But I am wandering from what I was intending to do, that is, make plainer than perhaps appears in the previous chapters some of the peculiar requirements of the science of piloting [a Mississippi steamboat]. First of all, there is one faculty

Topic Sentence

which a pilot must incessantly cultivate until he has brought it to absolute perfection. Nothing short of perfection will do. The faculty is memory. He cannot stop with merely thinking a thing is so and so, he must *know* it, for this is eminently one of the "exact" sciences. With what scorn a pilot was looked upon in the old times, if he ever ventured to deal in that feeble phrase "I think," instead of the vigorous one, "I know!" One cannot easily realize what a tremendous thing it is to know every trivial detail of twelve hundred miles of river and know it with

Comparison

absolute exactness. If you will take the longest street in New York and travel up and down it, conning its features patiently until you know every house and window and lamppost and big and little sign by heart, and know them so accurately that you can instantly name the one you are abreast of when you are set down at random in that street in the middle of an inky black night, you will then have a tolerable notion of the amount and the exactness of a pilot's knowledge who carries the Mississippi River in his head. And then, if you will go on until you know every street-crossing, the character, size, and position of the crossing-stones, and the varying depth of mud in each of these numberless places, you will have some idea of what the pilot must know in order to keep a Mississippi steamer out of trouble. Next, if you will take half of the signs in that long street and *change their places* once a month, and still manage to know their new positions accurately on dark nights, and keep up with these repeated changes without making any mistakes, you will understand what is required of a pilot's peerless memory by the fickle Mississippi.

I think a pilot's memory is about the most wonderful thing in the world. To

Comparison

know the Old and New Testaments by heart and be able to recite them glibly, forward or backward, or begin at random anywhere in the book and recite both ways and never trip or make a mistake, is no extravagant mass of knowledge and no marvelous facility, compared to a pilot's massed knowledge of the Mississippi and his marvelous facility in the handling of it. I make this comparison deliberately, and believe I am not expanding the truth when I do it. Many will think my figure too strong, but pilots will not.*

Comparison and Contrast: Develop Differences Point by Point

Your comparisons present helpful illustrations of your subject by emphasizing similarities. Contrasts, on the other hand, compare similar things to emphasize

*Mark Twain, *Life on the Mississippi*, in *The Portable Mark Twain*, ed. Bernard De Voto (New York: Viking Press, Inc., 1956): 109–11.

their differences—West Germany as against East Germany, for example—usually to persuade your reader that one is in some or most ways better than the other.

The problem in paragraphing such comparative contrasts is exactly what we have already seen with the sheep and goats in Chapter 3 and in the paragraph comparing the outgoing father and quiet mother: the problem of keeping both sides before the reader, of not talking so long about West Germany that your reader forgets all about East Germany. Again, the rule is to run your contrasts point by point, and this you may do in one of two ways: (1) by making a topic sentence to cover one point—agriculture, let us say—and then continuing your paragraph in paired sentences, one for the West, one for the East, another for the West, another for the East, and so on; or (2) by writing your paragraphs in pairs, one paragraph for the West, one for the East, using the topic sentence of the first paragraph to govern the second, something like this:

> **West Germany's agriculture is far ahead of the East's. Everywhere about the countryside, one sees signs of prosperity.** Trucks and tractors are shiny. Fences are mended and in order. Buildings all seem newly painted, as if on exhibit for a fair. New Volkswagens buzz along the country roads. The annual statistics spell out the prosperous details. . . .
>
> **East Germany, on the other hand, seems to be dropping progressively behind.** The countryside is drab and empty. On one huge commune, everything from buildings to equipment seems to be creaking from rusty hinges. . . . The annual statistics are equally depressing. . . .

Topic Sentence
West

Contrast, East

In an extended contrast, you will probably want to contrast some things sentence against sentence, within single paragraphs, and to contrast others by giving a paragraph to each. Remember only to keep your reader sufficiently in touch with both sides.

Here are two paragraphs from a student's paper neatly contrasted without losing touch:

> **In fact, in some respects the commercials are really better than the shows they sponsor.** The commercials are carefully rehearsed, expertly photographed, highly edited and polished. They are made with absolute attention to detail and to the clock. One split-second over time, one bad note, one slightly wrinkled dress, and they are done over again. Weeks, even months, go into the production of a single sixty-second commercial.
>
> **The shows, on the other hand, are slapped together hastily**

Topic Sentence

First Subject

The Contrast

**by writers and performers who have less than a week to put to-
gether an hour show. Actors have little time to rehearse, and
often the pieces of a show are put together for the first time in
front of the camera. Lighting, sound reproduction, and editing
are workmanlike, but unpolished; a shadow from an overhead
microphone on an actor's face causes no real concern in the
control room. A blown line or a muffed cue is "just one of
those things that happen." In all, it often takes less time and
money to do an hour show than to do the four sixty-second
commercials that sponsor it.**

EXERCISES

7. **(a)** *Write a paragraph developed by contrasts, running them point by point, as "students" are contrasted with "athletes" in this paragraph:*

> The most essential distinction between athletics and education lies in the in-
> stitution's own interest in the athlete as distinguished from its interest in its other
> students. Universities attract students in order to teach them what they do not
> already know; they recruit athletes only when they are already proficient. Stu-
> dents are educated for something which will be useful to them and to society
> after graduation; athletes are required to spend their time on activities the useful-
> ness of which disappears upon graduation or soon thereafter. Universities exist
> to do what they can for students; athletes are recruited for what they can do for
> the universities. This makes the operation of the athletic program in which re-
> cruited players are used basically different from any educational interest of col-
> leges and universities.*

(b) *Write two paragraphs contrasting something like high school and college, small
town and city, football and baseball, men and women—the first paragraph describing
one, the second the other, and the two using parallel contrasting terms, as in the example contrasting the two Germanys or the television commercials and shows on 89–90.*

Cause and Effect: Trace Back or Look Ahead

Because is the impulse of your thinking here: "Such and such is so *because. . . .*" You think back through a train of causes, each one the effect of
something prior; or you think your way into the future, speculating about the
possible effects of some present cause. In other words, you organize your paragraph in one of two ways:

---

*Harold W. Stoke, "College Athletics: Education or Show Business?" *Atlantic Monthly* (March 1954):
46–50. Copyright © 1954 by Harold W. Stoke. Reprinted by permission.

1. You state a general effect, then deal with its several causes.

2. You state a general cause, then deal with its possible effects.

In Arrangement 1, you know the effect (a lost football game, or the solar system, let us say), and you speculate as to causes. In Arrangement 2, you know the cause (a new restriction, or abolishing nuclear weapons, let us say), and you speculate as to the effects.

Arrangement 1: Effect Followed by Causes

An unusual cluster of bad luck lost the game. Many blamed Fraser's failure to block the tackler who caused the fumble that produced the winning touchdown. But even here, bad weather and bad luck shared the blame. Both teams faced a slippery field, of course. But Fraser was standing in a virtual bog when he lunged for the block and slipped. Moreover, the storm had delayed the bus for hours, tiring and frustrating the team, leaving them short of sleep and with no chance to practice. Furthermore, Hunter's throwing arm was still not back in shape from his early injury. Finally, one must admit, the Acorns were simply heavier and stronger, which is the real luck of the game.

You will probably notice, as you try to explain causes and effects, that they do not always run in a simple linear sequence, one thing following another, like a row of falling dominoes. Indeed, mere sequence is so famously untrustworthy in tracing causes that one of the classical errors of thought has been named *post hoc, ergo propter hoc* ("after this, therefore because of this"). In other words, we cannot reasonably suppose that *A* caused *B* simply because *A* preceded *B*. The two may have been entirely unrelated. But the greatest danger in identifying causes is to fasten upon a single cause while ignoring others of equal significance. Both your paragraph and your persuasiveness will be better if you do not insist, as some did, that only Fraser's failure to block the tackler lost the game.

In the lost ball game, you were interested in explaining causes, but sometimes your interest will lie with effects. When describing a slum problem, for instance, your topic sentence might be *The downtown slum is a screaming disgrace* (the effect), and you might then in a single sentence set aside the causes as irrelevant, as water over the dam, as so much spilt milk: "perhaps caused by inefficiency, perhaps by avarice, perhaps by the indifference of Mayor Richman." Your interests will dictate your proportions of cause and effect. You might well write an entire essay that balances the slum's causes and effects in equal proportions: a paragraph each on inefficiency, avarice, and the mayor's indifference, then a paragraph each on ill health, poor education, and hopelessness.

Here is how a brief essay, in three paragraphs, can deal with cause and effect alone. I have begun and ended with the *effect* (the peculiar layout of a town). First, I located the *immediate cause* (cattle) as my thesis, and then, in the middle paragraph, I moved through the cause and its *conditions* up to the *effect* again—the town as it stands today:

NORTH OF THE TRACKS

If you drive out west from Chicago, you will notice something happening to the towns. After the country levels into Nebraska, the smaller towns are built only on one side of the road. When you stop for a rest, and look south across the broad main street, you will see the railroad immediately beyond. All of these towns spread northward from the tracks. Why? As you munch your hamburger and look at the restaurant's murals, you will realize that the answer is cattle.

These towns were the destinations of the great cattle drives from Texas. They probably had begun at the scattered watering places in the dry land. Then the wagon trails and, finally, the transcontinental railroad had strung them together. Once the railroad came, the whole Southwest could raise cattle for the slaughter-houses of Chicago. The droves of cattle came up from the south, and all of these towns reflect the traffic: corrals beside the tracks to the south, the road for passengers and wagons paralleling the tracks on the northern side, then, along the road, the row of hotels, saloons, and businesses, with the town spreading northward behind the businesses.

The cattle-business itself shaped these one-sided Nebraska towns. The conditions in which this immediate cause took root were the growing population in the East and the railroad that connected the plains of the West, and Southwest, with the tables of New York. The towns took their hopeful being north of the rails, on the leeward side of the vast cattle drives from the south. The trade in cattle has now changed, all the way from Miami to Sacramento. But the great herds of the old Southwest, together with the transcontinental railroad and man's need to make a living, plotted these Western towns north of the tracks.

Margin labels: Effect, Cause, Conditions, Cause, Effect

Arrangement 2: Cause Followed by Probable Effects

Arrangement 2 is the staple of deliberative rhetoric, of all political and economic forecasting, for instance. Your order of presenting cause and effect is reversed. You are looking to the future. You state a known cause (a new restriction on dormitory hours) or a hypothetical cause ("If this restriction is passed"), and then you speculate about the possible, or probable, effects. Your procedure will then be much the same as before. But for maximum persuasiveness, try to keep your supposed effects, which no one can really foresee, as nearly probable as you can. Occasionally, of course, you may put an improbable hypothetical cause to good use in a satiric essay, reducing some proposal to absurdity: "If all restrictions were abolished. . . . " "If no one wore clothes. . . . " Or the improbable *if* may even help clarify a straightforward explanation of real relationships, as in the following excerpt from *Time* magazine's report on Fred Hoyle, the British astronomer and mathematician who has been modifying Newton's gravity and Einstein's relativity. The paragraph states the general condition, proposes its hypothetical cause with an *if*, then moves to the effects, first in temporal order and then in order of human interest:

> **The masses, and therefore the gravity, of the sun and the earth are partly due to each other, partly to more distant objects such as the stars and galaxies. According to Hoyle, if the universe were to be cut in half, local solar-system gravitation would double, drawing the earth closer to the sun. The pressure in the sun's center would increase, thus raising its temperature, its generation of energy, and its brightness. Before being seared into a lump of charcoal, a man on earth would find his weight increasing from 150 to 300 lbs.**

EXERCISES

8. *Below is a list of statements about the population of the United States, some general, some particular. First arrange them in a suitable order for Arrangement 1 (91); then arrange them again in a suitable order for Arrangement 2. Remember that subordinate points should also follow the order of ascending importance.*

1. An expanding population quickly expends resources and energy for new housing, and often neglects existing housing.
2. The annual death rate has declined slightly since 1960 (a decrease of slightly over one death per thousand of population).
3. Rapidly increasing population overstrains the classrooms in public schools, and has forced enlarged classes and, in some instances, half-day sessions.
4. The birth rate, which had declined from 1965 to 1975 (19.4 to 14.8), began to rise again in 1978 (15.3). By 1981, it had increased 1.3 percent to 15.5.
5. Despite our more recent concern and awareness, and some annual decreases, the total population in the United States has continued to increase since the 1960s.
6. The annual birth rate per thousand of population has declined (16.2 in 1980 compared with the 1960 rate of 23.7). Nevertheless, 3.6 million babies were

born in 1980, almost exactly the same number as in 1965, fifteen years previously.

7. An increasing population strains college facilities; the number of college students doubled between 1960 and 1970 and may be half again as large by 1990.

8. Immigration has increased in recent years: 2,515,479 in the decade 1951–1960; 3,321,770 in 1961–1970; 4,348,998 in 1971–1980, with many thousands of illegal aliens not included.

9. An expanding population forces cities to fill land once used for recreation and crops with shopping centers, streets, and houses.

10. A rapidly expanding population eventually crowds more people into less space, increasing their vulnerability to disease, to squalor, and to strife.

11. The population of the United States was 226,504,825 in 1980, an increase of 11.4 percent since 1970.

9. *Write a paragraph following Arrangement 1, with effect as the topic sentence, followed by causes.*

10. *Write a paragraph following Arrangement 1 that sets causes aside in a sentence or phrase and concentrates on effects.*

11. *Write a paragraph following Arrangement 2, with some cause followed by its probable effects. Work in a hypothetical effect if you can.*

12. *Work up any one of these into a three- or four-paragraph essay, handing in your original paragraph as well.*

CLASSIFICATION

Use the Natural Divisions

Many subjects fall into natural or customary classifications, as if they were blandly jointed, like a good roast of pork ready for carving, contrasting one joint with the next: freshman, sophomore, junior, senior; Republicans, Democrats; right, middle, left; legislative, executive, judicial. You can easily follow these divisions in organizing a paragraph, or you can write one paragraph for each division, and attain a nicely coherent essay. Similarly, any manufacturing process, or any machine, will already have distinct steps and parts. These customary divisions will help your reader, since he knows something of them already. Describe the Democratic position on inflation, and he will naturally expect your description of the Republican position to follow. If no other divisions suggest themselves, you can often organize your paragraph—or your essay—into a consistent series of parallel answers, or "reasons for," or "reasons against," something like this:

> **A broad liberal education is best:**
> 1. **It prepares you for a world of changing employment.**
> 2. **It enables you to function well as a citizen.**
> 3. **It enables you to make the most of your life.**

Many problems present natural classifying joints. Take the Panama Canal, for instance. Its construction divided into three nicely jointed problems, political, geological, and biological, each with its solutions, as the following paragraph shows:

> **Building the Panama Canal posed problems of politics, geology, and human survival from the beginning. A French company, organized in 1880 to dig the canal, repeatedly had to extend its treaties at higher and higher prices as the work dragged on. Uneasy about the French, the United States made treaties with Nicaragua and Costa Rica to dig along the other most feasible route. This political threat, together with the failure of the French and the revolt of Panama from Colombia, finally enabled the United States to buy the French rights and negotiate new treaties, which, nevertheless, continue to cause political trouble to this day. Geology also posed its ancient problems: how to manage torrential rivers and inland lakes; whether to build a longer but more enduring canal at sea level, or a shorter, cheaper, and safer canal with locks. Economy eventually won, but the problem of yellow fever and malaria, which had plagued the French, remained. By detecting and combating the fever-carrying mosquito, William Gorgas solved these ancient tropical problems. Without him, the political and geological solutions would have come to nothing.**

Problem 1

Solution 1

Problem 2

Solution to 2
Problem 3

Solution to 3

You could easily organize this into three paragraphs of problem and solution, with topic sentences like these:

> **The Panama Canal posed three major problems, the first of which was political.**
> **The second problem was geological, a massive problem of engineering.**
> **The third problem, that of human survival, proved the most stubborn of all.**

Any problem and its solution can produce a neatly ordered paragraph—or essay, for that matter: choosing a college, or something to wear (if you want to be light-hearted), making an apartment or a commune work, building the Eiffel Tower or the pyramids. You can often similarly classify sets of comparisons and contrasts, causes and effects, combining your tactics with magnified force.

EXERCISES

13. *Here are a number of topics that fall conveniently into natural divisions. For each topic, list the divisions that occur to you.*

   1. Causes affecting the rate at which a population grows.
   2. Levels of government.
   3. The lunatic fringe.
   4. Undersea exploration.
   5. Geological eras.
   6. Mathematics in public schools.
   7. Governmental response to the Depression.
   8. Inequities in the tax structure.

14. *Write a paragraph using one of the topics and the divisions you have worked out in Exercise 13.*

DESCRIBING PROCESSES

Follow the Natural Steps

Describing a process combines description and narration with classification. This is probably exposition at its most basic intent: explaining how to assemble the Christmas toy, the new hibachi or deck chair, how to build a sun dial or plant a vegetable garden or write an essay. Your subject will again offer natural sequences in space and time and natural divisions in classification. As always, you will find a topic sentence to govern the job. Then you proceed through those steps that will most clearly help your reader to do the job:

> **Growing the iris, the poor man's orchid, is easy. Irises grow almost like weeds in well drained soil, but a little care pays glorious dividends. Plant your rhizomes—the iris root—in early fall. First, enrich your soil with an organic fertilizer low in nitrogen, at about one ounce to the square foot, three weeks before planting. Then plant the rhizomes almost even with the surface. Spruce up each plant in the spring with a quarter of a**

cup of superphosphate. In the fourth or fifth year, dig them up
in late July or early September. Cut off the old tubers with a
sharp knife. Let the hardy tubers harden in the sun for a day.
Then replant them. They bloom long in the spring, and their attractive fans of leaves stand green until fall.

Another passage describing a process is one we looked at in the first chapter:
Sir Isaak Walton's fine one about dressing a chub (16).

In the following paper, a student has nicely amalgamated description, narration, and the classification implied in a problem and its solution to analyze
a fascinating process.

NOTHING PRIMITIVE ABOUT IT

Stonehenge, the gigantic prehistoric construction on Salisbury
Plain in England, cannot fail to fascinate us with a number of
nearly unanswerable questions. How long has it been there?
Who built it? Why? But of all the questions Stonehenge
raises, none is more intriguing than *"How* was it built?"
How did these primitive people, whose only tools were
rock, bone, or crudely fashioned sticks, who had not yet even
discovered the wheel, manage to transport the huge rocks, most
of them more than twenty feet in length and weighing over
thirty tons, more than twenty miles overland? And by what ingenuity did they manage, having transported the rocks, to stand
them on end and support them so that now, thousands of years
later, most of them still stand? What primitive engineering ge-
niuses were these?

    Transporting the stones from their original site at Marlbor-
ough Downs, some twenty miles to the north of Stonehenge,
must have been, by any of the possible means, a very slow process. One possibility is that hundreds of men, some pulling on
the rock, some cutting down trees and filling in holes as they
went, simply dragged the stones over the bare ground. Or perhaps they used snow or mud to "grease" the path. Foot by foot,
and day by day, they may have dragged the rocks all the way
from Marlborough Downs to Stonehenge. Another guess is that
these primitive men, even though they had not yet invented the
wheel, knew about using logs as rollers. If so, perhaps they
mounted each stone on a sledge, and rolled the sledge slowly

Thesis

Problem 1
Description and
Narration

Problem 2

Narrating the
Process

Solutions to 1
First Classification

Second
Classification

forward, workmen placing logs in its path as it moved. Such a method, while a good deal easier than dragging the rock along the ground, would still have required as many as seven or eight hundred men, and perhaps as much as a decade to move all the stones. A third possibility is that the stones were moved along riverbeds, the shallow water helping to buoy the weight, and the muddy banks helping to slide the weight along. Though much less direct than the overland route, the riverbed route would have provided these primitive men with a relatively clear path that ran approximately halfway from the stones' point of origin to their final location. Of course, the point is that any of these three means of transporting the stones must have been an incredibly laborious task, occupying as many as a thousand men, year after year after year.

Lifting the stones into an upright position, once they had been transported, was another triumph of ingenuity and brute strength. Apparently, the workmen dug closely fitted holes where they wanted the stones eventually to stand. Probably they cut away one side of the hole, the side nearest the stone, to form a ramp. Perhaps they also lined the hole with wooden skids. Then gradually they eased the stone down the ramp until it rested in a tilted position at the bottom of the hole. Next, they used brute strength, some men pushing, some pulling on primitive ropes, to raise the rock into a vertical position. If we suppose each man lifted only his own weight, say 150 pounds, it might have taken as many as 400 men to stand the stones upright. Finally, while some workers held the rock in position, others quickly filled in the excavation left by the ramp. For many months afterward they probably refilled and pounded the dirt until it was completely firm. They probably placed the huge transverse pieces across the tops of columns by similarly dragging them up long earthern ramps. The fact that most of the rocks are still standing after thousands of years is testimony of their planning and workmanship.

We may never know quite why these primitive men chose to build Stonehenge, or who the men were. We may never know where they came from, or where they went. In Stonehenge,

however, they have left a testament to their perserverance and their ingenuity. Clearly, they rivaled any of the builders of the ancient world.

EXERCISES

15. *Write a paragraph describing a process you know well—how to make a bracelet, a belt, a cake, how an internal combustion engine works.*

16. *Now find a thesis that will change this described process into an argument making some statement about the subject: making a cake is no child's play; what's under the hood is really no mystery. Rewrite your descriptive-narrative paragraph into a brief three-paragraph essay, using everything you said before and expanding your points with comments rising from your thesis, and with further descriptive and narrative details. Hand in your original paragraph with your essay.*

17. *Using the classifications of problem and solution, write a three- or four-paragraph paper in which you describe the process behind some particularly interesting architectural or engineering accomplishment. Choose any topic you wish. For example, how did architects design the high-rise buildings in San Francisco so that they would withstand the shock of the severe earthquakes of 1971? Or how did medieval man make a suit of armor? Or how do you plan to convert your VW bus into a camper that will sleep four people? In the first paragraph, state the problem as your thesis sentence. Then go on to describe how the problem could be, or was, solved.*

DEFINITION

Clear Up Your Terms

Definition is another mode of classification, in which we clear away hidden assumptions along with unwanted categories. What the Russians and Chinese call a People's Democracy is the very opposite of what the Americans and British call democracy, assumed also to be of and for and by the people. Ideally, your running prose should make your terms clear to your reader, avoiding those definitions that seem too stiff and stuffy, and especially those quoting the dictionary: "As *Webster's* says. . . ." Nevertheless, what we mean by *egotism, superiority, education,* or *character* may need laying on the table.

Richard Hofstadter, for instance, found it necessary in his essay "Democracy and Anti-Intellectualism in America" to devote a number of paragraphs to defining both *democracy* and *intellectual,* each paragraph examining the evidence and clarifying one aspect of his term. Coming early in his essay, after he has set his thesis and surveyed his subject, his section of definition begins with the following paragraph:

But what is an intellectual, really? This is a problem of definition that I found, when I came to it, far more elusive than I

Topic Sentence as Question

What It Is *Not*

What It *Is*

Con: Examples

Pro: Examples

Con: Detailed
Opposition

had anticipated. **A great deal of what might be called the journeyman's work of our culture—the work of engineers, physi-
cians, newspapermen, and indeed of most professors—does not
strike me as distinctively intellectual, although it is certainly
work based in an important sense on ideas. The distinction that
we must recognize, then, is one originally made by Max Weber
between living *for* ideas and living *off* ideas. The intellectual
lives for ideas; the journeyman lives off them. The engineer or
the physician—I don't mean here to be invidious—needs to
have a pretty considerable capital stock in frozen ideas to do
his work; but they serve for him a purely instrumental purpose:
he lives off them, not for them. Of course he may also be, in his
private role and his personal ways of thought, an intellectual,
but it is not necessary for him to be in order to work at his profession. There is in fact no profession which demands that one
be an intellectual. There do seem to be vocations, however,
which almost demand that one be an anti-intellectual, in which
those who live off ideas seem to have implacable hatred for
those who live for them. The marginal intellectual workers and
the unfrocked intellectuals who work in journalism, advertising,
and mass communication are the bitterest and most powerful
among those who work at such vocations***

Try Different Kinds of Definition

Your subject will prompt you in one of two ways, toward inclusiveness or toward exclusiveness. Hofstadter found that he needed to be inclusive about the
several essentials in *democracy* and *intellectual*—terms used commonly, and often
loosely. Inclusiveness is the usual need, as you will find in trying to define *love*
or *loyalty* or *education.* But you may sometimes need to move in the opposite
direction, toward exclusiveness, as in sociological, philosophical, or scientific
discussion, when you need to nail your terms firmly to single meanings: "By
reality, I mean only that which exists in the physical world excluding our ideas
about it."

Such exclusive defining is called *stipulative,* since you stipulate the precise
meaning you want. But you should avoid the danger of trying to exclude more
than the word will allow. If you try to limit the meaning of the term *course* to
"three hours a week a semester," your discussion will soon encounter courses

---

**The Michigan Alumnus Quarterly Review* 59 (1953): 282. Copyright © 1953 by the University of
Michigan.

with different hours; or you may find yourself inadvertently drifting to another meaning, as you mention something about graduating from an "engineering course." At any rate, if you can avoid the sound of dogmatism in your stipulation, so much the better. You may well practice some disguise, as with *properly speaking* and *only* in the following stipulative definition: "Properly speaking, the *structure* of any literary work is only that framelike quality we can picture in two, or three, dimensions."

Definitions frequently seem to develop into paragraphs, almost by second nature. A sentence of definition is usually short and crisp, seeming to demand some explanation, some illustration and sociability. The definition, in other words, is a natural topic sentence. Here are three classic single-sentence kinds of definition that will serve well as topics for your paragraphs:

1. DEFINITION BY SYNONYM.   A quick way to stipulate the single meaning you want: "Virtue means moral rectitude."

2. DEFINITION BY FUNCTION.   "A barometer measures atmospheric pressure"—"A social barometer measures human pressures"—"A good quarterback calls the signals and sparks the whole team's spirits."

3. DEFINITION BY SYNTHESIS.   A placing of your term in striking (and not necessarily logical) relationship to its whole class, usually for the purposes of wit: "The fox is the craftiest of beasts"—"A sheep is a friendlier form of goat"—"A lexicographer is a harmless drudge"—"A sophomore is a sophisticated moron."

Three more of the classic kinds of definition follow, of broader dimensions than the single-sentence kinds above, but also ready-made for a paragraph apiece, or for several. Actually, in making paragraphs from your single-sentence definitions, you have undoubtedly used at least one of these three kinds, or a mixture of them all. They are no more than the natural ways we define our meanings.

4. DEFINITION BY EXAMPLE.   The opposite of *definition by synthesis.* You start with the class ("crafty beasts") and then name a member or two ("fox"—plus monkey and raccoon). But of course you would go on to give further examples or illustrations—accounts of how the bacon was snitched through the screen–that broaden your definition beyond the mere naming of class and members.

5. DEFINITION BY COMPARISON.   You just use a paragraph of comparison to expand and explain your definition. Begin with a topic sentence something like: "Love is like the sun." Then extend your comparison on to the end of the paragraph (or even separate it, if your cup runneth over, into several paragraphs), as you develop the idea: love is like the sun because it too gives out warmth,

makes everything bright, shines even when it is not seen, and is indeed the center of our lives.

6. DEFINITION BY ANALYSIS.   This is Hofstader's way, a searching out and explaining of the essentials in terms used generally, loosely, and often in ways that emphasize incidentals for biased reasons, as when it is said that an *intellectual* is a manipulator of ideas.

Here are four good steps to take in reaching a thorough definition of something, assuring that you have covered all the angles. Consider:

1. What it *is not like*
2. What it *is like.*
3. What it *is not.*
4. What it *is.*

This program can produce a good paragraph of definition:

1

2

3

4

> **Love may be many things to many people, but, all in all, we agree on its essentials. Love is not like a rummage sale, in which everyone tries to grab what he wants. It is more like a Christmas, in which gifts and thoughtfulness come just a little unexpectedly, even from routine directions. Love, in short, is not a matter of seeking self-satisfaction; it is first a matter of giving and then discovering, as an unexpected gift, the deepest satisfaction one can know.**

The four steps above can also furnish four effective paragraphs, which you would present in the same order of ascending interest and climax. The same tactics also work well in reverse order:

What It *Is*

Definition by
Example

Definition by
Analysis

> **Black Power means, for example, that in Lowndes County, Alabama, a black sheriff can end police brutality. A black tax assessor and tax collector and county board of revenue can lay, collect, and channel tax monies for the building of better roads and schools serving black people. In such areas as Lowndes, where black people have a majority, they will attempt to use power to exercise control. This is what they seek: control. When black people lack a majority, Black Power means proper representation and sharing of control. It means the creation of power bases, of strength, from which black people can press to change local or nation-wide patterns of oppression—instead of from weakness.**

> **It does not mean *merely* putting black faces into office. Black visibility is not Black Power. Most of the black politicians around the country today are not examples of Black Power. The power must be that of a community, and emanate from there. The black politicians must start from there. The black politicians must stop being representatives of "downtown" machines, whatever the cost might be in terms of patronage and holiday handouts.***

What It *Is Not*

What It *Is*

Avoid the Pitfalls

1. Avoid echoing the term you are defining. Do not write "Courtesy is being courteous" or "Freedom is feeling free." Look around for synonyms: "Courtesy is being polite, being attentive to others' needs, making them feel at ease, using what society accepts as good manners." You can go against this rule to great advantage, however, if you repeat the *root* of the word meaningfully: "Courtesy is treating your girl like a princess in her *court.*"

2. Don't make your definitions too narrow—except for humor ("Professors are only disappointed students"). Do not write: "Communism is subversive totalitarianism." Obviously, your definition needs more breadth, something about sharing property, and so forth.

3. Don't make your definition too broad. Do not go uphill in your terms, as in "Vanity is pride" or "Affection is love." Bring the definers down to the same level: "Vanity is a kind of frivolous personal pride"—"Affection is a mild and chronic case of love."

EXERCISES

18. *Work out a paragraph defining some term like barometer, computer, class, humanities, intelligence. Avoid the scent of the dictionary. Consider, and use if possible: (1) what it is not like, (2) what it is like, (3) what it is not, and, finally, (4) what it is. See 102.*

19. *Write two independent paragraphs, each defining some term. Use a single-sentence definition (synonym, function, or synthesis) as the topic sentence of the first (see 101). Use a broader definition (example, comparison, or analysis) in your second paragraph (see 101–02). Here is an example to consider as model, along with Carmichael's on 102–03.*

---

*Stokely Carmichael and Charles V. Hamilton, *Black Power, the Politics of Liberation in America* (New York: Random House, 1967): 15.

As the sun was going down, we saw the first specimen of an animal known familiarly over two thousand miles of mountain and desert—from Kansas clear to the Pacific Ocean—as the "jackass rabbit." He is well named. He is just like any other rabbit, except that he is from one third to twice as large, has longer legs in proportion to his size, and has the most preposterous ears that ever were mounted on any creature *but* a jackass. When he is sitting quiet, thinking about his sins, or is absent-minded or unapprehensive of danger, his majestic ears project above him conspicuously; but the breaking of a twig will scare him nearly to death, and then he tilts his ears back gently and starts for home. All you can see, then, for the next minute, is his long gray form stretched out straight and "streaking it" through the low sage-brush, head erect, eyes right, and ears just canted a little to the rear, but showing you where the animal is, all the time, the same as if he carried a jib. Now and then he makes a marvelous spring with his long legs, high over the stunted sage-brush, and scores a leap that would make a horse envious. Presently he comes down to a long, graceful "lope," and shortly he mysteriously disappears. He has crouched behind a sage-bush, and will sit there and listen and tremble until you get within six feet of him, when he will get under way again. But one must shoot at this creature once, if he wishes to see him throw his heart into his heels, and do the best he knows how. He is frightened clear through, now, and he lays his long ears down on his back, straightens himself out like a yard-stick every spring he makes, and scatters miles behind him, with an easy indifference that is enchanting.*

Term

Definition by Synthesis

Function

Comparison

---

*Mark Twain, *Roughing It* (New York: Holt, Rinehart and Winston, 1964): 12–13.

CHAPTER 6

Straight and Crooked Thinking: Working with Evidence

All along, you have been working with evidence to support your thesis and persuade your reader. Evidence is an example, or several examples. Your thesis has, in fact, emerged from the evidence. It has evolved from thinking about the specific things you have experienced, seen, heard, in person, in reading, or on TV. To support that thesis, you have simply turned the process around, bringing in those same specific things, and others, as evidence—descriptive, narrative, and expository. You have been deciding logically on the weight and shape of that evidence, comparing, working out causes and effects, classifying, defining. But your evidence and its connections are always liable to certain logical fallacies that may defeat its persuasiveness.

DEGREES OF EVIDENCE

Write as Close to the Facts as Possible

The nature of *fact*, and of *belief, opinion,* and *preference* poses some problems for the writer. You cannot really present the "hard facts" themselves. You cannot reach through the page to hand out actual lumps of coal and bags of wheat. You can only tell *about* these things, and then persuade the reader to see them as you believe they should be seen. Facts are the firmest kind of thought, but they are *thoughts* nevertheless—verifiable thoughts about the coal and wheat

105

and other entities of our experience. The whole question of fact comes down to verifiability: things not susceptible of verification leave the realm of factuality. Fact is limited, therefore, to the kinds of things that can be tested by the senses (verified empirically, as the philosophers say) or by inferences from physical data so strong as to allow no other explanation. "Statements of fact" are assertions of a kind provable by referring to experience. The simplest physical facts—that a stone is a stone and that it exists—are so bound into our elementary perceptions of the world that we never think to verify them, and indeed could not verify them beyond gathering testimonials from the group. With less simple and tangible facts, verification is simply doing enough to persuade any reasonable person that the assertion of fact is true, beginning with what our senses can in some way check.

Measuring, weighing, and counting are the strongest empirical verifiers; assertions capable of such verification are the most firmly and quickly demonstrated as factual:

> **Smith is five feet high and four feet wide.**
> **The car weighs 2300 pounds.**
> **Three members voted for beer.**

In the last assertion, we have moved from what we call physical fact to historical fact—that which can be verified by its signs: we have the ballots. Events in history are verified in the same way, although the evidence is scarcer the farther back we go.

Facts, then, are those things, states, or events of a kind susceptible of verification. Notice: *of a kind* susceptible of verification. Some perfectly solid facts we may never be able to verify. The place, date, and manner of Catullus's death; whether a person is guilty as accused or innocent as claimed—these may never be known to us, may never be established as "facts," because we lack the evidence to verify them. But we would not want to remove them from the realm of factuality; they are the *kind* of thing that *could* be verified, if only we could get at the evidence.

Believe What You Write—but Learn the Nature of Belief

Facts, then, are things susceptible of verification. Belief presents an entirely different kind of knowledge: things believed true but yet beyond the reach of sensory verification—a belief in God, for instance. We may infer a Creator from the creation, a Beginning from the beginnings we see around us in the natural world. But a doubting Thomas will have nothing to touch or see; judging our inferences wrongly drawn, he may prefer to believe in a physical accident, or in a flux with neither beginning nor end. The point is that although beliefs are unprovable, they are not necessarily untrue, and they are not unusable as you discourse with your reader. Many beliefs, of course, have proved false as new evidence turns up. Nevertheless, you can certainly assert beliefs in your writing, establishing their validity in a tentative and probable way, so long as you do not assume you have *proved* them. State your convictions; support them with the best reasons you can find; and don't apologize. But, for both politeness and persuasion, you may wish to qualify your least demonstrable convictions with "I believe," "we may reasonably suppose," "perhaps," "from one point of view," and the like—unless the power of your conviction moves you beyond the gentilities, and you are writing heart to heart.

Don't Mistake Opinion for Fact

Halfway between fact and belief is *opinion.* An opinion is a candidate for fact or belief, something you believe true but about whose verification or support you are still uncertain. All the facts are not in, you are not sure of the tests, and you may not be sure that there are tests; but you can at least present tentative verification. The difference between fact and opinion, then, is simply a difference in verifiableness. One opinion may eventually prove true, and another false; an opinion may strengthen into belief and then, through verifying tests, into accepted fact, as with Galileo's opinion that the earth moved.

The testing of opinions to discover the facts is, indeed, the central business of argumentation. When you assert something as fact, you indicate (1) that you assume it true and easily verified, and (2) that its truth is generally acknowledged. When you assert something as opinion, you imply some uncertainty about both these things. Here are two common opinions that will probably remain opinions exactly because of such uncertainty:

Girls are brighter than boys.
Men are superior to women.

Although these statements are in *kind* susceptible of verification, we know we will probably never verify them satisfactorily. We know that the necessary tests are difficult, not merely to administer and control, but to agree upon, and we know that the terms *brighter* and *superior* have a range of meaning hard to pin down. Even when agreeing upon the tests for numerical and verbal abilities, and for memory and ingenuity, we cannot be sure that we will not miss other kinds of brightness and superiority, or that our tests will measure these things in any thorough way. The range of meaning in our four other terms, moreover, is so wide as virtually to defy verification. We need only ask "At what age?" to illustrate how broad and slippery the terms *girls, boys, men,* and *women* really are. So in these slippery regions of opinion, keep your assertions tentative with *may* and *might* and *perhaps,* cheerfully admitting the inherent uncertainty of your evidence.

Dispute Your Preferences with Care

Preferences are something else again. They are farther from proof than opinions—indeed, beyond the pale of proof. And yet they are more firmly held than opinions, because they are primarily subjective, sweetening our palates and warming our hearts. *De gustibus non est disputandum:* tastes are not to be disputed. So goes the medieval epigram, from the age that refined the arts of logic. You can't argue successfully about tastes, empirical though they be, because they are beyond empirical demonstration. Are peaches better than pears? Whichever you choose, your choice is probably neither logically defensible nor logically vulnerable. The writer's responsibility is to recognize the logical immunity of preferences, and to qualify them politely with "I think," "many believe," "some may prefer," and so forth.

But that preferences are subjective does not eliminate their general interest, nor remove them from discussion. Because they are immune, because they are strong, and because everyone has them, preferences have a certain validity that repays investigation. The medieval logicians notwithstanding, tastes are indeed worth disputing, because discussing them may lead to assertions demonstrable enough to be, in some measure, persuasive. You will probably never convince a pear person, but you may make a fairly sound case for peaches. I would guess that the annual consumption of peaches exceeds that of pears three to one. And in a best-selling cookbook, recipes for peaches outnumber those for pears three to one. Of course, popularity is no criterion for quality: but a continued preference by large numbers of people, if you can establish that as fact, shows that what had seemed a private preference actually has a public acceptance worth analyzing. Your private taste for peaches may then translate into a perfectly demonstrable thesis: "People seem to prefer peaches to pears." You could probably make even a qualitative judgment stand up, with a thesis something like: "Although chilled pears are delicious, Americans seem to consider peaches more satisfying, as the annual sales figures would indicate."

So go ahead, dispute over tastes, and you may find some solid grounds for them. Shakespeare is greater than Ben Jonson, his friend and greatest competitor. Subjective tastes have moved all the way up beside fact: the grounds for Shakespeare's margin of greatness have been exhibited, argued, and explored over the centuries, until we accept his superiority, as if empirically verified. Actually, the questions that most commonly concern us are beyond scientific verification. But you can frequently establish your preferences as testable opinions by asserting them reasonably and without unwholesome prejudice, and by using the secondary evidence that other reasonable people agree with you in persuasive strength and number.

ASSUMPTIONS AND IMPLICATIONS

Check Your Statements, Root and Branch

Your statements spring from assumptions below the surface and sprout all kinds of unwritten sprigs. These latter, the implications, you can more readily control. Actually, language is at its best when implying more than it says. Irony, for instance, is a constant shadow-play of implication. When you say, "As an officer, he certainly had command of his tailor," you clearly imply that he could command little else. The danger in implications is in not seeing them yourself. If you say "The demonstration was unfair to the management," you must face your implication that the management has been fair to the customers and the help. Keep your eyes open for where your words are pointing, and either trim the pointers or follow them out.

Language naturally looks ahead, so we look for our implications almost by second nature. But we do not naturally check our assumptions, because our whole lives rest on acquired assumptions we hardly think to question: love is better than hate; life is better than death; self-preservation is primary; giving your life for others is good; security is good; success is good; and so on and on. Many of our assumptions conflict, as when our approvals of selfless dedication and of self-sufficiency clash. Sacrifice can be truly selfless, or morbidly self-serving; and selfishness can have a certain forthright honesty that works not too badly in the social mix. As when you first shaped your thesis in Chapter 2, you should continue to check your assumptions to see what your readers, or your opponents, will take for granted, and what they will not grant until proved. If you assume, simply, that football builds character or that socialism ruins it, that some races are inferior or all men equal, you may find your platform shot from under you as the opposition hits the narrowness of your assumptions.

Assumptions and implications can be seen as different ends of the same idea. By assuming that football builds character, you may overlook your implications that other things do not and that "character" means, for you, only a healthy competitive tenacity and a measure of physical courage. Overlooking the full width of the term, you may assume its meaning too narrowly; "character" also means a sense of responsibility, honesty, and humanity, which, along with tenacity and courage, may come readily from other sources. If you acknowledge this breadth of assumption behind your term, you can very well go ahead with the case, arguing that football does indeed build character in certain ways. Perhaps you need merely change your thesis to something like: "Although no magical guarantee, football contributes certain valuable disciplines toward the development of character." You immediately show that you are neither claiming nor assuming more than the reasonable truth. You have found a solid premise.

Assumptions and implications have to do with your thesis, or with any subordinate assertion you make in demonstrating it. Your proof is what makes your assertions stick. Proof is just enough of evidence and reasoning to persuade your readers that what you are saying is true. Usually, as I have already said, all you need is common sense and enough delicacy not to shout "proved" too loudly. Anything within reason goes; but keep in mind the kinds of proving within reason, and the traps beyond reason.

EXERCISES

1. *After each of the following assertions, write two or three short questions that will challenge its assumptions, questions like "Good for what? Throwing? Fertilizer?" For example: Girls are brighter than boys. "At what age? In chess? In physics?" In the questions, probe and distinguish among your facts, opinions, beliefs, and preferences.*

   1. Men are superior to women.
   2. The backfield made some mistakes.
   3. Communism means violent repression.
   4. Don't trust anyone over thirty.
   5. All men are equal.
   6. The big companies are ruining the environment.
   7. Travel is educational.
   8. Our brand is free of tar.
   9. The right will prevail.
   10. A long run is good for you.

ASSESSING THE EVIDENCE

Logical Fallacies: Trust Your Common Sense

From the first, in talking about a valid thesis, about proof, about assumptions and implications and definition, we have been facing logical fallacies—that is, flaws in thought, things that do not add up. Evidence itself raises the biggest question of logic. Presenting any evidence at all faces a logical fallacy that can never be surmounted: no amount of evidence can *logically* prove an assertion because *one* and *some* can never equal *all*. Because the sun has gotten up on time every morning so far is—the logicians tell us—no logical assurance that it will do so tomorrow. Actually, we can take comfort in that fallacy. Since we can never *logically* produce enough evidence for certitude, we can settle for a reasonable amount and call it quits. One piece of evidence all by itself tempts us to cry, "Fallacy! *One* isn't *all* or *every.*" But three or four pieces will probably suit our common sense and calm us into agreement.

Cite Authorities Reasonably

An appeal to some authority to prove your point is really an appeal beyond logic, but not necessarily beyond reason. We naturally turn to authorities to confirm our ideas. "Einstein said . . . " can silence many an objection, since we believe Einstein knew more about physical fact than anyone. "According to Freud" may win your point on human personality, as may an appeal to Winston Churchill or Matthew Arnold or H. W. Fowler on English usage. Shakespeare, the Bible, and Samuel Johnson can authenticate your claims about the ways of the world and the spirit.

Since authority has long since proved itself right, appeals to authority are not beyond reason. But they are beyond logic, because the logical proof that first established the authority has long since retired to the bookshelves. What Einstein said, we tend to take on faith, without demanding proof, which may well be beyond us. The greatest men in the field have accepted Einstein's logic and acknowledged his achievement. Who are we to question that? In this apparent infallibility, of course, reside the hazards of relying upon authority.

Appeals to authority risk four common fallacies. The first is in appealing to the authority outside of his field, even if his field is the universe. Although Einstein had a powerful intellect, we should not assume he knew all about economics too. Even if a chance remark of Einstein's sounds like the quantum theory of banking, you will do best to quote it only for its own rational merits, using Einstein's having said it only as a bonus of persuasive interest; otherwise, your appeal to his authority will seem naïve in the extreme. The good doctor, of the wispy hair and frayed sweater, was little known for understanding money.

The second fallacy is in misunderstanding or misrepresenting what the authority really says. Sir Arthur Eddington, if I may appeal to an authority myself, puts the case: "It is a common mistake to suppose that Einstein's theory of relativity asserts that everything is relative. Actually it says, 'There are absolute things in the world but you must look deeply for them. The things that first present themselves to your notice are for the most part relative.' "* If you appeal loosely to Einstein to authenticate an assertion that everything is "relative," you may appeal in vain—since *relative* means relative *to* something else, eventually to some absolute.

The third fallacy is in assuming that one instance from an authority represents him accurately. Arguments for admitting the split infinitive (see 531–32) to equal status with the unsplit, for instance, often present split constructions from prominent writers. But they do not tell us how many splits a writer avoided, or how he himself feels about the construction. A friend once showed me a split infinitive in the late Walter Lippmann's column after I had boldly

---

The Nature of the Physical World (Ann Arbor: University of Michigan Press, 1958): 23.

asserted that careful writers like Lippmann never split their infinitives. Out of curiosity, I wrote Mr. Lippmann: after all, he might have changed his tune. He wrote back that the split had been simply a slip, that he disliked the thing and tried to revise it out whenever it crept in.

The fourth fallacy is deepest: the authority may have faded. New facts have generated new ideas. Einstein has limited Newton's authority. Geology and radioactive carbon have challenged the literal authority of Genesis. Jung has challenged Freud; and Keynes, Marx.

The more eminent the authority, the easier the fallacy. Ask these four questions:

1. Am I citing him outside his field?
2. Am I presenting him accurately?
3. Is this instance really representative?
4. Is he still fully authoritative?

Do not claim too much for your authority, and add other kinds of proof, or other authorities. In short, don't put all your eggs in one basket; write as if you knew the market and the risks. Every appeal to authority is open to logical challenge.

EXERCISES

2. *Each of the following statements contains at least one fallacious citation of authority. Identify it, and explain how it involves one or several of these reasons: "Outside Field," "Not Accurately Presented," "Not Representative," "Out of Date."*

1. According to Charles Morton, a distinguished seventeenth-century theologian and schoolmaster, the swallows of England disappear to the dark side of the moon in winter.
2. Einstein states that everything is relative.
3. "Nucular" is an acceptable pronunciation of "nuclear." President Eisenhower himself pronounced it this way.
4. War between capitalists and communists is inevitable, as Karl Marx shows.
5. The American economy should be controlled in every detail; after all, economist John Kenneth Galbraith comes out for control.
6. "Fluff is America's finest bubble bath," says Jimmy Connors.

Handle Persistences as You Would Authorities

That an idea's persistence constitutes a kind of unwritten or cumulative authority is also open to logical challenge. Because a belief has persisted, the appeal goes, it must be true. Since earliest times, for example, man has believed in some kind of supernatural beings or Being. Something must be there, the persistence seems to suggest. But the appeal is not logical; the belief could have persisted from causes other than the actuality of divine existence, perhaps only from man's psychological need. As with authority, new facts may vanquish persistent beliefs. The belief that the world was a pancake, persistent though it had been, simply had to give way to Columbus and Magellan. For all this, however, persistence does have considerable validating strength. Shakespeare's supremacy, upheld now for three centuries, and by people of many nations, has considerable force in upholding the assertion that he is, so far, supreme. As with appeals to authority, appeals to persistence are most effective when acknowledged as *indications* of validity rather than as logical proofs and validities themselves.

Inspect Your Documentary Evidence Before Using

Documents are both authoritative and persistent. They provide the only evidence, aside from oral testimony, for all that we know beyond the immediate presence of our physical universe, with its physical remains of the past. Documents point to what has happened, as long ago as Nineveh and Egypt and as recently as the tracings on last hour's blackboard. But documents are only records or traces, not events themselves, and you must be wary of presenting them at face value. Documents vary in reliability. The inscription on tombstone and monument would seem a firmer testimonial than the name in a legend; the diplomat's diary firmer than the public announcement; the eyewitness's description firmer than the historian's summary. You must consider a document's historical context, since factuality may have been of little concern, as with stories of heroes and saints. You must allow, as with newspapers, for the effects of haste and limited facts. You should consider a document's author, his background, his range of knowledge and belief, his assumptions, his prejudices, his probable motives, his possible tendencies to suppress or slant the facts.

Finally, you should consider the document's data. Are the facts of a kind easily verifiable or easily collected? Indeed, can you present other verification? For example, numerical reports of population can be no more than approximations, and they are hazier the farther back you go in history, as statistical methods slacken. Since the data must have been selected from almost infinite possibilities, does the selection seem reasonably representative? Are your source's conclusions right for the data? Might not the data produce other conclusions? Your own data and conclusions, of course, must also face questioning.

Statistics are particularly persuasive evidence, and because of their psychological appeal, they can be devilishly misleading. To reduce things to numbers seems scientific, incontrovertible, final. But each "1" represents a slightly different quantity, as one glance around a class of 20 students will make clear. Each student is the same, yet entirely different. The "20" is a broad generalization convenient for certain kinds of information: how many seats the instructor will need, how many people are absent, how much the instruction costs per head, and so forth. But clearly the "20" will tell nothing about the varying characteristics of the students or the education. So present your statistics with some caution so that they will honestly show what you want them to show and will not mislead your readers.

Averages and percentages can be especially misleading, carrying the numerical generalization one step farther from the physical facts. The truth behind a statement that the average student earns $10 a week could be that nine students earn nothing and one earns $100. A statement in an eminent professional journal that 73 percent of the "cultivated informants" in the North Central States say "ain't I" is actually reporting on a group of only 31 cultivated informants, a mere 11 of whom answered the question about "ain't I"—and only 8 of these used "ain't I." Dividing 8 by 11 does give .73. But put "73 percent" in print, and you seem to have scientific proof that 73 of every 100 cultivated persons say "ain't I," whereas the figure represents merely 8 people in a population of some 35 million. How many of 35 million persons are cultivated, and how we test for cultivation, are questions not easily answered. The statistic also ignores how often the "ain't I" people said "ain't" as against the other alternatives they used, and whether humorously, or accidentally, and so forth. Be wary in presenting your statistics, especially when each number, so firm and final, can conceal variations beyond the reach of calipers and scales.

EXERCISES

3. *Each of the following statistical statements is fallacious in one or several ways, either omitting something necessary for full understanding or generalizing in unsupported ways. Identify and explain the statistical fallacies.*

   1. This car gets thirty-five miles per gallon.
   2. Fifty percent of his snapshots are poor.
   3. Twenty-nine persons were injured when a local bus skidded on an icy road near Weston and overturned. Two were hospitalized. Twenty-seven were treated and released.
   4. Women support this book one hundred percent, but fifty percent of American males are still antifeminist. (In a class of five girls and ten boys, all the girls and five of the boys vote to write about a book entitled *The Stereotyped Female.*)

4. *If baseball is in season, go to the sports page and write a brief explanation of the statistics on batting averages, RBI's, and so forth. Can you find any fallacies—things the statistics do not tell? Or do the same with another sport or subject where statistics are common.*

LOGICAL PROOF: INDUCTION

Keep Your Hypothesis Hypothetical

Induction and deduction are the two paths of reasoning. Induction is "leading into" (*in* + *ducere,* "to lead"), thinking through the evidence to some general conclusion. Deduction is "leading away from" some general precept to its particular parts and consequences. All along, you have been *thinking inductively* to find your thesis, and then you have turned the process around, *writing deductively* when you present your thesis and support it with your evidence. Both modes have their uses, and their fallacies.

Induction is the way of science: one collects the facts and sees what they come to. Sir Francis Bacon laid down in 1620 the inductive program in his famous *Novum Organum, sive indicia vera de interpretatione naturae* ("The New Instrument, or true evidence concerning the interpretation of nature"). Bacon was at war with the syllogism; its abstract deductions seemed too rigid to measure nature's subtlety. His new instrument changed the entire course of thought. Before Bacon, the world had deduced the consequences of its general ideas; after Bacon, the world looked around and induced new generalizations from what it saw. Observed facts called the old ideas into question, and theories replaced "truths." As you may know, Bacon died from a cold caught while stuffing a chicken's carcass with snow for an inductive test of refrigeration.

Induction has great strength, but it also has a basic fallacy. The strength is in taking nothing on faith, in having no ideas at all until the facts have suggested them. The fallacy is in assuming that the mind can start blank, with no prior ideas. Theoretically, Bacon had no previous ideas about refrigeration. Theoretically, he would experiment aimlessly until he noticed consistencies that would lead to the icebox. Actually, from experience, one would already have a hunch, a half-formed theory, that would suggest the experimental tests. Induction, in other words, is always well mixed with deduction. The major difference is in the tentative frame of mind: in making a hypothesis instead of merely borrowing an honored assumption, and in keeping the hypothesis hypothetical, even after the facts seem to have supported it.

Use Analogies to Clarify, Not to Prove

The simplest kind of induction is analogy: because this tree is much like that oak, it too must be some kind of oak. You identify the unknown by its analogy to the known. You inductively look over the similarities until you conclude that the trees are very similar, and therefore the same kind. Analogies are tremen-

dously useful indications of likeness; analogy is virtually our only means of classification, our means of putting things into groups and handling them by naming them. Analogy also illustrates the logical weakness of induction: assuming
that *all* characteristics are analogous after finding one or two analogous. We
check a few symptoms against what we know of colds and flu, and conclude
that we have a cold and flu; but the doctor will add to these a few more symptoms and conclude that we have a virulent pneumonia.

Similarity does not mean total identity, and analogies must always make
that shaky assumption, or clearly demonstrate that the mismatching details
are unimportant. In your writing, you may use analogy with tremendous effect, as we saw when E. B. White compares Thoreau to a gun-slinging cow-
boy (87). But watch out for the logical gap between *some* and *all.* Make sure
that:

1. A reasonably large number of details agree.
2. These details are salient and typical.
3. The misfitting details are insignificant and not typical.

If the brain seems in some ways like a computer, be careful not to assume it
is in all ways like a computer. Keep the analogy figurative: it can serve you well,
as any metaphor serves, to illustrate the unknown with the known, but not to
prove.

Look Before You Leap

The hypothetical frame of mind is the essence of the inductive method, because it acknowledges the logical flaw of induction, namely, the *inductive leap.*
No matter how many the facts, or how carefully weighed, a time comes when
thought must abandon the details and leap to the conclusion. We leap from
the knowledge that *some* apples are good to the conclusion: "[All] apples are
good." This leap, say the logicians, crosses an abyss no logic can bridge, because *some* can never guarantee *all*—except as a general *probability.* The major
lesson of induction is that *nothing* can be proved, except as a probability. The
best we can manage is a *hypothesis,* while maintaining a perpetual hospitality
to new facts that might change our theory. This is the scientific frame of mind;
it gets as close to substantive truth as we can come, and it keeps us healthily
humble before the facts.

Probability is the great limit and guarantee of the generalizations to which
we must eventually leap. You know that bad apples are neither so numerous
nor so strongly typical that you must conclude: "Apples are unfit for human
consumption." You also know what causes the bad ones. Therefore, to justify
your leap and certify your generalization, you base your induction on the following three conditions:

1. Your samples are reasonably numerous.
2. Your samples are truly typical.
3. Your exceptions are explainable, and demonstrably not typical.

The inductive leap is always risky because all the data cannot be known. The leap might also be in the wrong direction: more than one conclusion may be drawn from the same evidence. Here, then, is where the inductive frame of mind can help you. It can teach you always to check your conclusions by asking if another answer might not do just as well. Some linguists have concluded that speech is superior to writing because speech has many more "signals" than writing. But from the same facts one might declare writing superior: it conveys the same message with fewer signals.

The shortcomings of induction are many. The very data of sensory observation may be indistinct. Ask any three people to tell how an accident happened, and the feebleness of human observation becomes painfully apparent. If the facts are slippery, the final leap is uncertain. Furthermore, your hypothesis, which must come early to give your investigation some purpose, immediately becomes a *deductive* proposition that not only will guide your selection of facts, but may well distort slightly the facts you select. Finally, as we have seen with statistics and averages, scientific induction relies heavily on mathematics, which requires that qualities be translated into quantities. Neither numbers nor words, those two essential generalizers of our experience, can adequately grasp all our particular diversities. The lesson of induction, therefore, is the lesson of caution. Logically, induction is shot full of holes. But it makes as firm a statement as we can expect about the physical universe and our experience in it. It keeps our feet on the ground, while it makes remarkable sense of our evidence. The ultimate beauty of science is perhaps not that it is efficient (and it is), but that it is hypothetical. It keeps our minds open for new hypotheses. The danger lies in thinking it absolute.

EXERCISES

5. *Explain the following fallacious analogies and inductive leaps.*

1. The brain is like a computer. Scientists have demonstrated that it, like the computer, works through electrical impulses.
2. This girl has ten sweaters; that girl has ten sweaters. They are equally rich in sweaters.
3. At sixty, Kirk retires with investments and savings worth more than $500,000. He has nothing to worry about for the rest of his life.
4. Every time the Boilers play a post-season game, they lose. They will lose this one.
5. English majors are poor mathematicians.
6. I studied hard. I answered every question. None of my answers was wrong. I have read my exam over again and again and can still see no reason for getting only a C.

LOGICAL PROOF: DEDUCTION

Establish Your Premise

De-ductive reasoning, like the deductive organization of the essay that borrows its structure, leads *away from* your premise, your basic assumption. A premise is a kind of weathered hypothesis, a general idea so well fitted and durable as to seem part of the natural order of things and beyond question: *life is essentially good,* for instance. Deductive reason characteristically operates in those areas of *values* and *qualities* where factual induction finds little to grasp. Induction starts with the particulars and sees what general proposition they make. Deduction, the only other possible way to reason, starts with the general proposition and sees what it implies for the particulars: granted that such and such is true, then these things also must be true. Both methods can fall down when the numbers or words they employ generalize too far from the skin of physical and mental actuality—which we can scarcely reach without them. Like induction, deduction can make some notorious mistakes. The greatest mistake may be in the premise itself. Since deductive reasoning *depends* on your premise—literally "hangs from" it—you must bolt your premise to solid assumptions, or your whole chain of logic will fall in a heap. First check your assumptions with an eye for termites; then attend to the logical linkage.

Deductive reasoning has produced the syllogism, the deducer's standard computer. We are sometimes put off by syllogisms, since they seem a ponderous device for producing what we already know. And when the input is faulty, they tell us that all men are Socrates or that Republicans wear blue neckties. But if you take the syllogism as a machine to test your logical alignment, or to attack the illogic of your adversaries, you will certainly improve the quality of the thoughts you commit to paper.

The *standard categorical syllogism* tests the validity of your classifications—your "categories." When you prove that all men are Socrates, something has gone wrong with your sorting: you should have "Socrates" in some larger class, like "men," and not the other way around. A syllogism does its classifying in three steps, as with this famous example (the typeface differentiates the size of the classes):

> **All MEN are MORTAL CREATURES.**   (major premise)
> *Socrates* **is a MAN.**   (minor premise)
> **Therefore,** *Socrates* **is a MORTAL CREATURE.**   (conclusion)

Socrates (the *minor term*) fits in the larger class of MEN (*middle term*), which fits in the still larger class of MORTAL CREATURES (*major term*).

The first step in classifying by syllogism is to construct a "categorical proposition"—an assertion containing a subject, a linking *is (are, were),* and a predicate nominative (a noun or noun clause that completes the linking *is*), the "predicate term." Your verb, I repeat, must be *is (are, were)* and no other; and it must be completed by a noun or noun clause (the predicate term). Both your subject and your predicate term must be nouns or noun clauses. You must change "Socrates is mortal" *(noun-*is-*adjective)* to "Socrates is a mortal creature" *(noun-*is-*noun);* otherwise you cannot manipulate your predicate term on the same logical plane with your subject. Similarly, to put into a syllogism the assertion that "you can't teach an old dog new tricks," you must manufacture the categorical proposition: "All new tricks are things that you can't teach old dogs." Such prose is atrocious, of course, but syllogisms often must untune the language to get at the logic. If you need to state a syllogism directly in your writing, there it must stand, clumsy or not. But more often you use the syllogism to check a question of logic on the side, and what appears in your paper will be a recasting of the same idea in your best-tuned language.

Now, there are only four kinds of categorical propositions: (texts on logic label them A, E, I, and O):

1. All students are pragmatists, (A).
2. No students are pragmatists, (E).
3. Some students are pragmatists, (I).
4. Some students are not pragmatists, (O).

As you have seen with Socrates, a syllogism has three propositions: (1) a major premise, (2) a minor premise, and (3) a conclusion. Our Socrates-syllogism takes its three propositions from Category 1 ("Socrates" is naturally "all Socrates"). Furthermore, a syllogism always uses three and only three terms: a MAJOR term, a *minor* term, and a MIDDLE term. The syllogism must always begin with the major premise (1), which contains the MAJOR term and the MIDDLE term. It must then assert the minor premise (2), which links the *minor* term with the MIDDLE term. Thus the MIDDLE term appears in both major and minor premises to help relate the *minor* term to the MAJOR term. That relationship is finally expressed in the conclusion (3), which must always state the *minor* term as its subject and the MAJOR term as its predicate, and which must not mention the MIDDLE term at all.

Unfortunately, classification by size does not work out so neatly in syllogisms using propositions of Categories 2, 3, and 4. In these, size of class may be irrelevant. Your minor class could well be larger than your major, as in the conclusion "No men [minor] are workhorses [major]," or "Some girls [minor] are sophomores [major]": the world obviously contains more men than workhorses, and more girls than sophomores. Nevertheless, except for our negative statements, we tend to think uphill, putting smaller into larger

("Some sophomores are girls"), as the traditional terms themselves suggest:
minor ⎯⎯⎯⎯⎯→ MAJOR.

EXERCISES

6. *To warm up, list the major, minor, and middle terms in each of the following syllo-gisms. Remember that the bottom line, the conclusion, will always give you "minor is MAJOR." You will notice (in the third syllogism) that the middle term may serve as either subject or predicate in the major and minor premises.*

   1. All knowledge is something useful.
      Awareness of death is knowledge.
      Therefore, awareness of death is something useful.
   2. No human being is a perpetually happy person.
      All teachers are human beings.
      Therefore, no teacher is a perpetually happy person.
   3. All poisonous plants are things to be avoided.
      Some things to be avoided are mushrooms.
      Therefore, some mushrooms are poisonous plants.

7. *Supply the missing terms for the following valid syllogisms.*

   1. All creatures aware of crime are human beings.
      Criminals are _____.
      Therefore, criminals are human beings.
   2. No fish are mammals.
      Some _____ are sea creatures.
      Therefore, some _____ are not fish.
   3. All respecters of Marx are potential Communists.
      Some faculty members are respecters of Marx.
      Therefore, some _____ are _____.
   4. No _____ are great-grandmothers.
      Girls are people under thirty.
      Therefore, no _____ are great-grandmothers.
   5. Some realists are idealists well seasoned.
      All _____ are _____.
      Therefore, some people of mature years are realists.
   6. No _____ is an astronaut.
      All _____ are teenagers.
      Therefore, no fifteen-year-old is an astronaut.
   7. All beasts of burden are _____.
      _____ are vegetarians.
      Therefore, no tigers are _____.
   8. _____ are carers for their young.
      _____ are mammals.
      Therefore, no fish are _____.

DISTRIBUTING YOUR TERMS

Syllogisms have one more requirement beyond placing major, middle, minor terms. Here for instance is one from Category 3:

Some elected officials are bribe-takers.
Smith is an elected official.
Therefore, Smith is a bribe-taker.

How was that again? Good old honest John Smith? Never! The syllogism follows the rules: (1) major term in major premise, (2) minor term in minor premise, (3) middle term in those two premises only, (4) conclusion stating *"minor* is MAJOR." What has gone wrong? We have another and final principle of classification, a most important one, concerning the "distribution" within each class.

The question of *all* and *some* is at the center of classifying ideas in syllogisms. Indeed, confusing *some* for *all* is at the bottom of most logical fallacies, deductive or inductive, so some practice with distribution will strengthen your logic. In syllogisms, the rules for distributing and not distributing your terms—that is, for making them assert information about *all* members, or only *some* members, of a class—are a little tricky. A term is "distributed," logically, when it includes ("is distributed throughout") *all* members of the group it describes. In the syllogism on 118, "All MEN" is *distributed* ("Some MEN" would be undistributed). MORTAL CREATURES is *undistributed* because it affirms nothing about all mortal creatures. "Socrates" is *distributed,* because he is "all Socrates"; but "MAN" is *undistributed* because it asserts nothing about the entire class of man. Two rules ensure against faulty distribution:

1. Your middle term *must* be distributed at least once.
2. Your minor term may not be distributed in the conclusion ("All," "No") if it is undistributed ("Some") in its premise.

In our elected officials syllogism, we have not kept our eyes on the *all* and *some.* Our middle term, "elected officials," is not distributed in either premise: "Some elected officials" asserts nothing about *all* elected officials; and "Smith is "an elected official" similarly asserts nothing about *all* elected officials. In short, we have fallen into that common fallacy known as "THE UNDISTRIBUTED MIDDLE."

Here are two simple summaries to help you check your distribution:

1. Distributed: "All" terms, and "No" terms, and any terms following "is not" or "are not."
2. Undistributed: Any terms following "some" or "is."

EXERCISES

8. *Copy out the following propositions. Over each term write "D" or "U" for "Distributed" or "Undistributed," and put a 1, 2, 3, or 4 after the proposition to indicate to which
category it belongs.*

1. All mice are warm-blooded creatures.
2. Some teenagers are voters.
3. Some men are not fighters.
4. No activist is a college president.
5. Some air creatures are not birds.
6. All motorists are potential killers.
7. No girls are varsity football players.

THE SIX STANDARD RULES OF THE SYLLOGISM

To round off your practice in deductive logic and the syllogism, and to help
you to sniff out the fallacies in your writing, here are the six RULES OF THE SYL-
LOGISM:

RULE 1.   Use only three terms—*with no shift in sense,* letting a term like *man,*
for instance, shift from meaning "human kind" to "male person." This shift
is called the *Fallacy of Four Terms,* one to be wary of in anything you write.

> Stars are bright creations.
> Some girls are bright creations.
> Therefore, some girls are stars.

That one actually gives us a double four-term fallacy, since some girls *are* stars,
in the movies and elsewhere. This is the point: *don't let your terms shift meaning*—
unless you intentionally shift for a humorous point. Always and ever: make
your words mean what they say, or play meaningfully.

RULE 2.   Distribute your middle term at least once, to avoid the prevalent FAL-
LACY OF THE UNDISTRIBUTED MIDDLE. In other words, that middle term must
at least once affirm something about *all* of its class. The syllogism that made
honest John Smith take bribes failed to distribute *elected officials,* saying something about *all* of them. If we distribute that middle term, saying something
about *all* elected officials, not just some of them, our syllogism becomes
logical:

Elected officials are potential bribe-takers.
Smith is an elected official.
Therefore, Smith is a potential bribe-taker.

Note that in the minor premise, introducing Smith, our *elected official* is undistributed, but that does not matter: we have already distributed it the required once. Note further that every subject *not qualified by "Some"* (or equivalents like *Most, Nearly all, A few, Twenty percent*) is distributed: "Socrates" is "All Socrates"; "Smith" is "All Smith"; "elected officials" is "All elected officials."

RULE 3.   Do not distribute your minor term ("All") in the conclusion *if undistributed* ("Some") *in its premise* (the FALLACY OF ILLICIT PROCESS):

Some Wimbledon winners are Americans.
Some sixteen-year-olds are Americans.
Therefore, all sixteen-year-olds are Wimbledon winners.

RULE 4.   Use only one negative premise, otherwise you conclude with a nonsensical double negative like "Therefore, no pears are not apples."

RULE 5.   If either premise is negative, the conclusion must be negative. The following two examples illustrate how either a "not fish" or a "No _____" in the conclusion would bring them to their senses:

No fish are warm-blooded creatures.
Warm-blooded creatures are air-breathers.
Therefore, air breathers are fish.

Fish are open-eyed sleepers.
No open-eyed sleepers are mammals.
Therefore, mammals are fish.

RULE 6.   If the conclusion is "particular" ("Some"), the syllogism may have only one "universal" ("All" or "No") premise. "Some collectables" would cure the nonsense in the following syllogism:

All collectables are inexpensive items.
All stamps are collectables.
Therefore, some stamps are inexpensive items.

EXERCISES

9. *Evaluate the following syllogisms, indicating which fallacy each contains ("Four Terms," "Undistributed Middle," or "Illicit Process"), or certify it "Valid."*

1. All paper money is a medium of exchange.
   Some beads are a medium of exchange.
   Therefore, some beads are paper money.

2. All media of exchange are tokens of value.
   Some beads are a medium of exchange.
   Therefore, all beads are tokens of value.

3. All media of exchange are commercially useful.
   Some beads are a medium of exchange.
   Therefore, some beads are commercially useful.

4. No cheaters are fair people.
   All blonds are fair people.
   Therefore, no blonds are cheaters.

5. No trustworthy people are people over thirty.
   Some people over thirty are alcoholics.
   Therefore, no alcoholics are trustworthy people.

6. Some meat-eaters are reptiles.
   Some reptiles are constrictors.
   Therefore, some constrictors are meat-eaters.

7. No vegetarians are meat-eaters.
   Some reptiles are meat-eaters.
   Therefore, no reptiles are vegetarians.

8. Some puzzles are nervewrackers.
   All syllogisms are puzzles.
   Therefore, all syllogisms are nervewrackers.

9. All good cooks are seasoners.
   Some seasoners are not girls.
   Therefore, no girls are good cooks.

10. All good cooks are seasoners.
    Some girls are not seasoners.
    Therefore, no girls are good cooks.

10. *Construct syllogisms on the following major premises.*

   1. All good cooks are seasoners.
   2. No cheaters are fair people.
   3. No trustworthy people are people over thirty.
   4. Some puzzles are nervewrackers.
   5. Some meat-eaters are reptiles.

THE CLASSIC FALLACIES

The syllogism helps to display our fallacies, including its special deductive three: the FOUR TERMS, the UNDISTRIBUTED MIDDLE, the ILLICIT PROCESS. But most fallacies in writing—our own and others'—we can uncover simply by knowing they are lurking and using our heads. We must constantly ask if our words are meaning what they say, and saying what we mean. Then we must ask if we are inadvertently taking *some* for *all,* or making that inductive leap too soon or in an errant direction. But logicians have identified six classic fallacies that sum up most of our muddles:

1. EITHER-OR.   You assume only two opposing possibilities: "Either we abolish requirements or education is finished." Education will probably amble on, somewhere in between. Similarly, IF-THEN: "If I work harder on the next paper, then I'll get a better grade." You have overlooked differences in subject, knowledge, involvement, inspiration.

2. OVERSIMPLIFICATION.   As with *either-or,* you ignore alternatives. "A student learns only what he wants to learn" ignores all the pressures from parents and society, which in fact account for a good deal of learning.

3. BEGGING THE QUESTION.   A somewhat unhandy term: you assume as proved something that really needs proving. "Free all political prisoners" assumes that none of those concerned has committed an actual crime.

4. IGNORING THE QUESTION.   The question of whether it is right for a neighborhood to organize against a newcomer shifts to prices of property and taxes.

5. NON SEQUITUR ("IT DOES NOT FOLLOW").   "He's certainly sincere; he must be right." "He's the most popular; he should be president." The conclusions do not reasonably follow from sincerity and popularity.

6. POST HOC, ERGO PROPTER HOC.   ("After this, therefore because of this.") The non sequitur of events: "He stayed up late and therefore won the race." He probably won in spite of late hours, and for other reasons.

EXERCISES

11. *Name and explain the fallacy in each of the following:*

1. Jones is rich. He must be dishonest.
2. He either worked hard for his money, or he is just plain lucky.
3. The best things in life are free, like free love.
4. Sunshine breeds flies, because when the sun shines the flies come out.
5. If they have no bread, let them eat cake. Cake is both tastier and richer in calories.
6. This is another example of American imperialism.
7. Smith's canned-soup empire reaches farther than the Roman empire.

8. *Chips* is America's most popular soap. It is clearly the best.
9. The draft is illegal. It takes young men away from their education and careers at the most crucial period of their lives. They lose thousands of dollars' worth of their time.
10. Women are the most exploited people in the history of the world.

12. *To conclude our excursion into the realms of reason, here is a short essay by a university professor with a law degree. Naturally, it is not unreasonable. Yet it does rest on some unexamined assumptions, and a fallacy or two. Question it as rigorously and reasonably as you can. Some questions at the end will help you turn up some fallacies and crooks in the thinking.*

BILINGUALISM*

The pledge that we are "one nation, indivisible" (let alone "with liberty and justice for all") has always masked an anxiety that the unity of the United States might rest on sand. Depending on one's ideological preferences, one can emphasize cleavage—and thus disunity—based on region, religion, class, or ethnicity. Yet if there is one assumption of commonality most of us share, it is that we speak the same language. Whatever other cleavages separate us, the United States has at least been spared the linguistic conflict of countries like Canada, Belgium, and India. To be "American" has meant, in this century at least, to speak English.

One of the major political issues of the 1980s will be the tenability of this assumption of a common language. *Time* magazine has pointed out that blacks are no longer this nation's largest minority group but rather brown-skinned persons of Hispanic or Puerto Rican descent. (Indeed, it is difficult even to find a common word suitable for use, since Chicano, Mexican-American, Hispanic, Cuban-American and Puerto Rican are used by different groups and carry different meanings.) And the one common attribute of many of these Americans is that they do not speak English. Southern California, South Texas, and South Florida all contain many American citizens who are monolingual in Spanish. During his recent trip to Mexico City, President Carter began a speech with "As President of the fourth largest Spanish-speaking nation. . . ." Increasingly, we shall be asked whether we wish to recognize the legitimacy of such monolingualism by moving, in at least these states, to a truly bilingual polity.

Most bilingual programs are now based on the assumption that they are aids to those persons who wish (or are required) to learn English. This might be termed "instrumental" bilingualism, and the non-English language is recognized only to the extent that it aids in learning English. But it is obviously open to question whether it is legitimate to expect all American citizens to master English, especially if the numbers of Spanish speakers are large enough. One can read Spanish newspapers, listen to Spanish radio and television programs, and otherwise lead a rich life in a number of American cities without needing to know the culturally dominant language.

---

*This is Sanford Levinson's contribution to "Bilingualism: A Symposium," *The Nation,* 17 March 1979. Reprinted by permission of *The Nation.*

Do we wish to encourage this? Let me suggest several forms that future controversies might take. Does government, whether state or Federal, have a duty to print its materials in Spanish as well as English? Does it deny equal protection of the laws by assuming that all American citizens are responsible for knowing English? A dozen years ago, Congress casually passed a statute that had the effect of enfranchising many Puerto Rican-Americans living in New York State by making completion of six grades of Spanish-language schools in Puerto Rico sufficient to meet the literacy requirements. One doubts that such a bill would sail through so easily today. Nor should it, since at the very least we should debate the implications of such bilingualism.

In this light, one might reconsider some of the issues raised by the Bakke case and the problem of affirmative action.* The University of California Medical School at Davis gave some preference to Mexican-Americans in regard to admission. The rationale was underrepresentation of Mexican-Americans in the medical field in California. Given this rationale, no effort was made to distinguish between the claims of Mexican-Americans, blacks, Asian-Americans, or Native Americans, the other beneficiaries of Davis's plan.

But consider the following proposal: Given the number of American citizens who speak only Spanish—and the relative shortage of Spanish-speaking doctors—it is thoroughly justifiable that Davis (or any other medical school) give an affirmative preference to those applicants, otherwise qualified, who score well on a language test based on the Spanish spoken, say, in Los Angeles, San Antonio, or Miami. The rationale is *not* compensation for past injustice; rather, it is based on the recognition that good medical service depends on the ability of a doctor to understand the patient. If ordinary citizens are not to be required to learn English, then the state can (indeed, *must*) take this into account in allocating its resources, including medical training. It is not even unthinkable that classes be taught in Spanish—if, that is, we become a truly bilingual nation.

Racial or ethnic identity would play no part in admissions to such a program; Spanish-speaking Anglos would presumably be free to apply. It would, therefore, seem to be immune to the constitutional criticisms leveled by Justice Powell against the Davis plan in his Bakke opinion. But determining the constitutionality of a program does not decide its wisdom.

Conversations I have had with all manner of people from high school students to professors of law lead me to believe that few issues are more volatile than bilingualism. Almost none of the arguments that apply to affirmative action are transferable, in part because most of the advocates of affirmative action remain integrationist in their vision of America's future. To accept the premises of strong bilingualism means accepting the fact that large numbers of one's fellow citizens simply have no desire (or ability) to communicate in the most effective manner possible—the speaking of a common language. It means an ultimate rejection of the premise that we are indeed a united nation in favor of the recogni-

---

*On 28 June 1978, the U.S. Supreme Court ruled in favor of Allan Bakke in his suit for admission to medical school at the University of California's Davis campus. Bakke, a white, claimed racial discrimination because the school refused him but admitted several minority students with scores lower than his. Bakke graduated with an M.D. on 4 June 1982.

tion that we are a congeries of groups joined together, often uneasily, in a political alliance.

The last twenty years have not seen the triumph of a vision of one world (or even one nation); instead, we are seeing a repeat of the nineteenth-century infatuation with nationalism. It remains to be seen how the United States will respond to its new largest minority—or how this minority will respond to the linguistic hegemony of the majority.

Write a critique of Levinson's reasoning, or an essay in reply. Consider the following questions. Where does the author stand? What would be his answer to "Do we wish to encourage this?" (fourth paragraph). Why is this question rhetorically misleading—in other words, what response does such a question usually invite? How about the other questions in this paragraph? What fallacy do you see in the phrase a rich life?

What unexamined assumptions and what non sequitur do you see in the assertion that a large Spanish-speaking minority, containing "many American citizens who are monolingual in Spanish," will produce "one of the major political issues of the 1980s"? How tenable is the assumption that the common language of the United States is English? What does the author assume about the legitimacy of requiring English for citizenship? What is the fallacy in Levinson's assumption that all monolingual Spanish-speakers are qualified for citizenship?

In speaking of the Bakke case, what does the author assume about "applicants otherwise qualified"? (Bakke demonstrated that he was excluded though better qualified.) What fallacy do you see in Levinson's assumption that giving preference to Spanish-speaking medical students would provide better communication between doctor and patient? What does bilingualism suggest for other non-English-speaking minorities? For speakers of Black English? How valid is Levinson's claim that racial or ethnic identity would play no part in preferring Spanish-speakers? How relevant is Levinson's assumption that admitting Bakke was unwise? What fallacy do you see in his assumption about nationalism?

CHAPTER 7

Getting Things in Order: Outlining

OUTLINES FOR WRITING: FIRST STEPS

The first thing to grasp about outlines is that they seldom work out to the letter. The second is that they always help. The third is that the headings do not represent equal space in the finished essay: one heading may become two paragraphs and the next only two sentences. The fluid pressure of writing will always force revision of your best-laid plans. An incidental sentence may swell into an entire section; a scheduled section may end up scrapped. But an outline helps you lay things straight. It helps you to spot gaps in your own argument and in the arguments of others, to test the relationships of parts, to certify a thesis, to validate an assertion. Outline your reading, and you will really grasp it. Outline the plan of your essay, and you straighten out your thinking for your reader to grasp.

We think and write largely by free association, but to explain these thoughts fully to our readers, and to ourselves, we need to discover and outline their logical pattern. Since shorter papers usually grow by themselves, once the thesis is set, an outline is an excellent test of the first draft for structure, for logic, for *pros* and *cons*, for ascending interest, and for helping us to revise to perfection. For longer papers, outlining before writing helps immeasurably, generating aspects for consideration and research, and straightening out our logic. With the logic down on paper, we can write from heading to heading, sure of our direction, with an order of ascending interest. We can push aside the good ideas constantly crowding in: our outline has already scheduled a place for them up ahead, each where it will be most logical and effective.

129

Begin Your Paper with a Jotted Outline

With a firm thesis and a short paper, you may need no outline at all, or one to check your first draft, as I have said. Nevertheless, even with only three points to make, jotting them down will help you arrange them for ascending interest, and will probably turn up another point or two as well. Take a sheet of paper. Think up a good title. Put down your thesis. If it is firm and assertive, it will win much of your battle with logic at the very beginning. Jot down your points, rearranging as you go. And, lo and behold, you almost have a completed essay. One tactical point: adjusting your headings to make them grammatically parallel will keep your reasoning running clearer as you write, all *-ing* phrases for instance: *Getting up, Going to class, Organizing free time;* or *Income, Expenses, Taxes, Savings.* Explanatory phrases after each of these headings, also grammatically parallel, make your jotting complete. Here is a jotted outline for a paper favoring a flat-rate income tax. The student, being an economics major, saw the moral objections as taking a smaller portion of her data and ideas, thus more suitably coming first.

THE FAIREST TAX: FLAT IS BEST

THESIS: Despite some personal and economic objections, taxing all income at a flat rate for everyone is both fairer and more feasible than the present graduated system.

1. **Moral objections—unfairness, taxes middle brackets more, upper brackets less.**
2. **Economic objections—reduction in necessary sheltered investments, like oil, synfuels, rental property, and in support for charities, churches, universities.**
3. **But moral benefits—fair-sharing, reduces cheating, improves responsibility.**
4. **Economic benefits—nontaxed underground economy diminished, less costly, lower interest rates, more money to spend and save.**

Notice how easily you may now convert this outline into an essay. The subordinate clause—"Despite . . . objections"—in your thesis has set aside the concessions you must make to the opposition, and the main clause—"flat rate . . . is . . . fairer and . . . more feasible"—has asserted the main point. The jotted main headings fall neatly into place, each grammatically parallel, each a noun with its adjective ("moral objections"), each structurally equal, and the four effectively balanced—two for opposition, two for affirmation. The lesser elements of your explanation are also in parallel—*unfairness, reduction, fair-sharing,* for example—to indicate equivalent treatment. With your paper's structure firmly before you, now you are free to write it out.

Outline Your Exam Answers

The jotted outline helps immensely in answering essay questions, particularly because it hangs on a thesis, which is the real secret of organizing any information whatever. Find your Big Idea; then jot down the points you want to cover, quickly saving best for last—the one you know best and can cover most fully.

Here is the trick: MAKE YOURSELF ANSWER THE QUESTION IN ONE SENTENCE. However well or poorly you are prepared, this forces all you know on the subject to its widest dimension. If you start your answer with this sentence, even desperately throwing in any old detail as it comes (as I used to do until I hit on the one-sentence idea), every detail will seem to illustrate your opening declaration, and your instructor will say, "Now *this* one is organized—a real grasp of the subject." So, start your answer with your seminal sentence, and your answer will sound like an essay. With a few points jotted to attain an ascending order of importance, it will sound even more so. It will indeed *be* an essay, in seminal form. Your instructor, after all, needs no introduction.

Next point: incorporate the language of the question in your one-sentence opener. This works even with the broadest kind of question—those barn doors opened so wide you can drive in any kind of load:

1. **Discuss the fall of the Roman Empire.**
2. **What is the most valuable thing you have learned in this course?**
3. **Demonstrate your knowledge of the materials of this course.**

Your one-sentence openers might go like this:

1. **The Roman Empire fell because of decay from within and attack from without.**
2. **The most valuable thing I have learned this semester is that people usually conceal their true motivations from themselves.**
3. **The materials of this course illustrate biological evolution, particularly the role of mutation in the survival of the fittest.**

Jot down your points, quickly arranging for ascending order, and you are off and running.

EXERCISES

1. *Write an essay from the outline on taxes on 130, if you wish, or make a comparable jotted outline on a subject you prefer. Then write an essay from it, handing in both.*

THE TOPIC OUTLINE

The topic outline is the most common, an arranging of your jotted thoughts into heads and subheads, each rank in parallel phrasing. The major headings rise in ascending importance, but their minor headings descend in smaller and smaller components. You alternate numbers and letters, proceeding from Roman numeral *I* through capital *A* to Arabic *1* and little *a,* until you reach, if you need them, parenthesized *(1)* and *(a)*, and finally lower-case Roman numerals. You indent equal heads equally, so that they fall in the same column, Roman under Roman, capital under capital, and so on:

I. _____

   A. _____

      1. _____

      2. _____

   B. _____

      1. _____

         a. _____

           (1) _____

              (a) _____

              (b) _____

                 i _____

                 ii _____

           (2) _____

         b. _____

      2. _____

II. _____

You will probably need no more than the Roman headings—*I, II, III*—with an *A, B,* and perhaps a *C* under each, but you arrange the *1*'s and *a*'s, the *(1)*'s and *(a)*'s, and the *i*'s and *ii*'s on the same scheme if you need them.

Check Your Outline for Balance

Ideally, every *I* should have its *II*, every *A* its *B*, every *1* its *2*, since an unpaired heading suggests that it is a detail too small for separate treatment, really a part of the larger heading above. For instance:

POOR	**GOOD**
II. Value of cats **A. As pets**	**II. Value of cats as pets**

III. Kinds of cats
    A.____
    B.____
	III. Kinds of cats
	    A.____
	    B.____

One of your first revisions should be to absorb any such unpaired heading into its related major heading. Then see that each heading is a noun (or noun phrase), with or without modifiers: "Benefits," for instance, or "Benefits to the individual." This will keep your outline parallel. You can signal your major turns by adding a *But* or *Nevertheless.* Note that "Introduction" and "Conclusion" are *not,* repeat *not,* headings in your outline. You are outlining ideas, not parts of structure.

Now for a topic outline of your projected essay on taxes. This will produce a bigger paper than your jotted outline, one with more thought and probably some reading and research added. Looking at your jotted outline and working it into topical order will suggest all sorts of things to include and look into. Suppose we start with the title and thesis and see where sorting and matching the topical headings will take us.

THE FAIREST TAX: FLAT IS BEST

THESIS: Although a graduated income tax relieves the poor and does not hurt the rich, taxing everyone at a flat rate is generally fairer and economically better.

I.   **Adverse effects**
   A.   **Ethical objections**
      1.   **Disproportionate burden**
         a.   **Poor**
         b.   **Middle-income**
         c.   **Rich**
      2.   **Disproportionate hardship**
         a.   **Charities**
         b.   **Churches**
         c.   **Universities**
         d.   **Social reforms**
   B.   **Economic objections**
      1.   **Reduction in benefits**
         a.   **Decrease in governmental income**
         b.   **Decrease in some private expenditure**

        (1) **Personal spending now interest-deductible**
           (a) **Cars**
           (b) **Housing**
        (2) **Decrease in investment now sheltered**
           (a) **Exploration for oil and gas**
           (b) **Alternate energy**
              i.   **Synfuel**
              ii.   **Solar energy**
           (c) **Rental construction**
              i.   **Government-supplemented housing**
              ii.   **Office space**
              iii. **Factories**
              iv. **Warehouses**
     c. **Decrease in some economic stimulation**
        (1) **Jobs**
        (2) **Business**
        (3) **Raw materials**
II. **But: beneficial effects**
  A. **Ethical benefits**
    1. **Fair sharing**
      a. **Elimination of resentment**
      b. **Reduction of cheating**
      c. **Reduction of underground economy**
        (1) **Greenback payments**
        (2) **Trades**
           (a) **Goods**
           (b) **Services**
      d. **Exemptions for the poor**
    2. **Responsibility**
  B. **Economic benefits**
    1. **Reduction of costs**
      a. **Personal**
        (1) **Time**
        (2) **Expert assistance**
      b. **Governmental**
        (1) **Printing forms and instructions**
        (2) **Mailing**
        (3) **IRS staffing**
           (a) **Advisory**
           (b) **Investigative**
           (c) **Legal**
        (4) **Prosecution**
    2. **Increase in income**
      a. **Governmental increases**

                 (1) Increases from reduced evasion
                      (a) In filing
                      (b) In underground economy
                 (2) Increases in number of payments
            b. Personal increases
                 (2) Increases from reduced taxes
                 (3) Increases in pay as the economy is stimulated
        3. Stimulated economy
            a. Reduction in interest rates
                 (1) Less personal borrowing for taxes
                 (2) Less governmental borrowing for administration
            b. Increase in personal income
                 (1) Spending
                 (2) Saving
                 (3) Investing

    We have discovered quite a number of things as we sought out matching topical headings, and will discover more as we write them out. Our balanced topics will coalesce as we argue *pro* and *con,* picking up items from *"II"* to answer objections in *"I,"* but we have the topics pretty well sorted before us. You will notice some necessary repetition, as the underground economy, for instance, figures both ethically and economically. You will also notice that under *"B. Economic benefits"* we have switched the order of *"Personal"* and *"Governmental"* under *"1"* to *"Governmental"* and *"Personal"* under *"2"* because the personal benefits become the more compelling as we move to conclusion. Note, too, that the stimulated economy serves as a transition from personal higher pay to the generally happy economy we see as the triumphant result of our flat-rate tax.

EXERCISES

2. *Work up a topic outline on some subject that interests you—affirmative action, nuclear power, the draft, regular exercise. Save it for Exercise 3.*

THE SENTENCE OUTLINE

In the sentence outline, you phrase each heading as a complete sentence. Such an outline lays out the plan of your essay as no other can, giving the fullest statement of your ideas, and showing clearly and explicitly the logical relation of parts. Often a required procedure in the assigned research paper, the sentence outline is useful for leading you through organizational intricacies and saving you from logical snares. Because it forces you to think out your plan so thoroughly beforehand, a good sentence outline can speed the actual writing of any essay that depends greatly on logical structure. But outlining in sentences consumes your time—and therein lies the danger. The outlining may leave too little time for the writing. A few experiments in the form, however, should help you decide when to use it to your advantage. An initial topic outline is often helpful, though not always necessary.

A sentence outline for your tax essay would begin like this:

THE FAIREST TAX: FLAT IS BEST

THESIS: Although a graduated income tax relieves the poor and does not hurt the rich, taxing everyone at a flat rate is generally fairer and economically better.

I.   **A flat-rate tax raises both ethical and economic objections.**
    A. **The fairness it claims is far from perfect.**
        1. **The burden remains disproportionate.**
            a. **The poor, unless exempted, would pay by far the largest portion of their buying power.**
            b. **Middle-income earners would also pay a larger portion than the rich.**
            c. **The rich, though paying many more dollars, would nevertheless pay much the smallest portion of their buying power.**

Remember, each heading, whether in a jotted, topic, or sentence outline, will require widely differing amounts of space as you write out your essay. Your second paragraph, in which you enter your Middle by facing the opposition, would probably absorb everything but heading *b* in its first two sentences:

> **Of course, a flat-rate tax raises both ethical and economic objections. The fairness it claims is far from perfect, burdening the poor, unless exempted, and letting the rich off very lightly. . . .**

Your next paragraph might combine four headings in its topic sentence:

> **Admittedly, a flat-rate tax would visit some budgetary stringencies on charities, churches, universities, and other worthy causes now inviting tax-exempt gifts.**

And then your next paragraph would probably begin with admitting reductions in certain economic benefits governmental and private. But the outline, as always, helps you to think and write your way through the logical framing of your problem with its answering parts and partitions.

EXERCISES

3. *Take your topic outline from Exercise 2 and make it into a sentence outline. Then convert the whole into an essay, handing in all three.*

OUTLINES FOR READING

Outlining is additionally useful in analyzing the logical structure of a printed essay and coming to understand it. Having first read for meaning, you then outline the structure of that meaning, discovering ideas, connections—and lapses—not at first apparent. First, you boil the essay down to its true thesis, in one sentence. Then you go through the essay, writing out a series of topics that identify the key ideas as they come along. Finally, to make a full topic outline, you grade and group your topics into what seem to be their major and minor hierarchies, probably recasting some *A*'s for *I*'s, some *I*'s for *B*'s, and so forth.

Making a sentence outline really masters an essay for you. You discover the essay's parts; you summarize them in clear sentences; you work out their logical relationships—and probably discover those logical lapses. Sometimes you use the author's words, but usually you compress them into a sentence of your own for greater clarity. You will have made the writer's thoughts and their relationships your own.

Let's consider a sentence outline of a remarkable piece by a remarkable man: Benjamin Lee Whorf (1897–1941), graduate of MIT, chemical engineer, officer of Hartford Fire Insurance Company. His compelling interest in life's overwhelming question, in meaning, and in Biblical translation, turned him into one of America's most seminal linguists. This brief handwritten essay,* found among his papers at his death at forty-four, written probably in 1927, is clearly incomplete: he wanted to explain the symbolic importance of language. Nevertheless, it illustrates how well the literate mind organizes its

---

*Entitled "On Psychology" by Whorf's editor. In *Language, Thought, and Reality,* ed. John B. Carroll (Cambridge, Mass.: The MIT Press, 1956): 40–42. Copyright © 1956 by the Massachusetts Institute of Technology. Reprinted by permission of the MIT Press, Cambridge, Massachusetts.

thoughts. Read it as if you were assigned to outline it. Then check your ideas against my sentence outline that follows.

Psychology has developed a field of research that may no doubt be useful or valuable in itself, but it throws little or no light on problems of the normal human mind or soul. The person who wishes to understand more fully the laws and, so to speak, topography, of the inner or mental life is as much thrown back on his own difficultly acquired store of wisdom and his native judgments, intuitions, sympathies, and common sense as though the science of psychology did not exist. Such a one, for instance, is the teacher, educator, sociologist, anthropologist, trainer, coach, salesman, preacher, manager, diplomat, executive: anyone who must deal with human intangibles, especially the man concerned in leadership of any sort. If he seeks aid from books, he will get far more information about this field from literature not intended to be scientific, that is, from the best works of the novelists, playwrights, and poets, than he will from any textbook of psychology. There are certain courses that psychology has elected to follow that have estranged it, perhaps permanently, from the truly mental field.

First, the "old school" of experimental laboratory psychology has rather definitely assumed the character of a branch of physiology. Its findings and their value all redound back to physiology. It is undoubtedly valuable to the student of mental phenomena to know the mechanisms of the body, but rather in the character of auxiliary information than anything else; and knowledge about the oxidation of the blood and the details of brain and nerve responses, sense perceptions, and association times are equally of this character. Moreover, one is impressed (and depressed) by the appalling sterility of the vast mass of minutiae that this science accumulates, and the dearth of integrating principles.

Second, the school of behaviorism has begun to appear in its true character as simply the old experimental psychology over again in a more pick-and-shovel aspect. That it is in many ways an improvement on the old school and has enlarged our understanding in certain fields I personally believe. It has been of service by teaching us to think more in terms of behavior,

but, when all is said and done, it can teach us little that is new. It has shown us how behavior may be conditioned by physical means, but along much the same lines that we already knew although they have been more systematically explained. It has become apparent that we may "condition" either with or against the cooperation of truly psychic considerations. This we already knew, but we are particularly interested in "conditioning" WITH the cooperation of and in accordance with the particular laws of the psychic. No doubt the same process of stimulus and response "conditions" a man into being a scientist or a maniac, a leader of men or a nervous wreck, a good workman or one who cannot hold a job, an inspiring helper or a resentful cog in the machine; but behaviorism does not show us which lines to work upon in order to be really in accord with human intangibles, except by way of announcing in behavioristic terms things already obvious to common sense.

Gestalt psychology* does seem to me to have discovered an important truth about mind, the importance of configurations in the mental domain. At the same time, the Gestalt psychologists have their hands full with the manifold mechanical, experimental, and personal data required to develop this large subject, most of which data are chiefly valid on the animal level. When we attempt to apply the configurative principle to the understanding of human life, we immediately strike the cultural and the linguistic (part of the cultural), especially the latter, as the great field par excellence of the configurative on the human level. Here the Gestalt psychologists let the matter drop. They have neither the time nor the linguistic training required to penetrate this field; moreover their ideas and terminology inherited from the old laboratory psychology are a liability rather than an asset.

Psychoanalysis is the one school that really deals with mental material, and it sometimes gets results, but it works only in the sphere of the abnormal and the deranged, and it is becoming evident that the abnormal is not the key to the normal. Moreover, it is so resolute in its determination to deal with intangibles that it shows almost a contempt for the external world

---

Gestalt is German for "form." This theory holds that a total configuration of impressions and concepts has a significance not derivable from any of its parts.

and strays continually into the realms of phantasm. It is too heavily stamped with the signature of its founder, Freud, an erratic genius with a faculty of apperceiving deep but obscure truths, and is notion-obsessed and cluttered with weird dogma. As an empirical tool for the clinic it may serve for a while, but I do not see how it can possibly be a means for the careful scientific scrutiny of the normal mind.

All the schools then have been surveyed and found wanting, and the seeker for knowledge about the human mind is forced to fall back on the long-collected mass of empirical observations sometimes called "the wisdom of the ages," on the works of keenly intuitive authors, on his own insight, and on what few general truths he can cull here and there from all the above schools.

One fact that stands out to a detached viewpoint, but is not stressed by any of the schools, is the great perhaps basic importance of the principle we denote by the word "meaning." Meaning will be found to be intimately connected with the linguistic: its principle is symbolism, but language is the great symbolism from which other symbolisms take their cue.

ON PSYCHOLOGY

THESIS: Although psychology may be valuable in itself, it throws little light on the normal mind and soul because it has followed courses estranging it, perhaps permanently, from the truly mental field.

I. Psychology throws little light on the laws by which the inner life operates.
   A. We are thrown back on acquired wisdom, intuition, and common sense.
   B. Those who deal with human intangibles—teachers, sociologists, executives, salesmen, preachers, coaches—find little help in psychological textbooks.
   C. Literature gives better guidance.
II. Experimental laboratory psychology gives no help.
   A. It has become a branch of physiology.
   B. Knowing physiological mechanisms is at best only an auxiliary for the student of mental phenomena.
   C. This mass of scientific minutiae is appallingly sterile as to integrating principles.

III. Behavioral psychology is some, but not much, improvement.
    A.   It is really only a workaday version of old experimental psychology.
    B.   Nevertheless, it has enlarged our understanding in some fields.
        1.   It has taught us to think in more behavioral terms.
        2.   It has shown us how we may condition behavior by physical means.
            a.   We can condition behavior with the cooperation of psychic considerations.
            b.   We can condition behavior against psychic considerations.
    C.   But behaviorism merely states in behavioristic terms things already obvious to common sense.
        1.   The same process of stimulus and response conditions a person as scientist or maniac, leader or nervous wreck, good or poor workman, inspiring helper or resentful cog.
        2.   Behaviorism does not show us which lines will harmonize with human intangibles.
IV. Gestalt psychology, considering wholes, is more promising.
    A.   It has discovered an important truth: the importance of mental configurations.
    B.   But most of its complex data remains on the animal level.
    C.   In the human configuration, cultural and linguistic phenomena are of the essence.
    D.   Gestalt psychologists cannot operate here.
        1.   They do not have the time.
        2.   They lack linguistic training.
        3.   They have inherited the ideas and vocabulary of the old experimental psychology.
 V. Psychoanalysis, dealing solely with mental material, comes closer still.
    A.   It serves for a while as a clinical tool.
    B.   But it studies abnormality, not the ways of the normal mind.
        1.   The abnormal is not the key to the normal.
        2.   Psychoanalysis is so mentalist that it virtually shuns the external world for intangibles and phantasms.
        3.   It is heavily stamped by Freud's erratic genius.
            a.   It inherits his gift for apperceiving deep but obscure truths.
            b.   It is notion-obsessed.
            c.   It is cluttered with weird dogma.

VI. **We have surveyed here all the psychological schools and found them wanting, so we must look elsewhere for knowledge of the normal mind.**

   A. **We must fall back on unscientific sources.**
   1. **We must use "the wisdom of the ages"—empirical observations accumulated over the centuries.**
   2. **We must turn to the literature of keenly intuitive authors.**
   3. **We must use our own insights.**
   4. **We must combine all this with the few general truths we can cull from the psychological schools.**

   B. **We must search for what the psychologists do not stress: the great and basic importance of meaning.**
   1. **Meaning is intimately connected with linguistic phenomena.**
   2. **The principle of meaning is symbolism.**
   3. **Language is the great symbolism from which all other symbolisms take their cue.**

As you can see, Whorf's writing is remarkably orderly. He may have written this piece straight out at one sitting, but it scans as if he had outlined it. I moved only one point out of the order in which it fell, the first point under "Psychoanalysis"—"It serves a while as a clinical tool"—which I lifted up from the end of the paragraph for a little better order. You may disagree with Whorf, of course. Psychology has changed in the fifty years since he wrote. But you can hardly help admiring the clarity of his thinking, and the way in which a sentence outline makes it apparent.

OUTLINING BY TOPIC SENTENCES

You can also outline a published essay paragraph by paragraph, to strengthen your ability to organize by topic sentences—as you also strengthen your grasp of the essay and of the essayist's own organizing skills. After formulating a thesis for some published essay—and also formulating headings for its main sections, if it doesn't have them—you simply write a topic sentence for each paragraph, filling out the author's own topic sentences for greater clarity. Since your paragraphs are many and your headings few, a combination of Roman and arabic numerals is most convenient. A topic-sentence outline of Whorf's essay would go like this:

ON PSYCHOLOGY

THESIS: **Although psychology may be valuable in itself, it throws little light on the normal mind and soul because it has followed courses estranging it, perhaps permanently, from the truly mental field.**

I. **All psychological schools fail to explore the ways of the mind in relation to the most important truths. [This is a general heading, not a topic sentence.]**
    1. **The old school of experimental laboratory psychology has become virtually a branch of physiology.**
    2. **Behavioral psychology, though showing us how behavior can be conditioned, is simply another version of the old experimental psychology, announcing in behavioristic terms what we already know from common sense.**
    3. **Gestalt psychology adds the importance of whole mental configurations, but remains at the animal level, unable to penetrate the cultural and linguistic phenomena that distinguish the human configuration.**
    4. **Psychoanalysis, though getting results, concerns the abnormal, shunning both the normal and the external world for the wholly mentalistic, intangible, and phantasmic.**
    5. **All these schools are wanting, forcing us to fall back on tradition, literature, intuition, and the general truths scattered here and there in the different psychological schools.**
II. **Symbolism is basic to these important truths. [Another general heading.]**
    1. **No psychological school has stressed the most important truth: meaning.**
    2. **Meaning is intimately connected with the linguistic.**
    3. **Language is the basic symbolism by which we project and interpret what the psychologists neglect: the meaning of life and the universe.**

My outline, as you see, has expanded Whorf's condensed last paragraph into what would have been at least three paragraphs, and probably many more, in a fully developed essay. But the outlining process, by extruding topic sentences to their fullest explicitness, has again helped us to grasp Whorf's thinking and to improve our own.

EXERCISES

4. *Work out a topic-sentence outline for the following essay.*

SNELL PUTNEY AND GAIL J. PUTNEY

THE CONFORMIST IN AMERICA*

After a careful appraisal of Americans, an observer writes: "In that immense crowd which throngs the avenues to power in the United States, I found very few men who displayed that manly candor and masculine independence of opinion which frequently distinguished the Americans in former times. . . . When I survey this countless multitude of beings, shaped to each other's likeness . . . the sight of such universal uniformity saddens and chills me, and I am tempted to regret that state of society which has ceased to be . . . every citizen, being assimilated to all the rest, is lost in the crowd."†

Familiar words! But they were not written by David Riesman,‡ not even in the twentieth century. They were written by Comte Alexis de Tocqueville after his visit to the United States in 1831. He found much that he admired, but he recoiled from the "tyranny of the majority" which seemed to be engulfing this country a quarter of a century before the Civil War.

De Tocqueville's reflections underscore the point that the American conformist is not, as many seem to believe, a new breed. Most Americans, influenced by the televised glorification of Western frontier life, think of their forebears as free spirits characterized by a crusty independence. But, except for the restless minority who moved the edge of the frontier westward, most early Americans were so tied to the life of small rural communities that they hardly perceived their bonds. A man is not free to do that which he cannot imagine doing, and if in the past Americans had a limited awareness of pressures to conform, it was only because they could not grasp the possibility of behaving in ways fundamentally different from those of their fellows. For that matter, when nonconformance occurred, it was likely to be considered heretical or sinful and dealt with summarily—those who wax nostalgic about the individualism of the American past might recall that dissenters were whipped out of the early colonies.

The startling change in conformity in America is thus not in the degree of conformity, but in the general *consciousness* of conformity. Despite their provincial reputation, Americans are becoming a cosmopolitan people and can no longer view their particular way of life with the insularity that characterized their ancestors. The isolation which produced and sustained the narrow horizons of an earlier era has all but disappeared. Mass communication, rapid transportation,

---

*From pp. 1–5 in *Normal Neurosis: The Adjusted American* by Snell Putney, Ph.D. and Gail J. Putney, Ph.D. Copyright © by G. J. Putney and Snell Putney. By permission of Harper & Row, Publishers, Inc.

†Alexis de Tocqueville, *Democracy in America,* tr. Phillips Bradley (New York: Alfred A. Knopf, 1951), 1:267; 2:332.

‡Author of *The Lonely Crowd* (1950).

and the requirements of commerce have created a mobile people intimately acquainted with regional differences. Moreover, the bulk of the population now lives in cities, where social classes mingle, ethnic groups interact, and differences in life style are a matter of daily experience.

Nor is the American's awareness of diversity limited to variations within his own society. In the last half century, three vast citizen armies have been sent abroad and hundreds of thousands of American civilians have gone into Europe, Asia, Africa, and Latin America. Other troops—and the Peace Corps—follow in their wake today. Like ancient Romans, Americans now man far-flung outposts at points determined by the exigencies of world trade and politics. And, of course there is the ubiquitous American tourist.

Exposure to different, often exotic, modes of existence has made Americans more aware of the patterns in their own culture. The English-speaking student who struggles with French verb conjugation becomes conscious of English verb forms which he has never before recognized—although he has used them continuously since childhood. By an analogous process, the American who becomes familiar with other ways of living acquires a heightened awareness of the pattern of his own life. The age of cultural innocence is passing; the American is beginning to recognize the patterns to which he conforms.

Moreover, for a decade and more, social critics from David Riesman to Vance Packard to the Sunday supplement writers have presented to an ever-widening audience a portrait of the American as an "other-directed," status-seeking conformist. The American finds this portrait consistent with his new consciousness of conformity, but he is uncomfortable with the image. He was reared in a tradition which taught that the ideal man chose his life without bending his knee to convention, and the fact that his ancestors did not necessarily measure up to this ideal is beside the point. His concern is with the fact that *he* does not. He is troubled by a feeling that he has exchanged mastery of himself for a place in the faceless ranks of a mass society.

Such a negative attitude toward conformity is not universal. There were, for example, the European enclaves in the Orient, small islands of conscious and proudly maintained conformity to patterns that originated thousands of miles away. Somerset Maugham portrays vividly the English colonial official at his post on some muddy Southeast Asian river, wearing formal dinner dress every evening, opening in daily sequence the issues of the *Times* of London that arrives in month-old batches—preserving to the last possible detail and by ingenious means a way of life that was his very being. Such a man hardly finds conformity a matter for shame; on the contrary, he is proud of conforming to the culture of a group with which he intensely identifies.

Thus the American's discomfort on perceiving that he, too, conforms cannot be dismissed as an inevitable reaction. We must account for why he feels uneasy. Lacking the Englishman's sense of tradition, the American pictures the conformist not as a correct gentleman but rather as a vacuous sheep. But perhaps the major source of his discontent is the scanty reward he receives through conforming. If the pattern of his life fulfilled him, he would be inclined to cherish it. But a growing number of Americans express a sense of emptiness and discontent that sits oddly with the affluent complacency ascribed to them.

Some of the discontented have tried to embrace the emptiness they encounter in their lives. This is not a new phenomenon. In the early decades of this century, disaffected young French and German intellectuals elevated "nothingness" to a prime value. Having experienced the destruction of old ideals and purposes, they made destruction itself an ideal and a purpose. They expressed their nihilism in a series of literary ventures and art exhibits, a notable example being the exhibition in Cologne where the public was invited to attack the exhibits with axes thoughtfully provided for the purpose. These disillusioned young men called themselves "Dadaist"; their mid-century American counterparts called themselves "Beat." Finding the patterns of life empty and obscene, they enshrined emptiness and obscenity. Their cultural heirs are the disaffected who reject the very symbols of the "American Way of Life" for which the conformist reaches greedily.

Although many other Americans are uneasy about conforming, most have too large a stake in the prevailing culture to turn their backs on it in angry protest. They may enjoy an occasional rebellious spree, envy what they imagine to be the sex life of the bohemian fringe. But they shrink from the nonconformist label, fearing loss of respectability even more than they regret the loss of individuality.

Besides, they doubt that the nonconformist has made a good bargain. They wonder if the bohemian is free to bathe or only not to bathe, and they smile knowingly when hearing of beards shaved off because a Founder's Day celebration has made beards respectable. The price of nonconformity seems great, and the freedom gained little more than conformity turned inside out.

Thus the American who has become uneasy about being a conformist is typically unwilling to become a nonconformist. And yet his discontent remains. It seems to him that conformity has diminished his enjoyment of life and of himself, but he does not see anything he can do about it.

FURTHER CONVENTIONS OF OUTLINING

Most of the outline's formal conventions have emerged during our survey, but some further details and reminders will be useful.

1. TITLE.   Keep your title independent of the text of your outline. Do not number it in with the text; do not use it as a heading for subheads; do not refer to it by pronouns. Do *not* do this:

I. THE ADVANTAGES OF THE BIKINI
A. Its convenience in packing

2. THESIS.   To keep your logical structure straight, make as explicit a thesis as you can.

3. CAPITALIZATION.   Capitalize only the first word of each heading (and other words normally capitalized).

4. PUNCTUATION.   Omit periods after your title and your headings, but put one after your thesis-sentence. If outlining in sentences, include periods, of course.

5. HEADINGS.   (a) Do NOT use "Introduction" and "Conclusion" as headings. (b) For the topic outline especially, use all nouns (or noun phrases), with modifiers accompanying as needed. Do not mix kinds of headings: some nouns, some sentences, some fragments. Keep headings equivalent:

A. **Ethical benefits**
B. **Economic benefits**
    1. **Reduction of costs**
    2. **Increase in income**
        a. **Governmental increases**
        b. **Personal increases**

CHAPTER 8

Writing Good Sentences

All this time you have been writing sentences, as naturally as breathing, and perhaps with as little variation. Now for a close look at the varieties of the sentence. Some varieties can be shaggy and tangled indeed. But they are all off-shoots of the simple active sentence, the basic English genus *John hits Joe,* with action moving straight from subject through verb to object.

This subject-verb-object sentence can be infinitely grafted and contorted, but it really has only two general varieties: (1) the "loose, or strung-along," in Aristotle's phrase, and (2) the periodic. English naturally runs "loose," or "cumulative." Our thoughts are by nature strung along from subject through verb to object, with whatever comes to mind simply added as it comes—a word order happily acquired from French as a result of the Norman Conquest. The loose sentence puts its subject and verb early. But we can also use the periodic sentence characteristic of our German and Latin ancestry, where ideas hang in the air like girders until all interconnections are locked by the final word, at the period: *John, the best student in the class, the tallest and most handsome, hits Joe.* A periodic sentence, in other words, is one that suspends its meaning until the end, usually with subject and verb widely separated, and the verb as near the end as possible.

So we have two varieties of the English sentence, partly because its old Germanic oak was first limbered by French and then cured by Latin, but mostly because (as Aristotle observed of Greek) the piece-by-piece and the periodic species simply represent two ways of thought: the first, the natural stringing of thoughts as they come; the second, the more careful contrivance of emphasis and suspense.

THE SIMPLE SENTENCE

Use the Simple Active Sentence, Loosely Periodic

Your best sentences will be hybrids of the loose and the periodic. First, learn to use active verbs (*John* HITS *Joe*), which will keep you within the simple active pattern with all parts showing (subject-verb-object), as opposed to verbs in the passive voice (*Joe* IS HIT *by John*), which put everything backwards and use more words: IS HIT *by John* is "passive voice" because it makes the real doer, John, seem to be inactive, or "passive," resting at the end of the sentence instead of starting the action, right at the beginning. So, keep active. Then learn to give your native strung-along sentence a touch of periodicity and suspense.

Any change in normal order can give you unusual emphasis, as when you move the object ahead of the subject:

> **That I like.**
> **The house itself she hated, but the yard was grand.**
> **Nature I loved; and next to Nature, Art.**
> **The manuscript, especially, he treasured.**

You can vary the subject-verb-object pattern more gently by interruptive words and phrases, so that the meaning gathers excitement from the delay. The *especially* does more for the manuscript than the words themselves could manage: the phrase postpones the already postponed subject and predicate. Put the phrase last, and the emphasis fades considerably; the speaker grows a little remote: "The manuscript he treasured, especially." Put the sentence in normal order—"He especially treasured the manuscript"—and we are, in fact, back to normal.

We expect our ideas one at a time, in normal succession—*John hits Joe* —and with anything further added, in proper sequence, at the end—*a real hay-maker.* Change this fixed way of thinking, and you immediately put your reader on the alert for something unusual. Consequently, some of your best sentences will be simple active ones sprung wide with phrases coloring subject, verb, object, or all three, in various ways. You may, for instance, effectively complicate the subject.

> **King Lear, proud, old, and childish, probably aware that his
>   grip on the kingdom is beginning to slip, devises a foolish
>   plan.**
> **To come all this way, to arrive after dark, and then to find the
>   place locked and black as ink was almost unbearable.**

Or the verb:

> **She made her way, carefully at first, then confidently, then with reckless steps, along the peak of the smoldering roof.**
> **A good speech usually begins quietly, proceeds sensibly, gathers momentum, and finally moves even the most indifferent audience.**

Or the object:

> **He finally wrote the paper, a long desperate perambulation, without beginning or end, without any guiding idea—without, in fact, much of an idea at all.**
> **Her notebooks contain marvelous comments on the turtle in the back yard, the flowers and weeds, the great elm by the drive, the road, the earth, the stars, and the men and women of the village.**

These are some of the infinite possibilities in the simple active sentence as it delays and stretches and heightens the ordinary expectations of subject-verb-object.

EXERCISES

1. *Give each of the following sentences a touch of periodicity by changing the normal word order, by adding interruptive words or phrases, or by complicating one of the three principal elements of the sentence: the subject, the verb, the object.*

   EXAMPLE   She made her way along the smoldering roof. She made her way, carefully at first, then confidently, then with reckless steps, along the peak of the smoldering roof.

   1. Commune residents are often escapees from solidly middle-class families.
   2. Former friends are often embarrassed when they meet and find they have little in common.
   3. Some firemen began carrying guns when they were frightened by the chaos of the riots.
   4. The bottleneck in education is that the teacher can listen and respond to no more than one student at a time.
   5. The car wheezed to a stop.
   6. The editorial in the *New York Times* suggested that tight control of governmental spending might check inflation.
   7. It was wholly unlike his father to give up without trying.
   8. The inspector discovered a window that had been forced open.
   9. We certainly remember that first night in the new house!
   10. The escaped convict offered only token resistance when a private citizen captured and disarmed him after a short chase.

11. We must note that some parents have misgivings about the schools.
12. The house sits at the edge of town in the middle of large grounds.

2. *Cull through your papers and find five of your own simple sentences. Revise them as in Exercise 1, handing in your original sentences paired with their revisions.*

COMPOUND SENTENCES

Learn the Difference Between Compound and Complex Sentences

You make a compound sentence by linking together simple sentences with a coordinating conjunction *(and, but, or, nor, yet, so, still, for)* or with a colon or a semicolon. You make a complex one by hooking lesser sentences onto the main sentence with *that, which, who,* or one of the many other subordinating connectives like *although, because, where, when, after, if.* The compound sentence *coordinates,* treating everything on the same level; the complex *subordinates,* putting everything else somewhere below one main self-sufficient idea. The compound links ideas one after the other, as in the basic simple sentence; the complex is a simple sentence elaborated by clauses instead of merely by phrases. The compound represents the strung-along way of thinking; the complex frequently represents the periodic.

Avoid Simple-minded Compounds

Essentially the compound sentence *is* simple-minded, a set of clauses on a string—a child's description of a birthday party, for instance: "We got paper hats and we pinned the tail on the donkey and we had chocolate ice cream and Randy sat on a piece of cake and I won third prize." *And . . . and . . . and.*

But this way of thinking is necessary, even in postgraduate regions. It is always useful simply for pacing off related thoughts, and for breaking the staccato of simple statement. It often briskly connects cause and effect: "The clock struck one, and down he run." "The solipsist relates all knowledge to his own being, and the demonstrable commonwealth of human nature dissolves before his dogged timidity." The *and* can link causes with all sorts of different effect and speed, can bring in the next clause as a happy afterthought or a momentous consequence. Since the compound sentence follows the most enduring of colloquial patterns—the simple sequence of things said as they occur to the mind—it has the pace, the immediacy, and the dramatic effect of talk. Hemingway, for instance, often gets all the numb tension of a shell-shocked mind by reducing his character's thoughts all to one level, in sentences something like this: "It was a good night and I sat at a table and . . . and . . . and. . . ."

With *but* and *or,* the compound sentence becomes more thoughtful. The mind is at work, turning its thought first one way then another, meeting the reader's objections by stating them. With semicolon and colon (or, if the clauses are very short, with comma), the compound grows more sophisticated still:

> **John demands the most from himself; Pete demands.**
> **I came, I saw, I conquered.**
> **Economic theorists assume a common man: he commonly wants**
> **more than he can supply.**

Think of the compound sentence in terms of its conjunctions—the words that yoke its clauses—and of the accompanying punctuation. Here are three basic groups of conjunctions that will help you sort out and punctuate your compound thoughts.

GROUP 1.   The three common coordinating conjunctions: *and, but,* and *or (nor).* Put a comma before each.

> **I like her, and I don't mind saying so.**
> **Art is long, but life is short.**
> **Win this point, or the game is lost.**
> **We will not be coerced, nor will we be bought.**

GROUP 2.   Conjunctive adverbs: *therefore, moreover, however, nevertheless, consequently, furthermore.* Put a semicolon before, a comma after, each.

> **Nations indeed seem to have a kind of biological span like**
> **human life, from rebellious youth, through caution, to decay;**
> **consequently, predictions of doom are not uncommon.**

GROUP 3.   Some in-betweeners—*yet, still, so*—which sometimes take a comma, sometimes a semicolon, depending on your pace and emphasis.

> **We long for the good old days, yet we never include the disad-**
> **vantages.**
> **People long for the good old days; yet they rarely take into ac-**
> **count the inaccuracy of human memory.**
> **The preparation had been halfhearted and hasty, so the meeting**
> **was wretched.**
> **Rome declined into the pleasures of its circuses and couches; so**
> **the tough barbarians conquered.**

Try Compounding with Semicolon and Colon

Though the conjunction usually governs the compound sentence, two powerful coordinators remain—the semicolon and the colon. These strong punctuations can replace both the comma, with its *and,* and the period. The semicolon most effectively coordinates by *contrasts;* the colon, by *amplification.* You will notice in the preceding sentence how the semicolon pulls the contrasting clauses together for close inspection, so closely, in fact, that we can drop the verb in the second clause, substituting a comma, and so tighten the contrast still further. For contrasts, the semicolon is the prince of coordinators:

> **The dress accents the feminine; the pants suit speaks for freedom.**   Contrast
> **Golf demands the best of time and space; tennis, the best of personal energy.**
> **The government tries to get the most out of taxes; the individual tries to get out of the most taxes.**

The colon similarly pulls two "sentences" together without blessing of conjunction, period, or capital. But it signals amplification, not contrast: the second clause explains the first.

> **A house with an aging furnace costs more than the asking price suggests: ten dollars more a month in fuel means about eighty dollars more a year.**   Amplification
> **A growing population means more business: more business will exhaust our supply of ores in less than half a century.**
> **Sports at any age are beneficial: they keep your pulses hopping.**

As a corollary to its role as amplifier in the compound sentence, the colon also introduces lists:

> **The following players will start: Corelli, Smith, Jones, Baughman, and Stein.**

EXERCISES

3. *Convert the following pairs of sentences into compound sentences with the coordinator you think most appropriate to the sense and style of the sentences.*

   1. He couldn't go on. He was just too tired.
   2. The crime commission recommended a number of such programs. Federal funds have been made available for putting them into operation.

3. The governor told the President that the state could not cope with the disaster. The President dispatched federal troops.

4. The first plant generating electricity by reactor began operating in 1956. Nuclear technology has been growing rather slowly since then.

5. We can probably never perfect the process beyond its present state. We should still try.

6. In some instances, the seminar for freshman courses would be extremely helpful. In other instances, it might be of little value.

7. The thought of quitting his job excited him. The idea had been in the back of his mind for a long time.

8. Most schools are just now starting courses in computers for freshmen. To evaluate those programs will take several years.

9. In his manuscripts, F. Scott Fitzgerald's sentences are often haphazard and careless. His spelling is often atrocious.

10. On small farms, labor was not specialized. On medium farms, labor was partially specialized. But large farms carefully divided their workers into teams of specialists.

11. Few recipients of Social Security benefits can actually live on that income alone. Most supplement their incomes with savings or by selling the possessions of a lifetime.

12. Mark Twain's book *The Gilded Age* attempts too much. It attempts to satirize an age.

13. Within the past few years, many kinds of jobs open to recent graduates have steadily shrunk. As a result, students are increasingly challenging the curriculum to provide them marketable skills.

14. We have made some progress in controlling exhaust. We still have a long way to go.

15. Statistically, your chances of being killed or injured in an airplane are lower than in an automobile. Most of us, however, are more nervous in planes than in cars.

COMPLEX SENTENCES

Learn to Subordinate

You probably write compound sentences almost without thinking. But the subordinations of the complex usually require some thought. Indeed, you are ranking closely related thoughts, arranging the lesser clauses so that they bear effectively on your main clause. You must first pick your most important idea. You must then change mere sequence into subordination—ordering your lesser thoughts "sub," or below, the main idea. The childish birthday sentence, then, might come out something like this:

Subordinating by
Adverbs "After"

**After we got paper hats and chocolate ice cream, after Randy
sat on a piece of cake and everyone pinned the tail on the donkey, I WON THIRD PRIZE.**

Depending on your interests, you might have made virtually any of the other
items predominant over the subordinates:

**After pinning the tail on the donkey, after I won third
prize, after everyone got paper hats and chocolate ice cream,
Randy sat on a piece of cake and ran home crying.**

Your interests will select your main idea, and the means of subordinating others to it are several, as we shall see.

You do the trick with connectives—with any word, like *after* in the preceding sentence, indicating time, place, cause, or other qualification:

If **they try,** *if* **they fail, THEY ARE STILL GREAT** *because* **their spirit
is unbeaten.**

You daily achieve subtler levels of subordination with the three relative pronouns *that, which, who,* and with the conjunction *that. That, which,* and *who* connect thoughts so closely related as to seem almost equal, but actually each tucks
a clause (subject-and-verb) into some larger idea:

Relative Pronouns

Conjunction

The car, which runs perfectly, is not worth selling.
The car that runs perfectly is worth keeping.
He thought that the car would run forever.
**He thought [that omitted but understood] the car would run
forever.**

But the subordinating conjunctions and adverbs (*although, if, because, since, until,
where, when, as if, so that*) really put subordinates in their places. Look at *when*
in this sentence of E. B. White's from *Charlotte's Web:*

Adverbs

**Next morning when the first light came into the sky and the
sparrows stirred in the trees, when the cows rattled their chains
and the rooster crowed and the early automobiles went whispering along the road, Wilbur awoke and looked for Charlotte.**

Here the simple *when,* used only twice, has regimented five subordinate
clauses, all of equal rank, into their proper station below that of the main
clause, "Wilbur awoke and looked for Charlotte." You can vary the ranking
intricately and still keep it straight:

Conjunctions
> **Although some claim that time is an illusion, because we have no absolute chronometer, although the mind cannot effectively grasp time, because the mind itself is a kind of timeless presence almost oblivious to seconds and hours, although the time of our solar system may be only an instant in the universe at large, WE STILL CANNOT QUITE DENY that some progression of universal time is passing over us, if only we could measure it.**

Complex sentences are, at their best, really simple sentences gloriously delayed and elaborated with subordinate thoughts. The following beautiful and elaborate sentence from the Book of Common Prayer is all built on the simple sentence "draw near":

> **Ye who do truly and earnestly repent you of your sins, and are in love and charity with your neighbors, and intend to lead a new life, following the commandments of God, and walking from henceforth in his holy ways, draw near with faith, and take this holy sacrament to your comfort, and make your humble confession to Almighty God, devoutly kneeling.**

Even a short sentence may be complex, attaining a remarkably varied suspense. Notice how the simple statement "I allowed myself" is skillfully elaborated in this sentence by the late Wolcott Gibbs of *The New Yorker:*

> **Twice in my life, for reasons that escape me now, though I'm sure they were discreditable, I allowed myself to be persuaded that I ought to take a hand in turning out a musical comedy.**

Once you glimpse the complex choreography possible within the dimensions of the simple sentence, you are on your way to developing a prose capable of turns and graceful leaps, one with a kind of intellectual health that, no matter what the subject or mood, is always on its toes.

EXERCISES

4. *Here are some pairs of sentences, some of them the same pairs you converted to compound sentences in the previous exercise. This time, convert them into complex sentences, trying to use a variety of subordinators.*

   1. He couldn't go on. He was just too tired.
   2. The crime commission recommended a number of such programs. Federal funds have been made available for putting them into operation.
   3. We can probably never perfect the process beyond its present state. We should still try.

4. Many schools are just now starting courses in computers for freshmen. To evaluate those programs will take several years.

5. On small farms, labor was not specialized. On medium farms, labor was partially specialized. But large farms carefully divided their workers into teams of specialists.

6. Few recipients of Social Security benefits can actually live on that income alone. Most supplement their incomes with savings or by selling the possessions of a lifetime.

7. We desperately need more judges and more staff. Courts are as much as twenty-six months behind schedule, with little hope of catching up.

8. A large reduction in the prime interest rate is not likely. House seekers, therefore, must choose either mortgages with interests as high as eighteen percent, or no purchases.

9. Within the past few years, many kinds of jobs open to recent graduates have steadily shrunk. As a result, students are increasingly challenging the curriculum to provide them marketable skills.

10. An independent candidate for President has little chance of becoming a serious contender. He cannot rely upon large party machinery, and he has little money for advertising.

11. Two motorists were killed last night when their car hit a guard rail, overturned, and caught fire. Police were unable to determine the cause of the accident.

12. Plants can obtain the elements necessary for photosynthesis from water in the soil and from carbon dioxide in the air. Nevertheless, they need many other elements.

13. Federal control of prices could have encouraged a switch to coal. The government could have let the price of oil and gas soar with the market while monitoring pollution.

14. You may be familiar with our facilities and resources already. If not, simply fill out the enclosed form and return it to us, and we will send you a free brochure.

15. True scientific knowledge is no longer accessible to the majority of us. We wish it were, but it just isn't. It's too complicated for most of us.

5. *Supply five pairs of simple sentences from your previous papers, and subordinate one to the other so as to revise the pairs into complex sentences.*

6. *Write a one-hundred-word sentence with only one independent clause and with everything else subordinated. You can get started with a string of parallel clauses: "When I get up in the morning, when I look at my bleary eyes in the mirror, when I think of the paper still to be done . . . ," or "After . . . , after . . . , after. . . ." See how far you can run on before you must bring in your main subject and verb.*

Try for Still Closer Connections: Modify

Your subordinating *if*'s and *when*'s have really been modifying—that is, limiting the meaning of the things you have attached them to. But there is a smoother way. It is an adjectival sort of thing, a shoulder-to-shoulder opera-

tion, a neat trick with no need for shouting, a stone to a stone with no need
for mortar. You simply put clauses and phrases up against a noun, instead of
attaching them with a subordinator. This sort of modification includes the following constructions, all using the same close masonry: (1) appositives, (2) relatives understood, (3) adjectives-with-phrase, (4) participles, (5) absolutes.

APPOSITIVES.   Those phrases about shoulders and tricks and stones, above,
are all in apposition with *sort of thing,* and they are grammatically subordinate
to it. The phrases are nevertheless nearly coordinate and interchangeable.
They are compressions of a series of sentences ("It is an adjectival sort of
thing. It is a neat trick . . . ," and so forth) set side by side, "stone to stone."
Mere contact does the work of the verb *is* and its subject *it.* English often does
the same with subordinate clauses, omitting the *who is* or *which is* and putting
the rest directly into apposition. "The William who is the Conqueror" becomes "William the Conqueror." "The Jack who is the heavy hitter" becomes
"Jack the heavy hitter." These, incidentally, are called "restrictive" apposi-
tions, because they restrict to a particular designation the nouns they modify,
setting this William and this Jack apart from all others (with no separating commas). Similarly, you can make nonrestrictive appositives from nonrestrictive
clauses, clauses that simply add information (between commas). "Smith, who
is a man to be reckoned with, . . . " becomes "Smith, a man to be reckoned
with,. . . . " "Jones, who is our man in Liverpool, . . . " becomes "Jones, our
man in Liverpool,. . . . " Restrictive or nonrestrictive, close contact makes your
point with economy and fitness.

RELATIVES UNDERSTOOD.   You can often achieve the same economy, as I have
already hinted, by omitting any kind of relative and its verb, thus gaining a
compression both colloquial and classic:

> **A compression [that is] both colloquial and classic. . . .**
> **The specimens [that] he had collected. . . .**
> **The girl [whom] he [had] left behind. . . .**

But be careful after verbs that easily take direct objects. Omitting *that* may lead
to confusion:

> **She felt his ears were too big.**
> **He saw her nose was too small.**
> **This does not deny his daily habits and thoughts are his own.**

ADJECTIVES-WITH-PHRASE.   This construction is also appositive and adjectival.
It is neat and useful:

The law was passed, *thick with provisions and codicils, heavy with implications.*
There was the lake, *smooth in the early air.*

EXERCISES

7. *Streamline the following sentences by using appositives wherever you can.*

   1. The security guard, who must have been a very frightened man, fired point-blank into the crowd.
   2. Professor Stanley, who is now associate vice-president and director of business operations, has been named a vice-president at the University of Nebraska.
   3. The book, which has been a best-seller for several months, will be made into a movie.
   4. American social mores have undergone staggering changes since the early 1950s. These changes are so great in quality and number as to constitute a virtual revolution.
   5. The Globe Theatre, which was immediately acclaimed the best designed and appointed playhouse in London, was completed in 1599.

8. *Eliminate relatives and their accompanying verbs from the following sentences:*

   1. The freeze on wages and prices that was announced by the President shocked European investors.
   2. *Pygmalion,* which had first been popular as a play, and which had later been rewritten as a popular musical comedy, was finally done as a movie.
   3. Although Picasso executed the original design, he had nothing to do with erecting the sculpture which is now standing in front of the Hancock Building in Chicago.
   4. The studded tire, which has long been popular for winter driving in some states, is now being outlawed in many states because of damage to roads.
   5. Because of the recession, the renovation that we had all hoped for has been postponed.
   6. Students who are now being admitted to the master's program will not have to pass the foreign language proficiency test that has always been required in the past.

9. *In the following sentences, insert the adjectival phrases ("pure terror in her eyes") next to the nouns they modify, within appropriate commas.*

   1. The young girl cowered in the corner. There was pure terror in her eyes.
   2. This construction is also appositional and adjectival. It is a neat trick for the beginning writer to remember.
   3. Its deck was splintered and peeling. Its rigging was nearly all frayed and rotted. The boat obviously hadn't been cared for at all.
   4. Griswell had neither eaten nor slept, and when he stumbled into the bar he was trembling with fatigue.
   5. The ladder was sagging with his weight, and at last it collapsed.

6. The commission's final report will probably not be ready for Friday's meeting. After all, the report is over three hundred pages long and has more than seventy charts.
7. The street in Lawrence was completely familiar to Andrews. It was firmly rooted in his memory even after three years in the Army.
8. The narrator in *Autobiography of an Ex-Colored Man* was so light-skinned that he could easily pass for white, and when he finally decided to give up his black identity, he found it easy to do. Still, the choice left him bitter and embarrassed.

PARTICIPLES.   Participles—when acting as adjectives—are extremely supple subordinators. Consider this sequence of six simple sentences:

He had been thrown.
He had accepted.
He felt a need.
He demanded money.
He failed.
He chose not to struggle.

Now see how Richard Wright, in *Native Son,* subordinates with participles the first five of these to the sixth. He elaborates the complete thought into a forceful sentence that runs for eighty-nine words with perfect clarity:

Having been thrown **by an accidental murder into a position where he had sensed a possible order and meaning in his relations with the people about him;** *having accepted* **the moral guilt and responsibility for that murder because it had made him feel free for the first time in his life;** *having felt* **in his heart some obscure need to be at home with people and** *having demanded* **ransom money to enable him to do it—***having* **done all this and** *failed,* **he chose not to struggle any more.**

The following participles have the same adjectival force:

Dead to the world, *wrapped* **in sweet dreams,** *untroubled* **by bills, he slept till noon.**

Notice that the participles operate exactly as the adjective *dead* does.
Beware of dangling participles. They may trip you, as they have tripped others. The participle, with its adjectival urge, may grab the first noun that comes along, with shocking results.

Dangling Participles

<u>Bowing to the crowd</u>, the bull caught him unawares.

<u>Observing quietly from the bank</u>, the beavers committed several
    errors in judgment.

What we need is a list of teachers <u>broken down alphabetically</u>.

The passive voice, by omitting the true subject, frequently invites a dangle:

<u>Squandering everything at the track</u>, the money was never paid.

<u>By bending low</u>, the snipers were avoided by the retreating
    squad.

<u>Tired and discouraged</u>, half the lawn was still uncut.

Move the participle next to its intended noun or pronoun. You will have to
supply this word if inadvertence or the passive voice has omitted it entirely.
Recast the sentence for good alignment when necessary. You may also save
the day by changing a present participle to a past, as in the fourth example.

The bull caught him unawares as he bowed to the crowd.

Observing quietly from the bank, they saw the beavers make
    several errors in judgment.

What we need is an alphabetical list of teachers.

Squandered at the track, the money was never repaid.

By bending low, the retreating squad avoided the snipers.

Tired and discouraged, she had cut only half the lawn.

Here is a sentence from Jane Austen's *Persuasion* that illustrates the adjectival and subordinating power of the participle—*delighted* twice modifying *She*
and subordinating everything to the one basic four-word clause that begins
the sentence:

She always watched them as long as she could, delighted to
fancy she understood what they might be talking of, as they
walked along in happy independence, or equally delighted to
see the Admiral's hearty shake of the hand when he encountered an old friend, and observe their eagerness of conversation
when occasionally forming into a little knot of the navy, Mrs.
Croft looking as intelligent and keen as any of the officers
around her.

This sentence ends so gracefully because, with the phrase *Mrs. Croft looking*,
it achieves the ultimate in participial perfection—the ablative absolute, which
we will consider in the next section.

EXERCISES

10. *Keeping an eye out for dangling participles, revise the following sentences by transforming as many verbs as reasonably possible into participles.*

1. Apparently the boxer thought the bell had sounded. He dropped his guard, and he was immediately knocked out.
2. He settled into a Bohemian life in the French Quarter. He started publishing in all the appropriate little magazines. And at last he found himself presiding over a colony of artists and writers.
3. The prisoners were obviously angered by the news that no guards were fired. They felt cheated and betrayed. And so on August 4, they seized three guards as hostages to force the warden to reconsider.
4. Trumbo was blacklisted in Hollywood; he was vilified in the press; and he was forced to write scripts under an assumed name until nearly 1960.
5. The student-designed rocket functioned perfectly. It rose one hundred miles above the earth, flew for ten minutes, traveled some fifty miles down range, and splashed down precisely on target.
6. After 100 miles, Hunt showed his winning style. He came out of each turn at 6000 rpm, accelerated to 8000 rpm on the following straight, then braked and shifted down for the next turn.
7. Nineteenth-century women were isolated and unenfranchised; they were sexually "used" and relegated to the kitchen and the nursery; in essence, society regarded them as brainless decorations.
8. He didn't check the charts for the water's depth and consequently ran aground thirty minutes after the race started.
9. The assembly line was invented by Ford. It was institutionalized by the UAW. It is now extensively automated. It produces many components that are untouched by human hands.
10. It depends on the smoothness and porosity of the surface. It will also vary with the kind of wood. You should test the color of this stain on a small inconspicuous area and then thin it to the shade you desire.

ABSOLUTES.   The absolute phrase has a great potential of polished economy. Many an absolute is simply a prepositional phrase with the preposition dropped:

> **He ran up the stairs, [with]** *a bouquet of roses under his arm,* **and rang the bell.**
> **She walked slowly, [with]** *her camera ready.*

But the ablative absolute (*ablative* means "removed") is absolutely removed from grammatical connection with the main clause, modifying only by proximity. If you have had some Latin, you will probably remember this construction as some kind of brusque condensation, something like *"The road completed,* Caesar moved his camp." But it survives in the best of circles. Somewhere E. B. White admits to feeling particularly good one morning, just having brought off an especially fine ablative absolute. And it is actually more common than you may suppose. A recent newspaper article stated that "the Prince has fled the country, *his hopes of a negotiated peace shattered."* The *hopes shattered* pattern (noun plus participle) marks the ablative absolute (also called, because of the noun, a "nominative absolute"). The idea might have been more conventionally subordinated: "since his hopes were shattered" or "with his hopes shattered." But the ablative absolute accomplishes the subordination with economy and style.

Take a regular subordinate clause: *"When* the road *was* completed." Cut the subordinator and the finite verb. You now have an ablative absolute, a phrase that stands absolutely alone, shorn of both its connective *when* and its full predication *was: "The road completed,* Caesar moved his camp." Basically a noun and a participle, or noun and adjective, it is a kind of grammatical shorthand, a telegram: *ROAD COMPLETED CAESAR MOVED*—most said in fewest words, speed with high compression: this is its appeal and its power. Here are further examples:

> **The cat stopped, its** *back arched,* **its** *eyes frantic.*
> **The whole company,** *God willing,* **soon will return to normal.**
> *All things considered,* **the plan would work.**
> **The** *dishes washed,* **the** *baby bathed* **and** *asleep,* **the last** *ashtray*
> *emptied,* **they could at last relax.**

It is certainly a construction you should use with caution. It can sound exactly like a bad translation. But able writers come to it sooner or later, whether knowingly or through discovering for themselves the horsepower in a subordinate clause milled down to its absolute minimum of noun and participle, or noun and adjective, or even noun and noun. Hemingway uses it frequently. Here is one of the noun-noun variety at the end of a sentence about pistols in *To Have and Have Not:* " . . . their only *drawback the mess* they leave for relatives to clean up." And here are two noun-participle ones *(he playing* and *the death administered),* in a passage that will serve as a closing illustration of how a complex sentence can subordinate as many as 164 words to the 7 of its one main clause ("they will put up with mediocre work"):

> **If the spectators know the matador is capable of executing a**
> **complete, consecutive series of passes with the muleta in which**
> **there will be valor, art, understanding and, above all, beauty**
> **and great emotion, they will put up with mediocre work, cow-**
> **ardly work, disastrous work because they have the hope sooner**

Subordinating
Conjunction

Main Clause

Sub. Conj.

Sub. Adv.
Relatives

Participles
Absolute

Absolute

or later of seeing the complete faena; the faena that takes a
man out of himself and makes him feel immortal while it is proceeding, that gives him an ecstasy, that is, while momentary, as
profound as any religious ecstasy; moving all the people in the
ring together and increasing in emotional intensity as it proceeds, carrying the bullfighter with it, he playing on the crowd
through the bull and being moved as it responds in a growing
ecstasy of ordered, formal, passionate, increasing disregard for
death that leaves you, when it is over, and the death administered to the animal that has made it possible, as empty, as
changed, and as sad as any major emotion will leave you.*

EXERCISES

11. *Try turning prepositional phrases and subordinate clauses in the following sentences into absolutes.*

1. With examinations coming and with the temperature dropping, students are beginning to show up at the health service with all sorts of nebulous ailments, most
of them purely imagined.
2. Ted left the room, where his things were still scattered over the floor.
3. Even though the tank was filled with gas and the ignition was working perfectly,
the engine still wouldn't start.
4. Even though the stock market had collapsed, and fifteen percent of the workers
were jobless, Hoover nonetheless felt the economy would eventually right itself
without tinkering.
5. With mud splattered all over her stockings, she looked as if she had been out
playing in puddles.
6. When his three minutes were up, he deposited another quarter.

PARALLEL CONSTRUCTION

Use Parallels to Strengthen Equivalent Ideas

Hemingway's 171-word sentence could not have held together without parallel
construction—putting equivalent ideas in matched grammatical forms, laying
them parallel, so to speak, so that they reinforce each other, as with Heming-

---

*Reprinted with the permission of Charles Scribner's Sons from *Death in the Afternoon:* 206–07.
Copyright 1932 Charles Scribner's Sons; renewal copyright © 1960 Ernest Hemingway.

way's "a faena *that takes . . . , that gives. . . .*" No complex sentence can hold up very long without it. Actually, Hemingway's "that is" after "ecstasy" makes a false parallel, throwing his sentence briefly out of line (he should have used "which is" or something like "an ecstasy as profound, though momentary, as any . . ."). You have also seen examples of parallel ranking in White's *when* sentence (155) and in the sentence that followed, dealing with time. The sentence about the cat and the one about the relaxing couple (163) have shown you ablative absolutes laid parallel.

Paralleling can be very simple. Any word will seek its own kind, noun to noun, adjective to adjective, infinitive to infinitive. The simplest series of things automatically runs parallel:

> **shoes and ships and sealing wax**
> **I came, I saw, I conquered**
> **to be or not to be**
> **a dull, dark, and soundless day**
> **mediocre work, cowardly work, disastrous work**

But they very easily run out of parallel too, and this you must learn to prevent. The last item especially may slip out of line, as in this series: "friendly, kind, unobtrusive, and *a bore*" (boring). The noun *bore* has jumped off the track laid by the preceding parallel adjectives. Your train of equivalent ideas should all be of the same grammatical kind to carry their equivalence clearly—to strengthen it: either parallel adjectives, *friendly, kind, unobtrusive,* and *boring,* or all nouns, *a friend, a saint, a diplomat,* and *a bore.* Your paralleling articles and prepositions should govern a series as a whole, or should accompany *every* item:

> **a hat, cane, pair of gloves, and mustache**
> **a hat, a cane, a pair of gloves, and a mustache**
> **by land, sea, or air**
> **by land, by sea, or by air**

Verbs also frequently intrude to throw a series of adjectives (or nouns) out of parallel:

> **FAULTY: He thought the girl was** *attractive, intelligent,* **and** *knew* **how to make him feel needed.**
> **IMPROVED: He thought the girl was** *attractive, intelligent,* **and** *sympathetic,* **knowing how to make him feel needed.**

Here is an example from one of my students that illustrates how faulty paralleling obscures equivalent ideas:

> **He stated two ways in which man could hope to continue sur-
> vival. (1) World citizenship, or 2) destroying most of the inven-
> tions that man is uncertain of and go back to where we can un-
> derstand ourselves and progress.**

The most glaring error is the period in the first line and the capitalized *World.*
This not only seems to start a new sentence, leaving the reader hanging in air
at the end, still waiting for a verb to complete the thought, but also breaks
the two parallel solutions away from the *two ways* that have set them up. A colon
and small *w* will pull the sentence together, and a full parenthesis at "(2)" will
make the parallel visibly equivalent. Next, we must bring the ideas themselves
to the surface as equals by putting them into the same kind of grammatical
slot, using either two nouns, as in the first solution below, or two participles,
as in the second:

> **(1) world citizenship, or (2) destruction . . .**
> **(1) seeking world citizenship, or (2) destroying . . .**

But the sentence goes farther out of parallel still: *go back* needs to be parallel
with *destroying* (or *destruction,* if you choose the noun). And what are we to make
of that blurred parallel at the end? Are we to understand *ourselves* and the nature of *progress* (two nouns)? Or are we to *go back* and then begin to *progress*
all over again (two verbs)? We do not know to which of the two choices *progress*
is parallel, nor whether to accent it as a verb or a noun. Parallel construction
would have told us. I found out by asking the student. The solution we worked
out, with parallel ideas underlined, was this:

> **He stated two ways in which man could hope to survive: (1) cre-
> ating some kind of world government, or (2) destroying most of
> our inventions, going back to where we can understand our-
> selves as simple human beings, and beginning the painful his-
> tory of progress all over again.**

The speaker, of course, was arguing for world government (not *citizenship*), and
he saw the present nuclear predicament as so threatening that the only parallel
alternative to world government was scrapping everything and beginning
again. We discovered that *creating* was the thought really parallel to *destroying.*
By searching out the parallel ideas and putting them into grammatically equivalent structures, we brought the writer's idea clearly up to visibility where both
he and I could understand it fully for the first time. Actually, only by first reaching for the grammatical parallels did we discover the really crucial parallel between *creating* and *destroying.*

Repeat Your Paralleling Connectives

When your series consists of phrases or of clauses, you should repeat the preposition or conjunction introducing them, to ensure clarity:

> *By* weeks of careful planning, *by* intelligence, *by* thorough training, and *by* a great deal of luck. . . .
> *Since* all things are not equal, *since* consequences cannot be foreseen, *since* we live but a moment. . . .
> He looked *for* clean fingernails and polished shoes, *for* an air of composure with a quick wit.

Watch the Paralleling of Pairs

Pairs should be pairs, not odds and ends. Notice how the faulty pairs in these sentences have been corrected:

> She liked *the lawn and gardening* (the lawn and the garden).
> They were *all athletic or big men on campus* (athletes or big men on campus).
> They wanted *peace without being disgraced* (peace without dishonor).
> She liked *to play well and winning before a crowd* (to play well and to win; playing well and winning).
> He was *shy but a creative boy* (shy but creative).

Check your terms on both sides of your coordinating conjunctions (*and, but, or*) and see that they match:

> Orientation week seems both worthwhile [adjective] and
>   necessary
>   ~~a necessity~~ [noun].
>   that
> He prayed that they would leave and ∧ the telephone would
>   not ring.

Learn to Use Paralleling Coordinators

The sentence above about "Orientation week" employs one of a number of useful (and tricky) parallel constructions: *Both/and; either/or; not only/but also; not/but; first/second/third; as well as.* This last one is similar to *and*, a simple link between two equivalents, but it often causes trouble:

> **One should take care of one's physical self [noun]** *as well as*
> **being [participle] able to read and write.**

Again, the pair should be matched: "one's *physical self* as well as one's *intellectual self*," or "one's physical *self* as well as one's *ability* to read and write"—though this second is still slightly unbalanced, in concept if not in grammar. The best cure would probably extend the underlying antithesis, the basic parallel:

> **One should take care of one's physical self as well as one's intellectual self, of one's ability to survive as well as to read and write.**

With the *either/or*'s and the *not only/but also*'s you continue the principle of pairing. The *either* and the *not only* are merely signposts of what is coming: two equivalents linked by a coordinating conjunction (*or* or *but*). Beware of putting the signs in the wrong place—too soon for the turn.

> **Either he is an absolute piker or a fool.**

> **Neither in time nor space. . . .**

> **He not only likes the girl, but the family, too.**

In these examples, the thought got ahead of itself, as in talk. Just make sure that the word following each of the two coordinators is of the same kind, preposition for preposition, article for article, adjective for adjective—for even with signs well placed, the parallel can skid:

> **The students are not only organizing [present participle] social**
>   **discussing**
> **activities, but also** ~~**are interested**~~ **[passive construction]** ~~**in**~~ **political questions.**

Put identical parts in parallel places; fill in the blanks with the same parts of speech: "not only _____, but also _____."

Beginning with *Not only,* a common habit, always takes more words as it duplicates subject and verb, inviting a comma splice and frequently misaligning a parallel:

> **POOR:** *Not only* **is man limited in his mind and in his position in the universe, he is also limited in his physical powers.**
> **IMPROVED: Man is limited** *not only* **in his mind and in his position in the universe,** *but also* **in his physical powers.** [*21 words for 23*]

The following sentence avoids the comma splice but still must duplicate subject and verb:

> POOR: *Not only* are the names similar, but the two men share some similarities of character.
> IMPROVED: The two men share similarities *not only* in name *but* in character. [*12 words for 15*]

The following experienced writer avoids the usual comma splice with a semicolon but makes a dubious parallel:

> POOR: *Not only* was the right badly splintered into traditional conservatives, economic liberals, and several other factions; the Communists were the weakest they had been in half a century.
> IMPROVED: The right was badly splintered . . . , *and* the Communists. . . .

Again, move that eager *Not only* along into the sentence until you can put the same parts of speech into the blanks—"not only_____, but also_____"—or abandon the parallel.

You similarly parallel the words following numerical coordinators:

> However variously he expressed himself, he unquestionably thought, first, that everyone could get ahead; second, that workers generally were paid more than they earned; and, third, that laws enforcing a minimum wage were positively undemocratic.
> For a number of reasons he decided (1) that he did not like it, (2) that she would not like it, (3) that they would be better off without it. [Note that the parentheses around the numbers operate exactly as any parentheses, and need no additional punctuation.]
> My objections are obvious: (1) it is unnecessary, (2) it costs too much, and (3) it won't work.

Numerical
Coordinators

In parallels of this kind, *that* is usually the problem, since you may easily, and properly, omit it when there is only one clause and no confusion:

> . . . he unquestionably thought everyone could get ahead.

If second and third clauses occur, as your thought moves along, you may have to go back and put up the first signpost:

that
. . . he unquestionably thought ∧ **everyone could get ahead,**
that workers . . . , and that laws. . . .

Enough of *that.* Remember simply that equivalent thoughts demand parallel constructions. Notice the clear and massive strategy in the following sentence from the concluding chapter of Freud's last book, *An Outline of Psychoanalysis.* Freud is not only summing up the previous discussion, but also expressing the quintessence of his life's work. He is pulling everything together in a single sentence. Each of the parallel *which* clauses gathers up, in proper order, an entire chapter of his book (notice the parallel force in repeating *picture,* and the summarizing dash):

> **The picture of an ego which mediates between the id and the external world, which takes over the instinctual demands of the former in order to bring them to satisfaction, which perceives things in the latter and uses them as memories, which, intent upon its self-preservation, is on guard against excessive claims from both directions, and which is governed in all its decisions by the injunctions of a modified pleasure principle—this picture actually applies to the ego only up to the end of the first period of childhood, till about the age of five.**

Such precision is hard to match. This is what parallel thinking brings—balance and control and an eye for sentences that seem intellectual totalities, as if struck out all at once from the uncut rock. Francis Bacon also can seem like this (notice how he drops the verb after establishing his pattern):

> **For a crowd is not company, and faces are but a gallery of pictures, and talk but a tinkling cymbal, where there is no love.**
> **Reading maketh a full man; conference a ready man; and writing an exact man.**

And the balance can run from sentence to sentence through an entire passage, controlled not only by connectives repeated in parallel, but by whole phrases and sentences so repeated, as in this passage by the Victorian historian T. B. Macaulay:

   To sum up the whole: we should say that the aim of the Platonic philosophy was to exalt man into a god. The aim of the Baconian philosophy was to provide man with what he requires while he continues to be man. The aim of the Platonic philosophy was to raise us far above vulgar wants. The aim of the Baconian philosophy was to supply our vulgar wants. The former aim was noble; but the latter was attainable.

EXERCISES

12. *Review the discussion of parallel coordinators on 167–70. Then write two sentences apiece for each of the following sets of coordinators. Try different parts of speech, but keep your parallels true by filling the blanks in any one sentence with the same parts of speech.*

    both _____ and _____
    either _____ or _____
    not only _____ but also _____
    (1) _____, (2) _____, (3) _____
    _____ as well as _____

13. *Correct the faulty parallelism in the following sentences from students' papers, and clean up any wordiness you find.*

    1. Twain seems eventually to become completely cynical, seemed to doubt even that any human life could be happy.
    2. The Hemingway hero is a man who moves from one affair to another, who seeks adventure, enjoys bullfights, did a great deal of drinking, who was involved in activities we all wish we could try at least once.
    3. In this way not only the teacher needs to be concerned with the poorest student, but every class member helped.
    4. A student follows not only a special course of training, but among his studies and social activities finds a liberal education.
    5. Either the critics attacked the book for its triteness, or it was criticized for its lack of organization.
    6. By driving carefully, by making sure the engine was tuned, keeping the tires carefully filled, we were able to increase the gas mileage by about 18 percent.
    7. When they go to church, it is only because they have to go and not of their own desire.
    8. Many people argue that the so-called virtues of man belong to the age of chivalry, and they do not apply to the present.
    9. This is not only the case with the young voters of the United States but also of the adult ones.
    10. Certain things are not actually taught in the classroom. They are learning how to get along with others, to depend on oneself, and managing one's own affairs.
    11. Not only did he delight in youth, but he had an almost pathological fear of growing old.

12. Knowing Greek and Roman antiquity is not just learning to speak their language but also their culture.
13. I think fraternities are sociable as well as the dormitories.
14. We have seen that Wright was always fascinated by violence, that he had often seen violence first-hand, and he was himself a potentially violent person.

14. (**a**) *In the following famous sentence of Bacon's, straighten the faulty parallels and fill out all the phrasing implied by them:*

Histories make men wise; poets witty; the mathematics subtle; natural philosophy deep; moral grave; logic and rhetoric able to contend.

(**b**) *Now write three sentences on the Baconian pattern: "Jack would eat no fat; his wife no lean; the old dog only soup . . .; the young. . . . "*

15. *To discover how far parallelism might take you, write a parody of the following passage from Samuel Johnson, matching him phrase for phrase and sentence for sentence. Pick out two ball players, two TV actresses, two rock stars, or the like, and have some fun. You simply substitute your terms for Johnson's, leaving everything else as it is, where it fits. ("Of genius, that power that constitutes a ball player, that quality without which fielding is cold and batting is inert. . . . " "Of glamour, that power which constitutes an actress. . . . ")*

Of genius, that power which constitutes a poet; that quality without which judgement is cold and knowledge is inert; that energy which collects, combines, amplifies, and animates—the superiority must, with some hesitation, be allowed to Dryden. It is not to be inferred that of this poetical vigour Pope had only a little, because Dryden had more, for every other writer since Milton must give place to Pope; and even of Dryden it must be said that if he has brighter paragraphs, he has not better poems. Dryden's performances were always hasty, either excited by some external occasion, or extorted by domestick necessity; he composed without consideration, and published without correction. What his mind could supply at call, or gather in one excursion, was all that he sought, and all that he gave. The dilatory caution of Pope enabled him to condense his sentiments, to multiply his images, and to accumulate all that study might produce, or chance might supply. If the flights of Dryden therefore are higher, Pope continues longer on the wing. If of Dryden's fire the blaze is brighter, of Pope's the heat is more regular and constant. Dryden often surpasses expectation, and Pope never falls below it. Dryden is read with frequent astonishment, and Pope with perpetual delight.

THE LONG AND SHORT OF IT

Your style will emerge once you can manage some length of sentence, some intricacy of subordination, some vigor of parallel, and some play of long against short, of amplitude against brevity. Try the very long sentence, and the very short. The best short sentences are meatiest:

Money talks.
A stitch in time saves nine.
The mass of men lead lives of quiet desperation.
The more selfish the man, the more anguished the failure.

Experiment with the Fragment

The fragment is close to conversation. It is the laconic reply, the pointed afterthought, the quiet exclamation, the telling question. Try to cut and place it clearly (usually at beginnings and ends of paragraphs) so as not to lead your reader to expect a full sentence, or to suspect a poor writer:

Not at all.
First, a look behind the scenes.
Expert within limits, that is.
Enough of that.

The fragment, of course, usually counts as an error. The reader expects a sentence and gets only a fragment of one: you leave him hanging in air, waiting for the second shoe to fall, or the voice to drop, with the thought completed, at the period. The *rhetorical* fragment—the effective and persuasive one—leaves him satisfied: *Of course.* The *grammatical* fragment leaves him unsatisfied: *When the vote was counted.* A question hangs in the air: *what* happened? who won? who got mad? Each of the following typical grammatical fragments—italicized—could be cured by attaching it, with a comma, to its governing sentence:

He dropped his teeth. *Which had cost five hundred dollars.*
A good example is Hawthorne. *A writer who could dramatize abstract moral theories.*
Cleopatra is the stronger. *Trying to create Antony in her own Egyptian image.*

The grammatical, or *accidental,* fragment usually follows its governing sentence, as in the examples above.

Here is a paragraph with rhetorical fragments placed at the surest and most emphatic places, beginning and end, with a faulty grammatical fragment, to illustrate the difference, still wandering in the middle (all fragments in italics):

Not quite. **The battle, as it proved, still had two bloody hours to run. B Company, presumed lost by allies and enemy alike, had finally worked through the jungle and flanking outposts, virtually intact.** *Tired but fully equipped.* **They now brought the full force of surprise and weaponry to bear on the attackers' weakened right flank. The attack turned to meet the surprise. The defenders, heartened, increased their pressure. Reinforcements by helicopter completed the flaming drama.** *Curtains for the assault on Won Thang.*

That floating fragment in the middle needs to be attached to the sentence of which it is really a part, either the one before or the one following.

> EITHER: **B Company, presumed lost by allies and enemy alike, had finally worked through the jungle and flanking outposts, virtually intact, tired but fully equipped.**
> OR: **Tired but fully equipped, they now brought the full force. . . .**

But the point here about rhetorical fragments is to use their short, conversational staccato as one of your means to vary the rhythm of your long and longer sentences, playing long against short.

Develop a Rhythm of Long and Short

The conversational flow between long and short makes a passage move. Study the subordinations, the parallels, and the play of short and long in this elegant passage of Virginia Woolf's—after you have read it once for sheer enjoyment. She is writing of Lord Chesterfield's famous letters to Philip Stanhope, his illegitimate son:

Subordinate
Long

Short
Long

Short
Shorter

> **But while we amuse ourselves with this brilliant nobleman and his views on life we are aware, and the letters owe much of their fascination to this consciousness, of a dumb yet substantial figure on the farther side of the page. Philip Stanhope is always there. It is true that he says nothing, but we feel his presence in Dresden, in Berlin, in Paris, opening the letters and poring over them and looking dolefully at the thick packets which have been accumulating year after year since he was a child of seven. He had grown into a rather serious, rather stout, rather short young man. He had a taste for foreign politics. A**

little serious reading was rather to his liking. And by every post — Longer
the letters came—urbane, polished, brilliant, imploring and — Long
commanding him to learn to dance, to learn to carve, to consider the management of his legs, and to seduce a lady of fashion. He did his best. He worked very hard in the school of the — Short
Graces, but their service was too exacting. He sat down halfway — Longer
up the steep stairs which lead to the glittering hall with all the
mirrors. He could not do it. He failed in the House of Com- — Short
mons; he subsided into some small post in Ratisbon; he died — Parallel
untimely. He left it to his widow to break the news which he
had lacked the heart or the courage to tell his father—that he — Long
had been married all these years to a lady of low birth, who had
borne him children.

     The Earl took the blow like a gentleman. His letter to his — Short
daughter-in-law is a model of urbanity. He began the education — Longer
of his grandsons. . . .*

Those are some sentences to copy. We immediately feel the rhythmic play of
periodic and loose, parallel and simple, long and short. Such orchestration
takes years of practice, but you can always begin.

EXERCISES

16. *Write a paragraph beginning and ending with a deliberate rhetorical fragment, and
containing one or two clearly faulty grammatical ones, on the model of the paragraph
on 174. Then show how you would correct the faulty fragments.*

17. *Write an imitation of the passage (just preceding) from Virginia Woolf, choosing your
own subject but matching the patterns, lengths, and rhythms of her sentences, sentence for sentence, if you can. At any rate, aim toward effective rhythms of long and
short.*

18. *Here is an awkward and monotonous passage. One after another, the sentences
march along for nearly the same number of words. Rewrite the passage, giving its
sentences variety in both pattern and length.*

    In 1911, Cal Rodgers was the first American pilot to attempt a successful
coast-to-coast flight across the United States. He was tempted by the $50,000
prize offered by the Hearst papers to the first man to fly coast-to-coast in under

---

30 days. But as it turned out, poor Rodgers had to endure a lot of trouble and hardship and still did not win any of the prize money. First, he had to pay all of his own expenses for the trip, and that included the very high cost of having a train follow his route with spare parts. Admittedly, he was able to sell some advertising space on the side of his plane to a beer manufacturer, but he still finished the trip deeply in debt. Next, he had to travel an especially long and zigzag route because his tiny plane was not powerful enough to fly directly over the mountains. And to top it off, he had to put up with long delays for repairs both to his plane and to himself. He had 68 stops and 19 crashes and incurred a broken ankle as well as numerous cuts and bruises. When he arrived in California the plane he was flying was almost entirely different from the plane he had started with. In all, the trip took him 49 days and Rodgers covered the 3,390-mile distance in 82 hours of flying. His average speed was 40 miles per hour and his longest hop was 133 miles. And in the end, the Hearst papers did not award him the prize because he was 19 days over the stipulated time.

CHAPTER 9

Correcting Wordy Sentences

Now let us contemplate evil—or at least the innocently awful, the bad habits that waste our words, fog our thoughts, and wreck our delivery. Our thoughts are naturally roundabout, our phrases naturally secondhand. Our satisfaction in merely getting something down on paper naturally blinds us to our errors and ineptitudes. It hypnotizes us into believing we have said what we meant, when our words actually say something else: "Every seat in the house was filled to capacity." Two ways of expressing your thought, two clichés, have collided: *every seat was taken* and *the house was filled to capacity.* Cut the excess wordage, and the absurd accident vanishes: "Every seat was taken." Good sentences come from constant practice in correcting the bad.

Count Your Words

Writing is devilish; the general sin is wordiness. We put down the first thought that comes, we miss the best order, and we then need lengths of *is*'s, *of*'s, *by*'s and *which*'s—words virtually meaningless in themselves—to wire our meaningful words together again. Look for the two or three words that carry your meaning; then see if you can rearrange them to speak for themselves, cutting out all the little useless wirings:

> **This is the young man who was elected to be president by the
> class.** [**This is the young man the class elected president.** *Or:*
> **The class elected this young man president.** *9 words, or 7 words,
> for 14*]

See if you can't promote a noun into a verb, and cut overlaps in meaning:

> **Last week, the gold stampede in Europe reached near panic proportions. [Last week, Europe's gold speculators almost stampeded.** *7 words for 11*]

When you convert the noun, *stampede,* into a verb, *stampeded,* you suddenly discover that you have already said "near panic proportions" and you can drop it entirely: stampedes *are* panics. That ungrammatical and ubiquitous *near* (which, incidentally, should be either *nearly* or *almost*) is usually a symptom of wordiness, probably because it reveals a general inattention to meanings: the writer is not, as his word seems to say, visualizing a hand reaching near something called "panic." Frequently you can reduce tautologies, those useless repetitions of the same idea in different words (see 187):

advance notice	**notice**
each separate incident	**each incident**
many different ways	**many ways**
dash quickly	**dash**

As these examples show, the basic cure for wordiness is to count the words in any suspected phrase or sentence—and to make each word count. If you can rephrase to save even one word, your sentence will be clearer. And seek the active verb: *John* HITS *Joe.*

EXERCISES

1. *Clear up the blurred ideas, and grammar, in these sentences from students' papers and official prose, making each word say what it means, and counting your words to make sure your version has fewer.*

   1. Tree pruning may be done in any season of the year. [11 words]
   2. After reading a dozen books, the subject is still as puzzling as ever. [13]
   3. The secret teller vote used in the past was this time a recorded teller vote. [15]
   4. I awoke at midnight, my bones aching and my back felt as if it were being pricked with electric needles. [20]
   5. The courses listed herein are those which meet the college level requirements which were stated above. [16]
   6. Summer is a time in which more engines overheat than any other. [12]
   7. They were unable to locate my check, as well as their cashier department. [13]
   8. Records can be used in the Audio Room by individual students for their suggested listening assignments. [16]
   9. My counter was for refunds for which the customer had already paid for. [13]
   10. Entrance was gained by means of the skylight. [8]

11. The reason we give this test is because we are anxious to know whether or not you have reflexes that are sufficiently fast to allow you to be a safe worker. [31]
12. The final upshot is whether or not the students have actually grasped the basic essentials, or just merely bare facts. [20]
13. What we have recently called early beginnings is now past history. [11]

2. *From magazines, newspapers, or your own papers, collect ten sentences you can improve. Cut excess words, promote nouns to verbs, convert to active voice, and generally economize by attending to what the words say. Hand in the wordy sentences with your revisions, indicating the number of words saved.*

Shun the Passive Voice

The passive voice is more wordy and deadly than most people imagine, or it would not be so persistent.

> **It was voted that there would be a drive for the cleaning up of the people's park.** [*passive voice—17 words*]
> **We [the town, the council] voted a drive to clean up the people's park.** [*active voice—10 or 11 words, depending on subject*]

The passive voice puts the cart before the horse: the object of the action first, then the harnessing verb, running backwards, then the driver forgotten, and the whole contraption at a standstill. The passive voice is simply "passive" action, the normal action backwards: object-verb-subject (with the true subject usually forgotten) instead of subject-verb-object—*Joe was hit by John* instead of *John hit Joe.*

The passive voice liquidates and buries the active individual, along with most of the awful truth. Our massed, scientific, and bureaucratic society is so addicted to it that you must constantly alert yourself against its drowsy, impersonal pomp. The simple English sentence is active; it *moves* from subject through verb to object: "The dean's office has turned down your proposal." But the impersonal bureau usually emits instead a passive smoke screen, and the student sees no one at all to help him:

> **It has been decided that your proposal for independent study is not sufficiently in line with the prescribed qualifications as outlined by the college in the catalog.**

Committees always write this way. Perhaps the basic rule should be to write like a person, not like a bureau or a committee.

I reluctantly admit that the passive voice has certain uses. It can, in a string of active sentences, give more variety, although phrasal and clausal variations are better. It can also vary the emphasis, and the interest, by inverting normal order. *Joe was hit by John* throws selective light on Joe, by inverting regular consequences and distinguishing him from all other unfortunates, and it gives John a certain dubious distinction too. The passive voice can, indeed, omit the doer with meaningful effect, especially when the doer is unknown: *Joe was hit.* ("I was sunk." "It was done.")

In fact, your meaning sometimes demands the passive voice: the agent may be better under cover—insignificant, or unknown, or mysterious. The active "Shrapnel hit him" seems to belie the uncanny impersonality of "He was hit by shrapnel." The broad forces of history similarly demand the passive: "The West was opened in 1848." Moreover, you may sometimes need the passive voice to place your true subject, the hero of the piece, where you can modify him conveniently: *Joe was hit by John, who, in spite of all.* . . . And sometimes it simply is more convenient: "This subject-verb-object sentence can be infinitely contorted." You can, of course, find a number of passive constructions in this book, which preaches against them, because they can also space out a thought that comes too fast and thick. In trying to describe periodic sentences, for instance (148), I changed "until all interconnections lock in the final word" (active) to " . . . are locked by the final word" (passive). The *lock* seemed too tight, especially with *in,* and the locking seemed contrary to the way buildings *are built.* Yes, the passive has its uses.

But most of the time, it is simply wordy. It puts useless words in a sentence. Its dullness derives as much from its extra wordage as from its impersonality. *Joe was hit by John* says no more than *John hit Joe,* but takes 66 percent more words! The passive's inevitable *was* and *by* do nothing but connect; worse, all the *was*'s and *by*'s and *has been*'s actually get in the way of the words carrying the meaning, like underbrush slowing you down and hiding what you want to see.

The best way to prune is with the active voice, cutting the passive and its fungus as you go. Notice the effect on the following typical, and actual, samples:

> PASSIVE: **Public concern** *has* **also** *been given* **a tremendous impetus** *by* **the findings of the Hoover Commission on the federal government, and "little Hoover" commissions to survey the organizational structure and functions of many state governments** *have been established.*
>
> ACTIVE: **The findings of the Hoover Commission on federal government** *have* **also greatly stimulated public concern, and many states** *have established* **"little Hoover" commissions to survey their governments.** [*27 words for 38*]
>
> PASSIVE: **The algal mats** *are made up of* **the interwoven filaments of several genera.**

ACTIVE: **The interwoven filaments of several genera** *make up* **the algal mats.** [*11 words for 13*]

PASSIVE: **Many of the remedies** *would* **probably** *be shown to be* **faith cures.**

ACTIVE: **Many of the remedies** *are* **probably faith cures.** [*8 words for 12*]

PASSIVE: **Anxiety and emotional conflict** *are lessened* **when latency sets in. The total personality** *is oriented* **in a repressive, inhibitory fashion so as to maintain the barriers, and what Freud has called "psychic dams," against psychosexual impulses.**

ACTIVE: **When latency sets in, anxiety and emotional conflict** *subside.* **The personality** *inhibits* **itself, maintaining its barriers—Freud's "psychic dams"—against psychosexual impulses.** [*22 words for 36*]

The passive voice, in its wordiness alone, is always a bit unclear even on the surface; but, if it eliminates the real subject of the verb, as it usually does, it is intrinsically unclear as well. "This passage has been selected because . . . ," the student will write, and the reader cannot tell who did the selecting. Does he mean that he, the writer, has picked it, or does he describe some process of natural or popular selection? We surmise he means himself, of course. He has omitted himself because his teachers have told him to keep his eye on the subject and not on the "I." But if the subject *is* the selection, he could save a word, and avoid confusion: "I selected this passage because. . . . "

Any form of the verb *is* may reveal a passive construction. Our language must use some form of *is* so frequently in stating that things *are* and in forming its compound verbs (*is falling, were playing*) that you should drop as many *is*'s and *was*'s as possible, simply to avoid monotony. But when they are—as they often are—signs of the passive voice, you can also avoid rigor mortis by replacing your *is*'s with active verbs, along with their true subjects, the real doers of the action.

EXERCISES ————————————————————————

3. *Write five sentences in the passive voice, and change each to its active equivalent.*

4. *Recast these sentences in the active voice, clearing out all passive constructions, saving as many words as you can, and indicating the number saved:*

   1. The particular topic chosen by the instructor for study in his section of English 2 must be approved by the Steering Committee. [Start with "The Steering Committee," and don't forget the economy of an apostrophe-*s*. I managed 14 words for 22.]

2. Recommendations concerning the type of study needed to assure adequate definition of the larger problem and develop feasible options in programs designed to eliminate or greatly reduce both the direct and indirect effects within a reasonable time and at acceptable cost were presented in the report. [Begin with "The report"; cut "type of"; try adverbs for "within a reasonable time and at acceptable cost." I made it 30 words for 46.]

3. Avoidance of such blunders should not be considered a virtue for which the student is to be commended, any more than he would be praised for not wiping his hands on the tablecloth or polishing his shoes with the guest towels. [Begin "We should not"; try *avoiding* for *avoidance,* and *virtuous* for *virtue.* I managed to score 27 for 41.]

4. Collaborative analytical determinations were utilized to assess the probable consequences of mechanical failure. [Start with "Analysts." I scored 10 for 13.]

5. The difference between restrictives and nonrestrictives can also be better approached through a study of the different contours that mark the utterance of the two kinds of element than through confusing attempts to differentiate the two by meaning. ["One can differentiate restrictives"—I managed 13 for 38.]

6. Individuals whose income is insufficient to lift them above poverty must be provided with assistance from public sources. [Start active, and try "supplement"—11 for 18.]

7. In the next thirty-five years it is expected that there will be more engineering work to be done than has been done in all of recorded history. [Make "The next thirty-five years" the subject—14 for 27.]

8. If expansion is not accomplished, then two less-efficient alternatives must be acted upon: either the book sales will have to be in separate quarters or else the whole enterprise will have to be moved to a new location. [Try "we"—18 for 38.]

9. Trees on average sites are expected to be about twenty inches in diameter when they are eighty years old if they are managed properly since youth. [Start "Managed properly"—16 for 26.]

10. Any amended declaration should be filed with the Internal Revenue Office with whom the original declaration was filed even if you move to another district. [Keep it clear, but repeat no words—19 for 25.]

5. *Pick three obese and passive passages from your textbooks (including this one, if I have slipped). Change them to clean active sentences, indicating the number of words saved in each passage.*

Check the Stretchers

To be, itself, frequently ought not to be:

He seems [to be] upset about something.
She considered him [to be] perfect.
This appears [to be] difficult.

Above all, keep your sentences awake by not putting them into those favorite stretchers of the passivists, *There is . . . which, It is . . . that,* and the like:

> **Moreover, [there is] one segment of the population [which]
>   never seeks employment.**
> **[There are] many women [who] never marry.**
> **[There] is nothing wrong with it. [Nothing is . . .]**
> **[It is] his last book [that] shows his genius best.**
> **[It is] this [that] is important.**

The bracketed words can disappear without a ripple. Furthermore, *It is* frequently misleads your reader by seeming to mean something specific (*beer,* in the following example):

> **Several members voted for beer. *It is* hard to get *it* through ·
>   some people's heads that minors can't buy it.**
> **REVISED: Some people never learn that minors can't buy it.**

Cut every *it* not referring to something, if you can. Some *it*'s and *there*'s are immutably idiomatic, of course: *It is raining. There is nothing to do.* But you can cut most of them for a real gain. Next to activating your passive verbs, and cutting the passive *there is*'s and *it is*'s, perhaps nothing so improves your prose as to go through it systematically also deleting every *to be,* every *which, that, who,* and *whom* not needed for utter clarity or for spacing out a thought. All your sentences will feel better.

Beware the Of-and-Which Disease

The passive sentence also breaks out in a rash of *of*'s and *which*'s, and even the active sentence may suffer. Diagnosis: something like sleeping sickness. *With*'s, *in*'s, *to*'s, and *by*'s also inflamed. Surgery imperative. Here is a typical, and actual, case:

> **Many biological journals, especially those *which* regularly
> publish new scientific names, now state *in* each issue the exact
> date *of* publication *of* the preceding issue. *In* dealing *with* jour-
> nals *which* do not follow this practice, or *with* volumes *which*
> are issued individually, the biologist often needs *to* resort *to* in-
> dexes . . . *in order to* determine the actual date *of* publication *of*
> a particular name.**

Note *of publication of* twice over, and the three *which*'s. The passage is a sleeping beauty. The longer you look at it the more useless little attendants you see.

Note the inevitable passive voice *(which are issued)* in spite of the author's active efforts. The *of*'s accompany extra nouns, *publication* repeating *publish,* for instance. Remedy: (1) eliminate *of*'s and their nouns, (2) change *which* clauses into participles, (3) change nouns into verbs. You can cut more than a third of this passage without touching the sense (using 39 words for 63):

> **Many biological journals, especially those regularly *publishing* new scientific names, now give the date of each preceding issue. With journals not *following* this practice, and with some books, the biologist must turn to indexes . . . *to date* a particular name.**

I repeat: you can cut most *which*'s, one way or another, with no loss of blood. Participles can modify their antecedents directly, since they are verbal adjectives, without an intervening *which:* "a car *which was* going south" is "a car going south"; "a train *which is* moving" is "a moving train." Similarly with the adjective itself: "a song *which was* popular last year" is "a song popular last year"; "a person *who is* attractive" is "an attractive person." Beware of this whole crowd: *who are, that was, which are.*

If you need a relative clause, remember *that. Which* has almost completely displaced it in labored writing. *That* is still best for restrictive clauses, those necessary to definition: "A house that faces north is cool" (a participle would save a word: "A house facing north is cool"). *That* is tolerable; *which* is downright oppressive. *Which* should signal the nonrestrictive clause (the afterthought): "The house, which faces north, is a good buy." Here you need *which.* Even restrictive clauses must turn to *which* when complicated parallels arise. "He preaches the brotherhood of man *that* everyone affirms" elaborates like this: "He preaches the brotherhood of man *which* everyone affirms, *which* all the great philosophies support, but *for which* few can make any immediate concession." Nevertheless, if you need relatives, a *that* will often ease your sentences and save you from the *which*'s. Rule: NEVER USE A WHICH WITHOUT A COMMA IN FRONT OF IT—unless you have no other choice, as with the *brotherhood of man* above.

Verbs and their derivatives, especially present participles and gerunds, can also help to cure a string of *of*'s. Alfred North Whitehead, usually of clear mind, once produced this linked sausage: "Education is the acquisition *of* the art *of* the utilization *of* knowledge." Anything to get around the three *of*'s and the three heavy nouns would have been better: "Education instills the art of using knowledge"—"Education teaches us to use knowledge well." Find an active verb for *is the acquisition of,* and shift *the utilization of* into some verbal form: the gerund *using,* or the infinitive *to use.* Shun the *-tion*'s! Simply change your surplus *-tion*'s and *of*'s—along with your *which* phrases—into verbs, or verbals *(to use, learning).* You will save words, and activate your sentences.

EXERCISES

6. *Eliminate the italicized words in the following passages, together with all their accompanying wordiness, indicating the number or words saved (my figures again are merely guides; other solutions are equally good, or better).*

   1. *There is* a certain tendency to defend one's own position *which* will cause the opponent's argument to be ignored. [13 for 19]
   2. *It is* the other requirements *that* present obstacles, some *of which* may prove insurmountable in the teaching of certain subjects. [11 for 20]
   3. In the sort of literature-centered course being discussed here, *there* is usually a general understanding *that* themes will be based on the various literary works *that* are studied, the theory being *that* both the instruction in literature and *that* in writing will be made more effective by this interrelationship. [21 for 49]
   4. The person *whom* he met was an expert *who was* able to teach the fundamentals quickly. [13 for 16]
   5. They will take a pride *which is* wholly justifiable in being able to command a prose style *that is* lucid and supple. [13 for 22]
   6. This is a book on social status in America *that* has the benefit of sure insight into the revolutionary changes *that* have taken place in the political and economic structure since the New Deal. [18 for 34]
   7. *It is* expected *that* the new schedule will be announced by the bus company on Monday morning. [11 for 17]
   8. In our company *there are* wide-open opportunities for professional growth with a company *that* enjoys an enviable record for stability in the dynamic atmosphere of aerospace technology. [21 for 27]
   9. A minority finds it difficult to progress in such a society due to the fact *that* a majority can perpetuate inequality by simply insuring *that* the vast majority of its members acquire the positions *that* pay the greater amounts of money and carry the greatest authority. [23 for 46]
   10. It is not really any act *which* Julian commits *which* turns all his friends against him, but the fact *that* his sins are exposed publicly *that* makes him unforgiveable. [17 for 29]

7. *To cap your editorial skills, here are two of my favorites, two official statements, one from an eminent linguist, one from an eminent publisher. Clear up the wordiness, especially the italicized patches.*

   1. The work *which is* reported *in this* study *is* an investigation *of* language *within* the social context of the community *in which it is spoken. It is* a study *of* a linguistic structure *which is* unusually complex, but no more than the social structure of the city in which it functions. [22 for 52]
   2. Methods *which are* unique to the historian *are illustrated* throughout the volume *in order to* show how history *is written* and how historians work. The historian's approach to his subject, *which* leads to the asking of provocative questions and to a new understanding of complex events, situations, and personalities *is probed*. The manner *in which* the historian reduces masses of chaotic fact—and occa-

sional fancy—to reliable meaning, and the way *in which* he formulates explanations and tests them *is examined and clarified* for the student. *It is its* emphasis on historical method *which* distinguishes this book from other source readings in western civilization. The problems *which are examined* concern *themselves with* subjects *which* are *dealt with by* most courses in western civilization [66 for 123. The all-time winner from a student is 45 words.]

Beware "the use of"

In fact, both *use,* as a noun, and *use,* as a verb, are dangerously wordy words. Since *using* is one of our most basic concepts, other words in your sentence will already contain it:

> **He uses rationalization. [He rationalizes.]**
> **He uses the device of foreshadowing. [He foreshadows.]**
> **Through [the use of] logic, he persuades.**
> **His [use of] dialogue is effective.**

The utilization of and *utilize* are only horrendous extremes of the same pestilence, to be stamped out completely.

Break the Noun Habit

Passive writing adores the noun, modifying nouns with nouns in pairs, and even in denser clusters—which then become official jargon. Break up these logjams, let the language flow, make one noun of the pair an adjective:

> *Teacher militancy* **is not as marked in Pittsburgh. [***Teachers* **are not so** *militant* **in Pittsburgh.** *7 words for 8*]

Or convert one noun to a verb:

> *Consumer demand* **is falling in the area of services. [Consumers** *are demanding* **fewer services.** *5 words for 9*]

Of course, nouns have long served English as adjectives, as in "*rail*road," "*railroad* station," "*court*house," and "*noun* habit." But modern prose has aggravated the tendency beyond belief; and we get such monstrosities as *child sex education course* and *child sex education curriculum publication deadline reminder*—whole strings of nothing but nouns. Education, sociology, and psychology produce the worst noun-stringers, the hardest for you not to copy if you take these courses. But we have all caught the habit. The nouns *level* and *quality,* used as adjectives, have produced a rash of redundancies. A meeting of "high officials" has now unfortunately become a meeting of "high-*level* officials." The "finest cloth" these days is always "finest *quality* cloth." Drop those two redundant nouns and you will make a good start, and will sound surprisingly original. In fact, using the noun *quality* as an adjective has become almost obsessive —*quality food, quality wine, quality service, quality entertainment, high-quality drilling equipment*—blurring all distinctions of *good, fine, excellent, superb, superior,* in one dull and inaccurate cliché. A good rule: DON'T USE NOUNS AS ADJECTIVES. You can drop many an excess noun:

WORDY	DIRECT
advance notice	notice
long in size	long
puzzling in nature	puzzling
of an indefinite nature	indefinite
of a peculiar kind	peculiar
in order to	to
by means of	by
in relation to	with
in connection with	with
1981-model car	1981 car

Wherever possible, find the equivalent adjective:

of great importance	important
highest significance level	highest significant level
government spending	governmental spending
teaching excellence	excellent teaching
encourage teaching quality	encourage good teaching

Or change the noun to its related participle:

advance placement	advanced placement
charter flight	chartered flight
uniform police	uniformed police
poison arrow	poisoned arrow

Or make the noun possessive:

reader interest	reader's interest
factory worker wage	factory worker's wage
veterans insurance	veterans' insurance

Or try a cautious *of:*

STACKED NOUNS	IMPROVED
color lipstick	color of lipstick
teaching science	science of teaching
production quality	quality of production
high quality program	program of high quality
significance level	level of significance

Of all our misused nouns, *type* has become peculiarly pestilential and trite. Advertisers talk of *detergent-type cleansers* instead of *detergents;* educators, of *apprentice-type situations* instead of *apprenticeships;* newspapermen, of *Marxist-type organizations* instead of *Marxist organizations.* Don't copy your seniors; write boldly. We have become a nation of hair-splitters, afraid of saying *Czechoslovakia's Russian tanks* for fear that the reader will think they really belong to Russia. So the reporter writes *Russian-type tanks,* making an unnecessary distinction, and cluttering the page with one more *type-type* expression. We have forgotten that making the individual stand for the type is the simplest and oldest of metaphors: "Give us this day our daily bread." A twentieth-century supplicant might have written "bread-type food."

The simple active sentence transmits the message by putting each word unmistakably in its place, a noun as a noun, an adjective as an adjective, with the verb—no stationary *is*—really carrying the mail. Recently, after a flood, a newspaper produced this apparently succinct and dramatic sentence: **Dead animals cause water pollution.** (The word *cause,* incidentally, indicates wasted words.) That noun *water* as an adjective throws the meaning off and takes 25 percent more words than the essential active message: **Dead animals pollute water.** As you read your way into the sentence, it seems to say *dead animals cause water* (which is true enough), and then you must readjust your thoughts to accommodate *pollution.* The simplest change is from *water pollution* (noun-noun) to *polluted water* (adjective-noun), clarifying each word's function. But the supreme solution is to make *pollute* the verb it is, and the sentence a simply active message in which no word misspeaks itself. Here are the possibilities, in a scale from most active and clearest to most passive and wordiest, which may serve to chart your troubles if you get tangled in causes and nouns:

Dead animals pollute water.
Dead animals cause polluted water.
Dead animals cause water pollution.
Dead animals are a factor in causing the pollution of water.
Dead animals are a serious factor in causing the water pollution situation.
Dead farm-type animals are a danger factor in causing the post-flood clearance and water pollution situation.

So the message should now be clear. Write simple active sentences, out-maneuvering all passive eddies, all shallow *is*'s, *of*'s, *which*'s, and *that*'s, all over-lappings, all rocky clusters of nouns: they take you off your course, delay your delivery, and wreck many a straight and gallant thought.

EXERCISES

8. *Clear these passages of passives, "the use of," noun-nouns, and any other congestions that may block the reader's understanding.*

1. Actually, "thinking" was included in the later treatments of the communications arts and the language arts because of the eventual realization by both communica-tionists and language arts educationists of the merely mechanical interpretation which could be and was given to a pure "arts" orientation. The segregation of thought from expression by the exile of logic, dialectic, and rhetoric from the field of English is probably the most serious defect of the present composition situation in both college and high school. [44 for 80]

2. Still another problem concerns the comprehensiveness of exercise content in the several assessments. As noted from the outset, the exercises actually used in any one assessment constitute only a sample of those required to exhaustively measure attainment of assessment objectives, which are global in scope. No claims for comprehensive representativeness of the exercise samples can be made. In fact, there is no way to decide the question of comprehensiveness except by reference to particular instructional models designed by individual schools or teachers to im-plement given sets of objectives. [49 for 88]

3. Economic policy-making with respect to persons earning low incomes must center around making such individuals more productive. Particularly, it should work to-ward removing impediments to geographic and to upward mobility. This is, of course, the aim of much recent antipoverty legislation. As impediments are re-moved, the price system should become more effective in performing its realloca-tion functions. [33 for 57]

4. The purpose of every control system is to maintain a certain "desired value" (also known as the "reference value" or "index value") of the controlled condition. This is very clearly exemplified by the thermostat, a device for the regulation of temperature. Thermostats are extensively used in connection with present-day heating appliances, refrigerators, and so on. In most cases, the actual tempera-ture-sensing element is a bimetallic strip, a composite strip which is formed when two metals, having different coefficients of thermal expansion, are bonded to-gether. [44 for 84]

Give Your Writing Warmth

I have been urging condensation, to get rid of useless and obstructive phrases, especially those that, along with the passive voice, harden into habitual jargon in almost every profession. But your sentences can be *too* short and dense.

Many thoughts need explanation and an example or two. Many need the airing of *and*'s and *of*'s. Many simply need some loosening of phrase. In fact, colloquial phrasing, which is as clear and unnoticed as a clean window, is usually longer than its formal equivalent: *something to eat* as compared to *dinner.* By all counts, *dinner* should be better. It is shorter. It is more precise. Yet "Let's have something to eat" is friendlier than the more economical "Let's have dinner." We don't want to push our friends around with precise and economical suggestions. We want them at their ease, with the choices slightly vague. Consequently, when we write *what we are after* for *object* and *how it is done* for *method,* we give our all-too-chilly prose some social warmth. These colloquial phrases use more words, but they are not wordy if they pull with the rest of the sentence. What we want to avoid is redundancy, the clutter of useless words and tangential ideas—"the accumulation of words that add nothing to the sense and cloud up what clarity there is," as Aristotle says. What we write should be easy to read.

Avoid Excessive Distinctions and Definitions

Too many distinctions, too many nouns, and too many big Latinate words make pea soup:

> **Reading is a processing skill of symbolic reasoning sustained by the interfacilitation of an intricate hierarchy of substrata factors that have been mobilized as a psychological working system and pressed into service in accordance with the purpose of the reader.**

This comes from an educator, with the wrong kind of education. He is saying:

> **Reading is a process of symbolic reasoning aided by an intricate network of ideas and motives. [16 words for 40]**

Except with crucial assumptions and implications (see 109–10), try *not* to define your terms. If you do, you are probably either evading the toil of finding the right word, or defining the obvious:

> **Let us agree to use the word signal as an abbreviation for the phrase "the simplest kind of sign." (This agrees fairly well with the customary meaning of the word "signal.")**

That came from a renowned semanticist, an authority on the meanings of words. The customary meaning of a word *is* its meaning, and uncustomary meanings come only from careful punning. Don't underestimate your readers, as this semanticist did.

The definer of words is usually a bad writer. Our semanticist continues, trying to get his signals straight and grinding out about three parts sawdust to every one of meat. In the following excerpt, I have bracketed his sawdust. Read the sentence first as it was written; then read it again, omitting the bracketed words:

> **The moral of such examples is that all intelligent criticism [of any instance] of language [in use] must begin with understanding [of] the motives [and purposes] of the speaker [in that situation].**

Here, each of the bracketed phrases is already implied in the others. Attempting to be precise, the writer has beclouded himself. Naturally, the speaker would be "in that situation"; naturally, a sampling of language would be "an instance" of language "in use." *Motives* may not be *purposes,* but the difference here is insignificant. Our semanticist's next sentence deserves some kind of immortality. He means "Muddy language makes trouble":

> **Unfortunately, the type of case that causes trouble in practice is that in which the kind of use made of language is not transparently clear. . . .**

Clearly, transparency is hard. Writing is hard. It requires constant attention to meanings, and constant pruning. Count your words, and make your words count.

EXERCISES

9. *Here are some wordy, awkward, and flat passages from students' papers, with their wordage indicated in parentheses. Improve their diction by making their meaningful words count, cutting all the waste, and indicating your own wordage. Make it less, and grow rich with economy.*

1. Machines are merely amplifiers of the abilities of workmen, and exist only as they can do man's bidding effectively. (19)
2. Clearly, the only way to deal with machines is to neither flee from them nor surrender to them, but to use them as means to ends appointed not by them but by ourselves. (33)
3. The question is pertinent today, and painfully practical, as people examine the premises of their personal morality. (17)
4. Civil disobedience, then, is not the product of a recalcitrant minority intent on abolishing law and order, but exists in consequence of and as an important inte-

gral part of the give-and-take in democratic adjustment. It serves as a kick in the pants for legislators and the unconcerned majority, making them aware of faults in the democratic system. (57, *give-and-take* counted as one word)

5. The criticism of the military in connection with the draft needs not be of only its character, which overshadowed the draft machinery, but also of its direct involvement with the selective service system. The draft, an institution created by Congress with the intention that it might be civilian-operated, administered by civilians for civilians, became what it was through the gradual infusion of the military. (64)

6. The ability to rapidly handle enormous amounts of data and make rapid decisions often enables the computer to do control applications, such as the generation of power at an electrical power plant. (32)

7. It is wrong to assume, although many criticisms are being raised against technology as it affects human values, that the author does not appreciate its great capacity for good. (29)

8. As the establishment filled with people, an air of stuffiness and a feeling of being uncomfortable permeated the room. (19)

9. This reviewer, after reading about a dozen reviews of the book, was struck by the lack of perception and openmindedness that the critics showed. (24)

10. With all the loud activity in the next apartment, the thinness of the walls became painfully apparent, and sleeping became impossible. (21)

11. The most essential prerequisite that any student group must have in order to be recognized as a power is a leader that acts both as a mouthpiece of the students' ideas and as an originator of students' strategy in their war against the administrators. (44)

12. When a student becomes a member of the Student Government Council, it is expected that he give up much of his spare time for the council. However, it is not, or at least should not, be expected that he quit school to take on the responsibility of a council member. (50)

13. Another fact which is revealed by the census statistics is that 72.4 percent of the total nonwhite population lives in urban areas. (22)

14. It is with the different classifications and different designations for the classes that the most immediately obvious departures from traditional and school grammars can be seen in the work of the linguists and the structural grammarians. Minor differences can easily be magnified and major points overlooked. (46)

15. There are two major results of the increasing mechanization of industry. One is a great reduction in the number of simple, repetitive jobs where all you need is your five senses and an untrained mind. The other result is a great increase in the number of jobs involved in designing, engineering, programming, and administering these automatic production systems. (58)

10. *To culminate this chapter on wordiness, write a* TERRIBLE ESSAY. *Have some fun with this perennial favorite, in which you reinforce your sense of clear, figurative, and meaningful language by writing the muddiest and wordiest essay you can invent, gloriously working out all the bad habits. Make it a parody of the worst kind of sociological and bureaucratic prose—the kind you have been editing in the previous exercises. Pick some trivial subject, like dripping faucets, and then write, in good essay form but with terribly abstract and jargonish language,* A Report of a Study of the Person

Sociology and Night Loss Cost Economics of the Faucets Which Drip in the Second Floor North Corner Woman Dormitory Lavatory, *or some similarly inflated piece of nonsense. Here are the rules:*

1. Put EVERYTHING in the passive voice.
2. Modify nouns *only* with nouns, preferably in strings of two or three, never with adjectives: *governmental spending* becomes *government level spending;* an *excellent* idea becomes *the excellence of conception of program.*
3. Use only big abstract nouns—as many *-tion*'s as possible.
4. Use no participles: not *dripping faucets* but *faucets which drip,* and use as many *which*'s as possible.
5. Use as many words as possible to say the least.
6. Work in as many trite and wordy expressions as possible: *needless to say, all things being equal, due to the fact that, in terms of, as far as that is concerned.*
7. Sprinkle heavily with *-wise*-type and *type*-type expressions, say *hopefully* every three or four sentences, make *quality* your only commendatory adjective (remember each time that it's really a noun). Likewise *near* ("near perfect").
8. Compile and use a basic terrible vocabulary: *situation, aspect, function, factor, phase, utilize, the use of,* and so on. The class may well cooperate in this.

One class has had great success with a three-paragraph terrible essay, incorporating each terrible error only once, and then having everyone rewrite the winning worst essay into the best prose possible.

CHAPTER 10

Words

Here is the word. Thesis, structure, paragraph, sentence, thought—our thoughts live in words. Our concepts are words. Sesquipedalian or short, magniloquent or low, Latin or Anglo-Saxon, Celtic, Danish, French, Spanish, Indian, Hindustani, Dutch, Italian, Portuguese, Choctaw, Swahili, Chinese, Hebrew, Turkish, Greek—English contains them all, a million words at our disposal, if we are disposed to use them. No language is richer than English. But our spoken vocabularies average only about 2800 words daily, our expository vocabularies probably fewer than 8000. We all have a way to go to possess our heritage.

We can realize that heritage only through reading and writing—discovering the words for what we have in mind to know, writing them out to express our thoughts, enriching our concepts as we enrich our vocabulary. Our written words uncoil the data of our perceptions and lay them out reasonably straight on paper so we can see them.

So we can see them—here is the key to the power of written words. We want to see them as well as hear them; we want Space to collaborate with Time—so we may have time and space to think. The ancient world designated sight as the chief of the five senses—superior to hearing, smell, taste, and touch. And certainly most of us would still agree. We would probably rather be deaf than blind, and *light* is our commanding metaphor for intelligence *(illumination, enlightenment, throw light on the subject)*. Because the spoken word, or the mind's idea, spins away as soon as it comes, we want to get it down on paper where it will stay put, where, by seeing it, we come to understand. Writing, then, both records and straightens our thoughts.

WORDS AND THINGS

Learn the Multiple Meanings of Words

Speech, in a sense, is virtually "wordless," since our meaningful utterances are words blended together in a fluid sweep of sound, with their meanings selected for us by their position and emphasis and pitch. You have probably heard about the difference between "HEzaLIGHThousekeeper" and "HE-zalightHOUSEkeeper," and about the subtle differences in stress, pitch, and pause by which we select from a word's several meanings the one we want. When conversing, we enjoy a total context of understanding, complete with shrugs and *you know*'s, that makes individual words and sentences of minimal importance. We actually speak as much in fragments as in sentences, and we constantly repeat and circle, even after we know we have been understood. In a sense, the other person doesn't hear a word we say: he gets the meaning without necessarily noticing the words at all.

But on the silent printed page, you must place your words with care: the pitch, the stress, the general context of understanding—all the elements that free our speech from care—are gone. And the visible presence of words heightens our awareness of them *as* words. So much so, indeed, that we sometimes think them physical things, confusing them with the actual sticks and stones of this world.

Words are not things, nor are they symbols of things: words are symbols of our *ideas* of things. The primary fact about words is that they are the abstractions or generalizations by which we pick up the particular sticks of this world. A word is a symbol for a generalization in our heads. Since we like our words to be as concrete as possible, the idea of generalization may bother us. But a word's function is to name a general class of things, or states, or thoughts, or whatever, and we want a word's limits no narrower. When I say *bed*, I mean the general idea of "bed." The physical bed you may picture will be different from mine, but we will understand each other sufficiently. You will get the general idea, and you will also know that I do not specifically mean your little bunk at the dorm, though I mean something like it.

So: words are symbols for our general ideas of things. They are classifiers not only of the sticks and stones of the physical world, but of all the qualities, movements, functions, and conditions we know—*cold, grateful, walk, marry, mother, president, slow, exactly.* Many words refer to nothing in the physical world, though we may infer the entity by its effects—*anger, confidence, peace,* for example; and many words seem to symbolize a kind of mental gesture, the grammar with which we connect our thoughts or describe the connections of the physical world, as with *of, by, in, with, when.*

Words, like other symbols, usually represent a multiplicity of things, not all closely related to each other. A *log* is something for cabins or hearths, a gadget towed behind a ship, or a book on its bridge. A *bridge* may be not only on a ship, but in someone's mouth, or across the Golden Gate (which has neither gold nor hinges). The skipper could take out his bridge while sailing under the bridge and playing bridge on the bridge. Context is usually sufficient to select the wanted meanings automatically from the unwanted. That words have varieties of meanings bothers no one but the theoreticians—or your readers, if you are careless.

Try a Little Punning

To master words, you must keep alert to all their possibilities of meaning. Hence the punster usually makes the good writer: he forestalls any diabolical misreading because he has already seen the possibility himself. He would never accidentally write: "The situation was explosive, and he was no match for it." Nor: "The girls were barely attractive." A certain devilish eye for meanings will keep your words straight, and save you from innocent damnation.

Words are full of deviltry. *Pale* means bloodless of complexion (from Latin *pallidus*); and *pale* means a region staked out for one's reign (from Latin *palus*, or stake). Add such homophones ("same-sounders") as *rain* and *reign* to *pail* (bucket) and *pale* (bloodless; region), and you can see what Shakespeare could do as in this, one of the best of his songs, from *The Winter's Tale:*

> **When daffodils begin to peer,**
> **With heigh! the doxie over the dale—**
> **Why, then comes in the sweet o' the year,**
> **For the red blood reigns in the winter's pale.**

A good writer revels in multiple meanings, letting the ones he doesn't want just linger around the edge of the fun, to show that he knows them but decrees them temporarily insignificant.

A word acquires multiple meanings as it drifts into a new general usage and its specific meaning fades. A circle is a circle, but in expressions like *well known in artistic circles* the word has faded until it means no more than "group." It is a dead metaphor, ready for the touch of the good writer's pencil. The first user was making a metaphor—describing one thing in terms of another—in which he pictured admirers literally standing around an artist in a ring; he called them not people but a *circle,* naming them by something logically similar. In ordinary thoughtless parlance, we certainly do not see the circle; the physical, literal origin has faded. But the good writer will turn up the color a little, will bring the physical origin back for the reader to see: "The artist found in his circle a charmed protection from the world." Or he will at least prevent any unwanted physical or literal meanings, never writing, for instance, "The

artist painted his circle." The writer's best control of a word's multiple meanings lies in respecting the essentially physical thing it says, and in keeping an
impudent eye open for all transferred and metaphorical meanings.

EXERCISES

1. *Find as many meanings as you can, in your head and dictionary, for each of the following words.* **EXAMPLE:** *bridge—a structure over a river; false teeth; a card game; the
navigating platform on a ship.*

   hatch, hitch, runs, fair, case, draft, lock, down, prove, club, grave, fashion, fast,
   light, medium, joint, sole, cross, term, check

VOCABULARY

Build Your Vocabulary

As you build your sense of multiple meanings, build your vocabulary. If you
can increase your hoard, you increase your chances of finding the right word
when you need it. Read as widely as you can, and look words up the second
or third time you meet them. I once knew a man who swore he learned three
new words a day from his reading by using each at least once in conversation.
I didn't ask him about *polyphiloprogenitive* or *antidisestablishmentarianism.* It depends a little on the crowd. But the idea is sound. Keeping the commerce flowing through your reading, your speech, and your writing not only builds your
vocabulary but develops your style, with your speech and writing working together in a kind of mutual body building. The bigger the vocabulary, the more
various the ideas one can get across with it—the more the shades and intensities of meaning.

   The big vocabulary also needs the little word. The vocabularian often
stands himself on a Latin cloud and forgets the Anglo-Saxon ground—the
common ground between him and his audience. So do not forget the little
things, the *stuff, lint, get, twig, snap, go, mud, coax.* Hundreds of small words not
in immediate vogue can refresh your vocabulary. The Norse and Anglo-Saxon
adjectives ending in *-y (muggy, scrawny, drowsy),* for instance, rarely appear in
sober print.* The minute the beginner tries to sound dignified, in comes a
misty layer of words a few feet off the ground and nowhere near heaven, the

---

*See 327–32, Section A, "The English Language," for the early background of English.

same two dozen or so, most of them verbs. One or two will do no harm, but any accumulation is fatal—words like *depart* instead of *go:*

accompany—go with	**place—put**
appeared—looked *or* **seemed**	**possess—have**
arrive—come	**prepare—get ready**
attempt—try	**questioned—asked**
become—get	**receive—get**
cause—make	**relate—tell**
cease—stop	**remain—stay**
complete—finish	**remove—take off**
continue—keep on	**retire—go to bed**
delve—dig	**return—go back**
discover—find	**secure—get**
locate—find	**transform—change**

I add one treasured noun: *manner* for *way.* The question, as always, is one of meaning. *Manner* is something with a flourish; *way* is the usual way. But the beginner makes no distinction, losing the normal *way,* and meaning, in a false flourish of *manners.* Similarly, "she *placed* her cigarettes on the table" is usually not what the writer means (*place* connotes *arrange*). *Delve* is something that happens only when students begin to meditate. *Get* and *got* may be too colloquial for constant use in writing, but a discreet one or two can limber many a stiff sentence. Therefore, use the elegant Latin and the commonplace Anglo-Saxon, tastefully fitted; but shun the frayed gentility of *secure* and *place* and *remain,* whose shades of meaning you can find in your dictionary.

THE DICTIONARY

The dictionary is the best invention since writing, which made it possible, and indeed necessary. Here you can clarify those multiple meanings of words, tracing their origins, gathering synonyms, and stretching your vocabulary. Any good collegiate edition will do—*Random House, Funk & Wagnall's, Merriam-Webster, Webster's New World, The American Heritage.* The big unabridged dictionaries are richer, of course, with over 450,000 entries as against about 165,000 or so in the collegiates. No dictionary ever has, nor will, contain all the words and meanings in the language as they mutate and drop in and out of vogue yet remain in a printed record that now stretches back to Old English and the Anglo-Saxons.

The Oxford English Dictionary, known as the *OED,* records in its many volumes the earliest appearance of a word in print, giving date and source, then illustrates its variations in meaning through the years by later quotations. If you were writing on horse racing, for instance, the *OED* would give you some useful and impressive facts: a racing calendar first mentioned a *handicap* in 1754, and the verb "to handicap" did not appear for another century, in 1850. Furthermore, you would pick up some interesting details about the term, the sport, and its origin.

But the collegiates are remarkably informative, nevertheless. Each one gives you a "Guide to the Dictionary" to tell you what it can tell. Study it, and then open your dictionary at random to see how it works. Page 200 shows an entry on *shake* and its relatives in *The American Heritage Dictionary.* *

1. *Spelling, pronunciation, syllabication.* Spelling and pronouncing **shake** is no problem, but people open their dictionaries most frequently to check those two things, along with a word's syllabication—to find out where to hyphenate it: **syl·lab/·i·ca/·tion.** The light and heavy accent marks show exactly what to stress in pronouncing. We would also find **to·ma· to** (tə-mā/ tō, -mä/ tō), for instance, as a typical entry: the word spelled and syllabicated in bold-face type; the usual pronunciation, followed by its secondary variant, in parentheses. The key to pronunciation at the bottom of the page would show us the ə (called the *schwa*) sounding like the *a* in *about,* the long *a* in m*ā* sounding like the *a* in *pay,* the ō sounding like *toe,* and the secondary m*ä* sounding like the *a* in *father.*

2. *Parts of speech.* **Shake** is most frequently a verb *(v.),* so here its uses as a verb come first. Its eleven transitive *(tr.)* meanings, being more frequent, take precedence over its five intransitive *(intr.)* ones. Then follow its eleven meanings as a noun *(n.).*

3. *Forms.* The forms of **shake** in past and present, with their varied spellings and pronunciations (**shook, shaken, shaking, shakes**), follow immediately after the entry, showing again what people most frequently look for. With nouns, the dictionary gives plurals when they raise questions beyond adding a simple *s.*

    child (chīld) *n., pl.* **children** (chĭl/ drən).
    crocus (krō/kəs) *n., pl.* **-cuses** or **-ci** (-sī/).
        With adjectives, comparative and superlative forms follow the entry:
    queer (kwîr) *adj.,* **queerer, queerest.**

4. *Definitions.* The most common meanings come first, again satisfying the most frequent need. Brief quotations and phrases illustrate the usual, special, informal, and slang meanings where helpful. A few dictionaries

---

Past participle

Third person present tense

Pronunciation

Past tense

Present participle

Spelling

Transitive meanings

Definition as verb

General usages and illustrations

Intransitive meanings

Special usages

Definition as noun

Informal and slang usages

Etymology: the word history

Related forms

Synonyms and their shades of meaning

Related forms

Comment on usage

shake (shāk) *v.* **shook** (shŏok), **shaken** (shā'kən), **shaking, shakes.** —*tr.* **1.** To cause to move to and fro with short jerky movements. **2.** To cause to quiver or tremble; vibrate or rock: *A severe tremor shook the ground.* **3.** To cause to stagger or waver; unsettle. **4.** To remove or dislodge by jerky movements: *shake the dust out.* **5.** To bring to a specified condition by or as if by jerky movements: *"It is not easy to shake one's heart free of the impression"* (John Middleton Murry). **6.** To disturb or agitate; unnerve. Often used with *up.* **7.** To brandish or wave: *shake one's fist.* **8.** To clasp (hands or another's hand) in greeting or leave-taking or as a sign of agreement. **9.** To free oneself from: get rid of. Usually used with *off.* **10.** *Music.* To trill (a note). **11.** *Dice.* To rattle and mix (the dice) before casting. —*intr.* **1.** To move to and fro in short jerky movements. **2.** To tremble, as from cold or in anger. **3.** To totter or waver; become unsteady. **4.** *Music.* To trill. **5.** To shake hands. —*n.* **1.** An act of shaking. **2.** A trembling or quivering movement. **3.** *Informal.* An earthquake. **4.** A fissure in rock. **5.** A crack in timber caused by wind or frost. **5.** *Slang.* A moment or instant; trice: *I'll do it in a shake.* **7.** *Music.* A trill. **8.** A beverage in which the ingredients are mixed by shaking: *a milk shake.* **9.** A rough shingle used to cover barns and other rustic buildings. —**give (someone** or **something) the shake.** *Slang.* To escape from or get rid of. —**get a fair** (or **good) shake.** *Slang.* To be treated with fairness. —**no great shakes.** *Slang.* Unexceptional; ordinary; mediocre. —**the shakes.** *Informal.* **1.** The chill accompanying intermittent fever. **2.** Uncontrollable trembling, especially as a symptom of alcoholism. [Shake, shook, shaken; Middle English *schaken, schook, schaken,* Old English *sceacan, sceōc, sceacen,* from Germanic *skakan* (unattested).] —**shak'a-ble, shake'a-ble** *adj.*

Synonyms: *shake, tremble, quake, quiver, shiver, shudder, wobble.* These verbs mean to give evidence of agitation in the form of involuntary vibratory movement. *Shake,* the most general, applies to any such pronounced movement in a thing or a person, especially one moved by strong emotion. *Tremble* implies quick and rather slight movement like that of a person affected by fear, anger, or awe. *Quake* refers to violent convulsive movement caused by physical or emotional upheaval. *Quiver* suggests a slight and tremulous movement. *Shiver* involves rapid and rather slight movement, as of a person experiencing chill or fear. Whereas *trembling* implies localized movement in persons, *shivering* affects a wide area of the body. *Shudder* chiefly applies to sudden strong, convulsive shaking in a person, caused by fear, horror, or a revolting sight or thought. *Wobble* refers to pronounced and very unsteady movement.

shake down. *Informal.* **1.** To extort money from. See Usage note at **shakedown.** **2.** To make a thorough search of. **3.** To subject to a shakedown cruise.

shake·down (shāk'doun') *n. Informal.* **1.** An extortion of money by blackmail or other means. **2.** A thorough search of a place or person. **3.** A period of appraisal followed by adjustments to improve efficiency or functioning. —*adj.* Designed to test the performance of a ship or airplane and familiarize the crew with the operation: *a shakedown cruise.*

Usage: *Shakedown* (noun) in the sense of extortion and the related verb form *shake down* are not appropriate to deliberately formal usage, but have won increasing acceptance on all other levels. As examples in writing, the following are acceptable to majorities of the Usage Panel: *The committee found no evidence of a shakedown* (accepted by 80 percent). *He was convicted of shaking down three film executives* (accepted by 67 per cent).

shak·er (shā'kər) *n.* **1.** One that shakes. **2.** A container used for shaking something out: *a salt shaker.* **3.** A container used to mix or blend by shaking: *a cocktail shaker.*

Shak·er (shā'kər) *n.* A member of a religious sect originating in England in 1747, practicing communal living and observing celibacy. The official name of the sect is "The United Society of Believers in Christ's Second Coming." [From the former custom of dancing with shaking movements during ceremonies.]

rank their definitions chronologically from earliest to current, but this ranking is less useful. The historical *OED* is the great exception.

5. *Usage labels.* These give the definitions their greatest richness, and help the writer tune his diction, mixing in tasteful touches of slang and the colloquial for some extra life. Dictionaries differ as to what they label, and their labels differ also. *The American Heritage Dictionary* uses *informal,* for instance, probably a more useful label than *colloquial,* which means primarily "what is spoken." In addition to the many special labels, like *Dice* and *Music* for **shake,** or *Botany, Medicine, Psychoanalysis,* and *Nautical,* some other common ones are:

WORD	LABEL	MEANING
ain't	*Nonstandard*	am (are, is, has, have) not
critter	*Regional*	domestic animal, especially a steer or horse
croft	*British and Scottish*	small enclosed field near a house
Od's bodkins	*Archaic*	euphemism for "(by) God's body"
pee	*Vulgar*	urinate

If a word you want to use has a specialized label, you should probably clarify it for your reader:

There was a croft, or small enclosed field, by the house.
The plant's gametophyte, or reproductive agent, alternates sex
    each generation.

6. *Transitive and intransitive usages.* Transitive usages *(tr.)* take objects; intransitive *(intr.)* do not. You *shake a leg (tr.),* but *shake with cold (intr.).* These labels are especially helpful with troublesome distinctions like that between *lay (tr.)* and *lie (intr.).* You lay a carpet but lie down. Some dictionaries use *v.t.* and *v.i.*

7. *Etymology.* A word's derivation and history, in brackets, closes the definition. Some dictionaries put this first, but this is usually not the first thing you want to know. Our **shake** goes back through Middle English to Old English and Germanic, and has not changed much these 1500 years or so.

8. *Related forms.* These include, for the verb **shake,** the adjective **shakable,** with its two acceptable spellings, and the nouns **shaker** and **Shaker** as separate entries. The noun **water,** for instance, includes the adjective **water** and the noun **waterer** and almost four full columns of separate entries running from **waterage** through **water hole** and down to **watery.**

9. *Synonyms.* Here we can tell a **shake** from a *quake* and a *shiver* and a *shudder,* with their distinctions neatly defined. These distinctions usually run from

the most general to the particular and offer a nice range from which to choose the word to say what you mean. *Webster's New Dictionary of Synonyms* offers an even broader range, but a good collegiate usually suffices. Owning a thesaurus, a "treasury" of synonyms, is also a good idea. Its graded lists of synonyms often help you find a word you don't know or couldn't think of. But you must check it in your dictionary for its definition and levels of usage to make sure it's the one you want.

10. *Usage.* Here you can ponder, and decide for yourself, those levels of usage to which the editors could not fix a firm label. Their notes on usage give educated opinions from which you may judge your choice.

EXERCISES

2. *Pick five common words now in slang or dialectal usage—joint, or roach, or grass, for a marijuana cigarette, for instance. Write a clear definition of each in Standard English anyone could understand, then look up the word's origin in the dictionary. Put this origin, together with a brief speculation on how the slang term may have derived, in parentheses after your definition.*

> **EXAMPLE** *joint.* Slang. A cigarette made from dried flower clusters and leaves of the hemp plant, *cannabis sativa,* usually rolled loosely in paper by the user. (Middle English, from Old French, from the past participle of *joindre,* "to join," possibly because the user "joins" the materials.)

   If your term is not in the dictionary, try another that is. If you can see no connection between its origin and its slang usage, say "slang origin obscure."

3. *Look up each of the following words and use it in a sentence:*

   1. disinterested
   2. ardent
   3. effete
   4. sycophant
   5. ingenuous
   6. surrogate
   7. consummate *(adj.)*
   8. mordant
   9. somnolent
   10. equine

FAMILIES OF WORDS

Abraham Lincoln read the dictionary from cover to cover, and you really can browse it with pleasure, looking at the pictures of shagbarks and shakos and finding out about aardvarks and axolotls, jerboas and jerkins. But as you build up your knowledge with your vocabulary, you can, as we have seen, also acquire from a word's etymology a quick sense of our linguistic history, of families of words and ideas, of how some meanings have changed and some others have persisted through centuries and across continents. *Mid,* for instance, is still what it has been for the last five thousand years, persisting in most of the Indo-European languages all the way from Sanskrit to Old Norse and giving English a whole family of words from *middle* to *Mediterranean* to *intermezzo.* Acquaintance with a family can make you feel at home, can strengthen your vocabulary and your ability to use it. You can know and use a *ramp,* or a *rampage,* or a lion *rampant* familiarly, once you see the Old French for *climb* in all three. You can cut your meaning close to the old root, as in "He was *enduring* and *hard* as nails," where the Latin *durus* ("hard") has suggested its Anglo-Saxon synonym and given you a phrase your readers will like, though most of them won't know why.

Through the centuries, English has added Latin derivatives alongside the Anglo-Saxon words already there, keeping the old with the new: after the Anglo-Saxon *deor* (now *deer*) came the *beast* and then the *brute,* both from Latin through French, and the *animal* straight from Rome. Although we use more Anglo-Saxon in assembling our sentences *(to, by, with, but, is),* well over half our total vocabulary comes one way or another from Latin. The things of this world tend to be Anglo-Saxon *(man, house, stone, wind, rain)*: the abstract qualities, Latin and French *(value, duty, contemplation).*

Our big words are Latin and Greek. Your reading acquaints you with them; your dictionary will show you their prefixes and roots. Learn the common prefixes and roots (see Exercises 4, 5, and 6 at the end of this section), and you can handle all kinds of foreigners at first encounter: *con-cession* (going along with), *ex-clude* (lock out), *pre-fer* (carry before), *sub-version* (turning under), *trans-late* (carry across), *claustro-phobia* (dread of being locked in), *hydro-phobia* (dread of water), *ailuro-philia* (love of cats), *megalo-cephalic* (big-headed), *micro-meter* (little-measurer). You can even, for fun, coin a word to suit the occasion: *megalopede* (big-footed). You can remember that *intramural* means "within the (college) walls," and that "intermural sports," which is the frequent mispronunciation and misspelling, would mean something like "wall battling wall," a physical absurdity.

EXERCISES

4. *Browse your dictionary and find three families of words, like* ramp-rampage-rampant. *Give the root-idea of each family, and a word or two in definition of each word.*

5. *Make a permanent reference list by looking up in your dictionary each of the Latin and Greek prefixes and constituents listed below. Illustrate each with several English derivatives, and put in parentheses after each derivative its close literal English translation, as in these two examples:*

con- (with): convince (conquer with), conclude (shut with) concur (run with)

chron- (time): chronic (lasting a long time), chronicle (a record of the time), chronometer (time-measurer)

LATIN: *a- (ab-), ad-, ante-, bene-, bi-, circum-, con-, contra-, di- (dis), e- (ex-), in- (two meanings), inter-, intra-, mal-, multi-, ob-, per-, post-, pre-, pro-, retro-, semi-, sub- (sur-), super-, trans-, ultra-*

GREEK: *a- (an-), -agogue, allo-, anthropo-, anti-, apo-, arch-, auto-, batho-, bio-, cata-, cephalo-, chron-, -cracy, demo-, dia-, dyna-, dys-, ecto-, epi-, eu-, -gen, geo-, -gon, -gony, graph-, gyn-, hemi-, hepta-, hetero-, hexa-, homo-, hydr-, hyper-, hypo-, log-, mega-, -meter, micro-, mono-, morph-, -nomy, -nym, -pathy, penta-, -phag, phil-, -phobe (ia), -phone, poly-, pseudo-, psyche-, -scope, soph-, stereo-, sym- (syn-), tele-, tetra-, theo-, thermo-, tri-, zoo-*

6. *Think up several more words (omitting parts of speech, like* acts, acted, acting) *to add to the list of derivations already started after each of the following Latin verbs and their past participles. Add a note explaining particularly interesting ones, like* actuary *(an insurance expert).*

agere, actus (do)—agent, act . . .
audire, auditus (hear)—audit . . .
capere, captus (seize)—capable . . .
cedere, cessus (go)—concede . . .
claudere, clausus (shut)—close, include . . .
currere, cursus (run)—recur, course . . .
dicere, dictus (say)—dictate . . .
ducere, ductus (lead)—produce . . .
facere, factus (make)—infect . . .
ferre, latus (carry)—infer, relate . . .
fidere, fisus (trust)—confide, Fido . . .
fundere, fusus (pour)—refuse, refund . . .
gradi, gressus (step)—grade, digressions . . .
ire, itus (go)—exit, tradition . . .
jacere, jactus (throw)—reject . . .
legere, lectus (choose, read)—legible, elect . . .
loqui, locutus (speak)—circumlocution . . .
mittere, missus (send)—permit, mission . . .
pellere, pulsus (drive)—impel, repulse . . .
pendere, pensus (hang)—depend, pension . . .
plicare, plicatus (fold)—implication, complex . . .
ponere, positus (put)—response, position . . .
portare, portatus (carry)—import . . .
rumpere, ruptus (break)—rumpus, erupt . . .
scribere, scriptus (write)—scribble, script . . .
sedere, sessus (sit)—sedentary, assess . . .
sentire, sensus (feel)—sense . . .
specere, spectus (look)—speculate . . .
tendere, tensus (stretch)—tend, tense . . .
tenere, tentus (hold)—content . . .

trahere, tractus (drag)—tractor . . .
venire, ventus (come)—convene, invent . . .
vertere, versus (turn)—diverting, verse . . .
videre, visus (see)—divide, visible . . .
vocare, vocatus (call)—vocation . . .

DENOTATION AND CONNOTATION

When we look at those synonyms in our dictionary—*shake, tremble, quake, quiver, shiver, shudder, wobble*—we see that all of them specify, or *denote,* the same thing: a shaking motion. But each also *connotes* a different kind of shake. We move from the *denotation,* "a shaking," to the *connotations* of different shakings. These connotations have certain emotional attachments: *tremble* (fear), *quiver* (excitement), *shiver* (coldness), *shudder* (horror), *wobble* (imbalance). In short, words *denote* things, acts, moods, whatever: *tree, house, running, anger.* But they also *connote* an attitude toward these things. *Tree* is a purely neutral denotation, but *oak* connotes sturdiness and *willow* sadness, in addition to denoting different trees. Contexts also add connotations. *Christ died on the tree,* for instance, connotes the whole expanse of agony and sacrifice with which medieval Christianity endowed the word. *A House Is Not a Home,* wrote a certain lady, playing on the warm connotation of *home* and a specific denotation: a house of prostitution. *Woman* and *lady* both denote the human female, but carry connotations awakened in differing contexts:

A *woman* usually outlives a man. (Denotation)
She is a very able *woman.* (Connotation positive)
She is his *woman.* (Connotation negative)
She acts more like a *lady* than a *lady* of pleasure. (Connotations plus and minus)

Usage changes denotations: *a gay party* changes from a festive to a homosexual gathering. Usage and contexts also change connotations. *Negro,* once polite, is now taboo for the once impolite *black. Chairman,* once a neutral denoter, now has acquired enough negative connotations to change a number of letterheads and signatures to *chairperson.* Even the denotative *chairwoman* has picked up negative connotations.

EXERCISES

7. *Replace each of the italicized negative connotations with a positive or inoffensive one, using helping words as necessary.* **EXAMPLE:** He is *stingy* (thrifty, frugal).

1. The party was *stuffy.*
2. She was very *garrulous.*
3. The army *fled.*
4. A *skinny* little tree grew by the walk.
5. The restaurant *stank* of garlic.
6. The attack on the machine-gun implacement was *foolhardy.*
7. A *sluggish* little stream ran through the pasture.
8. The game was *boring.*
9. They *interrogated* the prisoners.
10. Someone had *blundered.*

EUPHEMISM

Substituting positive for negative connotations is *euphemism* ("good speaking"). Ironically, it is an effective kind of understatement: "She drove *a little fast*"; "He *imbibed occasionally.*" But it also grows straight and unadorned from our social tact as we avoid hurting others and from our private defenses as we sugar-coat our shortcomings. We constantly say *passed away* for *died* and, with our pets, *put to sleep* for *killed.* A cripple is a *handicapped person.* Dull children go to classes for *exceptional students.* Politics, as George Orwell points out, is a constant game of euphemism to cover mistakes and atrocities:

> **Things like the continuance of British rule in India, the Russian purges and deportations, the dropping of the atomic bombs on Japan, can indeed be defended, but only by arguments which are too brutal for most people to face, and which do not square with the professed aims of political parties. Thus political language has to consist largely of euphemism, question-begging, and sheer cloudy vagueness. Defenceless villages are bombarded from the air, the inhabitants driven out into the countryside, the cattle machine-gunned, the huts set on fire with incendiary bullets: this is called *pacification.* Millions of peasants are robbed of their farms and sent trudging along the roads with no more than they can carry: this is called *transfer of population* or *rectification of frontiers.* People are imprisoned for years without trial, or shot in the back of the neck, or sent to die of**

scurvy in Arctic lumber camps: this is called *elimination of unreliable elements.* *

Since euphemism veils stark particulars in generality, we should steer clear if we can, except for irony. Give the particulars as clearly as possible without hurting or antagonizing your readers. Your writing, as Orwell suggests, will be livelier and truer.

EXERCISES

8. *Rewrite the following euphemistic sentences in clear English:*

1. Some personnel will be discontinued owing to adverse gains in the company's overall economic situation.
2. The driver's ability was impaired because of some sociable refreshment in which he partook prior to leaving.
3. He passed away suddenly by his own hand leaving his disconsolate widow, children, and grandchildren a considerable fortune consisting of one hundred million dollars.
4. I acknowledge that the examination was of a moderately difficult level, but I believe that your son considerably underestimated the time necessary for preparation. I regret that you are disturbed by the results and that you are unsatisfied with the level of the questions.
5. He has not yet found a position suitable to his talents, though several opportunities in the manufacturing and shipping processes have been offered.

ABSTRACT AND CONCRETE

Every good stylist has perceived, in one way or another, the distinction between the general and the particular, the abstract and the concrete. Tangible things—things we can touch—are "concrete"; their qualities, along with all our emotional, intellectual, and spiritual states, are "abstract." The rule for a good style is to be as concrete as we can, to illustrate tangibly our general propositions, to use *shoes* and *ships* and *sealing wax* instead of *commercial concomitants.* But this requires constant effort: our minds so crave abstraction we can hardly pin them down to specifics.

---

*From "Politics and the English Language" from *Shooting an Elephant and Other Essays,* by George Orwell. Copyright © 1946 by Sonia Brownell Orwell; renewed 1974 by Sonia Orwell. Reprinted by permission of Harcourt Brace Jovanovich, Inc. , the estate of the late Sonia Brownell Orwell, and A.M. Heath & Company Ltd. Published in Great Britain by Martin Secker & Warburg Ltd.

Abstraction, a "drawing out from," is the very nature of thought. Thought moves from concrete to abstract. In the strictest sense, *all* words are abstractions. *Stick* is a generalization of all sticks, the crooked and the straight, the long and the short, the peeled and the shaggy. No word fits its object like a glove, because words are not things: words represent *ideas* of things. They are the means by which we class eggs and tents and trees so that we can handle them as ideas—not as actual things but as *kinds* of things. A person can hold an egg in his hand, but cannot think about it, or talk about it, unless he has some larger idea with which his mind, too, can grasp it, some idea like *thing,* or *throwing thing,* or *egg*—which classes this one white ellipsoid with all the eggs he has known, from ostrich to hummingbird, with the *idea* of egg. One word per item would be useless; it would be no idea at all, since ideas represent not items, but *classes* of items.

But what we call abstract words—*virtue, abstract, concrete*—can attain a power of their own, as the rhetorician heightens attention to their meanings. This ability, of course, does not come easily or soon. First, and for the present, I repeat, you need to be as concrete as you can, to illustrate tangibly, to pin your abstractions down to specifics. But once you have learned this, you can move on to the rhetoric of abstraction, which is, indeed, a kind of squeezing of abstract words for their specific juice.

Lincoln does exactly this when he concentrates on *dedication* six times within ten sentences—in his dedication at Gettysburg. Similarly, Eliot refers to "faces/Distracted from distraction by distraction" *(Four Quartets).* Abstractions can, in fact, operate beautifully as specifics: "As a knight, Richard the Lion-Hearted was a *triumph;* as a king, he was a *disaster."* Many rhetorical patterns likewise concentrate on abstract essences:

> **. . . tribulation works patience, and patience experience, and experience hope. (Rom. v.3–4)**
> **The humble are proud of their humility.**
> **Care in your youth so you may live without care.**

An able writer like Samuel Johnson can make a virtual poetry of abstractions, as he alliterates and balances them against each other (I have capitalized the alliterations and italicized the balances):

> **Dryden's performances were always hasty, either *Excited* by some *External occasion,* or *Extorted* by some *domestic necessity;* he ComPosed without Consideration, and Published without Correction.**

Notice especially how *excited* ("called forth") and *extorted* ("twisted out"), so alike in sound and form, so alike in making Dryden write, nevertheless contrast their opposite essential meanings. Johnson thus extorts the specific juice of each abstract word.

So before we disparage abstraction, we should acknowledge its rhetorical power; and we should understand that it is an essential distillation, a primary and natural and continual mental process. Without it, we could not make four of two and two. So we make abstractions of abstractions to handle bigger and bigger groups of ideas. *Egg* becomes *food,* and *food* becomes *nourishment.* We also classify all the psychic and physical qualities we can recognize: *candor, truth, anger, beauty, negligence, temperament.* But because our thoughts drift upward, we need always to look for the word that will bring them nearer earth, that will make our abstractions seem visible and tangible, that will make them graspable—mentioning a *handle,* or a *pin,* or an *egg,* alongside our abstraction, for instance. We have to pull our abstractions down within reach of our reader's own busily abstracting headpiece. In short, we must pin our abstractions down with constant comparisons to the concrete eggs from which they sprang.

The writer's ultimate skill perhaps lies in making a single concrete object represent its whole abstract class. I have paired each abstraction below with its concrete translation:

> *Friendliness* **is the salesman's best asset.**
> *A smile* **is the salesman's best asset.**
>
> *Administration of proper proteins* **might have saved John Keats.**
> **A** *good steak* **might have saved John Keats.**
>
> **To** *understand* **the world by** *observing geological details.* . . .
> **To** *see* **the world in** *a grain of sand.* . . .

EXERCISES

9. *Write three sentences using abstractions concretely, as in "As a knight, Richard was a* triumph; *as a king, he was a* disaster."

10. *Write three sentences in which a single concrete item represents its whole abstract class, as in "A good steak* might have saved John Keats."

11. *Revise the following sentences to make them more vivid and distinct by replacing as many of the abstract terms as possible with concrete terms.*

    1. Unhappy because of their lack of recognition, the Wright brothers temporarily quit flying in October, 1905.
    2. For the better part of the year, he was without gainful employment.

3. Of the students who go to college outside their own state, 70 percent do not go back after completing their studies.

4. A sizable proportion of those people who use long-distance movers are large corporation employees whose moving expenses are entirely underwritten by their companies.

5. His great-grandfather once ran successfully for high public office, but he never served because his opponent mortally wounded him in a gunfight.

6. There was a severe disturbance in Jackson prison one day in the spring of 1952.

7. Convicts, armed with makeshift weapons, took some of the prison personnel hostage.

8. Her husband had one extramarital relationship after another and finally disappeared with a hotel dining room employee in one of our larger midwestern cities.

9. The lava issued slowly from the openings in the ground along the side of the trail.

10. Rejected by the military because of an impairment of his vision, Ernest became a journalist with a midwestern newspaper.

11. Hemingway was gravely injured when a trench mortar shell exploded directly behind him.

12. Several prominent labor leaders were entertained at the White House today.

13. Disadvantaged people are often maltreated by the very social-service agencies ostensibly designed to help them.

14. The newspaper reported that a small foreign car had overturned on the expressway just north of town.

15. The new contract offers almost no change in the fringe-benefit package.

METAPHOR

As you have probably noticed, I frequently use metaphors—the most useful way of making our abstractions concrete. The word is Greek for "transfer" (*meta* equals *trans* equals *across; phor* equals *fer* equals *ferry*). A metaphor treats something as if it were something else, ideas as if all of them were eggs, abstractions as if they were chickens that are also vaguely like flowers springing, thought as if it were rising steam. Metaphors illustrate, in a word, our general ideas. I might have written at length about how an idea is like an egg. I did, in fact, follow each declaration with an example, and I illustrated the point with a person holding an egg (208). But the metaphor makes the comparison at a stroke. I used our common word *grasp* for "understanding," comparing the mind to something with a hand, *transferring* the physical picture of the clutching hand to the invisible mental act.

Almost all our words are metaphors, usually with the physical picture faded. *Transfer* itself pictures a physical portage. When the company *transfers* its employees, it is sending them about the country as if by piggyback, or raft, or whatever. But mercifully the physical facts have faded—*transfer* has become a "dead metaphor"—and we can use the word in comfortable abstraction. Now, precisely because we are constantly abstracting, constantly letting the picture fade, you can use metaphor to great advantage—or disastrously, if your eyes aren't sharp. With metaphors, you overcome the nonpictorial quality of most of our writing; you make your writing both vivid and unique. As Aristotle said, the metaphor is clear, agreeable, and strange; like a solved riddle, it is the most delightful of teachers.

Metaphor seems to work at about four levels, each with a different clarity and force. Suppose you wrote "he swelled and displayed his finery." You have transferred to a man the qualities of a peacock to make his appearance and personality vivid. You have chosen one of the four ways to make this transfer.

> 1. SIMILE: **He was like a peacock.**
> **He displayed himself like a peacock.**
> **He displayed himself as if he were a pea-**
> **cock.**
> 2. PLAIN METAPHOR: **He was a peacock.**
> 3. IMPLIED METAPHOR: **He swelled and displayed his finery.**
> **He swelled and ruffled his plumage.**
> **He swelled, ruffling his plumage.**
> 4. DEAD METAPHOR: **He strutted.**

1. SIMILE. The simile is the most obvious form the metaphor can take, and hence would seem elementary. But it has powers of its own, particularly where the writer seems to be trying urgently to express the inexpressible, comparing his subject to several different possibilities, no one wholly adequate. In *The Sound and the Fury,* Faulkner thus describes two jaybirds (my italics):

> [they] **whirled up on the blast** *like gaudy scraps of cloth or paper*
> **and lodged in the mulberries, . . . screaming into the wind that**
> *ripped* **their harsh cries onward and away** *like scraps of paper or*
> *of cloth* **in turn.**

The simile has a high poetic energy. D. H. Lawrence uses it frequently, as here in *The Plumed Serpent* (my italics):

> **The lake was quite black,** *like a great pit.* **The wind suddenly**
> **blew with violence, with a strange ripping sound in the mango**
> **trees,** *as if some membrane in the air were being ripped.*

2. PLAIN METAPHOR.   The plain metaphor makes its comparison in one imaginative leap. It is shorthand for "as if he were a peacock." It pretends, by exaggeration *(hyperbole),* that he *is* a peacock. We move instinctively to this kind of exaggerated comparison as we try to convey our impressions with all their emotional impact. "He was a maniac at Frisbee," we might say, or "a dynamo." The metaphor is probably our most common figure of speech: *the pigs, the swine, a plum, a gem, a phantom of delight, a shot in the arm.* It may be humorous or bitter; it may be simply and aptly visual: "The road was a ribbon of silver." Thoreau extends a metaphor through several sentences in one of his most famous passages:

> **Time is but the stream I go a-fishing in. I drink at it; but while I drink I see the sandy bottom and detect how shallow it is. Its thin current slides away, but eternity remains. I would drink deeper; fish in the sky, whose bottom is pebbly with stars.**

3. IMPLIED METAPHOR.   The implied metaphor is even more widely useful. It operates most often among the verbs, as in *swelled, displayed,* and *ruffled,* the cocky verbs suggesting "peacock." Most ideas can suggest analogues of physical processes or natural history. Give your television system *tentacles* reaching into every home, and you have compared TV to an octopus, with all its lethal and wiry suggestions. You can have your school spirit *fall below zero,* and you have implied that your school spirit is like temperature, registered on a thermometer in a sudden chill. William F. Buckley, Jr., mentioning the dangers of chatting before a lecture, indirectly pictures a balloon, or tire: "This lets a little air out of the speaker, who very well may need all the air he has." In a metaphor concerning words, Lewis Thomas implies that our minds are like cities with junkyards at their fringes, by courtesy of an assisting simile:

> **We keep stores of discarded words around, out beyond the suburbs of our minds, stacked like scrap metal.**

Malcolm Cowley also thinks metaphorically about words in describing Hawthorne's style. He develops his explicit analogy first into a direct simile *(like a footprint)* and then into the metaphor implying that phrases are people walking at different speeds:

> **He dreamed in words, while walking along the seashore or under the pines, till the words fitted themselves to his stride. The result was that his eighteenth-century English developed into a natural, a *walked,* style, with a phrase for every step and a comma after every phrase like a footprint in the sand. Some-**

times the phrases hurry, sometimes they loiter, sometimes they march to drums.*

Cowley's implied metaphor about hurrying and loitering phrases is in fact a kind of extended pun, to illustrate the *walked* style he italicizes. You can even pun on the physical Latin components in our abstract words, turning them back into their original suggestions of physical acts, as in "The *enterprise* grabbed everything" (some beast or army is rushing in), for *enterprise* means in Latin something like "to rush in and grab." Too subtle? No, the contrast between *enterprise* and *grabbed* will please anyone, and the few who see it all will be delighted.

4. DEAD METAPHOR.   *Enterprise* is really a dead metaphor, and the art of resuscitation is the metaphorist's finest skill. It comes from liking words and paying attention to what they say. The punster makes the writer, if he can restrain himself. Simply add onto the dead metaphor enough implied metaphors to get the circulation going again: "He strutted, *swelling and ruffling his plumage.*" *He strutted* means by itself "walked in a pompous manner." By bringing the metaphor back to life, we keep the general meaning but also restore the physical picture of a peacock puffing up and spreading his feathers. We recognize *strut* concretely and truly for the first time. We know the word, and we know the man. We have an image of him, a posture strongly suggestive of a peacock.

Perhaps the best dead metaphors to revive are those in proverbial clichés. See what Thoreau does (in his *Journal*) with *spur of the moment:*

I feel the spur of the moment thrust deep into my side. The present is an inexorable rider.

Or again, when in *Walden* he speaks of wanting "to improve *the nick of time,* and notch it on my stick too," and of not being *thrown off the track* "by every nutshell and mosquito's wing that falls on the rails." In each case, he takes the proverbial phrase literally and physically, adding an attribute or two to bring the old metaphor back alive.

You can go too far, of course. Your metaphors can be too thick and vivid, and the obvious pun brings a howl of protest. Jane Austen disliked metaphors and reserved them for her hollow characters. I have myself sometimes advised scholars not to use them because they are so often overworked and so often tangled in physical impossibilities. "The violent population explosion has paved the way for new intellectual growth" looks pretty good—until you realize that explosions do not pave, and that new vegetation does not grow up

---

**The Portable Hawthorne* (New York: The Viking Press, 1948).

through solid pavement. *Cleared* instead of *paved* would have made the metaphor consistent. The metaphor, then, is your most potent device. It makes your thought concrete and your writing vivid. It tells in an instant how your subject looks to you. But it is dangerous. It should be quiet, almost unnoticed, with all details agreeing, and all absolutely consistent with the natural universe.

EXERCISES

12. *Write two sentences illustrating each of the following (six sentences in all): (1) the simile, (2) the metaphor, (3) the implied metaphor.*

13. *Write a sentence for each of the following dead metaphors, bringing it to life by adding implied metaphorical detail, as in "She* bridled, *snorting and* tossing her mane," *or by adding a simile, as in "He was* dead *wrong,* laid out like a corpse on a slab."

    dead center, pinned down, sharp as a tack, stick to, whined, purr, reflected, run for office, yawn, take a course, pull up stakes

14. *Revise the following sentences so as to clear up the illogical or unnatural connections in their metaphors and similes.*

    1. The violent population explosion has paved the way for new intellectual growth.
    2. The book causes a shock, like a bucket of icy water suddenly thrown on a fire.
    3. The whole social fabric will become unstuck.
    4. The tangled web of Jack's business crumbled under its own weight.
    5. His last week had mirrored his future, like a hand writing on the wall.
    6. The recent economic picture, which seemed to spell prosperity, has wilted beyond repair.
    7. They were tickled to death by the thunderous applause.
    8. Stream-of-consciousness fiction has gone out of phase with the new castles in the air of fantasy.
    9. The murmured protests drifted from the convention floor to the podium, cracking the facade of his imperturbability.
    10. Richard was ecstatic with his success. He had scaled the mountain of difficulties and from here on out he could sail with the breeze.

ALLUSION

Allusions illustrate your general idea by referring it to something else, making it take your reader as Grant took Richmond, making you the Mickey Mantle of the essay, or the Mickey Mouse. Allusions depend on common knowledge. Like the metaphor, they illustrate the remote with the familiar—a familiar place, or event, or personage. "He looked . . . like a Japanese Humphrey Bogart," writes William Bittner of French author Albert Camus, and we instantly see a face like the one we know so well (a glance at Camus's picture confirms how accurate this unusual allusion is). Perhaps the most effective allusions depend on a knowledge of literature. When Thoreau writes that "the winter of man's discontent was thawing as well as the earth," we get a secret pleasure from recognizing this as an allusive borrowing from the opening lines of Shakespeare's *Richard III:* "Now is the winter of our discontent/Made glorious summer by this sun of York." Thoreau flatters us by assuming we are as well read as he. We need not catch the allusion to enjoy his point, but, if we catch it, we feel a sudden fellowship of knowledge with him. We now see the full metaphorical force, Thoreau's and Shakespeare's both, heightened as it is by our remembrance of Richard Crookback's twisted discontent, an allusive illustration of all our pitiful resentments now thawing with the spring.

Allusion can also be humorous. For instance, the hero of Peter De Vries's "The Vale of Laughter"* (an allusion to the biblical "vale of tears") contemplates adultery but decides for home and honor:

> **If you look back, you turn into a pillar of salt. If you look ahead, you turn into a pillar of society.**

He alludes, of course, to Lot's wife, who looked back on the adulterous city of Sodom, against orders, and was turned into a pillar of salt (Gen. 19.26). De Vries begins his book with a wildly amusing allusion to Melville's already allusive beginning of *Moby Dick,* the archetypal whale hunt. Melville's narrator says to call him "Ishmael," the biblical outcast (Gen. 16.11–12). De Vries throws a devilish comma into Melville's opening sentence, then turns allusion into metaphor:

> **Call me, Ishmael. Feel absolutely free to. Call me any hour of the day or night at the office or at home, and I'll be glad to give you the latest quotation with price-earnings ratio and estimated dividend of any security traded in those tirelessly tossing, deceptively shaded waters in which we pursue the elusive whale of Wealth, but from which we come away at last content to have hooked the twitching bluegill, solvency. And having got me, call me anything you want, Ish baby. Tickled to death to be of service.**

---

*From *Blood of the Lamb* (Boston: Little, Brown and Company) Copyright 1953 © 1962, 1964, 1967 by Peter De Vries. The two excerpts are reprinted by permission of Little, Brown and Company.

EXERCISES

15. *Write a sentence for each of the following, in which you allude either humorously or seriously to:*

    1. A famous—or infamous—person (Caesar, Napoleon, Barnum, Lincoln, Stalin, Picasso, Bogart)
    2. A famous event (the Declaration of Independence, the Battle of Waterloo, the landing on Plymouth Rock, the Battle of the Bulge, the signing of the Magna Carta, Custer's Last Stand, Watergate)
    3. A notable place (Athens, Rome, Paris, London Bridge, Jerusalem, the Vatican)
    4. This famous passage from Shakespeare, by quietly borrowing some of its phrases:

        To be, or not to be—that is the question:
        Whether 'tis nobler in the mind to suffer
        The slings and arrows of outrageous fortune,
        Or to take arms against a sea of troubles,
        And by opposing end them.

DICTION

"What we need is a mixed diction," said Aristotle, and his point remains true twenty-three centuries and several languages later. The aim of style, he says, is to be clear but distinguished. For clarity, we need common, current words; but, used alone, these are commonplace, and as ephemeral as everyday talk. For distinction, we need words not heard every minute, unusual words, large words, foreign words, metaphors; but, used alone, these become bogs and vapors of gibberish. What we need is a diction that weds the popular with the dignified, the clear current with the sedgy margins of language and thought.

Not too low, not too high; not too simple, not too hard—an easy breadth of idea and vocabulary. English is peculiarly well endowed for this Aristotelian mixture, with the long abstract Latin words played against the short concrete Anglo-Saxon. Most of our ideas have Latin and Anglo-Saxon partners. In fact, many have a whole spectrum of synonyms from Latin through French to Anglo-Saxon, from general to specific—from *intrepidity* to *fortitude* to *valor* to *courage* to *bravery* to *pluck* to *guts*. You can choose the high word for high effect, or you can get tough with Anglo-Saxon specifics. But, again, you do not want all Anglo-Saxon, and you must especially guard against sobriety's luring you into all Latin. Tune your diction agreeably between the two extremes.

Indeed, the two extremes generate incomparable zip when tumbled side by side, as in *incomparable zip, inconsequential snip, megalomaniacal creep,* and the like. Rhythm and surprise conspire to set up the huge adjective first, then to add the small noun, like a monumental kick. Here is a passage from Edward Dahlberg's *Can These Bones Live,* which I opened completely at random to see how the large fell with the small (my italics):

> **Christ walks on a** *visionary sea;* **Myshkin . . . has his ecstatic premonition of infinity when he has an** *epileptic fit.* **We know the inward size of an artist by his** *dimensional thirsts.* **. . .***

This mixing of large Latin and small Anglo-Saxon, as John Crowe Ransom has noted, is what gives Shakespeare much of his power:

> **This my hand will rather**
> **The multitudinous seas incarnadine,**
> **Making the green one red.**

The short Anglo-Saxon *seas* works sharply between the two magnificent Latin words, as do the three short Anglo-Saxons that bring the big passage to rest, contrasting the Anglo-Saxon *red* with its big Latin kin, *incarnadine,* which Shakespeare invented here for the occasion. William Faulkner, who soaked himself in Shakespeare, gets much the same power from the same mixture. He is describing a very old Negro woman in *The Sound and the Fury* (the title itself comes from Shakespeare's *Macbeth,* the source of the *multitudinous seas* passage). She has been fat, but now she is wrinkled and completely shrunken except for her stomach:

> **. . . a paunch almost dropsical, as though muscle and tissue had been courage or fortitude which the days or the years had consumed until only the indomitable skeleton was left rising like a ruin or a landmark above the somnolent and impervious guts. . . .**

The impact of that short, ugly Anglo-Saxon *guts,* with its slang metaphorical pun, is almost unbearably moving. And the impact would be nothing, the effect slurring, without the grand Latin preparation.

A fully worded sentence, each word in place and pulling its weight, is a joy to see. But a sentence full of words is not. Words should count, I say again. And again, the best way to make them count is to count the words in each suspi-

---

*Ann Arbor: University of Michigan Press, Ann Arbor Paperbacks, 1967.

cious case. Suspect every *by,* every *of,* every *which,* every *is,* and especially that impersonal passive voice. Any shorter version will be clearer. I once counted the words, sentence by sentence, in a thirty-page manuscript rejected as "too loose." In some sentences, I cut no more than one or two words. I rephrased many, but I think I cut no entire sentence. In fact, I added a considerable para-graph; and I still had five pages fewer, and a better essay. If you cut only one word from every sentence, you will in ten pages (if you average ten words a sentence) save your reader one whole page of uselessness and obstruction and wasted time.

A good diction takes work. It exploits the natural, but does not come natu-rally. It demands a wary eye for the way meanings sprout, and the courage to prune. It has the warmth of human concern. It is a cut above the commonplace, a cut above the inaccuracies and circumlocutions of speech, yet within easy reach. Clarity is the first aim; economy, the second; grace, the third; dignity, the fourth. Our writing should be a little strange, a little out of the ordinary, a little beautiful, with words and phrases not met every day but seeming as right and natural as grass. A good diction takes care and cultivation.

It can be overcultivated. It may seem to call attention to itself rather than to its subject. Suddenly we are aware of the writer at work, and a little too pleased with himself, reaching for the elegant cliché and the showy phrase. Some readers find this very fault with my own writing, though I do really try to saddle my maverick love of metaphor. If I strike you in this way, you can use me profitably as a bad example along with the following passage. I have italicized elements that individually may have a certain effectiveness, but that cumulatively become mannerism, as if the writer were watching himself gesture in a mirror. Some of his phrases are redundant; some are trite. Everything is somehow cozy and grandiose, and a little too nautical:

> *There's* **little excitement** *ashore* **when merchant ships from** *faraway* **India, Nationalist China, or Egypt** *knife through the gen-tle swells* **of Virginia's Hampton Roads. This** *unconcern* **may sim-ply reflect the** *nonchalance* **of people who live by** *one of the world's great seaports.* **Or perhaps** *it's just* **that** *folk* **who** *dwell* **in the** *home towns* **of atomic submarines and Mercury astronauts are not likely to be impressed by a visiting freighter,** *from how-ever distant a realm.* . . . *Upstream a bit* **and also** *to port,* **the mouth of the Elizabeth River leads to Portsmouth and a major naval shipyard.** *To starboard lies* **Hampton, where at Langley Air Force Base the National Aeronautics and Space Administration prepares to send a man** *into the heavens.*

EXERCISES

16. **(a)** *As a warmup, clear the preceding example of its overdone phrases. Then* **(b)** *look for similar passages in your own papers written thus far for this course, and do the same for several of your most overblown paragraphs.*

17. *Write a paragraph in which you mix your diction as effectively as you can, with the big Latin word and the little Anglo-Saxon, the formal word and just the right touch of slang, working in at least two combinations of the extremes, on the pattern of* mul-titudinous seas, diversionary thrust, incomparable zip, *underlining these for your in-structor's convenience.*

CHAPTER 11

Writing About Literature

Writing about literature (or film or music or painting) is really no different from writing about life—though literature and life are distinctly different. Writing about either art or life is a way to discover meanings and then to deepen them for ourselves as we try to make them clear and meaningful to others. The significant difference lies not between literature and life, but between expository argument and literature, between the essay you write and the story, between the essay you write and the poem.

An essay states its point; literature implies its point. Poem, short story, novel, play, or motion picture, each acts out in its particular way some underlying idea that probably remains unstated. Even the brief lyric poem is really a dramatized moment, a voice speaking intensely and beautifully from some larger drama, which is probably life itself. So, poem or novel, each enacts and demonstrates—each *presents,* or represents—something about life, but usually does not tell exactly what. These are the *mimetic* arts—actions imitating life, grand mimickings of the human predicament.

So, to write about literature, you must first discover, and decide for yourself, what it is about. What point, or points, *does* it imply, or act out? Poems make statements, of course, and characters in plays, novels, or films also make statements. A poem or a character may even state the author's thesis explicitly. Even so, you must select the stated thesis from all the other things said, and then interpret it in the light of all the other statements, or of the entire action. When Hamlet says "the readiness is all," we know we have a thesis. Hamlet has found an important answer to both his brooding inaction and his impetuosity. Yet, is it *the* thesis? Perhaps—but certainly we need to qualify it with something about murderous ambitions, about thinking too little and too much, about appearance and reality, about the strange, dark web of thought and circumstance in which all life in this play seems caught beyond control.

Your first step, then, is to find the action's thesis, even though—and precisely because—the writer may have bent his best efforts to avoid stating a thesis or seeming to have one. The writer has wanted to *dramatize* his problem, or his mood, not to state it flatly, to display it in action, not merely to describe it. He has not wanted to tack a moral to his tale. That is the reader's job: to find the one idea toward which all these statements, all these moral and immoral actions, point.

To write an essay about literature, then, you first try to discover its point—or the significance of some part or feature—and assert something *about* it, probably that this *is* the point, that this feature *is* significant. *Your* thesis is an *aboutness* asserted.

EXPLICATION

Explication is an unfolding of meanings (from *ex,* "out," and *plicare,* "to fold")—detail by detail, pleat by pleat. You unfold for your reader what this play, or novel, or poem, is about. Your *aboutness* may be simply that the unfolding is necessary for full understanding, or it may find some commanding detail or pattern or metaphor and assert its preeminence, showing how all the others fit under it. Poetry, intense and compressed, metaphoric and symbolic, especially invites explication, invites an explanation and demonstration of what it is all about. But a scene or a passage in a novel or play also may evoke a valuable explication as you argue for its importance to the work as a whole in all its details and levels of suggestion. You may not wish to, or need to, unfold everything.

Now let me explicate as fully as I can a well-known poem by Emily Dickinson (1830–1886), so you can see something of the range of possibilities—some of the questions you might ask and write about.

> I like to see it lap the Miles—
> And lick the Valleys up—
> And stop to feed itself at Tanks—
> And then—prodigious step
>
> Around a Pile of Mountains—
> And supercilious peer
> In Shanties—by the sides of Roads—
> And then a Quarry pare

To fit its Ribs
And crawl between
Complaining all the while
In horrid—hooting stanza—
Then chase itself down Hill—

And neigh like Boanerges—
Then—punctual as a Star
Stop—docile and omnipotent
At its own stable door—*

The first line poses the first question. What is *it?* The poem is indeed a riddle, one of the most ancient literary forms, an inherently attractive verbal game, judging from its long history and its currency among children and TV quizzes. This riddling poem thus represents the cryptic quality that evidently attracts us in *all* poetry. We like *not* to know, *not* to be told, and to solve the puzzle by our triumphant ingenuity. As with fiction, we do not want the whole story right at the beginning, with all answers spelled out. Dickinson's unnamed *it* consumes miles, along valleys, around mountains, laboring through closely quarried passes, uttering harsh noises, speeding downhill, and at last stops punctually. All of Dickinson's readers were familiar with this creature, as fewer and fewer of us are. But clearly, *it* is a train.

But the poem is also an implied metaphor, posing a secondary riddle. What is the train *like,* as Dickinson's figurative imagination pictures it for us? Her *neigh* and *stable,* along with the quality of docile power, in the last stanza clearly project the dominant image of a horse. *The train is like a horse,* says the poet. Some poems fail, or remain cryptically blurred, because the poet does not clearly distinguish the object from its metaphor. But here we know that the train is real and the horse figurative, that the poet is not saying, *a horse is like a train.*

But other metaphors here raise problems. They are mixed, though all concern animals, or animals who are in turn like human beings—a train like an animal like a human being. *Lap,* with *Miles,* suggests horse racing all right (we immediately reject the lap we have when sitting) but, with the *lick up* following, a cat lapping up milk and licking the saucer pretty well obliterates the horse in the first two lines. Stopping to "feed itself at Tanks," the train again becomes horsy as it takes on water for its boilers—if you have ever seen a horse munching down leaves from a tree or hay from a feeder taller than itself. We can next see a gigantic horse stepping around a pile of mountains, and then lowering its head haughtily to peer, like a person, into the windows of poor roadside and railroad-side shanties. But next we have some kind of snake that

---

*From *The Complete Poems of Emily Dickinson,* edited by Thomas H. Johnson. Copyright © 1960 by Mary L. Hampson. Reprinted by permission of Little, Brown and Company.

can pare (now like a person with a paring knife) a quarry through a rocky moun-
taintop, crawling through and complaining (a horse cannot crawl, obviously).
Here we shift the picture again, the snake is complaining like some terrible
owl *(hooting)* turned poet *(stanzas).* But the way a train's whistle would reverber-
ate in a rocky defile as it sends its warning ahead does seem to come through
clearly, in spite of the flickering pictures. Then we seem to have our cat back,
chasing its tail down hill. And at last the horse, who neighs like ranting preachers *(Boanerges)*—again the train whistles as it comes into the station right on
time, with the railroader's proverbial punctuality—and who stands steaming
and puffing and magnificent in its power, yet docile, exactly like a horse, at
the door of its stable, arrived, and perhaps waiting to be unharnessed. That
the stable would properly be the engine's roundhouse rather than the station—at which it finally arrives as punctually as sidereal time, but with something of the glory of a star—is another small metaphorical inaccuracy, which
probably bothers us not at all. I suppose that the allusion to Boanerges (ranting
preachers) is effective enough, especially for Dickinson's immediate audience.
A horse's neigh is nasal, of course, and New England preachers, having de-
scended in the Puritan tradition, would tend to nasalize their fire and brim-
stone (on this quality of pronunciation, see remarks in "The English Language," 340). In Mark 3:17, Jesus calls the Apostles John and James
"Boanerges," or "Sons of Thunder," and the term evidently passed from Mark
to apply humorously to all pulpit thunderers. The word has a certain attraction
in the poem from its unusualness, and it sounds well with the *An, ne,* and *en*
of *And neigh . . . Then.*

The poem starts with a standard iambic ballad stanza of fours and threes,
with the three-beat lines rhyming. But immediately the pattern begins to vary
to suggest the train speeding and slowing with the irregularities of the countryside. The two two-beat lines clearly help the train squeeze through its tight
passage. And reestablishing the full metrical beat in the last two lines makes
both the poem and the train slow down and stop majestically.

Many will think Dickinson is not rhyming at all, but others will see that
she is slant-rhyming lines two and four, with the especially close consonance
of *peer* and *pare,* and that the effect is pleasantly similar to what the meter is
doing with both pattern and variety.

Now the question: *Is it a good poem?* I would say yes, in spite of what seems
some inattentive jumbling of metaphor. It conveys the excitement and power
of a train cruising the countryside, and of the speaker's evident pleasure in
it. Certainly the metaphorical mixing and layering (train-is-horse;
horse-is-person) is no fatal defect. And train-is-snake-is-owl-is-poet may be a
little too thick to bear close inspection. But the imagination can easily see the
train as "the iron horse" of the conventional metaphor imaginatively expanded.

But I find the cat metaphor of the first two lines and *chase itself* a mistake,
a blemish—one we hardly notice at all as the poem sweeps us along, but a

blemish nevertheless. A train is not naturally like a cat, and a huge stationary cat lapping up and licking up the cream of miles and valleys is even more inconsistent with the speeding train. And to chase itself down hill, though consistent with a string of railroad cars, is inconsistent with a horse and carriage, and it tempts our cat of the first two lines to spin around even more inconsistently with a train.

If Emily Dickinson were a student of mine (ah, we all can dream), I would suggest that *lick* is the culprit, invited by the ambiguity of *lap* and the line's three alliterating *l*'s, and that the cat jumped in where we don't want it. Find another horsy word, I'd say, to keep that horse-racing *lap* alive—even if you must change your rhyme and picture a bit: changing *lick* to *pace* or *race* might do, without disturbing anything else. And then I would get rid of that *chase* and its latent inconsistencies: *race the road down Hill* perhaps. I would probably let the *stable* stand, because a freight train would probably stop punctually at the door of its roundhouse at the end of its run.

EXERCISES

1. *Here are two love poems, one old and famous, one modern, the first by a man, the second by a woman.*

UPON JULIA'S CLOTHES
Whenas in silks my *Julia* goes,
Then, then (me thinks) how sweetly flowes
That liquefaction of her clothes.

Next, when I cast mine eyes and see
That brave Vibration each way free;
O how that glittering taketh me!
                    Robert Herrick, 1648

KIDNAP POEM
ever been kidnapped
by a poet
if i were a poet
i'd kidnap you
put you in my phrases and meter
you to jones beach
or maybe coney island
or maybe just to my house
lyric you in lylacs
dash you in the rain
blend into the beach
to complement my see
play the lyre for you

       ode you with my love song
       anything to win you
       wrap you in the red Black green
       show you off to mama
       yeah if i were a poet i'd kid
       nap you
               Nikki Giovanni, 1970*

   (a) *Write an explication of either one you prefer, or* **(b)** *write a comparison, on any point you wish, between Herrick's poem and Giovanni's.*
     Here are some questions on Herrick. What is the connection between silks, flowes, *and* liquefaction? *What is the implied metaphor? In what way are sounds significant? What does the wearing of silk suggest about the possible occasion in which the lover thrills at his lady's presence? What contrast between the first and second stanza becomes apparent with* when I cast mine eyes and see? *What is* that brave Vibration?— check brave *in your dictionary. Why do these words go well together?*
     *Here are some questions on Giovanni. In what way does any poet kidnap the beloved in a love poem? What image of the poet emerges from Giovanni's lower-case letters—*i, jones beach, coney island—*and her omission of punctuation? Why is* Black *the only capitalized word? (The poet is black.) What is her pun on* meter? *On* see? *On* lyre? *Perhaps on* ode? *Who blends into the beach? What is the metaphor implied in* wrap, show you off to mama, kid, *and* nap? *Do the two poems show anything typical about male and female attitudes?*

STEPS AND QUESTIONS

Each work stirs its own interest, and, as with Dickinson's iron horse, or Julia's clothes or Giovanni's kidnapping, presents us with questions, and more questions, as we become more interested. These questions are what you write about. We want ultimately to possess what the author wanted us to possess, since each literary work is, after all, a communication from author to reader. A writer may wish only to express himself, yes, but he expects us to understand and value that self-expression as he does. So the questions will arise, almost of themselves, from each different work. But in writing, and explaining, a questioning mind will help. Why does the author do this? Why that? What does he intend that vase on the mantle to signify?
   This first natural onrush of questions can perhaps be controlled so as to provide us with a kind of system for our explication. How can we formulate questions whose answers will indeed help our reader's understanding? What

*From *Re:Creation.* Copyright © 1970 by Nikki Giovanni; Broadside/Crummell Press, Detroit, Michigan.

particularities of a work will most likely provoke the questions you will want to answer in your essay?

To Summarize, Paraphrase

The simplest way to start the questions and find the answers is to summarize, letting the process of writing do its fundamental job of discovering our ideas for us. A paraphrase is the closest kind of summary. Paraphrasing a poem—translating it into clear English prose in your own words—is an excellent way to come to grips, in your own mind, with exactly what it says, raising the primary questions as to which of the possible meanings the author seems to intend. Shakespeare writes (Sonnet 116):

> **O, no; [love] is an ever-fixed mark**
> **That looks on tempests and is never shaken;**
> **It is a star to every wandering bark,**
> **Whose worth's unknown, although his height be taken.**

One student paraphrases like this:

> **O, no; love is an object that always needs fixing, that looks on**
> **storms and is never shaken; it is a moon barked at by every**
> **wandering dog, who is probably worthless and homeless, al-**
> **though his height is taken into account.**

In class, he defends his paraphrase by saying that the moon is a kind of star, and Shakespeare is saying that love is like the moon, which wears away and fixes itself up each month. Love is also always in need of repair. The moon looks down on storms untouched; dogs always bark at the moon. Other students argue that *bark* means a ship, and that love is like an actual star, fixed and stationary above storms, which a wandering ship would use in navigating, taking its height with a sextant but never knowing its actual physical nature or worth. The first student says, "Well, I guess *bark* threw me off." The practice of paraphrasing has pinpointed the ambiguous words, and has made them yield the meaning the author probably intended, since it fits better, as we put aside the less probable meanings.

A summary of a poem, a novel, or a play will yield much the same kind of clarification; we might summarize a hypothetical story like this:

> **The story opens with an unnamed "he" alone in a dingy**
> **room. One door of a cabinet is hanging from a single hinge. A**
> **spring and some stuffing stick up through a sofa cushion. We**

soon learn that his wife has just left him. He is angry and bitter. Piece by piece, from his thoughts, we learn what has happened—their high-school romance, their fashionable wedding, his "bad luck," as he calls it, losing one job after another only because he likes "to have a little fun." In the end, he finishes wrecking the cabinet, his wife's special treasure, and stamps off to the local bar, never learning what a hopeless fool he is, and will continue to be.

Such a summary has crystallized the story clearly and whole. Use such a summary in your own essay, to help your readers see the story as you see it. Some thesis about the story in general, or particular, a little more detail and illustration, and you would have a complete essay.

Explain the Metaphors

Metaphor is the heart of poetry—and that is a metaphor, as if poetry were a living being with a heart for vital life and feeling. All poems, even the most starkly pictorial, present their meanings in some kind of metaphorical *as if.* Ted Hughes, for instance, begins a poem about a dead pig in straight description:

VIEW OF A PIG
The pig lay on a barrow dead
It weighed, they said, as much as three men.
Its eyes closed, pink white eyelashes.
Its trotters stuck straight out.*

But very soon Hughes's description reaches for a metaphorical analogy. In fact, he has already moved toward metaphor in his second line: *as much as three men.* Already the dead pig represents more than itself. And soon comes a full simile: *like a sack of wheat.* Others come, as Hughes tries to convey the pig's startling deadness, so dead as to arouse neither guilt nor pity, as the butchers prepare to *Scald it and scour it like a doorstep*—the simile with which he ends his poem. He has not only found several metaphorical *as if*'s, but entailed a vaster one, *as if* this one pig represents the total enigma of lifelessness.

This metaphorical process is everywhere in poetry. Herrick hears Julia's

---

*From *New Selected Poems* by Ted Hughes. Copyright © 1960 by Ted Hughes. By permission of Harper & Row, Publishers, Inc., and Faber and Faber Ltd.

silks rustling *as if* they were turning to water. Nikki Giovanni would like to possess someone *as if* in a kind of verbal and cuddly kidnapping. Emily Dickinson sees a train *as if* it were a horse. For Shakespeare, love is a star, firm above tempests and wandering ships, and thought is a courtroom summoning up past deeds and debts. Whether in direct similes *(like a sack of wheat),* or in plain metaphor *(love is a star),* or implied metaphor *(the sessions of sweet silent thought),* the metaphorical process needs to be spelled out for your readers, as you explain your poem's spell. (See 210–14 in "Words" for fuller discussion of these terms.)

Because they need spelling out for full understanding and appreciation, metaphors probably give you more to write about than anything else in a poem. You can write a good paper comparing how two poets, or several, spin their metaphors from the same thing—love, death, or the same physical object, as in these two examples:

> **Slowly, silently, now the moon**
> **Walks the night in her silver shoon.**
> *Walter de la Mare, from* **"Silver"***

> **Greatly shining,**
> **The Autumn moon floats in the thin sky;**
> **And the fish-ponds shake their backs and flash their**
> **dragon scales**
> **As she passes over them.**
> *Amy Lowell,* **"Wind and Silver"**†

In de la Mare's metaphor the moon is a woman, mysterious because she walks slowly and silently through the night, majestic and magical because of her archaic "shoon" of silver. Amy Lowell's moon is also mysterious, rendered medieval and magical by the dragons, also with something of the mysterious East as fish-ponds become dragons. De la Mare's passive and silent lady goes on to turn windows, doves, and fish to silver with her beams. But Lowell's moon radiates a more magical power. It shines "greatly," and the ponds respond in mysterious obedience, as if they were fish-scaled dragons arching their backs at the water's surface, flashing back their respect for the moon's sovereignty. Lowell's moon, like de la Mare's, is a "she." But is it also a woman? Probably not, since we already see that it "floats in the thin sky," like an airy ship in a very thin kind of water, of which the ponds are a denser kind at the bottom

---

*Reprinted by permission of The Literary Trustees of Walter de la Mare and The Society of Authors (London).

†From *The Complete Poetical Works of Amy Lowell.* Copyright © 1955 by Houghton Mifflin Company. Reprinted by permission of the publisher.

of the sky. Ships, we know, are traditionally *she*. "Autumn" also gives Lowell's moon a more somber and shivery presence than de la Mare's, since autumn suggests winter and a change for the worse, and the dragons suggest dire things in the offing. Finally, Lowell's title fills out her metaphorical picture in a way de la Mare's does not. His "Silver" appears again in his verses. Lowell's "Wind and Silver" are not repeated, and by that very economy they underline her metaphor-making. Wind has actually rippled the fish ponds. The moon-light has actually caught the ripples in little silver points, making the water momentarily look like fish-scales, or dragon-scales. Out of this actual sight, evidently, Lowell has made her metaphor and her poem, creating her autumnal moon-ship with its mysterious influence that reaches down through its thin sea to its depths in this world with its denser waters. Clearly, Lowell's metaphor is more imaginative and exciting than de la Mare's. But the smooth meter and attractive sound of his language have carried his couplet, with its attractive metaphor, into dictionaries of familiar quotations, where we do not find Amy Lowell's lines.

EXERCISES

2. *Explain the metaphors in the following two poems by Carl Sandburg,* and compare their effectiveness.*

> FOG
> The fog comes
> on little cat feet.
> It sits looking
> over harbor and city
> on silent haunches
> and then moves on.

> LOST
> Desolate and alone
> All night long on the lake
> Where fog trails and mist creeps,
> The whistle of a boat
> Calls and cries unendingly,
> Like some lost child
> In tears and trouble
> Hunting the harbor's breast
> And the harbor's eyes.

---

*From *Chicago Poems* by Carl Sandburg, copyright 1916 by Holt, Rinehart and Winston, Inc.; renewed 1944 by Carl Sandburg. Reprinted by permission of Harcourt Brace Jovanovich, Inc.

In which poem is the metaphor most concentrated? Which of these words work meta-phorically, which not?—trails, creeps, whistle, Hunting. If you were Sandburg's editor, would you suggest changes in either poem? If so, what?

3. *Explain the contrasting metaphors in these two poems:*

> THE BATH TUB
> As a bathtub lined with white porcelain,
> When the hot water gives out or goes tepid,
> So is the slow cooling of our chivalrous passion,
> O my much praised but-not-altogether-satisfactory lady.*
>   *Ezra Pound*

> A DECADE
> When you came, you were like wine and honey,
> And the taste of you burnt my mouth with its sweetness.
> Now you are like morning bread,
> Smooth and pleasant.
> I hardly taste you at all for I know your savor,
> But I am completely nourished.†
>   *Amy Lowell*

VERSIFICATION

Find the Sound in Poetry

Poetry heightens the sounds of language in six major ways, each depending on some kind of repetition-with-variation. Perceiving and enjoying these will help you write about poetry.

1. *Meter*—the regular measure, as varied by the language flowing over it. See "Meter," below.
2. *Rhyme*—line-ends the same, with a necessary difference: *bird/third.*
3. *Reiteration*—the same word repeated, often with different force: "Of hammered *gold* and *gold* enameling" (Yeats).
4. *Alliteration*—first sounds of words or first accented syllables the same: "a *little lost alliteration.*"
5. *Assonance*—middle vowel-sounds the same: sm*o*ky l*oa*m, gl*a*d r*a*g, h*o*t r*o*d.

---

6. *Consonance*—middle- or end-consonant sounds the same, but vowels different (also called "slant rhyme" at line-ends): p*eer*/p*are*, st*ar*/d*oor*, *supple*/*apple, love*/*over.*

METER.   English has one dominant meter—iambic—and three others that lend iambic an occasional foot, for variety, and produce a few poems. (Modern verse is predominantly "free," with no regular pattern.)

RISING METERS

Iambic: ᴗ —
Anapestic: ᴗ ᴗ —

FALLING METERS

Trochaic: — ᴗ
Dactylic: — ᴗ ᴗ

The number of these metrical units, or feet, in a line also gives the verse a name: (1) monometer, (2) dimeter, (3) trimeter, (4) tetrameter, (5) pentameter, (6) hexameter. All meters will show some variations, and substitutions of other kinds of feet, but three variations in iambic writing are virtually standard:

Inverted foot: — ᴗ (a trochee)
Spondee: — —
Ionic double foot: ᴗ ᴗ | — —

Examples of scansion:

IAMBIC TETRAMETER

ᴗ — | ᴗ — | ᴗ — | ᴗ   — |
An-ni-hil-a-ting all that's made
ᴗ ᴗ | —   — | ᴗ ᴗ | —   — |
To a green thought in a green shade.
Andrew Marvell, "The Garden"

IAMBIC PENTAMETER

—   — | —   — | ᴗ   — | ᴗ — | ᴗ   — |
Love's not Time's fool, though ros-y lips and cheeks
ᴗ — | ᴗ   — | ᴗ   — | ᴗ   — | ᴗ   — |
With-in his bend-ing sick-le's com-pass come
Shakespeare, Sonnet 116

—   ᴗ | ᴗ   — | ᴗ   — | ᴗ   — | ᴗ   — |
When to the ses-sions of sweet si-lent thought
[or]
—   ᴗ | ᴗ   — | ᴗ   ᴗ | —   — | ᴗ   — |
When to the ses-sions of sweet si-lent thought
Shakespeare, Sonnet 30

Finally, here is a basic metrical variant pleasing to observe and report: the *cae-sura* (si-ZHUR-a), the "cutting off." The metrical march, holding its footage beneath all frisks and fanfares, cuts off and suspends for a breathless moment, as when the conductor, his wand in midair, suspends the beat for a dramatic pause before he sweeps on. Punctuation signals the caesura's pause. The *masculine caesura* suspends the meter at the foot's end:

$$— \quad \cup \ | \cup \ — \ \| \cup \quad — \ | \cup \quad — \ | \cup \quad — \ |$$
Things fall a part; the cen-ter can-not hold

The *feminine caesura* suspends mid-foot:

$$\cup \quad — \ | \cup \quad — \ | \cup \| — \ | \cup \quad — \ | \cup \quad — \ |$$
The Dog-star rage-s! nay 'tis past a doubt

These are the major sounds of poetry, which you can appreciate, and describe for your readers, as they contribute to the poem's pleasures and emphasize its meanings.

EXERCISES

4. *Here is a stanza of Yeats's to explore for sounds.*

> That is no country for old men. The young
> In one another's arms, birds in the trees
> —Those dying generations—at their song,
> The salmon-falls, the mackerel-crowded seas,
> Fish, flesh, or fowl, commend all summer long
> Whatever is begotten, born, and dies.
> Caught in that sensual music all neglect
> Monuments of unageing intellect.*
> > *From "Sailing to Byzantium"*

Scan it. What is the meter? Can you find an inverted foot? A spondee? A double ionic? A masculine and a feminine caesura? Examples of alliteration? Of a line containing assonance? Consonance? Any kind of reiteration?

What are the rhymes? The slant rhymes? Counting full rhymes and slant rhymes as the same, mark the first rhyming-sound a, the second b, the third c. What is the stanza's rhyme scheme? Does Yeats gain anything by writing in a patterned stanza rather than in free verse? Why is the phrase Fish, flesh, or fowl *significant? Why is that country no*

---

*From *Collected Poems*, by William Butler Yeats. Copyright 1928 by Macmillan Publishing Company, renewed 1956 by Georgie Yeats. Reprinted by permission of Michael Yeats, Anne Yeats, and Macmillan London Ltd. Reprinted with permission of Macmillan Publishing Company, Inc. (New York).

in free verse? Why is the phrase Fish, flesh, or fowl *significant? Why is that country no place for old men?*

THE NOVEL AND THE DRAMA

Determine the Genre

Tragedy and comedy are our largest literary genres. Recognizing to which one a story, novel, or play belongs, or where it lies between, will help you to describe it. Romance is a special genre on the comic side, ending happily, like comedy, but without the laughs and comic foolery and with a high coloration of the wishful and the far away in time and place. Satire, again on the comic side, though more cruel, pokes fun at some social absurdity, allegedly to cure it by laughing it out of countenance. Fantasy is unreality made real, with perhaps a touch of comic fear, as when *Alice in Wonderland* engages our psychic misgivings, or of grim humor, as when Vonnegut's *The Cat's Cradle* freezes to death man's scientific irresponsibility. Fantasy, indeed, may be the predominant characteristic of contemporary literature, as writer after writer projects our overreachings and shortcomings into some horrifying future. Placing any work in its genre will help your reader to understand it.

Analyze Titles, Names, Allusions

A work's title or its characters' names can carry part of the message. Look here for clues to explain to your reader. The "cat's cradle" of Vonnegut's title simultaneously informs us and raises a question. We see in our minds the loops of string interlaced between two hands; we know it is some kind of game, or pastime. In the end, we see it as a symbol of man's aimless and dangerous scientific ingenuity, and its meaninglessness: "See, no cat, no cradle," as one character says. Browning's "My Last Duchess" tells us, by his title alone, that a duke is speaking, and that he has had several duchesses (a servant could be speaking, of course, but the poem itself soon puts that possibility aside). Look out for these details—and explain them to your reader.

An author may deliberately look for neutral and natural names for his characters, and this in itself tells us that he aims toward realism. If his names seem somehow merely contrived, as in a story that begins "Stephanie Marsh had spoken to Stephen Blair only once," we suspect the slick and shallow. But an author may also name his characters to tell us what kinds of people they are, or what he wishes them to represent. Fielding's Mr. Allworthy is clearly the ideal worthy man; his Tom Jones, in the very commonness of his name, represents the common human lot. Dickens is a genius at making his names suggestive without labeling his people directly: Podsnap, Gradgrind, Murdstone, Steerforth, Uriah Heep. Gradgrind, for instance, is a schoolmaster grinding down his graduates. Murdstone is murderously stony. Introduce your reader to these possibilities. Show how they support your author's meanings.

Names may also be allusions. Look up *Uriah* in your dictionary, and you will discover Uriah the Hittite, an officer in King David's army, whom David ordered deserted and left to the enemy in the forefront of battle, so that David could marry Uriah's wife, Bathsheba. A good dictionary will also tell you that *Uriah* means "Yahweh [God] is my light." Explain this, and apply it to the story at hand. The creepy Uriah Heep is certainly the ironic opposite of his namesake: *he* is the treacherous one, as he heaps up swindles that he hopes will finally include the boss's daughter. Dickens has alluded, ironically, to one of the Bible's most famous stories. Likewise, almost any garden may prompt an author to allude to the Garden of Eden, strengthening his meaning from an even more famous biblical source. Shakespeare also is a frequent source. When Faulkner names his novel *The Sound and the Fury,* he wants us to remember, or discover, Macbeth's eloquent despair, which ends: "[Life] is a tale/Told by an idiot, full of sound and fury/Signifying nothing" (5.5 26–28). Faulkner's first section is literally "told by an idiot," the thirty-three-year-old Benjy, whose impressions and memories flow in sometimes incoherent sounds and frustrated furies, and the whole novel is a somber comment on life's fruitless struggles, which seem to signify nothing. Allusions are myriad in their variety, of course, but keeping alert for them will turn them up, and will help you explain to your reader what this is all about. Look up every biblical name—Timothy, Tobias, even Elizabeth—to see if the author may have had something allusive in mind. Catching an allusion will expand understanding both for you and your reader.

Recognize Symbols

Symbols are a kind of concrete allusion—a physical object that calls to mind, or acquires, a cluster of meanings—asking you for explanation. In *The Sound and the Fury,* again, clocks and watches recurringly symbolize the passage and the waste of time, and sometimes the elegance of good times past as against the tawdry present, sometimes the measure of time as against the fluid and insubstantial life of memory and thought. Similarly, a soiled wedding slipper symbolizes spoiled aspirations, empty institutions, and the failures and hopeless yearnings of love.

Symbols arise naturally from the natural world. Some have become traditional, accumulating layers of association over the ages—eagles, doves, snakes, for instance. Others are even more generally and immediately symbolic. A rose, or any flower, immediately symbolizes the beautiful and transitory. White and black come directly from all our days and nights. In a poem entitled "Design," for instance, Robert Frost tells of seeing a white spider with a dead white moth on an unusually white flower, all having come together in black night, and thus seeming to symbolize some eerie design in the universal way of things.

But unless the author brings his object into sufficient prominence to become a symbol, be cautious: it may be just one more of several objects that together suggest wealth, good taste, bad taste, acquisitiveness, carelessness, or the like. These are not symbols but merely parts of the setting, which you describe as a total impression.

Identify the Written Voice: Point of View

Every word speaks. In literature, every word is dramatic, since it conveys a human personality, its speaker's, whether that speaker is the author or a character, whether that word speaks from an essay, a poem, a story, or a play. Locate the speaker, assemble in your mind the personality speaking, and then describe it for your reader. The first question any text poses is: "Who is speaking?" The author? A dramatized voice of authority? A character? With Herrick's poem on Julia's clothes, the question of whether the speaker is actually Robert Herrick or some imagined lover is not immediately significant. But in poems or stories where the speaker seems markedly different from the author, the question becomes significant. We know instantly, for example, that Faulkner is dramatizing an idiot distinct from himself. But frequently we must wait some time for certainty as to whose voice utters the enchanting words from the first sentence onward: "She looked around. The world was all white velvet, with nothing beyond. Where were the walls? . . ." The voice may represent one of four speakers:

1. The omniscient narrator
2. A character observing
3. A character participating
4. The protagonist

THE OMNISCIENT NARRATOR.   The "all-knowing" narrator speaks in the third person: "she thought; he went; they arrived." The omniscient narrator speaks in a godlike voice, knowing all that has happened, recounting the story, quoting the characters ("she said"), summarizing their thoughts: *Where were the walls?* This third-person narrator—who may be very different from the actual author who is putting him on paper—tells us exactly what he wants us to know, taking us into one character's thoughts, describing another only from the outside, giving us a third only as another character sees him. The voice thus gives us the station—the point—from which we view everything. The narrator seems to locate himself, and us, just behind the shoulder of one character, or indeed within his consciousness, describing what goes on there, so that our third-person "she" comes through to us almost like a first-person protagonist. The narrator may also follow several persons, like a TV camera that can also transcribe thought. But the narrator and his omniscient voice can also move off, again like the camera and its commentator, to survey the large scene or to probe a small detail somewhere else. His reportage is godlike, and our interpretation must include both the reportage and the godlike reporter.

FIRST-PERSON OBSERVER.   A character observes the action. His first-person "I" tells us the tale. This "I" is close enough to the principal characters to know the details, but not so close as to be badly caught in their troubles. Dramatic irony—in which the speaker does not understand the full implications of what he reports—carries much of the impact. The barber who tells the story in Ring Lardner's "Haircut" is a classic example. The employer who tells Melville's "Bartleby, the Scrivener" is another. You, as the explicator, explain these implications.

FIRST-PERSON PARTICIPANT.   The participating first-person is also observing, of course. The narrating "I" is part of the action, but not the main character. Conrad's "The Heart of Darkness" is about Mr. Kurtz, but Marlowe, the first-person narrator, goes through considerable miles of Congo and throes of activity to get at the enigma of Kurtz. The participating-observing Nick tells us the story of Fitzgerald's *Great Gatsby.* The author must weave his participant into the story to get the information we need, and his skill in making this plausible and evolving his speaker's personality are what you need to watch and then unfold for your reader.

FIRST-PERSON PROTAGONIST.   Defoe's Crusoe tells us all that happened to him, with some touches of verbal irony at his former mistakes and limitations. But the first-person protagonist is most effective, again, as the voice of dramatic irony: he does not understand the full import of what he does and tells and explains. The speaker, like Browning's duke in "My Last Duchess," or Henry James's literary thief in *The Aspern Papers,* or Iris Murdoch's Bradley Pearson in *The Black Prince,* unknowingly reveals his meanness or other shortcomings in the very act of explaining or excusing himself. This inadvertent revelation, this dramatic irony, may be grim, as with Browning, or comic, as with James and Murdoch.

Your analytical question, then, is simply *Who is speaking?* From there, you unfold for your reader what the point of view is—whether third-person-omniscient or one of the three first-persons—and what that implies for the reportage. How limited is the view? How reliable the report? How deep the dramatic irony, if any?

Identify the Written Voice: Tone and Style

Tone and style come through together, of course, from the first sentence onward, giving us the author's, or speaker's, tone of voice and the attitude toward his story that this tone conveys. Hemingway's is like a sad bell that strikes a note and floats on in the same mellow resonance from first word to last. Joyce's is immediately ironic, as he looks down on his Leopold Bloom with amused detachment and a touch of scorn. Jane Austen's tone is also that of irony, as she describes her Emma, but warmer and more affectionate. Virginia Woolf's is the yearning inner voice of sensitive perception responding to the wonder and evanescence of life as it passes before us and we pass through it. Their various styles convey these various tones. Look for the typical sentence, the favorite words, and describe them, giving examples, if they are unusual and meaningful enough. You may not need, or want, to describe this for your reader, but you should ask yourself if it is distinctive enough to warrant description.

Determine the Setting

Where are we? As the voice implies its person, it also conjures up a place, even if only some lost mist of nonbeing. Frequently the setting is as dense as a Victorian sitting room, and it conveys the stuffiness of the people who sit in it. Sometimes the setting is so vaguely implied that we must fill it in only with the utmost tentativeness, as with the courtly surroundings that Julia's silks suggest. The setting may signify little or nothing, but you should at least ask yourself *where* and *when* it is, and what, if anything, it does signify—or you may miss a point your reader should know.

Describe the Plot

What happens? Nothing? That, too, is a significant happening. Describe it. Probably the happening is all in the past, put together by recollections—"flashbacks"—like flashes of lightning vivifying a moment along the trail of the past. Or the story may be highly plotted, one move causing another, invariably different from what the mover intended or we expected, though it may fulfill our general fears or expectations. Describe this too, trying to see how much the author emphasizes chance as against human intention and error. Whether the story is static and open-ended or active and conclusive, something is in conflict. Find out exactly what *is* in conflict. What motives, wishes, beliefs, assumptions collide? Who are the good guys and the bad guys, and what do they represent? Then locate those crucial events, mistakes, moments that determine the outcome, and ask what the people might have done differently—what and where the crucial mistakes are. These may be the very center of your essay.

In plot, irony of circumstance rides high, since life's contrariness seems to intrigue us. When things go as expected, we hardly notice, and we have little of interest to report. But buy a new car and have it dented, buy a watch for a lifetime and have it stolen the first hour, and you have a tale to tell. Plots are usually a chain of intentions ironically backfiring, or veering off, to the worst, or funniest, consequences. Romeo intends to stop a fight and end a feud, but his intervention kills his friend and seals his own doom. In describing any plot, comic or tragic, or in between, note the force and turn of these circumstantial ironies.

Distinguish Plot and Plotting*

An author rations his material. The *plot* is everything that happened—what we would summarize in straight chronological order after we learned the full story—and the storyteller knows its entirety before he begins. The *plotting* is his strategy of letting us discover, eventually, everything that happened, and probably not in the sequence of happening. He must keep us in suspense, in the dark, letting in the light only a bit at a time until the final illumination. What side-trips does he take? How does he delay even as he informs? What red herrings does he drag across the trail to draw us from the scent? Keeping the plot and the plotting distinct will help you to describe the story's effect as it unfolds, and finally achieves its end.

Look especially for those things the author lets us misinterpret. In Austen's *Emma,* Frank Churchill goes all the way to London for a haircut. Everyone, including us, takes this as a sign of his frivolity. He (and Jane Austen) lightheartedly lets everyone cultivate this impression. In the end, we surmise the truth the author never tells us directly: he got his haircut, of course, but he really went to London to buy the slightly mysterious piano everyone has explained in another way. This is plot, after we have assembled all the details. The plotting is in dissociating the two significant details so that we miss their connection, and infer it only after we have learned all the facts of the plot. The author has indulged in, and enjoyed at our expense, the necessary deception of plotting, allowing room to deepen her characterization of Churchill as well. And we, too, enjoy the deception, as we take in the full light at the end, admiring her deftness and economy, and her accuracy in depicting human personality and human misperceptions. This is the charm of storytelling: the excitement in not knowing, in waiting to learn, in trying to guess and being surprised, until the master storyteller finally lets us fully into the secret. This is the strength

---

*This distinction between plot and plotting originated in my "Bridget Allworthy: The Creative Pressures of Fielding's Plot." *Papers of the Michigan Academy of Science, Arts, and Letters* (Ann Arbor, 1967), 52: 345–356, reprinted in *Tom Jones,* Norton Critical Edition, ed. Sheridan Baker (New York: W. W. Norton & Co., 1973): 906–16.

of plotting. Your readers will appreciate your pointing it out to them, if it is notably good, as it certainly is in *Emma*.

Characters: Individuals or Stereotypes?

"Begin with an individual," writes F. Scott Fitzgerald, "and before you know it you find that you have created a type: begin with a type, and you find that you have created—nothing."* The writer has not *created,* in other words; he has merely borrowed a stereotype, a figure so thin and conventional as to be uninteresting or, worse, irritating, because the author thinks he has offered something new when he has given us only the fixed outline of the rich man, the poor man, the merchant, the chief, the Negro, the Jew, the Scotsman, the Irishman—all reflecting the haughty prejudices that produced them. A fully convincing character does seem an individual, a real person, however fanciful the setting, on whatever mission impossible.

But a character must also seem typical of something in the human spectrum, or he will mean nothing. Minor characters usually come in as types, and they are effective exactly because they represent something we immediately recognize as characteristically human. Actually, Fitzgerald is wrong about starting with a type. Probably all good writers often start precisely there—the young lover, the worried parent—and individualize the type as they go, as with Chaucer's marvelous array of types, each vividly individual. The greater the character, the more individualized, the more complex in motives and traits, and yet the more universally typical too, perhaps even *archetypical,* becoming a universal model forevermore, like Don Quixote or Falstaff or Hamlet or Huckleberry Finn.

In analyzing and describing characters, then, look first for their type. Labeling them may help you describe them for your readers—their names may tell something: *Flora* (the goddess of flowers), *Pinchpenny* (the ultimate tightwad). So try to find a label: the budding adolescent, the ineffectual old man, the pushy matron, the wily lawyer. Now you can present them a little more clearly, and show more clearly what energies are conflicting in this fictional drama. Then ask if the author individualizes them or leaves them merely typical. E. M. Forster divided characters into "round" and "flat," and the contrast has remained highly useful.† The round character has complexities, contradictions, depths, which make him seem fully rounded into life. The flat character we see only from the outside and from one side, knowing only a few of his typical traits, which remain the same, since his purpose is only to represent something typical. So tell your reader if a character is round or flat, and

---

*Opening sentence, "The Rich Boy," first published in two parts, *Redbook Magazine,* January and February, 1926, and now widely anthologized.

†*Aspects of the Novel* (New York: Harcourt Brace Jovanovich, Inc., 1927): 103.

whether we learn something of his inner life or see him solely in one dimension.

Finally, try to say what individualizes this person, who is, of necessity, also a type. In *Ulysses,* for example, Joyce's Bloom is the typical alienated modern man. He is also Ulysses, tossed on strange shores and seeking home. He is also an Irishman, and also the Wandering Jew. He is a sensualist, who loves scented soap, and eats "with relish the inner organs of beasts and fowls," each sensuality putting a slight but different mark on the negative side of Bloom's ledger. Bloom is also a father seeking the son he has lost, and a jolly good fellow in the pub. In Bloom, we see surprisingly that individuals are bundles of typical traits, the naming of which helps us to define the individual. We apparently individualize the typical by mixing in more typicalities. Any detail of dress, any mannerism that particularizes, any "human touch," as we say, engages our attention because it is typically human. Pinpoint these details for your reader.

Types may also operate powerfully in stylized contexts, as in Japanese No plays, or in those several modern satirical fantasies with characters named Boy, Girl, Stenographer, Machine, and so forth. Describe the odd stamp of these machined abstractions. Conversely, one sign of the great writer is to vitalize some insignificant and momentary character who would usually remain no more than a shadowy type. A highwayman in *Tom Jones* will pay an old woman a saucy compliment as he robs her, and will live forever in her memory, and ours. Shakespeare will let us glimpse an apothecary in Mantua so poor he will sell a deadly poison against his better will, or a soldier in Denmark who knows a piece of farmland when he sees one. These glimpses of vitalized types at the story's edges make its life broader and more solid. Describe them.

Analyze Characterization

We should therefore explain *how* the author presents his characters. He may tell us about them directly. D. H. Lawrence, for instance, frequently begins with a brilliant, almost breathtaking, summary of his protagonist's situation and personality.

> **There was a woman who was beautiful, who started with all the advantages, yet she had no luck. She married for love, and the love turned to dust. She had bonny children, yet she felt they had been thrust upon her, and she could not love them. They looked at her coldly, as if they were finding fault with her. And hurriedly she felt she must cover up some fault in herself. Yet what it was that she must cover up she never knew. Nevertheless, when her children were present, she always felt the cen-**

tre of her heart go hard. This troubled her, and in her manner
she was all the more gentle and anxious for her children, as if
she loved them very much. Only she herself knew that at the
centre of her heart was a hard little place that could not feel
love, no, not for anybody. Everybody else said of her: "She is
such a good mother. She adores her children." Only she herself, and her children themselves, knew it was not so. They read
it in each other's eyes.*

Lawrence's summarizing characterizations are straight from storyland,
with modern psychology added. Most authors shy away from such straight storytelling, describing their characters' appearance—note Lawrence's omission of
physical detail—and adding the psychological shading through dialogue and
action. But watch out for irony in the author's tone, as when Joyce says "inner
organs" instead of liver.

The first question, then, and perhaps the last, is the narrator's attitude
toward his character. Then tell whether he sketches out his portrait gradually,
or fills in and colors an initial outline. For your description of an author's method, ask how we come to know his main characters, whether by one or several
of the following: (1) how they look, (2) what they do, (3) what they say, (4)
what others say of them, or (5) how others react to them. Note especially how
your author introduces his characters. Description followed by speech and action? Other characters talking about them first? Dialogue? Inner monologue?
These questions will help you explain how your author works, how he puts
his portraits together.

Describe the Author's Blend of Narration and Scene

The author tells us what he wants us to know, describes what he wants us to
see, and gives us "scenes" of dialogue, in which his story seems much like a
play. Each author's proportion of narration to scene, of "telling" to "showing," is different.† Lawrence's tremendously effective "telling," for instance,

---

*"The Rocking-Horse Winner" from *The Complete Short Stories of D. H. Lawrence.* Copyright 1933
by the Estate of D. H. Lawrence. Copyright renewed 1961 by Angelo Ravagli and C. Montague
Weekley, Executors of the estate of Freida Lawrence Ravagli. Reprinted by permission of Vi-
king-Penguin Inc.

†This popular and useful distinction originates with Percy Lubbock, *The Craft of Fiction* (London:
Jonathan Cape, 1921), 62: ". . . the art of fiction does not begin until the novelist thinks of his
story as a matter to be *shown,* to be so exhibited that it will tell itself." But Joseph Warren Beach,
also writing on Henry James and acknowledging his debt to Lubbock in general, probably popular-
ized the terms: "I like to distinguish between novelists that *tell* and those that *show* ("Introduction:
1954," *The Method of Henry James* [Philadelphia: Albert Saifor, 1954]: xxix–xxx).

is much on the side unpopular with modern critics, but his scenes of dialogue are equally compressed and sharp, as in the generalized scene he so swiftly sketches in his opening paragraph: "Everybody else said of her: 'She is such a good mother. She adores her children.' "

So explain how your storyteller handles his scenes. Do they proceed mostly in the author's voice, with astute pinpoints of dialogue? Or are they briefly set, with dialogue carrying almost everything thereafter? In Fielding's *Joseph Andrews,* Lady Booby asks Joseph, her footman, to bring up her teakettle. Notice how Fielding's first sentence moves from description to dialogue with an indirect quotation in italics; his second places it within quotation marks. Then the dialogue becomes direct, with only an occasional descriptive touch, as with Joseph's "Confusion" (Fielding's capitals and italics are typical of the eighteenth century).

> **The Lady being in Bed, called** *Joseph* **to her, bad him sit down, and having accidently laid her hand on his, she asked him,** *if he had never been in Love? Joseph* **answered, with some Confusion, 'it was time enough for one so young as himself to think on such things.' 'As young as you are,' reply'd the Lady. . . .***

Each author moves into his scenes in a slightly different way. So try to describe these transitions especially, and then notice how much, or how little, the author's descriptive comments are present as he sets his dialogue before us.

Consider the Structure

Simply step back from the work for a moment and see how it is built. What follows what? What are the high points, what the transitions? Since all temporal works must begin somewhere, must arch through, or sag through, some middle ground, and then must end somewhere, consider Beginning, Middle, and End. You may find a work neatly proportioned and architectural, constructed in three equal parts, with the center of complexity almost at the exact mathematical center, as in *Tom Jones* or *Emma,* or in the central scene in the central third act in Shakespeare's five-act plays. Or you may find a work that flows, breaks off, and resumes, to be structured around some physical point, like Virginia Woolf's *To the Lighthouse* or Faulkner's *Light in August.* However it may be, consider the physical construction, and how it contributes to our

---

*Wesleyan ed., 1.5.29. First published 1742.

comprehension of the work. Structure, in itself, may stir you to an essay—it really is, fundamentally, fascinating.

Note the Similarities and Differences of Drama and Fiction

As our terms—plot, character, scene—suggest, fiction and the drama (and film, a vividly pictorial form of drama) share the same stuff of life and its mimesis. The drama tells a story, and the storyteller dramatizes his tale. Our impressions of both, especially if we *read* a play, are so similar that we hardly notice the differences of presentation. But two differences are essential:

1. Drama unfolds in the immediate present; fiction reports something already past.
2. The drama presents directly what fiction can only describe through a narrator.

Drama is present tense; fiction is past tense. Drama is first person ("I"); fiction is, most frequently, third ("he, she"). The play is before us, minute by minute. The story tells us things that have already happened. Even the narrator's dramatic scenes, which seem to unfold directly before us, as if on a stage, are actually reports from the past (he *said,* she *said*), with the storyteller mimicking the speakers' voices superbly well. But characters in plays (and films) speak *now.* "Now *I am* alone," says Hamlet. "Now *he was* alone," writes the storyteller.

As the narrator's scenes borrow "presentness" from the drama, so the dramatist must fill in some of the narrator's past. How he manages this exposition of past events is an index of his skill. A professional bore called a *nuntius* may come puffing in from Marathon to narrate triumph or disaster, or Shakespeare's repetitive Nurse may fix Juliet's birthday and age so amusingly in our minds that we do not notice the exposition. Or stark secrets may emerge from the past in intensely dramatic moments, as they do from the lips of Strindberg's Miss Julie, almost at the play's, and her own, tragic end. So look for background from the past (or from across the street a few moments before), and explain how well the playwright disguises its essentially undramatic exposition.

Finally, the drama's "presentness" is physical; it is visual and aural. Music, the dance, gesture, spectacle—royal processions with crowns bestowed or torn asunder—have added emphasis and symbolic meaning to the spoken words ever since the Greeks evolved their drama from pagan ritual. And modern theater, with lighting and sights and sounds at its fingertips, has evoked effects that earlier theaters could approximate only in words, if they could imagine them at all. Your estimate of any play must ponder these wordless effects, or must visualize them from stage directions, estimating what they add to the spoken drama.

EXERCISES

5. *Here is a scene that has proved widely effective on the stage, yet it is almost entirely narrative. It comes from Edward Albee's one-act play* The American Dream, *which he describes as "an examination of the American scene." The curtain rises on Mommy and Daddy sitting on opposite sides of a very dismal living room. From the exposition, as they talk, we gather that, years ago, they bought a child who proved "unsatisfactory" and eventually died. Now they want their money back, and are waiting for satisfaction.*

   Write a brief explanation of what Albee is saying about "the American scene" through this stylized "examination" of it. Note especially what he implies by his setting and his brief stage directions. Why "Mommy" and "Daddy" rather than names? How would you have them look and act? What is their relationship like? What is Mommy's relationship with "the chairman of our woman's club"? Why is her husband "adorable"? Why the indistinguishable colors? Why the repeated "lovely"? What is the point about buying and selling? What is the satisfaction Daddy says you can't get today, and what is Mommy's satisfaction? Finally, what does Albee gain or lose by having Mommy narrate the hassle of the hat rather than staging it directly?

   ### From THE AMERICAN DREAM*

   MOMMY *(giggles at the thought; then):* All right, now. I went to buy a new hat yesterday and I said, "I'd like a new hat, please." And so, they showed me a few hats, green ones and blue ones, and I didn't like any of them, not one bit. What did I say? What did I just say?

   DADDY: You didn't like any of them, not one bit.

   MOMMY: That's right; you just keep paying attention. And then they showed me one that I did like. It was a lovely little hat, and I said, "Oh, this is a lovely little hat; I'll take this hat; oh my, it's lovely. What color is it?" And they said, "Why, this is beige; isn't it a lovely little beige hat?" And I said, "Oh, it's just lovely." And so, I bought it. *(Stops, looks at* DADDY*)*

   DADDY *(to show he is paying attention):* And so you bought it.

   MOMMY: And so I bought it, and I walked out of the store with the hat right on my head, and I ran spang into the chairman of our woman's club, and she said, "Oh, my dear, isn't that a lovely little hat? Where did you get that lovely little hat? It's the loveliest little hat; I've always wanted a wheat-colored hat *myself.*" And, I said, "Why, no, my dear; this hat is beige; beige." And she laughed and said, "Why no, my dear; that's a wheat-colored hat . . . wheat. I know beige from wheat." And I said, "Well, my dear, I know beige from wheat, too." What did I say? What did I just say?

---

*Copyright © 1960, 1961 by Edward Albee. Reprinted by permission of Coward, McCann & Geoghegan, Inc.

DADDY *(tonelessly):* Well, my dear, I know beige from wheat, too.

MOMMY: That's right. And she laughed, and she said, "Well, my dear, they certainly put one over on you. That's wheat if I ever saw wheat. But it's lovely, just the same." And then she walked off. She's a dreadful woman, you don't know her; she has dreadful taste, two dreadful children, a dreadful house, and an absolutely adorable husband who sits in a wheel chair all the time. You don't know him. You don't know anybody, do you? She's just a dreadful woman, but she *is* chairman of our woman's club, so naturally I'm terribly fond of her. So, I went right back into the hat shop, and I said, "Look here; what do you mean selling me a hat that you say is beige, when it's wheat all the time . . . wheat! I can tell beige from wheat any day in the week, but not in this artificial light of yours." They have artificial light, Daddy.

DADDY: Have they!

MOMMY: And I said, "The minute I got outside I could tell that it wasn't a beige hat at all; it was a wheat hat." And they said to me, "How could you tell that when you had the hat on the top of your head?" Well, that made me angry, and so I made a scene right there; I screamed as hard as I could; I took my hat off and I threw it down on the counter, and oh, I made a terrible scene. I said, I made a terrible scene.

DADDY *(snapping to):* Yes . . . yes . . . good for you!

MOMMY: And I made an absolutely terrible scene; and they became frightened, and they said, "Oh, madam; oh, madam." But I kept right on, and finally they admitted that they might have made a mistake; so they took my hat into the back, and then they came out again with a hat that looked exactly like it. I took one look at it, and I said, "This hat is wheat-colored; wheat." Well, of course, they said, "Oh, no, madam, this hat is beige; you go outside and see." So, I went outside, and lo and behold, it *was* beige. So I bought it.

DADDY *(clearing his throat):* I would imagine that it was the same hat they tried to sell you before.

MOMMY *(with a little laugh):* Well, of course it was!

DADDY: That's the way things are today; you just can't get satisfaction; you just try.

MOMMY: Well, *I* got satisfaction.

EVALUATION

Evaluation sums up the questions we have been asking. Ultimately, all writing about literature—all criticism, in fact—entails evaluation. Merely selecting a story or poem to write about is an act of evaluation, since you are distinguishing it from others of its kind as exceptional, good or bad, outstanding in some ways, faulty in others. I would not have selected Dickinson's "I Like to See It Lap the Miles,'' for instance, had I not thought it good, and wanted to find out and explain exactly why. You may wish to explain a novel's point, making your thesis an assertion of what the novel's implied thesis is, and this would seem a perfectly neutral kind of exposition. But your selection has already made the initial evaluation, and your essay will assume that treating this particular novel, whether good or bad, will produce more illumination than would treating another. Or you may wish explicitly to take the final step and make your thesis openly evaluative: "This novel is unusually significant because. . . ."

To discover the implied thesis of your novel (or poem, play, or film), you may ask yourself the four essential critical questions:

1. What?
2. How?
3. How well?
4. So what?

These are handy abbreviations for the questions:

1. What is *there?*—describe it.
2. How is it presented?—tell us the author's characteristic ways of putting his *there* before us. This is the question of technique.
3. How well does the author succeed in hitting what he seems to be aiming at with his technical choices?
4. What does all this effort amount to, really?

The first two questions take you into the area of description, the last two into evaluation. As you make notes toward answering these questions, you will develop not only your thesis, but also all the evidence you need to illustrate it. The many ways of addressing the *What?* and *How?* questions, the many elements of a novel, play, or poem to which you direct these questions, we have just surveyed. Now, the most important *what* of all—what does the author imply through these elements? What is his implied thesis, his purpose?

The first of your two evaluative questions—*How well?*—is perhaps a lesser one, of technique and aesthetic effect, of means rather than ends. You may in fact not need to answer it, unless the means—the style, organization, and general management of the book—contribute noticeably to the end, to the book's final power and meaning. Most books are reasonably well written, and you may need little beyond a sentence observing the fact. The *How well?* becomes important only when technique makes an unusual contribution, or when it is noticeably at odds with content, as with a book that is skillfully written but empty, like a clever advertisement. On the other hand, you will occasionally find a book whose lack of art is forgivable because it has something to say. Although Defoe's *Moll Flanders,* for example, is an awkward and cluttered book, its moral vitality has enabled it to endure these two centuries and a half. If you know *Moll Flanders* at all, you understand that by *moral vitality* I do not mean simply "goodness," but any instructive and vital display of the various heavens and hells of existence.

Evaluate Firmly—Reach a Judgment

The ultimate evaluative question, *So what?*, is one we like to ask but hate to answer. Evaluation is extremely hard, and it is dangerous. When it applies inappropriate standards to something new, it may go badly wrong, as when critics decried Beethoven's dissonance. But warmth of judgment, even though wrong, is better than an eternal freeze of indecision. A mind gathered firmly around a reasoned conviction is better than no mind at all. Try to reach a judgment. Is it a good book (or movie) or a poor one? What does it amount to? What do its particulars tell you about life in general?

Here is a film that takes place in three hours in Hoboken, as two characters search for a lost train and relive their lives, seem to fall in love, but then move off on different tracks, both richer for the experience. It is ably done, perfectly believable, and the characters look and speak like real people. It seems to say that we are all on trains that pass in the night. Well—so what? You know it is good. But to explain to your readers *why* it is good, you must go beyond the movie to what man seems to value in life itself—love over hate, compassion over vindictiveness, sympathy over selfishness, understanding over ignorance—to some perception of the whole agony and wonder of being human.

Here is a book. It has held your attention and moved you, and you feel that it is good. But what has it said, what has it amounted to? What, in short, is its thesis and the worth of its thesis? The story is about a boy in prep school who has run away to the city because everything at school has suddenly turned to ashes in his mouth. Everyone and everything—the whole system—seems false, as if they would turn to dust when touched. He finds the same in the city's more devious ways. But he also comes to see that life, at its center, can sustain its false surfaces if one can give something of himself to others equally lost, if one can find some mutual support in the family. He may not have a stable center himself, but he sees that life does have this center, whereas he formerly saw only a void.

You have been describing, of course, Salinger's amusing and moving *The Catcher in the Rye.* You have summarized *what is there* until you have come to a statement of the novel's thesis. Although working unseen among the details, the thesis also has been *there* for you to find and state, if you are to grasp the novel as anything more than a series of serio-comic episodes. Now you can write your first paragraph:

J. D. Salinger's *The Catcher in the Rye* at first seems no more than a humorous, slangy tale about an adolescent boy in a hunt-

ing cap, which he wears turned backward for some obscure adolescent reason. We follow Holden Caulfield's escapades in New
York City with amusement, and we listen to his wild, earnest
slang with delight. How can anyone resist such good entertainment? But as we read on, we discover that the story is not simply funny: it is also pathetic. For all his distraught immaturity,
Holden is a very decent person. We soon find ourselves believing he is right and the world is wrong, until finally we discover,
with him, that the wrong, empty world can have a center after
all, that the center consists in helping the still more helpless, in
an act of protective love much like a parent's for a child. In
short, at the center of the sham and chaos is a simple affection
and understanding that begins at home, in the family.

In Criticism, Write in the Present Tense

You will notice that that paragraph describes *The Catcher in the Rye* in the present tense. You should continue in the present tense throughout the rest of your
paper. The custom and the rule is this: in describing events in plays or novels,
or in writing about a poem, *write in the present tense.* Write "Holden *goes* to New
York" not "Holden *went* to New York." Likewise you would write "Dickinson
slants her rhyme" not "Dickinson *slanted* her rhyme." To say "he *was* an adolescent" implies that he is one no longer. The past tense unveils you, as a student
and amateur, experiencing the book last night, now in your own past. The present tense testifies to the timeless present in which literature lives, and it also
exhibits your own sophistication as critic in recognizing that timeless present.
Dickinson will still slant, and Holden will still go, tomorrow and tomorrow and
tomorrow (when you and I can no longer do either), and at the same place
in the poem or book. And be careful not to drift into the past without noticing,
as you recall reading by the midnight lamp, or think of Dickinson herself as
long since dead. Now, in the present tense, we can continue with Holden.

Describe and Explain

The middle of your "Holden" paper may now well begin by summarizing the
What, describing the story and the people, in more detail.

> **The story begins at Holden's prep school, on a Saturday
> night, when ends are especially loose. . . .**

You tell just enough to establish the book for your reader without telling him
everything. But do not assume that he has read the book, or you will refer to

things he cannot know. Fill in the necessary details: "Then he goes to New York City."

Next you will probably want to say something about the *How*, since the book's language is not only striking but important. Holden's improper idiom carries us to the truth, which the proper world has apparently lost. Proper speech seems a sham, and the only true language left is Holden's yearning, vivid, improper slang. So you give an example or two of this.

Another important *How* about the book, one that immediately moves into the question of *How well*, arises at the end. There we discover that Holden's entire story has been a monologue addressed to his psychiatrist. His telling of his story has presumably straightened out his perspectives. You would certainly point out this unusual technical feature to your reader, and comment on whether it works. Salinger gives some clues in the first chapter, but are they sufficient to forestall the reader's surprise at the end? Perhaps you think the end a bit too much the gimmick to come off with complete conviction. Nonetheless, you think the book stands up under the sudden strain of its ending. Explaining the strain and the survival will lead you to the heart of the book's value. You will have come from describing contents and technique to answering the question *So what?*, to which your thesis addressed itself, though briefly, at the start.

Here you are, then, at the last section of your middle and just before your conclusion, ready to answer the question that will give your thesis its fullest explanation: how, exactly, does the book assert its thesis that familial affection triumphs over social chaos? Here you explain the title: Holden's hunting cap symbolizes his role. He is hunting for something, and going about it backwards, running away from, rather than pursuing, his problem. More specifically, his cap symbolizes his role as "catcher" in the rye: he wears it backward, like a baseball catcher's cap, though he does not know why he likes it that way. You explain his curious misunderstanding of the song "Coming Through the Rye," his seeing the little boy on a Sunday stroll with his father and mother, happily walking the gutter's edge, his imagining himself waiting in the rye, the savior of little children, ready to catch them just before they fall over cliffs. Then, of course, you describe his little sister, "old Phoebe," and tell how he gives her his hunting cap, and how *she* saves *him*.

Notice that you have not needed to answer directly the devastating final question of value. You have implied its answer. From the very first, everything you have said has implied, "This book is valuable." You have asserted the grounds for its value: its thesis that love, and familial love, can hold the world together. Few would think to dispute that assertion very strenuously. Furthermore, your paper has shown, without directly saying so, that this valid thesis is convincingly acted out, in Salinger's superb mimesis.

Now I have sketched out a number of the various ways you may write about literature, and the questions to ask to get started. Don't feel that you must answer all of them, all at once, for any one paper. I have tried to cover the possibilities, to make them available if, and when, you may need them. Actually, you write in much the same terms whatever you choose to discuss: the importance of a minor character, let us say, or of a particular speech or scene, the prominence of a particular metaphor, the balance and emphasis of form, the force of a style, the difference between two similar stories or poems. You simply assert that something is significant, then explain how this is so, describing what you see and quoting for illustration. And you shape your essay in the usual way, following the essential psychology of how we take things in, through time: a thesis to guide and organize, a beginning, middle, and end.

EXERCISES

6. *Here is a story by Joyce Cary, conveniently good and short. Enjoy it, with one eye open for significant details to write about. Then check your impressions against my explicating essay, which follows it.*

EVANGELIST*

John Pratt, fifty-five, on holiday at the sea, gets up one sunny morning, looks from the window, says, "It won't last," and picks from his seven suits the only dark one. He dresses himself with care, and eats for breakfast one piece of dry toast.

"A touch of liver," he says to himself, takes his umbrella and a bowler, and goes for his morning walk along the Parade.

"Why the bowler?" he asks himself, "I'm not going back to town." And suddenly it strikes him that he is bored. "Impossible," he says; "I've only been here a week and my regular time is always a fortnight."

He looks about him to discover some usual source of pleasure in this charming old place; and immediately he is seized, possessed, overwhelmed with boredom, with the most malignant and hopeless of all boredoms, holiday boredom. It rises from his stomach, it falls from the lukewarm air. Everything in sight is instantly perceived as squalid, mercenary, debased by mean use and vulgar motives. The Regency facades whose delicate taste he has so much admired, which bring him year after year to a place neither smart nor quiet, seem to leer at him with the sly, false primness of old kept women on the lookout for some city lecher, willing to set off cracked plaster against lewd dexterity.

He looks at the sea for freshness. But it appears thick, greasy: he murmurs with horror, "The cesspool of the whole earth." He sees the drains discharging from a million towns, the rubbish unbucketed from ten thousand years of ships, wrecks full of corpses; the splash of glitter beyond the pier is like the explosion of some hidden corruption. The ozone comes to his nose like a stench.

---

*"Evangelist" in *Spring Song and Other Stories* (New York: Harper & Row, Publishers). Copyright 1952 by Arthur Lucius Michael Cary and David Alexander Ogilvie, Executors of the Estate of Joyce Cary. Reprinted by permission of Harper & Row, Publishers, Inc., and Curtis Brown Ltd., on behalf of the Estate of Joyce Cary.

He sees from the distance a friend, the Colonel in his light gray suit, stepping briskly. He is whirling his stick—it is plain that he is in his usual high spirits.

Pratt crosses the road to avoid him. A taxi hoots in an angry and distracted manner, but he does not hurry, he would rather be killed than betray the dignity of his despair. The taxi's brakes squawk like Donald Duck—it comes to a stop at his elbow—a furious young man with upstanding black hair and red-rimmed eyes, thrusts out his neck and bawls insults. Bystanders laugh and stare. Pratt does not turn his head or quicken his walk. He accepts these humiliations as appropriate to such a morning in such a world.

The shopping housewives with their predatory eyes and anxious wrinkled foreheads fill him with a lofty and scornful pity, as for insects generated by a conspiracy of gases and instinct to toil in blind necessity for the production of more insects.

Yes, he thinks, humanity is like the maggots on a perishing carcass. Its history is the history of maggots; the fly, the buzz, the coupling of flies, the dropping of their poison on every clean thing, the hunt for some ordure, some corpse, the laying of eggs, and another generation of maggots. Foulness upon foulness. Tides of disgust and scorn rise in his soul; he stalks more grandly; he has become a giant for whom all history is meaner than the dust on his boot soles.

Suddenly he is accosted by a red-faced man, an hotel acquaintance, who starts out of a shop and seizes him by the hand—impossible to avoid this person. The red-faced man is in a fluster. Has Mr. Pratt seen the news? Is there going to be a war, is this it? Should he sell out his investments and pay his debts; should he fetch back his family from abroad?

Pratt draws himself up and out of mere wrath at this intrusion, utters in severe tones such banalities as amaze his own ears. If war comes, he says, it will come, and if not, then not. There are good arguments on both sides of the question. If we believe our freedom is worth defending, then we should be ready to defend it at all costs. For faith is not faith, not what we truly believe, unless we are prepared to die for it. And in a conflict of faith those alone who are prepared to die for what they believe deserve to win. As for bombs, one can die but once. One will die anyhow and possibly much worse than by a bomb.

And all these panic-mongers, are they not more than foolish? Panic is not only useless, it is a treachery—a defeat—an invitation to the enemy within as well as without.

The red-faced man is taken aback by this rigamarole of eloquence. He listens with surprised attention in his green eyes—then with respect. Pratt's unmoved solemnity, his severe tone born of scornful indifference, impress him. He ejaculates murmurs of approval. He says that this is just what he himself has always thought. And this is probably true. He could scarcely have escaped such reflections.

At last he is greatly moved. He turns even redder, his gooseberry eyes shine. He grasps Pratt's hand with fervor and a glance that means, "This is an important, a solemn occasion. You are a bigger man than I took you for. Men of sense and courage, like ourselves, should be better acquainted." He departs exalted.

Pratt walks on alone, his step is still majestic but full of spring. He is exhilarated; he looks at the sea and it appears to him noble in its vastness, transcendent in its unconcern, venerable in its intimation of glorious deeds. The houses are like veteran soldiers in line, meeting with stoic pride the injuries of time. The housewives, striving, saving for their families, wear the brows of angels; the battered angels roughly carved on some primitive church. He salutes with heroic elation a world made for heroes. He perceives with joy that it is going to be a fine day, that he is hungry. He whirls his umbrella.

CARY'S METAPHORICAL EVANGELIST

Opening Orientation
with Setting

Joyce Cary's brief story, "Evangelist," gives us a picture of a typical English seaside resort, and a typical British personality. We see the unnamed seaside village through the eyes and disposition of middle-aged John Pratt during a short span in one morning of his annual vacation. Cary's story is a gem of playful comic irony.

Thesis

It shows us with unusual wit and clarity how our disposition colors the world and generates our metaphors.

Describing
Characterization

Cary makes Pratt very amusingly British. Pratt's reference to "town," together with his bowler and umbrella, denote the man from the "City," London's financial district, the heart of London, of England, of former empire. Pratt is a proper bachelor on a proper holiday, scheduled for two weeks annually, at the same time, to the same place. He is affluent and orderly, with seven suits, one for each day of the week, and, one might surmise, worn in proper succession. All are appropriately light in color for the summer holidays, except one, presumably for Sunday. Pratt has awakened to a sunny day but a gloomy mood. He selects his only dark suit to suit his dark spirits.

Summarizing and
Describing Events

He breakfasts only on one piece of dry toast. He feels that he has indigestion. He puts on his bowler, inappropriate for a holiday stroll, and takes his umbrella, inappropriate for a sunny day, since he thinks it cannot last. He goes out in the full black formal rigging of the City for his routine morning walk. He feels boredom rising from his stomach. Consequently, he sees the village, a "charming old place," as the epitome of mercenary corruption and squalor. The calm sea seems the cesspool of the world.

He turns quickly across the street to avoid his friend, the Colonel, whom he sees at a distance stepping along in a light gray suit, swinging his stick in high spirits, the living opposite of Pratt's black gloom. Pratt, disdainful in his mood, almost steps in front of a taxi, "whose brakes squawk ridiculously like Donald Duck," bringing laughter from the bystanders as the uncouth and weary young cab-driver shouts insults. This raises Pratt's contempt for the world, as he stalks grandly on, generating more metaphors of corruption. Life seems nothing but a senseless toil of flies breeding maggots on corpses.

Explication

In this mood, Pratt faces a red-faced acquaintance, with opaque green eyes, like gooseberries, evidently not very bright, who is worried about an impending war. From the story's date (1952) and the talk of bombs, we can surmise that Cary is placing Pratt's day in the late 1930s, on the verge of World War II. Pratt's contempt for the world, and for his worried acquaintance, now produces a string of platitudes about facing the inevitable. Pratt's platitudes begin to amaze even himself, and indeed they do sound impressive. His friend's green eyes shine even more comically in his even redder face as, his worries relieved, he looks on Pratt as a savior.

More Describing

Pratt is now the comically ironic "evangelist" of Cary's title, the bringer of good news to lift the spirits. "Evangelist" means exactly that, combining Greek *eu* ("good") and *angelos* ("messenger") to designate a preacher of the gospel ("good news"), a "Good Angel." Now the evangelist has converted himself. His accidental triumph, which ironically sprang from his sour mood, lifts his picture of himself into heroic majesty, and his metaphors change to match. Now, like the Colonel whose sprightliness grated against Pratt's mood, Pratt has a spring in his step, and he whirls his inappropriately moody umbrella, as the Colonel had whirled his stick. Pratt sees with joy that the day, sunny from the first, will indeed be fine, because now his spirits are fine.

More Explication

The point of the story is the comically ironic fact that we think we have rational charge of ourselves, and that we think of reality as steadily one thing, out there, at the very time we are demonstrating that accidents of bodily chemistry and chance are controlling us and coloring reality a great deal more than we admit. The actual façades of the buildings along the seafront work nicely in the story to suggest Pratt's, and our, changing façades. They had formerly seemed delicate to Pratt. Now, to his gloomy eyes, they seem like lewd old women, an extreme of moral decay. Next, in his heroic mood, they seem like old soldiers, holding their ranks stoically and proudly against the "injuries of time." His metaphorical projection of old women as bad and old soldiers as good, neatly mirrors his conservative bachelorhood. The sea is now vast and transcendent, made for heroes. The housewives have changed from flies to angels "roughly carved on some primitive church," as the new evangelist walks on. His sourness has turned to joy, and we see the cause he does not: he is hungry. His spirits have cleared up his stomach, which they had probably soured to begin with.

Analysis

More Explication

Cary's economy makes his story especially attractive. It is barely 1000 words, as against, let us say, 5000 for stories that still seem quite short. He deftly sketches a very amusingly British Britisher, as he also gives us vividly and amusingly the comic fact of how our moods work, in spite of us, and how insignificant and transitory they are. The story's short scope highlights Cary's skill, making its appreciation part of our enjoyment. We see in clear detail his unusually well-educated and pictorial imagination at work on the image-making few achieve so fully. We see clearly his psychological perception and his comic view of the human lot. Pratt—a comic, impudent name—proves to be an evangelist of nothing but the comic human ego.

Conclusion, including the "How"

Restatement of Thesis

Now, with this story and its analysis for suggestion and encouragement, see what you can do to analyze in a brief essay some story you like.

7. *Pick two of Shakespeare's sonnets and demonstrate that one is better than the other.*

8. *Pick two stories from James Joyce's* Dubliners, *from John Cheever's* Stories, *or from any similar collection of stories by another author, and demonstrate that one is better than the other.*

9. *Write an essay on a novel you have read recently, or a movie you have seen, checking your analysis against the four critical questions: What? How? How well? So what?*

10. *Following the same procedure, write an essay on a work of nonfiction—a book of ideas, political, sociological, philosophical, an autobiography, a biography, a history.*

CHAPTER 12

Beginning Research: Using the Library

Now to consolidate and advance. Instead of one thousand words, you will write three thousand. Instead of a self-propelled debate or independent analysis, you will write a scholarly argument. You will also learn to use the library, and to take notes and give footnotes. You will learn the ways of scholarship. You will learn to acknowledge your predecessors as you distinguish yourself, to make not only a bibliography, but a contribution.

The research paper is very likely not what you think it is. *Research* is searching again. You are looking, usually, where others have looked before; but you hope to see something that they have not. Research is not combining a paragraph from *The Encyclopaedia Britannica* and a paragraph from *The Book of Knowledge* with a slick pinch from *Time.* That's robbery. Nor is it research even if you carefully change each phrase and acknowledge the source. That's drudgery. Even in some high circles, I am afraid, such scavenging is called research. It is not. It is simply a cloudier condensation of what you have done in school as a "report"—sanctioned plagiarism to teach something about ants or Ankara, a tedious compiling of what is already known. That such material is new to you is not the issue: it is already in the public stock.

CHOOSING YOUR SUBJECT

Pick Something that Interests You

You need not shake the world. Such subjects as "Subsidized College Football," "Small College Versus Big University," or the worth of "A Best-Selling Novel"

255

well suit the research paper—a threefold elaboration of the simple essay involving: (1) the handling of your argument, (2) the citation of others' facts and arguments *as part of your own argument,* and (3) the managing of citations, footnotes, and bibliography. Bigger subjects, of course, will try your mettle: subjects like nuclear power, abortion, federal funding, endangered species as against public need. The whole question of governmental versus private endeavors affords many lively issues for research and decision, perhaps in your own locality and your own local newspaper.

You can stir your own interests and turn up a number of good ideas for research by reading the newspapers—*The Christian Science Monitor* is especially fruitful—and by browsing the current magazines such as *Time, Newsweek, Psychology Today, Scientific American, Harpers, Atlantic Monthly, Saturday Review,* and many another. Other good sources are interviews on TV, film documentaries, and even arguments in the coffee shop or bar.

Find a Thesis

Well, then, since you will be dealing mostly with facts in the public stock and with ideas with other people's names on them, what can you do to avoid copycatting? You move from facts and old ideas to new ideas. In other words, you begin by inquiring what is *already* known about a subject; then, as you collect inferences and judgments, you begin to perceive fallacies and to form conclusions of your own. Here the range is infinite. Every old idea needs new assertion. Every new assertion needs judgment. Here you are in the area of values, where everyone is in favor of virtue but in doubt about what is virtuous. Your best area of research is in some controversial issue, where you can add, and document, a new judgment of "right" or "wrong." I have put it bluntly to save you from drowning in slips of paper. Remember that an opinion is not a private fancy; it is an opinion *about* what the right is, what the truth is, what the facts mean. It is a judgment of what *is*—out there somewhere, not merely in somebody's head. An opinion, when careful and informed, is usually as close as you will get to truth: a statement of what the truth of the matter seems to be. Your opinion may be just as accurate as anybody else's, and the major task of the research paper is to sift opinions.

Your sifter, as always, is your thesis, right there at the neck of your beginning paragraph. Your thesis may be an authentic argumentative proposition, for or against abortion, let us say. Or it may be a question to be considered, its sides to be weighed for the reader, and the question left at the end as one of the vital issues of the day. This kind of question-thesis, in short, asserts and then demonstrates that abortion, or capital punishment, or gun control, is indeed a current and important issue stirring and requiring public attention, discussion, and eventual resolution from the opinions and alternatives you have put before your readers. Your thesis, as always, is your essay in miniature.

Make your thesis as soon as you can from what you already know and think about your subject. Take a side if you can. Call it a hypothesis (a "subthesis") if that will make you comfortable. It does seem unscientific. But it is nearer the scientific method than it looks. The scientist, too, plays his hunches. James Watt saw the steam condenser in the lid of his aunt's teakettle; Donald Glaser saw the tracks of atomic particles in the bubbles of his beer. As with scientific experiment and the simple essay, if the hypothesis proves wrong, the testing will have furnished means to make it more nearly right. With the research paper, if you do not have a thesis or a significant question to lead you through the twists and turns of print, you will never come out the other end. Unless you have a working hypothesis to keep your purpose alive as you collect, or at least a clear question to be considered, you may collect forever, forever hoping for a purpose, If you have a thesis, you will learn—and then overcome—the temptations of collecting only the supporting evidence and ignoring the obverse facts and whispers of conscience. Your thesis will no doubt modify and shift as your research proceeds. If further facts and good arguments persuade you completely to the other side, so much the better. You will be the stronger for it.

Persuade Your Reader

You do not search primarily for facts. You do not aim to summarize everything ever said on the subject. You aim to persuade your reader that the thesis you believe in is right, or the question you consider is important. You persuade him by: (1) letting him see that you have been thoroughly around the subject and that you know what is known of it and thought of it, (2) showing him where the wrongs are wrong, and (3) citing the rights as right. *Your* opinion, *your* thesis, is what you are showing; all your quotations from all the authorities in the world are subservient to *your* demonstration. You are the reigning authority. You have, for now, the longest perspective and the last word.

Pick an Argument

The tactics of the research paper, then, are exactly those of any argumentative essay, even though it asserts no more than "This question is current and vital." Any straight exposition can take a helpful argumentative edge: not "House Cats" but "House cats are more intelligent than most people realize." You can find something to prove even in straight description: "See," you say, "this has been overlooked; this has not been appreciated; this has been misunderstood." But you will be stronger yet in dealing with a controversial topic. Therefore: (1) pick a subject in which much is to be said on both sides; (2) take the side where your heart is if you can; (3) write a thesis-sentence with a *because* in it: (4) gather your material around and about the *pro* and the *con;* (5) write an essay with beginning, middle, and end, and with a *pro-*and-*con* structure like one of those described on 36–38.

ORGANIZING YOUR RESOURCES

Now you are ready to dig in. You have decided on your subject and your tentative thesis. Now for the library—which is rationally organized for research and conveniently staffed with experts to help you. You can easily learn the ways of this organization and apply fundamental procedures to virtually any subject you will ever want to investigate. Research in a library is really no more than the logical discovering of information to answer specific questions, a very reasonable lamp with which you play both Aladdin and the genie at the same time. As with all engagements of mind and matter—like the process of writing itself—the process of research permits, and often inspires, creativity. Only when you are confidently in touch with the existing sources of knowledge about a topic can you resolve the age-old ambiguities, make the educated guesses, and ask the questions out of which new knowledge and insights are born.

Getting Around*

Take a tour of the building. Your instructor may have arranged one. If not, see what your library does for its public. Some provide self-guided walking tours through brochures or even earphones and recorded voice. Others have videotape programs to explain their facilities, policies, and services. Every library will have some form of handout to help you. In any case, find (1) the circulation desk, (2) the reference room, (3) the card catalog, (4) the course-reserve area, (5) the microform and documents collections, and (6) the current newspapers and periodicals. And get a general idea of where books on various subjects are shelved. Ask someone how to find out if a book is checked out to another person and what to do to have it held for you when returned. Since many campuses have more than one library, pick up a list or map specifying what and where the other collections are. Explore the library in your dormitory. And find out about the local public library: it may be both superb and uncrowded.

---

*For advice and help in the writing of this section on research, I am heavily indebted to Mary W. George, Reference Librarian, Princeton University.

Getting Equipped

For efficiency and peace of mind, you need two kinds of equipment for any but the briefest kind of research: (1) a supply of notecards and (2) a notebook. The 3″ × 5″ cards used for cataloging are perhaps most handy, but some people like the larger sizes (4″ × 6″ or 5″ × 7″) affording more room for publication data and evaluative comments like "Nothing new." Cards in several colors can help you segregate information on various subtopics in your research. On these cards, you record both your bibliography and your notes—summaries in your own words and direct quotations.

The notebook has another purpose altogether: to help you keep track of your progress. For a brief paper researched in a single day, this is no problem. But for any extended investigation, an informal running diary is indispensable. It will prevent you from wasteful repetitions—going through the same periodical index twice, for instance—a common pitfall when several days elapse between trips to the library. A notebook gives you a handy checklist of your steps, from first analyzing your problem to your final double-check of citations. You can cross off the steps completed, rearrange subsequent ones, jot down relevant subject headings, questions arising, new ideas and insights, and generally keep tabs on how your work and thoughts are flowing. Keeping the same notebook for research projects over several terms gives you a kind of homemade research guide of your own. Finally, your research diary is there for that crucial moment when you ask your professor or reference librarian for help, and they say, "What have you done so far?" No one wants to suggest what you have already tried, so you can help them and help yourself by recapitulating your steps. In general, your entries should record the date, what you did, how it worked, and any ideas or leads it gave you.

Start your notebook with a statement of your subject—with your tentative thesis, if you can manage one. Then jot down which disciplines would seem most productive of the answers you seek—psychology, literary history, anthropology, geography, biography. Then go to the library. In the card-catalog room, you will find the two-volume *Library of Congress Subject Headings,* from which you can jot down in your notebook the likely headings to look under in the catalog. Many of the periodical indexes use the same subject-words. By jotting these terms in your notebook, you will save a great deal of trial and error. You may miss whole areas, or think your library has no books on your subject, because you are looking under the wrong headings. A notorious example is the Library of Congress's custom of listing books on World War I under "EUROPEAN WAR, 1914–1917." Suppose you were researching some phase of cybernetics, the study of biological and automated systems of control. Here is the relevant section from the *Library of Congress Subject Headings,* giving you no less than nineteen headings under which you might find what you are looking for:

Subject heading used by library of Congress (note heavy type face)	**Cybernetics**
	sa **Biological control systems**
	Bionics
	Computers
	Conscious automata
"sa" means "see also": all of these......	**Information theory**
terms can also be	**Information theory in aesthetics**
looked under for	**Information theory in psychology**
other aspects of	**Perceptrons**
the same idea.	**Self-organizing systems**
	System analysis
	Systems engineering
	x **Mechanical brains**
Ignore terms	*xx* **Automatic control**
preceded by "x"	**Calculating-machines**
or "xx" (these are	**Communication**
for use by	**Electronics**
catalogers).	**System theory**
These subheadings can	**—Juvenile literature**
be added to basic	**—Research** *(Direct)* *(Q317)*
term.	

Analyze the Problem

Your tentative thesis has formulated your problem. But the research-problem needs some analysis into its components to discover what kinds of information it requires and what kinds of places to look for it. Suppose you have decided to research the following thesis:

> **Small colleges provide a better education than large universities because they emphasize excellence in teaching.**

This suggests a number of areas to research. Jot them down in your notebook as you think of them:

1. Statistical evidence: relative enrollment, student-teacher ratios, demographic characteristics, grade point averages. . . .
2. Profiles of typical small colleges and large universities: matched geographically, by public funding, private funding. . . .
3. Comparison of curricula and degrees offered.
4. Placement in jobs, representative careers of graduates.
5. Surveys of opinions of administrators, faculty, students, and parents.

You can probably think of others. Your list, of course, would depend on your emphasis and the length of your paper. The point is not to begin researching haphazardly, without thinking your topic through in some detail, looking for possibilities. You won't use them all, of course. But some of them may provide you solid and unexpected information, and give your paper an air of original and creative thinking. If you have trouble coming up with varying approaches, talk with your teacher, or your librarian, or have a friend brainstorm with you. Discussing your thesis with someone with a different point of view is bound to open new possibilities to explore.

Now jot down in your notebook, for preliminary strategy, the disciplines or fields that seem most likely to yield the information you want. Here "Education" and "Sociology" would seem most central. Then jot down what forms of information you will probably need: books, learned journals, governmental reports, statistics, college catalogues. Now you will have something firm to go on.

Distinguish Your Sources: Primary, Secondary, Tertiary

Distinguishing the kinds of sources of information simplifies your researching. A *primary source* most closely and accurately records whatever phenomenon is being studied—a book, a document, an observer's report. A *secondary source* is one step removed, deriving from one or several primary sources. A *tertiary source* describes secondary sources. We might represent them like this:

PHENOMENON	PRIMARY SOURCE
Speed of light	Equation
Depth of the ocean	Measurement
Tribal puberty rites	Data from observation
Speed of human reflexes	Data from experiment
Hamlet	Edition of text
Baseball game	Videotape, newspaper account, box score

SECONDARY SOURCES

Discussion or commentary on primary source: textbooks, treatises, journal articles, conference papers. . . .

TERTIARY SOURCES

Syntheses and lists of primary and secondary sources: reference tools, bibliographies, indexes

To get the best coverage, to identify your secondary and primary sources, and to get a synthesis or clarification of the information they contain, you must start with the tertiary sources and move up the chart to the more and more specific. This is exactly the logical procedure you have probably followed many times in the past. Suppose you want to buy an elaborate stereo set, bringing together components of various makes to achieve the ultimate. You begin with catalogues to find out what is available, your tertiary sources. You then read through consumers' guides and the recommendations of experts, your secondary sources. You then draw up a list of the components to investigate further, based on quality, cost, and compatibility. Finally, you go to a stereo store and spend hours listening and asking questions—examining and evaluating your primary sources. When at last you decide on exactly the equipment you want—the primary data of your research, selected and arranged—you go back to the tertiary level again, turning the yellow pages and watching the sales and shopping the stores to get the very best piece of primary data at the most attractive price. Research in the library follows this same everyday procedure, investigating, narrowing, and selecting as the researcher focuses more and more closely on the phenomenon in question.

Get Acquainted with the Tools

The tertiary sources are your reference tools. Like a good tourist bureau, they either give you information directly or tell you where to go to get it—they are what the librarians call either fact tools or finding tools. You have certainly already used a number of them:

FINDING TOOLS

Bibliographies
Catalogs
Indexes
Lists of book reviews,
   paintings, sound
   recordings. . . .

HYBRIDS

Encyclopedias
Directories
Textbooks
Gazetteers

FACT TOOLS

Dictionaries
Almanacs, yearbooks
Handbooks, companions
Summaries of current events
Histories, chronologies
Biographical sketches
Statistical tables
Collections of quotations

Encyclopedias and dictionaries are very handy hybrids because of their dual nature. An article in an encyclopedia will give you not only a vast number of facts and a thorough background, but also citations and a brief bibliography of the most important books and articles, thus serving as a finding tool, too.

If someone's initials appear at the end, this is also an important "find." He is an authority. Look him up in the index or contributors' list, which may also cite his important works. You can find more by looking him up in the card catalog. The index also helps you find data scattered through all the volumes. Under "Medicine," for instance, it directs you to such topics as "Academies," "Hypnotism," "Licensing," "Mythology," and so on.

Your desk dictionary is primarily a factual tool, of course, but it also is a handy finder locating people and things in their areas of geography, time, and thought, for further investigation. Along with the usual meanings and derivations of words, your dictionary can give you quickly some needed biographical details, like the birth and death dates of Harriet Beecher Stowe or the real name of Voltaire. As we have seen, the great *Oxford English Dictionary* (twelve volumes and a supplement, abbreviated *OED* in your footnotes) gives the date a word like *highwayman* first appeared in print, and traces changing usages through the years, points both factual and suggestive of other things to investigate.

In a somewhat different sense, a directory—whether a phone book or a list of schools that teach bee-keeping—is also a hybrid, since it indicates not only who or what does something but where to find him or it. Textbooks function like encyclopedias; gazetteers (geographical dictionaries), like dictionaries. These are your finders. In general, you cite fact tools in your "Works Cited," but not your finding tools, unless, like encyclopedic articles by authorities, they turn out to be sources themselves.

Follow a Basic Strategy

In researching, as in buying your stereo, you start with a general analysis and then move in for the particulars. Once you have defined your problem and jotted down its components and possibilities, the intelligent manipulation of factual and finding tools will provide an efficient and creative strategy. You move back and forth, merging the two. You begin with those seminal hybrids, the encyclopedias. You then go to the factual tools for background. You move to the finding tools for your primary and secondary sources, for your raw data and its interpretation by others. You move back again to the factual tools for support and embellishment. Your procedure might look like this:

1 NOTEBOOK	**2 FACT TOOLS**
The problem analyzed	The possibilities clarified
3 FINDING	**4 FACT TOOLS**
Relevant primary and	Your argument
secondary sources	embellished
discovered	

Your topic will require only a few of the many tools available. You have two super-tools. The first is your reference librarian. Come with your problem blocked out in your notebook, and your librarian will probably hand you the tools in fur-lined geniality. The second is the librarian's librarian, the constantly revised *Guide to Reference Books.* You can ask for it at the reference desk, and use it for your preliminary list of sources for your topic. You will probably see your librarian reach for it to suggest tertiary and secondary sources to get you started. The *Guide to Reference Books* follows the logical pattern of research, first sources by discipline, then types of tools in each discipline, finally those beautiful hybrids, dictionaries and encyclopedias.

The Encyclopaedia Britannica, now based at the University of Chicago after two centuries in London (begun, 1768), still reigns. Find it, and you are well on your way. Its new *Micropaedia,* in ten volumes, provides index and quick reference. Its *Macropaedia,* in nineteen volumes, adds authoritative depth. Here you can survey your subject as nowhere else. But it can't do everything. The *Encyclopedia Americana, Collier's Encyclopedia, Chambers's Encyclopedia,* and the *Columbia Encyclopedia* can fill in many a small gap and challenge *Britannica*'s reign.

Here are some encyclopedias on special subjects, which can also fill in the facts:

AGRICULTURE

Yearbook of Agriculture. 1894–. [U.S. Department of Agriculture]

THE ARTS

Encyclopedia of Painting. 1955.
Encyclopedia of World Art. 1959–1968.
Sadie, Stanley, ed. *The New Grove's Dictionary of Music and Musicians.* 20 vols. 1980.
The New Oxford History of Music. 1954–.
Thompson, Oscar. *International Cyclopedia of Music and Musicians.* 10th ed., revised, 1975.

EDUCATION

Encyclopedia of Educational Research. 4th ed. 1969.
International Yearbook of Education. 1948–1969.
Monroe, Paul, ed. *Cyclopedia of Education.* 5 vols. 1911–1913, repr. 1926–1928.

HISTORY

Adams, J. T., ed. *Dictionary of American History.* 6 vols. 1940–1963.
An Encyclopedia of World History, Ancient, Medieval, and Modern. 1972.

LITERATURE

Burke, W. J., and William D. Howe. *American Authors and Books: 1640 to the Present Day.* Revised by Irving Weiss. 1962.
Hart, James D. *The Oxford Companion to American Literature.* 4th ed., 1965.

Harvey, Sir Paul. *The Oxford Companion to English Literature.* 4th ed. Revised by Dorothy Eagle. 1967.

Steinburg, S. H., ed. *Cassell's Encyclopedia of World Literature.* 2 vols. 1954.

RELIGION

Catholic Encyclopedia. 17 vols. 1907–1922. Revised 1936–, with looseleaf supplements.

New Catholic Encyclopedia. 15 vols. 1967–1974.

Hastings, James, ed. *Dictionary of the Bible.* 5 vols. Revised 1963.

———. *Encyclopedia of Religion and Ethics.* 13 vols. 1908–1927.

The Interpreter's Dictionary of the Bible. 4 vols. 1962.

Encyclopaedia Judaica. 16 vols. 1972.

New Schaff-Herzog Encyclopedia of Religious Knowledge. 13 vols. 1949–1950.

Twentieth-Century Encyclopedia of Religious Knowledge. 2 vols. 1955.

SCIENCE

McGraw-Hill Encyclopedia of Science and Technology. 15 vols. 3rd ed. 1971.

Van Nostrand's Scientific Encyclopedia. 6th ed. 1982.

SOCIAL SCIENCE

Baldwin, J.M., ed. *Dictionary of Philosophy and Psychology.* 1901–1905, repr. 1960.

Encyclopedia of Social Sciences. 15 vols. 1930–1935.

International Encyclopedia of Social Sciences. 17 vols. 1968.

Munn, Glenn G. *Encyclopedia of Banking and Finance.* 6th ed. 1962.

BIOGRAPHICAL ENCYCLOPEDIAS

Current Biography. Monthly. 1940–. Index to 1970.

Dictionary of American Biography. 20 vols., index. 1928–1937, plus current supplements. [Abbreviated as *DAB* in citations.]

Dictionary of National Biography [British]. 22 vols. 1908–1909, indexes, plus current supplements. [Abbreviated as *DNB* in citations.]

International Who's Who. 1935–. Annual.

Kunitz, S. J., and Howard Haycraft. *American Authors, 1600–1900.* 1938.

———. *British Authors of the Nineteenth Century.* 1936.

———. *Twentieth-Century Authors.* 1942. Supplement, 1955.

———. *British Authors Before 1800.* 1952.

Wakeman, John. *World Authors, 1950–1970.* 1975.

Webster's Biographical Dictionary. 1971.

Who's Who [British]. 1848–. Annual.

Who's Who in America. 1899–. Biennial.

Investigate the Almanacs

Benjamin Franklin compiled a collection of pithy sayings to see us through the year—*Poor Richard's Almanac.* But more useful to research will be the modern almanacs of facts, statistics, and events, year by year. If you want to know what the population of Nevada was in 1950, what the wheat crop was in 1960, what the rainfall was in 1970, or who your senator was in 1980—these are the books for you. Suppose you are writing about Eugene O'Neill's *Mourning Becomes Electra.* You could say many different kinds of things about that play: what each character represents in the play's diagram of forces, how the play relates to O'Neill's other plays, or to the Greek drama, which its title invokes. But if you want a glimpse of the play's career on Broadway, go to *The World Almanac and Book of Facts,* which has led the field yearly since 1868. Here you will find what other plays were running, how long O'Neill's play ran, who played the leading roles, when and where the actors were born, whether O'Neill won a Pulitzer Prize (he did) and for which play (not this one). This is not all on one page, of course; but the index will lead you. For almost any subject, you can find interesting facts and figures in the almanacs. Here are some others:

> *American Year Book.* 1910–.
> *Americana Annual.* 1923–.
> *Annual Register of World Events* [British]. 1759–.
> *Britannica Book of the Year.* 1938–.
> *Economic Almanac.* 1940–.
> *Facts on File* [weekly]. 1940–.
> *Information Please Almanac, Atlas, and Yearbook,* 1947–.
> *Keesing's Contemporary Archives* [British, weekly]. 1931–.
> *Statesman's Year-Book.* 1864–.
> *Statistical Abstract of the United States.* 1878–.
> *Yearbook of World Affairs.* 1947–.

EXERCISES

1. *To get a sense of how research changes knowledge in quantity and esteem, and of how encyclopedias differ in personality, compare two articles on the same subject in two different encyclopedias. The 1911 edition of the* Britannica *and the most recent one, published and continually updated by the University of Chicago, make interesting contrasts on such subjects as* Egoism, Poetry, Public Health, *or almost anything. Or you may contrast an article in one of the specialized encyclopedias, such as the* Catholic Encyclopedia, *the* Encyclopedia of World Art, *or the* Cyclopedia of American Government, *with an article on the same subject in one of the general encyclopedias like the* Britannica *or* Collier's. *Write an analysis that compares and evaluates the differing treatments.*

2. *Consult the current* World Almanac and Book of Facts *for the date of some memorable event: the sinking of the* Titanic *or the* Lusitania, *Lindbergh's flight over the Atlantic, the United States' entry into war, the founding of the United Nations, the great stock-market crash, or the like. Now go to another collection, such as* Facts on File, *and some of the other almanacs for the year of your event, and write an essay entitled,*

let us say, "1929"–a synopsis of the monumental and the quaint for that year, as lively and interesting as you can make it.

3. *Go to the* World Almanac *and see what you can find out about the items listed below. Remember that if you want details about 1983, you must go to the* World Almanac *for 1984. Each succeeding year's* Almanac *will repeat many of the same facts, of course, but it will also drop many, such as last year's postal rates and former presidents of small countries: you must go back to the pertinent year for these.*

1. To whom were the first five Pulitzer Prizes in American Poetry awarded?
2. What was the best selling nonfiction book in 1982?
3. What was the best selling book of fiction in 1982?
4. Who is the head of state, and with what title, of: Afghanistan? Algeria? Canada? Kenya? Mali?
5. Who is the premier or prime minister of: Canada? China? Japan? North Vietnam? Yugoslavia?
6. Find the following facts about Canada: the capital, the population in 1982, the largest group by ethnic origin, the second largest, the smallest.
7. Write a paragraph on the history of Canada, being particularly cautious not to plagiarize (see 280).

INSIDE THE SYSTEM

Now Go to the Card Catalog

The card catalog contains the library's system. Its 3×5 cards list all the library's holdings—books, journals, newspapers, atlases, microfilms, microfiches—with approaches by (1) author, (2) title, and (3) subject. The card catalog tells you the primary fact of whether the library has the magazine, newspaper, or book at all. No card, no book. The catalog also tells you a great deal about each item it has. The next page illustrates the three kinds of cards (filed alphabetically) on which the catalog lists the same book—by author, by title, and by subject. Some libraries file all cards in one alphabet, so that you will find *Adams, John* and *The Anatomy of Melancholy* and *Atomic Energy* in that order, in the *A* drawers. Other libraries divide their catalog into separate alphabets for authors, titles, and subjects. In any case, drawers will be clearly marked, and cross-references will direct you around.

On the cards in the illustration, notice the call number, the same on all cards for that book, typed by your library according to its system of classification. This number locates the book on the shelves, leads you to it (in open stacks), and identifies it on your call slip, if you wish to "call" for it. Notice that the subject card is made simply by adding the subject to the top of an extra author card. Title cards are made in the same way. The author card is filed

Author Card: the "Main Entry"

call number:

Dewey class

author's initial

author's name and dates

title

place, publisher, and date of publication

number of pages

size of book

subject heading

Library of Congress call number

Dewey Decimal class number

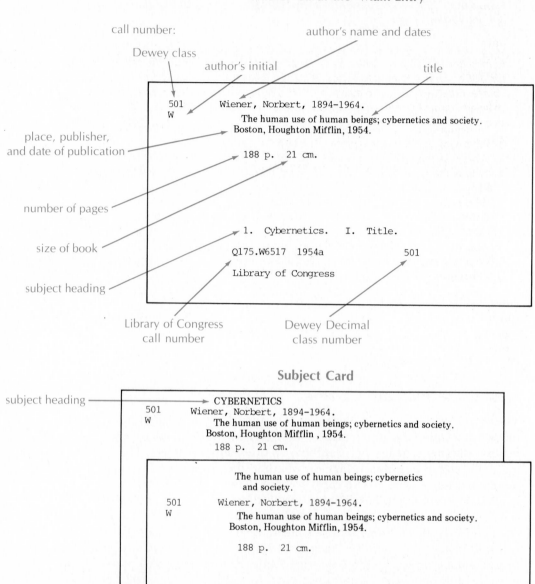

```
501        Wiener, Norbert, 1894-1964.
W               The human use of human beings; cybernetics and society.
             Boston, Houghton Mifflin, 1954.

                188 p.   21 cm.




                1.  Cybernetics.   I.  Title.

             Q175.W6517  1954a                    501

             Library of Congress
```

Subject Card

subject heading

```
           CYBERNETICS
501        Wiener, Norbert, 1894-1964.
W               The human use of human beings; cybernetics and society.
           Boston, Houghton Mifflin , 1954.
                188 p.   21 cm.
```

```
                The human use of human beings; cybernetics
                and society.
501        Wiener, Norbert, 1894-1964.
W               The human use of human beings; cybernetics and society.
           Boston, Houghton Mifflin, 1954.

                188 p.   21 cm.




                1.  Cybernetics    I.  Title.

           Q175.W6517  1954a                    501

           Library of Congress
```

Title Card

under W (for Wiener), the subject card under C (cybernetics), and the title card under H (Human). You will notice that the bottom of the card shows the Library of Congress's cataloging number (Q175.W6517) and the number from the older Dewey Decimal System (501), devised by Melvil Dewey in 1876, and still broadly in use, as this card shows (501/W).

The following table shows the Dewey system, with its ten divisions of knowledge, easily subdivided by decimals. Bringing order out of confusion, it became virtually standard throughout the United States, and made considerable headway in Great Britain.

THE DEWEY DECIMAL SYSTEM

000 General Works	500 Natural Sciences
100 Philosophy	600 Useful Arts
200 Religion	700 Fine Arts
300 Social Sciences	800 Literature
Government, Customs	900 History, Travel, Biography
400 Philology	

But Library of Congress is now predominant, particularly in the larger collections. Big libraries need more and more subdivisions, to place a book among hundreds of a class. The Library of Congress, using letters for its general headings, offers twenty categories for Dewey's ten, and additional possibilities by combining letters with numbers.

THE LIBRARY OF CONGRESS SYSTEM

A General Works	M Music
B Philosophy, Religion	N Fine Arts
C History	P Language and Literature
D Foreign History	Q Science
E,F American History	R Medicine
G Geography, Anthropology	S Agriculture
H Social Sciences	T Technology
J Political Science	U Military Science
K Law	V Naval Science
L Education	Z Library Science, Bibliography

Letters present some difficulties, of course. *I* and *O* have been skipped to avoid their confusion with numerals, and only three letters stand as initials for their categories. But in the older and the newer systems, you can see some interesting changes in the shape of human knowledge. "Religion" has lost some distinction, now sharing a category with "Philosophy"; "Philology" has become "Language" and has moved in with "Literature"; "History" has proliferated; "Politics" has become a science, with a category of its own. The newer system is far from perfect: "American History" has two letters, for instance, but "Anthropology" shares one with "Geography," which no longer seems its nearest relative. Knowledge, and the categories of knowledge, will change; the stock of books, and microfilms, will fluctuate in proportion; and our librarians will adjust their systems, endlessly and faithfully keeping their cards up to date.

Learn How Libraries Alphabetize

If you have ever tried to find your library's file of *The New Yorker,* or the *New York Times,* your heart probably sank before the drawers and drawers in the N-section labeled "New York." The alphabet seems to have collapsed under the dominance of our city of cities. You discover that you need to know a little more than the alphabet to find your way. Here are some finer details of arrangement in the card catalog:

1. Not only men, but organizations and institutions, can be "authors" if they publish books or magazines, as do the following:

Parke, Davis & Company, Detroit
The University of Michigan
U.S. Department of State

2. Initial *A, An, The,* and their foreign equivalents (*Ein, El, Der, Une,* and so forth) are ignored in alphabetizing a title. *A Long Day in a Short Life* is alphabetized under *L.* But French surnames are treated as if they were one word: De la Mare as if *Delamare,* La Rochefoucauld as if *Larochefoucauld.*

3. Cards are usually alphabetized *word by word: Stock Market* comes before *Stockard* and *Stockbroker.* "Short before long" is another way of putting it, meaning that *Stock* and all its combinations with other separate words precede the longer words beginning with *Stock-.* Whether a compound word is one or two makes the apparent disorder. Hyphenations are treated as two words. The sequence would run thus:

Stock
Stock-Exchange Rulings
Stock Market
Stockard

4. Cards on one subject are arranged alphabetically by author. Under *Anatomy,* for instance, you will run from "Abernathy, John" to "Yutzy, Simon Menno," and then suddenly run into a title—*An Anatomy of Conformity*—which happens to be the next large alphabetical item after the subject *Anatomy.*

5. Identical names are arranged in the order (a) person, (b) titles and places, as they fall alphabetically.

Washington, Booker T.
Washington, George
Washington (State)
Washington, University of

Washington, D.C.
Washington Square **[by Henry James]**

"Washington," the state, precedes the other "Washingtons" because "State" (which appears on the card only in parentheses) is not treated as part of its name. The University of Washington precedes "Washington, D.C." because no words or letters actually follow the "Washington" of its title.

6. Since *Mc, M', and Mac* are all filed as if they were *Mac,* go by the letter following them: *M'Coy, McDermott, Machinery, MacKenzie.*

7. Other abbreviations are also filed as if spelled out: *Dr. Zhivago* would be filed as if beginning with *Doctor; St. Joan* as if with *Saint; Mrs. Minniver* as if with *Mistress*—except that many libraries now alphabetize *Mr. and Mrs.* as spelled, and *Ms.* has found its place in the alphabet.

8. Saints, popes, kings, and people are filed, in that order, by name and not by appellation (do not look under *Saint* for St. Paul, nor under *King* for King Henry VIII). The order would be:

Paul, Saint
Paul VI, Pope
Paul I, Emperor of Russia
Paul, Jean

9. An author's books are filed first by collected works, then by individual titles. Different editions of the same title follow chronologically. Books *about* an author follow the books *by* him.

That is the system. Now you can thumb through the cards filed under your subject—"cancer," or "television," or "Hawthorne"—to see what books your library has on it, and you can look up any authorities your encyclopedia has mentioned. Two or three of the most recent books will probably give you all you want, because each of these will refer you, by footnote and bibliography, to important previous works.

The computer is rapidly augmenting this system with computer-output-microfiche catalogues, agreeably known as "COM cats." These are not standardized. Each library will have its own instructions and, as always, its librarians to help you.

EXERCISES

4. *Go to the card catalog and pick a card at random. Write down everything you can learn from it about the author and the book. Is it classified according to Dewey Decimal or the Library of Congress? Whichever way, what would its number be in the other system? What general category is it in—Philosophy, Agriculture? What can you surmise from the other numbers and letters of the call number? What other cards have probably been made for it? Record everything you can learn or guess from the single card.*

Now, find the book itself, and report everything else you learn about it from the title page and the back of the title page.

5. *Select some well-known literary work:* Walden, David Copperfield, Huckleberry Finn, Alice in Wonderland, The Wind in the Willows, A Farewell to Arms. *Describe how thoroughly it is cataloged by your library. Check cards for author, title, and subject. How many editions does the library have? Is the work contained within any* Works? *How many cards treat it as a subject? Does your library own a first edition? This last may require that you find the date of the first edition by looking up your author in an encyclopedia, checking available books about him, and perhaps checking in the British Museum's* General Catalogue of Printed Books, *or, for a twentieth-century book,* United States Catalog of Printed Books *or* Cumulative Book Index *to discover the earliest cataloging.*

INDEXES TO PERIODICALS AND NEWSPAPERS

Indexes to periodicals do for articles what the card catalog does for books. Some index by subjects only, others by subjects and authors. They, too, will probably be in your reference room. The card catalog or list of magazine holdings will tell you whether your library has a particular magazine, and where the bound volumes of it are shelved. Issues for the current year will be available, unbound, in some kind of periodical section, or room. But to find what is in the popular magazines, bound or unbound, you start with the *Reader's Guide to Periodical Literature.*

This is a long file of fat volumes, beginning in 1900, and kept current with supplements, now issued twice monthly, running only a few weeks behind the flood of articles in the magazines they index. They list these magazines inside the front cover; check this list first if, for instance, you are trying to find an article you once read at the barbershop in some magazine called *Thrill.* You will discover that *Thrill* is not indexed, which is probably just as well, and you can shift your search to another sector. Also inside the front cover is a list of the abbreviations used in describing the articles. Studying them will enable you to read an entry such as this:

> **GAMBLING**
>   **It's bye! bye! blackjack. D. E. Scherman.**
>   **il Sports Illus 20:18–20+ Ja 13 '64**

—and to translate it into this:

> **Scherman, D. E., "It's Bye! Bye! Blackjack,"** *Sports Illustrated,*
> **13 January 1964, 18–20. . . .**

You learn that the article is illustrated ("il") and in volume 20, containing the issue for January 13, 1964, which you may need for finding it. You also learn that the article continues on back pages: "18–20+"—which you would complete after you had found the article and read it through, as: "18–20, 43, 46–47." And you will learn that the author is "David E. Scherman." You will do well to write out as full a translation as you can on your own bibliographical card, or you may not understand the abbreviations when going to find the magazine or writing your bibliography. Other important general indexes are:

Annual Magazine Subject-Index. 1908–1949. [Particularly for history.]
Biological and Agricultural Index. 1916–. [Monthly]
Book Review Digest. 1905–.
Essay and General Literature Index. 1900–. [Very useful for locating particular subjects within books of essays.]
General Science Index. 1978–.
Humanities Index. 1974–. [See *Social Sciences Index* below.]
The New York Times Index. 1913–. [A wonderful guide to the news. Get the date, and you can read about the incident in most other newspapers for the same day, if your library lacks the *Times.*]
The New York Times Book Review Index, 1896–1970. [A remarkable mine of information on most of what we consider modern literature.]
Nineteenth Century Readers' Guide. . . . 1890–1899, with supplementary indexing, 1900–1922.
Poole's Index to Periodical Literature. 1802–1906. [By subject only, but admirably supplemented by Marion V. Bell and Jean C. Bacon, *Poole's Index, Date and Volume Key* (Chicago, 1957). If you want to know what the reviewers thought of Webster's first *Dictionary,* or Hawthorne's *Scarlet Letter,* dip into *Poole's.*]
Social Sciences Index and *Humanities Index.* 1974–. [These were both formerly *International Index to Periodicals,* 1907–1964, then *Social Sciences and Humanities Index,* 1964–74, doing for scholarly journals what the *Reader's Guide* does for popular ones.]
The Subject Index to Periodicals. 1915–1951. [Covers more than 450 periodicals in all fields, American and British. In 1961, it split into two, limited to Britain: *British Humanities Index* and *British Technology Index.*]

The *Guide to Reference Books* can lead you to the many indexes in the various fields you might be researching—*Art Index, Environmental Index, Index Medicus, Psychological Index*—as well as to the many "abstracts," the indexes that also briefly summarize articles: *Biological Abstracts, Chemical Abstracts, Geological Abstracts.* Katz's *Magazines for Libraries* and Farber's *Classified List of Periodicals for the College Library* evaluate the magazines you have discovered and can help you to the best ones for your subject. For literature, probably all you will ever need is *The Essay and General Literature Index,* and the "Annual Bibliography" in the April issue of the quarterly journal *PMLA* (Publications of the Modern Language Association of America). This last one gives you both an index and a collection of abstracts. Since 1957, its international coverage has made it the supreme literary bibliography.

EXERCISES

6. *Look up "Ecology" in the* Reader's Guide, *March 1983–February 1984, and translate the entries into complete statements by writing out the abbreviations. This will help you to use the table of abbreviations in the front of the book, and accustom you to getting the complete information before you go to the card catalog and stacks to find the articles themselves. Then, below each written-out translation, write a full bibliographical entry, as it would appear in your finished bibliography, your "Works Cited," looking up the article itself to complete the details.*

7. *Choose some subject like "Dog Racing," "Saudi Arabia," "Bowling," "Mushrooms," —anything that interests you—and write a short statistical report on the listings under this subject in the* Reader's Guide to Periodical Literature *over the past ten years. Does your subject have unusually fat or lean years? What kinds of magazines treat the subject? Can you infer anything from your data about fashions in magazines, or happenings in the world? Go to one article in the most prolific year to discover the reason for your subject's popularity.*

8. *Choose a subject like the origin of man, the PLO, tennis, apartheid—anything that interests you—and compile a bibliographical list of the articles given in the* Reader's Guide, *beginning with the most recent issue and going backward in time until you have eight or ten titles. You may have to look under several headings, such as "archeology," "anthropology," and "evolution," for the origin of man; under "Israel," "Lebanon," and others in addition to "PLO" itself; and under "South Africa," "racism," and "apartheid" itself for apartheid. Then look in the* Humanities Index *and the* Social Sciences Index, *and make another bibliographical listing of your subject for the same period. Which articles appear in the* Humanities *or* Social Sciences Index *(or both) only? Which articles appear in the* Reader's Guide *only? Which appear in both the* Indexes *and the* Guide? *Write a brief commentary about the differences in coverage in these two (or three) indexes. What does comparing them tell you about research?*

9. *Look up some event of the recent past (after 1913) in the* New York Times Index. *Write a paper on how the event is reported in the* Times *and in one or two other newspapers available in your library.*

10. *Learn to use the valuable* Essay and General Literature Index *by taking the following steps:*

   1. What essays on "Skepticism" appeared in books published between 1941 and 1947? Give the author, the essay's title, the book's title, the book's editor if different from the essay's author, and the pages.
   2. Now, go to the card catalog and record the call numbers and full bibliographical data on three of these.
   3. Look up an essay entitled "Pornography, Art, and Censorship" that appeared in a book of essays published sometime after 1969. Record the entry given in the *Essay and General Literature Index,* then give below it the call number of the

book, together with the book's editor, title, place of publication, publisher, and date, all from the card catalog.

4. Find an essay on the moon by Harold Urey, published in a collection sometime after 1968. Again, record the entry in the *Essay and General Literature Index,* and full information from the card catalog.

5. Look up three essays published in anthologies between 1965 and 1969 on Gerard Manley Hopkins, recording each entry in the *Essay and General Literature Index,* and then following it by full data on the book, with call number, from the card catalog.

MAKING YOUR CARDS

Your notebook will have formulated your problem, blocked out the likely areas to investigate, and listed some of the tools for the initial dig. It will be a diary of your progress, a log of what you have done on each trip, and the luck you have had. But your actual notes, from which you will write your paper, your citations, and your "Works Cited" will go on two sets of cards: (1) source cards, (2) note cards.

Suppose you are assigned a three-thousand-word paper, about twelve pages of double-spaced typescript. Some ten or fifteen sources will probably suffice for ample information and solid coverage, giving your thesis an air of conviction and your reader a sense that you have been thoroughly around the question. As an animal lover who has read about talking chimpanzees in the newspaper, you decide to research the question of animal communication. As you pick up an author or two, and some titles, start a source card for each: *one card for each title.* Leave space to the left to put in the call number later, and space at the top for a label of your own, if needed. Put the author (last name first) on one line, and the title of his work on the next, leaving space to fill in the details of publication when you get to the work itself—for books, place of publication, publisher, and date; for magazine articles, volume, number, date, and pages. Italicize (that is, underscore) titles of books and magazines; put titles of articles *within* books and magazines in quotation marks. The card catalog will supply the call numbers, and much of the other publishing data you need; but check and complete all your publishing data when you finally get the book or magazine in your hands, putting a light ✓ in pencil to assure yourself that your card is authoritative, that all your publishing data are accurate, safe to check your finished paper against. Get the author's and the publisher's names as they appear on the title page, adding details in brackets, if they would be helpful: Smith, D[elmar] P[rince]. Get all the information, to save repeated trips to the library. Make sure especially that the call number is complete and accurate to help you and the librarian find, and refind, the book. See the completed cards for a book and an article.

When picking up bibliographical items from encyclopedias and indexes, be sure to get all the information they have, translating out fully on your source-card their abbreviations. "Nat. Geog. 154:438–65. O. 78" becomes *"National Geographic Magazine* 154 (October 1978):438–65." When you cite this in your "Works Cited," you will drop the month, but on your card it is handy in locating unbound issues or in getting xeroxes from other libraries through

Source-card, Book

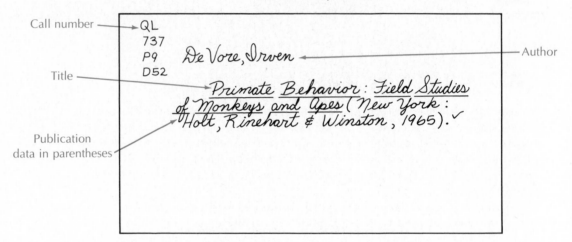

Call number — QL 737 P9 D52

Author

Title — *Primate Behavior: Field Studies of Monkeys and Apes* (New York: Holt, Rinehart & Winston, 1965).

De Vore, Irven

Publication data in parentheses

Source-card, Article

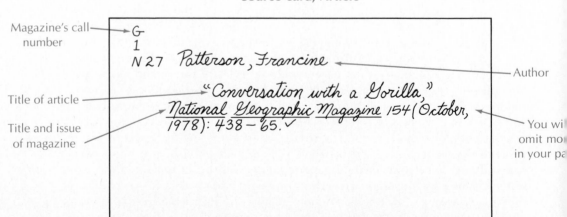

Magazine's call number — G 1 N27

Author

Patterson, Francine

Title of article — "Conversation with a Gorilla,"

Title and issue of magazine — *National Geographic Magazine* 154 (October, 1978): 438–65.

You wi
omit mo
in your pa

your reference librarian. Two sample source-cards, one for a book, one for an article, appear on 276.

Take Brief Notes

Taking notes on 3 × 5 cards or slips has the advantage of enforcing brevity and of making neat packets topped by your source-card. Using 4 × 6 or 5 × 7 note-cards has the advantage of keeping them distinct from your source-cards when organizing, and of affording more room, especially for your own commentary, added below a dividing line to distinguish it. Either way, brevity is the soul of wit. Summarize as ardently as possible, crystalizing three or four pages—or a chapter or a book—into one comprehending sentence that may eventually go straight into your paper: "Primates' cries reflect no more than emotions and their intensities" (596–98). Make only one entry per card, and only on one side, so you can spread out and rearrange everything you need.

Read quickly, with an eye for the general idea and the telling point. Some of your sources will need no more than the briefest summary: "Wholly disbelieves in the possibility." This dogmatic and undistinguished author will appear in your paper only among several others in a single sentence: "Ward, Cohen, and Smithers remain wholly skeptical." You can abbreviate to save space and time—*w* for "with," + for "and," *F* for a frequently repeated "Freud," for instance—as long as you remember that they are your own, standing for full words in your source.

Quote as little as possible. The temptation is always to copy out at length. Resist it for the crucial and colorful remark. Quote phrases, or sentences, or more, only when you cannot effectively paraphrase and condense without losing something striking, or when you need to quote for authority. Paraphrasing as far from the author's words as possible will save you from unconscious plagiarism and, more important, will compel you to look closely at what he is really saying, what he really means.

To distinguish quotations from your summaries, surround them with strong quotation marks: " . . . our mischievous charge finally leaned back on the counter and executed a perfect drink sign—in her ear" (456). If your quotation is paragraphed, mark the paragraphing with a ¶. Otherwise, you may want to insert the whole thing in your paper and be uncertain whether to paragraph it or not, requiring another trip to the library. You can, of course, also quote telling phrases *within* your summaries, and, if your thesis is clear, label your cards *pro, con,* or for information, as you go, as shown in the examples on 278. Since you have full information on your source-cards, all you need is the author's identity and page at the foot. Check your quotations word for word—*slippage is all too easy*—and put a ✓ at the end, and after the page-number, to assure yourself your card is solid.

Chimp talk. Info.

    V's first word "mama," next "papa," then
"cup," all coached by modifying her natural
sounds, getting her to imitate her natural
sounds on request, putting fingers on lips
to make _m_, etc. At 30 mos. learned and
frequently used her 3 wds. but "not always
appropriately." ✓

_____
                                Hayes, 144 ✓
But just how frequently is she
right as against that "not always"?

Chimp talk. Con

    "The significance of Viki's speech training
lies not in the ⎡241 fact that she has learned
a few wds., but rather in her great
difficulty in doing so, and in keeping
them straight afterward." — probably
because can't retain _any_ great number
of "arbitrary associations." ✓

                          Hayes, 240-41 ✓

Porpoises. Pro

    Dr. John Lilly, pioneering experimenter,
writes (apparently to author) "_these_ _cetacae_
w huge brains are more intelligent than
any man or woman." ✓

                          Parfit, 73 ✓

_____

A bit extreme. Neglects ratio of
brain to overall size and weight.

Take care with page numbers. When your passage runs from one page to the next—from 29 over onto 30, for instance—put *"(29–30)"* after it, *but also mark the exact point where the page changed.* You might want to use only part of the passage and then be uncertain as to which of the pages contained it. An inverted L-bracket and the number "30" after the last word of page 29, will do nicely: "All had ⌐30 occurred earlier." Do the same even when the page changes in mid-word with a hyphen: "having con- ⌐21 vinced no one."

When preparing a research paper on a piece of literature, you would also make a source-card for the edition you are using, and would probably need a large number of note-cards for summaries and quotations from the work it-self—again, one card for each item, for convenience in sorting.

Condense with Ellipses; Clarify with Brackets

You can make an important long quotation more manageable by dropping the lesser phrases. You mark these drops by three spaced dots . . . , the ellipsis mark. When you cut the end of a sentence, or a whole sentence, you put in a period (no space) and add the three spaced dots. . . . Be careful, of course, not to distort your author's meaning by cutting a negation or an important qualification: "though always very tentative." Conversely, if you want to clarify a point for your reader, you do so within brackets: "This research [culminating 500 experiments] was conclusive." For more on brackets and ellipsis, see 405, 409–11. Here is a passage from Eugene Linden's *Apes, Man, and Language* (New York: Saturday Review Press; Dutton, 1974), followed by a note-card illustrating the ellipsis and brackets:

> **The symposium had set out to explore whether the differ-ence between human language and animal communication was the result of saltation in evolution or an illusion resulting from an approach to animal and human communication that assumed such saltation. In other words, the topic was whether Washoe demanded the abandonment of the traditional paradigm or, if not, whether she could be explained by distinctions derived from that paradigm. The dispute over Washoe could not be summarized more concisely: The Gardners never argued that Washoe could do everything a person does in using language; rather, they sought to determine whether there was "overlap," continuity, between animal and human communication, which an evolutionary view of behavior would suggest. (273)**

> *Chimp talk   PRO – THE CRUX*
>
> *# "The symposium had set out to explore whether the diff. between human language and animal communication was the result of saltation [a leap] in evolution or an illusion.... The Gardners [Beatrice and R. Allen] never argued that Washoe could do everything a person does in using language; rather, they sought to determine whether there was "overlap," continuity, between animal and human communication, which an evolutionary view of behavior would suggest." ✓*
>
> *Linden, 273 ✓*
>
> _____
> *And they did!*

Take Care Against Plagiarism

Plagiarism is presenting someone else's work as your own. Since in research you will be dealing with what others have written, and with a number of ideas already stated and shared, plagiarism, inadvertent or intentional, may seem hard to avoid. But simple honesty will guide you, and care in your note-taking will protect you. Actually, care against plagiarizing will make your research self-evidently more solid and thorough. If you borrow an idea, declare your source (see 289–301 for citation). If you have an idea of your own and then discover that someone has beaten you to it, swallow your disappointment and mention your predecessor, seeing what more you can add to get back some of your own. Or you can keep even more of your own by saying, in footnote, "I discover that James Smith agrees with me on this point," explaining, if possible, what Smith has overlooked, or his differing emphasis, and again giving a full citation of Smith's article for all future reference.

In taking notes, copy out possible quotations accurately, with full details of source and page, and mark them clearly so that you will know they are quotations later. Quote them directly in your paper, and include the page number from the work your "Works Cited" will fully identify:

```
According to Freud, establishing the ego is a kind of

"reclamation work, like the draining of the Zuyder Zee"

(112).
```

Notice that I have quoted the shortest possible segment of Freud's sentence to get the sharpest focus, and that I have run it into my own sentence within quotation marks. You would indent and single-space a long quotation, and omit the quotation marks: for further details, see 406–09.

Or you may quote indirectly, rephrasing unmistakably in your own words:

`Freud likens psychotherapy to reclaiming territory from`

`the sea (112).`

The danger lies in copying out phrases from your source as you summarize what it says, and then incorporating them in your essay, with or without realizing that those phrases are not yours. The solution is, again, to take down and mark quotations accurately in your notes, or to summarize succinctly in your own words, words as far away from the original as possible, keeping the two as distinct as you can, so that nothing from your source will leak through your notes, unmarked, into your paper, arousing your reader's suspicions. Remember that the word *plagiarism* comes from the Latin word for kidnapping (from *plaga,* "net"), and that it is indeed a crime—one that can bring lawsuits and expulsions from college. Remember, too, that your instructor can almost invariably detect changes in your vocabulary and style that indicate a kidnapping of someone else's brainchild. Be honest, and your papers and prose will reflect that honesty.

EXERCISES

11. *Take a passage of about 150 words from one of your sources, or a handy textbook. Reproduce it, and then make a note-card from it containing at least one ellipsis and a bracket.*

12. *Go to the card catalog and find* PMLA: Publications of the Modern Language Association of America. *(This contains the world's most comprehensive literary bibliography, listing the annual international crop of scholarly articles and books on literary subjects.) Then, from the shelf, pick Vol. 84 (1969), which contains the "1968 MLA International Bibliography." Now, give the full bibliographical form of the first four entries concerning Emily Dickinson. Again, you will have to consult the list of abbreviations at the front of the magazine, completing your entries—and checking them—by consulting the works themselves. Do the same for any British author of your own choosing.*

CHAPTER 13

Writing the Research Paper

YOUR FIRST DRAFT

Plot Your Course

Formal outlines made too early in the game can take more time than they are worth, but a long paper with notes demands some planning. First, draft a beginning paragraph, incorporating your thesis. Then read through your note-cards, arranging them roughly in the order you think you will use them, getting the opposition off the street first. If your thesis is strongly argumentative, you can sort into three piles: *pros, cons,* and *in-between*'s (often simply facts). Now, by way of outlining, you can make three or four general headings on a sheet of paper, with ample space between, in which you can jot down your sources in the order, *pro* and *con,* that is best for your argument. The very act of ordering your thoughts and notes through such an arrangement will bring your thesis to sharp focus, if its edges have been uncertain before. Our paper on animal communication would block out something like this:

```
    I. Animals use language.

          PRO                                    CON

                                   Only spontaneous cries (De
                                      Vore)


        But differing signals
        Pilbeam, Seyfarth
```

                           Still not clearly
                             perceptual Seyfarth

But generalizing
   powers Sherman &
   Austin (Seyfarth)

II. Volition
    Lyn Miles

                           But Hediger--deception
                             widespread. Chimps lack
                             speech centers. Clever
                             Hans (Hahn)

III. Understanding
    Much evidence in
      general
    Peg the poodle (Hahn)
    Dolphins
    Parfit
    McIntyre

                           But Norris (Parfit)

    Lilly
    Louis Herman (Parfit)

IV. Talking Apes
    Monboddo, Garner,
      Witmer
    Furness, Hayes,
      Laidler

 V. Ameslan
    Gardners
    "George smell Roger"
      (Miles)
    "Roger tickle Lucy"
      (Linden)
    Patterson

                         But Terrace and Nim

    Patterson's reply
    Koko's drink

```
                              But Morgan on volition

        Fred the cockatoo
          (Terry)
```

Outline More Fully for the Finished Product

You can easily refine this rough blocking into a full topic outline, one that displays your points logically, not necessarily in the actual sequence of your writing. You can make this outline best after your first draft has stretched and squeezed your material into handsomer shape. The principle of outlining is to rank equivalent headings—keeping your headings all as nouns, or noun phrases, to make the ranks apparent (see 130, and the full outline on 133–35).

But *begin to write soon.* You have already begun to write, of course, in getting your thesis down on paper, and then drafting a first paragraph to hold it. Now that you have blocked out your argument or your course, however roughly, plunge into your first draft.

Put in Your References as You Go

The Modern Language Association of America, in conformity with many journals in the social and natural sciences, recommends a system of citations that simplifies your job considerably. A list of "Works Cited" at the end of your paper—the usual bibliography—now replaces all footnotes merely identifying a work. Previously, on first mention, you would have made the following footnote:

```
    [1] Irven De Vore, Primate Behavior: Field Studies of

Monkeys and Apes (New York: Holt, 1965), p. 598.
```

Now you save all that for your "Works Cited," where you would have had to repeat it anyway. You skip the footnote altogether, putting in your paper no more than the author's name and the page number, omitting the old and unnecessary *p.*:

```
        Irven De Vore, for instance, concludes that pri-

mates' cries express no more than emotional states and de-

grees of arousal (598). Samuelson believes. . . .
```

More details on the new system will follow in a moment. But the old problem of handling footnotes and numbering them in your first draft has vanished. All you do is mention your author's name—last name alone suffices after first mention—and then add the page number in parenthesis where you usually would have put a footnote number. Now you limit your footnotes to your own commentary or explanation, which of course may include other authors and even quotations handled in the same way. These few footnotes you may type directly into your draft, surrounding them with triple parentheses: (((. . .))) —the easiest distinction you can make.

YOUR FINAL DRAFT

Reset Your Long Quotations

Your final draft will change in many ways, as the rewriting polishes up your phrases and turns up new and better ideas. But some changes are merely presentational. The triple parentheses of your first draft will disappear, along with the quotation marks around the *long* quotations, since you will single-space and indent, *without quotation marks,* all quotations of more than fifty words, to simulate the appearance of a printed page. You will do the same with shorter quotations, if you want to give them special emphasis, and also with passages of poetry. Some instructors prefer, and some handbooks recommend, that you double space your long inset quotations, setting them off by triple spacing, above and below, as you would in an essay submitted for publication.

Differentiate Those Page Numbers

Notice that you cite, or quote, in three different ways: (1) indirect quotation or reference, (2) direct quotation in your running text, (3) direct quotation set apart from your running text and single-spaced. Accordingly, you punctuate the page-parenthesis in three slightly different ways.

1. With an indirect quotation or reference, you simply include the parenthesis, like any parenthesis, *within* the sentence, or within the phrase—that is, *before* any and all punctuation marks:

```
. . . as Anderson (291) and others believe, but not. . . .
```

```
. . . as others, including Anderson (291), believe.
```

```
Anderson believes the evidence inconclusive (291).
```

2. With a direct quotation in your running text, put the page-parenthesis *after* the closing quotation mark but *before* the punctuation, thus including the parenthesis within *your* sentence.

```
He thinks them "quite daffy" (213), but concedes. . . .
```

```
As Belweather says, "Many of these proposals for investi-

gation are quite daffy" (213).
```

3. But when you inset and single-space a quotation, you *omit* quotation marks, and put the page-parenthesis *after* the final period and a few spaces farther along—with no period following it:

```
     the same sound may have subtly different meanings
for members of different troops of the same species. .
(111)
```

```
     a culture, a commonly shared, learned, and
remembered history as a group, which it transmits
through the generations. (218)
```

EXERCISES

1. *Devise examples to illustrate how you would handle the page number in your text when citing (1) an indirect quotation or reference, (2) a direct quotation in your running text, (3) an inset quotation.*

Paragraph for Balance

Since some of your paragraphs will contain quotations single-spaced and set apart, try to make the paragraph contain them in a way pleasing to the eye. Indent these quotations the value of your paragraph indentation (i.e., five spaces), preferably triple-spacing above and below to set them off clearly. With short-lined poetry, you will probably need to indent even more to center it attractively. To keep your paragraph clear as a whole, try to conclude, after your inset quotation, by coming back out to the margin with a sentence or two of your own. With a very long quotation, however, which may take up a full block of paragraphing and more, you had best let the paragraph go at that, and start again with your own text in a new paragraph.

For clear paragraphing with long quotations, which you may want to introduce with no more than a sentence of your own, try to make that introductory sentence long enough to come back out to the margin, making the opening notch of your paragraph clearly visible to your reader. If your quotation itself begins in a paragraph, indent it *one more* full indentation, to show your reader just how it stands in its original text. But, in general, avoid long quotations. Quote to the point.

One more point: if you are quoting and insetting blocks of poetry, you may need "hanging indentation" for the longer lines, indenting their endings three or four letter-spaces under the line-head to keep the line standing clear—perhaps even several times, as you would in quoting Walt Whitman's "There Was a Child Went Forth":

```
There was a child went forth every day,         Indented Quotation
And the first object he looked upon he became,
And that object became part of him for the
        day or a certain part of the day,      Hanging Indentation
Or for many years or stretching cycles of years.
The early lilacs became part of this child,
And grass and white and red morning glories,
        and white and red clover, and the song  Hanging Indentation
    of the phoebe-bird,
And the third-month lambs. . . .
```

When quoting poetry in your running text, however, you enclose it in quotation marks, and indicate the line-end with a virgule (slant):

```
"That is no country for old men. The young/In one anoth-

er's arms. . . ."
```

A FURTHER NOTE ON MECHANICS

Type, or write, on good 8½-by-11-inch paper. If writing by hand, use white paper with broad lines. Use one side only. Keep your type clean of fuzz and your handwriting neat, in a good dark ink. Double-space your typing and skip every other line in handwriting. Unless otherwise instructed, follow the customs of publication by putting your name and identifications, double-spaced, in the upper *right* corner of your first page (unnumbered), an inch down and an inch in, leaving a one-inch margin at the right. Double-space down for your title, centering it and putting it in regular type with the main words beginning with capitals. DO NOT: (1) capitalize the whole thing, (2) put it in quotation marks, (3) underline it, (4) put a period after it. Double-space titles of more

A first page without title-page

No page number

1"

Sherman Clark
English 123
Mr. Baker
16 April 1984

1"

Double space

Can Animals Talk?

Quadruple space

Indent five spaces

My Golden Retreiver speaks for food. He tells

1"

any of my family what he wants, whether just to go

A title page

4"

Can Animals Talk?

Quadruple space

Sherman Clark

[12 to 15 lines of space]

English 123

Mr. Baker

16 April 1984

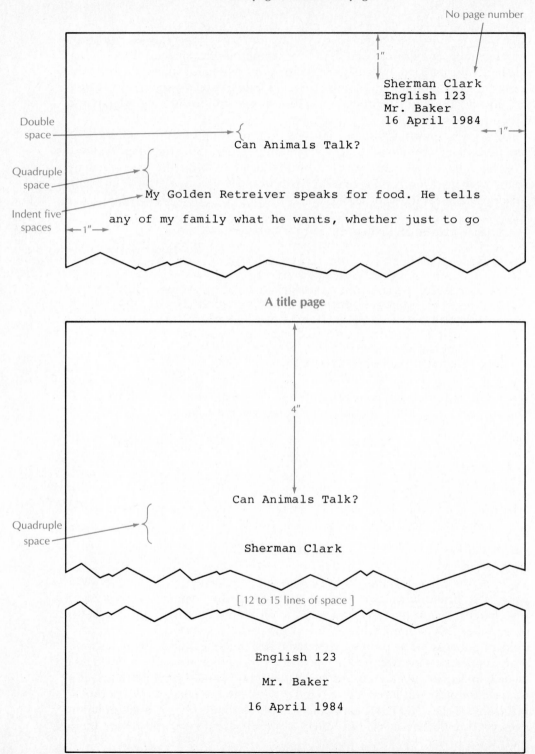

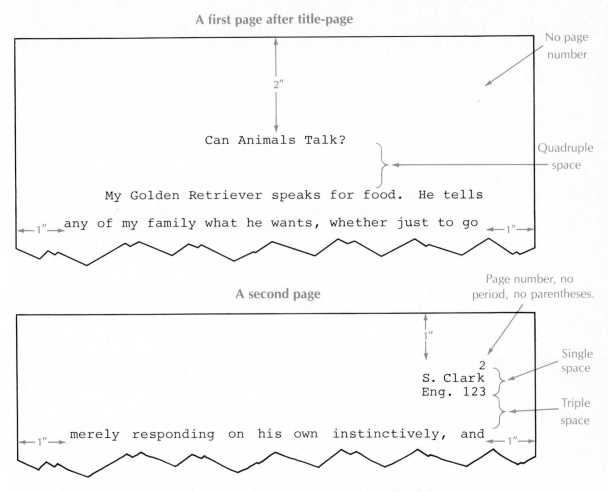

A first page after title-page

2″

Can Animals Talk?

Quadruple space

No page number

My Golden Retriever speaks for food. He tells

1″ any of my family what he wants, whether just to go 1″

A second page

Page number, no period, no parentheses.

1″

2
S. Clark
Eng. 123

Single space

Triple space

1″ merely responding on his own instinctively, and 1″

than one line. In your title, put titles of books in italics by underlining them; put titles of poems and other "quoted" phrases in quotation marks:

The Problem of Time in Faulkner's The Sound

and the Fury

Heaven in Frost's "After Apple Picking"

They All Said "Nuts"

Quadruple-space to start your text. Set up your margin an inch in from the left edge, and indent five spaces more for your paragraphs. If you use a separate title page, omit your name from your first page of text, which will nevertheless still carry your title two inches down from the top, with the page still unnumbered. Number subsequent pages an inch down and an inch in, putting your name and your course, abbreviated, below the page number (no period) to identify any pages going adrift in handling.

DOCUMENTING YOUR FINDINGS

With your "Works Cited" replacing the full citation formerly required in a first-mention footnote, your footnoting is reduced to a very few and perhaps none at all in the usual research paper. This saves space, and time, and money in publication, and it saves you a great deal of work and fussing about fitting in your notes. Your footnotes now consist only of your own commentary and explanation—anything useful that nevertheless does not fit well in the flow of your text.

Some instructors like footnotes gathered together in a page headed "Notes" at the end, which would come before your "Works Cited." You would do this in a manuscript prepared for the printer. Others prefer them at the foot, where the reader can see them. Since your notes, if you need them, will now probably run for several lines, allow plenty of space. You will begin your note four spaces below your text, to set it off from your double-spacing. Do *not* type a solid line between text and note: this indicates a footnote continued from the preceding page, when space ran out. Single-space your note, but double-space between notes if you need another one on the same page. In your text, roll up a half-space, preferably after the period of the relevant sentence, and strike your number:

. . . incapable of the necessary range of vowels.[2]

Your footnote might then cite a group of authors to exhibit your coverage, but ones who add little to the discussion. Quadruple-space after your last line of text, indent for a paragraph, and strike your "2." Now roll down about half the height of a capital letter, strike a letter-space, and begin typing your note:

> [2] Samuelson, Czapinski, Rapp, and Honeywell all similarly assert that subhuman primates are incapable of language because of their neural or oral physiology, or both.

Notice that you come back out to the margin after your initial footnote paragraphing. Notice also that you need include no detail about these authors' works, because they will be fully displayed in your "Works Cited."

What if an author has more than one item in your "Works Cited"? Simply devise a convenient short label to identify each. Suppose Samuelson, above, has both a book and an article you want to cite—I'm making these up: *Physiological Differences in Simian Primates* and "The Oral and Nasal Physiology of *Pongo Pygmaeus.*" Your note above then might read "Samuelson (*Physiological,* "Oral"), Czapinski . . . ," or, if you like, *Simian* and "Pongo"—anything that would help the reader identify them easily on your list. If you had cited these in your text, they would have come out something like this:

Samuelson finds the neocortex inadequate for language

(Physiological 291).

. . . the larynx is too high, according to Samuelson

("Oral" 13).

Notice that you omit punctuation between title and page.

Omit Unnecessary Abbreviations

DO NOT USE these old favorites:

ibid.—*ibidem* ("in the same place"), meaning the title and page recently cited. Instead, *use the author's last name and page,* preferably phrased as part of your text: ". . . as Claeburn also makes clear (28)."

op. cit.—*opere citato* ("in the work cited"), meaning a work referred to again after several others have intervened. Again, *use the author's last name and page:* ". . . too small for vocalization (Adams 911)."

loc. cit.—*loco citato* ("in the place cited"). Simply repeat the page number: ". . . as Smith says (31). He cites, however, some notable exceptions (49)."

p., pp.—"page, pages." These old standbys are now redundant: *Omit them completely.* As we have seen, the number alone within parentheses suffices in the text, as it does in "Works Cited" as well.

l., ll.—"line, lines." These you would probably not need anyway, since they concern certain kinds of literary and textual scholarship, but, as you see, they are confusing, since they look like the numerals 1 and 11. If you ever need them, just write "line" and "lines."

Use Only the Convenient Abbreviations

The following conventional abbreviations remain useful (do *not* italicize them):

cf.—*confer* ("bring together," or "compare"); do not use for "see."

et al.—*et alii* ("and others"); does not mean "and all"; use after the first author in multiple authorships: "Ronald Elkins et al."

Two more Latin terms, also not italicized, are equally handy:

passim—Not an abbreviation, but a Latin word meaning "throughout the work; here and there." Use when a writer makes the same point in many places within a single work; use also for statistics you have compiled from observations and tables scattered throughout his work.

sic—a Latin word meaning "so"; "this is so"; always in brackets—[sic]—because used only within quotations following some misspelling or other surprising detail to show that it really was there, was "so" in the original and that the mistake is not yours. But don't use [sic] snidely to nudge your reader and say in effect, "what a bone-head."

Other useful abbreviations are:

c. or *ca.*	*circa,* "about" (*c.* 1709)
ch., chs.	chapter, chapters, with Arabic numerals, "ch. 12."
ed.	edited by, edition, editor
ms, mss	manuscript, manuscripts
n.d.	no date given
n.p.	no place of publication given
rev.	revised
tr., trans.	translated by
vol., vols.	volume, volumes (use only with books: *Forsyte Saga,* vol. 3.)

A footnote using some of these might go like this (Allenberg has two titles on your list):

3 See Donald Allenberg et al., Population 308-12; cf. Weiss 60. Dillon, passim, takes a position even more conservative than Weiss's. See also A. H. Hawkins 71-83 and ch. 10. Records sufficient for broad comparisons begin only ca. 1850.

Abbreviate Books of the Bible, Even the First Time

The Bible and its books, though capitalized as ordinary titles, are never italicized. Spell them out in your running text: "The Bible begins with Genesis." You refer to them also directly in your text, within parentheses—abbreviated, with no commas, and with Arabic numerals: Mark 16.6; Jer. 4.24; 1 Sam. 18.33. No comma—only a space—separates name from numbers; periods separate the numbers, *with no spacing.* The dictionary gives the accepted abbreviations: Gen., Exod., Lev., Deut. Make biblical references like this:

There is still nothing new under the sun (Eccl. 1.9); man

still does not live by bread alone (Matt. 4.4).

As Ecclesiastes tells us, "there is no new thing under the

sun" (1.9).

Abbreviate Plays and Long Poems After First Mention

After first mention, handle plays and long poems like biblical citations. Your "Works Cited" will contain the edition you are using. Italicize the title (underscore on typewriter or in handwriting): Merch. 2.4.72–75 (this is *The Merchant of Venice,* Act II, scene iv, lines 72–75), Caesar 5.3.6, Ham. 1.1.23; Iliad 9.93 (=Book IX, line 93), PL 4.918 (=*Paradise Lost,* Book IV, line 918). Notice: no comma between short-title and numbers; periods and no spaces between numbers. Use the numbers alone if you have already mentioned the title, or have clearly implied it, as in repeated quotations from the same work.

EXERCISES

2. *Write a summarizing footnote, including the following phrases and abbreviations—c., cf., ed., see also, ch., ff., et al., passim—and dealing with the following supposed items:*

   1. An essay entitled Too Many Cars by L. A. Crump, who also has a book you have cited entitled Money Machines.
   2. Certain statistics have become available only from about 1920.
   3. Wilma Smithers says something on her page four that the reader should compare with Crump, and the reader should also look at her sixth chapter.
   4. Claudia Griffin takes a generally hostile view of Crump's work.
   5. You want the reader to consult also the entry about automobiles in the Encyclopaedia Britannica, volume dated 1980.

3. *Abbreviate the following items for suitable parenthetical documentation in your text:*

   Measure for Measure, Act III, scene 4, lines 10 to 20.
   The Faerie Queene, Book II, Canto IX, stanza xxix.
   The first epistle to the Corinthians, New Testament, second chapter, eleventh verse.
   Ezekiel, chapter forty-seven, verse five.
   Tom Jones, Book VIII, Chapter IV, pages 313 to 314.

THE DETAILS OF "WORKS CITED"

Handle with care, so your readers can find what you found, and you too can find it again. Note that the new system asks for condensing the names and designations of publishers, as long as they remain clear. Thus "Holt, Rinehart & Winston" becomes "Holt," and "Dunne Press, Inc." becomes "Dunne." The form is the usual one for bibliographies, spaced like this:

Books

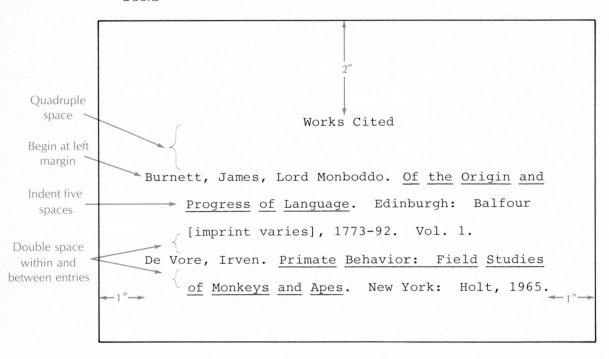

You indicate books that give no place or date of publication as follows:

```
Segal, Annette. The Question of Rights. N.p.:

    Bell Press, n.d.
```

The point is to give the fullest information available, and to indicate what the title page and its back omit to assure your reader that this is how things stand and that the omissions are not your negligences.

When listing other works by the same author or authors, use three hyphens and a period instead of repeating the names:

Jones, Bingham, and Samuel Maher. The Kinescopic

  Arts and Sciences. Princeton: Little House,

  1970.

---. "Television and Vision: The Case for

  Governmental Control." Independent Review 7

  (1969): 18-31.

Two Authors; More
Than One Entry for
Same Author(s)

Jones and Maher also wrote the second entry, which alphabetizes second with its *T* following the *K* of *Kinescopic.* If Jones alone had written "Television and Vision," it would come first, with his name in full, and the "*Kinescopic*" entry would follow as it stands, showing both authors' names. Note that the three-hyphens-and-period is the sign for a repeated authorship, single or multiple.

Books that are monographs in a series look like this:

Thornbury, Ethel Margaret. Henry Fielding's The-

  ory of the Comic Prose Epic. Univ. of Wiscon-

  sin Studies in Language and Literature, 37.

  Madison: Univ. of Wisconsin Press, 1931.

Magazines

With scholarly journals that number their pages consecutively throughout the year, you give volume number, the year, and the pages an article covers, with no comma following title, but with spaces between numbers and punctuations:

Solovyov, Vladimir. "The Paradox of Russian

  Vodka." Michigan Quarterly Review 21 (1982):

  406-19.

Here you have condensed the magazine's designation of volume, issue, and date, "Vol. XXI, No. 3, Summer 1982," into "21 (1982)," followed by a colon (the sign for "page" or "pages"), and then the inclusive pages, omitting "Vol.," "No. 3," and "Summer." Rule: put everything into Arabic numbers.

  With weekly and monthly magazines that begin numbering their pages anew with each issue, give the date, which appears on the cover and is the only practical means of finding the issue again, for both you and your readers:

```
Hahn, Emily. "Getting Through to Others." Part 1.

    The New Yorker 17 April 1978: 38-103.
```

```
Jason, Artemus. "World Communication." Atlantic

    Monthly Mar. 1984: 20-31.
```

Newspapers

Newspaper articles sometimes need more detail. Since many are anonymous, you usually alphabetize them by the first significant word of the title—by *Trouble* in the following item:

```
"The Trouble with Fiction." Editorial. New York

    Times 10 Apr. 1984, sec. 4: 8.
```

You have added Editorial by way of helpful explanation. Here again the full date is necessary. The "sec. 4: 8" indicates "section 4, page 8" in this newspaper that numbers pages anew with each section. With newspapers that letter their sections—*A, B, C, D*—and also letter their page numbers within sections, you need give only the page—*8B* or *D*-4—however the paper does it.

If the article has a by-line, you of course include the author. If the article is mostly an interview with one authority, like the one below, you had better bracket that authority as your key, since you will be quoting him in your essay:

```
[Mills, Jay.] "Chipmunks Are Funny People." Asso-

    ciated Press News Release. Back Creek Eve-

    ning Star 15 Oct. 1983: D4, D8.
```

You alphabetize anonymous articles by the first significant word of the title, omitting "Anon.," which is self-evident. This title would go under *V:*

```
"A Visit with Prarie Dogs." Western Scientist 10

    (1981): 256-73.
```

Here are some further complications:

Source Within Source

> Caldwell, Abraham B. "The Case for a Streaming
>
> Consciousness." American Questioner 62
>
> (1979): 37-49. Qtd. in Albert N. Mendenhall.
>
> Modern Commentary. Princeton: Little House,
>
> 1980.

You have found Caldwell in Mendenhall's book.

> Hill, D.C. "Who Is Communicating What?" In Essays
>
> for Study. Ed. James L. McDonald and Leonard
>
> P. Doan. New York: Appleton Hall, 1978.
>
> 214-25. Rpt. from Era 12 (1972): 9-21.

McDonald and Doan have edited this collection, or casebook, reprinting Hill's article from *Era*. A period, not a colon, follows the "1978" before the article's pages within the book, since we already have a colon after "New York."

> Small, David R. "The Telephone and Urbanization."
>
> In Annals of American Communication. Ed. Wal-
>
> ter Beinholt. Boston: Large, Green, 1969. 3:
>
> 401-18.

The *Annals of American Communication* is a series of bound volumes, not a magazine. Therefore, the volume-number follows the date. Had this been a magazine, the entry would have read, omitting the "In": . . . *Annals of American Communication* 3 (1969): 401–18.

> Peters, Arnold. "Medicine." Encyclopaedia Bri-
>
> tannica. 11th ed. 1911.

"Jackal." Encyclopaedia Britannica: Micropaedia.

    1980 ed.

You need neither volume nor page numbers in alphabetized encyclopedias, only the edition you are citing. The entry on "Medicine" was initialed "A.P.," and you have looked up the author's name in the contributors' list. The article on the "Jackal" was anonymous, to be alphabetized in your "Works Cited" under *J*.

Editions

Alphabetize editions by the author's name, but cite the editor:

Shakespeare, William. Romeo and Juliet. In An Es-

    sential Shakespeare. Ed. Russell Fraser.

    New York: Prentice-Hall, 1972.

But alphabetize by the editor, when you have referred to his introduction and notes:

Cowley, Malcolm, ed. The Portable Hawthorne. With

    introduction and notes. New York: Viking,

    1948.

Quackenbush, Colby. Afterword. The Scarlet Let-

    ter. By Nathaniel Hawthorne. New York:

    Dunne, 1983.

In the second entry, Quackenbush has contributed only an "Afterword" to a printing of a novel with no editor specified, and you have referred only to his remarks. If, on the other hand, you quote from both the novel and Quackenbush, you would list by *Hawthorne:*

Hawthorne, Nathaniel. The Scarlet Letter. With

    Afterword by Colby Quackenbush. New York:

    Dunne, 1983.

Other Details

    Gillies, George L. "Henry Smith's 'Electra.' "

        Speculation 2 (1881): 490-98.

This example shows where to put the period when the title of an article ends in a quoted title. The original title would have had double quotation marks around the poem.

    Schwartz, P[aul] F[riedrich]. A Quartet of Thoughts.

        New York: Appleton Hall, 1943.

    [Lewes, George H.] "Percy Bysshe Shelley." Westmin-

        ster Review 35 (1841): 303-44.

These two entries show how to use brackets to add useful detail not actually appearing in the published work. Of course, famous initials are kept as initials: T. S. Eliot, H. G. Wells, D. H. Lawrence.

Pamphlets

Pamphlets, governmental publications, and other oddities just require common sense:

    "The Reading Problem." Mimeographed pamphlet.

        Center City, Ark.: Concerned Parents Commit-

        tee, 25 Dec. 1979.

    Racial Integration. House Committee on Health, Ed-

        ucation, and Welfare, U. S. Congress, 101st

        Cong., 2nd sess. Washington: GPO, 1969. H.

        Rep. 391 to accompany H. R. 6128.

Pamphlets like these you must play by instinct, including all the details, as briefly as possible, that would help someone else to hunt them down.

Audio-Visual Materials

Recordings, films, and tapes also require some ingenuity. Do not cite microfilms and other reproductions of things in print. Simply cite the book, article, or newspaper as if you had it in hand. But other media are forms of publication in themselves, to be cited as clearly as possible if you use them. The American Library Association recommends the following ways of citation:

MOTION PICTURE

Valley Forge. Motion Picture. New York: Steve

    Krantz Productions. Released by

    Encyclopaedia Britannica Educational Corp.,

    1972.

DISC

O'Neill, Eugene. Long Day's Journey into Night.

    Sound Recording. Caedmon, [1972]. 3 discs

    TRS350. Disc 3, Side 2.

FILMSTRIP

Limericks. Filmstrip. In Enjoying Poetry.

    Jamaica, N.Y.: Eye Gate House, 1964. Frame 27.

TAPE

York, Herbert Frank. The Missile Race Destination

    Unknown. Sound Recording. Santa Barbara,

    Calif.: Center for the Study of Democratic

    Institutions [1972]. Tape no. 576.

McDuff, Rachael. "Interpreting the Media." Sound

    Recording. Lecture presented at the

    Department of Journalism, Winston State

    College, 20 Apr. 1980.

Notice that York's formal production corresponds to a book (italicized) and that McDuff's lecture is like an article (within quotation marks).

CASSETTE

Bogard, Charles. "Ree-deep, ribbid":
Herpetologist Charles Bogard Studies the
Frog and Its Call. Sound Recording. N.p.:
Center for Cassette Studies, 1971. Cassette
010 13460.

I have based these instructions on *The MLA Handbook for Writers of Research Papers, Theses, and Dissertations* (compiled by the Modern Language Association of America), following the customs for work in literature and the humanities. Some of the social and natural sciences continue to use slightly different conventions. An article would look like this in a botanical bibliography (no quotation marks, no parentheses, fewer capitals):

Mann, K. H. 1973. Seaweeds: their productivity

    and strategy for growth. Science 182:975-81.

Entry in Scientific Bibliography

This article might be referred to in the text as (Mann, 1973), or simply as, say, (14), if the bibliographic entries are not alphabetized but numbered (for example, "14. K. H. Mann, *Science.* 182:975–81"—title of article omitted). For papers in the social and natural sciences, consult your instructor about the correct style, or style manual, to follow.

A good general manual is the current edition of Kate L. Turabian, *A Manual for Writers of Term Papers, Theses, and Dissertations* (Chicago and London: The University of Chicago Press). A larger reference popular with scholars is *A Manual of Style* (the "Chicago Style Manual"), also published by the University of Chicago Press. Both the *MLA Handbook* and the Chicago *Manual* list other manuals for the various disciplines—engineering, geology, linguistics, psychology, and medicine, for example.

EXERCISES ────────────────────────────────

4. *For the items below, concoct a sentence of citation in your imaginary text and then follow it with a full entry in your "Works Cited." (See 529 for help with Roman numerals.)* **EXAMPLE:**

Hall several times denies any connection (211, 304, 421).

Hall, Candleman. <u>The Obdurate Atom</u>. New York and

London: Donlevy, 1983.

1. You are citing a brief quotation from page 663 in an article with these characteristics:

Quarterly magazine entitled: *Scholastic Times*
Author: Adam Czerny
Volume number: XLIX
Number: Four
Date: Fall 1982
Title: "When Times Are
Trying"
Pages: 621 to 693

2. You refer to a point made on pages 79 and 80 in an article with these characteristics:

Monthly magazine entitled: *Schools and Scholars*
Author: Gladys P. Spencer
Volume number: CXVII
Number: Thirty-six
Date: March 30, 1979
Title: "Our Local Schools"
Pages: 68 to 81

3. In this same article, Spencer refers to a point made on page 90 of a book by Jarvis MacFarland entitled *The Red Schoolhouse,* published in Miami, Florida, by the Adamantine Press in 1980. Now add MacFarland to your "Works Cited."

4. Suppose you had found Spencer's article in an anthology entitled *Education for Educators,* edited by Featherbush Brown in Philadelphia in 1983 by the P. J. Slacks Company, Incorporated. Write an entry for your "Works Cited."

5. You cite an article entitled "What Makes Salmon Run?" by Lyall Pendergast on page 5 of section "C" in a newspaper, *The Crossroads Courier,* dated August 20, 1984.

6. You refer to a point made both in an article and a book by W. L. Cranberry.

Book: *The Dying Locomotive*
Publisher: Verity and Company
Place: Cambridge, Massachusetts
Date: 1978
Page: 200
Article: "Transportation No Problem"
Quarterly Magazine: *Automotive Motion*
Volume: LXVI
Number: Four

Date: October 1969
Pages: 93 to 117

You want your readers to know that the author's name is really Walter Lightfoot Cranberry.

7. Using *The New York Times Index,* play researching detective on one of the following murder cases or historian on Indian uprisings, tracing your case or event through the newspapers and subsequent indexings, and any other sources you may discover.* Look under "Murders" and the victim's name both; for Indian uprisings, check "Editorials," "Political," "War," and "Miscellaneous." Write a paper (2000–3000 words) presenting and evaluating the case or the affair.

MURDERS (AN ASTERISK MARKS UNSOLVED CASES)

The Sickles Tragedy (1859)
John Smedick (1868)
C. M. Rogers (1869)
*Benjamin Nathan (1870)
William J. Sharkey (1872)
James Fisk (1872)
*Kelsey Tar and Feather Case (1873)
Coroner Croker (1874)
James Noe (1875)
Judge Chisolm (1877)
Staten Island Mystery (1878)
R. H. Smith (1878)
Judge Elliot (1879)
Capt. A. C. Nutt (1882)
*Rose Clark Ambler (1883)
Benjamin Pitzel (1884)
Mrs. H. H. Bliss (1885)
*Rahway Murder Mystery (1887)
Dr. P. H. Cronin (1889)
Josephine Barnaby (1891)

William Guedensuppe (1897)
Kate Adams (1898)
William Marsh Rice (1900)
Robert Thorpe (1900)
F. J. Young (1904)
Herman Rosenthal (1912)
Barnet Baff (1914)
Mrs. William Bailey (1914)
*Charles Murry (1915)
Charles F. Stielow (1915)
Arthur Warren Waite (1916)
Ruth Cruger (1917)
Virginia Rappe (1921)
Mills Hall (1922)
West End Bank Messenger (1923)
Red Cassidy (1929)
*The 3-X Murders (1930)
E. A. Ridley (1933)
Major Cofran et al. (1946)
Willie Earl (1947)

INDIAN UPRISINGS

Sioux Uprising (1862)
Genl. Sully, Indian Fighter (1862)
Black Kettle, Indian Chief (1868)
Spotted Tail, Indian Chief (1869)
Piegans Indians (1870)

Modoc War (1872)
Bannock War (1877)
Nez-Perce War (1877)
Poncas Indians (1879)
Ute Uprising (1879)

---

*I am indebted to W. Keith Kraus, Shippensburg State College, Pennsylvania, who invented the game and who provides enough cases for every member of the class ("The Research Paper Revisited," *The PCTE Bulletin.* Official Publication of the Pennsylvania Council of Teachers of English, No. 27, April, 1975: 14–20).

CHAPTER 14

The Full Research Paper

Here is a sample, a complete research paper to show what the final product can look like, with everything laid out in typescript and properly spaced, as if you had done it. The writer has followed out his own interest in pets, as anyone might explore an interest in automobiles, kites, or piccolos, or whatever. What is known about pets? What has man done with them? What ought to be done with them? The writer has found a lively argumentative area, right down the alley of his personal curiosity about his Golden Retriever's eloquent but speechless communication.

To convey an idea of the process, the back of the first page shows his note-cards for his first three citations, each one different: (1) a summarized reference, (2) a full quotation, single-spaced and inset, (3) a brief quotation followed by summarized information. Note that these citations occur on the third page of the research paper (308).

Our paper combines title-page with outline. Perhaps more common is the separate title-page already illustrated on 288. Notice especially how the footnotes contain only authorial amplification, and how the writer easily refers to his sources, both in his two footnotes and in his text, working names and titles into his prose so as to require no more than the page, in parenthesis, all easily affirmed in the "Works Cited."

Sherman Clark
English 123
Mr. Baker
April 16, 1984

Can Animals Talk?

Thesis: Although many remain skeptical, evidence shows
that animals are to some extent capable of
comprehending and using human language.

  I. Communication
     A. Natural communication
         1. Spontaneous general cries
         2. Differentiated cries
             a. Vervet monkeys' warnings
             b. Vervet monkeys' conversational grunts
     B. Volitional communication
         1. Deceptive signals
         2. Trained signals
             a. Clever Hans's failure
             b. Peg's success
 II. Animals' vocal language
     A. Natural vocal language
         1. McIntyre's porpoises
         2. Lilly's dolphins
         3. Norris's denial
     B. Trained vocal language
         1. Herman's dolphins
         2. Talking apes
             a. Belief from Monboddo to Laidler
             b. Physical deficiency
III. Animals' sign language
     A. Natural gestures
     B. Trained gestures
         1. The Gardners and Washoe
         2. Patterson's vocal and sign
         3. Terrace's skepticism
 IV. The cockatoo's spontaneous sentence

Chimp Talk. Con

    Monkey-cries and those of other non-human primates are involuntary, representing only immediate emotions and different intensities of arousal.

                De Vore 158 ✓

Baboons. Pro

    "Almost all behavior in monkeys and apes in-volves a mixture of the learned and the innate; almost all behavior is under some genetic control in that its development is channelled -- although the amount of channelling varies. Thus all baboons of one species will grow up producing much the same range of vocalizations; however, the same sound may have subtly different meanings for members of different troops of the same species." ✓

                Pilbeam 111 ✓

Monkey-cries. Pro

    Field studies "suggest that these natural signals may be more specific and wordlike than anyone ever imagined." ✓ 17
Tom Struhsaker discovered vervet cries:
    (1) raspy bark - leopard - take to trees.
    (2) short staccatto grunts - eagle - look up, then
         dive for cover (bushes, grass).
    (3) high-pitched chutter - snake - all stand
         and scan grass.

                Seyfarth 17 ✓

2
S. Clark
Eng. 123

Can Animals Talk?

<u>My Golden Retriever speaks for food</u>. He tells any of   Beginning

my family what he wants, whether just to go out or to go for

a walk. Everything about him--his different whines, his

eyes and the wrinkles between, his ears, his wagging

tail--conveys the message. <u>Some people similarly feel</u>   (Funneling to)

<u>that horses can almost talk</u>, as they talk to them. In

fact, researchers have discovered distinctive cries in

birds, wolves, and monkeys, and have even taught chimpan-

zees to use language on computers. <u>Although many remain</u>

<u>skeptical, a formidable body of evidence now shows that</u>

<u>some animals can use and comprehend language.</u>

   <u>The case against non-human linguistic comprehension</u>   Opposition (Con)

rests on defining it as the ability to generate new sen-

tences. <u>But clearly animals communicate in many ways in-</u>   Back to Pro

<u>cluding vocal sounds.</u> Their keen senses of smell, sight,

and hearing, their rising hackles and bared teeth, re-

ceive and send instant messages. Their cries tell clearly

of discovered food or danger. But are these language? <u>The</u>

<u>skeptics answer, "No."</u> When a bluejay sounds the alarm at   Con

a cat, or when a monkey barks if he whiffs a leopard, they

say, the animal is merely reacting on its own, and his fel-

lows react accordingly. This is all spontaneous, not

intentional language. Irven De Vore, for instance, con-

Source Cited with
Page in Parenthesis

cludes that primates' cries express only emotional states

and degrees of arousal (598), not the rational detachment

of a linguistic concept.

Topic Sentence
(Pro)

But others find something very like language in

non-human primates. David Pilbeam observes that

Ellipsis, Set-in
Quotation, Page in
Parenthesis Without
Following Period

> . . . all baboons of one species will grow up pro-
> ducing much the same range of vocalizations;
> however, the same sound may have subtly differ-
> ent meanings for members of different troops of
> the same species. (111)

Quotation Marks,
Page in Parenthesis,
Period

Robert Seyfarth, after studying vervet monkeys in Africa,

believes that "these natural signals may be more specific

and more wordlike than anyone ever imagined" (17). Ver-

vets have three alarms. A raspy bark for a leopard sends

the troop into the trees. Short staccato grunts for ea-

gles send everyone into the brush. A high-pitched chutter

for a snake brings all to their hind legs to scan the grass

(17). By playing their recorded alarms, Seyfarth demon-

strated that the sounds alone, not an actual snake or

leopard, sent the message.

Further Evidence

Furthermore, in the browsing vervet's grunts, Sey-

farth distinguished four varieties: (1) "You are domi-

nant; I am approaching cautiously"; (2) "You are subordi-

nate, but need not move off"; (3) "The group has begun to
move into an open plain"; (4) "Another group approaches"
(18).

But can vervets string sounds into a sentence? Sey-   Qualified Con
farth thinks not: " . . . the line that separates man from
other animals remains hazily drawn, somewhere between the
word and the sentence" (18).

The problem of volition--of intending a meaning--   Topic Sentence
(Con)
remains open to interpretation. Lyn Miles, at the   Pro
Institute for Primate Research, University of Oklahoma,
reports volitional "language." Bruno, a chimpanzee,
wanted a hose his cage-mate had. He went to the door and
uttered the chimpanzee's alarm. His companion dropped
the hose and ran to see while Bruno captured the hose (15).
Nevertheless, H. Hediger questions that teaching chim-   Con
panzees signs to get what they want is language, particularly the computerized system known as "Yerkish." He
points out that the animal brain lacks the human
speech-center, the Broca's Area and the Wernicke Area
(443), and that deceptive signals, which seem to indicate
volition, are widespread in creatures far below the rational threshold. Female glowworms emit the female signal of another species to catch and eat their incoming

males. Polar foxes and many birds give alarms to scare

their colleagues from choice morsels (441-42).

Further Opposition
(Con)

    Hediger suspects the "Clever Hans Effect," fre-

quently mentioned in criticizing animals' linguistic

achievements. Clever Hans, a German horse, mystified the

late nineteenth century by tapping out numbers and pick-

ing out words until his examiners discovered that he fol-

lowed his questioners' inadvertent signals--slight signs

Amplifying Footnote

of satisfaction at his reaching the right number of taps

or nuzzling the right placard.[1] Hediger sees little more

than a clever animal's sensing a human animal's involun-

tary signs to get what he wants.

Topic Sentence
Switching Back to
Pro

    Nevertheless, evidence that animals can understand

human language is plentiful. Emily Hahn cites Mrs. Eliza-

beth Mann Borgese, daughter of Thomas Mann, most

Evidence: Specific
Illustration

notably her testing of an Italian poodle named Peg

(54-59). To avoid Clever-Hansing, Mrs. Borgese took a

Amplifying Footnote

    [1] See Hahn, 46-48. Wilhelm van Osten, a mathematician, trained Hans and exhibited him privately to the scientifically interested in a courtyard adjoining his house in Berlin. Hans would nod or shake his head to yes-no questions, would indicate "up" or "down," would translate into a code of hoof-taps answers concerning letters, musical tones, and names of playing cards. He knew cardinal numbers up to 100 and ordinals up to 10. His examiners discovered that he failed completely when someone who did not know the answer read him a question, or when he was blindfolded, which he resisted vigorously.

6
S. Clark
Eng. 123

child's picture book, faced it away from her, and opened

it at random. She marked the place, closed the book, and

asked Peg, in her native Italian, "Did you see what I

showed you?" Peg barked three times, her "Yes." She then

chose from her cards "CAVALLI," or "horses." Mrs. Borgese

opened the book at her marker and discovered a picture of

two work horses. Peg could not only spell but could tell

plurals from singulars.

    This is training, which discounts Peg's natural

ability to talk. But Dr. John C. Lilly goes considerably   Additional Evidence:
                                    Expert Opinion

farther than Seyfarth in describing the boundaries be-

tween human and animal language. Lilly believes that dol-

phins have a language, culture, oral history, philosophy,

and system of ethics, as he told Michael Parfit (76). Joan

McIntyre agrees:

> [This school of porpoises] has had to instruct its   Bracket Substituting
> members in the specific lore and history of the   Reference to
> group, time-binding its lessons in a communica-   Original *It* in
> tion matrix that is specific to itself. . . . The   Quotation
> school, it seems, has a culture, a commonly
> shared, learned, and remembered history as a
> group, which it transmits through the genera-
> tions. (218)

Others find no evidence. Kenneth Norris, observing dol-   Opinion: Con

phins, told Parfit, "There isn't anything that even hints

at language" (77). Although Lilly could neither teach

dolphins English nor decipher their language after more   Return to Pro

than a decade, he nevertheless believes, as he told Par-

Pro Opinion

fit, that "these Cetacea with the huge brains are more in-telligent than any man or woman" (73).

Pro Documented

Though Lilly does not document his belief, Louis Herman at the University of Hawaii may be achieving Lilly's goal. Parfit reports that Herman has created a computerized code of whistles that his dolphins can un-derstand and use. One dolphin has a vocabulary of twen-ty-five nouns, adjectives, and verbs. Herman throws a ball into the pool. The dolphin whistles "ball." Herman whistles him to push the ball to a floating plastic pipe, then to push the pipe to the ball, demonstrating a grasp of subjects and verbs that bridges the gap between word and sentence (79).

Major Evidence: Pro

History of Belief and Experiment

The many apes now trained to use sign language and computers have also demonstrated this crucial grasp of the sentence. The belief that simian primates are capable of language has a long history, beginning with James Bur-nett, Lord Monboddo, in his Of the Origin and Progress of Language (1773-92). Monboddo speculates from an un-founded traveler's report of orangutans who played the flute that the orangutan was man in his primitive state, a creature who could learn to talk if he had the opportunity (346-47). In 1892, Richard L. Garner reported that he had discovered the language of monkeys in the Chicago zoo.

8
S. Clark
Eng. 123

Though he imitated only the sound he took for "milk," or

"food," he got something like a conversation (19-20), and

eventually concluded:

> Each race or kind of monkey has its own peculiar
> tongue, slightly shaded into dialects, and the
> radical sounds do not appear to have the same
> meaning in different tongues. (202-03)

Seyfarth and Pilbeam would agree.

In 1909, Lightner Witmer reported training a chim-   Historical

panzee to say "mama," though the ah was only whispered

(179-205). In 1916, William H. Furness achieved Monbod-   Further Experiment

do's goal by teaching a female orangutan to say "papa,"

and "cup" (283-84). Beginning in 1947 with a three-day-

old, Cathy and Keith Hayes taught their chimpanzee Viki   Contemporary
Evidence

three words in thirty difficult months: "mama," "papa,"

and "cup." After six years, they had added no more than

"up," and Viki's discrimination was far from accurate and

not always forthcoming (67, 108, 136, 240).[2]

By limiting the environment and following Furness's

method of molding lips, tongue, and breath, Keith Laidler

in England has accomplished more with his infant orang-

---

[2] Linden reports once that Viki achieved four words   Footnote
(15), and once that she was able "laboriously to produce   Summarizing Several
seven words" (68). But he gives no source, misspells Viki   Sources
"Vicki," and finally refers to the Hayeses as "Keith and
Virginia" (244). Elaine Morgan (132), Roger Fouts (23), and
Laidler (36, 162) all indicate that Viki's limit was four.

utan, Cody: four distinct words, for the naturally taci-
turn ape, at the age of fifteen months in less than eight
months of training: kuh, from the larynx with mouth open
("a drink"); puh, from pouted lips, unvoiced ("pick me
up"); fuh, from teeth over lower lip ("solid food"); and
thuh, from tongue between teeth ("brush me," which Cody
also used for "I'm sorry"). Cody became more than 70 percent accurate on most days, and even invented sheesh for
"come follow" (123-30, 144-45, 161-65).

But, in spite of limited success, Viki showed the way
to sign language. R. Allen and Beatrice Gardner noticed
in films that Viki was fluent in gestures as she agonized

Most Recent
Evidence

with words. Hence their famous experiments in teaching
the female chimpanzee, Washoe, American Sign Language, or
"Ameslan," which led to many similar projects. The Gard-
ners reinforced the chimpanzee's natural asking gesture,
the hand extended, palm up. They taught Washoe to flex her
wrist upward and back for the Ameslan sign "give me." In
Ameslan, both hands extended side by side, palms down,
then rotated outward, signify "open," which Washoe
learned to ask for opening doors and turning on faucets.
She can generate new words like "water bird" for "swan."
Her responses show a sense of syntax and an urge to communicate independent of physical needs. Hearing a dog bark,
she made two Ameslan signs, pointing to her ear for

10
S. Clark
Eng. 123

"hear," slapping her thigh for "dog." She was saying "I

hear a dog" (664-72).

Full Quotation
Marks Around
Writer's Own
Phrases

    Though ape-Ameslan omits the finger-spelling that
augments human signing, each animal and person has a
name-sign, usually his finger-spelt initial combined
with a characteristic gesture like pushing back the hair
or touching the moustache. Eugene Linden tells of watching Roger Fouts reversing the chimpanzee Lucy's habitual
"Roger tickle Lucy." Lucy, puzzled, signed, "No, Roger
tickle Lucy." Fouts signed back, "No, Lucy tickle Roger."
Linden "could see comprehension brighten in Lucy's eyes"
as she responded and enjoyed successive turn-abouts (99).
Finally, Lyn Miles tells of a chimpanzee, Allee, signing
to a trainer named George as another trainer (evidently
Fouts again) approached smoking a pipe, "George smell
Roger"--not only an original sentence but a remark showing sympathetic understanding of another, which is a good
conceptual step beyond a simple "I want," or even "I
smell" (15).

    Francine Patterson's work with her two gorillas, Koko
and Michael, reveals even more remarkable verbal ability.
Patterson, unlike the chimpanzee people, combines spoken
English with Ameslan. In "Conversation with a Gorilla,"
she matches Washoe's "water bird" with Koko's "white
tiger" for a zebra and "eye hat" for a mask (462). With a

Further Evidence

Title Given When
Author Has Two
Works Cited

computer that generates a female voice, Koko will punch
keys to enunciate "want apple eat" when shown an apple
(465). Patterson's recent The Education of Koko tells of
Koko, when asked if she can rhyme, signing "hair bear" and
"all ball," and pointing to a pig in a series of toys when
asked what rhymes with "big" (141). She also makes spontaneous metaphors, like "red mad gorilla" when angry.

Her junior partner, Michael, can also generate sentences, and he also reports past events. When a teacher
asked what he had been doing, he repeatedly signed anger,
hit, mouth, red, hair, and woman to tell of a red-haired
woman's fisticuffs in an office across the way, which Michael and Koko had watched from their window. When asked
about a bird, Michael signed bird good cat chase eat red
trouble cat eat bird, clearly another narrative of what he
had seen from his window (172-73).

Argument Con

Many have challenged the Ameslan signers, particularly Patterson, for Clever-Hansing and wishful interpretation, especially Herbert S. Terrace, a behaviorist
who trains pigeons to peck a sequence of four colors for
their corn. He raised from infancy a male chimpanzee
named Nim Chimsky in honor of Noam Chomsky, the Cartesian
linguist who disbelieves in animals' language. After
four years, Terrace returned Nim to his center of origin

12
S. Clark
Eng. 123

in Oklahoma believing that Nim could form sentences. But
after studying his evidence, he concluded that Nim was
just another clever behaviorist doing what he must to get
what he wanted. Nim's sign-sentences, Terrace believes,
were probably only "separate words related to a particular situation but not to each other" (169-70). Unlike a
child, Nim would frequently interrupt a question, showing
that he was not following the signaled sequence as a sentence. Unlike a child's lengthening sentences, Nim's remained an average of only 1.5 signs. The most Terrace will
admit is that chimpanzees "can master some aspects of
human language" (226).

Francine Patterson thinks Terrace too conservative,
and, with only four years, not nearly as close in rapport
and rich in evidence as she is after a decade. As she says
in her "Conversation," Patterson knows by her grin when
Koko is playfully deceitful, and by her straight face when
disobediently deceitful. When a trainer tried fruit-
lessly to get Koko to sign drink, "our mischievous charge
finally leaned back on the counter and executed a perfect
drink sign--in her ear," grinning all the while (456).

Many argue, however, that animals cannot conceptu-
alize. You may teach your dog to speak, writes Elaine Morgan, but you cannot get him to "Bark," "Whine," or "Growl"

Back to Pro

Title Shortened After
First Mention

on neutral command. These vocalizations are as involuntary as his rising hackles (131-32). If we ever discover,
she writes skeptically, that one of a dolphin's twenty-seven noises for food means "herring," then "we will
know for certain that we are not the only linguists on this
planet" (137).

Final Evidence Pro

Nevertheless, some animals in human environment
have proved remarkably capable of conceptual language.
Sara Terry reports an interview concerning a cockatoo
named Fred, one of those birds proverbial for parroting
human language. His trainer had prepared him for a TV se-
rial in which an actor was to carry him around upside down:

> "Fred started screaming at the top of his
> lungs, 'Stop! Stop! Don't hurt Fred!' He yelled
> this through the entire scene . . . and it was on a
> first-time basis. He had never been taught those
> words before. He put that phrase together all by
> himself." (B-7)

An intense emotion had produced not an animal's emotive
cry but spontaneous human sentences.

Thesis Restated

Clearly, then, animals have demonstrated themselves
capable of language, in a human environment and under intense training. In the wild, with their keener senses, environmental awareness, and involuntary signals, animals
have little need for conversation. But human communication, too, relies to a considerable extent on context, on

14
S. Clark
Eng. 123

tiny signals of mood, on smiles, nervous tics, and ges-

tures. <u>We are probably closer to the animals than we</u>   Clincher

<u>think,</u> and the whistling dolphins, talking Freds, and

signing Washoes have shown that they sometimes can in fact

talk to us on our own ground.

Works Cited

Burnett, James, Lord Monboddo. Of the Origin and Progress

of Language. Edinburgh: Balfour [imprint varies],

1773-92. Vol. 1.

De Vore, Irven. Primate Behavior: Field Studies of Mon-

keys and Apes. New York: Holt, 1965.

Fouts, Roger. "Talking Things Over With Chimps." Na-

tional Geographic World 38 (1978): 23-27.

Furness, W. H. "Observations on the Mentality of Chimpan-

zees and Orang-utans." Proceedings of the American

Philosophical Society (Philadelphia: The Am. Phi-

los. Soc., 1916) 65: 281-90.

Gardner, R. Allen, and Beatrice T. Gardner. "Teaching

Sign Language to a Chimpanzee." Science 165 (1969):

664-72.

Garner, Richard L. The Speech of Monkeys. London: Heine-

mann, 1892.

Hahn, Emily. "Getting Through to Others." Part 1. New

Yorker 17 Apr. 1978: 38-103.

Hayes, Cathy. The Ape in Our House. New York: Harper,

1951.

16
S. Clark
Eng. 123

Hediger, H[eini]. "Do You Speak Yerkish? The Newest Colloquial Language with Chimpanzees." In Sebeok and
Sebeok: 441–47.

Kellogg, Winthrop N. "Communication and Language in the
Home-Raised Chimpanzee." In Sebeok and Sebeok:
61–70.

Laidler, Keith. The Talking Ape. New York: Stein and Day,
1980.

Lilly, John C. Man and Dolphin. Garden City, N.Y.: Doubleday, 1961.

Linden, Eugene. Apes, Men, and Language. New York: Saturday Review Press; Dutton, 1974.

McIntyre, Joan. Mind in the Waters. New York: Scribner;
Sierra Club Books, 1974.

[Miles, Lyn]. "Chimpanzees Chat in Sign Language." Associated Press Release. Ann Arbor News 14 Nov. 1975:
15.

Morgan, Elaine. The Descent of Woman. New York: Bantam,
1973.

Parfit, Michael. "Are Dolphins Trying to Say Something,
Or Is It All Much Ado About Nothing?" Smithsonian
Oct. 1980: 72–81.

Patterson, Francine. "Conversation With a Gorilla." National Geographic Magazine Oct. 1978: 438-65.

Patterson, Francine, and Eugene Linden. The Education of Koko. New York: Holt, 1981.

Pilbeam, David. "An Idea We Could Live Without: The Naked Ape." Discovery 7 (1971). Rpt. in Ashley Montagu. Man and Aggression. 2nd ed. New York: Oxford, 1973. 110-21.

Sebeok, Thomas A., and Jean Umiker Sebeok. Speaking of Apes: A Critical Anthology of Two-Way Communication with Man. New York and London: Plenum, 1980.

Seyfarth, Robert. "Talking with Monkeys and Great Apes." International Wildlife Mar.-Apr. 1982: 12-18.

Terrace, Herbert S. Nim. New York: Knopf, 1978.

Terry, Sara. "All This and a Cockatoo Too!" Christian Science Monitor Service. Ann Arbor News 5 Mar. 1978: B-7.

Witmer, Lightner. "A Monkey with Mind." Psychological Clinic [Philadelphia] 3 (1909): 179-205.

THE HANDBOOK

The English Language

In your writing course, as in the rest of your life, you deal with and through an extraordinary language. The speech you are born to—or have since acquired—is rich and supple because of the many historic threads that constitute its weave. For a century or so it has been, and for at least the near future it will continue to be, a worldwide language, constantly absorbing greater variety of expression and enlarging its communicative power. This global language of ours began in the distant past among other peoples and other tongues. Fascinating in itself, this story can help you to understand your medium, and to use it more effectively.*

THE INDO-EUROPEANS

The story of English begins about 5000 B.C. with a late Stone Age people, perhaps in the Eurasian grasslands of what is now western Russia, where man first

---

*For this survey, I am basically indebted to a splendid course in philology with Professor Arthur Brodeur, University of California, 1947–48, and, in addition to Murray, Pyles, and Dillard, as cited, to Albert H. Marckwardt, *American English* (New York: Oxford University Press, 1958), Richard Middlewood Wilson, "English Language," *Encyc. Brit.* (1967), from whom I have selected a number of word-lists, James R. Hulbert, *Bright's Anglo-Saxon Reader,* revised and enlarged (New York: Henry Holt and Co., 1936), and Calvert Watkins, "Indo-European and the Indo-Europeans," *The American Heritage Dictionary* (1969), 1496–1502. I am also grateful to Professor John H. Fisher of the University of Tennessee and Professor William Labov of the University of Pennsylvania for informed and helpful comments.

domesticated the horse. Words surviving in many of the eight big groups of languages descending from their speech show that they were an inland people, living among rivers and lakes, among waterfowl and grazing animals, knowing wolves, bears, deer, and beavers, in open country with deciduous trees, and snow—all suggesting a Eurasian terrain, perhaps near modern Lithuania, rather than the deserts and jungles of the countries farther east and south where their language also eventually thrived.

They were hunters and herdsmen. They had horses, and were acquiring bronze and gold. They were also warriors, as the dominance and spread of their language suggest, since they had no writing. Their language spread very slowly, over thousands of years and many generations, as one segment or another moved to new grass and hunting grounds, displacing and absorbing other peoples before them, slowly separating into divers races and derivative languages. Their general movement to new territories was probably underway by 3500 B.C., when the Egyptians were just beginning to write a few pictograms and to build the world's first great civilization. The modern world has named these people *Aryans,* or, better, *Indo-Europeans,* a name indicating the ultimate span of their language from Europe to India.

Derivatives of Indo-European speech and people eventually covered Europe, and Russia, flowing gradually down the peninsulas and subcontinents of Spain, Italy, Greece, Asia, and India, and northward into Scandinavia, and westward into the British Isles—possibly dry-soled over ridges not yet sunken under the North Sea, or not broken at the Straits of Dover. The English language itself arrived several thousand years later, a very late comer, a division of a small subdivision that had evolved in Germany to become, today, the most widespread of all the Indo-European languages—virtually an international language. And, oddly, most of the basic Indo-European words modern scholars can reconstruct are still represented in modern English, through inheritance or borrowing from other Indo-European languages—words like *father, mother, east,* for instance, and *name* and *bear,* which combined to form *number.*

Here is a table of the Indo-European languages, to help you visualize this astonishing linguistic dispersal that eventually produced English:

INDO-EUROPEAN LANGUAGES

I.   Satem Languages*
    A.   Indo-Iranian
        1.   Indic: Sanskrit, Pakrit, Pali, Hindi, Urdu, Hindustani, Bengali, Gujarati, Marathi, Punjabi, Singhalese, Romany
        2.   Iranian: Avestan (the oldest of the Indo-Iranian group), Old Persian, Pahlavi (Middle Persian), Sogdian (ancient Central Asia), Scythian (ancient southeastern Europe and Asia), Baluchi (modern Baluchistan, India), Pashtu (Afghanistan), Persian, Kurdish, Ossetic (Russia, between the Black and Caspian seas)
    B.   Armenian: Classical Armenian, Eastern, and Western Armenian
    C.   Albanian: Thracian, Illyrian (ancient coastal Yugoslavia), Albanian

D. Balto-Slavic
  1. Slavic: Old Bulgarian, Bulgarian, Serbo-Croatian, Slovenian, Czech, Slovak, Polish, Wendish (ancient German area), Great Russian, White Russian, Ukrainian
  2. Baltic: Old Prussian, Lithuanian, Latvian

II. Centum Languages*
  A. Hellenic: Mycenean Greek, Attic, Ionic (ancient Greeks of western Asia Minor), Doric (ancient central Greece), Aeolic (ancient eastern Greece), Cyprian, Modern Greek
  B. Italic
    1. Oscan (ancient southern Italy)
    2. Umbrian (ancient central Italy)
    3. Latin: Faliscan (around prehistoric Rome), Latin, Italian, Provençal, French, Spanish, Catalan, Portuguese, Rumanian
  C. Celtic: Gaulish, Welsh, Cornish, Breton, Irish, Manx, Gaelic
  D. Germanic
    1. East Germanic (Gothic)
    2. North Germanic
      a. East Norse: Swedish, Danish, Gutnish
      b. West Norse: Norwegian, Faroese, Icelandic
    3. West Germanic
      a. High German: Alemannic, Bavarian, Yiddish
      b. Low Germanic (*Plattdeutsch*)
        i. Franconian: Flemish, Dutch
        ii. Frisian
        iii. English

THE ANGLO-SAXONS (449)

Before "English" came to Britain (named by the Romans for some of its inhabitants, the Brythonic Celts, a western Indo-European branch), the Roman Em-

---

*Linguists divide the Indo-European languages into two groups according to whether they have kept the Indo-European *k*-sound or changed it to *s*. Linguists arbitrarily chose the word for "hundred," *statem* in Avestan, *centum* in Latin, to designate the two groups. As you probably know, the Latin *c* is "hard," pronounced as *k*.

Sir William Jones, a learned orientalist and lawyer appointed to the British supreme court in Calcutta, took the first step toward uncovering the Indo-European languages. He put forward, for the first time with sufficient evidence and force (1786), the theory that Sanskrit had derived from the same source as Greek and Latin. Nineteenth-century German scholars—notably Jacob Grimm, who, with brother Wilhelm, wrote the famous fairy tales, and Karl Verner, whose law explains some changes beyond Grimm's law—completed the basic analysis, identifying the related languages and the principles by which they had changed the sounds of the consonants in the parent tongue.

Modern scholars identify two other small groups, separate from the Satems and Centums: (1) ancient Hittite and related Anatolian languages in Turkey about 2000 B.C. (the oldest), and (2) two Tocharian languages in Chinese Turkestan about 1000 B.C.

pire had risen, flourished, and begun to totter. Caesar had invaded Britain in 55 B.C., though serious conquest and colonization began almost a century later. Nevertheless, by the time that Angles, Saxons, and Jutes landed in southern England in A.D. 449, bringing the language that was to become "Old English," Romans had lived and died in Britain, representing the dominant culture, for almost five hundred years—a century longer than Europeans now have lived in America. Latin (a southern Indo-European branch) was the language of England. "English," under some other name, might well have become another Romance language, like Italian, Spanish, and French.

But the Roman Empire slipped. Alaric the Goth, after sieges in 408 and 409, finally sacked Rome in 410. Other Gothic tribes were raiding into Roman Gaul (modern France). Britain was the empire's farthest outpost. Emperor Honorius wrote the British cities in 409 that they must fend for themselves. The legions withdrew, and many citizens with them. The elegant resort city of Bath, abandoned, sank back into the sulphur marsh, totally lost and forgotten for another two hundred years. Native chieftains began to gather strength, and to squabble. One, Vortigern, invited two "Saxon" lords and their men to help him fend off raiding Picts and Irish. Hengist and Horsa, two brothers (the first means "stallion," the second, "horse's"), of the Jutes, sailed from their native Jutland—the Danish peninsula—to land at Ebbsfleet, Kent, on the coast south of the Thames, in 449. They continued to dominate Kent; and other Angles and Saxons—also from the Danish peninsula, all closely related in race and language—landed, first, on the southern coast, and later, on the eastern coast to the north. The invaders' power as well as their language prevailed over the scattered Celtish fragments left behind by the Romans.

ANGLO-SAXON BORROWINGS

The Anglo-Saxons picked up very few Celtic words, and even fewer from British Latin, probably because the Celts had mostly stayed clear of the Romans, and because the new invaders from Europe had the dominant culture. But many place-names in England survived from Roman-Celtic times, notably *ceaster* (from Roman *castrum,* fortified camp), which still remains in names like *Winchester, Westchester,* and *Worcester* (pronounced "Wooster" now, for more than four hundred years). Shakespeare's river Avon is a Celtish name for "river," as are others like Usk, Ouse, Stour, and Wye. London and York are Celtish names (the Romans had called the great city *Londinium,* from the Celtish *Londos,* for "wild"). Of the few other Celtish words the Anglo-Saxons adopted, even fewer remain today, among them *binn,* for "manger," now our flourbins and coalbins, and *cursian,* "to curse."

The Anglo-Saxons had already acquired a stock of Latin words from fighting and trading with the Romans in continental Europe, many of which are still in the language. *Copor,* "copper," from Latin *cuprum/coprum,* comes in very early, before the Latin in Gaul had shifted pronunciation to *covrum.* Similarly, *wĭn* ("wine," pronounced "ween") came in when classical Latin *vinum* was still pronounced "weenum." Our word *vine,* which grows the grapes for the wine, comes from the same Latin word, but six or seven centuries later, after the Norman Conquest, as the English borrowed the French word for the *vines* in the *vineyards* of Bordeaux, which were producing their *wines.* From the Romans, the continental Anglo-Saxons, with the other Germanic peoples, had also borrowed *naep,* now "turnip," *peose* "pea," *culter* "colter" (plowblade), *weall* "wall," *cēap* "to bargain" (hence "cheap"), *pund* "pound," and *mynet* "money" (hence "mint"). They also took the *flasce* for the *wĭn* they poured in their *cuppe* to put under their *belt,* and they bought from the Romans *cyse* "cheese," *pipor* "pepper," and *butere* for the *cycene* "kitchen." Roman *cealc* "chalk," *pic* "pitch," and *tigele* "tile" went into buildings. The early continental Germans also borrowed "street" from Roman *via strata* and "mile" from *mil*— a thousand paces of the marching Roman legions. *Segl* "sail" from Latin *sagulum* is the same in almost every Germanic language, as the northerners, especially the Vikings, saw how much it improved the Roman galley. A ruler became *cāsere,* after Caesar, which also produced the German *Kaiser* and the Russian *Czar* or *Tsar.* The last day of the week became *Saeternesdaeg,* "Saturn's day"—the only Roman among a week of Germanic sun, moon, and gods. Christianity, in 597, brought a new flood of Latin words into Anglo-Saxon England.

THE OLD ENGLISH PERIOD (450–1100)

The Anglo-Saxons referred to themselves and their language as *Anglisc* or *Englisc,* probably because the Angles in Northumbria, in northern England, developed the first literature, centuries earlier than any literature in any of the other Germanic languages. Their language was nearer modern German than English. It was a "synthetic," or inflected, language, signaling its grammar by word-endings, as in German or Latin. Here are the opening lines of the *Beowulf,* the greatest remaining Old English epic (pronounce the *ae* like *hat,* but the other vowels separately, with the qualities of Spanish or Italian; the *y* pronounces like the *u* in French *lune;* þ and ð are "th"):

> Hwaet, wē gār-Dena   in gēardagum,
> þēodcyninga,   þrym gefrūnon,
> hū ðā aeþelingas   ellen fremedon!

Literally:

> **What! we, of spear-Danes',   in yore-days,**
> **People-kings',   power have heard,**
> **how the noblings   valor performed!**

Only the simple words—*what, we, in, how, the*—remain in English today, pretty much as they were. Notice that we still pronounce the beginning of *what* in the Anglo-Saxon way, *hw,* although the Middle-English scribes changed it to *wh,* for some obscure reason. Here the Anglo-Saxon harper uses it as a call for the audience's attention: it is usually translated "Lo" or "Behold." The blocky half-lines, incidentally, pausing in the middle and alliterated across the gap, probably coordinated with the harper-reciter's sweeps across the strings, one sweep for each half-line. We can also recognize the outlines of modern *Dane, yore, day,* and *king,* but all the rest are entirely foreign to us, lost from the language along with the seemingly backward word-order, and the inflectional grammatical endings that support it. In its fifteen hundred years of history, English has changed from a "synthetic," inflected language to an "analytic," almost uninflected one, where position in the sentence (subject-verb-object), together with such indicators as *with, in, to, by,* expresses meaning, the former function of the vanished word-endings. And it has traded off a major portion of its old vocabulary for new.

THE NORSEMEN (789)

Because the Germanic languages characteristically accent the beginnings of words, Anglo-Saxon had already begun to slur and to lose older and more complicated inflectional endings before the Norsemen came. But invading Norsemen, in two waves three hundred years apart, accelerated the change from synthetic to analytic. The Norsemen, or Vikings, began their raids on England in 789, when, as *The Anglo-Saxon Chronicle* tells us, three ships, "the first ships of Danish men," raided a seaport on the southern coast. Raids continued on eastern and northern coasts, Scotland, and Ireland, until the Danes had settled the whole of central England as their territory, known as the "Danelaw." Alfred, the West Saxon king, who had held the Danes out of southern England and had established the last great period of Anglo-Saxon literature and culture, signed the Peace of Wedmore with them in 878. Since the Old Norse of the Danes and the Old English of the Anglo-Saxons were similar Germanic languages but with differing word-endings, people went for the word and forgot the endings, smoothing out the grammar. Nevertheless, only about forty

Norse words appear in the written language, still classically Anglo-Saxon under Alfred—notably *lagu* "law," *hūsbonda* "householder," and *þræl* "thrall" (slave, now in *enthrall*)—until after the next and very different Norse invasion, that of the Norman French.

THE NORMAN CONQUEST (1066)

The raids and settlement of Norsemen southward—the Age of the Vikings—lasted from the first appearance of Danish ships off southern England (789) until the treaty of St. Clair-sur-Epte (912), which established the Norsemen in Normandy, France. Some social upheaval, perhaps overpopulation, had turned the Nordic custom of sea-raiding ("Viking" means "sea-raider") into conquest. By land, the Norsemen pushed into western Russia, and southward into the Burgundy of modern France, which bears the tribal name of its Norse invaders and settlers. By sea, they raided the coasts of France and Spain, and pushed into the Mediterranean to settle in Sicily (where, at Monreale, near Palermo, you can still see a magnificent Norman cathedral built by their Christianized descendants).

But the most significant of the Norse settlements was in Normandy, which, like Burgundy, bears the invaders' name. While Alfred was fighting the Vikings in England, other Norsemen sailed up the Seine to Rouen, devastating the countryside and eventually repopulating it with a Nordic-Gallic admixture. But France (or French women) prevailed after all, for the conquerors lost their language, ultimately adopting both Christianity and French. When the Norman William, the Conqueror, landed at Hastings, in England, in 1066, about the only Norse remaining was his battle cry, *Tur ai!,* "Thor, aid!" The rest of the swearing was in French.

MIDDLE ENGLISH (1100–1500)

The language of English upper-class culture was now Norman French. Anglo-Saxon went underground, the speech of peasants. All the riches of Anglo-Saxon poetry, like *hron-rād,* "whale-road," for "sea," and *eard-stapa,* "earth-stepper," for a wandering outcast, never found in common prose, disappeared from the language. But all the Old Norse words acquired in common parlance in Anglo-Saxon days now begin to appear in writing, many of them eventually replacing their Old English synonyms with such central words as *sky, die, take, fellow, leg, low, egg, awe.* Some Old English words acquired an Old Norse synonym of slightly differing meaning: *rear/raise, from/fro, craft/skill, hide/skin, to/til, sick/ill,* and *shirt/skirt,* which became the female version of the belted Anglo-Saxon smock, or "shirt," worn by both sexes. Any *sk* word in modern English is very likely from Old Norse. Old Norse also endowed us with the pronoun *she,* a clearer distinction than the Old English *hēo,* and with the other pronouns *they, their, them,* for the same reason. Other important Old Norse words still with us, surfacing after the Norman Conquest, are *though, aloft, athwart,* and *seemly.*

But the Noresman's most significant imprint on English was not of Norse but of his more recent Norman French, which cut Anglo-Saxon off from writing and accelerated its incipient change from synthetic to analytic grammar, offering as reinforcement a language already analytic in structure. Many new words came in directly from Latin, still the language of learning and science, and many more French words derived directly from their ancestral Latin. English and French words, surviving side by side, give us some interesting opportunities for one-upmanship: *hearty/cordial, ask/demand, answer/reply, house/mansion, ghost/spirit, room/chamber, shun/avoid, seethe/boil, yearly/annual.* In most of these pairs, the French half, the second one, still carries an air of social superiority— *house/mansion,* for instance. While the Anglo-Saxon peasantry herded, in their own language, the *calves, steers, swine,* and *sheep,* and refrained from killing the *deer,* the French lords and ladies ate in French: *veal, beef, pork, mutton, venison.* Since Anglo-Saxon *lamb* is our word for both the animal and the meat, we may assume that the French lords liked their *mutton* mature, and that roast leg of lamb came into favor only after the lordly descendants of the Normans had shifted to English. Synonyms also borrowed later from both Norman and Parisian French give us some other interesting pairs: *catch/chase, canal/channel, real/royal, wage/gage, warden/guardian, warrant/guarantee.*

But although the Norman Conquest deposed and then largely rebuilt much of our vocabulary, English, as evolving from Anglo-Saxon, continued to work itself upward. By the reign of Edward III (1327–1377), the nobility were speaking English. About 1350, "John Cornwal, a maystere of gramere," changed the language of teaching in grammar school from "Freynsch into Englysch."* A statute of Edward's in 1362–1363 made English the language for pleadings in the lawcourts, though still recorded in Latin. And Chaucer's great works, beginning in 1359 and culminating in the *Canterbury Tales* (1387), though heavily influenced by French, are, of course, in Middle English. French is again a foreign language.

The opening lines of Chaucer's *Canterbury Tales* well show what has happened to the Old English inflectional endings, which had signaled subjects,

---

*John de Trevisa, translation of Ranulf Higden's *Polychronicon,* 1387, quoted in Sir James A. H. Murray, "English Language," *Encyc. Brit.,* 11th ed. (1910): 594.

objects, indirect objects, and so forth: they have all rounded down to a meaningless final *e,* pronounced "uh," or not pronounced at all when the meter (or the rush of conversation) crowds it against the vowel of a word following. *Aprille* is pronounced "Ah-PRILL-uh," and *shoures soote* is pronounced "SHOOR-uhs SOHT-uh"; but *veyne* is pronounced exactly like modern *vein* because the *i* of the following *in* absorbs the final *e,* or at least most of it. *Drought* sounded about like modern "looked" with a guttural *gh* for the *k,* like a clearing of the throat. I have scanned the lines into their iambic pentameter (which allows for an extra light syllable at the end of its usual ten-syllable line), so you can see how the word-endings work, and how Middle English sounded at its very best. Pronounce the *a*'s as in *ah,* long *e*'s as in "SWAYT-uh brayth," long *i* like the double *ee* in "peer," and long *u* and *o* as in "SHOOR-uhs SOHT-uh."

<pre>
   —   ∪ |∪ — |∪ — | ∪   — |∪ — |∪
</pre>
Whan that A pril le with his shour es soo te
<pre>
 ∪   — | ∪   — | ∪   — |∪ — | ∪   — |∪
</pre>
The droug ht of March hath per ced to the roo te.
<pre>
 ∪   — |∪ — |∪   — |∪   — | ∪ — |
</pre>
And bath ed eve ry veyne in swich lic our
<pre>
 ∪   — | ∪ — | ∪   — |∪ — |∪   — |
</pre>
Of which ver tu eng end red is the flour;
<pre>
   ∪   — |∪ — |—   ∪ |∪   — |∪   — |
</pre>
Whan Zep hir us eek with his swee te breeth
<pre>
 ∪ — |∪   — |∪ — |∪ — | ∪   — |
</pre>
In spir ed hath in eve ry holt and heeth
<pre>
 ∪   — |∪ — | ∪
</pre>
The tend re crop pes. . . .

(When April, with his sweet showers, has pierced the drought of March to the root, and bathed every vein in such liquor of whose strength the flower is engendered, when Zephyr, moreover, with his sweet breath has inspired the tender crops in every field and heath. . . .)

This opening sentence of Chaucer's runs on for another four and a half lines before reaching its main clause (*Thanne longen folk to goon on pilgrimages,* "Then folk long to go on pilgrimages"), and for another six lines beyond that before the period. His sentence is 128 words long. English has loosened, and flexed, and sophisticated considerably since the hardy, blocky phrases of the *Beowulf.*

To illustrate further the change from Old English to Middle English to Modern English, here are three translations of the same passage from the Latin Bible—New Testament, St. Mark 4. 2–9:

OLD ENGLISH WEST-SAXON GOSPELS (c. 1000)

(2) And hē hi fela on bigspellum lǣrde, and him tō cwæð on his
lāre, (3) Gehȳraþ: Ūt ēode sē sǣdere his sǣd tō sāwenne. (4)
And þā hē sēow, sum fēoll wið þone weg, and fugelas cōmon
and hit frǣton. (5) Sum fēoll ofer stānscyligean, þār hit næfde
mycele eorðan, and sōna ūp ēode; and for þām hit næfde
eorðan þiccnesse, (6) þā hit ūp ēode, sēo sunne hit forswǣlde,
and hit forscranc, for þām hit wyrtruman næfde. (7) And sum
fēoll on þornas; þā stigon ðā þornas and forðrysmodon þæt,
and hit wæstm ne bær. (8) And sum fēoll on gōd land, and hit
sealde ūppstīgendne and wexendne wæstm; and an brōhte
þrītigfealdne, sum syxtifealdne, sum hundfealdne. (9) And hē
cwæð, Gehȳre, sē ðe ēaran hæbbe tō gehȳranne.

MIDDLE ENGLISH JOHN WYCLIFF'S BIBLE (1382)

(ȝ = The Old English gutteral *gh*-sound; v = u, and u sometimes
= v, as in *heuene, up,* and ȝ*aue*)

And he tauȝte hem in parablis many thingis. And he seide to
hem in his techynge. Heere ȝee. Loo! a man sowynge goth out
for to sowe. And the while he sowith, an other seed felde ab-
oute the wey, and briddis of heuene, or of the eire, camen, and
eeten it. Forsothe an other felde doun on stony placis, wher it
had nat myche erthe; and anoon it sprong vp, for it hadde nat
depnesse of erthe. And whenne the sunne rose vp, it welwide
for heete, and it dried vp, for it hadde not roote. And an other
felde doun into thornes, and thornes stieden vp, and strangli-
den it, and it ȝaue not fruyt. And an other felde doun in to
good lond, and ȝaue fruyt, styinge vp, and wexinge; and oon
brouȝte thritty fold, and oon sixtyfold, and oon an hundridfold.
And he seide, He that hath eris of heeryng, heere.

MODERN ENGLISH KING JAMES VERSION (1611)

(2) And he taught them many things by parables, and he said
unto them in his doctrine, (3) Hearken; Behold, there went out
a sower to sow: (4) and it came to pass, as he sowed, some fell
by the wayside, and the fowls of the air came and devoured it
up. (5) And some fell on stony ground, where it had not much
earth; and immediately it sprang up, because it had no depth of
earth: (6) but when the sun was up, it was scorched; and because it had no root, it withered away. (7) And some fell among

**thorns, and the thorns grew up, and choked it, and it yielded
no fruit. (8) And other fell on good ground, and did yield fruit
that sprang up and increased, and brought forth, some thirty,
some sixty, and some a hundred. (9) And he said unto them, He
that hath ears to hear, let him hear.**

After English had firmly reestablished itself by the middle 1300s, a new
tide of Latin borrowings came in, alongside the French words, which also derived from Latin. From the days of the Roman Empire onward, steadily
through the Dark Ages, the Middle Ages, the Renaissance, and well into modern times, the international language of learning and science was Latin. All
discourse at the universities was in Latin. Today, ceremonial lectures at Oxford
and Cambridge continue to be delivered in Latin. The new tide of Latin
brought into Middle English such familiar words as *client, psalm, equivalent, alle-
gory, formal, library, dissolve, ascension, impediment, alienate,* and *dissent.* But it
reached its height in the fifteenth century with a number of self-conscious poetic inventions, like *dispone,* and *equipolent,* known as "aureate [that is, gilded]
diction." Most of these faded away, but some became permanent, like *laureate,
mediation, oriental,* and *prolixity.* From the early 1500s, as the Modern period
opened, and up through the days of Queen Elizabeth and Shakespeare, similar
immense borrowings from Latin came into English, many literary and
self-conscious, which were soon called, in reaction, "inkhorn terms." But most
came in naturally as the Renaissance moved into England, as interest in the
Greek and Roman classics revived under the stimulus of humanists like John
Colet, William Lyly, and Erasmus, and as scientists and voyagers expanded
their discoveries.

MODERN ENGLISH (1500 ONWARD)

The Modern period of the English language really begins when William Caxton brought the printing press to England, and London, in 1476. On the continent, where he learned the craft, he had already issued, probably in 1474 and
1475, the first two books printed in English: his translation of a French romance concerning the Trojan War, *Recuyell of the Historyes of Troye,* and *The Game
and Playe of Chesse,* also translated from the French. Setting up at Westminster,
he issued almost eighty books, many his own translations, in his remaining
fourteen years of life. His books confirmed the English of London as the national standard, though great variety in dialect and usage persisted as perfectly
acceptable well into the seventeenth century. Throughout the sixteenth century, the language "seems to be in a plastic, unformed state, and its writers, as

it were, experiment with it, bending it to constructions which now seem inde-fensible," writes Sir James A. H. Murray.* Nevertheless, Caxton did a great deal toward stabilizing a language even more fluid and diversified.

Nothing so well illustrates the English language at the outset of the Mod-ern period as Caxton's *Prologue* to his translation (from the French) of Vergil's *Aeneid,* which he spelled *Eneydos* (1490). What words should a person choose from such a conflict of dialects—when a countrywoman cannot understand *eggs* (from Old Norse) but can understand *eyren* ("eggs" in Old English)? And, of course, spelling, capitalization, and printing, which Caxton had just intro-duced, were far from stable. Printed *u* frequently stood for *v,* as in *ouer,* and printed *v* frequently stood for *u,* as in *vnderstande.* In his *y*ᵗ, Caxton is using *y* for the Old English thorn, þ, the *th-*sound, which, combined with the little superscript *t,* was an abbreviation for *that.* Caxton's *tamyse* is the river Thames; *zelande* is Zeeland (southern Holland); *forlond* is Foreland, the farthest tip of land on the southern shore of the Thames estuary, just north of where the Jutes landed in 449.

> . . . I delybered and concluded to translate it in-to eng-lysshe, And forthwyth toke a penne & ynke, and wrote a leef or tweyne whyche I ouersawe agayn to corecte it. And whan I sawe the fayr & straunge termes therin I doubted that it sholde not please some gentylmen whiche late blamed me, sayeing, yᵗ in my translacyons I had ouer curyous termes whiche coude not be vnderstande of comyn peple and desired me to vse olde and homely termes in my translacyons. and fayn wolde I satysfye euery man and so to doo, toke an olde boke and redde therin and certaynly the englysshe was so rude and brood that I coude not wele vnderstande it. And also my lorde abbot of westmyn-ster ded do shewe to me late, certayn euydences wryton in olde englysshe, for to reduce it in-to our englysshe now vsid. And certaynly it was wreton in suche wyse that it was more lyke to dutche than englysshe; I coude not reduce ne brynge it to be vnderstonden. And certaynly our langage now vsed varyeth ferre from that whiche was vsed and spoken whan I was borne. For we englysshe men ben borne vnder the domynacyon of the mone, whiche is neuer stedfaste but euer wauerynge, wexynge one season and waneth & dyscreaseth another season. And that comyn englysshe that is spoken in one shyre varyeth from a no-ther. In so moche that in my dayes happened that certayn mar-

---

Encyc. Brit., 11th ed. (1910): 601.

chauntes were in a shippe in tamyse, for to haue sayled ouer
the see into zelande and for lacke of wynde, thei taryed atte forlond, and wente to lande for to refreshe them; And one of
theym named sheffelde, a mercer, cam in-to an hows and axed
for mete; and specyally he axyd after eggys; And the goode wyf
answerde, that she coude speke no frenshe. And the marchaunt
was angry, for he also coude speke no frenshe, but wolde haue
hadde egges and she vnderstode hym not. And thenne at laste a
nother sayd that he wolde haue eyren. then the good wyf sayd
that she vnderstod hym wel. Loo, what sholde a man in thyse
dayes now wryte, egges or eyren. certaynly it is harde to playse
euery man by cause of dyuersite & chaunge of langage. For in
these dayes euery man that is in ony reputacyon in his countre,
wyll vtter his commynycacyon and maters in suche maners &
termes that fewe men shall vnderstonde theym. And som honest
and grete clerkes haue ben wyth me, and desired me to wryte
the moste curyous termes that I coude fynde. And thus bytwene
playn rude & curyous, I stande abasshed. but in my Iudgemente
the comyn termes that be dayli vsed, ben lyghter to be vnderstonde than the olde and auncyent englysshe.

By Shakespeare's day, English had somewhat settled down, but was still
exploring its riches, with a sense of freedom. The civil war that tore England
apart in the middle 1600s also shook the language into further transition, but
with the Restoration of 1660 and the general reaching out for postwar stability,
the language settled into a recognizably modern form, with the Bloodless Revolution of 1688 usually taken as the final watershed into modernity, as the language attained a new smoothness and fluency under the pen of John Dryden.

Samuel Johnson's *Dictionary* of 1755 helped to stabilize English spelling,
and Bishop Robert Lowth's *A Short Introduction to English Grammar* (1762) did
much the same for grammar, setting the pattern for school texts almost down
to our own time. Johnson and Lowth shared the age's wish for stability, definition, and clarity. Both looked at the classical languages, particularly Latin, as
fountainheads at which modern languages ought again to refresh themselves.
Their works, and others following, answered the urge of a new mercantile society moving upward to affluence and literacy, and wanting to know what was
deemed correct in cultivated circles. Nineteenth-century America, sprawling
rapidly to new and newer frontiers, pursued correctness in pronunciation and
usage even more persistently than England, toward which America continued
to feel secretly and chronically inferior.

The influence of Latin on English has been, from the first, considerable.
Some 60 percent of our modern vocabulary comes, one way or another, from

Latin, and many influential writers from the sixteenth through the nineteenth centuries have had Latin in their heads as they wrote their English. Schooling of every boy in England from Shakespeare through Fielding and on to about 1866, consisted basically of studying the classics and memorizing Lyly's *Latin Grammar* (c. 1513), used in all schools in England, and later in America, with almost no change for three and a half centuries. This classical cast of mind helped frame the Declaration of Independence and the U.S. Constitution—note the "Senate" straight from ancient Rome—and shaped the linguistic habits of those who wrote and spoke English well into the twentieth century. A certain learned eloquence persisted in correspondence and conversation, as men and women read George Eliot and Dickens aloud, quoted poetry to each other, and attended to the ornate oratory of the pulpit and the popular lecture platform. Before World War I, most American universities still required a proficiency in Latin for admission.

AMERICAN ENGLISH

The language the people of Jamestown and Plymouth first brought to America was not only ample in heritage and potential, but was in the especially fluid and fluent state of the late Renaissance. The most significant shift in pronunciation since 449, though almost completed, was still in progress. The English long vowels—*ah, ay, ee, oh, oo*—shifted from the "continental" quality they shared with their sister languages to the diphthongs of modern English, the double vowels all of us say, though we hear them as single letters: we think *a,* but pronounce it to rhyme with something like "May-ee." Beginning in the fifteenth century, *a* shifted from *ah* to the "May-ee" of *make.* Long *e,* which had sounded like modern *make,* shifted to *ee; i* became *ai; o* became *oh-oo; u* changed from *oo* to the *au* in *ouch.* In Virginia to this day, people retain something of the older *u,* because their ancestors came over before the *u* had fully shifted, calling a *house* a "huh-oos" and a *mouse* a "muh-oos," after the Old English *hūs* ("hoos") and *mūs* ("moos"). English-speaking Canadians, whose ancestors came largely from Scotland two centuries later, say these words very much like Virginians, because in Scotland the Old English *u* never fully shifted to *au.*

British and American pronunciations now differ considerably, with New England and the South being somewhat nearer to British in their dropping of the final *r,* but differing from educated British and from each other in many other ways. These areas were settled mostly by people from the old East-Anglian region—southeastern England, including London. The middle area—New Jersey, Delaware, Maryland, Pennsylvania, which now stretches to the west coast and northwest—came mostly from more northern English regions where the *r* remained hard, or even trilled. Consequently, most Americans say *water* not *watah.*

Aside from "New England" and "Southern," the vast majority of Americans can hardly detect regional differences among themselves, though these exist both in qualities of pronunciation and in vocabulary. Reading and writing, and more recently, radio, TV, and the movies have evened out American vocabulary and pronunciation considerably. Although levels of education and affluence still produce marked differences, as do the many minority dialects, particularly Black English, the lines between regional and social groups in America are not so explicitly drawn in pronunciation and vocabulary as they are between upper class and working class in England, or among the numerous regional and rural dialects of Britain, which retain many differing traces from old Anglo-Saxon-Nordic times—dialects that many Americans and some Britishers have great difficulty in understanding.

These Old English traces remain in American regional usages also. America keeps the Anglo-Saxon *dune,* but limits it to a sandhill; England uses the later vowel-shifted version, *down,* for its hills (which mixes Americans up). American English frequently retains these older forms that British has long since lost: *gotten,* for instance, as against British (and American) *got.* The British say "his attitude *to* sports"; Americans, "his attitude *toward* sports," keeping the more elaborate and less frequent of the two Anglo-Saxon alternatives. The Old Germanic habit of accenting beginnings and swallowing endings is stronger in England, producing what Americans call the "clipped" British way of speaking, with "Thank you" sounding like "kyup!" and *extraordinary* like *strórdnr,* and even *got* and *that* now swallowed back in the throat, in common parlance, to the briefest *ga'* and *tha',* so that the modern Londoner sounds like the traditional Scot with his "Will y' na' come back again." Americans have followed the printed word more closely than have the British, tending to pronounce syllables and letters slurred over by Britishers—evidently, as we have seen, from the early feeling of cultural inferiority and the drive to be educated. Nevertheless, in rural American speech, some words the city-dweller thinks mere country ignorance actually reflect the oldest forms, as they do also in rural England: *lookee,* for instance, from the archaic *look ye* that goes straight back to Anglo-Saxon, and *ax,* for "ask," which still seems to reflect the dominant Anglo-Saxon verb, *ācsian* or *āxian,* of which *āscian* was then only a minor variant.

Many such differences in American speechways reflect the region of England (and sometimes the historical period) from which a particular group of settlers came. But since most groups included people widely assorted from different old Anglo-Saxon dialectical areas, the reasons for one American region's saying, for instance, *pail* and another's saying *bucket* are obscure. *Pail* goes back to the Anglo-Saxons; *bucket,* to the Normans. But why one should prevail in Maine and the other in Pennsylvania is uncertain. The different choices in America simply demonstrate how language will develop independently in any region not consistently communicating with another. So an American's car has a *hood;* a Britisher's, a *bonnet.* One buys *gas;* the other, *petrol. Two-lane traffic* is a *dual carriageway;* an *overpass,* a *flyover;* a *drugstore,* a *chemist's shop. Corn,* in England, is wheat, or any grain; in America it's on the cob, or in something generally rural or *corny.* And an American's *crotch* is a Britisher's *crutch.*

American English has always been inventive, and highly absorptive, and many Americanisms have migrated to England and around the world. *O.K.* may be the world's most universal word.* Our Thomas Jefferson invented the ever-popular *belittle. Cocktail, jackpot, know-how, fizzle, bingo, honk* are all American innovations as are most of our terms of racial contempt, like *hunky* or *honky,* first applied (in the form *Bohunk,* "Bohemian-Hungarian") to Hungarian immigrants of the steel mills and coal mines by established whites, now often applied to all whites by blacks. *Honky-tonk,* which seems to have come from a tinking-tonking piano, and *jazz,* which arose, with the music, from the Black culture of New Orleans, both with an African origin (Pyles, 47), have become international English words. Another is *Yankee,* perhaps from *Janke,* a diminutive of *Jan* (Dutch for "John"), as a nickname for New York's early Dutch settlers.

But the most curious thing about American English is the great difference in pronunciation between New England and the South—areas both settled mostly from southeast England in the same span of history. New Englanders apparently tended to nasalize, especially the Puritans, whom an Englishman in 1770 reported as having a "whining cadence" in their speech (Pyles, 241). On the other hand, Southern speech seems to have mellowed, except for some Puritan nasalizing in the hills.

However one may attempt to explain this southern mellowing—the languid climate and slower pace in life, for instance—the greatest single distinction between North and South was, almost from the first, a considerable population of African slaves. Black slaves, often deliberately assorted from different tribes to minimize revolts on shipboard and ashore, had no common language.† The slave's greatest need was to talk with his fellow captives. The

---

*Allen Walker Read traces it to the O.K. Club, supporting Martin Van Buren against William Henry Harrison in the presidential campaign of 1840. "O.K." stood for "Old Kinderhook," Van Buren's nickname, from his birthplace, Kinderhook, New York. "The O.K. Club" first appeared in print on 23 March 1840. But the opposition decided to smudge the Democrats by an article "explaining" O.K. as an illiterate abbreviation of "All Correct" by the incumbent President, Andrew Jackson, Van Buren's sponsor ("The Evidence on O.K." *The Saturday Review of Literature* (19 July 1941), summarized and discussed by Thomas Pyles, *Words and Ways of American English* [New York: Random House, Inc., 1952]: 158–65). *O.K.* had indeed originated as an abbreviation for humorously misspelt "oll korrect" in a spate of abbreviations in the Boston newspapers in the 1830s, along with *N.G.* ("no go"), *R.T.B.S.* ("remains to be seen"), and *S.P.* ("small potatoes"), according to Merriam-Webster researchers (*Christian Science Monitor,* 2 December 1977). The O.K. Club was apparently exploiting a coincidence with popular slang. A later theory, that *O.K.* derived from Choctaw *hoke* ("it is so"), a theory much liked by President Woodrow Wilson, who wrote it *okeh,* gave the term a certain respectable boost.

†For this point and a number of others following, I am indebted to J. L. Dillard, *Black English* [New York: Random House, Inc., 1972]: 73 ff.

white master had little to say to him. A *git,* a *wuk,* a *come,* a *go,* and a whip, would probably suffice. For communication among themselves, slaves used whatever lingua franca they could acquire from their captors and each other. In the fourteenth century, Sabir, the French-Italian-Spanish pidgin of the Arab slavers, the oldest in the business, was current. When the Portuguese began to dominate world trade in the fifteenth and sixteenth centuries, the West African slaving areas began to acquire Pidgin Portuguese. *Pickaninny, savvy,* and *Negro* (reinforcing the earlier Sabir-Spanish) testify to their Portuguese origin. The simplified grammar of Pidgin Portuguese probably copied that of Sabir, and the simplified grammar of Pidgin English probably followed that of both.*

But African intonations and words were shaping whatever pidgin or creole a slave community acquired. In Louisiana, a French pidgin evolved into an indigenous French Creole. Slaves who escaped to islands offshore of South Carolina, Georgia, and Florida evolved from the pidgins of Portuguese and English, and their native African, an independent creole language known as Gullah, a language which in turn put many Africanisms first into Black English, then into general American usage: *jazz,* most notably, and *tote, gumbo, buckaroo, banjo, okra, juke, bozo, voodoo,* and probably other special usages like *hip, hep,* and *cat* (Dillard, 118–119). *Mon,* or "man," almost universal for address and exclamation in black dialects around the Caribbean, has now become almost equally universal in young American speech.

Thus, even as blacks were acquiring English, something of their intonations and idioms was tempering the English of their white masters. The white pidgin-speaker, when giving orders, would naturally imitate the black to make himself understood, and some of that imitation would eventually remain. Even more significant was the black mammy, and her children, with whom the white child spent much of his time from infancy onward. William Faulkner's short story "That Evening Sun" illustrates the process still at work in relatively modern times. Conversely, Southern vowels were changing in ways wholly unrelated to West African, Caribbean, or Gullah,† and blacks were acquiring them as they learned the white community's speech. From the first, the early pidgins and Plantation Creole moved steadily over toward the evolving Standard English,‡ and moved outward to virtually every state in the nation. The dual process continues from coast to coast, as whites acquire black idioms and intonations, and blacks acquire the shared standard usages.

Writing makes the ultimate selection, and is perhaps the ultimate educator. Like Caxton in 1490, the modern writer ponders which words will reach

---

*Keith Whinnon, "The Origin of the European-based Creoles and Pidgins," *Orbis* (1968): 509–26, cited Dillard: 21.

†William Labov, commenting on my earlier draft of this section.

‡Dillard notes that runaway slaves—people of nerve and ability—"were likely to be just those slaves who did attain a relative mastery of Standard English" (86); a runaway would need to communicate with a wide diversity of people who would not understand Plantation Creole, and being able to read and write Standard English was greatly to his advantage.

the widest audience, which will connect him with the largest sharing of culture, which will persuade, which may lose him the credit he needs to be convincing. His choices, and their social nuances, are richly varied, since English has gathered and kept synonyms not only from its Germanic-Latin-Norse-French mainstream but from most of the other languages one can name. English probably has the largest living vocabulary in the world, because its literature—the written language—keeps alive, in great works, those words that speech alone would have long since lost.

Literature continually breathes new life into the inevitable decay of daily usage as metaphors and precisions fade into gobbledegook, and prominent people can utter with satisfaction such densities as *fuel economy program success.* A word like *sanction,* for instance, which means "a blessing," comes in official jargon to mean also its opposite, a "penalty," its precision impaired, until some poet comes along to remind us again of what it means, at the root, in the holy sanctions of the heart. The spoken word dies on our breath. The written word endures—*litera scripta manet*—because the writer makes words mean what they say, and renews their durable life. As Auden reminds us, Time, who is

. . . indifferent in a week
To a beautiful physique,

Worships language and forgives
Everyone by whom it lives.*

To join that timeless crowd by whom language lives is the writer's secret obsession, as he searches the clutter of everyday usage for the real riches of the world's most extended language.

The process of writing, then, brings these riches into our personal usage, and our speech acquires the breadth and span of the written language, moving into the mainstream from whatever regional or dialectical point we may have started. This mainstream, this Standard English, is constantly gathering new vitalities from its edges and dropping others no longer of use. To use it well is to share a living entity, perhaps with some wonder at the strange energy in Indo-European that slowly flowed outward over Europe and Asia, and then, in a much changed and minor dialect, reached southern England in 449 to carry itself on around the world.

---

*W. H. Auden, from "In Memory of W. B. Yeats," in *Collected Shorter Poems 1927–1957* (New York: Random House, 1966). Copyright © 1940, renewed 1968 by W. H. Auden. Reprinted by permission of Random House, Inc.

A Writer's Grammar

Theories of grammar have proliferated in the twentieth century, but the familiar nouns, verbs, adjectives, and other entities persist simply because they are the most handy. Although structural linguistics and transformational-generative grammar have analyzed the workings of language with considerable precision, they are too complex to give most writers help when they need it. Traditional grammar, in spite of certain leaks in the system, can do the job quite well.

Grammar tells us how the language fits. When we speak casually, our ungrammatical ways probably get by: "He don't have nothing." But on paper, or in front of the TV cameras, many will put us down as uneducated—nice, sincere, but not so fully in command as the person who says, "He has nothing." Words mean what they say. You should too. Your grammatical mismatches will show you unaware, naïve, uninformed, not so fully worthy of attention as the person who gets things straight.

GRAMMAR AS MEANING

Grammar, simply, is a scheme for understanding how sentences fit together meaningfully. On paper, you can see where the meanings slide. Here are fifteen sliding sentences, each with slippage noted, each slippage discussed on the text pages given at the right.

343

They study hard, but *you* do not have to work
all the time. [*You* does not agree with *They.*]   352–53

Holden *goes* to New York and *learned* about life.   352–53
[*Learned* does not agree in tense with *goes.*]

A *citizen* should support the government, but *they*   352–53
should also be free to criticize it. [*They* does
not agree with *citizen.*]

The *professor,* as well as the students, *were* glad   353–55
the course was over. [*Were* does not agree
with *professor.*]

As *he looked up,* a *light could be seen* in the win-   351–52; 358–59
dow. [The subject has shifted awkwardly
from *he* to *light,* and the verbal construction
from active to passive.]

Now we knew: it was *him.* [*Him* does not agree in   366–67
case with the subject, *it.*]

Let's keep this between you and *I.* [*I* cannot be   366–67
the object of *between.*]

Can you and Shirley play doubles next Sunday   366–67
with *Bob and I?* [*I* cannot be the object of
with—*with I?*]

They accuse William Singleton Stone and *I* of   366–67
mismanaging their accounts. [*I* cannot be the
object of a verb—*accuse I?*]

The students always elect whomever is popular.   367–68
[*Whomever* cannot be the subject of the verb
is.]

She hated me leaving so early. [She hated not *me*   368–69
but the *leaving.*]

Bill told *Fred* that *he* failed the exam. [*He* can   370
mean either *Bill* or *Fred.*]

Each of the laborers performed *their* task. [*Each*   371–72
and *their* disagree in number.]

Father felt *badly*. [*Badly* describes Father's compe-   373
tence, not his condition.]

He *spoke friendly*. [The verb requires an adverb,   373
like *warmly*, and *friendly*, though ending in
-ly, is an adjective, not an adverb.]

She said *on Tuesday* she *would call*. [The position   374–75
of *on Tuesday* confuses the times of *saying*
and *calling*.]

Walking to class, her *book* slipped from her grasp.   377
[*Walking* refers illogically to *book*.]

While *playing* the piano, the *dog* sat by me and   377–78
howled. [Dogs don't usually play pianos.]

With each of these, you sense that something is wrong. With a little thought
you can usually find the trouble. But what to do may not be so readily apparent.
We first need to understand something of the basic structure of grammar.

Know the Basic Parts of Speech.

The parts of speech are the elements of the sentence. A grasp of the basic
eight—nouns, pronouns, verbs, adjectives, adverbs, prepositions, conjunctions, and interjections—will give you a sense of the whole.

NOUNS.   Nouns name something. A *proper noun* names a particular person,
place, or thing. A *common noun* names a general class of things; a common noun
naming a group as a single unit is a *collective noun*. A phrase or clause functioning as a noun is a *noun phrase* or a *noun clause*. Here are some examples:

> COMMON: **stone, tree, house, girl, artist, nation, democracy**
> PROPER: **George, Cincinnati, Texas, Europe, Declaration of Inde-**
> **pendence**
> COLLECTIVE: **committee, family, quartet, herd, navy, clergy, kind**
> NOUN PHRASE: *Riding the surf* **takes stamina.**
> NOUN CLAUSE: *What you say* **may depend on** *how you say it.*

PRONOUNS.   As their name indicates, pronouns stand "for nouns." The noun
a pronoun represents is called its *antecedent*. Pronouns may be classified as
follows:

PERSONAL *(standing for persons):* **I, you, he, she, we, they; me, him, her, us, them; his, our, and so on**

POSSESSIVE *(indicating ownership):* **my, mine, yours, his, hers, ours, theirs, whose, its—notice that none of them takes the usual possessive apostrophe-s:** *ours* **not** *our's,* *its* **not** *it's.*

REFLEXIVE *(turning the action back on the doer):* **I hurt** *myself.* **They enjoy** *themselves.*

INTENSIVE *(emphasizing the doer):* **He** *himself* **said so.**

RELATIVE *(linking subordinate clauses):* **who, which, that, whose, whomever, whichever, and so on**

INTERROGATIVE *(beginning a question):* **who, which, what**

DEMONSTRATIVE *(pointing to things):* **this, that, these, those, such**

INDEFINITE *(standing for indefinite numbers of persons or things):* **any, each, few, some, anyone, no one, everyone, somebody, and so on**

RECIPROCAL *(plural reflexives):* **each other, one another**

VERBS.   Verbs express actions or states of being, present, past, or future. A verb may be *transitive,* requiring an object to complete the thought, or *intransitive,* requiring no object for completeness. Some verbs can function either transitively or intransitively. *Linking verbs* link the subject to a state of being.

TRANSITIVE: **He** *put* **his feet on the chair. She** *sold* **her old car. They** *sang* **a sad old song.**

INTRANSITIVE: **He** *smiled.* **She** *cried.* **They** *sang* **like birds. They** *are coming.*

LINKING: **He** *is* **happy. She** *feels* **angry. This** *looks* **bad. It** *is* **she.**

ADJECTIVES.   Adjectives narrow and specify nouns or pronouns. An *adjectival phrase* or *adjectival clause* functions in a sentence as a single adjective would.

ADJECTIVES: **The** *red* **house faces west. He was a** *handsome* **devil. The** *old haunted* **house was** *empty.* **We saw a** *dancing* **bear. We walked at a** *leisurely* **pace.** *These* **books belong to** *that* **student. [In the last example, demonstrative pronouns serve as adjectives.]**

ADJECTIVAL PHRASE: **He had reached the end** *of the book.*

ADJECTIVAL CLAUSE: **Here is the key** *that unlocks the barn.*

ADVERBS.   Adverbs describe verbs, adjectives, or other adverbs, completing the ideas of *how, how much, when,* and *where.* An *adverbial phrase* or *adverbial clause* functions as a single adverb would.

ADVERBS: Though *slightly* fat, he runs *quickly* and plays *extremely*
   well. She runs *fast.*
ADVERBIAL PHRASE: He left *after the others.* He spoke *with vigor.*
ADVERBIAL CLAUSE: She lost the gloves *after she left the store.*

Certain forms of verbs, alone or in phrases, serve as nouns, adjectives,
and adverbs. *Participles* act as adjectives. *Present participles* are verbs plus *-ing,*
and *past participles* are regular verbs plus *-ed* (see 362–63 for *Irregular verbs*).
Gerunds, like present participles, are verbs plus *-ing* but work as nouns; past
participles occasionally function as nouns, also. *Infinitives*—*to* plus a
verb—serve as nouns, adjectives, or adverbs. Unlike participles and gerunds,
infinitives can have subjects, which are always in the objective case.

PRESENT PARTICIPLES: *Feeling* miserable and *running* a fever, she
   took to her bed. [adjectives]
PAST PARTICIPLES: The nurses treated the *wounded* soldier. [adjec-
   tive] The nurses treated the *wounded.* [noun]
GERUND PHRASE: *His going* ended the friendship. [noun, subject of
   sentence]
INFINITIVES: *To err* is human; *to forgive,* divine. [nouns, subjects
   of sentence]
   I saw *him* [*to*] *go.* [phrase serving as noun, object of *saw*;
   him subject of *to go*]
   Ford is the man *to watch.* [adjective]
   Coiled, the snake waited *to strike.* [adverb]

PREPOSITIONS.   A preposition links a noun or pronoun to another word in the
sentence. A preposition and its object form a *prepositional phrase,* which acts as
an adjective or adverb:

BY *late afternoon,* **Williams was exhausted.** [as adverb, modifying
   was exhausted]
He walked TO *his car* **and drove FROM** *the field.* [as adverbs, modifying *walked* and *drove*]
The repairman opened the base OF *the telephone.* [as adjective,
   modifying *base*]

CONJUNCTIONS.   Conjunctions join words, phrases, and clauses. *Coordinating*
conjunctions—*and, but, or, nor, yet, so, still, for*—join equals:

Mary *and* **I won easily.**
Near the shore *but* **far from home, the bottle floated.**
He was talented, *yet* **he failed.**

Subordinating conjunctions attach clauses to the basic subject-and-verb:

Since it was late, they left.
He worked hard *because* he needed an A.
They stopped *after* they reached the spring.

INTERJECTIONS.   Interjections interrupt the usual flow of the sentence to emphasize feelings:

But, *oh*, the difference to me.
Mr. Dowd, *alas*, has ignored the evidence.
The consumer will suddenly discover that, *ouch*, his dollar is cut
    in half.

SENTENCES

Learn to Identify the Simple Subject and Its Verb

Grammar conveniently classifies the words in your sentences into parts of speech. With the natural and logical joining of parts, thought begins. And the very beginning is the subject and its verb. A noun expresses a meaning, which, when expressed, gathers other meanings to it. The mere idea of *tree* moves on to include some idea of a verb: *tree is.* And other subject-verb thoughts are probably not far behind: *tree sways; it drops its leaves.* With *The poplar tree sways in the wind, dropping yellow leaves on the lawn,* you have a full-grown sentence. At its heart are *tree*—the simple subject (the subject shorn of all modifiers)—and *sways,* the verb. All the rest is filling out, or explaining, of the simple subject and its verb. You should accustom yourself to locating these two parts in an ailing sentence. They will help you see how its other parts are behaving—or ought to behave. First, find the verb, since that names the action: *sways.* Then ask *who* or *what.* The answer gives you your subject, *tree,* which, with modifiers cut away, is the simple subject. Having found the heart—*simple subject* plus *verb*—you are well on the way to understanding the rest of your sentence's anatomy.

Know the Structure—and Modifications—of the Simple Sentence

The simple English sentence can take one of three essential forms:

1. Subject-Verb
2. Subject-Verb-Object
3. Subject-Is-Something

These three incorporate the three major kinds of verbs (indicated in brackets):

1. SUBJECT-VERB [*INTRANSITIVE*]

She *smiles.*
He *laughs* like a perfect idiot.
The tree *sways* in the wind.

2. SUBJECT-VERB [*TRANSITIVE*]-OBJECT

Boy *meets* girl.
He *liked* her minibus.
They *cashed* the check.

3. SUBJECT-IS [*LINKING*]-SOMETHING

The temperature *is* up.
Maxine *is* president.
Max *is* jealous.
They *are* here.
This *tastes* salty.
The pie *smells* good.

Is is the most common linking verb; but, as you see, a number of other verbs may serve: *taste, smell, feel, look, seem, appear, act, get, grow, turn, become.*

Although the structure is simple, the simple sentence may exhibit considerable variation. It may contain compounds in subject or predicate:

The *boy and* the *girl,* the *aunt, and* the whole hypocritical *family* smile. [compound subject]
He *hit* the right note with her *and struck* a full sympathetic chord with her parents. [compound predicate]
The *president* of the company *and* the *chairman* of the board *stormed and raged.* [compounds in subject and predicate]

Simple Sentence

Or it may attach modifiers to subject and verb:

Beautiful beyond imagination, glowing with health, *she* won the contest. [*She* is the subject]
He *swam,* unaware of sharks, indifferent to snipers' bullets, as if merely racing again in the varsity pool. [*Swam* is the verb.]

Or put the verb before the subject:

Near the window *stood* a folding *screen.*
Behind it *was* the *murderer.*

> **There *is* a *problem*.** [The expletive *there* can never be a subject.]
> **It *was* too bad *that he quit*.** [*That he quit*, a noun clause, is the subject. Like *There, It* is an expletive introducing the sentence. You will write more concisely if you avoid these expletives altogether: *We have a problem. Unfortunately, he quit.*]

Or use a verbal form for subject:

> ***To see* it will be enough.**
> ***Seeing* it will convince you.**

Or omit the subject (*you* implied) in a command or request—an *imperative* sentence:

> **Get smart.**
> **As a courtesy to your reader, please take the trouble to punctuate accurately.**
> **Take, oh take, those lips away.**

Two or more simple sentences can combine into a *compound* sentence:

Compound
Sentence
> **He drove the car, and she did the talking.**
> **He liked the scenery, she liked the maps, and they both enjoyed the motels.**
> **The food was good; the prices were reasonable.**
> **Either the plan was bad, or the instructions failed.**

A simple sentence with one or more subordinate clauses added becomes a *complex* sentence:

Complex Sentence
> **When the weather cleared, they started their vacation.**
> **Although the weather was fine, although the timing was perfect, although expenses were no problem, their vacation was miserable.**
> **They returned home as soon as they could.**

Two or more simple sentences combined with one or more subordinate clauses become a *compound-complex* sentence:

**When the weather cleared, they started their vacation, but they
returned home as soon as they could.**

Compound-Complex
Sentence

EXERCISES

1. *Treat these ailing sentences. In your cured versions, underline the simple subject of
each clause once, and the subject's verb twice. Underline any other changes, and put
brackets around subordinate clauses where you find them.*

SIMPLE SENTENCES

 1. The old and the young, the feeble and the sprightly, joins the dance.
 2. John Stevenson liked everything about the old town, her relatives, and she most
    of all.
 3. There is one or two things left to do.
 4. Solving several specific problems are good exercise.
 5. Ann, as well as her mother, like to sew.

COMPOUND SENTENCES

 6. He drives the car, and she, a friendly girl, do the talking.
 7. Jim drove the car, and her friends think him crazy.
 8. They liked the dinner, but they forgot to thank Gertrude and I.
 9. Either the bed was too hard, or it is too expensive for one night.

COMPLEX SENTENCES

10. While leaving the stadium, the game was over.
11. Whenever he comes, a party could be expected to begin.
12. Them who gets there first gets the best seats.
13. After all these years, they still envied him succeeding in everything he tried.
14. Winding the grandfather clocks that stand in several rooms are easy, since they
    just pull the chains that lifts the weights.
15. All the people, whoever happened to be in the village, was welcome.

SUBJECTS

Avoid Awkward Changes of Subject in Midsentence

Unnecessary shifts in structure can confuse a sentence's vision and its sense
of direction. A needless change in subject may make a sentence appear unsure
whether it is coming or going.

FAULTY: As *I* entered the room, *voices* could be heard.
REVISED: As *I* entered the room, *I* could hear voices.

FAULTY: The *audience* was pleased by his performance, and *he* earned a standing ovation.
REVISED: *His* performance pleased the audience and earned *him* a standing ovation.

FAULTY: The first *problem* is political, but there are *questions* of economics that are almost entirely involved in the second problem.
REVISED: The first *problem* is political; the second, principally economic.

FAULTY: *Jim* rolled up his sleeves, the *axe* was raised, and the *sapling* came down with four powerful strokes.
REVISED: *Jim* rolled up his sleeves, raised the axe, and cut the sapling down with four powerful strokes.

Avoid Illogical Shifts in Person and Number

Person refers to the form a pronoun and verb take to indicate who is speaking, who is being spoken to, and who is being spoken about:

Person

I am—first person
You are—second person
He is, they are—third person

Number refers to the form a noun or pronoun and verb take to indicate one *(singular)* or more than one *(plural)*. A sentence that shifts illogically in person or number is almost completely unhinged: it cannot distinguish between persons, or it has forgotten how to count.

Number

FAULTY: *They* have reached an age when *you* should know better.
REVISED: *They* have reached an age when *they* should know better.

FAULTY: *The reader has* difficulty in following the argument. *You get* lost in qualifications.
REVISED: *The reader has* difficulty in following the argument. *He gets* lost in qualifications.

FAULTY: If *someone asks* her a question, *they get* a straight answer.
REVISED: If *someone asks* her a question, *he gets* a straight answer.

FAULTY: **A motion *picture can improve* upon a book, but *they* usually *do* not.**

REVISED: **A motion *picture can improve* upon a book, but *it* usually *does* not.**

EXERCISES

2. *Revise the following sentences, correcting the awkward shifts of subject, person, and number.*

Correcting Shifts

1. While Barbara sewed, a stitch was dropped, and she sighed.
2. Whenever a stitch was dropped while she sewed, Barbara would sigh.
3. First he investigated the practical implications, and then the moral implications that were involved were examined.
4. Sam sat down at the counter, catsup was poured on the hamburger, and there was hunger in his face as he ate it.
5. These statistics are impressive, but error is evident in them.
6. The United Nations is not so firmly established that they can enforce international law.
7. One should never assume that they have no faults.
8. A person is overwhelmed by the gardens. Everywhere you look is beauty.
9. The buffalo is far from extinct. Their numbers are actually increasing.
10. People distrust his glibness. One feels they are being taken in by him.

VERBS

Keep Your Verb and Its Subject in Agreement

Match singulars with singulars, plurals with plurals. You will have little trouble except when subject and verb are far apart, or when the number of the subject itself is doubtful. (Is *family* singular or plural? What about *none?*—about *neither he nor she?*)

Sidestep the plural constructions that fall between your singular subject and its verb:

FAULTY: **The *attention* of the students *wander* out the window.**

REVISED: **The *attention* of the students *wanders* out the window.**

Mistaken Plurals

FAULTY: *Revision* **of their views about markets and averages *are* mandatory.**

REVISED: *Revision* **of their views about markets and averages *is* mandatory.**

FAULTY: The *plaster,* as well as the floors, *need* repair.
REVISED: The *plaster,* as well as the floors, *needs* repair.

Collective Nouns

Collective nouns *(committee, jury, herd, group, family, kind, quartet)* are single units; give them singular verbs, or plural members:

FAULTY: Her *family were* ready.
REVISED: Her *family was* ready.

FAULTY: The *jury have disagreed* among themselves.
REVISED: The *members* of the jury *have disagreed* among themselves.

FAULTY: *These kind* of muffins *are* delicious.
REVISED: *This kind* of muffin *is* delicious.
REVISED: *These muffins are* delicious.

Remember that in clauses introduced by expletive *there* (which can never be a subject though it may look like one), the subject follows the verb and governs its number:

"There"

There *is* only one good *choice.*
There *are* several good *choices.*

But expletive *it* always takes a singular verb:

"It"

It *is* [was] the *child.*
It *is* [was] the *children.*

Watch out for the indefinite pronouns *each, either, neither, anyone, everyone, no one, none, everybody, nobody.* Each of these is (not are) singular in idea, yet each flirts with the crowd from which it singles out its idea: each of *these,* either of *them,* none of *them.* They all take singular verbs. *None of them are,* of course, is very common. From Shakespeare's time to ours, it has persisted alongside the more precise *none of them is,* which seems to have the edge in careful prose, since it follows the structure of English, matching singular with singular.

Indefinite Pronouns

FAULTY: *None* of these men *are* failures.
REVISED: *None* of these men *is* a failure.

FAULTY: *None* of the class, even those best prepared, *want* the test.
REVISED: *None* of the class, even those best prepared, *wants* the test.

FAULTY: *Everybody* on the committee *are* present.
REVISED: *Everybody* on the committee *is* present.

FAULTY: *Neither* the right nor the left *support* the issue.
REVISED: *Neither* the right nor the left *supports* the issue.

When one side, or both, of the *either-or* contrast is plural, the verb conventionally matches the closer side:

Either the players or the coach *is* bad.
**Neither the rights of man nor the needs of the commonwealth
are relevant to the question.**

In the first example, though, *players is* disturbs some feelings for plurality. The best solution is probably to switch your nouns:

Either the coach or the players *are* bad.

When a relative pronoun *(who, which, that)* is the subject of a clause, it takes a singular verb if its antecedent is singular, a plural verb if its antecedent is plural:

The *person* who *tries* cannot fail.
The *people* who *try* cannot fail.

Relative Pronouns

FAULTY: **Phil is one of the best *swimmers* who *has* ever been on
the team.**
REVISED: **Phil is one of the best *swimmers* who *have* ever been on
the team.**

FAULTY: **Phil is the only *one* of our swimmers who *have* won
three gold medals.**
REVISED: **Phil is the only *one* of our swimmers who *has* won
three gold medals.**

Don't let a plural noun in the predicate lure you into a plural verb:

FAULTY: **His most faithful rooting *section are* his girl and his family.**
REVISED: **His most faithful rooting *section is* his girl and his
family.**

Use the Tense That Best Expresses Your Idea

Tense means time (from Latin *tempus*). Using verbs of the right tense means placing the action in the right period of time. Usually, you have no trouble choosing the forms to express simple past, present, and future; but you may have trouble expressing "perfected" forms of past, present, and future—especially when they must appear in the same sentence or paragraph with the simpler forms.

Here, with active and passive examples, are the six principal tenses found in English:

TENSE	ACTIVE VOICE	PASSIVE VOICE
Present	He asks	He is asked
Past	He asked	He was asked
Future	He will ask	He will be asked
Present Perfect	He has asked	He has been asked
Past Perfect	He had asked	He had been asked
Future Perfect	He will have asked	He will have been asked

Each tense has its own virtues for expressing what you want your sentences to say.

Use the *present tense* to express present action:

Present Tense   **Now she *knows*. She *is leaving*.**

Use the present also for habitual action:

He *sees* her every day.

Or for future action:

Classes *begin* next Monday.

Or for describing literary events:

Hamlet *finds* the king praying, but he *is* unable to act; he *lets* the opportunity slip.

Or for expressing timeless facts:

The Greeks knew the world *is* round.

Or for the "historical present":

> **King Alfred *watches* as the spider *mends* her web. He *determines*
> to rebuild his kingdom.**

But reserve the historical present for such deliberate literary effect. In ordinary narration or exposition, *avoid* this kind of thing:

> **One day I *am* watching television when the phone *rings*; it *is*
> the police.**

Use the *past tense* for all action before the present:

Past Tense

> **He just *left*.**
> **One day I *was watching* television when the phone *rang*; it *was*
> the police.**

Use the *future tense* for action expected after the present:

Future Tense

> **He *will finish* it next year.**
> **When he *finishes* next year. . . . [the present functioning as fu-
> ture]**
> **He *is going to finish* it next year. [The "present progressive" *is
> going* plus an infinitive, like *to finish*, commonly expresses
> the future.]**

Use the *present perfect tense* for action completed ("perfected") but relevant to the present moment:

Present Perfect
Tense

> **I *have gone* there before.**
> **He *has sung* forty concerts.**
> **She *has driven* there every day.**

Use the *past perfect tense* to express "the past of the past":

Past Perfect Tense

> **When we *arrived* [past], they *had finished* [past perfect].**

Notice that the present perfect (*have* plus past participle) becomes the past perfect (*had* plus past participle) when you step from present to past. Everything moves back one step:

> **The flare *signals* that he *has started*.**
> **The flare *signaled* that he *had started*.**

Use the *future perfect tense* (or *the present perfect* tense if appropriate) to express "the past of the future":

When we *arrive* **[future], they** *will have finished* **[future perfect].**
You *will have worked* **thirty hours by Christmas [future perfect].**
The flare *will signal* **[future] that he** *has started* **[present perfect].**

Avoid Unnecessary Shifts in Tense, Voice, and Mood

Inconsistencies in verbal forms will bother your reader, and usually muddle your ideas as well. Choose your tense and stay with it, stepping away only when the thought demands some other tense to make a distinction of time.

FAULTY: **Then Antony** *looked up* **from the body and** *begins* **to speak.**
REVISED: **Then Antony** *looks up* **from the body and** *begins* **to speak.**

FAULTY: **King Alfred** *thanks* **the peasant, and** *went* **his way. He** *gathered* **his men. They** *are* **overjoyed.**
REVISED: **King Alfred** *thanks* **the peasant, and** *goes* **his way. He** *gathers* **his men. They** *are* **overjoyed.**

FAULTY: **While the executives** *stayed* **in the plant, the strikers** *picket* **outside.**
REVISED: **While the executives** *stayed* **in the plant, the strikers** *picketed* **outside.**

FAULTY: **Although the government** *has stated* **its policy [present perfect], the people** *have* **still** *been* **confused [present perfect].**
REVISED: **Although the government** *has stated* **its policy [present perfect], the people** *are* **still confused [present].**

AWKWARD: **We** *will have left* **[future perfect] by the time they** *will have arrived* **[future perfect].**
REVISED: **We** *will have left* **[future perfect] by the time they** *arrive* **[present functioning to express future action].**

English has only two "voices"—the active (I *see*) and the passive (I *am seen*)—of which, as we have seen, the active is by far the more efficient. But whether using active or passive, avoid awkward shifts, especially if they also bring awkward shifts of subject.

FAULTY: This plan *reduces* taxes and *has been proved* workable in three other cities.

REVISED: This plan *reduces* taxes and *has proved* workable in three other cities.

FAULTY: He *had paid* for the new tires and the new upholstery; and now even the car *was paid for*.

REVISED: He *had paid* for the new tires and new upholstery; and now he *had* even *paid* for the car.

FAULTY: After they *laid out* the pattern, electrical shears *were used* to cut around it.

REVISED: After they *laid out* the pattern, they *cut* around it with electrical shears.

Mood (also called *mode:* "manner") is the attitude of the speaker toward the action his verb names. English has three moods. The *indicative mood* declares a fact or asks a question:

This pie *is* good. Susan *baked* it.
Susan *baked* it? *Is* there any left?

The *imperative mood* expresses a command or request:

Get out. Please *be* careful. *Take* two aspirin.

The *subjunctive mood* expresses an action or condition not asserted as actual fact. Such conditional, provisional, wishful, suppositional ideas are usually subjoined (*subjunctus,* "yoked under") in subordinate clauses. The form of the verb is often plural, and often in a past-tense form, even though the subject is singular, and the condition is present or future.

He looked as if he *were* confident.
If I *were* you, Miles, I would ask her myself.
If this *be* error, and upon me [*be*] proved. . . .
Had he *been* sure, he would have said so.
I demand that he *make* restitution.
I move that the nominations *be closed*, and that the secretary *cast* a unanimous ballot.

Avoid awkward or faulty shifts of mood:

FAULTY: If I *was* you, John, I would speak for myself.
REVISED: If I *were* you, John, I would speak for myself.

FAULTY: If he *would have known,* he never would have said that.
REVISED: If he *had known*, he never would have said that.
REVISED: *Had* he *known,* he never would have said that.

FAULTY: He moved that the club buy the picture, and that the secretary *shall bill* the members.
REVISED: He moved that the club buy the picture, and that the secretary *bill* the members.

FAULTY: You *should read* carefully and *don't miss* his irony.
REVISED: You *should read* carefully *to avoid missing* his irony.
REVISED: *Read* carefully, and *don't miss* his irony.

Finally, be careful not to write *would of* or *should of* for *would have (would've)* or *should have (should've).*

Master the Tenses of the Troublesome Verbs

Six short verbs are among the most troublesome in English: *lie, lay; sit, set; rise, raise.* These are six separate verbs, with six separate meanings. Master their meanings and their "principal parts" (present tense, past tense, and past participle—the form used with *has* or *had* in compound verbs). Indeed, three of the six suggest the convalescing patient: *lie, sit, rise.* These three are intransitive: they never take an object. The other three function more aggressively, always transitively, always taking an object: *lay, set, raise.* Now for the meanings, principal parts, and uses of them all.

First, the intransitive verbs, *lie, sit, rise.*

Lie, lay, lain (present, past, past participle) means to recline, or to be at rest.

Intransitive

PRESENT: The patient *lies* quietly asleep.
The patient *is lying* quietly asleep.
PAST: After the visitors left, the patient *lay* quietly asleep.
The purse *lay* unnoticed on the chair.
PAST PARTICIPLE: He has *lain,* quiet and asleep, all afternoon.

Since this one gives the most trouble, memorize this simple set:

I *lie* down.
I *lay* down yesterday.
I have *lain* down often.

When someone says incorrectly "He is *laying* down," ask yourself the impudent questions "Who is Down?" or "Is he laying feathers?"—and you might remember to say, and write: "He is *lying* down."

Sit, sat, sat means to assume, or remain in, a sitting position.

> **PRESENT: I *sit* by the bed.**
> **A clock *sits* on the table near the bed.**
> **PAST: The patient *sat* in the sun today.**
> **PAST PARTICIPLE: He had *sat* by the window yesterday.**

Rise, rose, risen means to stand up, or to move upward.

> **PRESENT: When supply is short, prices *rise*.**
> **PAST: To my surprise, he *rose* to greet me.**
> **PAST PARTICIPLE: To my surprise, he had *risen* to greet me.**

Here are the transitive verbs, *lay, set, raise.*

Lay, laid, laid means to place or put something.

> **PRESENT: He *lays* the suitcase on the bed.**
> **He *is* already *laying* plans for a new life.**
> **PAST: Yesterday he *laid* new tile in the playroom.**
> **PAST PARTICIPLE: By now he has *laid* the cornerstone of the new city hall.**

Transitive

Set, set, set means to place something in position.

> **PRESENT: I *set* the chair near the window.**
> **He *sets* the checkerboard on the table.**
> **PAST: He *set* the chair near the window.**
> **PAST PARTICIPLE: He has *set* the checkerboard on the table.**

Don't confuse it with *sit* or *sit down:*

> **FAULTY: He *sat* the chair near the window.**
> **REVISED: He *set* the chair near the window.**

> **FAULTY: He *set* himself *down* by the entrance.**
> **REVISED: He *sat* himself *down* by the entrance**

Finally, *raise, raised, raised* usually means to make something move up or grow.

PRESENT: **When supply is short, businessmen** *raise* **prices.**
PAST: **He** *raised* **his hand in greeting.**
PAST PARTICIPLE: **She has** *raised* **three beautiful children.**

Check the Irregular Verbs

Part of the difficulty is that the first five of these six troublemakers are *irregular verbs*—verbs not forming the past and the past participle by adding the usual *-ed,* as in **work**ed, **graduat**ed, **danc**ed. Here are some more to watch; learn to control their past and past-participial forms. Alternate forms are in brackets, in italics.

> **arise, arose, arisen**
> **awake, awoke, awaked** [but *was awakened*]
> **bear, bore, borne** [but: "She was *born* in 1966."]
> **beat, beat, beaten**
> **begin, began, begun**
> **bid** ("order"), **bade** [pronounced "bad"], **bidden**
> **bid** ("offer"), **bid, bid**
> **burst, burst, burst**
> **drag, dragged, dragged** [not *drag, drug, drug*]
> **draw, drew, drawn**
> **drink, drank, drunk**
> **fit, fitted** [or *fit,* especially intransitively], **fitted**
> **fling, flung, flung**
> **get, got, got** (*gotten*)
> **hang** ("suspend"), **hung, hung** [but: *hang* ("execute"), *hanged, hanged*]
> **lead, led, led** [Don't let the *lead* in *lead pencil* trick your spelling.]
> **lend, lent, lent**
> **light, lit** [*lighted*], **lit** [*lighted*]
> **prove, proved, proved** [*proven*]
> **ride, rode, ridden**
> **ring, rang, rung**
> **sew, sewed, sewn** [*sewed*]
> **shine** ("glow"), **shone, shone** [distinct from "polish"—*shine, shined, shined*]
> **show, showed, shown** [*showed*]
> **shrink, shrank** [*shrunk*], **shrunk** [*shrunken*]
> **sing, sang, sung**
> **sink, sank, sunk**
> **sow, sowed, sown** [*sowed*]

slink, slunk, slunk
spring, sprang, sprung
swim, swam, swum
swing, swung [not *swang*], swung
wake, woke [*waked*], waked

EXERCISES

3. *Treat these troubles, mostly verbal:*

   1. Conservatism, as well as liberalism, are summonses for change in American life as we now know it.
   2. These kind of questions are sheer absurdities.
   3. The lion shall lay down with the lamb, and the hen will have lain the golden egg.
   4. The committee were miles apart.
   5. None of these proposals are unworkable.
   6. Neither the tweed of his jacket nor the silk of his tie impress us.
   7. The house set on a low hill. A brick patio had been lain in back.
   8. Neither the question nor the answers seems pertinent to the issue.
   9. None of us are perfect.
   10. He swang out of the upper bunk before he had really woke up.
   11. John was the second one of the fifty boys who has volunteered.
   12. Each who have come this far have shown real determination.
   13. His idea of fine foods are hamburgers and French fries.
   14. Toys were laying all over the floor, and the babysitter had laid down and fallen asleep.
   15. Doug is the only one of the tall boys who always stand straight.
   16. Last year we are warned of higher taxes and getting lower taxes. This year we are promised lower taxes and getting higher taxes. What next year is holding, we can only guess. But sooner or later we are being promised and taxed into disbelief.
   17. He looked like something the cat had drug in when he flang open the door.
   18. They laid on the beach all afternoon, talking and just laying around, until after the sun had sank in the ocean. A few may have swam a little.
   19. He had rang the bell and lead the posse that hung him.
   20. If our defense would of been tighter, we would of won.

4. *Clinch your mastery of* lie, lay, sit, set, rise, *and* raise *by writing three active sentences for each, the first using the present tense, the second using the past tense, the third using the past participle.*

5. *Straighten out the inconsistencies of tense, voice, and mood in this passage:*

   A third principle that industry should recognize was the need for constant appraisal by management of an employee's progress. Management would determine what a person, when he or she would of been hired, were expected by it to achieve; and it then judges whether it now had had that person poorly assigned. They probably know their own limitations, and jobs beyond their capacity are poorly handled by them. But it is not enough that a manager sit down periodically with employees and reviews their performance. The important thing is that the manager understands a person well enough and be articulate enough to make sure the person has become conscious of needs for further development. If the manager will have been sufficiently observant, he might have helped his employees to an accurate evaluation of their own potential.

PRONOUNS AS SUBJECTS AND OBJECTS

Match a Pronoun's Form to Its Function

Unlike nouns, pronouns change form when they change from subject to object. *John* remains *John,* whether on the giving or receiving end of the verb: *John* hits *Joe; Joe* hits *John.* But the pronoun changes from subjective to objective form: *He* hits Joe; Joe hits *him.* We all know the difference between *who* (subject) and *whom* (object), if only because we are so often uncertain about them. We tend to say, *"Who* did you see," because *who,* though really the object of the verb *see,* comes first—in the slot usually reserved for subjects. *"Whom* did you see" is historically correct. Though *who,* as object, is displacing *whom* in some uses, knowing the distinction will help your writing in tricky constructions. We are also sometimes skittish about "between you and me," which is solidly correct, *me* being the object of the preposition *between.* Pronouns can cause considerable uncertainty—but they need not if you merely remember which forms are subjective and which objective. Here are the pronouns that give trouble:

SUBJECTIVE	OBJECTIVE
I	me
he	him
she	her
we	us
they	them
who	whom
whoever	whomever

Use Subjective Pronouns for Subjective Functions

Compound subjects, like "Bill and I," are a common source of trouble. For an easy way to check whether *I* or *me (he* or *him)* is right, drop the "Bill" and see how well the pronoun alone stands as subject of the verb. You would not, for instance, say "Me reported the accident."

FAULTY: *Me* and Bill reported the accident.
REVISED: Bill and *I* reported the accident.

FAULTY: Sally and *her* rode up front.
REVISED: Sally and *she* rode up front.

FAULTY: *Us* and *them* should have cooperated on this.
REVISED: *We* and *they* should have cooperated on this.

FAULTY: Pierce, Finch, and *myself* have resigned.
REVISED: Pierce, Finch, and *I* have resigned. [Keep *myself* where it belongs, as an intensive (I *myself*) or reflexive (I hurt *myself*), and be unashamed of *me* where it properly fits.]

A *complement* is a word that "complements" or completes the meaning of a verb. *Subjective complements* are words that complete the meaning of a linking verb, like *is,* while referring back to the subject ("Tom is *chairman*"). Pronouns serving as subjective complements must, of course, be subjective in form:

FAULTY: This is *him*.
REVISED: This is *he*.

FAULTY: He discovered that it was *me*.
REVISED: He discovered that it was *I*.

FAULTY: It was *them* who signed the treaty.
REVISED: It was *they* who signed the treaty.

A pronoun *in apposition* with the subject (that is, positioned near, and meaning the same thing as, the subject), or in apposition with a subjective complement, must also take the subjective form:

FAULTY: *Us* students would rather talk than sleep.
REVISED: *We* students would rather talk than sleep.

FAULTY: Both of us—Mike and *me*—should have gotten the credit.
REVISED: Both of us—Mike and *I*—should have gotten the credit. [*Mike and I* are in apposition with the subject, *Both,* not with the object of the preposition, *us*]

FAULTY: They were both to blame—Lord Hervey and *him*.
REVISED: They were both to blame—Lord Hervey and *he*.

When a pronoun follows *than* or *as,* it must be subjective if it is the subject of an implied verb:

Implied Verb

FAULTY: She is taller than *me* [am].
REVISED: She is taller than *I* [am].

FAULTY: You are as bright as *him* [is].
REVISED: You are as bright as *he* [is].

FAULTY: She loves you as much as *me* [love you].
REVISED: She loves you as much as *I* [love you].

FAULTY: She loves you better than [she loves] *he*.
REVISED: She loves you better than [she loves] *him*. [Here the pronoun is objective, since it is the object of the implied verb.]

Use Objective Pronouns for Objective Functions

A pronoun functioning as a *direct object,* an *indirect object,* or an *object of a preposition* must be *objective* in form. Compound objects give most of the trouble. Again, *see if the pronoun would stand by itself.*

Object of
Preposition

FAULTY: The credit goes to *he* or *she* who tries.
REVISED: The credit goes to *him* or *her* who tries.

Compound Object

FAULTY: Can you have lunch with Mary and *I*?
REVISED: Can you have lunch with Mary and *me*?

FAULTY: She typed the letter for Stuart and *he*.
REVISED: She typed the letter for Stuart and *him*.

FAULTY: Between her and *I*, an understanding grew.
REVISED: Between her and *me*, an understanding grew.

FAULTY: Everyone but Mildred and *she* contributed.
REVISED: Everyone but Mildred and *her* contributed. [*But* is used here as a preposition with the meaning "except."]

FAULTY: The petition was drafted by Nielsen, Wright, and *myself*.
REVISED: The petition was drafted by Nielsen, Wright, and *me*.

FAULTY: The mayor complimented Bill and *I*.
REVISED: The mayor complimented Bill and *me*.

FAULTY: The clerk sold John and *I* the case.
REVISED: The clerk sold John and *me* the case. [*Case* is the direct object of *sold*.]

Pronouns in apposition with objects must themselves be objective:

FAULTY: The mayor complimented us both—Bill and *I*.
REVISED: The mayor complimented us both—Bill and *me*.

FAULTY: She gave the advice specifically to us—Helen and *I*.
REVISED: She gave the advice specifically to us—Helen and *me*.

FAULTY: Between us—Elaine and *I*—an understanding grew.
REVISED: Between us—Elaine and *me*—an understanding grew.

FAULTY: He would not think of letting *we* girls help him.
REVISED: He would not think of letting *us* girls help him.

Notice this one:

FAULTY: Will you please help Leonard and *I* find the manager?
REVISED: Will you please help Leonard and *me* find the manager?

Leonard and me are objective both as objects of the verb *help* and as subjects of the shortened infinitive *to find.* Subjects of infinitives are always in the objective case, as in "She saw *him* go"; "She helped *him* find his keys."

Use a Subjective Pronoun for the Subject of a Noun Clause

This is one of the trickiest of pronominal problems. When a pronoun is the subject of a noun clause, it will often follow a verb or preposition, and therefore look like an object. But it is the subject, after all, and it must take a subjective form:

FAULTY: The sergeant asked *whomever* did it to step forward.
REVISED: The sergeant asked *whoever* did it to step forward.
[*Whoever did it* is a noun clause functioning as direct object of the verb *asked.* But *whoever* is the subject of the clause.]

After Preposition

FAULTY: They promised the medal to *whomever* would go.
REVISED: They promised the medal to *whoever* would go.
[*Whoever would go* is a noun clause functioning as object of
the preposition *to*. But *whoever* is the subject of the clause.]

Similarly, parenthetical remarks like *I think, he says,* and *we believe* often
make pronouns seem objects when they are actually subjects:

Parenthetical Remark

FAULTY: Ellen is the girl *whom* I think will succeed.
REVISED: Ellen is the girl *who* I think will succeed.

FAULTY: Jim will vote for *whomever* they say is a winner.
REVISED: Jim will vote for *whoever* they say is a winner.

The *who* pronouns also match form to function in relative adjectival
clauses:

In Relative Clause

FAULTY: The man *whom* had lied to her came in.
REVISED: The man *who* had lied to her came in. [*Who* is the subject of the clause *who had lied to her*.]

FAULTY: The man *who* she hated came in.
REVISED: The man *whom* she hated came in. [*Whom* is the direct
object of the verb in the clause *whom she hated*.]
BETTER: The man she hated came in.

But the *subject of an infinitive—and its complements—*is objective in form:

With Infinitive

FAULTY: They guessed the author to be *I*.
REVISED: They guessed the author to be *me*.

FAULTY: They will pay *whoever* they find the artist to be.
REVISED: They will pay *whomever* they find the artist to be.

Use the Possessive Pronoun Before a Gerund

Gerunds are verbal forms used as nouns (*hunting, skating, reading, sleeping*). *Participles* look exactly the same, but serve as adjectives.

GERUND: *Hunting* is good exercise.
PARTICIPLE: *Hunting* the southern hills, he came upon an old
cabin.

A gerund accompanied by a pronoun often runs into trouble:

FAULTY: She disliked *him* hunting.
REVISED: She disliked *his* hunting.

The object of her dislike is not *him* but *hunting;* hence the possessive pronoun merely modifies the true object, the gerund. Sometimes, however, the choice is not so clear:

They caught *him* cheating on the first exam.
They caught *his* cheating on the first exam.

Here the difference is not one of correctness, since both examples are correct, but of meaning as expressed through grammatical structure. In the first sentence, the object of *caught* is *him,* which is modified by the participle *cheating.* In the second sentence, the object is the gerund *cheating,* which is modified by *his.* In the first sentence, he is caught in the act; in the second, they detect his cheating as they read the completed exam.

FAULTY: Her father disapproved of *me* dating her.
REVISED: Her father disapproved of *my* dating her.

FAULTY: I am bothered by *him* not asking me out.
REVISED: I am bothered by *his* not asking me out.

FAULTY: He consented to *them* making the trip.
REVISED: He consented to *their* making the trip.

EXERCISES

6. *Correct the pronouns:*

1. It was him all right.
2. She disliked him whistling the same old tune.
3. They cheered both of us—Andy and I.
4. I admit it was me to whom they first confided.
5. We all three like it—Helen, Ann, and myself.
6. Us sophomores should all sign the petition. Me and Pete will circulate it.
7. Both her and me were elected.
8. He blamed Winston Atterbury and I for his missing the plane.
9. They always elect whomever is popular.
10. They choose whoever they like.
11. My mother insists on me buying my own clothes.
12. Everybody thinks us girls should go.

13. Little love is lost between him and I.
14. In the end, it was them who succeeded.
15. The child who he adored finally broke his heart.
16. Gladys takes more responsibility than her, and everyone knows it but him.
17. Christmas Greetings from we Bradshanks—Marge, Dave, Pat, and Binkie. Everyone will add their own tale to this, our fifth annual newsletter.
18. Everything comes to he who waits, but not to you and I.
19. No one likes their friends talking behind their back.
20. The child who she had saved was reading a comic book, as calm as you or I.

PRONOUNS AND THEIR ANTECEDENTS

Keep Your Antecedents Specific, Unambiguous, and Close at Hand

An antecedent states your pronoun's meaning. If an antecedent is missing, ambiguous, vague, or too far away, the pronoun will suffer from "faulty reference" and throw your sentence into disarray. Here are some of the problems:

Missing

FAULTY: **In Texas *they* produce a lot of oil.**
REVISED: ***Texas* produces a lot of oil.**

FAULTY: **My father is a doctor, and *this* is the work I want to do too.**
REVISED: **My father is a doctor, and *medicine* is the profession I want to follow too.**

Ambiguous

FAULTY: **Peter told Sam that *he* had played terribly. [Is *he* Pete or Sam?]**
REVISED: **Pete said that *Sam* had played terribly.**
REVISED: **To Sam, Pete admitted having played terribly.**

FAULTY: **Adams told Andrews that he could send *him* to London.**
REVISED: **Adams threatened Andrews with being sent to London.**

FAULTY: **Paul smashed into a girl's car *who* was visiting his sister.**
REVISED: **Paul smashed into the car of a *girl* visiting his sister.**

FAULTY: **He aimed at the tiger's eye, but *it* ran away.**
REVISED: **He aimed at the eye, but *the tiger* ran away.**

FAULTY: He is an excellent guitarist. *This* is because he began studying *it* as a child.

REVISED: He is an excellent guitarist because he began taking lessons when a child.

FAULTY: Because Ann had never spoken before an audience, she was afraid of *it*.

REVISED: Because Ann had never spoken before an audience, she was afraid.

FAULTY: He shouted outside the window and pounded on the frame, *which* finally broke the glass.

REVISED: He shouted outside the window and pounded on the frame till he finally broke the glass.

FAULTY: The mayor's committee reported on the remaining problems of polluted air, poor traffic control, inadequate schools, and rat-infested slums. The mayor was proud of *it*.

REVISED: The mayor's committee reported on the remaining problems of polluted air, congested traffic, inadequate schools, and rat-infested slums. The mayor was proud of *the committee*.

FAULTY: The castle was built in 1337. The rooms and furnishings are carefully kept up for the eyes of tourists, and at the entrance stands a coin-fed turnstile. *It* still belongs to the Earl.

REVISED: The castle, which still belongs to the Earl, was built in 1337. The rooms and furnishings are carefully kept up for the eyes of tourists, and at the entrance stands a coin-fed turnstile.

With an Indefinite Antecedent, Use a Singular Pronoun

Prominent among the indefinite antecedents are *anybody, anyone, each, either (neither), everybody, everyone, no one, nobody*. Also included are generic nouns like *kind, sort, man, woman,* and *person,* and the collective nouns like *family, jury,* and *clergy.* All of these, collecting plural items under one head, retain a certain misleading plural feeling, which may wrongly tempt you to plural pronouns of reference.

FAULTY: Modern woman is frequently unable to pursue *their* true goals.

REVISED: Modern woman is frequently unable to pursue *her* true goal.

FAULTY: *Everybody* paid for *their* ice cream.
REVISED: *Everybody* paid for *his* ice cream.

FAULTY: Each of the students hoped to follow *their* teacher's footsteps.
REVISED: Each of the students hoped to follow *the* teacher's footsteps.

FAULTY: After *everybody* in the crowd had contributed, Stan thanked *him*. [The grammar is correct, but the meaning is wrong.]
REVISED: After *all* the crowd had contributed, Stan thanked *them*.

FAULTY: If the *clergy* dares to face the new philosophy, *it* should declare *themselves*.
CLEARER: If the *clergy* dares to face the new philosophy, *it* should declare *itself.*
REVISED: If the *clergy* dares to face the new philosophy, the *clergy* should declare *itself.*

EXERCISES

7. *Strengthen the faulty references:*

1. He sent him his high-school pictures.
2. He kicked the child's toy by accident who was visiting.
3. Everyone knows their own best interest.
4. He missed several classes, which in the end defeated him.
5. When industries fail to make plans far enough into the future decades, they often underestimate them.
6. She ended her performance, but it was too late.
7. He opened the bird's cage, and it flew away.
8. My family is always throwing their weight around.
9. Shakespeare has Edgar portray his essential position.
10. These sort of snakes are very deceptive in their coloring.
11. The roofers finished early, after last touches to the trim and shingles, and they had really made it sparkle.
12. She loves swimming especially in the surf, thinking it the best exercise in the world.
13. His article was accepted by *Sport* magazine, for which he acknowledged his gratitude.
14. People should insure themselves against death and accident. These provide for the welfare of their loved ones.
15. There is a sandwich shop by the police station, and we phone them when we get hungry.

16. Coaches sometimes ignore the best interests of their players for the sake of winning games, and they are angry if they lose them because of bad grades, after working them too hard.
17. When he had his last heart attack, it almost stopped beating.
18. A governor should know a little about law and a lot about people, and apply them diplomatically.

MODIFIERS MISUSED AND MISPLACED

Learn the Difference Between Adjectives and Adverbs

Adjectives describe nouns; adverbs describe verbs, adjectives, or other adverbs. ("He *very shrewdly* played a *really* conservative game.") But the adjective sometimes wrongly crowds out the adverb ("He played *real* well"). And the adverb sometimes steals the adjective's place, especially when the linking verb looks transitive but isn't *(feels, looks, tastes, smells),* making the sense wrong. "He feels *badly*" means incompetence, not misery. "It tastes *wonderfully*" means skill in *it*—some kind of tasting machine. And certain adjectives ending in *-ly (lonely, lovely, friendly)* tend to masquerade as adverbs:

> **WRONG: She swam lovely.**
> **DOUBTFUL: They talked friendly.**
> **WRONG: He brooded lonely.**

But notice how quickly you can restore the adjective if you press your words for their meanings:

> **She swam, lovely as a swan.**
> **They talked, friendly and thoughtful.**
> **I wandered lonely as a cloud.**

Or you can simply assert the adverbial:

> **She swam beautifully.**
> **They spoke softly.**
> **He brooded solitarily.**

Some words serve both as adjectives and adverbs: *early, late, near, far, only, little, right, wrong, straight, well, better, best, fast,* for example.

He waited *late* for the *late* train.
Think *little* of *little* things.
Go *straight* up the *straight* and narrow path.

Near is both an adverb of place *(near to it, near the barn)* and an adjective *(the near hill, the near future);* and *near,* the adverb of place, is often confused with *nearly,* the adverb of degree, which means "almost."

RIGHT: It was *near* Toledo. [adverb of place]
RIGHT: It was *nearly* perfect. [adverb of degree]

To avoid confusing the two, substitute *almost* or *nearly* for the *near* of degree that tends to slip wrongly into everyone's prose, or convert it into a proper *near* of place, actual or figurative:

FAULTY: He was near exhausted.
REVISED: He was nearly exhausted.
REVISED: He was near exhaustion.

FAULTY: It was a near treasonous statement.
REVISED: It was a nearly treasonous statement.
REVISED: The statement was almost treasonous.

FAULTY: We are nowhere near knowledgeable enough.
REVISED: We are not nearly knowledgeable enough.

FAULTY: With Dodge, he has a tie of near-filial rapport.
REVISED: With Dodge, he has a nearly filial rapport.
REVISED: With Dodge, he has an almost filial rapport.

Slow has a long history as an adverb, encouraged by its crisp antithesis to *fast* (and its convenience for street-signs), but *slowly* keeps the upper hand in print. Notice that adverbs usually go after and adjectives before:

The *slow* freight went *slowly.*

Put Your Modifiers Where Their Meaning Is Clear

Some modifiers seem to look in two directions at once—the so-called "squinting" modifiers. Put them in their proper places. Make clear which way you want them to face.

AMBIGUOUS: She said on Friday to phone him.
REVISED: On Friday, she said to phone him.
REVISED: She said to phone him on Friday.

AMBIGUOUS: They agreed when both sides ceased fire to open negotiations.

REVISED: They agreed to open negotiations when both sides ceased fire.

REVISED: When both sides ceased fire, they agreed to open negotiations.

AMBIGUOUS: Several delegations we know have failed.

REVISED: We know that several delegations have failed.

AMBIGUOUS: They hoped to try thoroughly to understand.

REVISED: They hoped to try to understand thoroughly.

AMBIGUOUS: He resolved to dependably develop plans.

REVISED: He resolved to develop plans dependably. He resolved to develop dependable plans. [See "Split infinitives," in "A Glossary of Usage and Common Errors."]

AMBIGUOUS: Prices moved upward sufficiently to virtually wipe out the loss.

REVISED: Prices rose almost enough to wipe out the loss completely. [And you can take out *completely* to save a word.]

Make Your Comparisons Complete

Both adjectives and adverbs have "comparative" and "superlative" forms:

ADJECTIVE: green, green*er*, green*est*
easy, easi*er*, easi*est*
ADVERB: smoothly, *more* smoothly, *most* smoothly
easily, *more* easily, *most* easily

All comparatives demand some completion of thought, some answer to the question *than what?*—"Greener than what?"; "More smoothly than what?"

FAULTY: The western plains are flatter.

REVISED: The western plains are flatter than those east of the Mississippi.

FAULTY: He plays more skillfully.

REVISED: He plays more skillfully than most boys his age.

FAULTY: He was as tall if not taller than his sister.
REVISED: He was as tall as his sister, if not taller.

FAULTY: Jane told her more than Ellen.
REVISED: Jane told her more than she told Ellen.

FAULTY: His income is lower than a busboy.
REVISED: His income is lower than a busboy's.

FAULTY: The pack of a paratrooper is lighter than a soldier.
REVISED: A paratrooper's pack is lighter than a soldier's.

The adjectives ending in *y* that have an adverbial companion—*easy, easily, handy, handily*—most frequently stray into the wrong comparative slot.

WRONG: so she can get around *easier.*
RIGHT: so she can get around *more easily.*

WRONG: and the new lathe works handier.
RIGHT: and the new lathe works more handily.
RIGHT: and the new lathe is handier.

Superlatives also sometimes need completion if the context is unclear:

UNCLEAR: This is the best painting.
REVISED: This is the best painting in this exhibit.

UNCLEAR: Here was the prettiest if not the fastest car.
REVISED: Here was the prettiest car in the show, if not the fastest.

EXERCISES

8. *Cure the faulty modifiers:*
    1. They asked after ten days to be notified.
    2. We wanted to win enough to cry.
    3. Everyone feels badly about it.
    4. She sang melancholy.
    5. The bidding began quietly and friendly.
    6. The work of a student is more intense than his parents.
    7. It was a near perfect shot.
    8. Some girls have expectations beyond a husband.
    9. The party planned to completely attempt reform.

10. Industry is as strong if not stronger than before the depression.
11. We were dancing slow when the alarm sounded louder, and we were asked to leave peaceful and quiet but as quick as possible.
12. A number of women she knew had driven trucks, so she could refute his argument easier in the recent negotiations.
13. It was a near perfect pass, but he was near exhausted and too tightly covered to really get it.
14. They agreed to pay last year on January 1, 1989, to fully complete the contract.
15. Eliot respected him more than Pound.

DANGLING VERBAL CONSTRUCTIONS

Connect a Modifier Clearly to What It Modifies

Verbals are those *-ing* words, the gerunds (verbal nouns) and participles (verbal adjectives): *laughing, cooking, concentrating.* The phrases and clauses growing out of these words have a tendency to slip loose from the main sentence and dangle. "Going home, the walk was slippery" indicates that the *walk* was going home. The writer has actually compressed two sentences:

I was going home.
The walk was slippery.

But the compression has accidentally omitted the true subject of *going,* which we can put back, to keep that *going* from dangling:

When **I was going home, the walk was slippery.**

Or we can give the main clause its true subject:

Going home, *I found* the walk slippery.

Make sure your modifying verbal connects with its true subject:

FAULTY: **When getting out of bed, his toe hit the dresser.**
REVISED: **When getting out of bed, he hit his toe on the dresser.**

The passive voice is a major offender:

FAULTY: **Slapping on a conclusion, the play was almost ruined.**
REVISED: **Slapping on a conclusion, she almost ruined her play.**

Infinitive phrases also can dangle badly:

> **FAULTY:** **To work well, keep your bike oiled.**
> **REVISED:** **To work well, your bike needs frequent oiling.**

> **FAULTY:** **To think clearly, some logic is important.**
> **REVISED:** **To think clearly, you should learn some logic.**

Any clause or phrase may dangle:

> **FAULTY:** **When only a freshman, Jim's history teacher inspired him.**
> **REVISED:** **When Jim was only a freshman, his history teacher inspired him.**

> **FAULTY:** **After he had lectured thirty years, the average student still seemed average.**
> **REVISED:** **After he had lectured thirty years, he found the average student still average.**

For more on dangling participles, see 160–61.

EXERCISES

9. *Mend these dangling constructions:*

1. What we need is a file of engineers broken down by their specialities.
2. Following the games on television, the batting average of every player was at his fingertips.
3. When entering the door, the lamp fell over.
4. It is still not safe to drink or bathe in the water without being boiled first.
5. After he arrived at the dorm, the dean phoned.

10. *Straighten these sentences:*

1. The only light coming from machine-gun fire and explosions, it is hard for the audience to see whom is hit.
2. The audience, as well as the cast, were glad when they were finished.
3. In 1965, blacks numbered only 14 out of 863 students at the Bronx High School of Science, 23 out of 629 students at Stuyvesant High School, 45 in 368 at the High School of Music and Art, and out of 907 at Brooklyn Technical School you could only find 22.
4. If the Republicans would have checked into the activities that were being done by the Democrats in an honest manner, they would have avoided the mess of Watergate.

5. Either the report is incomplete or deliberately lying to both the public and he personally.
6. Not only did he delight in youth, but he had an almost pathological fear that it was already too late to enjoy it.
7. They study hard here, but you do not have to work all the time.
8. The contest between Louise and I was decided by only the absentee ballots, and they totaled them inaccurately.
9. Walking to the game, it was decided to give the team their due, whether or not it was going to bring us the championship.
10. Speaking before the committee, everything he said damaged his case.
11. Every member of the committee had tried to keep their minds open.
12. He sat his briefcase carefully on the desk, hoping it would not be too late to use the evidence in it, and left it laying there when he answered the phone.
13. She was awakened by a loud knocking, which turned out to be across the hall where they were installing a new floor.
14. Bordered on each side by steep white cliffs, they entered the valley where Dieppe lays.
15. Norsemen may have lain out the first settlement here, finding it's *diep,* or inlet, right for their ships.
16. Disturbing the peace, the judge decided to leniently sentence them to consecutively work out their penalty on week ends.
17. I would wish that he would have resigned more graceful.
18. Give the award to he who earns it, whether or not someone else may have swam a better race than him.
19. The police drug the river but could of conducted a more thorougher investigation.
20. Everyone and their brother was there, but they always take forever to really start the fireworks.

Punctuating the Sentence

Punctuation gives the silent page some of the breath of life. It marks the pauses and emphases with which a speaker points his meaning and controls his sentences. Loose punctuators forget what every good writer knows: that even silent reading produces an articulate murmur in our heads, that language springs from the breathing human voice, that the beauty and meaning of language depend on what the written word makes us *hear,* on the sentence's tuning of emphasis and pause. Commas, semicolons, colons, periods, and other punctuation transcribe our meaningful pauses to the printed page, and make our sentences fully meaningful.

THE COMMA

The comma is the key to meaningful punctuation. Here are the four basic commas:

1. THE INTRODUCER—after introductory phrases and clauses.
2. THE COORDINATOR—between "sentences" joined by *and, but, or, nor, yet, so, for.*
3. THE INSERTER—a PAIR around any inserted word or phrase.
4. THE LINKER—when adding other words or phrases.

1. THE INTRODUCER.   A comma after every introductory word or phrase makes your writing clearer, more alive with the breath and pause of meaning:

Indeed, the idea failed.
After the first letter, she wrote again.
In the autumn of the same year, he went to Paris.

Without the introductory comma, your reader frequently expects something else:

After the first letter she wrote, she . . .
In the autumn of the same year he went to Paris, he . . .

Notice how the introducer changes the meaning of *However* in these two sentences:

However she goes, she goes in style.
However, she goes when she feels like it.

You can usually avoid the danger of forgetting the comma and spoiling the sense by substituting *but* for your introductory *however*'s: "But she goes . . ." Put your *however*'s within the sentence between commas:

She goes, however, when she feels like it.

But beware! What looks like an introductory phrase or clause may actually be the subject of the sentence *and should take no comma.* A comma can break up a good marriage of subject and verb. The comma in each of these is an interloper, and should be removed:

That handsome man in the ascot tie, is the groom.
The idea that you should report every observation, is wrong.
The realization that we must be slightly dishonest to be truly
      kind, comes to all of us sooner or later.

If your phrase or clause as subject is unusually long, or confusing, you may relieve the pressure by inserting some qualifying remark after it, between two commas:

The idea that you should report every observation, *however in-*
      ***significant,* is wrong.**
The realization that we must be slightly dishonest to be truly
      kind, *obviously the higher motive,* comes to all of us sooner or
      later.

Commas mark your meaning. A man inquires about bidding on a carload of coal. How does he read the telegram in reply?

No price too high.
No, price too high.

A comma would make a difference in the commissar's telegram:

Pardon impossible, to be sent to Siberia.
Pardon, impossible to be sent to Siberia.

EXERCISES

1. *Master* however *by writing two groups of three sentences on the following pattern:*

   However she tried, she could not do it.
   She tried, however, a very long time.
   She tried; however, she could not do it.

2. *Write three sentences with a long clause or phrase as subject, avoiding the temptation of putting a comma after the subject. Then repeat each of these sentences, but after each clause-or-phrase as subject insert a qualifying remark, between commas, thus setting the subject apart from its verb for clearer distinction.*

---

2. THE COORDINATOR—between "sentences" joined by coordinating conjunctions. You will often see the comma omitted when your two clauses are short: "He hunted and she fished." But nothing is wrong with "He hunted, and she fished." The comma, in fact, shows the slight pause you make when you say it.

Think of the "comma-and" **(, and)** as a unit equivalent to the period. The period, the semicolon, and the "comma-and" **(, and)** all designate independent clauses—independent "sentences"—but give different emphases:

He was tired. He went home.
He was tired; he went home.
, and   **He was tired, and he went home.**

A comma tells your reader that another subject and predicate are coming:

He hunted the hills and dales.
He hunted the hills, and she fished in the streams.
She was naughty but nice.
She was naughty, but that is not our business.
Wear your jacket or coat.
Wear your jacket, or you will catch cold.

It was strong yet sweet.
It was strong, yet it was not unpleasant.

Of course, you may use a comma in *all* the examples above if your sense demands it. The contrasts set by *but, or,* and *yet* often urge a comma, and the even stronger contrasts with *not* and *either-or* demand a comma, whether or not full predication follows:

It was strong, yet sweet.
It was a battle, not a game.
. . . a bird in the hand, or two in the bush.

Commas signal where you would pause in speaking.

The meaningful pause also urges an occasional comma in compound predicates, usually not separated by commas:

He granted the usual permission and walked away.
He granted the usual permission, and walked away.

Both are correct. In the first sentence, however, the granting and walking are perfectly routine, and the temper unruffled. In the second, some kind of emotion has forced a pause, and a comma, after *permission.* Similarly, meaning itself may demand a comma between the two verbs:

He turned and dropped the vase.
He turned, and dropped the vase.

In the first sentence, he turned the vase; in the second, himself. Your **, and** in compound predicates suggests some touch of drama, some meaningful distinction, or afterthought.

You need a comma before *for* and *still* even more urgently. Without the comma, their conjunctive meaning changes; they assume their ordinary roles, *for* as a preposition, *still* as an adjective or adverb:

She liked him still . . . [That is, either *yet* or *quiet!*]
She liked him, still she could not marry him.
She liked him for his money.
She liked him, for a good man is hard to find.

An observation: *for* is the weakest of all the coordinators. Almost a subordinator, it is perilously close to *because. For* can seem moronic if cause and effect are fairly obvious: "She liked him, for he was kind." Either make a point of the cause by full subordination—"She liked him *because* he was kind"—or flatter the reader with a semicolon: "She liked him; he was kind." *For* is effective only when the cause is somewhat hard to find: "Blessed are the meek, for they shall inherit the earth."

To summarize the basic point about the comma as coordinator: put a comma before the coordinator (*and, but, or, nor, yet, so, still, for,*) when joining independent clauses, and add others necessary for emphasis or clarity.

EXERCISES

3. *Write six pairs of sentences, using the six conjunctions* and, but, for, or, yet, still, *on the pattern:*

He hunted the hills and . . .
He hunted the hills, and . . .

4. *Write three pairs of sentences with compound predicates showing how a comma changes verbal meaning, briefly explaining the difference in meaning after each:*

He turned and dropped the vase.
He turned, and dropped the vase.

---

3. THE INSERTER.   Put a PAIR of commas around every inserted word, phrase, or clause—those expressions that seem parenthetical and are called "nonrestrictive." When you cut a sentence in two to insert something necessary, you need to tie off *both* ends, or your sentence will die on the table:

When he packs his bag, however he goes. [, however,]
The car, an ancient Packard is still running. [, an ancient Packard,]
April 10, 1989 is agreeable as a date for final payment. [, 1989,]
John Jones, Jr. is wrong. [, Jr.,]
I wish, Sandra you would do it. [, Sandra,]

You do not mean that 1989 is agreeable, nor are you telling John Jones that Junior is wrong. Such parenthetical insertions need a PAIR of commas:

The case, *nevertheless,* was closed.
She will see, *if she has any sense at all,* that he is right.
Sam, *on the other hand,* may be wrong.
Note, *for example,* the excellent brushwork.
Tom Flint, *M.D.,* and Bill Stone, *Ph.D.,* doctored the punch to perfection.
He stopped at Kansas City, *Missouri,* for two hours.

The same rule applies to all *nonrestrictive* remarks, phrases, and clauses—all elements simply additive, explanatory, and hence parenthetical:

John, *my friend,* **will do what he can.**
Andy, *his project sunk, his hopes shattered,* **was speechless.**
The taxes, *which are reasonable,* **will be paid.**
That man, *who knows,* **is not talking.**

Think of *nonrestrictive* as "nonessential" to your meaning, hence set off by commas. Think of *restrictive* as essential and "restricting" your meaning, hence not set off at all (use *which* for nonrestrictives, *that* for restrictives; see 184).

RESTRICTIVES:

    The taxes that are reasonable will be paid.
    Southpaws who are superstitious will not pitch on Friday
        nights.
    The man who knows is not talking.

NONRESTRICTIVES:

    The taxes, which are reasonable, will be paid.
    Southpaws, who are superstitious, will not pitch on Friday
        nights.
    The man, who knows, is not talking.

The difference between restrictives and nonrestrictives is one of meaning, and the comma-pair signals that meaning. Our first "Southpaw" sentence says that only the superstitious ones lie low on Fridays: our second one, that *all* of them do. Now, how many grandmothers do I have in the first sentence below (restrictive)? How many in the second (nonrestrictive)?

    My grandmother who smokes pot is ninety.
    My grandmother, who smokes pot, is ninety.

In the first sentence, I still have two grandmothers, since I am distinguishing one from the other by my restrictive phrase (no commas) as the one with the unconventional habit. In the second sentence, I have but one grandmother, about whom I am adding an interesting though nonessential, nonrestrictive detail within a pair of commas. Read the two aloud, and you will hear the difference in meaning, and how the pauses at the commas signal that difference. Commas are often optional, of course. The difference between a restrictive and a nonrestrictive meaning may sometimes be very slight. For example, you may take our recent bridegroom either way (but not halfway):

> **That handsome man, in the ascot tie, is the groom.** [nonrestrictive]
> **That handsome man in the ascot tie is the groom.** [restrictive]

Your meaning will dictate your choice. But use **PAIRS** of commas or none at all. Never separate subject and verb, or verb and object, with just one comma.

Some finer points. One comma of a pair enclosing an inserted remark may coincide with, and, in a sense, overlay, a comma "already there":

> **In each box, a bottle was broken.**
> **In each box, however, a bottle was broken.**

> **The team lost, and the school was sick.**
> **The team lost, in spite of all, and the school was sick.**

> **The program will work, but the cost is high.**
> **The program will work, of course, but the cost is high.**

Between the coordinate clauses, however, a semicolon might have been clearer:

> **The team lost, in spite of all; and the school was sick.**
> **The program will work, of course; but the cost is high.**

Beware: *however,* between commas, cannot substitute for *but,* as in the perfectly good sentence: "He wore a hat, *but* it looked terrible." You would be using a comma where a full stop (period or semicolon) should be:

WRONG:

> **He wore a hat, however, it looked terrible.**

RIGHT   *(notice the two meanings):*

> **He wore a hat; however, it looked terrible.**
> **He wore a hat, however; it looked terrible.**

But a simple **(, but)** avoids both the ambiguity of the floating *however* and the ponderosity of anchoring it with a semicolon, fore or aft: "He wore a hat, but it looked terrible."

Another point. *But* may absorb the first comma of a pair enclosing an introductory remark (although it need not do so):

> **At any rate, he went.**
> **But, at any rate, he went.**
> **But at any rate, he went.**
> **But [,] if we want another party, we had better clean up.**
> **The party was a success, but [,] if we want another one, we had better clean up.**

But avoid a comma *after* "but" in sentences like this:

> **I understand your argument, but [,] I feel your opponent has a stronger case.**

Treat the "he said" and "she said" of dialogue as a regular parenthetical insertion, within commas, and without capitalizing, unless a new sentence begins:

> **"I'm going," he said, "whenever I get up enough nerve."**
> **"I'm going," he said. "Whenever I get up enough nerve, I'm really going."**

And American usage puts the comma *inside* **ALL** quotation marks:

> **"He is a nut," she said.**
> **She called him a "nut," and walked away.**

Finally, the comma goes after a parenthesis, never before.

> **On the day of her graduation (June 4, 1985), the weather turned boiling hot.**

EXERCISES

5. *Write five pairs of sentences showing the difference between nonrestrictive and restrictive clauses on this pattern:*

The taxes, which are reasonable, will be paid.
The taxes that are reasonable will be paid.

4. THE LINKER.   This is the usual one, linking on additional phrases and after-thoughts:

> **They went home, <u>having overstayed their welcome.</u>**
> **The book is too long, <u>overloaded with examples.</u>**

It also links items in series. Again, the meaningful pause demands a comma:

> **words, phrases, <u>or</u> clauses in a series**
> **to hunt, to fish, <u>and</u> to hike**
> **He went home, he went upstairs, <u>and</u> he could remember noth-**
> **   ing.**
> **He liked oysters, soup, roast beef, <u>and</u> song.**

Put a linker before the concluding *and* in any series. We pause there in our speech, saying "Hawthorne, Dickens, and Thackeray" and keeping "Dickens and Thackeray" (no comma) from sounding like a comedy team. Again, commas signal those pauses by which the English language distinguishes meanings.

By carefully separating all elements in a series, you keep alive a final distinction long ago lost in the daily press, the distinction Virginia Woolf makes (see 175): "urbane, polished, brilliant, imploring and commanding him. . . ." *Imploring and commanding* is syntactically equal to each one of the other modifiers in the series. If Woolf customarily omitted the last comma, as she does not, she could not have reached for that double apposition. The muscle would have been dead. These other examples of double apposition will give you an idea of its effectiveness:

> **They cut out his idea, <u>root and branch.</u>**
> **He lost all his holdings, <u>houses and lands.</u>**
> **He loved to tramp the woods, <u>to fish and hunt.</u>**

A comma makes a great deal of difference, of sense and distinction.

But adjectives in series, as distinct from nouns in series, change the game a bit. Notice the difference between the following two strings of adjectives:

> **a good, unexpected, natural rhyme**
> **a good old battered hat**

With adjectives in series, only your sense can guide you. If each seems to mod-ify the noun directly, as in the first example above, use commas. If each seems to modify the total accumulation of adjectives and noun, as with *good* and *old* in the second phrase, do not use commas. Say your phrases aloud, and put your commas in the pauses that distinguish your meaning.

Finally, a special case. Dramatic intensity sometimes allows you to join clauses with commas instead of conjunctions:

She sighed, she cried, she almost died.
I couldn't do it, I tried, I let them all get away.
It passed, it triumphed, it was a good bill.
I came, I saw, I conquered.

Clauses Joined with Commas

The rhetorical intensity of this construction—the Greeks called it *asyndeton*— is obvious. The language is breathless, or grandly emphatic. As Aristotle once said, it is a person trying to say many things at once. The subjects repeat themselves, the verbs overlap, the idea accumulates a climax. By some psychological magic, the clauses of this construction usually come in three's. The comma is its sign. But unless you have a stylistic reason for such a flurry of clauses, go back to the normal comma and conjunction, the semicolon, or the period.

EXERCISES

6. *Write five sentences with concluding double appositives that might look like parts of a simple series but are not: "They cut out his idea, root and branch."*

FRAGMENTS, COMMA SPLICES, AND RUN-ONS

These are the most persistent problems in using the comma—either missing it or misusing it. We have already looked at the fragment (173–74), but one more look will consolidate your control. The rhetorical fragment may have great force: "So what." But the grammatical one needs repairing with a comma:

FAULTY: **She dropped the cup. Which had cost twenty dollars.**
REVISED: **She dropped the cup, which had cost twenty dollars.**

FAULTY: **He does not spell everything out. But rather hints that something is wrong, and leaves the rest up to the reader.**
REVISED: **He does not spell everything out, but rather hints . . . , and leaves. . . .**

FAULTY: **. . . and finally, the book is obscure. Going into lengthy discussions and failing to remind the reader of the point.**

REVISED: . . . and finally, the book is obscure, going into lengthy discussion. . . .

FAULTY: Yet here is her husband treating their son to all that she considers evil. Plus the fact that the boy is offered beer.
REVISED: Yet here is her husband treating their son to all that she considers evil, especially beer.

FAULTY: He points out that one never knows what the future will bring. Because it is actually a matter of luck.
REVISED: He points out that one never knows what the future will bring, because it is actually a matter of luck.

FAULTY: They are off. Not out of their minds exactly but driven, obsessed.
REVISED: They are off, not out of their minds exactly, but driven, obsessed.

Beware the Comma Splice, and the Run-On

The comma splice is the beginner's most common error, the exact opposite of the fragment—putting a comma where we need a period rather than putting a period where we need a comma—splicing two sentences together with a comma:

Comma Splice

The comma splice is a common <u>error, it</u> is the opposite of a fragment.

Of course, you will frequently see comma splices, particularly in fiction and dialogue, where writers are conveying colloquial speed and the thoughts come tumbling fast. Some nonfiction writers borrow this same speed here and there in their prose. But you should learn to recognize these as comma splices and generally avoid them because they may strike your reader as the errors of innocence. Like the rhetorical fragment, a comma splice between short labored clauses can be most effective (see *asyndeton,* 389, 458): "If speech and cinema are akin to music, writing is like architecture; *it endures, it has weight.*"*

The run-on sentence (fortunately less common) omits even the splicing comma, running one sentence right on to another without noticing:

*Italics added. Richard Lloyd-Jones, "What We May Become," *College Composition and Communication* 33 (1952): 205.

The comma splice is a common <u>error it</u> is the opposite of a fragment.   Run-On

Here the writer is in deeper trouble, having somehow never gotten the feel of a sentence as based on subject and verb, and thus needing special help. But most of us can see both the comma splice and run-on as really being two sentences, to be restored as such:

> **The comma splice is a common error. It is the opposite of a fragment.**

Or to be coordinated by adding a conjunction after the comma:

> **The comma splice is a common error, and it is. . . .**

Or to be subordinated by making the second sentence a phrase:

> **The comma splice is a common error, the opposite. . . .**

Here are some typical comma splices:

> **She cut class, it was boring.**
> **The class was not merely dull, it was useless.**
> **He was more than satisfied, he was delighted.**

Each of these pulls together a pair of closely sequential sentences. But a comma without its *and* or *but* will not hold the coordination. Either make them the sentences they are:

> **She cut class. It was boring.**

Or coordinate them with a colon or dash (with a semicolon *only* if they contrast sharply):

> **The class was not merely dull: it was useless.**
> **He was more than satisfied—he was delighted.**

Or subordinate in some way:

> **She cut class because it was boring.**
> **The class was not merely dull but useless.**
> **More than satisfied, he was delighted.**

Here are some more typical splices, all from one set of papers in advanced freshman composition dealing with Shakespeare's *The Tempest.* I have circled the comma where the period should be:

> **She knows nothing of the evil man is capable of, to her every man is beautiful.**
> **The question of his sensibility hovers, we wonder if he is just.**
> **Without a doubt, men discourage oppression, they strive to be free.**
> **Ariel is civilized society, besides being articulate, he has direction and order.**
> **Stephano and Trinculo are the comics of the play, never presented as complete characters, they are not taken seriously.**

You will accidentally splice with a comma most frequently when adding a thought (a complete short sentence) to a longer sentence:

> **The book describes human evolution in wholly believable terms, comparing the social habits of gorillas and chimpanzees to human behavior, it is very convincing.**

But your reader will be confused by your drift. Which way is that *comparing* phrase supposed to go? You must help him by repairing your splice with a period, either like this:

> **The book describes human evolution in wholly believable terms, comparing the social habits of gorillas and chimpanzees to human behavior. It is very convincing.**

Or like this:

> **The book describes human evolution in wholly believable terms. Comparing the social habits of gorillas and chimpanzees to human behavior, it is very convincing.**

In short, be sure to attach all accidental fragments—that *comparing* phrase, by itself, would be a fragment—to your main sentence. But be sure each complete sentence—*It is very convincing*—stands clear and alone with its own capital and period.

Conjunctive adverbs (*however, therefore, nevertheless, moreover, furthermore,* and others) may cause comma splices and trouble:

> **She continued teaching, however her heart was not in it.**

Here are three mendings:

> **She continued teaching, but her heart was not in it.**
> **She continued teaching; however, her heart was not in it.**
> **She continued teaching; her heart, however, was not in it.**

Similarly, transitional phrases *(in fact, that is, for example)* may splice your sentences together:

> **He disliked discipline, that is, he really was lazy.**

You can strengthen the weak joints like this:

> **He disliked discipline; that is, he really was lazy.**
> **He disliked discipline, that is, anything demanding.**

Meet the Press

Now, let's face the music of everyday print. A corporation recently told its stockholders, "Abilene, Kansas looks promising," as if the chairman were telling his wife that things looked good in Kansas. Much advertising copy is virtually all fragments, and commas in the popular press fall out at random. The following paragraph, from *Time* magazine, is representative:

> **The *Aquatic*, a noisy, diesel-driven 40-ft. private sub tender chugs out of Warwick Cove into a gray Rhode Island day. Past rows of boats with names like *Many-Ha-Ha's, Daddy's Girl, Lucy M* and *Gyp Sea*. Past a dock where burlap sacks of clams are bought and sold—the seller getting 55¢ per lb. for littlenecks, as high as 80¢ for big quahogs. Past a sandbar where a tourist drowned yesterday clamming in 3 ft. of water. Past the big shingled mansions that trim the shoreline at fashionable Warwick Neck. And so into Narragansett Bay, a body of water variously ravished by long-handled rakes, progress and history.***

Commas and a dash will turn this choppy passage into a smooth sentence that sweeps the panorama into cohesive view from capital to period:

---

*Copyright © 1978 Time Inc. All rights reserved. Reprinted by permission from *Time*.

Inserter

Linker

Linker

Dash as Paired
Inserter

Linker

Linker

Linker

The *Aquatic*, a noisy, diesel-driven 40-ft. private sub tender, chugs out of Warwick Cove into a gray Rhode Island
day, past rows of boats with names like *Many-Ha-Ha's*, *Daddy's
Girl, Lucy M,* and *Gyp Sea,* past a dock where burlap sacks of
clams are bought and sold—the seller getting 55¢ per pound for
littlenecks, as high as 80¢ for big quahogs—past a sandbar
where a tourist drowned yesterday clamming in 3 ft. of
water, past the big shingled mansions that trim the shoreline at
fashionable Warwick Neck, and so into Narragansett Bay, a
body of water variously ravished by long-handled rakes, progress, and history.

Commas keep your sentences coherent, meaningful, and attractive; they give
your prose some of the breath, and breadth, of life.

EXERCISES

7. *Find a fragmented passage similar to the preceding one and see what you can do to repair it, indicating in the margin which commas you are using.*

8. *Correct the following sentences, inserting commas where needed, removing them where not (and, in a few cases, inserting periods). Some of the sentences are correct as they stand.*

1. This report will discuss the equipment to be used, the procedure to be followed the data to be obtained and the format for presenting the results.
2. We find however that the greatest expense in renovation will be for labor not for materials.
3. This book, even after seventy-five years is still one of the finest examples of sociological scholarship available and it ought to be required reading in any elementary sociology course.
4. The French Revolution of 1789 sparked a similar revolution led by Toussaint L'Ouverture, in Haiti in 1791 and shortly thereafter, the French recognized the freedom of the slaves.
5. Remote sensing devices exploit parts of the electromagnetic spectrum invisible to the eye.
6. Will Sexton a long-time member of the department will become sales manager on July 1, 1987 but until that time he will remain on convalescent leave.
7. Tight money and a scarcity of jobs have given a boost to graduate school applications.
8. He depended for his quotations upon the Bible Shakespeare and Emerson.
9. A faithful sincere friend he remained loyal to his roommate even after the unexpected turn of events.
10. We were delayed by the heavy snow, and therefore did not arrive in time for the lecture.

11. Although few readers of *The Adventures of Huckleberry Finn* recognize it at first the book is really a somber story of treachery murder and brutality.
12. Robert E. Lee was born at Stratford Virginia on January 19 1807.
13. In America said the Chinese lecturer people sing "Home Sweet Home." In China they stay there.
14. Should the estimate be too high I will seek other bids.
15. Printed in London bound in New York and first released in Chicago the book cost so much its sales were very limited.
16. The jobs of these machine operators largely assembly-line workers have become as simple repetitive and mechanical as the functions of the machines themselves.
17. Readers of Joseph Heller's book *Catch-22* a comic novel about World War II seem to react in one of two ways. Either they love the book or they can't stand it, in either case the book seems to arouse their passions.
18. Depressed refusing to face the reality of his situation he killed himself, it was as simple as that.
19. Writing in a popular magazine the critic said that Rex Harrison as Henry Higgins and Wilfrid Hyde-White as Colonel Pickering stole the show.
20. Jill Crabtree, in her article, "Foreign Relations at Home" says that American students despite the campaign by the International Center to promote their interest are not interested in the foreign students on this campus.
21. I guess I could drive the truck myself, still I really don't want to.
22. Person-to-person calls collect calls credit-card calls and calls to be billed to another number must be placed through the operator.
23. With the advent of refrigeration both in the home and in conveyances, the housewife could feed her family fresh foods in any season, before that she had fresh foods available only in season, and her winter menus were nutritionally weak.
24. In "Indian Camp" Hemingway's short story the reader's attention is on Nick Adams an eight- or ten-year-old observer of the jackknife Caesarean that his father performs on the Indian woman. We watch the watcher so to speak.
25. Although there are areas of overlap this report is divided into five parts: General Activities Criteria The Committee's Influence Upon Classified Research Communications and Future Considerations.

THE SEMICOLON

Use the Semicolon Only Where You Could Also Use a Period, Unless Desperate

The dogmatic formula that heads this section, which I shall loosen up in a moment, has saved many a punctuator from both despair and a reckless fling of semicolons. Confusion comes from the belief that the semicolon is either a weak colon or a strong comma. It is most effective as neither. It is best, as we have seen (153), in pulling together and contrasting two independent clauses that could stand alone as sentences:

> **The dress accents the feminine. The pants suit speaks for free-**
> **dom.**
> **The dress accents the feminine; the pants suit speaks for free-**
> **dom.**

This compression and contrast by semicolon can go even farther, allowing us to drop a repeated verb in the second element (note also how here a comma marks the omission):

> **Golf demands the best of time and space; tennis demands the**
> **best of personal energy.**
> **Golf demands the best of time and space; tennis, the best of**
> **personal energy.**

Used sparingly, the semicolon emphasizes your crucial contrasts; used recklessly, it merely clutters your page. *Never* use it as a colon: its effect is exactly opposite. A colon, as in the preceding sentence, signals the meaning to go ahead; a semicolon, as in this sentence, stops it. The colon is a green light; the semicolon is a stop sign.

Consequently, a wrong semicolon frequently makes a fragment. *Use a semicolon only where you could also use a period*—forget the exceptions—or you will make semicolon-fragments like the underscored phrases following the erroneous semicolons circled below:

> **The play opens on a dark street in New York City; one street-**
> **light giving the only illumination.**
> **The geese begin their migration in late August or early Septem-**
> **ber; several families having started, in small stages, a week**
> **or so earlier.**

Each of those semicolons should have been a comma.

Of course, you may occasionally need to unscramble a long line of phrases and clauses, especially those in series and containing internal commas:

> **You should see that the thought is full, the words well cleaned,**
> **the points adjusted; and then your sentence will be ready to**
> **go. [*Note that the period rule would still guide you here:* ". . .**
> **adjusted. And then. . . ."]**
> **Composition is hard because we often must discover our ideas**
> **by writing them out, clarifying them on paper; because we**
> **must also find a clear and reasonable order for ideas the**
> **mind presents simultaneously; and because we must find, by**
> **trial and error, exactly the right words to convey our ideas**
> **and our feelings about them.**

But the semicolon is better when it pulls related sentences together, replacing the period (or the comma-plus-conjunction) for some unusual emphasis:

> **They worked hard; they never thought of failure; they were wholly self-sufficient.**

And better still when it pivots a contrast:

> **Work when you work; play when you play.**
> **The semicolon is a stop sign; the colon, a green light.**

Notice that the semicolon (like the colon) goes *outside* quotation marks:

> **This was no "stitch in time"; it was complete reconstruction.**

EXERCISES

9. *Write five compound sentences, using a semicolon between two contrasting independent clauses.* **EXAMPLES:**

Compound sentences are strings of thoughts; complex sentences envelop them.
The semicolon is a stop sign; the colon, a green light.

10. *The following selections include examples of both correct and incorrect semicolons. Insert them where needed; remove them where not. Adjust commas and periods as necessary.*

   1. The book deals with the folly of war, its stupidity, its cruelty, however, in doing this, the author brings in too many characters, repeats episodes over and over again, and spoils his comedy by pressing too hard.
   2. Despite these shortcomings; however the book has remained popular because it is fresh and wacky in its approach.
   3. Most men smoked either cigars or pipes, for a long time cigarettes were regarded as unmanly.
   4. Most men smokers used either cigars or pipes; most women smokers used cigarettes.
   5. Steinbeck's fictional strike in *In Dubious Battle* is not unique, in the 1930s, such strikes were very real indeed.
   6. The endowment provides stipends for periods of from six months to a year. The scope of support includes; language, both modern and classical, literature, jurisprudence, philosophy, ancient, historical, and modern, archaeology, history (of Western Europe only) and sociology.
   7. Your comments should be specific, pointed, and candid, you should not hold back anything.

8. We need to create a new kind of academic community, one with a spirit of openness, the student must be able to find meaning, coherence, and significance behind the jumble of experiences he gets.

9. Many graduating students are scared to death. The job market hasn't been so tight since the 1930s.

10. The law library will be open from 8 A.M. to 1 A.M., now through December 21; from 8 A.M. to 6 P.M., from December 24 to January 4, and closed Christmas Day and New Year's Day.

11. To let him go unpunished was unthinkable, to punish him, unbearable.

12. In McKay's novel, *Home to Harlem,* Jake's character remains rather constant, however, his friend Ray undergoes a fairly substantial change.

13. Although the story was written in 1933; it shows few of the characteristic marks of the period's popular literature.

14. On the one hand, it is obvious that Mr. Bisko disagrees with the company policy, on the other hand, if he wants to keep his job, he has to put up with it.

15. Probably only 5 percent of the potential jobs for naval architects and marine engineers are actually held by people who are trained for them, in fact, probably 50 percent of these jobs are held by people who aren't college-educated or technically trained at all.

THE COLON

Use a Colon as a Green Light, or Arrow.

The semicolon, as we have seen, makes a full stop; the colon waves the traffic on through the intersection: "Go right ahead," it says, "and you will find what you are looking for." The colon is like one of those huge arrows that say HERE IT IS after you have been following the signs for half a continent. It emphatically and precisely introduces the clarifying detail, the illustrative example, the itemized series, the formal quotation:

> **Pierpont lived for only one thing: money.**
> **In the end, it was useless: Adams really was too green.**
> **Now he speaks in the romantic mode: "Hasten, O damsel"**
>   **(1.2.24).**
> **The Lord helps those who help themselves: Jasper helped himself.**
> **Several things were missing: the silver service, his gold watch, Beth's pearls, and the moonstone.**
> **The committee considered three things: (1) how to reduce expenditures, (2) how to raise more money, and (3) how to handle Smith's unfortunate laxity.**

The point is precisely this: no one can win.
He thought not only of home: he thought of grandmother's oat-
meal cookies.

Use the Colon to Introduce Quotations

You naturally introduce long quotations with a colon, indenting them and setting them apart from your own words. Do the same with short quotations within your running text when they need your sentence but are not part of its grammar:

We remember Sherman's words: "War is hell."

You may use a comma informally:

We remember Sherman's words, "War is hell."

When a quotation is an integral part of your sentence, punctuate as necessary, but do not use a colon:

As Sherman implied, "war is hell" for all concerned.
We remember, as Sherman said, that "war is hell."

Notice that here you do not capitalize "war," although you would capitalize in the most careful scholarly writing, to preserve exactly all the details of your quotation.

Do not use a colon immediately after a verb, a preposition, or the conjunction *that,* where it would break up grammatical connections:

WRONG:

The trouble was: he never listened.
The trouble was that: he never listened.
She liked the simple things, like: swimming pools, diamonds,
and unadorned mink.
She was fond of: swimming pools, diamonds, and unadorned
mink.

Do not capitalize after a colon, unless what follows is normally capitalized, as with a proper name, a quotation beginning with a capital, a title of a work, or, occasionally, a sequence of several sentences.

RIGHT:

> **All effort is painful: pleasure comes with achievement.**
> **Again we may say with Churchill: "Never have so many owed**
>   **so much to so few."**
> **But several major considerations remain: Unending leisure is**
>   **no blessing for the ordinary mortal. We must be occupied,**
>   **and yet we cannot forever occupy ourselves. Further-**
>   **more, . . .**

I still prefer a period after *remain,* since the colon tends to tie the first two sentences too closely.

EXERCISES

11. *Write five sentences using the colon to introduce a complete clarifying "sentence"—that is, write your sentence so that the colon is clearly more meaningful than a period and new capitalization would have been:*

    In the end, it was useless: he really was too green.
    The point is precisely this: no one can win.

12. *In the following selections, some colons are right, some wrong, some missing: correct all errors, including misused periods, commas, and semicolons.*

    1. The music is generally excellent; the tunes are quite good and the singing clear and bright.
    2. Ralph Ellison, describing in *Shadow and Act* how he switched his interest from music to literature says; "Writing provided me a growing satisfaction and required, unlike music, no formal study. . . ."
    3. There's only one thing we need right now—more time.
    4. Remote sensing devices exploit the following parts of the electromagnetic spectrum; infrared radiation, ultraviolet radiation, gamma rays, and microwaves.
    5. We're out here for one reason only, to work with Dr. Ravelli.
    6. The semicolon, as we have seen, makes a full stop; the colon waves the traffic on through the intersection, "Go right ahead," it says, "and you will find what you are looking for."
    7. For assistance call any of the following staff members, Mr. Beatty, 714-1425; Mr. Greenway, 714-2829; Mr. Brooks, 714-4432.
    8. A project may be given a national security classification to provide researchers access to classified information, to facilitate visiting classified activities, counseling, and participating in advisory functions; or to allow freer exchange of ideas.
    9. There's one thing you can say: the plot is timely.
    10. This attitude is caused by two things; first, students in a large university tend to think of themselves as being lost in the crowd: and, second, students tend to

view administrators—as administrators sometimes view themselves—as substitute parents.

THE PERIOD

The period affirms your sentence, and should not break it into fragments. It
ends a declaration and makes it independent. It concludes each thought you
complete with subject, verb, and other attachments, even when you only imply
both subject and verb, as in the fragmentary sentence *Of course.* Notice that
you may change your declarations to questions and exclamations merely by
switching from the declarative period to a question mark or exclamation point:
Of course? Of course!

Use a Period After an Indirect Question

The following are not really questions, but declarations of what the question
was; hence the period.

> **She asked me when I was going to finish college.**
> **I wonder if you could come tomorrow.**
> **He wanted to know how I found it and why I hadn't told him.**

Use a Period After a Polite Command or Request; Use Exclamations Sparingly

The exclamation point shouts a little, and the question mark can grow a little
shrill. My page would startle you had I written: "Use a period after a polite
command or request!" Similarly, the question mark may seem too insistent:
"Will you kindly remit?"

> **But be careful.**
> **Come when you can.**
> **Will you kindly give this matter your earliest attention.**

May the council please have your comments at your convenience.

For periods in abbreviations, see 429–30.

EXERCISES

13. *Write five sentences containing indirect questions, ending them properly with periods.*

14. *Some of the following sentences have correct periods; some run together without punctuation; some fumble the period in various ways. Insert the proper punctuation in the faulty sentences.*

    1. I have only a faint recollection of the place of my childhood at times, I can close my eyes and call up vague images, but most of the time I just can't remember.
    2. Sitting down in front of the TV set, I kicked off my shoes and loosened my belt, still, I felt very nervous and tense.
    3. Two of these packages are headed for Washington, D.C., the third is going to Baltimore.
    4. Please climb down you'll hurt yourself.
    5. The International Brigades, which were formed by Comintern to fight in Spain, were a combination of displaced and dissatisfied people from all over the world, many of the first to join were people forced by Fascist governments to leave Germany and Italy.
    6. During the Depression, Wright held a number of jobs he was a hospital orderly, a counselor in a boys club, a newspaper correspondent.
    7. In studying the similarities in the courtroom strategies of Boris Max and Clarence Darrow, one can also find parallels between the characters themselves, their lives, their attitudes.
    8. Thank you for your answers to my questionnaire I will be able to use much of your response in my report.
    9. The law school has reached an all-time high in applications. With 13 applicants for each of its 370 openings.
    10. About 1000 scientists from 25 foreign countries are expected to attend the workshop. Where 180 papers will be presented.
    11. In order to gain a full understanding of any book. One ought to know something of the life and intellectual background of its author.
    12. People seldom form their own judgment about politics they let others form it for them.
    13. Although the lawyer knew that his client was guilty. He defended him vigorously so that he could gain a reputation for victory, if not for justice.
    14. I awoke at midnight, my bones were aching and my back felt as if it were being pricked with electric needles.
    15. Like space, time is a natural organizer. Ancient. And simple.

PARENTHESIS AND DASH

The dash says aloud what the parenthesis whispers. Both enclose interruptions too extravagant for a pair of commas to hold. The dash is the more useful—since whispering tends to annoy—and will remain useful only if not overused. It can serve as a conversational colon. It can set off a concluding phrase—for emphasis. It can bring long introductory matters to focus, as in Freud's sentence on 170. It can insert a full sentence—a clause is really an incorporated sentence—directly next to a key word. The dash allows you to insert—with a kind of shout!—an occasional exclamation. You may even insert—and who would blame you?—an occasional question. The dash affords a structural complexity with all the tone and alacrity of talk.

With care, you can get much the same power from a parenthesis:

> **Many philosophers have despaired (somewhat unphilosophical-**
> **ly) of discovering any certainties whatsoever.**
>
> **Thus did Innocent III (we shall return to him shortly) inaugu-**
> **rate an age of horrors. [Note no period after** *shortly,* **and no**
> **capital for** *we.* **]**
>
> **General Douglas MacArthur ("We shall return") accomplished**
> **his prediction in October, 1944, when American forces in-**
> **vaded the Japanese-held Philippines. [An exception to the**
> **previous rule—with quotation marks, a capital, but no peri-**
> **od.]**
>
> **Thus did Innocent III inaugurate an age of horrors. (We shall**
> **return to him shortly.) [A full sentence in parenthesis posi-**
> **tioned thus for more emphasis takes a period, and a capital**
> **for the first word.]**
>
> **But in such circumstances (see 34), be cautious.**
>
> **Delay had doubled the costs (a stitch in time!), so the plans**
> **were shelved.**

Phrase

Sentence in
Sentence

Quoted Sentence in
Sentence

Parenthetical
Sentence After a
Sentence

Cross-Reference

Interjection

But dashes seem more generally useful, and here are some special points. When one of a pair of dashes falls where a comma would be, it absorbs the comma:

> **If one wanted to go, he certainly could.**
> **If one wanted to go—whether invited or not—he certainly**
> **could.**

Dashes

Not so with the semicolon:

> **He wanted to go—whether he was invited or not; she had more sense.**

To indicate the dash, type two hyphens (--) flush against the words they separate—not one hyphen between two spaces, nor a hyphen spaced to look exactly like a hyphen.

Full Sentence

Put commas and periods *outside* a parenthetical group of words (like this one). (But if you make an entire sentence parenthetical, put the period inside.)

Change has had its way with the parenthesis around numbers. Formal print and most guides to writing, including this one, still hold to the full parenthesis:

Numbered Items

> **The sentence really has only two general varieties: (1) the "loose," or strung-along, in Aristotle's phrase, and (2) the periodic.**
> **For a number of reasons, he decided (1) that he did not like it, (2) that she would not like it, and (3) that they would be better off without it.**

Popular print and secretarial fashion now omit the first half of the parenthesis:

> **. . . decided 1) that he did not like it, 2) that she. . . .**

But for your papers—keep the full parenthesis. Don't put a comma before or after a parenthesis, unless the normal phrasing would require it.

> **WRONG: Don't put a comma (or a semicolon), before or after. . . .**
> **RIGHT: Don't put a comma before or after a parenthesis (it doesn't make sense), unless the normal phrasing would require it.**

EXERCISES

15. *Write four sentences, two containing a phrase or clause within dashes, two containing a phrase or clause within parentheses. Try to make your sentences more elaborate than the following simple models—as different from them as possible, and more interesting.*

He wrote a sentence containing a phrase—he could have used a clause—inserted between dashes.
He wrote hastily (he pretended to concentrate) as the boss looked over his shoulder.

BRACKETS

Brackets indicate your own words inserted or substituted within a quotation from someone else: "Byron had already suggested that [they] had killed John Keats." You have substituted "they" for "the gentlemen of the *Quarterly Review*" to suit your own context. You do the same when you interpolate a word of explanation: "Byron had already suggested that the gentlemen of the *Quarterly Review* [especially Croker] had killed John Keats." *Do not use parentheses:* they mark the enclosed words—that is, the parenthesis itself—as part of the original quotation. Don't claim innocence because your typewriter lacks brackets. Just leave spaces and draw them in later, or type slant lines and tip them with pencil or with the underscore key:

In the example below, you are pointing out with a *sic* (Latin for "so" or "thus"), which you should not italicize, that you are reproducing an error exactly as it appears in the text you are quoting:

> **"On no occassion [sic] could we trust them."**

Similarly, you may give a correction after reproducing the error:

> **"On the twenty-fourth [twenty-third], we broke camp."**
> **"In not one instance [actually, Baldwin reports several instances] did our men run under fire."**

Use brackets when you need a parenthesis within a parenthesis:

> **(***see*** Donald Allenberg, *The Future of Television* [New York, 1973], 15–16)**

Your instructor will probably put brackets around the wordy parts of your sentences, indicating what you should cut:

> **In fact, [the reason] he liked it [was] because it was different.**

EXERCISES

16. *Straighten out errors in parentheses, dashes, and brackets in the following sentences.*

1. Many skiers, (hardly the best) have given up Big Bear run.
2. Several members of the expedition (We name no names.) refused to go on.

3. The paper reported (the *Pinkley Currier,* sic) that Otis had had twenty-one [21] drinks before leaving.
4. When the alarm rang,—it had been tested only once—it sounded like a distant teapot.
5. "The night before the duel, (Hamilton) wrote his wife that he did not intend to kill Burr."
6. "Our tuition is the lowest *(College Index* lists three institutions lower) in the state."
7. *(See* Alexis Winsome, *All That Matters* (New Haven: Escapist Press, 1981), 32).
8. "Many young couples find a condominia (sic) convenient."
9. Quirk ran the option—he got out of the pocket and still had time to throw, and Coffin was wide open, but he at least picked up four yards.
10. Although some researchers have proved marijuana relatively harmless, others (even admitting its medicinal value for some patients) are pointing to the carcinogenic effects of inhalation.

QUOTATION MARKS AND ITALICS

Put quotation marks around quotations that "run directly into your own sentence" (like this), but *not* around quotations set off from your text and indented. You normally inset poetry as it stands, centering it on your page, without quotation marks:

> **An aged man is but a paltry thing,**
> **A tattered coat upon a stick, unless**
> **Soul clap its hands and sing. . . .**

But if you run it into your text, use quotation marks, with *virgules* (slants) showing the line-ends: "An aged man is but a paltry thing,/A tattered coat. . . ." *(See* 287). Put periods and commas *inside* quotation marks; put semicolons and colons *outside:*

Quotation Marks with Other Punctuation

> **Now we understand the full meaning of "Give me liberty, or give me death."**
>
> **"This strange disease of modern life," in Arnold's words, remains uncured.**
>
> **In Greece, it was "know thyself "; in America, it is "know thy neighbor."**
>
> **He left after "Hail to the Chief ": he could do nothing more.**

Although logic often seems to demand the period or comma outside the quotation marks, convention has put them inside for the sake of appearance, even when the sentence ends in a single quoted word or letter:

Clara Bow was said to have "It."
Mark it with "T."

If you have seen the periods and commas outside, you were reading a British book or a freshman's paper (or some of America's little magazines).

If you are quoting a phrase that already contains quotation marks, reduce the original double marks (") to single ones('):

ORIGINAL	**YOUR QUOTATION**
Hamlet's "are you honest?" is easily explained.	**He writes: "Hamlet's *'are you honest?'* is easily explained."**

Single Quotation Marks Within Double Quotation Marks

Notice what happens when the quotation within your quotation falls at the end:

A majority of the informants thought *infer* meant "imply."	**Kirk reports that "a majority of the informants thought *infer* meant 'imply.' "**

And notice that a question mark or exclamation point falls between the single and the double quotation marks at the end of a quotation containing a quotation:

"Why do they call it 'the Hippocratic oath'?" she asked.
"Everything can't be 'cool'!" he said.

But heed the following exception:

"I heard someone say, 'Is anyone home?' " she declared.

Do not use *single* quotation marks for your own stylistic flourishes; use *double* quotation marks or, preferably, none:

It was indeed an "affair," but the passion was hardly "grand."
It was indeed an affair, but the passion was hardly grand.
Some "cool" pianists use the twelve-tone scale.

Once you have thus established this slang meaning of *cool,* you may repeat the word without quotation marks. In general, of course, you should favor that slang your style can absorb without quotation marks.

Do not use quotation marks for calling attention to words as words. Use italics (an underscore when typing) for the words, quotation marks for their meanings.

This is taking *tergiversation* too literally.
The word *struthious* means "like an ostrich."

Similarly, use italics for numbers as numbers and letters as letters:

He writes a *5* like an *s*.

Use quotation marks for titles *within* books and magazines: titles of chapters, articles, short stories, songs, and poems, and for unpublished works, lectures, courses, TV episodes within a series. But use italics for titles or names of books, newspapers, magazines, plays, films, long poems, sculptures, paintings, ships, trains, airplanes, and TV programs.

Poe's description of how he wrote "The Raven" was attacked in the *Atlantic Monthly* [or: the *Atlantic*].
We saw Michelangelo's *Pietà*, a remarkable statue in white marble.
We took the Santa Fe *Chief* from Chicago to Los Angeles.
He read all of Frazer's *The Golden Bough*.
His great-grandfather went down with the *Titanic*.
She read it in the *New York Times*.

Handle titles within titles as follows:

"The Prelude" and Nature in Wordsworth [book]
" 'The Prelude' and Natural Imagery" [article]
"The Art of *Tom Jones*" [article]
The Art of **Tom Jones** [book]

In the last example, notice that what is ordinarily italicized, like the title of a book (*Tom Jones*), is set in roman when the larger setting is in italics.

Italicize foreign words and phrases, unless they have been assimilated into English through usage (your dictionary should have a method for noting the distinction; if not, consult one that has):

The statement contained two clichés and one *non sequitur*.
The author of this naïve exposé suffers from an *idée fixe*.

Other foreign expressions *not* italicized are: etc., e.g., et al., genre, hubris, laissez faire, leitmotif, mimesis, roman à clef, raison d'être, tête-à-tête.

Use neither quotation marks nor italics for the Bible, for its books or parts (Genesis, Old Testament), for other sacred books (Koran, Talmud, Upanishad), nor for famous documents like the Magna Carta, the Declaration of Independence, the Communist Manifesto, and the Gettysburg Address, nor for instrumental music known by its form, number, and key:

Beethoven's C-minor Quartet
Brahms's Symphony No. 4, Opus 98

When a reference in parentheses falls at the end of a quotation, the quotation marks *precede* the first parenthesis:

> **As Ecclesiastes tells us, "there is no new thing under the sun"**
>   **(i.9).**

ELLIPSIS

1. Use three spaced periods . . . (the ellipsis mark) when you omit something from a quotation. Do *not* use them in your own text in place of a dash, or in mere insouciance.
2. If you omit the end of a sentence, put in a period (no space) and add the three spaced dots. . . .
3. If your omission falls after a completed sentence, just add the three spaced dots to the period already there. . . . The spacing is the same as for case 2.

Here is an uncut passage, followed by a shortened version illustrating the three kinds of ellipsis (the numbers refer to the foregoing rules):

> **To learn a language, learn as thoroughly as possible a few everyday sentences. This will educate your ear for all future pronunciations. It will give you a fundamental grasp of structure. And start soon.**

> **(1)**
> **To learn a language, learn . . . a few everyday sentences. This**
>   **(2)**
> **will educate your ear. . . . It will give you a fundamental grasp**
>   **(3)**
> **of structure. . . .**

The three spaced dots of the ellipsis may fall on either side of other punctuation, to indicate exactly where you have omitted something from the text you are quoting:

With Other
Punctuation

In many instances . . . , our careful words are superfluous.
In many instances of human crisis, . . . words are superfluous.
We have the bombs . . . ; it looks as if they have the troops.
**Eighteenth-century prisons were vicious: . . . the people no less
than the rats and the fevers.**
Alas, poor Yorick! . . . a fellow of infinite jest.
**In this sonnet, Shakespeare is well aware of the foolishness of
self-pity: "And trouble deaf heaven with my bootless
cries,/ . . . and curse my fate. . . ."**

If you have no compelling reason to show the other punctuation, then you may
drop it, retaining the ellipsis only: "We have the bombs . . . it looks as if they
have the troops."

If you omit a line or more of poetry, or a paragraph or more of prose,
and *if the omission is significant,* use a whole line of elliptical dots:

In Poetry

When in disgrace with Fortune and men's eyes,
I all alone beweep my outcast state,
And trouble deaf heaven with my bootless cries,
· ·
Yet in these thoughts myself almost despising,
Haply I think on thee. . . .

If the omission had not been significant, the ellipsis would have followed *cries:*

And trouble deaf heaven with my bootless cries. . . .
Yet in these thoughts. . . .

Be sure that your omissions do not distort your author's meaning. And
remember this: *the shorter your quotation, the better.* A short quotation puts your
purpose into sharpest focus for your reader's attention. A long quotation may
require you to requote or paraphrase to make your point.

If you begin to quote in the middle of a sentence, place three elliptical
dots before the first quoted word:

Mid-Sentence

. . . learn as thoroughly as possible a few everyday sentences.
This will educate your ear for all future pronunciations. It will
give you a fundamental grasp of structure. . . .

But if you quote a full sentence that falls in the middle of a paragraph, omit
the initial elliptical dots:

Mid-Paragraph

> We have come to dedicate a portion of that field as a final rest-
> ing place for those who here gave their lives that that nation
> might live. It is altogether fitting and proper that we should do
> this.
>
> But, in a larger sense. . . .

When you use a short partial quotation within a sentence, you can omit
the beginning and ending ellipses:

> Lincoln was determined that the "brave men . . . who strug-
> gled here" should be redeemed by a strengthened nation.

In Quotations Only

Use the ellipsis in quoted material only. If you use it in your own text, you
will seem to drift, which is precisely what it means in a novel: the passage of
time, or the drifting of thought. Only most rarely can you work it into expository prose. It is dramatic, and risky. You risk seeming affected. I have used
it only once in this entire book (23), and I do not recall ever having used it
before. You put an ellipsis after your last word to stress the drift:

> Even the dog-lovers will be uninterested, convinced they
> know better than you. But the cat . . .

As I threw the cat in after the dogs to emphasize a point already made, the
ellipsis seemed right. But the exception does not overturn the rule: use ellipsis
marks in quoted material only.

EXERCISES

17. *Repair the following sentences with the necessary quotation marks, italics (underlining to indicate italics), and ellipses.*

   1. Like the farmer in Frost's Mending Wall, some people believe that Good fences
      make good neighbors.
   2. Germaine Greer's The Female Eunuch is a book to be remembered, especially
      in phrases like I'm sick of peering at the world through false eyelashes and I'm
      a woman, not a castrate.
   3. "The swimming pool. . . . desperately needs draining and resurfacing . . ."
   4. Some groovy singers seem stuck in one groove.
   5. Cleopatra's Husband, I come! seems out of character.
   6. Butterfield finds that Cleopatra's Husband, I come! seems out of character.
   7. The committee of twelve . . . was a total failure.
   8. The San Francisco Chronicle called it a goof.
   9. For him, the most important letter is I.

10. . . . In the evening, in the morning, at noon . . . and at 4 P.M. . . . they check the valves.
11. Their favorite books were Huckleberry Finn, the Bible, especially Ecclesiastes, and Henry David Thoreau's Walden.
12. Why does the raven keep crying Nevermore! he asked.
13. She hated what she called excess baggage; she loved the world from A to Z.
14. . . . yet the mains keep bursting, because they are half a century old. . . .
15. Here see means understand.

Spelling, Abbreviations, Numbers, Capitalization

Now for the needlepoint. Letter by letter, we stitch our words, and most of us have trouble with the lettering, and with questions of punctuating those words with apostrophes, hyphens, capital letters, and other small but meaningful pointings. As always, the details count, either impressing your reader with your mastery, or putting a beginner's sampler on exhibit. So get the stitches down, and don't let them get you down.

SPELLING IT OUT

You can conquer your troubles with spelling more easily than you think—once you put your mind to it. The dictionary is your best friend as you face the inevitable anxieties of spelling, but three underlying principles and some tricks of the trade can help immeasurably:

PRINCIPLE 1.   Letters represent sounds: proNUNciation can help you spell. No one proNOUNcing his words correctly would make the familiar errors of "similiar" and "enviorment." You can even improve your social standing by learning to say *envIRONment* and *goverNment* and *FebRUary* and *intRAmural.* Simply sound out the letters. Of course, you will need to be wary of some words *not* pronounced as spelled: *Wednesday,* pronounced "Wensdee," for instance. But sounding the letters can help your spellings. You can even say "convert*i*ble" and "indel*i*ble" and "plaus*i*ble" without sounding like a fool, and you can silently stress the *able* in words like "prob*able*" and "immov*able*" to remember the difficult distinction between words ending in *-ible,* and *-able.*

Consonants   Consonants reliably represent their sounds. Remember that *c* and *g* go soft before *i* and *e.* Consequently you must add a *k* when extending words like *picnic* and *mimic—picnicKing, mimicKing—*to keep them from rhyming with *slicing* or *dicing.* Conversely, you just keep the *e* (where you would normally drop it) when making *peace* into *peacEable* and *change* into *changEable,* to keep the *c* and *g* soft—otherwise they would sound like *peekable* and *hangable.*

Single *s* is pronounced *zh* in words like *vision, occasion, pleasure.* Knowing that *ss* hushes ("sh-h-h") will keep you from errors like *occassion,* which would sound like *passion.*

Vowels   Vowels sound short and light before single consonants: *hat, pet, kit, hop, cup.* When you add any vowel (including *y*) the first vowel will say its name: *hate, Pete, kite, hoping, cupid.* Notice how the *a* in *-able* keeps the main vowel saying its name in words like *unmistakable, likable,* and *notable.* Therefore, to keep a vowel short, protect it with a double consonant: *petting, hopping.* This explains the troublesome *rr* in *occuRRence:* a single *r* would make it say *cure* in the middle. *Putting* a golf ball and *putting* something on paper must both use *tt* to keep from being pronounced *pewting.* Compare *stony* with *sonny* and *bony* with *bonny.* The *y* is replacing the *e* in *stone* and *bone,* and the rule is working perfectly. It works in any syllable that is accented: compare *forgeTTable* as against *markeTable, begiNNing* as against *buttoNing,* and *compeLLing* as against *traveLing.*

Likewise, when *full* combines and loses its stress, it also loses an *l.* Note the single and double *l* in *fulFILLment.* Similarly, *sOULful, GRATEful, AWful—*even *spOONful.*

i Before e   **PRINCIPLE 2.**   This is the old rule of *i* before *e,* and its famous exceptions:

> *I* before *e*
> **Except after *c*,**
> **Or when sounded like *a***
> **As in** *neighbor* **and** *weigh.*

Memorize it, and use it to check your uncertainties. It works like a charm (*achieve, believe, receive, conceive*). Note that *c* needs an *e* to make it sound like *s.* Remember also that *leisure* was once pronounced "lay-sure," and *foreign,* "forayn." Memorize these exceptions: *protein, seize, weird, either, sheik, forfeit, counterfeit.* Note that all are pronounced "ee" (with a little crowding) and that the *e* comes first. Then note that another small group goes the opposite way, having a long *i* sound as in German "Heil": *height, sleight, seismograph, kaleidoscope. Financier,* another exception, follows its French origin with a hint of its original sound.

PRINCIPLE 3.   Most big words, following the Latin or French from which they came, spell their sounds letter for letter. Look up the derivations of the words you misspell (note that double *s,* and explain it). You will never again have trouble with *desperate* and *separate* once you discover that the first comes from *de-spero,* "without hope," and that *sePARate* divides equals, the PAR values in stocks or golf. Nor with *definite* or *definitive,* once you see the kinship of both with *finite* and *finish.* Derivations can also help you a little with the devilment of *-able* and *-ible,* since, except for a few ringers, the *i* remains from Latin, and the *-ables* are either French *(ami-able)* or Anglo-Saxon copies *(workable).* Knowing origins can help at crucial points: *resemblAnce* comes from Latin *simulAre,* "to copy"; *existEnce* comes from Latin *existEre,* "to stand forth."

The biggest help comes from learning the common Latin prefixes, which, by a process of assimilation *(ad-similis,* "like to like"), account for the double consonants at the first syLLabic joint of so many of our words:

AD- (toward, to): *abbreviate* (shorten down), *accept* (grasp to).
CON- (with): *collapse* (fall with), *commit* (send with).
DIS- (apart): *dissect* (cut apart), *dissolve* (loosen apart).
IN- (into): *illuminate* (shine into), *illusion* (playing into).
IN- (not): *illegal* (not lawful), *immature* (not ripe).
INTER- (between): *interrupt* (break between), *interrogate* (ask between).
OB- (toward, to): *occupy* (take in), *oppose* (put to), *offer* (carry to).
SUB- (under): *suffer* (bear under), *suppose* (put down).
SYN- ("together"—this one is Greek): *symmetry* (measuring together), *syllogism* (logic together).

Spelling takes a will, an eye, and an ear. And a dictionary. Keep a list of your favorite enemies. Memorize one or two a day. Write them in the air in longhand. Visualize them. Imagine a blinking neon sign, with the wicked letters red and tall—d e f i n I t e—d e f i n I t e. Then print them once, write them twice, and blink them a few times more as you go to sleep. But best of all, make up whatever devices you can—the crazier the better—to remember the tricky parts:

DANCE attenDANCE.

EXISTENCE is TENSE.

There's IRON in this enviRONment.

The resistANCE took its STANCE.

There's an ANT on the defendANT.

LOOSE as a goose.

LOSE loses an O.

ALLOT isn't A LOT.

ALready isn't ALL RIGHT.

I for gaIety.

The LL in paraLLel gives me *el.*

PURr in PURsuit.

When an unaccented syllable leads to misspelling, you can also get some help by trying to remember a version of the word that accents the troublesome syllable:

acad*e*my—acaDEMic	irrita ble—irriTATE
affirma tive—affirMAtion	labo ratory—laBORious
ange l—anGELic	libera l—libeRATE
apolo gy—apoLOGia	magne t—magNETic
compa rable—comPARE	medi cine—meDIcinal
compe tition—comPETE	melo dy—meLOdious
defini tely—defiNItion	persona l—personALity
degra dation—deGRADE	prepa ration—prePARE
democra cy—demoCRAT	preva lent—preVAIL
de spair—DESperate	repe tition—rePEAT
dormi tory—dorMIR	reser voir—reSERve
extravag ant—extravaGANza	reside nce—resiDENtial
fanta sy—fanTAStic	resto ration—reSTORE
ferti le—ferTILity	ridi cule—riDIculous
hypocri sy—hypoCRItical	Sabba th—sabBATical
imagina tive—imagiNAtion	vigila nce—vigiLANtes

Here are most of the perpetual headaches:*

- **accept, except**—you *accept* criticism, *except* from busybodies.
  accommodate—frequently misspelled *accomodate*.
  acknowledgment, judgment—don't add an extra *e;* that's British.
- **adverse, averse**—you are *averse* to *adversity*.
- **advice, advise**—you give *advice* when you *advise*.
  adviser, advisor—used interchangeably, with *adviser* preferred.
- **affect, effect**—you *affect* a British accent, and the *effect* is ridiculous.
- **allusion, illusion, disillusion, delusion**—an *allusion* refers to something; an *illusion* is unreal; *delusion* is a deception. *Disallusion* is the usual error.
  analysis, analyzing, annual—watch the *n*'s and that *z.*
  apologize—frequently misspelled *apollogize, appologize;* forget Apollo.
  argument—frequently misspelled *arguement.*
  athlete, athletics—often misspelled *athelete, atheletics. Athletics* is singular.

  balance—frequently misspelled *ballance:* think of that *l* balancing an *a* on each side.
  balloon—frequently misspelled *baloon:* it's like a *ball.*

---

*The entries marked by · indicate confusion in meaning as well as spelling, and are treated more fully in the "Glossary of Usage and Common Errors," 490–540.

beginning—frequently misspelled *begining,* which would rhyme with *shining.*

- **beside, besides**—"by the side of" often confused with "in addition to." **businessman, businesswoman**—frequently misspelled *businesman, busineswoman.*

- **capital, capitol**—every *capital* is *-al,* except those buildings in which Congress and your state legislature sit.
careful—frequently misspelled *carefull,* and even *carfull.*
challenge—frequently misspelled *challange.* Remember *revenge.*
- **cite, site, sight**—you *cite* an authority and build a house on a *site.*
committee—frequently misspelled *commitee* or *comittee.* Think of double *m*'s and *t*'s. Perhaps thinking *double m-t empty* will help.
- **complement, compliment**—*complement* completes; *compliment* flatters.
- **council, counsel, consul**—a *council* governs as a group; a *counsel* advises as a person, as a *counselor;* a *consul* is a foreign diplomat.
- **credible, creditable, credulous**—*credible* is believable; *creditable,* deserving esteem; *credulous,* believing too easily.
curriculum, career—watch the *r*'s.

dealt—often misspelled as it sounds: *delt.* Remember *deal.*
decide, divide, devices—watch the *i*'s and *e*'s.
defendant—frequently misspelled *defendent.* A person is usually an *ant.*
defies, deifies—*defies* stands up against; *deifies* turns something into a god.
definite—frequently misspelled *definate.* Remember *finIte, finIsh, infinIty.*
- **desert, dessert**—the first is sand; the second, ice cream.
despair—often misspelled *dispair,* or *despare.*
desperate, separate—one of the most common tangles in spelling. Remember what *desperate* means at the root: *de* (without)-*sperare* (hope). For *separate,* usually misspelled *seperate* on the pattern of *desperate,* remember the *par,* or equal, in golf. You sePARate equals.
detrimental—frequently misspelled *detramental.*
- **dilemma, condemn**—*dilemma* frequently, and wrongly, takes on the ending of *condemn: dilemna.* A *lemma* is a proposition; a *dilemma,* a double one.
disastrous—frequently misspelled *disasterous,* after *disaster.*
discrete, discreet—*discrete* is separate; *discreet,* diplomatic.
disillusion—not *disallusion.* See *allusion.*
dissatisfied—frequently misspelled *disatisfied.* Think of *satisfied* and *dis-satisfied.*
dissolve—not *disolve,* but *dis-solve,* "to loosen apart."
divide—not *devide.* Remember the Latin *dis,* and *di,* for "apart."

embarrassment—commonly misspelled by forgetting one of the *r*'s or *s*'s. Spelling it em*baras*ment is an *embarrassment.*
- **eminent, imminent, immanent**—*eminent* is prominent; *imminent* is soon forthcoming; *immanent* is indwelling.
environment—remember the *iron;* forget the *vior.*
exaggerate—frequently misspelled *exagerate.*
- **exalt, exult**—*exalt* is to raise; *exult* is to rejoice or gloat.
existence—often misspelled *existance* or *existense.*
explanation—*explain* often induces the misspelling *explaination.*

- **faze, phase**—watch the *s* and the *z.* His adolescent *phase* didn't *faze* him.
- **forward, foreword**—*forward* is a direction; *foreword* is a "word before," a preface.
fulfill, fulfillment—often misspelled *fullfil, fullfilment,* or with double *ll*'s all around.

genius, ingenious—*genius* is supreme talent; *ingenious* is inventive.
harassment—often misspelled *harrasment.*
height—frequently misspelled *heighth.* Think of *eight.*
hypocrisy—frequently misspelled *hypocracy,* like *democracy.* Remember *hypocrIte, hypocrItical.*

- **indite, indict**—to *indite* is to write; to *indict* is to charge with a crime.
- **inequity, iniquity**—an *inequity* is an unfairness; an *iniquity* is a sin.
irritable—not *iritable,* nor *irritible.* Remember *irritATE.*

lead, led—*led* is often misspelled *lead,* after the *lead* in pencils and pipes.
libel, liable—*libel* defames character; *liable* means likely, or obligated.
lonely, loneliness—often misspelled *lonly, lonliness,* which would sound like a *lawn.* Remember *alone* and *loner.*
- **loose, lose**—with a *loose* grip, you *lose* the ball.

- **mislead**—mistaking the *lead* in *lead pencil,* you probably mean *misled:* led astray. To *mislead* is to *lead* astray.
misspell—frequently misspelled *mispell.* Think of the meaning: *misspell.*

Negroes, heroes, tomatoes—remember the *e.*

obstacle—frequently misspelled *obsticle.*
occurred, occurring—frequently misspelled by omitting the second *r,* which you need to keep the *u*-syllable from sounding like *cure,* or *your.*
operate (opus, opera)—frequently misspelled *opperate.* Think of *opera.*

possession—frequently misspelled *posession* or *possesion.*

- **predominate, predominant**—to *predominate* is to dominate outstandingly; *predominant* is an adjective: "His *predominant* feature was his nose."
- **prejudiced**—not *prejudice,* as in "He was *prejudice*": you want the past participle, *prejudiced.*

primitive—often misspelled *primative.* That a primate is either an ape or a bishop confuses the issue a bit, since both *primitive* and *primate* derive from Latin *primus,* "first."

- **principal, principle**—the first heads a school; the second is a natural or moral law. Think of *pal* for the person.
- **proceed, precede, procedure**—the *e*'s are tricky.

pronunciation—frequently misspelled *proNOUNciation,* after *pronounce.* Remember *eNUNciation,* how one speaks his words.

pursue—frequently misspelled *persue,* aided by the idea of "through" in *per.* Remember *PURr* in *PURsuit.*

questionnaire—misspelled *questionaire.* Its French form, complete with two *nn*'s and an *e,* shows that it is a recent borrowing.

renown—frequently misspelled *reknown* or *renoun.* Remind yourself that you do not mean "to be *known again*" nor "to replace *nouns.*"

resistance—frequently misspelled *resistence,* on the pattern of *existence.* Remember, take a STANCE for resiSTANCE.

separate—frequently misspelled *seperate.* Remember PAR, and the idea of sepARating equals. See *desperate.*

similar—frequently misspelled *similiar,* on the pattern of *familiar.* Avoid the LIAR.

successful—frequently misspelled *sucessful.* Pronounce it.

suppressed—often misspelled *supressed.*

there's, theirs—the contraction of *there is* is very often misused for the possessive pronoun, *theirs,* which never takes an apostrophe (see 421).

till, until—watch the *l*'s. Both words are acceptable, but avoid *'til.*

truly—frequently misspelled *truely.*

unnoticed—frequently misspelled *unoticed.* Remember *un-noticed.*

EXERCISES

1. *To help you identify your likely errors, here are some sentences with a number of commonly misspelled words. Correct each misspelling you find. Then list the five words that give you the most trouble.*

1. Marriage seems to be loosing some of it's traditional signifigance as the devorce rate continues to climb and common-law relationships multiply.
2. Writting is neccessary in almost any proffession.
3. Many women feel there achievements go unrecognized.
4. Offering an explaination is uneccessary unless the personal director asks for one.
5. Certainly one of the most contraversial issues to come along in years, abortion reform has sparked heated arguements in most churches.
6. The proffessor said he would reccomend at least three possable sources.
7. I value your opinion, but your mistaken in principal.
8. He had a good sence of rythm but a terrible ear for pitch.
9. The preformance last night was embarassing, a suprise consideerring the ammount of rehersal time the actors had.
10. Environmental deterioration is probobly the single most disasterous consequence of overcrowding.
11. The wittness was able to supply a good discription.
12. Ammong the words on this page, your likely to find at least a few you commonly mispell.
13. There is really no point in studing the definations of words unless at the same time you make an effort to incorperate them into your speech.
14. Students who have transfered from other schools will recieve credit only for those courses in which their grades were above C.
15. The audiance wasn't conscience that anything unusual had occured, but during the third act the leading man broke his collarbone when he was topled back over the couch in the fight scene.
16. The principle reason for the written examinition is that it allows us to spot canidates who's work isn't likely to meet company standards.
17. The city counsel studied each of the items on the agenda seperately and in it's proper sequence.
18. George gets embarrassed whenever anyone pays him a complement.
19. The committee voted to except the treasurer's annual report, but decided to delay any final judgement on the new buget till after all the members had time to anilize the implications of the previous year's figures.
20. The sucessful businessman usually combines aggressiveness with caution; he is willing to take risks but carefull to minimize those risks as much as possible.
21. There's no point in exagerating the significants of Saturday's loss.
22. Heros are often apologetic about their accomplishments.
23. The curriculum has changed remarkably during the passed twenty years.
24. He may be ingenius, but he's certainly no genius.
25. To divide is to separate.
26. One of the curious side-affects of long contact with DDT seems to be an increased resistance to cancer.
27. Primative versions of the television receiver had tiny screens, barely four inches accross.
28. Children often become irratable in the late afternoon.
29. The acknoledgements and the forward precede the table of contents.
30. The Secretery sited the current drop in interest rates as an encouraging sign.

APOSTROPHE

It's may be overwhelmingly our most frequent misspelling as in "The dog scratched *it's* ear." No, no! *It's* means *it is. Who's* means *who is.* NO pronoun spells *its* possessive with an apostrophe: *hers, its, ours, theirs, yours, whose, oneself* (but *one's self,* if you are emphasizing the self).

For all other words, however, we do add aspostrophe-*s* to spell the singular possessive:

dog's life	**man's world**
hour's work	**day's end**
horse's mouth	**Marx's ideas**

Even to words already ending in *s:*

Yeats's poems	**Charles's crown**
Leavis's error	**Moses's law**
Pericles's Athens	**Vassilikos's work**

The same is preferred for French names ending in silent *s*-sounds:

Camus's works	**Marivaux's plays**
Delacroix's friends	**Berlioz's Requiem**

A few plurals also form the possessive by adding *'s:*

children's hour	**people's attitudes**
women's rights	**mice's feet**
sheep's bellwether	**fish's habits**

But most plurals take the apostrophe after the *s* (or *s*-sound) already there:

witches' sabbath	**ten cents' worth**
citizens' rights	**the Joneses' possessions**
The Beaux' Stratagem	**doctors' fees**

I repeat, the best rule for making singulars possessive is to add *'s,* regardless of length and previous ending, though many people and some authorities merely add the apostrophe to names of several syllables already ending in *s* (*Dickens' novels, Adams' horse*). And certainly there is colloquial and auditory cause for so handling the longest names, as with *Themistocles' death* and *Aristophanes' wit.*

But Sis' plans and the boss' daughter are not what we say. We say *Sissuz*   Singular Ending in *s* and *bossuz* and *Keatsuz,* and should say the same in our writing: Sis's, boss's, Keats's. Even with long words, I find the added *s* an improvement in euphony as well as in sense: Themistocleses DEATH, Aristophaneses WIT. The same is true for Horace's satires, Catullus's villa, Cummings's style, Dickens's Pip. The extra *s* makes no mistake, and you may prefer to distinguish Dickens from Dicken and Adams from Adam. If your page grows too thick with double *s*'s, substitute a few pronouns for the proper names, or rephrase: *the death of Themistocles, the Dickens character, Pip.*

String of Nouns   The apostrophe can help to clarify clusters of nouns, which are actually misspellings that have followed casual pronunciation. These I have actually seen: Alistair Jones Renown Combo, the church barbecue chicken sale, the uniform policeman training program, the members charter plane, and of course, teachers meeting and veterans insurance are spellings so common as to seem almost normal. But an apostrophe chips one more noun out of the block. It makes your meaning one word clearer, marking *teachers'* as a modifier, and distinguishing *teacher* from *teachers.* Inflections are helpful, and the written word needs all the help it can get: Jones's Renowned, church's barbecued, uniformed policeman's, members' chartered. Distinguish your modifiers, and keep your possessions.

Don't forget the *'s* in the possessive before a gerund:

She objected to Bill's smoking. [not *Bill smoking*]
The teacher's leaving upset our plans. [not *teacher leaving*]
He didn't like anyone's working overtime. [not *anyone working*]

Your *'s* makes clear that she is not objecting to Bill and that "He" is not disliking anyone: the smoking and the working are being disliked.

Compounds   Compound words take the *'s* on the last word only, mother-in-law's hat, the brothers-in-law's attitude (all the brothers-in-law have the same attitude), somebody else's problem, Governor Cass of Michigan's proposal. Joint ownerships may similarly take the *'s* only on the last word (Bill and Mary's house), but Bill's and Mary's house is more precise and preferable.

Double Possessive   The double possessive uses both an *of* and an *'s:* a friend of my mother's, a book of the teacher's, a son of the Joneses', an old hat of Mary's. Note that the double possessive indicates one possession among several of the same kind: mother has several friends; the teacher, several books. Note, further in the Joneses' example, that the apostrophe falls *before* the comma, instead of after as a single or double quotation mark would.

Omissions   Use the apostrophe to indicate omissions: the Spirit of '76, the Class of '02, can't, won't, don't.

Grammatical Endings   Finally, the apostrophe serves as a grammatical ending to a number, letter, sign, a word as word, or an abbreviation: 1920's; his 3's look like 8's; p's and q's; he got four A's; too many of's and and's; she X'd each box; K.O.'d in the first round. Contemporary usage now omits the apostrophe in some of these: 1920s, *8*s, two *t*s. Don't use an apostrophe when writing out a number: *the thirties.*

Be wary of the common mistake of writing *families* for *family's* and *societies* for *society's.*

EXERCISES

2. *Think up, or collect from observation, five strings of nouns an apostrophe -s (and perhaps an -ed) would help clarify; then clarify each string:*

the church barbecue chicken sale
the church's barbecued chicken sale
[They were not cooking the church.]

the sophomore cheesecake rally
the sophomores' cheesecake rally
[The cheesecake was no sophomore.]

3. *To strengthen your perception of the possessive before a gerund, write five pairs of sentences on the following pattern, explaining after each pair the difference in meaning:*

He didn't like anyone working overtime.
He didn't like anyone's working overtime.

4. *Handle the question of apostrophes and possessives in the following sentences.*

1. He is indignant about his students asking her advice.
2. She went to the governors convention. Its the place where state government gets it's chance to be heard.
3. Aiken objected to them leaving early, no matter who's work was finished.
4. They wont support Converse bid for nomination, even if she keeps running until 88.
5. The teachers lounge is a slum, with everything at 6s and 7s.
6. They Xd him from the list at Lois and Matthews apartment.
7. A friend of her brothers cant keep from prying into everybody else problems.
8. The President of the United States proposal carries some weight with Lewis supporters and Malraux enemies.
9. They stayed at Bates' house and met his boss' wife.
10. Some sponsor of their's complained of him appearing on the program, since it's purpose is educational.

HYPHEN

"Time abhors the hyphen," someone once said, and, ever since James Joyce's *hoofirons* and *steelyringing,* modern print has tended to compound the work of time, and *Time,* by squeezing the hyphens out of compounds. But the unfamiliar compound is hard on the eye, and the hyphens come back in—until another burst of editorial housekeeping.

The oldest and most useful compounds have coalesced from two words, first through hyphenation, then into one solid compound. *Housekeeping,* with the *housekeeper,* has scrubbed out the hyphen entirely. But many very common compounds live happily separated: *horse racing, Adam's apple, all right, blood pressure, stock market, girl friend.* And many very common compounds go steadily hyphenated, and go no farther: *blue-pencil* (verb), *clear-cut, deep-freeze, good-bye, mother-in-law.* Check your dictionary.

But one rule remains solid: hyphenate two or more words serving together as an adjective. Unhyphenated words acquire hyphens when moved to an adjectival position:

Compound Adjectives

She teaches in high school.
She is a high-school teacher.

He was sick of olive drab.
He was sick of his olive-drab uniform.

He was well known.
He was a well-known drifter.

His serve is red hot.
He has a red-hot serve.

It was never to be forgotten.
It was a never-to-be-forgotten gesture.

Some attitudes from the eighteenth century puzzle us.
Some eighteenth-century attitudes puzzle us.

Southern crocus blooms early, cheering us at winter's close.
Early-blooming southern crocus cheers us at winter's close.

You will have to check the hyphenation of prefixes and suffixes in your dictionary, but you can be sure of hyphenating prefixes to proper names:

Prefixes to Proper Names

anti-Semitism   trans-Russian
post-Crimean War   un-American

Similarly, hyphenate suffixes to single capital initials:

Suffixes to Capitals

F-sharp   **U-turn**

I-beam   **V-neck**

T-shirt   **X-ray**

Hyphenate *ex-*, meaning former, and *self-* (except *selfhood, selfish, selfless,* and *self-same* where *self* is the root):

Ex- Self-

ex-champion   **self-reliance**

ex-president   **self-respect**

Hyphenate to distinguish meanings:

For Meaning

co-op from coop   **re-collect from recollect**

re-cover from recover   **re-creation from recreation**

Hyphenate to avoid doubling *i*'s and tripling consonants:

Double *i*; Triple Consonants

anti-intellectual   **bell-like**

semi-invalid   **wall-less**

Hyphenate compound words expressing numbers:

Numbers

twenty-one   **three-fourths**

ninety-nine   **one ten-thousandth**

three hundred twenty-four   **twenty-one forty-fourths**

Use the "suspensive," or hanging, hyphen for hyphenated words in series:

In Series

We have ten-, twenty-five-, and fifty-pound sizes.

He still prefers the six- to the eight-cylinder model.

Or, with only two items, you can avoid the truncated look by using a few more words:

He still prefers the six-cylinder model to the eight-cylinder one.

When you must break a word at the end of a line, put your hyphen where your dictionary marks the syllables with a dot: *syl · lables, syl-lables.* If you must break a hyphenated word, break it after the hyphen: *self-/sufficient.* Don't hyphenate an already hyphenated word: *self-suf-/ficient.* It's hard on the eyes and the printer. When you write for print, underline those line-end hyphens you mean to keep as hyphens, making a little equals sign: self = / sufficient.

Hyphenate those slants that are popping up all over: not "psychic/social complex" but "psychic-social complex." See "Virgule" (below).

EXERCISES

5. *Write five pairs of sentences to show your control of the hyphen:*

She teaches in high school.
She is a high-school teacher.

It was never to be forgotten.
It was a never-to-be-forgotten gesture.

VIRGULE

Don't use the virgule, or slant-mark, for a hyphen: not "male/female conflict" but "male-female conflict." Spare this "little rod" (/), and don't spoil your work with the legalistic *and/or.* Don't write "bacon and/or eggs"; write "bacon or eggs, or both." Use the virgule to mark where a line ends when quoting poetry in your running text: "That time of year thou mayst in me behold/When yellow leaves. . . ."

DIACRITICAL MARKS

Many foreign words, though very common in English, retain their native markings, as in *naïveté.* Diacritical marks occasionally appear in spelling native words, as when a writer wishes to distinguish *the learnèd man* from what he has learned. (For italicizing foreign words, see 408.) Here are some specifics:

DIERESIS   (coöperation, coördinate, naïve, Chloë, Danaë). Let your dictionary be your guide. Newspapers tend to omit the dieresis, and some very common doubles go unmarked in the most meticulous print, as with *coordination* in this
ö, ü   book, and with *cooperation* and *zoology.* But coördination, coöperation, and zoölogy are perfectly acceptable. You also use the dieresis to indicate the umlaut in German words: über, Fräulein, Götterdämmerung.

ACUTE ACCENT. For spelling certain words borrowed from French. The *é* sounds like the *a* in *hay:*

attaché	fiancé, fiancée	é
blasé	habitué	
café	naïveté	
cliché	outré	
communiqué	passé	
décor	précis	
décolleté	protége, protégée	
éclat	résumé	
exposé	séance	

GRAVE ACCENT. For words from French. The *à* sounds like *a* in *ah;* the *è* like the *e* in *bet.*

à la carte	mise en scène	à; è
à la mode	Molière	
crème de la crème	pièce de résistance	

CIRCUMFLEX ACCENT. Also for words from French. The *â* sounds like *ah;* the *ê* like the *e* in *bet;* the *ô*, like the *o* in *holes:*

bête noire	raison d'être	ê; ô
coup de grâce	table d'hôte	
papier-mâché	tête-à-tête	

CEDILLA. For words from French, the *ç* being pronounced *s:*

aperçu	garçon	ç
façade	Provençal	
français	soupçon	

TILDE. For Spanish words pronouncing *n* like the *ny* in *canyon:*

doña, mañana, señor, vicuña.	ñ

Spelling foreign names requires their native diacritical markings: *Müller, Gödel, Göttingen, Poincaré, Brontë, García Lorca, Havlícek.* As always, your dictionary is your best guide, as it is, indeed, to all words transliterated to English from different alphabets and systems of writing (Russian, Arabic, Chinese, Japanese, and so on). French or Dutch *de* is included in monosyllabic surnames —*de Gaulle, De Vries*—with names beginning with a vowel—*D'Arblay*—and with others established by custom—*De Valera, de Soto.* But some names like Madeleine *de Scudéry* become *Scudéry* in last-name references.

NUMBERS

Spelling

In general, spell out numbers that take no more than two words: two, twelve, thirty-one dollars, one hundred, five hundred *percent,* forty thousand, six billion—forty-foot *sub tender,* three *feet of water.* You also spell out numbers with fractions: sixty-three and two-thirds. Use numerals for the rest: 101; 1976; 200,000. When a two-word number, like five hundred, for example, contrasts with a numeral, make them both numerals: Even with a short assignment of 500 words, you still have 490 to go.

Comparisons

Similarly, use numerals and signs in any statistical comparison: 14 as against 19; only 2 in 96; 30% as compared to 28.5% (otherwise, spell out "percent").

More Uses of Numerals

Also use numerals in dates, times, measurements, money, and percentages requiring more than two words, and for streets: April 1, 1984; 6:30 a.m. (but *half-past six*), 3 × 5 cards; 240 by 100 feet; 6'3″ (but *six feet tall); $4.99* (but *two dollars a ticket; 69 cents a bunch);* 8½ percent (but *four percent);* 42nd Street, 5th Avenue (but *Fifth Avenue* is equally frequent), 1st Street, 3rd Avenue.

Dates

Dates come with commas around the year: April 1, 1884, *was grim.* Or you may follow the European style without commas—1 April 1884—as long as you are consistent throughout. You may write either February 1918 (no commas) or February, 1918, but not both in the same paper. Centuries come uncapitalized: the twentieth century (hyphenated when an adjective: twentieth-century viewpoint). Put A.D. before the year, and B.C. after: A.D. 1066; 750 B.C. Times are in small letters: 2:10 a.m.; 3 p.m.

Commas with Numbers

As a rule, a comma goes with numbers of four or more digits: 1,386; $6,145; 11,669 (but the sciences usually omit the comma in four-digit numbers: 4589 kilometers [km]). Further exceptions are addresses—5112 Broadway; page numbers—page 1334; and years—2985 B.C. (but *32,000 B.C.*).

Page Numbers

When connecting page numbers, give all numbers, in full, up through ninety-nine: 88–99. For the hundreds and thousands, use only the last two digits of the second figure: 204–06, 1071–85 (but 296–304, 1098–1103).* (For Roman numerals, see 529.)

Numbered Points in Parentheses

Put full parentheses around numbered points in your text:

---

*Largely for less chance of error in reading or writing, some writers prefer full numbers for such connections. Whichever way you go, follow it consistently.

We will discuss (1) wages and hours, (2) fringe benefits, and (3) sick leave and vacation.

ABBREVIATIONS

Use only those conventional abbreviations your reader can easily recognize: *Dr., Mr., Mrs., Ms., Messrs.* (for two or more men, pronounced "messers," as in *Messrs. Adams, Pruitt, and Williams*), *Jr., St., Esq.* (Esquire, following a British gentleman's name, between commas and with *Mr.* omitted), *S.J.* (Society of Jesus, also following a name). All take periods. College degrees are equally recognizable: *A.B., M.A., Ph.D., D. Litt., M.D., LL.D.* Similarly, dates and times. *B.C., A.D., a.m., p.m.,* Though B.C. and A.D. are conventionally printed as small capitals, regular capitals in your classroom papers are perfectly acceptable. Write them without commas: *2000 B.C. was Smith's estimate; A.D.* precedes the year, and *B.C.* follows: *from 2000 B.C. until A.D. 2000.* A number of familiar abbreviations go without periods: *TV, FBI, USSR, USA, YMCA,* though periods are perfectly OK or O.K. Acronyms ("tip-names" made from the initials or "tips" of longer titles, as in NOW, or UNESCO) usually go without periods, as do radio and television stations (WQXR-FM, NBC-TV) and tuberculosis (TB). *U.N.* and *U.S. delegation* are customary. Note that *U.S.* serves only as an adjective; write out *the United States,* serving as a noun. Certain scientific phrases also go without periods, especially when combined with figures: *55 mph, 300 rpm, 4000 kwh.*

Abbreviations conventional in running prose, unitalicized, are e.g. (*exempli gratia,* "for example"), i.e. (*id est,* "that is"), etc. (*et cetera,* better written out "and so forth"), and viz. (*videlicet,* pronounced "vi-DEL-uh-sit," meaning "that is," "namely"). These are followed by either commas or colons after the period:

Conventional Abbreviations in Prose

> **The commission discovered three frequent errors in manage-ment, i.e., failure to take appropriate inventories, erroneous accounting, and inattention to costs.**
> **The semester included some outstanding extracurricular pro-grams, e.g.: a series of lectures on civil rights, three con-certs, and a superb performance of *Oedipus Rex.***

The abbreviation *vs* ., usually italicized, is best spelled out, unitalicized, in your text: "The antagonism of Capulet versus Montague runs throughout the play." The abbreviation *c.* or *ca* ., standing for *circa* ("around") and used with approxi-mate dates in parentheses, is italicized: "Higden wrote *Polychronicon* (*c.* 1350)."

For further abbreviations in citations, see 291–93.

Spelling in Full

Avoid making abbreviations of your own. In your running text, spell out names of persons, places, months, and such words as Street, Road, and Boulevard; for example, Oxford Street, not *Oxford St.* (Obvious exceptions are *St.* for *Saint, Mr., Ms.,* initials in names, and so on.) Corporate names should follow the firms' preferences. When in doubt, spell Company and Incorporated in full.

Here are some special problems:

1. An abbreviation at the end of a declarative sentence. End the sentence with the final abbreviating period.

He asked her to mail it C.O.D. [not C.O.D..]

2. An abbreviation at the end of a question or exclamation. Add the question mark or exclamation point after the abbreviating period.

C.O.D.? Yes—but not to Washington, D.C.!

3. An abbreviation inside a sentence. Let the abbreviating period stand as it comes, and add other punctuation as necessary.

All prices are F.O.B. at our nearest warehouse.
The joy of his life, i.e., his mother-in-law, arrived.

Note that common abbreviations like *i.e., etc., viz.,* and the like, are enclosed in commas, since they are parenthetical remarks. But, except for heavy irony, as with the *i.e.* before *mother-in-law,* your phrase will be smoother if you omit these abbreviations completely, or use *that is, and so on,* and *namely.*

4. Abbreviations like *Mr., Mrs., Ms., Mlle., Mme., Dr., St.* (Saint), *Co.,* and *Ltd.* occur without the period in some British papers and books. Follow U.S. usage, which requires the period.

EXERCISES ——————————————————

6. *Amend the errors in hyphenation, virgules, diacritical marks, numbers, and abbreviations in the following sentences.*

   1. At about 10000 BC, man made settlements appear, but probably 80 % of subsistence still came from hunting and gathering.
   2. At three P.M., the crowd dwindled, having lost its raison detre—tete a tete with the brass.
   3. A twenty ft. gap in the hedge marked the path of 10 tanks and 1222 soldiers, after the attache, protege of the chancellor, misinterpreted a communique while thinking of his fiancee over a soupcon of vichyssoise at the table d hote.

4. Here came the once in a life time piece de resistance, a 500 pound side of ox, roasted slowly by Godel for 24 hours over an open pit fire.
5. Each guest exhibited his/her naivete, as a learned observer observed, by squealing in delight at the never to be forgotten spectacle at two thirty one third ave.
6. He noticed among the crowd, three fourths of whom were strangers, a matron who taught in the local high-school, a noted antiintellectual, a semiinvalid selfreliant sculptress in a T shirt, and an ex president of the pta.
7. This house, the largest on Rivington Rd., has a living and/or dining area, ten or twelve foot ceilings, a three and a half acre lot, a three car garage, and 4500 square feet of flooring.
8. This is 1986 AD, almost 6000 years since writing was invented in Sumeria at some dim point beyond 3,500 B.C.
9. He had a PHD in herpetology and joined Messrs Wallach, Stein, and Crouch as their chief consultant with the UN and the US; eg, he solved the problem of frogs in fish weir cultures.
10. Polyphemus Goode, born April 1, 1789 accomplished 40 manuscript pages a day well into his 80s, VIZ almost one hundred and twenty pages/month, or about one hundred and eighty thousand scientific/philosophic pages in his last 30 yrs.

PROBLEMS IN CAPITALIZATION

You know about capitalizing most names and the first word of a sentence, certainly; but the following points are troublesome. Capitalize:

1. Names of races, languages, and religions—Negro, Caucasian, Mongolian, Protestant, Jewish, Christian, Roman Catholic, Indian, French, English, Black (as in Black English). But "blacks and whites in this neighborhood," "black entrepreneurs," "white storekeepers"—especially in phrases that contrast blacks and whites, since *white* is never capitalized.

2. Adjectives formed from names—the Shakespearean sonnet, a Joycean sentence, the Renaissance outlook, the American way. But when such adjectives become common allusions, they drop their capital: *jeremiad, draconian measures, platonic love, herculean effort.*

3. Titles of officers, *but not of offices:* "Dean Metzlar is the first dean to subscribe"; "District Attorney Whelan is everyone's district attorney." The President of the United States is generally capitalized: *He was our best President, from his Presidential address throughout his Presidency.* But *she was president of her class.*

4. The *complete* names of churches, rivers, hotels, and the like—the First Baptist Church, the Mark Hopkins Hotel, the Suwannee River (*not* First Baptist church, Mark Hopkins hotel, Suwannee river).

5. Nouns and pronouns of deity—God, our Father, Messiah, Son, Savior, He, His, Him, Allah, Krishna, Siva. Pronouns referring to gods in mythology and minor religions are usually not capitalized.

6. North, south, east, and west *only when they are regions*—the mysterious East, the new Southwest (but southwestern flora, midwestern farmland)—or parts of proper nouns: the West Side, East Lansing.

7. All words in titles, except prepositions, articles, and conjunctions. But capitalize even these if they come first or last, or if they are longer than five letters—"I'm Through with Love," *Gone with the Wind,* "I'll Stand By," *In Darkest Africa.* Capitalize all members in hyphenated compounds—*The Eighteenth-Century Background, The Anti-Idealist* (but *The Antislavery Movement*), *Pre-Engineered Parts for Heavy-Duty Make-Up.* But the names of numbered streets and the written-out numbers on your checks are *not* capitalized after the hyphen: *Forty-second Street. Fifty-four . . . Dollars.* When referring to magazines, newspapers, and reference works, you may drop *The* as part of the title—the *Saturday Evening Post,* the *Kansas City Star,* the *Encyclopaedia Britannica.*

8. References to a section of a work—the Index, his Preface, Introduction, Afterword, Chapter 1, Volume IV, Act II. But "scene iii" is usually not capitalized because its numerals are also in lower case. Smaller numbered items within a work are less certain: Table— and Figure— are customary, but Section [section], Problem [problem], and Exercise [exercise] often go either way. In such instances, capitalize (be sure to do so consistently) when in doubt.

9. Abstract nouns, when you want emphasis, serious or humorous— "The truths contradict, so what is Truth?"; Very Important Person; the Ideal.

10. The first word of a quoted phrase, if originally capitalized, falling within a sentence:

> **Horace Greeley advised, "Go west, young man," and stayed home to make a fortune.**

But do not capitalize, except for proper nouns, indirect quotations:

> **Horace Greeley advised young men to go west, and stayed home to make a fortune.**

For sentences in parentheses, see 403.

11. *Do not* capitalize the seasons—spring, winter, midsummer—except in titles like *The Summer Festival.*

12. *Do not* capitalize after a colon, unless what follows is normally capitalized (see 399–400):

> **Again we may say with Churchill: "Never have so many owed so much to so few."**

Culture, People, Nature: An Introduction to General Anthropology
   [title of book]
Many lost everything in the earthquake: their homes had vanished along with their supplies, their crops, their livestock.

13. *Do not* capitalize proper nouns serving as common nouns: *china, cognac, napoleon* (a pastry), *chauvinist, watt* (electricity). (Usage divides on some proper adjectives: *French [french] pastry, Cheddar [cheddar] cheese, German [german] measles, Venetian [venetian] blinds.* Breeds of animals, as in *Welsh terrier,* and products of a definite origin, as in *Scotch whiskey,* are less uncertain.) When in doubt, your best guide, as in spelling, is your dictionary.

14. Articles and prepositions not capitalized in full names become capitalized when used at the beginning of sentences: *De la Mare's poems* [Walter de la Mare]; *Von Neumann's computers* [John von Neumann]; *De Gaulle's policies* [Charles de Gaulle, *or* General de Gaulle]. (Within a sentence, the same articles or prepositions would be set in lower case: *Many disagreed with de Gaulle's policies.*) Some names have all parts capitalized; an excellent help is *Webster's Biographical Dictionary.*

EXERCISES

7. *Capitalize the following, where necessary:*

go west, young man.
the south left the union.
the east side of town
the introduction to
   re-establishing toryism
east side, west side
the tall black spoke french.
she loved the spring.
health within seconds [book]
clear through life in time
   [book]
a doberman pinscher
the methodist episcopal church

the missouri river
my christian name begins
   with *c*
the new york public library
the neo-positivistic approach
   [book]
the st. louis post-dispatch [add
   italics]
twenty-five dollars [on a check]
33 thirty-third street
the tundra occupies a large
   portion of northern canada.
bohr's and de broglie's theories

8. *Review the ways to italicize (407–08) and see if you can restore the original capitals and italics in the following paragraphs.*

1. the oldest independent black people in the western hemisphere are the bushmen of surinam on the north coast of south america, the descendants of negro slaves who escaped from their dutch masters early in the 1600s, according to the greenhill star-advertiser. They set up strategically scattered villages, raided plantations for black women and supplies, and successfully fought all campaigns against them, even those conducted by experienced european commanders. aphra behn, in her

novel oroonoko, or the royal slave (1688), especially in her preface, praises the handsomeness, intelligence, and bravery of the surinam negro. thomas southerne repeats the impression in oroonoko a tragedy (1695), a play based on mrs. behn's book, especially in act i, scene iii. two u.s. blacks from harvard, s. allen counter, jr., a neurobiologist, and david l. evans, admissions officer, have studied the bush people for five years and have produced a documentary film entitled the bush afro-americans of surinam and french guiana: the connecting link. "these people," says counter, "represent to american blacks a mirror of the best example of what we would have been like had we chosen not to live in slavery and had removed ourselves to another place."

2. religious wars are the worst, as we can see in both the near east and the british isles, specifically in lebanon and northern ireland. the german motto gott mit uns ("god is with us") of world war i becomes an attitude excluding the other side from all justification and humanity. it generates fanatical dedication and hatred, as a recent article in the new republic suggests. when moslem fights christian, and catholic fights protestant, each sees his side as right with a religious fervor, as un-like his enemy's as day and night, yet all are identical in their fanaticism unto death, like the ancient zealots, in their unquenchable dedication to revenge and ultimate victory for the cause even in the distant future. dr. roger shinn, reinhold niebuhr professor of social ethics at union theological seminary, new york city, points out that war and religion both ask dedication beyond self. when the two combine, the dedication doubles, and all compromise seems evil, a betrayal of truth, and faith, and the right way.

The Written Examination

When you receive a sheet of examination questions, be calm. Glance through the whole thing to get it and your time in perspective. Notice especially if you have choices. Many students run out of time by writing pell-mell on both questions of an "either 1 or 2." Read your questions carefully, looking for cues like *discuss, compare, summarize, consider, paraphrase.* We have already considered the essential strategic points in Chapter 7, on outlining, but they are worth repeating and illustrating:

1. To get started, answer your exam-question *in one sentence.*
2. Incorporate the question's language in your one-sentence answer.
3. Jot down the points you want to cover, quickly numbering them for ascending interest, saving best for last—the point you know best and can cover most fully.
4. Paragraph, with topic sentence if you can, about once a page.

Your one-sentence answer stretches your knowledge to its fullest, covering everything you have to say, like a good thesis. Then you are off and running as you expand your jotted points to complete your answer.

A LITERARY QUESTION

1. Discuss the role of the senses in Wordsworth's philosophy, identifying and analyzing the following passage:

435

> Therefore I am still
> A lover of the meadows and the woods,
> And mountains; and of all that we behold
> From this green earth; of all the mighty world
> Of eye, and ear,—both what they half create,
> And what perceive; well pleased to recognize
> In nature and the language of the sense
> The anchor of my purest thoughts, the nurse,
> The guide, the guardian of my heart, and soul
> Of all my moral being.

One-Sentence Answer

In this important passage from "Tintern Abbey," Wordsworth makes his clearest statement about the role of the senses perceiving the natural world and establishing — or "nursing" — the inner being.

Jotted Outline—on another sheet, or in margin

1. Outer nature — wild, cultivated (cottages)
2. Inner nature — world of eye and ear
3. Reality
4. Senses as creators
5. Senses as perceivers
6. Nature plus senses = soul and being
7. Perceived and created reality
8. Poetry — iambic pent — sincerity

Answer

In this important passage from "Tintern Abbey," Wordsworth makes his clearest statement about the role of the senses in perceiving the natural world and establishing — or "nursing" — the inner being. He has previously in this poem acknowledged the point with which he opens his "Immortality" ode: that the unconscious and joyful impressions of boyhood, when he ran and jumped through these hills, have faded to the calmer impressions of maturity, which have mixed a sense of humanity (a "sad music") with the youthful joys in wild non-human nature.

He has visited this same scene five years before, as he says at the beginning, and the impressions from that visit have nourished him as they recurred to his mind — actual pictures popping into his thoughts — in the frenzy of the city and times of depression (his own depressed feelings). These recollections have brought to him the same tranquil mood that now fills his soul and gives the impression of harmony with nature and a feeling that he "sees into the life of things." He says that his present recapturing of the scene and mood is made even better because he knows that this present visit, a kind of recharging of batteries, will similarly sustain him in the future.

In this quoted passage, he tries to analyze the psychological process and the nature of reality — a very important statement. Here the uninhabited wilds of youthful joy have become "meadows and the woods/and mountains." This is the more inhabited part of the view already mentioned in the cottages here and there among the woods, with smoke rising, still suggesting calm solitude, and the pastures divided by wild rows of heath. He refers to "this green earth," which again suggests cultivated fields and pastures rather than the surrounding wild woods.

All of this "mighty world," which is all of external reality, is perceived by eye and ear — the senses. But in fact, he says, these same senses "half-create" reality too. From this psychological exchange between external physical nature and the "language of the sense," which seems to half-perceive and half-create in a kind of dialogue, he nourishes his soul and moral being. He even seems to say, at the end, that this sensory experience _is_ his soul and moral being.

But he also speaks of this interchange with nature, through the senses, as an anchor, a nurse, a guide, and a guardian, implying that his soul and being are something separate that the sensory experience works on. He seems uncertain what this entity "nature and the language of the sense" really is — an anchor, a nurse, a guide (a leader), or a guardian (a protector). These lines, I think, show Wordsworth working very hard to explain something he feels deeply, but which is hard to explain. These lines, which seem almost like prose statements, yet scan as iambic pentameter, convey the deep sincerity so typical of Wordsworth's poetry and his ideas.

AN HISTORICAL QUESTION

2. Discuss Gibbon's reasons for the fall of the Roman Empire.

One-Sentence Answer

The Roman Empire fell because of decay from within and attack from without.

Jotted Outline

1. Augustus
2. Tiberius-Caligula-Nero
3. Nerva, Trajan, Hadrian, the Antonines
4. Commodus
5. Mercenaries
6. Overextension
7. Goths
8. Rome and Byzantium

Answer

The Roman Empire fell because of decay from within and attack from without. After the five good emperors who extended the Pax Romana to the end of the second century A.D. — Nerva, Trajan, Hadrian, and the two Antonines — Gibbon unfolds a long account of folly, luxuriance, insanity, and bloodshed. But he sees the seeds of decay already sown by the wily Augustus, as he calls him, who dissolved the remaining republican powers of the Senate under a fiction of senatorial authority that disguised a military dictatorship. This dictatorship of the emperor, now the "Caesar," expanded the borders but weakened the old Roman spirit of freedom and patriotic commitment.

Moral decay was also evident from the first years of empire. Augustus had tried to reform the profligacy of the upper classes, banishing both his wife and daughter for flagrant lewdness, as well as the poet Ovid, who was somehow implicated in the daughter's scandalous behavior, as the lecturer pointed out. That Rome could survive the inner decay displayed in the murderous orgies of Tiberius

(A.D. 14–37), or in the insane Caligula (37–41), who made his horse a senator, or in the almost equally mad and more bloody Nero (54–68), is a wonder.

But Commodus (180–192), the adolescent wastrel who thought he was Hercules and fought men and beasts in the arena in Herculean costume — the son of good Marcus Aurelius Antoninus — begins Rome's long decline, in Gibbon's eyes. The few good emperors along the line could not sustain the overextended empire, defended by mercenaries rather than patriots, the leading citizens who were now luxuriating at home and keeping the populace happy with bread and circuses. The empire broke in two, with two loosely cooperating caesars, one in Rome, one in Byzantium. The tail began to wag the dog, as Byzantium gained ascendancy, and at one time as many as six caesars divided the power and luxuriated on the taxes.

The pressure of attack from without was sustained from the first on all the empire's borders — Scotland, Gaul, the Danube, the East. But how outer attack conspired with inner decay is nowhere better illustrated than in the account of the Goths, whose future king Alaric conquered Italy and sacked Rome in 410. Driven to the north banks of the Danube by the Huns, the Goths begged Valens, the caesar of the East, for admittance into the empire in 376. Gibbon estimates a population of nearly a million men, women, and children from the 200,000 Gothic warriors reported by the contemporary historian. When agreement was reached that they would settle in Thrace and defend the empire, the Romans began to ferry this multitude across the badly swollen river in canoes and boats of all sizes for many days and nights, losing many in the rapid current. Valens and his counselors, whom Gibbon calls slaves decorated with the titles of prefects and generals, looked on the settlement as a rich bargain, since they could now keep and spend the gold the provinces sent in as taxes to hire mercenaries.

But this was only the beginning of Roman greed and moral decay in the Gothic story. Valens had decreed that the warriors must surrender their arms before crossing the river and that they must give up their children to be sent to distant cities where they would be civilized and would serve as hostages to keep the Goths in line. But the Goths, whose weapons were their hereditary honor, bribed the Roman officials with their wives, daughters, sons, carpets, and linen, and entered the boats with weapons in hand.

Then Roman greed went farther. Instead of feeding the Goths as Valens had ordered, the officials sold them bread, dog meat, and meat from cattle killed by disease at outrageous prices — a slave for a loaf of bread, a little bad meat for ten pounds of gold. The Goths finally rebelled, devastated the country, fought Valens to a standstill, and settled independently in Thrace, where, though they became Christians, their hatred for the Romans smoldered until Alaric led them westward to conquer Italy and sack the ancient capital in A.D. 410. Aside from other forays into Italy, Alaric's victory illustrates clearly how moral decay combines with outer attack to contribute a major plunge in the long continuing fall of the Roman Empire.

A QUESTION IN THE SOCIAL SCIENCES

3. Brewer and Brewer contrast Freudian and Jungian ideas as the essential poles of psychological theory. Describe the basic similarities and contrasts.

One-sentence Answer

Both Freud and Jung agree in the primacy of subconscious ideas, but Freud finds this realm of dreams and lost remembrances sexual and socially destructive, a negative pole whereas Jung finds it archetypical and positive.

Jotted Outline

1. Freud-hypnosis-dualistic psychology
2. Jung's buried treasure
3. Archetypes
4. Schubert
5. Dementia praecox (schizophrenia)
6. Superego-Ego-Id
7. Freud negative-Jung positive

Answer

Both Freud and Jung agree in the validity of unconscious or subconscious ideas, but Freud sets dreams and lost remembrances as a negative pole to social life whereas Jung finds them archetypal and positive. Freud, starting with hypnosis to get at suppressed traumas, became convinced that evidence from dreams was crucially informative. Jung, Adler, and others joined him. But Jung, analyzing his own dreams, as Freud had done, found joy, as if discovering buried secrets, rather than the fear and aversion in Freud's interpretations. Consequently, their polar split was between Freud's negative and Jung's positive views.

Freud had actually built on the predominating psychology of G. H. Schubert, which saw, as in Stevenson's <u>Dr. Jekyll and Mr. Hyde</u>, a good daytime personality suppressing a nocturnal and savage one. Freud adopted this as he described infantile sexuality as the seat of evil, or antisocial impulses, to be repressed in maturity — sexual love of one's mother, murderous hatred of one's father, the famous Oedipus complex. Freud converted the, to him, traditional two-level psychology into three. Instead of a good surface and a destructive subsurface, he described a <u>superego</u>, the socially acceptable good set of values, and the <u>id</u>, the hidden sexual and violent side of personality, with the <u>ego</u>, or personal identity, negotiating and defining itself between the two.

Jung, beginning with work on dementia praecox, or schizophrenia, evidently a deeper psychic trouble than hysteria, was attracted to Freud's work, joined him in editing a new journal, and in a new international psychoanalytic society. But Jung broke with Freud on the interpretation of dreams. Where Freud saw suppressed and unacceptable sexual drives, Jung saw archetypal patterns, built into the brain's caverns by evolution, up from savagery.

Jung sees two psychic levels in the unconscious where Freud sees only the libido (the <u>id</u>) containing rebellious infantile sexuality. Jung, like Freud, sees the unconscious retaining repressed drives, as expressed in dreams. But he sees these repressions as more broadly personal than explicitly sexual. This is the first level of Jung's unconscious, the somewhat negative and Freudian one. Beneath this is the collective unconscious, the positive reservoir of human experience built into the

brain by evolution, which all people share, beyond or beneath
the personal.

In short, Freud sees the unconscious as a threat, shared by all but
built from personal traumas. Jung sees it more positively, containing
personal and threatening suppressions, but supported by a positive and
archetypical human consciousness built into human awareness by
evolution, not so much suppressed as forgotten, a positive, universal, and
archetypical source of energy that can be tapped through dreams and
psychoanalysis.

Letters of Application

You will probably agree by now that writing is crucially important to you. It has evoked your growing intelligence through the years of learning. Now you face the real test, finding and expressing your position before the world's audience. Everything you put on paper speaks for you—spelling, commas, the flow of your prose that conveys your ideas and bespeaks your maturity. When applying for a job, or graduate school, or study abroad, or a fellowship, put yourself forward as sensible and able, describing your qualifications, interests, and aptitudes clearly, stating how the job or program will help fulfill your goals, and stating or implying how your work will be an asset to the company or the program. When asking for redress of justice, or urging votes for a worthy cause, make your points calmly and clearly, with an air of mature conviction and a prose that shows you in full command in every detail.

Whatever your purpose, type your letters on 8½ × 11 inch paper. Smaller personal stationery, or something "From the Desk of _____," seems either too chummy or too pretentious and gets lost in the files. Put your address and date in the upper right corner. Type out names and titles, addresses, and salutations in full, keeping a copy for reference. Single-space everything, double-spacing between salutations and paragraphs. Though official correspondence sometimes aligns everything flush with the left margin, including signature, such styling may seem too flashy from a private person. Space long names of institutions equally in two (or more) lines in your salutation:

```
Dr. Robert A. Nordham, President
Society for Developing
Countries in Asia and
the Western Hemisphere
9876 Central Street West
Clintdale, West Virginia 11213
```

Note that abbreviations for states—CA (California), TX (Texas), N.Y. (New York)—are also acceptable, and may improve your spacing. Use "Dear Sirs:" or "Dear Sir or Madam:" for salutation to organizations when you do not know a person to address. To women's organizations "Dear Madam:" is customary. "Sincerely" or "Sincerely yours" will meet most situations.

The following examples illustrate the form and spacing, and illustrate the kinds of information and the general tone you will need for letters that may change your life, beginning with a plea to change your grade.

Return Address
```
                                    12345 Elmwood Drive
                                    Tracy, Illinois 50123
```

Date
```
                                    July 1, 1984
```

Inside Address
```
Professor Alan Kurtz, Chairman
Department of English
University of Michigan
Ann Arbor, Michigan 48109
```

Salutation
```
Dear Professor Kurtz:
```

```
    You may remember me from your class in freshman com-
position, English 123, last spring.  I do not recall the
section number.  But perhaps you will remember that I did
not appear for the final examination.  My name in class was
Kathy Miller.

    I have recently received my grades, indicating a C in
English.  Since my average had been at least a strong B, or
even B+, as I remember, and since the emphasis was on the
weekly essay, I thought this was a little severe.

    I am writing to ask if I might make up the final, and
receive some adjustment in my grade.  I would be happy to
come to Ann Arbor, or to arrange some time early in the
fall term.  I hope to make and maintain a strong college
record for future employment.

    Please let me know what the regulations are, and if I
can hope for a second chance.  I apologize for missing the
final, but I had some extreme personal and emotional prob-
```

lems right at the end of the semester. I really enjoyed
the course.

                                    Sincerely yours,

Kathy Miller Albright

          (Mrs.) Kathy Miller Albright

Kathy Miller Albright
12345 Elmwood Drive
Tracy, Illinois 50123

          Professor Alan Kurtz, Chairman
          Department of English
          University of Michigan
          Ann Arbor, Michigan 48109

THE PERSONAL STATEMENT

Law schools, business schools, medical schools, and businesses will supply
forms to list your accomplishments. But they will usually also ask for a summary from *you,* the person. This may be your life's most vital writing. Here
is a sample of aspirations for law school.

          I was attracted to the law at an early age by the ca-

reer of my uncle, Rowland B. Nakian, one of those writing

to support my application to law school. I early recog-

nized the respect accorded him as a lawyer, and I loved him

as a person, but I hardly dreamed that a girl might be a lawyer.

In high school, however, I studied Shakespeare's <u>The Merchant of Venice</u>, where I encountered Portia, a mere girl who triumphed in court, and my dream began to form. At the University of Michigan, I majored in English, with a strong minor in history, but, as my transcript shows, I also have some basic economics and accounting, since, for a while, I was considering a career in business.

I have also gathered some experience that would be valuable in a business career or in the legal aspects of business. In my freshman year, I started to work as a waitress in Sally's Cellar, a popular restaurant near the campus. Being a waitress requires a good memory, diligence, and an ability to add up bills quickly and accurately. It teaches one to meet the public and to understand all kinds of people, a truly valuable asset for a legal career. Furthermore, I have been promoted to cashier, testifying to the management's confidence in my responsibility, accuracy, and tact.

In my first three summers after graduating from high school, I was also approaching a legal career unknowingly from another direction. I was counselor at Goose Lake Camp, a camp for girls from ten to fourteen years of age. I was responsible for groups of several different ages, in numbers ranging from five or six to as many as fifteen.

This position required an almost constant lawyer-like tact and leadership, adjudicating dozens of small claims and crises day and night and making adjustments as new girls entered the group and others finished their stay.

But my most valuable preparation for law school has been my major in English, which, in fact, began with my high-school teacher and my reading of Shakespeare. I realize now that both my dream of law and my love of literature and language began together in my high-school English class. Now I can analyze human motives, trace out causes and effects, and, above all, write a persuasive analysis, as I believe my grades and recommendations will show.

I am confident that I can be a lawyer. I hope that I can demonstrate my ability at your Law School, and eventually even add something to its preeminent reputation.

THE COVERING LETTER AND RÉSUMÉ

Your central statement, and its accompanying forms, requires an introductory letter, and a résumé of your career. Start your letter with your address and that of your addressee, as on 444–45. Then proceed something like this:

Dear Dean Gilbrich:

I am applying for admission to your Law School, and I enclose my application form, together with my transcript, my resume, and my personal statement as required.

I also list the ten people who are writing letters of recommendation.

As these letters, my statement, and my record will show, I have been keenly interested in the law for some time, while I have also broadened my background in English and history, which I believe are primary to a lawyer's achievement.

I sincerely hope that you will find me well qualified for the University of Michigan Law School and a career in the law.

Sincerely yours,

Nancy Nakian

Nancy Nakian

When you apply for an opening in business, or in academics, write a letter outlining your qualifications accompanied by a résumé (or, with colleges and universities, a "Curriculum Vitae"). Limit your résumé to one page, if possible, but if needed to include all good, important points, an extra page is acceptable. Suppose a Nancy Nakian with a different background wants a job in advertising. Her covering letter and her résumé (on a separate page) might look like this:

Dear Mr. Adsell:

I noticed in the *New York Times* that you have a vacancy. I am looking for a challenge in advertising with a dynamic firm, and I have also admired the recent one-column ads in *The New Yorker* and *Time,* which I have discovered were yours. They impressed me as exactly what I have been working toward in combining clear statement and graphic outlay.

I have been fascinated with this visual union of language and line since I was advertising manager (a one-person staff) for my high-school year book. I have majored in journalism, and have acquired further experience in graphic design on the advertising for the Campus Relief Drive, for the Friends of Art, and, on part-time salary, for the Record Center. I will send my dossier, and have letters of recommendation sent at your request.

I enclose my resume and hope you will find me worthy of your consideration. If you have no immediate opening,

I would appreciate your considering me for any opening on your staff. I am impressed by your style and quality, and I believe I can contribute to it effectively.

Sincerely yours,

Nancy Nakian

Nancy Nakian

RÉSUMÉ

Nancy Nakian
2304 River Street
Adams, Wisconsin 53814
(414) 293-1671

Objective

Beginning position in writing and designing advertising for magazines and newspapers.

Education
1981–85

The University of Michigan
Degree: A.B. (expected May 1985)
Major: Journalism

1977–81

Adams Central High School, Adams, Wisconsin
Academic degree

Experience
1984–85

Advertising staff, The Record Center, Ann Arbor, Michigan, three hours a week.

Summers
1981–84

Counselor, Goose Lake Camp, Goose Lake, Wisconsin

1981–84

Waitress, Sally's Cellar, Ann Arbor, Michigan

1982–84

Advertising staff, Friends of Art, Ann Arbor, Michigan, periodic posters and brochures

1981–83	Advertising staff, annual Campus Relief Drive, University of Michigan
1980–81	Advertising Manager, *The Clover Leaf,* year book, Adams Central High School

Extracurricular Activities

Forward, field hockey team, Winchester House, University of Michigan Winchester House Council (President, 1984–85)
Reporter and advertising staff, *The High Flier*, monthly newspaper, Adams Central High School (1978–81)

Special Interests

Sports, photography, writing

References

For academic dossier:

Career Planning and Placement
3200 Student Activities Building
The University of Michigan
Ann Arbor, MI 48109

Mr. George A. Ponder, Manager
The Record Center
209 South State Street
Ann Arbor, MI 48104

Mrs. Anita Mendelssohn, Manager
Sally's Cellar
315 Williams Street
Ann Arbor, MI 48104

Rhetorical Devices

The general strategies of rhetoric I have described in this book—even such familiar devices as parallelism—have all evolved through classical oratory, as it tested in its noisy forums the essentials of how one may persuade one's audience, how one may arrange one's phrases attractively, forcefully, and memorably. Both the structure and the devices are still with us, since, as Russian novelist and Nobel laureate Alexander Solzhenitsyn once remarked, human nature seems to change only about as fast as the geological surface of the earth. Consequently, we can strengthen our ideas of structure and phrasing by seeing how these devices have persisted, through differing ages and languages, in the essential dynamics of communication.

STRUCTURE: CLASSICAL AND MODERN

The classical form is still visible not only in the modern essay, but even in the modern scientific paper, which reproduces in most of its details the ancient Greek oratorical form that the Roman lawyer Cicero (first century B.C.) polished in his orations and outlined in his *De Oratore*.

You can detect this classic oratorical form almost anywhere you look in the literature and exposition of the Middle Ages and the Renaissance. Sir Philip Sidney turned to it automatically when he wrote *An Apologie for Poetrie*, as did John Milton for his famous *Areopagitica*. The great formal essayists, like John Henry Newman, followed it in more recent times. And today, as I have

451

said, it appears universally behind the structure of the essay and the scientific report.

The form was adjustable; parts were sometimes omitted, and subdivisions added. But the usual form, as set forth by Cicero, Quintilian, and their followers, with the first three items matching our "beginning," and the last one our "end," was more or less like this, under the traditional Latin headings:

1. *Exordium* (or *Proem*). The introduction.
2. *Narratio.* General description of subject and background.
3. *Propositio.* The thesis, the statement of what is to be demonstrated or proved.
4. *Partitio.* Statement of how the thesis is to be divided and handled.
5. *Confirmatio* (or *Argumentatio,* or *Explicatio*). The chief evidence in support of the thesis; the body, the longest part, of the oration. Roughly, our "middle."
6. *Reprehensio.* Knocking out the opposition. Although the ancients, with somewhat more leisure than we, saved their merriment until after their own case was firmly established, the *reprehensio* contained exactly the refutations that must always accompany an enumeration of the opposition's claims. The structure of the *reprehensio* was exactly that recommended in our discussion of *pros* and *cons:* setting up the opposition only to knock it flat.
7. *Digressio.* The name speaks for itself. The "digression" was intended to lighten the load. It could come anywhere between *exordium* and *peroratio,* with matters related, but not essential, to the subject.
8. *Peroratio.* The conclusion, summarizing the discussion and urging the thesis with greater eagerness and enthusiasm.

Shorter orations sometimes dropped the *reprehensio,* if no opposition needed refuting, and absorbed the *propositio* and *partitio,* the statements of thesis and method, into the *narratio,* coming very near to what we have described as our "beginning." *Digressio,* which is largely decoration or relief anyway, was also frequently dropped, or inserted at some different place. Since these parts were movable, we have in the ancient form, the larger framework of beginning-middle-end, of assertion and refutation, that we have already outlined for the modern essay in general. Here is how the modern scientific paper, or lab report, reflects the form of classical oration:

CLASSICAL	SCIENTIFIC
Exordium ⎱ *Narratio* ⎰	Introduction
Propositio	Purpose (thesis)
Partitio	Materials and methods
Confirmatio	Results
Peroratio	Discussion ⎱ Summary ⎰

The modern essayist has simply streamlined the classical form a little further than has the systematic scientist. The classical orator stated his case, faced the opposition, then stated his case again—and at some length—in his summative peroration. The essayist's only real alteration is in putting the *reprehensio*, the managing of the opposition, before his own argument rather than after it, for simple economy. By hitting the opposition first, he need state his own case but once, repeating only a little in his conclusion, which immediately follows.

CLASSICAL ORATION	**MODERN ESSAY**
Exordium	
Narratio	Beginning (with thesis)
Propositio	
Confirmatio	Middle *(reprehensio* followed by *confirmatio)*
Reprehensio	
Peroratio	End

RHETORIC AT GETTYSBURG

A famous and familiar rhetorical event illustrates classical rhetoric surprisingly well: "The Consecration of the National Cemetary at Gettysburg, Pa.," on 19 November 1863. Two very different speakers memorialized the occasion, but both reflected classical rhetoric in form as well as device.

Edward Everett, preacher, professor of Greek, president of Harvard, congressman, minister to Great Britain, secretary of state, senator, Orator of the Day, was the most distinguished orator of his time. By his oration on George Washington, delivered in all parts of the country, he had raised more than $100,000 to buy Mount Vernon for the nation.

Everett's two-hour analysis of the battles at Gettysburg is still one of the best, but his style, alongside that of Lincoln's two-minute dedication, seems enormously puffy:

> . . . whether this august republican Union, founded by some of the wisest statesmen that ever lived, cemented with the blood of some of the purest patriots that ever died, should perish or endure. . . .
> . . . those who sleep beneath our feet, and their gallant comrades who survive to serve their country on other fields of danger. . . .

These two quotations, as you will already have noticed, were echoed by Lincoln, who followed Everett on the program. Having read the press release of Everett's oration in advance, Lincoln recalled Everett's thoughts as he drafted his own brief dedicatory remarks, probably both to compliment Everett and to unify the program:

> **. . . whether that nation . . . can long endure.**
> **The brave men, living and dead, who struggled here. . . .**
> **. . . shall not perish. . . .**

Later, in Gettysburg, Lincoln reworked his address twice before the ceremony. The first version, with his subsequent alterations, is on the opposite page. Lincoln, with his speech in hand, nevertheless spoke mostly from memory and followed his text almost verbatim, adding only *under God,* as his speaking moved him. Even in his remarkably condensed speech, Lincoln, like Everett, follows the classical framework of beginning *(exordium-narratio-propositio),* middle *(confirmatio),* and end *(peroratio),* magnificently expanded in power. Lincoln, like Everett, elevates his language rhetorically. In one place, indeed, he may have elevated a touch too high: Matthew Arnold told friends that he could never get beyond "dedicated to the proposition." And by itself the phrase, rhyming a little slushily with "nation," does indeed sound like good old sociological jargon in full flower.

But the fault is ever so slight, and it consorts unnoticed with the general rhetorical heightening the occasion required. Note Lincoln's slightly inverted order of words in the famous opening sentence, and the tying of words beginning in *f* and *s* and *c*—all elevating the language above the ordinary in the classical device of *alliteration.* Note his repetitions (classical *ploce*), some merely emphatic, some worked for extra meaning—especially *lives-live,* and *dedicated,* which came only after revision. Note the new "fitting and proper" sentence, where the purely rhetorical need of bringing the paragraph to rest demands the redundant comfort of a cliché. Finally, notice how Lincoln dignifies and intensifies his thought by echoing the biblical "threescore years and ten" *(paradiorthosis)*—the traditional span of a human life—to resonate his idea of the uncertain life of the nation at that moment, a nation that had perhaps already outlived its divinely appointed time in its present, ominous, internal war. "Eighty-seven years ago" would have seemed too short, too insignificant, and Lincoln would have lost not only the biblical solemnity but also the idea of the span of life—of birth, life, and death—which he beautifully elaborates in the first sentence with *fathers, brought forth,* and *conceived,* and in the last with *new birth of freedom,* as the life cycle starts again.

I have bracketed the portions Lincoln deleted as he revised, and I have underlined his additions. The phrase *who fought here* and the word *advanced* (indicated in italics) he added for publication at some time after the event.

Four score and seven years ago our fathers brought forth [up]on this continent, a new nation, conceived in [liberty] <u>Liberty</u>, and dedicated to the proposition that ["]all men are created equal.["]

Now we are engaged in a great civil war, testing whether that nation, or any nation so conceived, and so dedicated, can long endure. We are met on a great battle-field of that war. We have come to dedicate a portion of [it] <u>that field</u>, as a final resting place for those who [died here, that the] <u>here gave their lives</u> that that nation might live. [This we may, in all propriety do.] It is altogether fitting and proper that we should do this.

But, in a larger sense, we can not dedicate—we can not consecrate—we can not hallow—this ground. The brave men, living and dead, who struggled here, have [hallowed] <u>consecrated</u> it, far above our poor power to add or detract. The <u>world</u> will little note, nor long remember what we say here [; while], but it can never forget what they did here. It is [rather] for us, <u>the living</u> [to stand here ‖ we here be dedicated], <u>rather,</u> to be dedicated here to the unfinished work which they *who fought here* have thus far so nobly [carried on] *advanced.* It is rather for us to be here dedicated to the great task remaining before us—that from these honored dead we take increased devotion to that cause for which they [here] gave the last full measure of devotion—that we here highly resolve that these dead shall not have died in vain—that [the] <u>this</u> nation, under God, shall have a new birth of freedom—and that government of the people, by the people, for the people, shall not perish from the earth.*

There, indeed, is rhetoric. Coming after Everett's two hours of orotundity, it has always seemed simplicity unadorned, the homespun prose of Honest Abe, the noble backwoodsman. But note again the rhetorical force accumulating behind the word *dedicated,* used (with *dedicate*) six times in the ten sentences. The whole purpose was to *dedicate* a national cemetery. The nation, which the Civil War was cruelly testing, had been *dedicated* to the equality of men. We

---

Abraham Lincoln's Gettysburg Address: The First and Second Drafts Now in the Library of Congress (Washington, D.C.: U.S. Government Printing Office, 1950), as compared against Lincoln's final fair copy—his fifth and last holograph, known as the "Bliss" copy (Joseph Tausek, *The True Story of the Gettysburg Address* [New York: Lincoln MacVeagh, The Dial Press, 1933], facsimile fold-out facing page 36).

who have come to *dedicate* a portion of that battlefield cannot match the personal *dedication* of those who died there. We must again *dedicate* ourselves to equally shared freedom. Lincoln has punned in a serious way to extract from the word its shades of meaning and to emphasize the essential democratic ideal, which requires the dedication of all. He briefly works a similar rhetorical emphasis with the word *devotion*, before his final rhetorical repetition and parallel—*of the people, by the people, for the people*—alliterating beautifully and meaningfully with the *perish* he had borrowed from Everett. There classical *ploce* and *alliteration* rise to perfection.

Here also we can see how a command of grammar takes its rhetorical effect. Grammar is necessary, of course, merely to steer clear of any error that would throw the audience off track, or lose its respect. But Lincoln uses his grammar rhetorically as well, not only in the slightly heightened inversion at the beginning *(brought forth on this continent a new nation)* but in a number of grammatical parallels: his contrast of *remember what we say here* as against *forget what they did here*, for instance, a classical *antithesis*. But the grammatical parallels with which he closes are the most striking: two triple parallels, one within the other, achieving a magnificent and moving finality. He puts equivalent thoughts into the same grammatical structure, again accumulating an emphasis: we are to resolve (1) that these dead shall not have died in vain, (2) that this nation shall have a new birth, (3) that democratic government shall not perish. And within this third parallel we learn, again in a triple grammatical parallel, that government of the people (any government at all) is, in a democracy, government *by* the people, but more especially *for* the people, as grammar effects the rhetorical point.

Behind both rhetoric and grammar is logic, since rhetoric accents the logical point, and grammar puts it in logical order. Grammar, logic, and rhetoric, the first three of the seven liberal arts, formed the basic *trivium* ("three roads, meeting") of education for over two thousand years, from old Roman schools almost down to our own day. Lincoln here exhibits their union, probably through insight, since his formal schooling was nil. Here he works straight through a logical unfolding from the Liberty in which the nation began, through the war over secession and liberty not achieved because some men were slaves and some thought themselves at liberty to own slaves, and on to the new birth of freedom that will reaffirm the original political ideal. The grammar, logic, and rhetoric are here inseparable, fused together by Lincoln's deep conviction. The truly right message is the best rhetorical device after all, and the truth the best persuader.

But even the simple truth needs a vehicle. It cannot just hover in midair, like a disembodied glow. It must arrive in some procession, preceded by a few heralds and attended by visible evidence. Hence the rhetorical heightening, the biblical allusion and metaphor, the parallels, the repetitions, the emphases, in what is sometimes taken as Lincoln's simple, and simply moving, statement.

RHETORICAL DEVICES: A GLOSSARY

Sooner or later, the natural dynamics of expression will get you to many of the devices the Greeks long ago discovered and named. But the terms, commonplace during ancient times, are today difficult to find listed in one place; and the devices, still more common than one might think, are such pleasant invigorators of the linguistic circulation, that it seems good to have them grouped and handy. I have had great pleasure in seeing the rhetorical modes just as active in modern English as in ancient Greek and Latin, and in trying them out in my own idiom. Here they are, arranged for your convenience within functional categories (by no means mutually exclusive), and with pronunciations suggested for those your desk dictionary may not include. You can indeed increase your power by making these venerable devices your own, by having them ready, by learning through them the fair and beautiful play of language.

Alluding to the Familiar

anamnesis (AN-am-NEE-sis). "A remembering." You remind your reader of former success or catastrophe to emphasize your point.

> **This is the very day we lost last year. Again we meet a stronger team in our own stadium. Again injuries have wiped out our strongest hope. Again the weather looks hopeless.**

parachresis (para-KREE-sis). You bring another's words into your own context, with new emphasis or effect.

> **As Ovid says of the sun: Ann sees all things.**
> **Bill constantly follows John around, like Plato's shadow of a shadow.**
> **When Thoreau said that the mass of men lead lives of quiet desperation he must have had Butch in mind.**

paradiorthosis (para-die-or-THO-sis). You quote famous words with your own twist and without identifying them: a witty, subtle, and learned game much played by the Greek poets and T. S. Eliot.

> **The boredom, the horror, and the glory of life [Eliot's allusive twisting of "the kingdom, the power, and the glory"].**

paroemia (pa-REE-mi-a). You apply proverbs to a new situation.

Even the rose has thorns [when a plan has drawbacks, or a girl
    a temper].
Every dog has its day. [Your opponent has just won the elec-
    tion.]
Man shall not live by bread alone. [He has just ordered steak.]
Never look a gift-horse in the mouth. [Someone has criticized
    the doorway of a new building given the university.]

Building to Climax

asyndeton (a-SIN-de-ton). "Without joining." You rush a series of clauses
    together without conjunctions, as if tumbled together by emotional
    haste.

> **They tried, they fought, they did their best.**

climax. You repeat the same word or sound in each succeeding phrase or
    clause—an intensified form of *anadiplosis* (see 464).

> **Knowing that tribulation works patience, and patience experi-
> ence, and experience hope. (Rom. 5.3–4)**

incrementum (in-kre-MENT-um). You arrange items from lowest to highest.

> **The law will be kept in the shacks of the farms, in the tene-
> ments of the slums, in the bungalows and homes of the sub-
> urbs, and in the mansions of the countryside.**

polysyndeton. You repeat connectives in close succession for emphasis.

> **Here and there and everywhere. . . .**

synonymy (si-NON-i-me). You repeat, by synonyms, for emphasis.

> **A miserable, wretched, depressed neighborhood.**

Intensifying

anacoenosis (ana-see-NO-sis). You heighten your style as if in urgent
    consultation with your audience, and with frequent rhetorical
    questions. You gain an urgent mixture of intimacy and elegance.

> If then I be a father, where is mine honor? And if I be a mas-
> ter, where is my fear? (Mal. 1.6)
> Would we really want freedom? Would we really want liberty of
> all kinds? Would we really want anarchy more than peace
> of mind? We would, I think you will agree, gladly accept a
> restricted peace for some measure of quiet.

apodioxis (apo-die-ox-is). You reject an idea emphatically.

> Absurd! Now really! Well, after all!
> Can anything be less practical?

aposiopesis (apo-sigh-o-PE-sis). "A silence." You stop suddenly in
mid-sentence, as if words fail, or as if a word to your wise reader has
been completely sufficient.

> But the cat. . . .
> Do you believe that he can cope . . . ?
> And in the name of common sense—!

apostrophe (a-POS-tro-fee). "A turning away." You "turn away" from your
audience to address someone new—God, the angels, heaven, the dead,
or anyone not present.

> Hear, O heavens.
> Death, where is thy sting?
> Blush, America, for this stupidity.

ecphonesis (ek-fo-NEE-sis). Also called **exclamatio.** You cry out against
something—usually in an apostrophe.

> O wicked speed, to post/With such dexterity to incestuous
> sheets.

erotesis (ero-TEE-sis). This is what we know as the rhetorical question.

> Is this the best course? Will this pave the streets?

Irony

antonomasia (antono-MAY-zhia). You substitute an epithet, a label, for a
person's real name, usually with ironic emphasis.

The Philosopher. The Blowhard. A Solomon. A Castro. A Mickey Mouse. The Swede.

apophasis (a-POF-a-sis). Also called **paralepsis** or **preteritio.** "A passing over." You pretend not to mention something in the very act of mentioning it. The effect is strongly, and sometimes hilariously, ironic. It was a favorite of Cicero's.

> **I shall not mention the time he failed to come home at all, or his somewhat wobbly condition at breakfast.**
> **I shall not go into all his broken promises, his campaign speeches, or his scandalous treatment of his aged mother.**
> **I pass over. . . .**
> **We had perhaps better forget. . . .**
> **I shall not mention. . . .**

aporia (a-POR-i-a). "Doubting." You hesitate ironically between alternatives.

> **Whether he is more stupid than negligent, I hesitate to guess.**
> **One hardly knows what to call it, folly or forgetfulness, ignorance or ignominy.**

epitrope (e-PIT-ro-pe). You ironically grant permission.

> **Let her go, let her go, God bless her!**
> **All right, go on, have a good time, kill yourself.**

euphemism (YOU-fe-mizm). You substitute less pungent words for harsh ones, with excellent ironic effect.

> **The schoolmaster corrected the slightest fault with his birch reminder.**
> **After a gallon of whisky, he was slightly indisposed.**

ironia (eye-RO-ni-a). Also called **antiphrasis** (an-TIF-ra-sis). You say the contrary of what you mean, in what is usually designated "verbal irony" (see 514).

> **He was a beauty.**
> **She is so kind to her friends.**
> **How thoughtful!**

litotes (LIE-toh-teez). "Simplifying." You assert something by denying its opposite.

> **Not bad.**
> **This is no small matter.**
> **My house is not large.**
> **She was not supremely happy.**
> **He is not the wisest man in the world.**

oxymoron (ox-i-MOR-on). "Pointed stupidity." You emphasize your point by the irony of an apparent contradiction or inconsistency.

> **A wise fool, a fearful joy, a sweet sadness, a quiet orgy.**
> **Their silence is eloquent.**
> **This somebody is nobody.**

paralepsis (or **preteritio**). *See* **apophasis**, 460.

zeugma (ZYEWG-ma). "Yoking." You yoke two words so that one is accurate and the other an ironic misfit (a favorite irony of Edward Gibbon's in *The Decline and Fall of the Roman Empire*).

> **Waging** *war* **and** *peace.*
> **Laws the wily tyrant** *dictated* **and** *obeyed.*
> **Pacified by** *gifts* **and** *threats.*
> **A position they** *enjoyed* **and** *feared.*

Overstating, Understating

auxesis (awk-SEE-sis). You ironically use an overly weighty or exaggerated term for the accurate one.

> **She is an angel.**
> **He is a devil.**
> **That pig ate all the olives.**

hyperbole (high-PER-bo-lee). You exaggerate for emphasis, humorous or serious.

> **She cried like a banshee.**

hypothesis. You illustrate with an impossible supposition.

> **If salt lose its savor, wherewith shall it be salted?**
> **Even if he had a million dollars, he would be unhappy.**
> **I'll come to thee by moonlight, though Hell should bar the way.**

meiosis (my-o-sis). You make big things seem trifles, or substitute a lighter word for ironic effect. The opposite of **auxesis** (see above).

> **He had three sandwiches and a quart of milk for his** *snack.*
> **It was** *nothing; a pinprick.*
> **He had a mansion in the country and another** *little place* **in town.**

Posing Contrasts

antithesis. You strongly and closely contrast your ideas.

> **From rags to riches, from beans to beef, from water to wine.**
> **Man proposes, God disposes.**
> **A world in a grain of sand, a heaven in a wild flower.**
> **The world will** *little note nor long remember* **what** *we say* **here, but it can** *never forget* **what** *they did* **here.**
> **It was the best of times; it was the worst of times.**

chiasmus (ky-AZ-mus). "A crossing"—from the Greek letter *chi,* X, a cross. (Also called **antimitabole.**). You "cross" the terms of one clause by reversing their order in the next.

> **Ask not what your country can do for you: ask what you can do for your country.**
> **What you write may mark your place in society—or place your mark on it.**

comparison. In an extended and balanced comparison, you match your clauses almost syllable for syllable.

> **My years are not so many, but that one death may conclude them, nor my faults so many, but that one death may satisfy them.**
> **He who loves pleasure shall be a poor man; he who loves wine and oil shall not be rich.**

dilemma. You catch the argument both ways, in a pair of opposing suppositions.

> **If you're so smart, why aren't you rich? If you're rich, why act**
> **so smart?**
> **If he is right, why disparage him? If he is wrong, why pay at-**
> **tention to him at all?**

dissimile. You emphasize the condition of something by saying how dissimilar it is from the usual run of things.

> **The foxes have holes, and the fowls of the air their nests, but**
> **the son of man has nowhere to lay his head. (Luke 9.58)**
> **One generation passeth away, and another generation cometh;**
> **but the earth abideth forever.**

enantiosis (en-AN-ti-o-sis). Also called **contentio.** You emphasize contraries, often with **chiasmus.**

> **One wouldn't hurt her; the other couldn't help her.**
> **Could not go on, would not go back.**
> **Serious in silly things, and silly in serious.**

Refining, Elaborating

epanorthosis (EP-an-or-THO-sis). "A correction." You seem to "correct" yourself to reinforce your idea.

> **Written not in tables of stone but in the fleshy tables of the**
> **heart. (II Cor. 3.3.)**
> **He asks, or rather demands, an answer.**
> **A gift-horse—no, a white elephant.**

exegesis (ek-suh-JEE-sis). Also called **explicatio.** You clarify a thought in the same sentence.

> **Time is both short and long, short when you are happy, long**
> **when in pain.**

exergasia (eks-er-GAY-zhia). "A polishing." You put the same thing several ways.

A beauty, a dream, a vision, a phantom of delight.

hirmos (HIR-mos). "A series." You heap appositives together.

All men, rich, poor, tall, short, young, old, love it.

horismos (ho-RIZ-mos). You elaborate a concept by defining it.

Beauty is transitory, a snare for the unwary, an invitation to disaster.

Repeating

alliteration. You repeat the initial letter or sound in two or more nearby words.

The morning air was _c_ool and _c_risp.
They have _b_ribed us with promises, _b_lackmailed us with threats, _bl_udgeoned us with prohibitions, and _bl_ed us with taxes.
_Sp_eak the _sp_eech, I _pr_ay you, as I _pr_onounc'd it to you, _t_rippingly on the _t_ongue. . . .

anadiplosis (ana-di-PLO-sis). You repeat early in a clause a significant word from the end of the preceding clause.

They rode in on a _wave_ of fear, but the _wave_ took them up the beach.
Learn as though you would _live_ forever; _live_ as though you would die tomorrow.

anaphora (a-NAF-or-a). "A bringing again." You begin successive clauses with the same word or sound.

The voice of the Lord is powerful. The voice of the Lord is full of majestie. The voice of the Lord breaks the cedars. (Psa. 29.4–5)
The game is lost. The game was finished before it began. The game was a farce from the first.

antanaclasis (anta-NAK-la-sis). You repeat the same word in a different sense, punning on it to drive home your point.

> **Learn a *craft* so you may live without *craft*.**
> ***Care* in your youth so you may live without *care*.**

epanalepsis (EP-ana-LEP-sis). You end your second clause with the same word or sound that began your first clause.

> **A fool with his friends, with his wife a fool.**
> **In sorrow was I born, and will die in sorrow.**

epistrophe (e-PIS-tro-fee). You end several sentences alike for emphasis.

> **They loved football. They ate football. They slept football.**

epizeuxis (EP-i-ZYEWK-sis). You double the same word for emphasis.

> **Romeo, Romeo, wherefore art thou Romeo?**
> **Oh John, John.**
> **It is not, believe me, it is not.**
> **War, war after war.**

homeoteleuton (homeo-TEL-yu-ton). You end successive clauses or phrases with the same sound.

> **In activity commendable, in commonwealth formidable, in war terrible.**
> **He spoke wittily, praised the principal mightily, and ended happily.**

paregmenon (pa-REG-meh-non). You play upon derivatives of a word.

> **A discrete discretion.**
> **A marvel of the marvelous.**
> **The humble are proud of humility.**

paronomasia (parono-MAY-zhia). You pun by changing a letter or syllable.

> **His *sword* is better than his *word*.**
> ***Errors* cause *terrors*.**
> **Bolder in the *buttery* than in the *battery*.**
> ***Friends* turned *fiends*.**
> ***Repining* but not *repenting*.**

ploce (PLO-see). You repeat a word emphatically to bring out its literal meaning.

A *man's* a *man*, for a' that.
A *player* who is really a *player*.
In that battle *Caesar* was *Caesar*.

Substituting

hendiadys (hen-DIE-a-dis). "One through two." You divide what would be an adjective-and-noun into two nouns connected by *and*.

We drank from cups and gold [golden cups].
He looked with eyes and anger [angry eyes].

metaphor. "A carrying across." You describe something as if it were something else (see 210–14).

All flesh is grass.
He was a horse.
She preened her feathers.

metonymy (meh-TON-i-me). A kind of metaphor, in which you substitute an associated item for the thing itself.

The *White House* declares [for "the *President* declares"].
The *crown* decides [for "the *king* decides"].
The *hot rod* is here [for "the young man who drives a car in which the piston rods run at high temperatures is here" —*hot rod* is already a synecdoche for *car*].

parabola (pa-RAB-o-la). You illustrate with a slight narrative touch, or "parable." This is an **hypothesis** (see 462) somewhat nearer the possible.

It is as if a man were to hit the bull's-eye without aiming, or indeed without even seeing the target.
But this is to count your chickens before they hatch.

paradiastole (para-die-ASS-to-lee). In a kind of euphemism, you substitute a term remotely similar to the real idea, as in calling a reckless driver "playful" to underline his recklessness ironically.

The *generous* **Mr. Smith [actually improvident].**
The general's tactics were *cautious* **[downright timid or coward-**
ly].
Bill played a *conservative* **game [obviously stupid].**
She is *considerate* **of her appearance [does nothing but work on**
it].

prosopopoeia (pro-so-po-PE-ya). You personify an inanimate object. Originally, the idea was pretending that an inanimate thing, an imaginary
being, or an absent person (especially the illustrious dead) was speaking; now, more broadly, it is the general endowing of inanimate objects with human attributes.

This car is a sweetheart.
Thou still unravished bride of quietness.
The stadium settled back for a lonely week.
"What," Lincoln might ask, "are we still withholding citizen-
ship?"

synecdoche (si-NEK-do-kee). You put (1) the part for the whole, (2) the
whole for the part, (3) the species for the genus, (4) the genus for the
species, (5) the material for the object it constitutes.

1. **He is a good** *hand.*
2. **Here comes** *Michigan* **[for only the football team of one uni-**
   versity within the state].
3. **a** *cutthroat* **[for any kind of murderer].**
4. **the** *felines* **[for lions].**
5. **He handles his** *irons* **well [for golf clubs made of metal].**

Miscellaneous

hyperbaton (high-PER-ba-ton). You transpose the normal order of words
for elegance.

That the lady will surely enjoy.
Him the crowd adores.

martyria (mar-TIR-i-a). "Witnessing." You confirm something from your
own experience.

I have seen thousands standing with their rice bowls.
Many times I have found the stadium only half filled.

metabasis (meh-TAB-a-sis). "Transition." Briefly reminding the reader where you and he are, where you have been, and where you are going.

> **We have just seen some of radiation's immediate effects; now let us consider the long-term problems.**
> **I have already mentioned property taxes; now I shall consider those that hit everybody.**

mimesis (mi-MEE-sis). "Imitation." You imitate the language of others for ironic effect.

> **The cracker-barrel politician is just about *done gone* from the Southern scene.**
> **Try *to never split* your infinitives, if you wish *to further improve* your diction and *to really understand* good writing.**

synchoresis (SIN-ko-REE-sis). You concede something, usually ironically, in order to retort with greater force.

> **I admit that we have no business in their affairs, except the business of helping them, at their request, toward freedom and justice.**
> **They are surly, unmanageable, ungrateful. I admit it. But I deny that society can afford not to help them.**

A Glossary of Grammatical Terms

Absolute phrase. A phrase modifying a whole sentence—noun plus participle, present or past.

> *Flags waving,* **the band marched in.**
> **We'll win,** *God willing.*
> *All forgiven,* **they came home**

Active voice. See **voice.**

Adjective. A word modifying a noun (or a pronoun), telling which, how many, what kind.

> **The** *tall* **tree, with** *many* **branches, was very** *old.*

Adjective phrase. A phrase acting as an adjective.

> **Here is a book** *of great interest.*
> **The house** *at the end of the road* **is our favorite.**

Adjective (relative) clause. A subordinate clause acting as an adjective—beginning with *who (whom, whose), which, that, where.*

> **Jeddley,** *who has just published his third novel,* **is a writer to be watched.**
> **The house [***that***]** *you liked* **burned down.**

469

The street, *which the city recently paved,* has always been
   charming.
This is the town *where I was born.*

Adjective-with-phrase.   A subordinate, modifying phrase built this way:

There was the lake, *smooth in the morning air.*

Adverb.   A word modifying a verb, an adjective, or another adverb, supplying information as to *how, when, where, why,* and the like.

She swam *strongly.*
He was *always* punctual.
The table was *very* attractive.
The freed prisoners shouted *joyously.*

Adverbial clause.   The usual subordinate clause, beginning *although, since,
when, before, after,* and the like, modifying main-sentence units.

Although they played their hearts out, they lost.
Laughing when the first glass broke, he grew grimmer *as time went
   on,* finally leaving *before things really went wild.*

Adverbial phrase.   A phrase acting as an adverb to modify a verb, adjective, or another adverb.

He left *in the nick of time.*
The house was cool *for most of the summer.*
Careful *by habit,* she called the police.
On a sunny afternoon, the park is always crowded.

Agreement of pronoun and antecedent.   Singular pronouns must match
the singular nouns they represent; plurals must match plurals.

Everyone knows *his* [not *their*] own interests.
The *committee* reached *its* [not *their*] decision unanimously.
Many *thousands* of individuals proclaimed *their* [not *his* or *her*]
   personal freedom.

Agreement of subject and verb.   Singular verbs match singular subjects;
plurals match plurals. The present tense is the only problem, and only
in the third person singular *(he, she, it),* which adds an *-s* or *-es* to the
basic verb.

Jerome *writes* **every day.** [I *write;* they *write*]

The verb *to be* also complicates the system.

PRESENT TENSE	**PAST TENSE**
I *am* hungry	I *was* hungry
You *are* hungry	You *were* hungry
He	He
She	She
It } *is* hungry	It } *was* hungry
Everyone	Everyone
The worker	The worker
We	We
You	You
They } *are* hungry	They } *were* hungry
Many	Many
The workers	The workers

Antecedent.   The word a pronoun refers to.

> *Abigail,* **the oldest of the group, said that** *she* **would try.** [*Abigail* is the antecedent of *she.*]
> **The** *leaves* **turn in** *their* **season.** [*leaves* is the antecedent of *their.*]
> *Everything* **works out in** *its* **own way.** [*Everything* is the antecedent of *its.*]

Appositive.   A noun or noun phrase explaining another noun or pronoun.

> **El Greco,** *preeminent painter of Toledo,* **was born in Crete.**
> **The quarterback,** *a master at running the option,* **was sacked three times in the first quarter.**
> **All of them—***father, mother, children, cousins***—worked in the restaurant.**

Article.   *A, an,* or *the.*

> *a* **hat,** *an* **ostrich,** *the* **ocean**

Auxiliary (helping) verb.   The words introducing a two- or three-part verb.

is **going,** *have* **gone,** *was* **entered,** *am* **looking,** *might have* **been** [*May, can, must, will, do, would, should* **are the other basic auxiliaries.**]

Bare form.   The basic verb in the present tense, to which *he, she,* and *it* add *-s* or *-es.*

I *go;* you *go;* we *go;* they *go;* he (she, or it) *goes.*

Base sentence.   A sentence without modifiers. The simple subject plus verb.

Trees grow.
Adams won [five dollars].
All is [lost].

Base verb. The main verb in a two- or three-part verb.

will have *gone,* **might have** *been,* **would have** *played,* **is** *trying,* **was** *talking*

Case.   The part a noun or pronoun plays in a sentence as its subject, its object, a possessive, a reflexive, or intensive.

SUBJECT: **The** *cat* **licked her paws.**
   She **then cleaned her whiskers.**
OBJECT: **The right tackle sacked the** *quarterback.*
   He hit *him* **very hard.**
POSSESSIVE: **The** *women's* **singles begins in fifteen minutes.**
   Her **backhand is amazing.**
REFLEXIVE: **He pampers** *himself.*
INTENSIVE (EMPHATIC): **She** *herself* **thinks nothing of it.**

Clause.   Part of a compound or complex sentence, complete with subject and predicate—a noun (or pronoun) with its finite verb.

INDEPENDENT CLAUSE (COORDINATE CLAUSE):

The president called the meeting to order, **and** *the room grew deathly still.*

SUBORDINATE CLAUSE (DEPENDENT CLAUSE):

After the president called the meeting to order, ...
They have no rights, *when all is said and done.*

Collective noun.   A word naming groups as single units:

family, quartet, herd

Comma splice (comma fault).   Joining two sentences with a comma.

FAULTY: **The comma splice is an error, it is the exact opposite of
a fragment. (See 390–93.)**
REVISED: **The comma splice is an error. It is the exact opposite
of a fragment.**

Common form.   The verb's basic form:

go, work, swim, think

Common noun.   A word identifying, or naming, things:

pen, hay, horse

Comparative and superlative.   Adjectives and adverbs making contrasts.

COMPARATIVE: **Men are *taller* than women.**
Women live *longer* than men.
Geller's passes are *more accurate* than Smith's.
Barbara plays *more consistently* than Jim.
SUPERLATIVE: **He is the *tallest* player.**
Geller's passes are the *most accurate*.
Barbara plays the *most consistently*.

Comparison.   Detailing similarities, with contrasting differences.

**Jonson, like Shakespeare, dominated the stage in both tragedy
and comedy, but Jonson was essentially a classicist and Shakespeare a romantic.**

Complete subject.   See **subject.**

Complex sentence.   A sentence combining subordinate and independent
clauses.

Because he was too optimistic, he is bankrupt.

Compound-complex sentence.   One or more subordinate clauses and two or more independent clauses.

When I submitted my application, when they had reviewed it forever, they finally wrote that I was admitted, and I immediately caught a plane.

Compound phrase.   Phrases joined by a conjunction.

She played the course *carefully but with great confidence.*
He was *by far the best but most underestimated contender.*
In this course, a student must *either go all out or be content with barely passing.*
By going outside and running the option, **he made the crucial first down.**

Compound predicate.   Two or more verbs for the single subject.

Andrea *went* **to Africa and** *became* **a missionary.**

Compound sentence.   Two or more independent clauses joined by a comma-and-conjunction, a semicolon, or a colon.

He was dedicated, and the company appreciated him. They had many opportunities, but none like this. They valued him: he really understood the market.

Conditional sentence.   One beginning with a subordinate clause, an *If* . . . , *When* . . . , *Provided that* . . . , OR EQUIVALENT.

If something isn't done soon, Social Security will collapse.

Compound subject.   Two or more nouns, or noun phrases, governing one verb.

Jack and Jill **went up the hill.**
Going to work every day and having to commute for an hour each way **leaves little time for fun.**

Conjunction.   Conjunctions join words, phrases, and clauses. *Coordinating* conjunctions—*and, but, or (nor), yet*—join equals (*for* and *so* join equal clauses only):

Mary *and* I won easily.
Near the shore *but* far from home, the bottle floated.
He was talented, *yet* he failed.
He upset everyone, *for* the exam had just begun.
He left the room, *so* everyone was relieved.

Subordinating conjunctions attach clauses to the basic sentence (independent clause):

Since it was late, they left.
He worked hard *because* he needed an A.
They stopped *after* they reached the spring.

Conjunctive adverb.   Conjunctions that modify a whole clause adverbially —*therefore, moreover, however, nevertheless, consequently, furthermore.*

Therefore, to thine own self be true.
He thinks well; the job, *however,* is beyond his experience.
Consequently, they must move.

Connotation.   See **denotation.**

Contrast. Pointing out differences.

A play, unlike a novel, unfolds in the immediate present of its situation; a novel recalls past events, however immediate they may seem.

Coordinating conjunction.   See **conjunction.**

Coordination.   Putting two or more parts of a sentence in equal rank.

The birds and *the bees* know how.
He ran, and *she kept pace* on her bicycle.

Copulative verb.   A linker, an equals sign, like *is, seems, smells, looks, tastes.* It takes a predicate adjective. (*Is* also takes a predicate nominative.)

The turtle is *dead.* This tastes *good.* That smells *bad.* Ed is *mayor.*

Correlatives.   Pairs of paralleling coordinators: *both/and; either/or; neither/nor; not only/but also; whether/or.*

The food was *both* good *and* plentiful.
They watched *not only* the game *but also* all the discussion and
replays.
Neither the book *nor* the movie was worth much.

Dangling modifier. An introductory phrase dangles, with nothing to relate to: "Bowing to the crowd, the bull caught him unawares"; "Driving across country, the prices get higher and higher." You have left
out the real subject your modifier modifies: "Bowing to the crowd, the
toreador . . . ", "Driving across country, we. . . . " Other mismatches
are frequent: "Having broken the dam, the sandbags could not hold
the water" ("The water, having broken the dam, rushed through the
sand bags"); "Born in Hungary, his knowledge of American folklore
was minimal" ("Born in Hungary, he knew little about American folklore"). For further details see 160–61, 377–78.

Deduction. In logic, leading away from some general precept to its particular parts and consequences. See 118–23. In composition, setting up
your thesis in your Beginning, and then presenting your arguments
and evidence for it in your Middle. See 45–46.

Definite pronoun. See **Pronoun.**

Denotation, connotation. A word **denotes** something specific: *tree, stone,
chair.* Its **connotation** conveys an attitude, generally of good or bad.
Tree merely denotes. *Willow* denotes a kind of tree but also connotes
sadness. See 205.

Demonstrative adjective. *This, that, these, those,* when modifying a noun:
This hat; *these* people. Some grammars call these *determiners* or *noun
markers.*

Dependent clause. See **Clause.**

Direct object. See **Object.**

Emphatic case. See **Case** (Intensive).

Expletive. A grammatical filler, like *there* in "There are frequent errors"
("Errors are frequent") and *it* in "It is easy to win" ("Winning is
easy").

Fallacy. An undetected error in logic. See 124–25.

Faulty parallelism. Parallel thoughts put in unparallel grammatical constructions.

FAULTY: She liked the *garden, cleaning* the house, and *paying* the
bills.

REVISED: She liked *gardening,* . . .
FAULTY: He thought the girl was *attractive, intelligent,* and *knew* how to make him feel needed.
REVISED: He thought the girl was *attractive, intelligent,* and *sympathetic,* knowing how to make him feel needed.

Faulty predication.   Linking an independent and a subordinate clause with an *is (are, was, were).*

FAULTY: What gripes me is when they leave.
REVISED: When they leave, I'm griped.
What gripes me is their leaving.

Faulty shift of tense.   Shifting from past to present, or vice versa, when moving from one clause to another.

FAULTY: They *like* the film, and *went* every day.
REVISED: They *like* the film, and *go.* . . .
FAULTY: When he *went* into the room, it *is* as black as coal.
REVISED: When he went into the room, it *was.* . . .

Finite verb.   A verb complete in itself, in past, present, or future, serving as predicate.

He *came.* He *saw.* He *will conquer.*
Next year, he *would have been* eighty. She *is* right.

Fragment.   A subordinate part of a sentence made to stand as a complete sentence, usually incorrectly. See 389–90.

When they go.
Wanting to succeed.
Because I cannot understand.
As anyone would think.

Fused sentence.   A run-on sentence (see **Run-on**).

Future perfect tense.   See **Tense.**

Future tense.   See **Tense.**

Gender.   The male, female, and neuter pronouns—*he, she, it, his, hers, its* —must match the gender of their antecedents.

Gerund.   An *-ing* word (one of the verbals) working as a noun.

Going to the blackboard embarrassed her.
He does not like *passing* out campaign leaflets.

Headword.   The noun or noun-phrase heading a sentence, clause, or phrase.

Going to bat, *Blivens* tripped on the dugout steps.

I do not believe that this *team* will ever win.

The *girl* running the diner is my sister.

Helping verb.   See **Auxiliary.**

Idiomatic.   The habitual way of a language. *To rely on* is idiomatic English; *To rely in* is not.

Imperative mood.   See **Mood.**

Indefinite pronoun.   See **Pronoun.**

Independent clause.   See **Clause.**

Indicative mood.   See **Mood.**

Indirect object.   See **Object.**

Induction.   In logic, leading up to a general proposition by adding up the particular pieces of evidence. (See 115–17.) In composition, starting with questions and particulars and leading your reader up to your thesis. See 43–45.

Infinitive.   The verb in its basic form, not yet defined in time and action, designated by *to: to run, to think, to be,* which change, in their finite forms, to *he runs, I thought, they are.*

I hate *to see* that evening sun go down.
To think is *to be* alive.

Infinitive phrase.   An infinitive plus an object and its modifiers.

To be a mockingbird is not everything.
She likes *to rule as queen of the hive.*
He wants *to live on easy street soon.*

Often the infinitive *to* is understood: *We can make the car* [*to*] *run more smoothly.* See **Split infinitive,** 111–12, 375, 531–32.

Intrasitivive verb.   See **Transitive.**

Irregular verb.   See **Regular verbs.**

Linking verb.   A Verb that links the subject to a state of being.

> She *is* champion.
> This *smells* good.
> That *looks* wonderful.
> He *feels* fine.

See **Copulative verb.**

Main clause.   The basic sentence, with subordinate clauses attached.

> However she tries to be sophisticated, *she is still Annie from next door.*
> The ship finally sailed *after the government cleared it.*

Main verb.   The base verb, the hub of the action, or state of being, in sentences that have other finite verbs in their subordinate clauses.

> He *cleaned* the gutters before winter clamped down.
> After the market closed, we *bought* some beautiful lettuce.

Misplaced modifier.   It mistakenly modifies something else, as do dangling modifiers.

> *Bowing to the crowd,* the bull caught him unawares. [*Bowing to the crowd,* he let the bull catch him.]
> She *only* loved her mother. [She loved *only* her mother.]
> They decided *when the teams tied* to end the game. [*When the teams tied,* they decided to end the game.]
> [They decided to end the game *when the teams tied.*]
> He liked people *in his way.* [*In his way,* he liked people.]

Modal auxiliary.   See **Auxiliary.** A helping verb in the subjunctive mood, one urging *should, would, can, may, might, must, ought:*

> They *ought* to go; if they *can* [go], they *must* [go].
> Who *would* think otherwise?

Modifier.   A word, phrase, or clause that qualifies a basic term.

> The *wily* emperor. . . .
> He ruled *severely.*
> He ruled *like an adolescent.*

He *frequently* fought *in the arena.*
The *low white* house dominates the *green and tangled* park *like a quiet observer.*

Mood.   The aspect of a verb that carries the speaker's attitude as to factuality or likelihood.

Indicative mood.   Indicates actuality or strong likelihood.

He *won.*
He *will win.*
They *gave* up.

Imperative mood.   Commands or requests something.

Win, or your name is mud.
Please *win,* for my sake.
Let us *go* now, you and I.
Come here.

Subjunctive mood.   Expresses a hypothetical condition in conditional, provisional, wishful, or suppositional subordinate clauses. The verb is often a plural form or past-tense form.

If I *were* you, . . .
If this *be* error, . . .
Had he *been* sure, . . .
I demand that he *make* restitution.

Nonrestrictive.   See **Restrictive.**

Noun.   Nouns name something—persons, animals, places, things, concepts, activities.

Noun adjunct.   A noun modifying another noun: *stone* wall; *education course* selection. See **Break the Noun Habit,** 186–88.

Noun clause.   A clause functioning as a noun.

Everyone who went enjoyed it.
Home is *where he hangs his hat.*
They saw *that something was wrong.*
He was pleased by *what she had done.*

Noun equivalent.   A verbal noun (gerund) or noun clause.

Noun phrase.   (1) A phrase serving as a noun.

He hated *going to class.*

(2) In transformational grammar, a noun plus its modifiers, if any.

Ben **called this morning.**
The long black car **stopped by the mailbox.**
He stepped on *a slippery rock.*

Number.   The singular or plural: *horse, horses; is, are.*

Object.   Whatever receives the action of a verb, verbal (participal or gerund), or infinitive, or that completes a preposition.

She slammed *the door.*
Giving *the party* **was fun.**
He didn't want to shoot *the elephant.*
His wallet was under *the table,* **by** *the waiter's foot.*

Direct object.   The object of the main verb.

He wasted *his inheritance.*

Indirect object.   The indirect recipient of the action, the object of a preposition understood *(to, for, of).*

They gave their *son* **a new car.**
The sheriff asked *him* **several questions.**

Objective case.   See **Case** (Object).

Objective complement.   A noun, adjective, or clause completing a direct object.

They elected Washington *President.*
We painted the house *white.*
They named their daughter *what her grandmother had wished.*

Parallel construction.   Putting equivalent ideas in matching grammatical patterns, balancing noun with noun, participle with participle, clause with clause. See 164–71.

An *attractive, considerate,* **and** *intelligent* **girl.** . . .
By **weeks of planning,** *by* **careful training, and** *by* **luck.** . . .

Since all things are not equal, *since* consequences cannot be foreseen, *since* we live but a moment. . . .

They are *not only organizing* social activities *but also discussing* political issues.

Participle.   A verbal form ending in *-ing* (present) or, usually, *-ed* (past), which joins with verbal auxiliaries to form some past, progressive, and future tenses, and which acts independently as an adjective. Present participle: *walking, going, singing, throwing.* Past participle: *walked, gone, sung, thrown.* A perfect participle joins *has (have, having)* to a past participle: *having walked, having been gone, will have taken.*

Participial phrase.   A participle with its object and other modifiers.

Launching the boat through heavy surf, they lost some tackle but survived.

Exhausted from hours of rowing, they reached the ship.

The fire engine, *having missed the right turn,* arrived a little late.

She made a delicious stew, *simmering it slowly for two hours.*

Parts of speech.   The grammatical types, like *nouns, adjectives, verbs.*

Passive voice.   See **Voice.**

Past participle.   See **Participle.**

Past tense.   See **Tense.**

Perfect participle.   See **Participle.**

Person.   Whether a pronoun represents *first person* ("I"), *second person* ("you"), or *third person* ("they").

Phrase.   A unit of thought without complete subject and predicate—a subordinate part of a sentence: *By the way; Thinking all the time; of no importance.*

Possessive case.   See **Case.**

Predicate.   The verb and its modifiers.

The book *was not on the shelf.*

He *makes lasagna beyond your wildest dreams.*

The **base predicate,** above, is *was* and *makes:* the basic finite verb.

Predicate nominative (predicate noun).   The noun, on the far side of a linking verb, that describes or qualifies the subject.

She is a *freak.*
Tadpoles become *frogs.*

Predication, faulty.   See **Faulty predication.**

Preposition.   A word like *by, from, to, for, in, of, with, at* connecting a noun
with another noun, a verb, or an adjective.

The house *with* seven gables was Hawthorne's.
She swam *for* five miles.
The bricks were a uniform red *from* top to bottom.

Prepositional phrase.   A phrase starting with a preposition. It functions as
either adjective or adverb.

She was a girl *of many hidden resourses.*
She swam *with unbelievable stamina.*

Present participle.   See **Participle.**

Present perfect tense.   See **Tense.**

Present tense.   See **Tense.**

Principal parts.   The verb's basic forms: present, past, present participle,
past participle.

PRESENT (BARE FORM)	PAST	PRESENT PARTICIPLE	PAST PARTICIPLE
go	**went**	**going**	**gone**
walk	**walked**	**walking**	**walked**

Progressive form.   The verb's form indicating continuing action: *am going,
are walking, were thinking.*

Pronoun.   Those little words stand for *(pro)* a noun: *I, he, she, it; hers, his,
theirs* and the like. **Indefinite pronouns** have no antecedents: *one, some,
none, any, each, all, many, few, much, more, most, everybody, somebody, nobody,
nothing, everyone,* and the like. See 346 for the roster of various kinds.

Reflexive case.   See **Case.**

Regular and irregular verbs.   **Regular verbs** form the past and past participle by adding *-ed* or *-d: talk, talked, talked; cook, cooked, cooked; say, said,
said.* **Irregular verbs** retain a variety of older forms: *be (am, is), was
(were), been; go, went, gone; swim, swam, swum.*

Relative clause.   See **Adjective clause,** and **Restrictive** and **nonrestrictive clauses.**

Relative pronoun.   One introducing a relative (adjective) clause: *who (whom, whose), that, which, whoever, whatever,* and the like.

Relative understood.   Omitting the *that* or *who* effectively.

> **The books he collected. . . .** [*that* **omitted**]
> **The girl he liked best. . . .** [*whom* **omitted**]

Restrictive and nonrestrictive clauses.   **Restrictive clauses** are essential, restricting the meaning of the word they modify.

> **The taxes that are reasonable will be paid.**

Nonrestrictive clauses are nonessential to meaning, merely adding some information, within commas. See 184, 385–86.

> **The taxes, which are reasonable, will be paid.**

Run-on sentence.   Two or more sentences run together as one, with no punctuation where a period or semicolon should go. See **Comma splice** and 390–93.

RUN-ON	REPAIRED
The hero can no longer think he nearly goes insane.	The hero can no longer think. He nearly goes insane.
The book is well written it is full of fascinating information.	The book is well written. It is full of fascinating information.
The novel fails to make Gatsby convincing the movie brings him to life.	The novel fails to make Gatsby convincing; the movie brings him to life.

Sentence.   A grammatical unit with at least one independent subject and predicate (finite verb), beginning with a capital and ending with a period, question mark, or exclamation mark: *I am here. Are you there? Go!* (the subject *You* is understood). *After he left the room, all hell broke loose.*

Sentence fragment.   See **Fragment.**

Sequence of tenses.   Verbs following one another in the same tense—present, past, or future.

When this cannon *goes* [future, in present form] off, the ships
   will have entered [future] the harbor.
When the cannon *goes* [present] off, everyone *knows* [present]
   the fleet is in.
Everywhere he *went,* the crowds *gathered* and *cheered.*

Shift of tense.   See **Faulty shift of tense.**

Simple sentence.   A sentence of one independent clause.

The fleet is in.
Every dog has its day.

Simple subject.   See **Subject.**

Split infinitive.   An infinitive, like *to read,* split by an adverb or two: *to carefully and thoroughly read.* See 111–12, 375, 531–32.

Subject.   What a sentence is about—the topic.

Rats are a nuisance.
Going to church was not his bag.
Does *anything* happen as planned?

A **simple subject** is the subject considered without any of its modifiers.

The tall and luminous poplar *tree* swayed in the wind.

The **complete subject** includes the modifiers.

The tall and luminous poplar tree swayed. . . .

Subjective case.   See **Case** (Subject).

Subject-verb agreement.   See **Agreement of subject and verb.**

Subjunctive mood.   See **Mood.**

Subordinate (dependent) clause.   A clause amplifying the main (independent) clause, hooked on with *that, who, which,* or one of the many other
subordinators like *although, because, where, when, after, if.*

Although they tried, they lost badly.
They started fishing *where the water ran smooth.*
The gift *that pleased her most* was her grandmother's ring.

Subordinate verb.   The verb in a subordinate clause:

> **Although they** *tried,* . . .
> . . . **where the water** *ran* **smooth.**
> . . . **that** *pleased* **her most.** . . .

Subordinating conjunction.   The *that* in sentences like *I think that she will win,* plus all the adverbial conjunctions like *when, until, although, because, after, if.*

Subordination.   Ordering your lesser thoughts "sub," or below, the main idea of your independent clause with subordinators, appositives, relatives understood, or adjectives-with-phrase. See 154–56.

Subordinator.   Any of the subordinating conjunctions (*although, after, because,* and so forth) and the relative pronouns *who, that, which,* and the like.

Substantive.   A noun or its equivalent (a phrase or clause serving as a noun). See **Noun clause** and **Noun phrase.**

Superlative.   See **Comparative and superlative.**

Tense.   The time of a verb's action.

> PRESENT: **She sings.**
> PAST: **She sang.**
> FUTURE: **She will sing.**
> PRESENT PERFECT: **She has sung.**
> PAST PERFECT: **She had sung**
> FUTURE PERFECT: **She will have sung.**

Transition.   A word or phrase helping the reader to make the step from one paragraph to the next, or from one sentence to the next: *also, of course, but, to be sure,* and the like. See 56–58, 60–62, 66–67.

Transitive and intransitive verbs.

> TRANSITIVE: **A verb that takes an object: She** *hit* **him.**
> INTRANSITIVE: **A verb without an object: Jesus** *wept.*

Transform, transformation.   In transformational grammar, one of the versions generated from the same kernel-sentence:

> **I like candy.**
> **Candy I like.**
> **Candy is liked by me.**

Verb.   Words expressing actions or states of being.

He *swims* every day.
This *is working* well.

Verbals.   Forms of the verb acting as adjectives (present and past participles) or nouns (gerunds and infinitives).

Verbal noun.   Gerunds and infinitives serving as nouns.

Swimming **was his primary recreation.**
He liked *to swim.*

Verb phrase.   (1) A base verb with its auxiliaries: *may graduate, could have written, ought not to have gone.* (2) In transformational grammar, the predicate, whether a single verb or a verb with its object and modifiers:

He *eats.*
He *eats oysters by the dozen.*

Voice.   The verb's statement as to whether the subject is doing something or being done to.

ACTIVE VOICE: **They built the boat.**
PASSIVE VOICE: **The boat** *was built.*
       Is the job *finished?*

A Glossary of Usage and Common Errors

A NOTE ON USAGE

Speech keeps a daily pressure on writing, and writing returns the compliment, exacting sense from new twists in the spoken language and keeping old senses straight. Usage, generally, is "the way they say it." Usage is the current in the living stream of language; it keeps us afloat, it keeps us fresh—as it sweeps us along. But to distinguish yourself as a writer, you must always swim upstream. You may say, *hooja-eatwith?;* but you will write: *With whom did they compare themselves? With the best, with whoever seemed admirable.* Usage is, primarily, talk; and talk year by year gives words differing social approval, and differing meanings. Words move from the gutter to the penthouse, and back down the elevator shaft. *Bull,* a four-letter Anglo-Saxon word, was unmentionable in Victorian circles. One had to use *he-cow,* if at all. Phrases and syntactical patterns also have their fashions, mostly bad. *Like unto me* changes to *like me* to *like I do; this type of thing* be comes *this type thing; -wise,* after centuries of dormancy in only a few words (*likewise, clockwise, otherwise*), suddenly sprouts out the end of everything: *budgetwise, personalitywise, beautywise, prestigewise. Persuade them to vote* becomes *convince them to vote.* Suddenly, everyone is saying *hopefully.* As usual, the marketplace changes more than your money.

But the written language has always refined the language of the marketplace. The Attic Greek of Plato and Aristotle (as Aristotle's remarks about local usages show) was distilled from commercial exchange. Cicero and Catullus and Horace polished their currency against the archaic and the Greek. Mallarmé claimed that Poe had given *un sens plus pur aux mots de la tribu*—which Eliot rephrases for himself: "to purify the dialect of the tribe." It is the very nature of writing so to do; it is the writer's illusion that he has done so:

I have laboured to refine our language to grammatical purity, and to clear it from colloquial barbarisms, licentious idioms, and irregular combinations. Something, perhaps, I have added to the elegance of its construction, and something to the harmony of its cadence.

—wrote Samuel Johnson in 1752 as he closed his *Rambler* papers. And he had almost done what he hoped. He was to shape English writing and speech for the next hundred and fifty years, until it was ready for another dip in the stream and another purification. His work, moreover, lasts. We would not imitate it now; but we can read it with pleasure, and imitate its enduring drive for excellence.

Johnson goes on to say that he has "rarely admitted any word not authorized by former writers." Writers provide the second level of usage, the paper money. But even this usage requires principle. If we accept "what the best writers use," we still cannot tell whether it is valid: we may be aping their bad habits. Usage is only a court of first appeal, where we can say little more than "He said it." Beyond that helpless litigation, we can test our writing by asking what the words mean, and by simple principles: clarity is good, economy is good, ease is good, gracefulness is good, fullness is good, forcefulness is good. As with all predicaments on earth, we judge by appeal to meanings and principles, and we often find both in conflict. Do *near* and *nearly* mean the same thing? Do *convince* and *persuade? Lie* and *lay?* Is our writing economical but unclear? Is it full but cumbersome? Is it clear but too colloquial for grace? Careful judgment will give the ruling.

Which is right, "I feel *bad*" or "I feel *badly*"? "The dress looks *good* on her" or "The dress looks *well* on her"? The man on the street would say, "I feel *bad*" and "The dress looks *good*," and he would be right: because *badly* would indicate shaky fingers and *well* a dress with good eyes. "Tie it tight" means "Tie it so that it is tight." Unfortunately, people trying to be proper follow the pattern of "He writes badly" and fall into the errors of "I feel badly" and "Tie it tightly." But *writes badly* is a verb with an adverb telling how the action is done, and *feel bad* is a verb with a predicate adjective modifying the subject and telling how the subject is. The predicate adjective describes existences, as in *ring true* and *come thick:* "they ring, and they are true"; "they come, and they are thick." So it is with other verbs pointing to states of being—*seem, appear, become, grow, sound, smell, taste*—on which "good usage" might rule the wrong way. English simply has an unresolved problem between usage and logic: *he doesn't feel well* says that his feelers are faulty but means that his health is hurting him. Just remember that you don't say "I feel goodly," and let reason be your guide.

Likewise with *the reason . . . is because.* You can find this colloquial redundancy on many a distinguished page. But everything a good writer writes is not necessarily good. The phrase is a collision between two choices, as the mind rushes after its meaning: between (1) *the reason is that . . .* and (2) *it is . . . because.* Delete the *reason . . . is,* the colloquial pump primer, and you save three words, sometimes four (the following eminent sentence, in which I have bracketed the surplus words, also suffers some redundancy of the *be*'s):

> **In general it may be said that [the reason why] scholasticism was held to be an obstacle to truth [was] because it seemed to discourage further inquiry along experimental lines.**

And so, usage is perhaps where we begin; but if we end there, we may end in wordiness and mediocrity. Remember that usage sanctions all those horrors of dense nouns like *personnel application clearance center manager* and *teacher credentialization,* and all those nouns turned overnight into verbs: *to host, to parent, to finalize.* Clarity and economy are better guides than mere usage. Make your words mean what they say.

The following prescriptions are just about what the doctor ordered to keep you ticking, and in good company. They summarize the practices of the most careful writers—those who constantly attend to what words mean. They provide tips on avoiding wordiness, and avoiding those slips in diction that sometimes turn your reception a little chilly. I have also included comments on common problems with meanings, contradictions, and tautologies, and on other informational things like "Irony" to supplement the discussions in the text.

THE GLOSSARY

A, an.   Use *a* before *h* sounded in a first syllable: *a hospital, a hamburger.* Use *an* before a vowel or a silent *h: an atom, an error, an honor, an heir, an hour. An hypothesis,* accented on the second syllable, presents a problem, since the *h* is also sounded: *a hypothesis* is fully acceptable. But the *h* is very light. Most ears prefer *an hypothesis,* as well as *an historical* and *a history.* For the distinction between *a (an)* and *the,* see **The.**

Abbreviations.   See 291–93, 429–30.

Above.   For naturalness and effectiveness, avoid such references as "The above statistics are . . . ," and "The above speaks for itself." Simply use "These" or "This."

Abrogated, arrogated.   To *abrogate* is to abolish authority; to *arrogate* is to claim haughtily.

Accept, except. Frequently mistaken for each other in writing. *Accept* is to receive willingly; to *except* is to exclude, to make an *exception.* As a preposition, except means "other than," "but."

Action. A badly overused catchall: "He was sentenced for his action." Go colloquial: "for what he did." Or, better, be specific: *negligence, murder, robbery, rape.*

A.D., B.C. A.D. (*anno Domini,* "the year of the Lord") goes *before* its year: A.D. 1984. B.C. ("before Christ) goes *after* its year: 320 B.C.

Adapt, adopt. To *adapt* is to modify something to fit a new purpose. To *adopt* is to take it over as it is.

Adverse, averse. Both turn away. But *adverse* means bad luck, and *averse* means opposed.

Advice, advise. Frequently confused. *Advice* is what you get when advisers *advise* you.

Aesthetic. An adjective: *an aesthetic judgment, his aesthetic viewpoint. Aesthetics* is singular for the science of beauty: "Santayana's *aesthetics* agrees with his metaphysics."

Affect, effect. *Affect* means "to produce an *effect."* Avoid *affect* as a noun; just say *feeling* or *emotion. Affective* is a technical term for *emotional* or *emotive,* which are clearer.

Aggravate. Means to add gravity to something already bad enough. Avoid using it to mean "irritate."

WRONG	**RIGHT**
He *aggravated* his mother	He *irritated* his mother. The rum *aggravated* his mother's fever.

Agreement. Usage aligns singulars with singulars, plurals with plurals. A pronoun should agree with its antecedent; a verb with its noun; a demonstrative adjective, with its noun. See 353–55, 370–72.

FAULTY	**REVISED**
Everyone should roll *their* own.	*Everyone* should roll *his* own.
It was *her.* [Disagreement in case]	*It* was *she.* [Both *It* and *she* are subjective case]
A *politician* should be fair, but *they* usually are not.	*Politicians* should be fair, but *they* usually are not.
Those kind of sausages *are* bad.	*That kind* of sausage *is* bad.

Revision **of their views about markets and averages** *are* **mandatory.**	*Revision* **of their views about markets and averages** *is* **mandatory.**

All, all of.   Use *all* without the *of* wherever you can to economize: *all this, all that, all those, all the people, all her lunch.* But some constructions need *of: all of them, all of Faulkner* (but *all Faulkner's novels*).

All ready, already.   Two different meanings. *All ready* means that everything is ready: *already* means "by this time."

All right, alright.   *Alright* is not *all right;* you are confusing it with the spelling of *already.*

Allusion, illusion, disillusion, delusion.   The first two are frequently confused, and *disillusion* is frequently misspelled *disallusion.* An *allusion* is a reference to something; an *illusion* is a mistaken conception. You disillusion someone by bringing him back to hard reality from his illusions, or *delusions*—madly mistaken beliefs.

Alot.   Wrong. You mean *a lot,* a whole *lot* of things, not *allot.*

Also. Do not use for *and,* especially to start a sentence; not *"Also,* it failed," but simply "And it failed."

Ambiguous.   If your instructor marks *Amb* in the margin, he means "this has two meanings," one of which you probably have not noticed. Have you said, "Socrates admitted he was wrong"? This could mean that Socrates admitted that he, Socrates, was wrong, or it could mean that Socrates admitted that Crito was wrong. Check your statements to see that they cannot mean something else to the innocent reader.

Among.   See **Between.**

Amount of, number of.   Use *amount* with general heaps of things; use *number* with amounts that might be counted: *a small amount of interest, a large number of votes.* Use *number,* never *amount,* with living creatures: *a number of people, a number of voters, a number of squirrels.*

And/or.   An ungainly hairsplitter and thought stopper. You never say it. Don't write "for stage and/or screen"; write "for stage or screen, or both." Or just write "for stage and screen," and skip the finer possibilities.

Ante-, anti-.   *Ante-* means "before": *an antebellum house* (a house built before the [Civil] War); *antedate* (to date before). *Anti-* means "against": *antifeminine, antiseptic.* Hyphenate before capitals, and before *i* and other vowels that confuse the reading: *anti-American, anti-intellectual, anti-acid, anti-ego.*

Anxious. Use to indicate *Angst,* agony, and anxiety. Does not mean cheerful expectation: "He was *anxious* to get started." Use *eager* instead.

Any. Do not misuse as a modifier:

POOR	GOOD
She was the best of *any* senior in the class.	She was the best senior in the class.
If *any* people know the answer, they aren't talking.	If *anyone* knows the answer, he's not talking.

Add *other* when comparing likes: "She was better than *any other* senior in the class." But "This junior was better than any senior."

Anybody. Don't write it as two words—**any body**—unless you mean "any corpse," or other inanimate object (stellar body, body of water).

Any more. Written as two words, except when an adverb in negatives and questions:

She never wins *anymore.*
Does she play *anymore?*

Anyone. Don't write it as two words—*any one*—unless you mean "any one thing."

Anyplace, someplace. Use *anywhere* and *somewhere* (adverbs), unless you mean "any *place*" and "some *place.*"

Appear. Badly overworked for *seem.*

Appearing. Don't write "an expensive-appearing house." "An expensive-looking house" is not much better. Write "an expensive house," or "the house looked expensive."

Apostrophe-*s.* It signals possession. Use it as pronounced: *boss's daughter, Kraus's great idea.* Use it to distinguish the possessor's name: *Adams's, Dickens's, Jones's.* Use it to indicate the plurals of letters, numbers, and words as words: four *a's,* two *8's,* too many *which's.* See also 421–23.

Appreciate. Means "recognize the worth of." Do not use to mean simply "understand."

LOOSE	CAREFUL
I *appreciate* your position.	I *understand* your position.
I *appreciate* that your position is grotesque.	I *realize* that your position is grotesque.

Apt to, likely to, liable to.   *Apt* is the more colloquial and dubious choice, but acceptable for known physical tendencies: *He is apt to overshoot his volleys. Likely to* is for general probabilities: *It is likely to rain; She is likely to succeed. Liable to* implies vulnerability: *He is liable to lose on powder snow; Overconfidence is liable to end in disappointment.* Don't use *liable* or *apt* for mere probability: *She is liable [apt] to come tomorrow* for *She may come tomorrow.*

Area.   Drop it. *In the area of finance* means *in finance.* Be specific.

POOR	GOOD
This chart is conclusive in all *areas.*	This chart is conclusive.
	This chart thoroughly displays all departments.

Around.   Do not use for *about:* it will seem to mean "surrounding."

POOR	GOOD
Around thirty people came.	*About* thirty people came.
He sang at *around* ten o'clock.	He sang at *about* ten o'clock.

As.   This is the right one, where many have *like:*

FAULTY	REVISED
Nobody loves you *like* I do.	Nobody loves you *as* I do.

Use where the cigarette people have *like:*   "It tastes good, *as* a goody should." (See also *Like.*)

Do not use for *such as:*   "Many things, *as* nails, hats, toothpicks. . . ." Write "Many things, *such* as nails. . . ."

Do not use *as* for *because* or *since;* it is ambiguous:

AMBIGUOUS	PRECISE
As I was walking, I had time to think.	*Since* I was walking, I had time to think.
	Because I was. . . . [even clearer]

Do not use *as* to mean "that" or "whether" (as in "I don't know *as* he would like her").

As . . . as. Use positively, not forgetting the second *as:*

WRONG	RIGHT
as **long if not longer than the other.**	*as* **long** *as* **the other, if not longer.**

Negatively, use *not so . . . as;* it is clearer (but more formal) than *as . . . as:*

It is *not so* **long** *as* **the other.**
His argument is *not so* **clear** *as* **it ought to be.**
His argument is *neither so* **clear** *nor so* **thorough** *as* **it ought to be.**

As far as. A wordy windup.

WORDY	IMPROVED
As far as **winter wraps are concerned, she is well supplied.**	**She has a good supply of winter wraps.**

As if. Takes the subjunctive:

as if he *were* **cold**

As of, as of now. Avoid, except for humor. Use *at,* or *now,* or delete entirely.

POOR	IMPROVED
He left *as of* **ten o'clock.** *As of now,* **I've sworn off.**	**He left at ten o'clock.** **I've just sworn off.**

As to. Use only at the beginning of a sentence: "As to his first allegation, I can only say. . . ." Change it to *about,* or omit it, within a sentence: "He knows nothing *about* the details"; "He is not sure [as to] [whether] they are right."

As well as. You may mean only *and.* Check it out. Avoid such ambiguities as *The Commons voted as well as the Lords.*

Aspect. Overused. See **Jargon.**

Assignment, assignation. An *assignment* is a job to be done; an *assignation* is a rendezvous.

At. Do not use after *where.* "Where is it at?" means "Where is it?"

Awake, awakes. See **Wake.**

Awhile, a while. You usually want the adverb: *linger awhile, the custom endured awhile longer.* If you want the noun, emphasizing a period of time, make it clear: *the custom lasted for a while.*

Bad, badly. Remember that *bad* is an adjective: *a bad trip, a bad book,* and that *badly* is an adverb: *he traveled badly, he wrote badly.* Confusion arises with the linking verbs. *He is bad* is clear enough. But the logic extends to *he looks bad, he smells bad, he acts bad, the dress looks bad, the air seems bad, I feel bad.* These are right! Don't be tricked into using *badly.*

Back of, in back of. *Behind* says it more smoothly.

Balance, bulk. Make them mean business, as in "He deposited the balance of his allowance" and "The bulk of the crop was ruined." Do not use them for people.

POOR	IMPROVED
The *balance* of the class went home.	The *rest* of the class went home.
The *bulk* of the crowd was indifferent.	*Most* of the crowd was indifferent.

Basis. Drop it: *on a daily basis* means *daily.*

B.C. See **A.D.**

Be sure and. Write *be sure to.* See **Try and.**

Because of, due to. See **Due to.**

Behalf—in your behalf, on your behalf. A nice distinction. "He did it *in your behalf*" means he did it in your interest. "He did it *on your behalf*" means he was representing you, speaking for you.

Beside, besides. *Beside* means "by the side of." *Besides* means "in addition to," not "other than."

POOR	IMPROVED
Something *besides* smog was the cause [unless smog was also a cause].	Something *other than* smog was the cause.

Better than. Unless you really mean *better than,* use *more than.*

POOR	**IMPROVED**
The lake was *better than* two miles across.	The lake was *more than* two miles across.

Between, among.   *Between* ("by twain") has *two* in mind; *among* has several. *Between,* a preposition, takes an object; *between us, between you and me.* ("Between you and I" is sheer embarrassment; see **Me,** 519.) But words sometimes fail us. "Between you and me and the gatepost" cannot conform to the rule and become "among you and me and the gatepost." *Between* connotes an intimate sharing *among* all concerned, each to each. *Between* also indicates geographical placing: "It is midway between Chicago, Detroit, and Toledo." "The grenade fell between Jones and me and the gatepost"; but "The grenade fell among the fruit stands." Keep *between* for two and *among* for three or more—unless sense forces a compromise. "*Between* every building was a plot of petunias" conveys the idea, however nonsensical "between a building" is. "Between all the buildings were plots of petunias" would be better, though still a compromise.

Bimonthly, biweekly.   Careless usage has damaged these almost beyond recognition, confusing them with *semimonthly* and *semiweekly.* For clarity, better say "every two months" and "every two weeks."

But, cannot but.   "He can but fail" is old but usable. After a negative, however, the natural turn in *but* causes confusion:

POOR	**IMPROVED**
He cannot *but* fail.	He can only fail.
He *could not* doubt *but* that it. . . .	He could not doubt that it. . . .
He *could not* help *but* take. . . .	He could not help taking. . . .

Similarly, *but*'s too close or frequent keep your reader spinning:

POOR	**IMPROVED**
The campaign was successful *but* costly. *But* the victory was sweet.	The campaign was costly, but victory was sweet.

When *but* means "except," it is a preposition.

WRONG	**RIGHT**
Everybody laughed *but* I.	Everybody laughed *but* me.

But rather.   Acceptable, though sometimes redundant and open to ambiguity: *She was aloof, but rather nice.* It can be effective following negatives: *The course offers no amusement, but rather information and insight.*

But that, but what.   Colloquial redundancies.

POOR	IMPROVED
There is no doubt *but that* John's is the best steer.	**There is no doubt *that* John's is the best steer.** **John's is clearly the best steer**
There is no one *but what* would enjoy it.	**Anyone would enjoy it.**

c., ca.   Indicates an approximate date, used only in a parenthesis with numerals, always italicized: "(*c.* 1496)." It stands for *circa,* "around."

Can, may (could, might).   *Can* means ability; *may* asks permission, and expresses possibility. *Can I go?* means, strictly, "Have I the physical capability to go?" In speech, *can* usually serves for both ability and permission, though the salesgirl will probably say, properly, "May I help you?" In assertions, the distinction is clear: "He can do it." "He may do it." "If he can, he may." Keep these distinctions clear in your writing.

Could and *might* are the past tenses, but when used in the present time they are subjunctive, with shades of possibility, and hence politeness: *"Could* you come next Tuesday?" "*Might* I inquire about your plans?" *Could* may mean ability almost as strongly as *can:* "I'm sure he could do it." But *could* and *might* are usually subjunctives, expressing doubt:

Perhaps he *could* make it, if he tries.
I *might* be able to go, but I doubt it.

Cannot, can not.   Use either, depending on the rhythm and emphasis you want. **Can not** emphasizes the *not* slightly.

Can't hardly, couldn't hardly.   Use *can hardly, could hardly,* since *hardly* carries the negative sense.

Can't help but.   A marginal mixture in speech of two clearer and more formal ideas *I can but regret* and *I can't help regretting.* Avoid it in writing.

Capability.   Often "scientific" jargon. Say *it does* or *can do,* not *it has a capability for.*

Capital, capitol.   Frequently confused. You mean *capital,* the head thing (from Latin *capitalis,* "of the head"), whether writing of the head city of a state or national government, the head letter of a sentence, or the top (the "head") of a Greek column, the money that heads your investment, or the offense that once would have gotten your head chopped off—capital punishment. *Capitol,* always capitalized, is the special name of the Temple of Jupiter on the Capitoline Hill in Rome, and also of the Capitol building where Congress sits in Washington, D.C., or the Capitol Hill in Washington on which the Capitol stands (the American founders named their new headquarters, and the hill they stood on, after the Roman ones). The distinction extends to the states: legislators sit in their *capitols* (buildings; lower case *c*). Confusion comes especially when you think of Washington:

WRONG	RIGHT
Washington, D.C., is the *capitol* of the United States.	Washington, D.C., is the *capital* of the United States.

Capitalization.   Capitalize the first letters of sentences, the names of people, places, books, magazines, organizations, races, nationalities, religions, languages, a Supreme Deity and pronouns referring to Him, the first-person pronoun *I.* For further details, see 431–33.

Case.   Chop out this deadwood:

POOR	IMPROVED
In many cases, ants survive.	Ants *often.* . . .
In such a case, surgery is recommended.	*Then* surgery is recommended.
In case he goes. . . .	*If* he goes. . . .
Everyone enjoyed himself, *except in a few scattered cases.*	*Almost* everyone enjoyed himself.

Cause, result.   Since *all* events are both causes and results, suspect yourself of wordiness if you write either word.

WORDY	ECONOMICAL
The invasion *caused* depopulation of the country.	The invasion depopulated the country.
He lost *as a result* of poor campaigning.	He lost *because* his campaign was poor.

Cause-and-effect relationship.   Verbal adhesive tape. Recast the sentence, with some verb other than the wordy *cause:*

POOR	IMPROVED
Othello's jealousy rises in a *cause-and-effect relationship* **when he sees the handkerchief.**	**Seeing the handkerchief** *arouses* **Othello's jealousy.**

Censor, censure.   Frequently confused. A *censor* cuts out objectionable passages. *To censor* is to cut out or prohibit. *To censure* is to condemn: "The *censor censored* some parts of the play, and *censured* the author as an irresponsible drunkard."

Center around.   A physical impossibility. Make it *centers on,* or *revolves around,* or *concerns,* or *is about.*

Character development.   A common cliché, literary jargon. Avoid it. It is ambiguous and cumbersome (noun-on-noun). You mean either *characterization,* the way an author fills out his portraiture, or something like *maturity, evolution, growth in perception or integrity*—the way a literary personality develops. Make clear to your reader which you mean, and avoid the term altogether. See **Jargon.**

Circumstances.   *In these circumstances* makes more sense than *under these circumstances,* since the stances are standing around *(circum),* not standing under. Often jargon: *The economy is in trouble* (not *in difficult circumstances*).

Cite.   See **Site, sight, cite.**

Clichés.   Don't use unwittingly. But they can be effective. There are two kinds: (1) the rhetorical—*tried and true, the not too distant future, sadder but wiser, in the style to which she had become accustomed;* (2) the proverbial —*apple of his eye, skin of your teeth, sharp as a tack, quick as a flash, twinkling of an eye.* The rhetorical ones are clinched by sound alone; the proverbial are metaphors caught in the popular fancy. Proverbial clichés can lighten a dull passage. You may even revitalize them, since they are frequently dead metaphors (see 213). Avoid the rhetorical clichés unless you turn them to your advantage: *tried and untrue, gladder and wiser, a future not too distant.*

Colloquial, colloquialism.   A characteristic of speech, frequently too personal, informal, or unclear for writing.

Come and, try and, go and, be sure and.   All colloquial ways of saying *come to, try to, go to, be sure to. Come and see us* means "Come to see us," and so forth.

Comma splice, comma fault. The most common mistake in writing: putting a comma where you need a period, or, occasionally, a colon, dash, or semicolon. See 390–93.

COMMA SPLICE	**REPAIRED**
The car, already ten years old, and looking twenty, collapsed in a heap of oily steam, it had run its last mile.	The car, already ten years old, and looking twenty, collapsed in a heap of oily steam. It had run its last mile. . . . oily steam, having run its last mile.

Compare to, compare with. To compare *to* is to show similarities (and differences) between different kinds; to compare *with* is to show differences (and similarities) between like kinds.

Composition has been compared *to* architecture.
He compares favorably *with* Mickey Spillane.
Compare Shakespeare *with* Ben Jonson.

Comparisons. Make them complete; add a *than:*

It is more like a jigsaw puzzle *than a rational plan.*
They are more thoughtful *than the others.*
The first is better *than the second.* (Or "The first is *the* better.")

Complement, compliment. Frequently confused. *Complement* is a completion; *compliment* is a flattery: "When the regiment reached its full *complement* of recruits, the general gave it a flowery *compliment.*"

Comprise, compose, is comprised of. A frequent confusion. Say "The federal government *comprises* [not *is comprised of*] the legislative, judicial, and executive branches." Here, *compose* is correct: "The legislative, judicial, and executive branches *compose* the federal government." Or, as a slightly more wordy passive, "The federal government *is composed of* the legislative, judicial, and executive branches." *Comprise,* because it denotes only the whole containing the parts, lacks a passive voice; that is, it is transitive.

Concept. Often jargonish and wordy.

POOR	**IMPROVED**
The *concept* of multiprogramming allows. . . .	Multiprogramming allows. . . .

Connected with, in connection with.   Always wordy. Say *about, with,* or *in.*

POOR	IMPROVED
They discussed several things *connected with* history.	They discussed several historical questions.
They liked everything *in connection with* the university.	They liked everything *about* the university.
He is *connected with* the Smith Corporation.	He is *with* the Smith Corporation.

Consensus.   *A consensus of opinion* has seemed redundant to many stylists, since consensus means "feeling together," or "an agreed opinion." But you can write "they reached a consensus" and "they reached a consensus of opinion" with equal confidence that your words are meaning what they say. *They agreed* or *Their opinions coincided* would be original and economical, however.

Consider, consider as.   The first means "believe to be"; the second, "think about" or "speak about": "I consider him excellent." "I consider him first as a student, then as a man."

Contact.   Don't *contact* anyone: get in touch with him, call him, write him, find him, tell him. Don't make a good *contact,* make a helpful friend.

Contemptible, contemptuous.   *Contemptible* is deserving contempt; *contemptuous* is giving it.

Continual, continuous.   You can improve your writing by *continual* practice, but the effort cannot be *continuous.* The first means "frequently repeated"; the second, "without interruption."

It requires continual practice.
There was a continuous line of clouds.

Contractions.   We use them constantly in conversation: *don't, won't, can't, shouldn't, isn't.* Avoid them in writing, or your prose will seem too chummy. But use one now and then when you want some colloquial emphasis: *You can't go home again.*

Contrast.   See **Compare to.**

Convince, persuade. *Convince* THAT and *persuade* TO are the standard idioms: *I am convinced that he is right.* Resist the frequent *convince . . . to:*

POOR	IMPROVED
He *convinced* him *to* run.	He *persuaded* him *to* run.
	He *convinced* him *that* he should run.

Could, might.   See **Can, May.**

Could care less.   You mean *couldn't care less.* Speech has worn off the *n't,* making the words say the opposite of what you mean. A person who cares a great deal could care a great deal less; one who does not care *"couldn't* care less."

Could of, would of.   Phonetic misspellings of *could've* ("could have"), and *would've* ("would have"). In writing, spell them all the way out: *could have* and *would have.*

Couldn't hardly.   Use *could hardly.*

Council, counsel, consul.   *Council* is probably the noun you mean: a group of deliberators. *Counsel* is usually the verb "to advise." But *counsel* is also a noun: an adviser, an attorney, and their advice. Check your dictionary to see that you are writing what you mean. A *counselor* gives you his *counsel* about your courses, which may be submitted to an academic *council.* A *consul* is an official representing your government in a foreign country.

Couple.   Use *two, a few,* or *several.* In some breezy moments, you can lighten your prose with *a couple of.*

Credible, creditable, credulous.   Sometimes confused. *Credible* means "believable." *Creditable* means "worthy of praise"—putting something down to your credit: "His catching the pass at third hand was *credible,* but not really *creditable,* since after Jones's fumble he hardly knew he had the ball." *Credulous* means gullible, believing too naïvely.

Curriculum.   The plural is *curricula,* though *curriculums* will get by. The adjective is *curricular.*

> **The school offers three separate curricula.**
> **Extracurricular activities also count.**
> **The dean has asked for curricular innovations.**

Dangling modifier.   See 160–61, 377–78.

Data.   A plural, like *curricula, strata, phenomena:*

> **The data are inconclusive.**

Defies, deifies.   Frequently misspelt. *Defies* resists; *deifies* turns into a god.

Definitely.   A high-school favorite, badly overused. Avoid "I definitely want to go"; "I want to go" is strong enough.

Depreciate, deprecate.   *Depreciate* is to talk something down; *deprecate* is to "pray away," to wish the removal of. You usually mean *depreciate* ("reduce the price of").

Desert, dessert.   Frequently confused. You usually mean *desert,* either the sandy place, running away, or getting what you deserve, your "just deserts." *Dessert* comes after dinner. Remember one *s* for sand, two *ss*'s for the sweet stuff.

Different from, different than.   Avoid *different than,* which confuses the idea of differing. Things differ *from* each other. Only in comparing several differences does *than* make clear sense: "All three of his copies differ from the original, but his last one is *more* different *than* the others." But here *than* is controlled by *more,* not by *different.*

WRONG	RIGHT
It is different *than* I expected.	It is different *from* what I expected.
	It is not what I expected.
This is different *than* all the others.	This is different *from* all the others.

Dilemma.   Frequently misspelled *dilemna,* or *dillema.* A *lemma* is a proposition in logic, an argument; a *di-lemma* is a two-pronged proposition of equal choices that leave one puzzled.

Discreet, discrete.   Frequently confused. *Discreet* means someone careful and judicious; *discrete* means something separate and distinct: "He was discreet in examining each discrete part of the evidence."

Disinterested.   Does not mean "uninterested" nor "indifferent." *Disinterested* means impartial, without private interests in the issue.

WRONG	RIGHT
You seem *disinterested* in the case.	You seem *uninterested* in the case.
	The judge was *disinterested* and perfectly fair.
He was *disinterested* in it.	He was *indifferent* to it.

Disprove, disapprove.   "To prove wrong" as against "to dislike."

Dissemble, disassemble.   "To pretend" as against "to take apart."

Double negative.   A negation that cancels another negation, making it accidentally positive: "He couldn't hardly" indicates that "He could easily," the opposite of its intended meaning. "They can't win nothing" really says that they *must* win something.

The double negative was standard in Middle English, patterned as it was on French, notably the French *ne . . . pas ("no . . . not")* that frames the verb. Chaucer's Absolon, the young priest in "The Miller's Tale," for instance, liked the women so well *That of no wyf ne took he noon offrynge* ("that of no wife no took he none offering"). We still double our negatives to intensify: "No, no, not so." And the habit most languages share of putting affirmative questions in the negative—"Isn't that so?" when we mean it *is* so *(N'est-ce pas? Nicht wahr?)*—makes some other double negatives also emphatic: "Don't think he couldn't care" means something like "He cares a great deal, but you seem to think he doesn't." A doubled negation carries the same kind of indirect emphasis—a mild irony, really—in such tentative assertions as "One cannot be certain that she will not prove to be the century's greatest poet," or "a not unattractive offer." But make sure your negatives don't cancel each other out, as in *couldn't hardly,* or land you in some mind-boggling absurdity like *No Trespassing Without Permission.*

Due to.   Never begin a sentence with *"Due* to circumstances beyond his control, he. . . ." *Due* is an adjective and must always relate to a noun or pronoun: "The catastrophe *due* to [modifies *catastrophe*] circumstances beyond his control was unavoidable," or "The catastrophe was *due* to circumstances beyond his control" (predicate adjective). But you are still better off with *because of, through, by,* or *owing to. Due to* is usually a symptom of wordiness, especially when it leads to *due to the fact that.*

WRONG	RIGHT
He resigned *due to* sickness.	He resigned *because of* sickness.
He succeeded *due to* hard work.	He succeeded *through* hard work.
He lost his shirt *due to* leaving it in the locker room.	He lost his shirt *by* leaving it in the locker room.
The Far East will continue to worry the West, *due to* a general social upheaval.	The Far East will continue to worry the West, *owing to* a general social upheaval.

Due to the fact that.   A venerable piece of plumbing meaning *because.*

JARGON	IMPROVED
The program failed *due to the fact that* a recession had set in.	The program failed *because* a recession had set in.

Economic, economical.   *Economic* deals with the economy, with business: *an economic disaster; economical* saves money: *an economical purchase.*

Effect.   As a noun, it means "result"; as a verb, "to bring about" (not to be confused with *to affect,* meaning "to concern, impress, touch, move"—or "to pretend." See **Affect.**

What was the *effect?*
He *effected* a thorough change.
How did it *affect* you?

But note that "He effected a change" is wordy for "He changed."

E.g.   "For example" *(exempli gratia).* Not in italics. Preceded by a comma, followed by comma or colon. "They lost through errors, e.g., Wilson's fumble, Mitchell's miscall." See **Abbreviations,** 429.

Either, neither.   One of two, taking a singular verb: *Either is a good candidate, but neither speaks well. Either . . . or (neither . . . nor)* are paralleling conjunctions (see 168).

Eminent, imminent, immanent.   Often confused. *Eminent* is something that stands out; *imminent* is something about to happen. *Immanent,* much less common, is a philosophical term for something spiritual "remaining within, indwelling." You usually mean *eminent.*

Enormity.   Means "atrociousness"; does not mean "enormousness."

the *enormity* of the crime
the *enormousness* of the mountain

Enthuse.   Don't use it; it coos and gushes:

WRONG	**RIGHT**
She *enthused* over her new dress.	She gushed on and on about her new dress.
He was *enthused.*	He was enthusiastic.

Environment.   Frequently misspelled *enviorment* or *envirnment.* It is business jargon, unless you mean the world around us.

WORDY	**IMPROVED**
in an MVT *environment*	in MVT; with MVT; under MVT
He works in the *environment* of cost analysis.	He analyzes costs.

| We need to improve the landscaping in the *environment* of the offices. | We must improve the landscaping around the offices. |

Equally as good.   A redundant mixture of two choices, *as good as* and *equally good.* Use only one of these at a time.

Erring, errant.   *Erring* makes mistakes; *errant* wanders.

Eruption, irruption.   An *eruption* is a bursting out, as with lava from a volcano, or a tooth through a gum; an *irruption* is a breaking up of things, like a bull in a china shop.

Etc.   Substitute something specific for it, or drop it, or use something like "and so forth." See "Abbreviations," 429.

POOR	**IMPROVED**
She served fruit, cheese, candies, *etc.*	She served fruit, cheese, candies, and little sweet pickles. She served fruit, cheese, candies, *and the like.*

Ethic.   A mannered rendition of *ethics,* the singular and plural noun meaning a system or science of moral principles. Even poorer as an adjective for *ethical.*

POOR	**IMPROVED**
The Muslim *ethic* forbids interest on loans.	Muslim *ethics* forbids interest on loans.

Everyday, every day.   You wear your *everyday* clothes *every day.*

Everyone, everybody.   Avoid the common mismatching *their:*

Everyone does *his* [or *her* but not *their*] own thing.

Evoke, invoke.   To *evoke* is to call forth the emotions; to *invoke* is to call upon gods for assistance.

Exalt, exult.   To *exalt* is to raise on high; to *exult* is to rejoice, or gloat.

Except.   See **Accept, Except.**

Exclamation.   *Exclaim* often induces the misspelling *exclaimation.* Avoid overusing exclamation marks!!!!

Exists.   Another symptom of wordiness.

POOR	IMPROVED
a system like that which *exists* at the university	a system like that at the university

Facet.   This means "little face," as on a diamond. Use metaphorically or not at all.

POOR	IMPROVED
This problem has several *facets.*	This problem has *five parts.*
	Each *facet* of the problem sparkles with implications.

The fact that.   Deadly with *due to,* and usually wordy by itself.

POOR	IMPROVED
The fact that Rome fell due to moral decay is clear.	*That* Rome fell through moral decay is clear.
This disparity is in part a result *of the fact that* some of the best indicators make their best showings in an expanding market.	This disparity arises in part *because* some of the best indicators look best in an expanding market.
In view of the fact that more core is installed. . . .	*Because* it has more core. . . .

Factor.   Avoid it. We've used it to death. Try *element* when you mean "element." Look for an accurate verb when you mean "cause."

POOR	IMPROVED
The increase in female employment *is a factor in* juvenile delinquency.	The increase in female employment *has contributed to* juvenile delinquency.
Puritan self-sufficiency *was an important factor in* the rise of capitalism.	Puritan self-sufficiency *favored* the rise of capitalism.

Farther, further.   The first means more actual or figurative distance; the second means more in time or degree. You look *farther* and consider *further,* before you go *farther* into debt.

Faze, phase.   See **Phase.**

Feasible. See **Viable.**

Fewer, less. See **Less, Few.**

The field of. Try to omit it—you usually can. It is trite and wordy.

POOR	**IMPROVED**
He is studying in *the field of* geology.	He is studying geology.
He changed from *the field of* science to fine arts.	He moved from science to the fine arts.

Firstly. Archaic. Trim all such terms to *first, second, third,* and so on.

Fix. The word means "to establish in place"; it means "to repair" in speech and colloquial writing, where it can occasionally help fix a ponderous passage.

Flaunt, flout. *Flaunt* means to parade, to wave impudently; *flout* means to scoff at. The first is metaphorical; the second, not: "She *flaunted* her wickedness and *flouted* the police."

For. Be sure to distinguish the conjunction with a comma, or it will look like a preposition.

MISLEADING	**ACCURATE**
He went *for* the time was ripe.	He went, *for* the time was ripe.

Former, latter. Passable, but they often make the reader look back. Repeating the antecedents is clearer.

POOR	**IMPROVED**
The Athenians and Spartans were always in conflict. *The former* had a better civilization; *the latter* had a better army.	The Athenians and Spartans were always in conflict. Athens had the better culture; Sparta, the better army.

Forward, foreword. The first is direction; the second, an introduction to a book, a "fore" word or two.

Fragment. An incomplete sentence. A piece of a sentence. Both those statements are, grammatically, fragments, since they contain no verb. Complete your sentences by giving each subject its existence, or its action: its verb. But you can use a *rhetorical* fragment, one that your reader will not mistake as a mistake, most effectively, especially at the beginning of a paragraph: *Not so. Overwhelmed completely. Of course.* These are forceful trimmings from a complete sentence, the rest of which is left understood. See 173–74, 389–90.

Frightened, afraid.   You are frightened *at* or *by;* you are afraid *of.*

Fun.   *Fun thing, fun time, fun party*—all popular jargon. Keep *fun* as a noun: "It was fun." Or try something more vivid and original: "The party was hilarious from start to finish."

Funny.   Avoid it, especially when you must explain "not funny 'ha-ha,' but funny queer."

Further.   See **Farther.**

Go and see, come and see, be sure and see, try and see. All conversational versions of *go to, come to,* and so forth.

Good, well.   *Good* is the adjective: *good time. Well* is the adverb: *well done.* In verbs of feeling, we are caught in the ambiguities of health. *I feel good* is more accurate than *I feel well,* because *well* may mean that your feelers are in good order. But *I feel well* is also an honest statement: "I feel that I am well." Ask yourself what your readers might misunderstand from your statements, and you will use these ambiguous terms clearly.

Got, gotten.   Both acceptable and equivalent. Your rhythm and emphasis will decide. America prefers the older *gotten* in many phrases; Britain goes exclusively for *got.*

Got to.   Use *must,* or *has to.*

Gray.   America prefers *gray;* England, *grey*—matching each country's initials.

Hand, on [the] one.   See **On [the] one hand.**

Hanged, hung.   *Hanged* is the past of *hang* only for the death penalty.

They hung the rope and hanged the man.

Hardly.   Watch the negative here. "I can't *hardly*" means "I *can* easily." Write: "One can hardly conceive the vastness."

Healthy, healthful.   Swimming is *healthful;* swimmers are *healthy.*

Height.   Not *heighth.*

His/her, his (her).   Shift to the neutral plural ("Students should sign their papers on the first page."), employ an *occasional* "his or her," or otherwise rephrase. But *his* is still respectable when standing for both sexes so long as your reader can reasonably infer both. Something like "Men and women in science" near your beginning will help. You should, however, avoid these traps: "Any *man* who has endured privation in service . . . ," or "The secretary trying to please *her* boss . . . ," unless you are clearly writing *only* about men or women.

Historically.   A favorite windy throat-clearer. Badly overused.

Historic, historical.   *Historic* means momentous, but avoid it. *Historical* means recorded, or like history—*an historical novel.*

History.   The *narrative,* written or oral, of events, not the events themselves. Therefore, avoid the redundancy "*recorded* history," likewise "*annals* of history," "*chronicles* of history." *History* alone can suffice, or even itself disappear:

PASSABLE	BETTER
Archeologists have uncovered evidence of events previously unknown to history.	Archeologists have uncovered evidence of events previously unknown.
World War II was the most devastating conflict in history.	World War II was the most devastating conflict the world had known.

Homogenous, homogeneous.   You probably mean *homogeneous,* "of the same kind, uniform throughout." To *homogenize* is to "make homogeneous." *Homogenous,* on the other hand, is a biological term meaning "of common origin."

Honorable.   See **Reverend.**

Hopefully.   An inaccurate dangler, a cliché. "Hopefully, they are at work" does not mean that they are working hopefully. Simply use "I hope": not "They are a symbol of idealism, and, hopefully, are representative," but "They are a symbol of idealism and are, I hope, representative."

Host.   A jargonish verb. Try *entertain, has invited, will hold, will preside.*

However.   Bury it between commas, or replace it with *But* or *Nevertheless.*

POOR	IMPROVED
However, the day had not been entirely lost.	*But* the day had not been entirely lost.
However, the script that Alcuin used became the forerunner of modern handwriting.	The script that Alcuin used, *however,* became the forerunner of modern handwriting.

Initial *however* should be an adverb:

However long it takes, it will be done.
However she did it, she did it well.

Humanism   (mistaken for "Human nature" or "humanitarianism"). The intellectual awakening in the late Renaissance when men like Erasmus (1466–1536) rediscovered the culture and literature of ancient Greece and Rome, and began to shift attention from God and eternity to man and his capacities. Since the term has this specific historical meaning, find something else when you want to express, more generally, some focus on human nature.

MISLEADING	**CLEARER**
This study will be based on *humanism*.	This study will focus on *human nature*.
They pardoned him for *humanistic* reasons.	They pardoned him for *humanitarian* reasons.

Hung.   See **Hanged.**

I (we, you, one).   See discussion, 9–11. Also see "Pronouns as Subjects and Objects," 364–72, and **Me,** 519.

The idea that.   Like *the fact that*—and the cure is the same.

POOR	**IMPROVED**
He liked *the idea that* she was going.	He was pleased she was going.
The idea that space is infinite is difficult to grasp.	That space is infinite is difficult to grasp.

Identify.   Give it an object:

He *identified the wallet.*
He *identified himself* with the hero. ("He identified with the hero" is acceptable but not preferred.)

I.e.   *Id est,* "that is." See "Abbreviations," 429.

If, whether.   *If* is for uncertainties; *whether,* for alternatives. Usually the distinction is unimportant: *I don't know if it will rain; I don't know whether it will rain [or not].* To be absolutely clear, use *if* unless you express an *or.*

Image.   Resist its popularity, make it mean what it says, and never make it a verb. Do NOT say, "The university should *image* the handsome intellectual."

Imminent, Immanent.   See **Eminent.**

Imply, infer.   The author *implies;* you *infer* ("carry in") what you think he means.

> He *implied* that all women were hypocrites.
> From the ending, we *infer* that tragedy ennobles as it kills.

Importantly.   Often an inaccurate (and popular) adverb, like *hopefully*.

INACCURATE	IMPROVED
More *importantly*, he walked home.	More *important*, he walked home.

He did not walk home importantly, nor more importantly.

In back of.   Use *behind.*

Includes.   Jargonish, as a general verb for specific acts.

POOR	IMPROVED
The report *includes* rural and urban marketing.	The report *analyzes* rural and urban marketing.

Indite, indict.   *Indite,* meaning "to write," is a common misspelling for *indict* (pronounced "indite") meaning "to charge with a crime."

Individual.   Write *person* unless you really mean someone separate and unique.

Inequity, iniquity.   "Injustice" as against "sin."

Infer.   See **Imply, Infer.**

Ingenious, ingenuous.   Sometimes confused. *Ingenious* means clever; *ingenuous,* naïve.

Inside of, outside of.   "They painted the *outside* of the house" is sound usage; but these expressions can be redundant and inaccurate.

POOR	IMPROVED
inside of half an hour	*within* half an hour
He had nothing for dinner *outside of* a few potato chips.	He had nothing for dinner *but* a few potato chips.

Instances.   Redundant. *In many instances* means *often, frequently.*

Interesting.   Make what you say interesting, but never tell the reader *it is interesting;* he may not believe you. *It is interesting* is merely a lazy preamble.

POOR	IMPROVED
It is interesting to note that nicotine is named for Jean Nicot, who introduced tobacco into France in 1560.	Nicotine is named for Jean Nicot, who introduced tobacco into France in 1560.

Intransitive.   A verb not taking an object: "She *weeps.*"

Irony.   Not the same as *sarcasm* (which see). A clash between appearance and reality. Irony may be either comic or tragic, depending on your view. But, comic or tragic, irony is of three essential kinds:

Verbal Irony.   You say the opposite of what you mean: "It's a *great* day," appearing to mean "great" but really meaning "terrible."

Dramatic Irony.   Someone unwittingly states, or acts upon, a contrariety to the truth. A character in a play, for example, might say "This is my great day," and dance a jig, when the audience has just seen his daughter abducted and the mortgage foreclosed. The dramatic irony projected through a naïve or imperceptive narrator, like Twain's Huck or Swift's Gulliver, is sometimes called *IRONY OF MANNER.*

Irony of Circumstance.   The opposite of what ought to happen happens (it rains on the day of the Weather Bureau's picnic; the best man of all is killed), and we are sharply aware of the contrast.

Irregardless.   A faulty word. The *ir-* (meaning *not*) is doing what the *-less* already does. You are thinking of *irrespective,* and trying to say *regardless.*

Is when, is where.   Avoid these loose attempts.

LOOSE	SPECIFIC
Combustion *is when* oxidation bursts into flame.	Combustion *is* oxidation bursting into flame.
"Trivia" *is where* three roads meet.	"Trivia" means the place three roads meet.

It. Give it a specific reference, as a pronoun. Avoid the expletive, non-referential *it:* it is wordy and often ambiguous (see also **There is**):

FAULTY	IMPROVED
She quit smoking. *It* is said that it is harmful.	**She quit smoking. Doctors say it is harmful.**

It's, its.   *It's* means "it is": *It's a nice day.* When you write *the book and ɪᴛ's message,* you are saying "the book and it is message." But *it's* for *its* may be our most popular error. Try to remember that ɴᴏ pronoun takes an apostrophe in the possessive: *yours, hers, ours, theirs, whose, its. Write the book and* ɪᴛs *message.*

Italics.   See 407–09.

-ize.   A handy way to make verbs from nouns and adjectives (*patron-ize, civil-ize*). But handle with care. Manufacture new *-izes* only with a sense of humor and daring ("they Harvardized the party"). Business over-does the trick: *finalize,* a relative newcomer, has provoked strong disapproval from writers who are not commercially familiarized.

Jargon.   A technical, wordy phraseology that becomes characteristic of any particular trade, or branch of learning, frequently with nouns modifying nouns, and in the passive voice. Break out of it by making words mean what they say:

JARGON	CLEAR MEANING
The *plot structure* of the play provides no *objective correlative.*	**The play fails to act out and exhibit the hero's inner conflicts.** **The plot is incoherent.** **The structure is lopsided.**
The *character development* of the heroine is excellent.	**The author sketches and deepens the heroine's personality skillfully.** **The heroine matures convincingly.**
Three *motivation profile studies* were developed *in the area of production management.*	**The company studied its production managers, and discovered three patterns of motivation.**

Jingles.   Avoid jingling your sounds together inadvertently.

Use ample *illumination* for every *examination.*
A *visionary revision* of the *decision.*
A *beautiful* example of *dutiful* bureaucrats.

Judgment, judgement.   Americans have made *judgment* standard; the British prefer *judgement,* along with *labour, colour,* and so forth.

Kind of, sort of.   Colloquialisms for *somewhat, rather, something,* and the like. "It is *kind of* odd" will not get by. But "It is a *kind of* academic hippopotamus" will get by nicely, because a *kind of* means a *species of.* Change "a kind of a poor sport" to "a kind of poor sport," and you will seem as knowledgeable as a scientist.

Lay.   Don't use *lay* to mean *lie. Lay* means "to put" and needs an object; *lie* means "to recline." Memorize both their present and past tenses, which are frequently confused (see 360–61):

> I *lie* down when I can; I *lay* down yesterday; I have *lain* down
> often [Intransitive—no object.]
> The hen *lays* an egg; she *laid* one yesterday; she has *laid* four
> this week. [Transitive—hen *lays* an object.]
> Now I *lay* the book on the table; I *laid* it there yesterday; I have
> *laid* it there many times.

Lead, led.   Because *lead* (being in front) is spelt like the *lead* in *lead* pencil, people frequently misspell the past tense, which is *led.*

Leave, let.   Interchangeable only with *alone: Leave him alone. Let him alone. Leave* is wrong in other senses of *let* as allowing: *Let me go. Let it lie. Let us now praise great men.*

Lend, loan.   Don't use *loan* for *lend. Lend* is the verb; *loan,* the noun: "Please *lend* me a five; I need a *loan* badly." Remember the line from the song: "I'll *send* you to a *friend* who'll be willing to *lend.*" But *loan* is displacing *lend* and may soon surpass it.

Less, few.   Do not use one for the other. *Less* answers "How much?" *Few* answers "How many?"

WRONG	RIGHT
We had *less* people than last time.	We had *fewer* people this time than last.

Level.   Usually redundant jargon. *High level officials* are *high officials* and *college level courses* are *college courses.* What is a *level official,* or a *level course* anyway?

POOR	IMPROVED
This high school offers a college level course in the senior year.	This high school offers a college course in the senior year.

Lie, lay.   See **Lay.**

Lighted, lit.   Equally good past tenses for *light* (both "to ignite" and "to descend upon"), with *lit* perhaps more frequent. Rhythm usually determines the choice. *Lighted* seems preferred for adverbs and combinations: *a clean well-lighted place; it could have been lighted better.*

Like, as, as if.   Usage blurs them, but the writer should distinguish them before he decides to go colloquial. Otherwise, he may throw his readers off.

> **He looks *like* me.**
> **He dresses *as* I do.**
> **He acts *as if* he were high.**

Note that *like* takes the objective case, and that *as,* being a conjunction, is followed by the nominative:

> **She looks like *her*.**
> **He is as tall as *I* [am].**
> **He is tall, like *me*.**

The pattern of the prepositional phrase *(like me, like a house, like a river)* has caused *like* to replace *as* where no verb follows in phrases other than comparisons *(as . . . as):*

> **It works *like* a charm. (. . . *as* a charm *works*.)**
> **It went over *like* a lead balloon. (. . . *as* a lead baloon *does*.)**
> **They worked *like* beavers. (. . . *as* beavers *do*.)**

Notice that *as* would give these three statements a meaning of substitution or disguise: "It works as a charm" (but it really isn't a charm); "It went over as a lead balloon" (disguised as a lead balloon).

Likely.   See **Apt to, likely to, liable to.**

Literally.   Often misused, and overused, as a general emphasizer: "We *literally* wiped them off the field." Since the word means "by the letter," a *literal* meaning is distinct from a *figurative* meaning. *His heart was stone* means, literally, that his blood pump was, somehow, made of stone; it means, figuratively, "He was cruel." Avoid *literally* unless you mean to show exactly what a word, or a statement, means: *To decapitate means literally to take the head off.*

Loan.   See **Lend.**

Loath, loathe.   You probably mean *loathe*, "to hate": *loath* is a slightly archaic word meaning "reluctant."

Loose, lose.   You will *lose* the game if your defense is *loose*.

Lots, lots of, a lot of.   Conversational for *many, much, great, considerable*. Try something else. See **Alot**.

CASUAL	IMPROVED
Henry VIII had *lots of* problems.	Henry VIII had *many* problems.
Latimer showed *lots of* courage.	Latimer showed *considerable* courage.
Their diet included *a lot of* pepper.	Their diet included *much* pepper.

Majority.   More than half the votes, sometimes loosely used for a plurality, the highest number of votes but less than half, when more than two are running. Erroneously applied to quantities rather than numbers.

ERRONEOUS	ACCURATE
He ate *the majority* of the watermelon.	He ate *most* of the watermelon.
The majority of the play is comic.	*Most* of the play is comic.

Often wordy, even when applied to numbers:

WORDY	IMPROVED
The majority of the students take composition.	*Most* students take composition.

Manner.   Drop this from your working vocabulary. *In a . . . manner* is a favorite redundancy. Replace it with an adverb: *in a clever manner* means "cleverly"; *in an awkward manner* means "awkwardly." *Manner* usually reveals your amateur standing, unless you really mean a mannerism in gesture or speech, or social manners, good and bad. Use *way,* or something else.

AMATEURISH	IMPROVED
In this *manner,* we learn . . .	In this *way,* we learn . . .
The play proceeds in this *manner* for three more acts.	The play goes on *like this* for three more acts.

Martial, marital.   *Martial,* meaning "military," is a frequent misspelling for those *marital* troubles that lead to divorce, embattled though they may be.

Maximum (minimum) amount.   Drop *amount.* The minimum and the maximum *are* amounts. Don't write *a minimum of* and *as a minimum:* write *at least.*

May.   See **Can, may.**

Maybe.   Conversational for **perhaps.** Sometimes misused for **may be.** Unless you want an unmistakable colloquial touch, avoid it altogether.

FAULTY	IMPROVED
The book *maybe* popular, but *maybe* it will endure.	The book *may be* popular, but perhaps it will endure.
It has sold *maybe* a million copies.	It has sold *perhaps* a million copies.

Me.   Use *me* boldly. It is the proper object of verbs and prepositions. Nothing is sadder than faulty propriety: "between you and *I,*" or "They gave it to John and *I,*" or "They invited my wife and *I.*" Test yourself by dropping the first member: "between I" *(no),* "gave it to I" *(no),* "invited I" *(no).* And do NOT substitute *myself.* See "Pronouns as Subjects and Objects," 364–69.

Medium, media.   The singular and the plural. Avoid *medias,* and you will distinguish yourself from the masses.

Might.   See **Can, may.**

Might of.   A mistake for *might have.*

Mislead, misled.   Frequently confused in spelling. To *mislead* is to *lead* astray. To be *misled* is to have been *led* astray.

Most.   Does not mean *almost.*

WRONG	RIGHT
Most everyone knows.	*Almost* everyone knows.

Must, a must.   *A must* is popular jargon. Try something else.

JARGON	IMPROVED
Beatup is really a *must* for every viewer.	Everyone interested in film should see *Beatup.*
This is a *must* course.	Everyone should take this course.

Myself.   Use it only reflexively ("I hurt *myself*"), or intensively ("I *myself* often have trouble"). Fear of *me* leads to the incorrect "They gave it to John and *myself.*" Do not use *myself, himself, herself, themselves* for *me, him, her, them.*

Nauseous.   Sickening: "The picture was *nauseous,* and I am *nauseated.*"

Nature.   Avoid this padding. Do not write *moderate in nature, moderate by nature, of a moderate nature;* simply write *moderate.*

Near.   Avoid using it for degree, though you see it everywhere:

POOR	IMPROVED
a *near* perfect orbit	a *nearly* perfect orbit
	an *almost* perfect orbit
We are *nowhere near* knowledgeable enough.	We are *not nearly* knowledgeable enough.
This tribe is *nowhere near* *self-sufficient.*	This tribe is *far from* *self-sufficiency.*
It was a *near* disaster.	It was *nearly* a disaster [*or: nearly* disastrous].

No one.   Two words in America, not *noone,* nor *no-one* (which the British prefer).

None.   This pronoun means "no one" and takes a singular verb, as do *each, every, everyone, nobody,* and other distributives. *None are* has been common and admissible for centuries, but *none is* holds its own, with a certain prestige, even in the daily newspaper. Another pronoun referring back to any of these must also be singular:

POOR	IMPROVED
None of them *are* perfect.	None of them *is* perfect.
Every one of the men *eat* a big breakfast.	Every one of the men *eats* a big breakfast.
None of the discoveries *appear* significant.	None of the discoveries *appears* significant.
Everybody thinks *they have* the worst of it.	Everybody thinks *he has* the worst of it.

Not . . . as, not . . . so.   See **As . . . as.**

Not un-.   *A not unwelcome interruption.* Some good writers—most notably George Orwell—find this construction redundant for *a welcome interruption.* It is nevertheless an example of *litotes,* a form of irony that has endured in our thinking for centuries—underlining an affirmative by a roundabout double negative: *not bad, no small achievement, not unusual mistake.* Use it for irony, where it works.

Noun habit, noun-on-noun.   Modifying nouns with nouns. Characteristic of wordy writing and jargon. If you find yourself writing *plot structure* or *character trait* or *production management* or *student survey,* suspect yourself of both. See **Jargon,** and the discussion on 186–88.

NOUN-ON-NOUN	REPAIRED
A lower volume of *product sales.* . . .	A lower volume *of sales.* . . .
His character involvement is. . . .	He *involves* his *characters.* . . .
At the root of *health care inflation* is the doctor.	At the root of the *inflating costs of illness* is the doctor.
. . . slashing *health care costs.*	. . . slashing the *costs of illness.*

Nowhere, noplace. Use *nowhere* (not *nowheres*), and reserve *no place* (not *noplace*) only for literal meanings: "He could find no place that would hold it."

Nowhere near. Use *not nearly,* or *far from,* unless you really mean *near:* "He was nowhere near the end." See **Near.**

AWKWARD	IMPROVED
It was *nowhere near* long enough.	It was *not nearly* long enough.
They had *nowhere near* enough food.	They had *far from* enough food.

Numbers. See 428, and *Roman numerals,* 529.

Number of. Usually correct. After *the, number* in singular: *the number of students failing is small.* After *a, number* is plural: *A number of people are disappointed.* See **Amount of.**

Off of. Write *from:* "He jumped *from* his horse."

On behalf, in behalf. See **Behalf.**

On [the] one hand. For one side of an issue, to be followed by *on the other hand* or *on the other,* to guide the reader. *On one hand* (*the* omitted) is more economical and preferable, as is *on the other,* if it follows closely and without confusion.

On one hand, **logging can leave land eroded and destitute of wildlife.** *On the other,* **trees prosper in forests thinned of competing and dying timber.**

Be careful to place *on one hand* to avoid an unwanted hand:

On one hand, she wore a hat.

What did she wear on the other?

On the part of.   Wordy.

POOR	IMPROVED
There was a great deal of discontent *on the part of* those students who could not enroll.	The students who could not enroll were very discontented.

One.   Avoid this common redundancy.

POOR	IMPROVED
One of the most effective ways of writing is rewriting.	The *best* way to write is to rewrite.
The Ambassadors is *one* of the most interesting of James's books.	*The Ambassadors* is James *at his best.*
The meeting was obviously a poor *one.*	The meeting was obviously poor.

In constructions such as "one of the best that . . ." and "one of the worst who . . ." the relative pronouns often are mistakenly considered singular. The plural noun of the prepositional phrase *(the best, worst),* not *the one,* is the antecedent, and the verb must be plural too:

WRONG	RIGHT
one of the best *players* who *has* ever swung a bat	*one* of the best *players* who *have* ever swung a bat

One (I, we, you).   See discussion, 9–11.

Only.   Don't put it in too soon; you will say what you do not mean.

WRONG	RIGHT
He *only liked* mystery stories.	He liked *only* mystery stories.

Outside of.   See **Inside of.**

Overall.   Jargonish. Use *general,* or rephrase.

DULL	IMPROVED
The *overall* quality was good.	The lectures were *generally* good.

Oversight. An unintentional omission: "Leaving you off the list was an *oversight*—I'm terribly sorry." Unfortunately, officialdom has started to use it for *overview* or *supervisory.* Congress, for instance, now has an Oversight Committee (perhaps several)—which sounds like a committee set up to catch omissions. Avoid this pompous ambiguity. Keep your *oversights* meaning *oversights.*

Parent. One of those nouns aping a verb: *to rear, to bring up, to supervise, to raise, to love, to be concerned.*

Participle for gerund Avoid this frequent confusion of the *-ing*'s. The participle works as an adjective; the gerund, as a noun. You want gerunds in the following constructions, and you can get them by changing the misleading noun or pronoun to the possessive case:

WRONG	RIGHT
Washington commended *him* **passing through the British lines.**	**Washington commended** *his* **passing through the British lines.**
Do you mind *me staying* **late?**	**Do you mind** *my staying* **late?**
She disliked *Bill smoking.*	**She disliked** *Bill's smoking.*
We all enjoyed *them singing* **songs and** *having* **a good time.**	**We all enjoyed** *their singing* **songs and** *having* **a good time.**

You can catch these errors by asking yourself if you mean that "You mind *me,*" or that "She disliked *Bill*" (which you do not).

Passed, past. *Passed* means "went by" or "handed something." *Past* is time gone by, or a preposition, meaning "later than" *(past noon),* or an adverb meaning to pass by or go beyond. Here lies the confusion. "He *passed* the house; he had gone *past* several times."

Per. Use *a:* "He worked ten hours *a* day." *Per* is jargonish, except in conventional Latin phrases: *per diem, per capita* (not italicized in your running prose).

POOR	IMPROVED
This will cost us a manhour *per* **machine** *per* **month a year from now.**	**A year from now, this will cost us a manhour a machine a month.**
As *per* **your instructions**	**According to your instructions**

Per cent, percent, percentage. *Percent* (one word) seems preferred though *percentage,* without numbers, still carries polish: "A large *percentage* of non-voters attended"; "a significant *percentage* of the students."

Use both the % sign and numerals only when comparing percentages as in technical reports; elsewhere, use numerals with *percent* when your figures cannot be spelled out in one or two words (2½ percent, 150 percent, 48.5 percent). Otherwise, spell out the numbers as well: *twenty-three percent, ten percent, a hundred percent.* See "Numbers," 428.

Perfect.   Not "more perfect," but "more nearly perfect."

Personal.   Change "personal friend" to "good friend," and protect him from seeming too personal.

Personally.   Always superfluous.

POOR	IMPROVED
I want to welcome them *personally.*	I want to welcome them [myself].
Personally, I like it.	I like it.

Phase.   *Phase* is not *faze* ("daunt"), nor does it mean *aspect* or *part;* it is a stage in a familiar cycle, like that of the moon or the caterpillar. Unless you can carry the specific metaphor, avoid it, along with *facet.*

Phenomena.   Frequently misused for the singular *phenomenon:* "This is a striking *phenomenon*" (not *phenomena*).

Phenomenal.   Misused for a general intensive: "His popularity was *phenomenal.*" A phenomenon is a fact of nature, in the ordinary nature of things. Find another word for the extraordinary: "His success was *extraordinary*" (*unusual, astounding, stupendous*).

Picket.   A pointed fence post, or a person so staked. *To picket* is to deploy people as pickets, or to join with others as a protesting fence against wrongs.

POOR	IMPROVED
They began *a picket* of. . . .	They began *to picket.* . . .
They began *their* picket. . . .	They began *picketing.* . . .
Until they withdraw their picket. . . .	Until they withdraw their pickets. . . .

Plan on.   Use *plan to.*

WRONG	RIGHT
He *planned on* going.	He *planned to* go.

Plot structure.   Jargon. See **Noun habit,** and **Jargon.**

Possessives.   See "Apostrophe," 421–23.

Power vacuum.   A physical contradiction, since a vacuum is the absence of power. Delete *power,* or put it where it belongs, and your phrase will be accurate. See **Noun habit.**

INACCURATE	IMPROVED
The junta rushed into the *power vacuum* **created when the big three withdrew their support.**	**The junta rushed into the** *vacuum* **left as the three big** *powers* **withdrew.**

Predominate, predominant.   A frequent confusion. To *predominate* means to dominate everything. *Predominant* is the adjective you probably mean—The *predominant* opinion, the *prevailing* opinion, the *major* opinion.

Prejudice.   When you write "He was *prejudice,*" your readers may be *puzzle.* Give it a *d*—"He was *prejudiced,*"—so they won't be *puzzled.*

Presently.   Drop it. Or use *now.* Many readers will take it to mean *soon:* "He will go *presently.*" It is characteristic of official jargon.

POOR	IMPROVED
The committee is meeting *presently.* **He is** *presently* **studying Greek.**	**The committee is meeting** *soon.* **He is studying Greek.**

Principle, principal.   Often confused. *Principle* is a noun only, meaning an essential truth, or rule: "It works on the *principle* that hot air rises." The *pal* is the *adjective:* remember the *a*'s, and the *pal* in the princi*pal* person at our schools. The high-school *principal* acts as a noun because usage has dropped the *person* the adjective once modified. Likewise *principal* is the principal amount of your money, which draws interest.

Our *principal* **is a woman of** *principle.*
If you withdraw your *principal* **from the bank, you will lose some interest.**
His *principal* **motive was greed.**
The committee formulated two basic *principles.*

Proceed, precede, procedure.   Continually mixed up in spelling. *Proceed* is to go ahead; *precede* is to go before. *Procedure* is a way of doing. The only solution here is memorizing, after you get the three meanings clearly in mind.

Process. Often verbal fat. For example, the following can reduce more often than not: *production process,* to *production; legislative* (or *legislation*) *process,* to *legislation; educational* (or *education*) *process,* to *education; societal process* to *social forces.*

Proof, evidence. *Proof* results from enough *evidence* to establish a point beyond doubt. Be modest about claiming proof:

POOR	IMPROVED
This *proves* that Fielding was in Bath at the time.	Evidently, Fielding was in Bath at the time.

Proved, proven. *Proved* is the preferred past participle, which may serve as an adjective meaning "successfully tested or demonstrated"; *proven* is best kept an adjective meaning "tested by time," immediately before a noun:

INACCURATE	IMPROVED
It has proven true. [past part.]	It has proved true.
The theory was proven. [same]	The theory was proved.
a proved remedy [pure adj.]	a proven remedy

Provide. If you *absolutely cannot* use the meaningful verb directly, you may say *provide,* provided you absolutely cannot *give, furnish, allow, supply, enable, authorize, permit, facilitate, force, do, make, effect, help, be, direct, cause, encourage.* . . .

Providing that. Use *provided,* and drop the *that. Providing,* with or without *that,* tends to make a misleading modification. See **Dangling modifier.**

POOR	IMPROVED
I will drop, *providing that* I get an incomplete.	I will drop, *provided* I get an incomplete.

In "I will drop, *providing* I get an incomplete," *you* seem to be providing, contrary to what you mean.

Put across. Try something else: *convinced, persuaded, explained, made clear. Put across* is badly overused.

Quality. Keep it as a noun. Too many *professional quality writers* are already producing *poor quality* prose, and *poor in quality* means *poor.* See **Noun habit** and **Jargon.**

Quite. An acceptable but overused emphatic: *quite good, quite expressive, quite a while, quite a person.* Try rephrasing it now and then: *good, very good, for some time, an able person.*

Quote, quotation. Quote your quotations, and put them in quotation marks. Distinguish the verb from the noun. The best solution is to use *quote* only as a verb and to find synonyms for the noun: *passage, remark, assertion.* See "Punctuating the Sentence," 406–07, for further details.

WRONG	RIGHT
As the following *quote* from Milton shows: . . .	As the following *passage* from Milton shows: . . .

Rarely ever. Drop the *ever:* "Shakespeare *rarely* misses a chance for comedy."

Real. Do not use for *very. Real* is an adjective meaning "actual":

WRONG	RIGHT
It was *real* good.	It was *very* good.
	It was *really* good.

Reason . . . is because. Knock out *the reason . . . is,* and *the reason why . . . is,* and you will have a good sentence.

[The reason] they have difficulty with languages [is] because they have no interest in them.

Regarding, in regard to. Redundant or inaccurate.

POOR	IMPROVED
Regarding the banknote, Jones was perplexed. [Was he *looking* at it?]	Jones was perplexed by the banknote.
He knew nothing *regarding* money.	He knew nothing *about* money.
She was careful *in regard to* the facts.	She respected the facts.

Regardless. This is correct. See **Irregardless** for the confusion.

Repetition. Avoid saying again what you have already said sufficiently. Avoid also inadvertent repetitions:

Of *course,* the *course* itself was boring.
By this time, people could *buy* some things *by* means of money.
The banking *interests* were *interested* in peace.

But you may repeat words and phrases for effective emphasis. See "Parallel Construction," 164–71, and "Reiteration," 230. Repeating a necessary word is far better than trying for synonyms that may mislead your reader by making nonexistent distinctions.

POOR	IMPROVED
In London, most *shops* were small. The owner frequently lived above *the establishment.* Some *stores* were large.	In London, most *shops* were small, though some were large. The owner frequently lived above his *shop.*

Reputed, reputable.   *Reputed* means "has the false reputation," or "rumored reputation." *Reputable* means respected. When you write "This is a *reputed* restaurant," you say that it is called a restaurant but really isn't one.

Respective, respectively.   Redundant.

POOR	IMPROVED
The armies retreated to their *respective* trenches.	The armies retreated to their trenches.
Smith and Jones won the first and second prize *respectively.*	Smith won the first prize; Jones, the second.

Reverend, Honorable.   Titles of clergymen and congressmen. Use both with first names or initials. "Reverend Smith" and "Honorable Jones" should be *Mr. Smith* and *Mr. Jones,* omitting the title altogether. The fully proper forms, as in the heading of a letter (*the* would not be capitalized in your running prose), are:

The Reverend Mr. Claude C. Smith
The Honorable Adam A. Jones [omit *Mr.*]

In running prose, *the Reverend Mr. Smith* is most proper; *Rev. Claude Smith* and *Hon. Adam Jones* will get by, but the best procedure is to give the title and name its full form for first mention, then to continue with *Mr. Smith* and *Mr. Jones.*

Rise, raise.   Frequently confused. *Rise, rose, risen* means to get up. *Raise, raised, raised* means to lift up. "He *rose* early and *raised* a commotion."

Roman numerals.   The following table includes most of the Roman numerals you will need:

ROMAN NUMERALS

(Subtract a smaller number preceding a larger: IV = 4, XL = 40)

1	I	14	XIV	30	XXX	110	CX
2	II	15	XV	40	XL	199	CIC
3	III	16	XVI	41	XLI	200	CC
4	IV	17	XVII	49	XLIX	400	CD
5	V	18	XVIII	50	L	500	D
6	VI	19	XIX	60	LX	900	CM
7	VII	20	XX	70	LXX	1000	M
8	VIII	21	XXI	90	XC	1500	MD
9	IX	22	XXII	91	XCI	1600	MDC
10	X	23	XXIII	98	XCVIII	1700	MDCC
11	XI	24	XXIV	99	IC	1865	MDCCCLXV
12	XII	25	XXV	100	C	1492	MCDXCII
13	XIII	29	XXIX	101	CI	1980	MCMLXXX

You may use Roman numerals together with Arabic to designate act, scene, and line in plays, and book, chapter, and page in the novels that use them:

Romeo lies on the floor and cries like a child (III.iii.69–90).
When Tom Jones finds the banknote (XII.iv.483), . . .

But the Modern Language Association now recommends Arabic numerals throughout: (3.3.69–90), (12.4.483). For further details, see 293.

Round. British for *around.*

Sanction.   Beautifically ambiguous, now meaning both "to approve" and "to penalize." But why contribute to confusion? Stick to the root; use it only "to bless," "to sanctify," "to approve," "to permit." Use *penalize* or *prohibit, penalty* or *restriction,* when you mean just that.

POOR	IMPROVED
They exacted *sanctions.*	They exacted *penalties.*

Sarcasm.   The student's word for irony. Sarcasm intends personal hurt. It may also be ironic, but need not be. "Well, little man, what now?" is pure sarcasm when a dwarf interrupts the class; it is ironic sarcasm when a seven-footer bursts in. See **Irony.**

Seldom ever.   Redundant. Cut the *ever.*

Set, sit.   Frequently confused. You *set* something down; you yourself *sit* down. Confine sitting mostly to people *(sit, sat, sat),* and keep it intransitive, taking no object. *Set* is the same in all tenses *(set, set, set).* See 360–61.

CONFUSED	CLARIFIED
The house *sets* too near the street.	The house *stands* [*sits*] too near the street.
The package *sat* where he left it.	The package *lay* where he *had set* it.
He *has set* there all day.	He *has sat* there all day.

Shall, will; should, would.   The older distinctions—*shall* and *should* reserved for *I* and *we*—have faded; *will* and *would* are usual: "I will go"; "I would if I could"; "he will try"; "they all would." *Shall* in the third person expresses determination: "They shall not pass." *Should,* in formal usage, is actually ambiguous: *We should be happy to comply,* intended to mean "would be happy," seems to say "ought to be happy."

Should of.   See **Could of, would of.**

[sic].   Latin for "so," put in brackets within a quotation, unitalicized, after some error or detail that might puzzle the reader. See "Brackets," 405.

Similar to.   Use *like:*

POOR	IMPROVED
This is *similar to* that.	This is *like* that.

Sit. See **Set, sit.**

Site, sight, cite.   Often confused. *Site* is a piece of land to put a building on, or holding a building. You do not see the *sites;* you see the *sights.* To *cite* is to quote or mention an authority, or other evidence.

Situate.   Usually wordy and inaccurate. Avoid it unless you mean, literally or figuratively, the act of determining a site, or placing a building.

FAULTY	IMPROVED
Ann Arbor is a town *situated* on the Huron River.	Ann Arbor is a town on the Huron River.

The building is *situated* in the slums.	The building is in the slums.
The control panel is *situated* on the right.	The control panel is on the right.
He is well *situated*.	He is rich.
The company is well *situated* to meet the competition.	The company is well *prepared* to meet the competition.

Situation.   Usually jargon. Avoid it. Say what you mean: *state, market, mess, quandary, conflict, predicament.* . . .

Size.   Often redundant. *A small-sized country* is *a small country. Large in size* is *large.*

Slash, slant-line (/).   See **Virgule,** and 426.

Slow.   GO SLOW is what the street signs and the men on the street all say, but write "Go slowly."

So.   Should be followed by *that* in describing extent: "It was so foggy *that* traffic almost stopped." Avoid its incomplete form, the gushy intensive —*so nice, so wonderful, so pretty*—though occasionally this is effective.

So . . . as.   See **As . . . as.**

Someplace, somewhere.   See **Anyplace.**

Sort of.   See **Kind of, sort of.**

Split infinitives.   Improve them. They are cliché traps: *to really know, to really try, to better understand.* They are misleaders: *to better* . . . , *to further* . . . , *to well* . . . , *to even* . . . , all look and sound like complete infinitives: *to further investigate* starts out like *to further our investigation,* throwing the reader momentarily off the track. *To better know* is to make *know* better, *to even like* is to make *like* even, all of which is nonsense. Indeed, in perverse moments *to eventually go* seems to say that *go* is being "eventualied." They are one of the signs of a wordy writer; they are usually redundant: *to really understand* is *to understand.* The quickest cure for split infinitives is to drop the adverb, giving *try* and *understand* their full weight. Or you can spell out your adverbial thought in a phrase.

Even the splitters do not recommend splitting as a rule. The rule remains DON'T SPLIT; and if you must, learn what you are doing—a little deviltry is better for the soul than ignorance. But I am convinced that you can always mend the split for a gain in grace, and often for a saving of words. You can sometimes change the adverb to an adjective, gaining force, saving letters and words:

POOR	IMPROVED
to better understand to really try	to understand completely to try, harder than ever

POOR	IMPROVED
to adequately think out solutions	*to think* out *adequate* solutions *to think adequately about* solutions
to enable us *to effectively plan* our advertising	to enable us *to plan effective* advertising

Or you can drop the adverb, or bring it forward, or move it along, or spell out your meaning in a phrase:

POOR	IMPROVED
I cannot bring myself *to* really *like* the fellow.	I cannot bring myself *to like* the fellow.

Here are some examples from eminent splitters, each of which can be improved:

EXAMPLE	IMPROVED
I wish the reader to clearly understand this. (Ruskin)	I wish the reader to understand this clearly.
. . . without permitting himself to actually mention the name. (Arnold)	. . . without permitting himself to mention the name.
. . . of a kind to directly stimulate curiosity. (Pater)	. . . of a kind to stimulate curiosity.
. . . to bravely disbelieve (Browning)	. . . bravely to disbelieve

Browning's full line (*The Ring and the Book,* 570) would have thumped somewhat less if he had dared bravely to vary his meter and mend his infinitive:

Whence need bravely to disbelieve report.

Stationary, stationery.   Sometimes confused. Remember that you get your station*ery* from a station*er,* whose shop is station*a*ry—fixed in place, not moving.

Structure.   A darling of the jargoneer, often meaning nothing more framelike than "unity" or "coherence." *Plot structure* usually means *plot,* with little idea of beams and girders. Use it only for something you could diagram, like the ribs of a snake, and never use it as a verb. See **Jargon.**

POOR	**IMPROVED**
He *structured* the meeting.	He *organized* (planned, arranged) the meeting.

Such.   Overused as a colloquial intensive: *She is such a good organizer.* Complete the implied relative clause: *She is such a good organizer that no one need worry.*

Note that as a demonstrative pronoun *such* may be followed by that:

The applause was *such* that he decided to run for governor.

Such is an effective demonstrative pronoun to conclude a summary or demonstration:

Such is life.
Such were the effects of unwarranted suspicion.

Such that.   An awkward slippage from *such . . . that.* Write *so.*

AWKWARD	**IMPROVED**
He wrote mannered poetry, *such that* his audience was small.	He wrote mannered poetry, *so* his audience was small.
	He wrote *such* mannered poetry *that* his audience was small.

Suppose to.   You mean *supposed to.*

Sure.   Too colloquial for writing: "It is *sure* a good plan." Use *surely* or *certainly,* or otherwise rephrase.

Tautology.   Several words serving where fewer—usually one—are needed, or wanted: useless repetition. Drop the bracketed words in these habitual tautologies:

attach [together]	**[final] completion**
[basic] essentials	**[final] upshot**
consecutive days [in a row]	**[first] beginnings**
[early] beginnings	**[just] merely**

mix [together]
[pair of] twins
  (but, two *sets* of twins)
[past] history

refer [back]
repeat [again]
sufficient [enough]
whether [or not]

That, which, who.   *That* defines and restricts; *which* is explanatory and nonrestrictive: *who* stands for people, and may be restrictive or nonrestrictive. See **Restrictive and nonrestrictive clauses,** 484; 184, 385–86; see also **Who, which, that.**

The faucet *that* drips is in the basement.
The faucet, *which* drips badly, needs attention.
Of all the Democrats *who* supported him at first, none was
    more ardent than Jones.
Of all the Democrats, *who* supported him at first, none was
    more ardent than Jones.

Here is the distinction: only some Democrats supported him in the first sentence, but all did in the second.

The, a (an).   *The* is the *definite* article, specifying particulars:

the book you want
the secretary in charge

A (an) is the *indefinite* article. It is *indefinite* because it makes a single item represent its whole general ("indefinite") class:

A tree gives shade.
A woman lives longer than *a* man.
A few people reverse *the* statistics.
An apple *a* day keeps *the* doctor away.
Not *a* penny in *the* house.

The progression from general to specific runs *books, a book, the book:*

Books can teach much.
A book can teach much.
The book sold millions of copies.

There is, there are, it is.   However natural and convenient—it is WORDY. Notice that *it* here refers to something specific, differing distinctly from the *it* in "It is easy to write badly." This indefinite subject, like *there is* and *there are,* gives the trouble. Of course, you will occasionally need an *it* or a *there* to assert existences:

There are ants in the cupboard.
There is only one Kenneth.
There are craters on the moon.
It is too bad.

But avoid *There is* and *It is,* and you will avoid some sludgy traps. They are part of the spoken language, like clearing the throat, and they frequently add just as little, especially when entailing a *that* or a *which:*

WORDY	IMPROVED
There are three men on duty.	Three men *are* on duty. *[5 words for 6]*
There is nothing wrong with this.	Nothing *is* wrong with this. *[5 words for 6]*
There are two things *which are* important here.	Two things *are* important here. *[5 words for 8]*
It is a habit *which* few can break.	Few can break *this* habit. *[5 words for 8]*
It is a shame *that* they had no lawyer.	*Unfortunately,* they had no lawyer. *[5 words for 9]*

These kind, these sort.   Should be *this kind, this sort.*

They.   A loose indefinite pronoun; tighten it:

POOR	IMPROVED
They are all against us, you know.	*Everyone* is against us, you know.
They launch our rockets at Cape Kennedy.	The *United States* launches its rockets from Cape Kennedy.

Do not use *they* with a singular antecedent:

WRONG	RIGHT
Everyone knows *they* should write correctly.	*Everyone* knows *he* should write correctly.
Every one of the students assumes *they* will pass.	*Every one* of the students assumes *he* will pass.

Too.   Awful as a conjunctive adverb: "Too, it was unjust." Also poor as an intensive: "They did not do too well" (note the difference in Shakespeare's "not wisely but too well"—he really means it). Use *very,* or (better) nothing: "They did not do well" (notice the nice understated irony).

Tool.   Overused for *means*. Also try *method, instrument.*

Toward, towards.   *Toward* is the better, though both are acceptable.

Trite.   From Latin *tritus:* "worn out." Many words get temporarily worn out and unusable: *emasculated, viable, situation,* to name a few. And many phrases are permanently frayed; see **Clichés.**

Try and.   Write *try to. To try and do* means "to try and to do," which is probably not what you mean. *Come and, go and, be sure and,* and so forth, should all likewise take *to: come to see, go to look, be sure to ask.*

Type.   Banish it, abolish it. If you must use it, insert *of:* not *that type person* but *that type OF person,* though even this is really jargon for *that kind of person, a person like that.* The newspapers have succumbed, and we hear of *commando-type forces* for *commando forces,* of *a Castro-type dictator* for *another Castro,* of *the force of a Hiroshima-type bomb* for *the force of the Hiroshima bomb.* The most accurate translations of *-type* are *-like, -ish, -esque,* and *-ate,* depending on sense and euphony: *Castro-like, Castro-ish, Russianesque, Italianate.* English has many ways of saying it:

WRONG	RIGHT
essay-*type* question	essay question
Mondrian's checkerboard-*type* painting	Mondrian's checkerboard painting
French-*type* dressing	French dressing
Italian-*type* spaghetti	Italian spaghetti *[Be bold!—we neither know nor care whether it's imported.]*
atomic-*type* submarine	atomic submarine
She was a Chris Evert-*type* girl.	She was *like* Chris Evert.
	She was a Chris Evert *kind of* girl.
	She was a Chris Evert *type.*
an apprentice-*type* situation	apprenticeship
a Puck-*type* person	a *Puckish* person, a *Puck-like* person

Unique.   Something *unique* has nothing in the world like it.

WRONG	RIGHT
The more unique the organization. . . .	The more *nearly* unique. . . .
the most *unique* man I know	the most *unusual* man I know
a very unique personality	a unique personality

Use, use of. A dangerously wordy word. "Through [the use of] personifi- cation, he asserts a theme." "In this sense, [the use of] physical detail is significant."

POOR	IMPROVED
He *uses* personification. . . .	He **personifies.** . . .
He *uses* inductive reasoning. . . .	He **reasons inductively.** . . .

Use to. A mistake for *used to.*

Utilize, utilization. Wordy. *Utilize* means *use* (verb). *Utilization* means *the use* (noun). And the whole idea of "using"—a basic, universal con- cept—is frequently contained in the other words of your sentence.

POOR	IMPROVED
He *utilizes* frequent dialogue to enliven his stories.	Frequent dialogue enlivens his stories.
The *utilization* of a scapegoat eases their guilt.	A scapegoat eases their guilt.

Viable. With *feasible,* overworked. Try *practicable, workable, possible.*

Very. Spare the *very* and the *quite, rather, pretty,* and *little.* I would hate to admit (and don't care to know) how many of these qualifiers I have cut from this text. You can do without them entirely, but they do ease a phrase now and then.

Virgule. Avoid it, except to mark lines of poetry (see 426). Replace it with a hyphen if you must use such lumps as "work/play problem," "science/religion controversy"—but rephrasing to avoid the jargon is better: "the choice of work or play."

Viz. Pronounced "vi-DEL-uh-sit," after *videlicet,* the Latin word it abbrevi- ates. It means "that is" or "namely." Put commas before and after it; do not italicize. See "Abbreviations," 429–30.

Wait for, wait on. You *wait for* someone, but *wait on* a table.

Wake, waken (awake, awaken). *Wake, woke, waked (awake, awoke, awaked)* are standard. *Waken, wakened, wakened (awaken, awakened, awakened)* are slightly different verbs meaning "to wake up" (intransitive) or "to cause to wake up" (transitive).

He *wakes* up early. He *woke* him up yesterday. He *has waked* them up every morning at seven.

Awake, awoke, awaked is usually intransitive:

She *awakes* **easily. They** *awoke* **with a start. The birds** *have* **already** *awaked.*

Waken and *awaken* are most frequently used transitively: "He *wakened (awakened)* his roommate." And they are more frequent in the passive voice: "He *was awakened* by loud knocking." Figurative usages prefer *awake* and *awaken: He was awake to the risk; his fears were awakened.*

We (I, you, one).   See discussion, 9–11.

Ways.   Avoid it. Means *way:* "He went a short *way* into the woods."

Weather, whether.   *Weather,* which means storms or breezes, rain or shine, is sometimes mistakenly written for *whether.* Whether the reader will smile or wince is problematical.

Well.   See **Good.**

Whereas.   Now a useful subordinating conjunction, preceded by a comma: "Hamlet is partly responsible for the tragedy, *whereas* Ophelia is wholly an innocent victim."

Whether.   See **If,** and **Weather.**

Which.   See **Who, that, which.**

While.   Reserve for time only, as in *"While* I was talking, she smoked constantly." Do not substitute for *although, whereas, and, but.*

WRONG	RIGHT
While I like her, I don't admire her.	*Although* I like her, I don't admire her.
The side roads were impassable, *while* the highways were clear.	The side roads were impassable, *but* the highways were clear.
The seniors eat in clubs, *while* the freshmen eat in their dormitories.	The seniors eat in clubs, *and* the freshmen eat in their dormitories.

Who, which, that.   Relative pronouns, *relating* an additional and subordinate clause to some preceding noun or pronoun:

She *who falls* **falls far.**
The fall *that hurts least* **is the last.**
The fall, *which was severe,* **was not serious.**

Who may be either restrictive or nonrestrictive (see **Restrictive and nonre-strictive clauses,** 484): "The ones *who win* are lucky"; "The players, *who are all outstanding,* win often." *Who* refers only to persons:

FAULTY	REPAIRED
The girl *that* so chooses may enter dentistry.	The girl *who* so chooses may enter dentistry.
Some of the characters *that* wander around the stage. . . .	Some of the characters *who* wander. . . .

Use *that* for all other restrictives; *which* for all other nonrestrictives. See "the *of*-and-*which* disease" (183–84), and the further discussion on 385–86; see also **That, which, who.**

Avoid *which* in loose references to the whole idea preceding, rather than to a specific word, since you may be unclear:

FAULTY	IMPROVED
He never wore the hat, which his wife hated.	His wife hated his going bareheaded.
	He never wore the hat his wife hated.

Whom, whomever. The objective forms, after verbs and prepositions; but each is often wrongly put as the subject of a clause.

WRONG	RIGHT
Give the ticket to *whomever* wants it.	Give the ticket to *whoever* wants it. [The whole clause is the object of *to; whoever* is the subject of *wants.*]
The president, *whom* he said would be late. . . .	The president, *who* he said *would be late.* . . . [Commas around *he said* would clear the confusion.]
Whom shall I say called?	*Who* shall I say called?

BUT:
They did not know *whom* to elect. [The infinitive takes an objective subject; see 368.]

Who's, whose. Sometimes confused in writing. *Who's* means "who is?" in conversational questions: *"Who's* going?" Never use it in writing (except in dialogue), and you can't miss. *Whose* is the regular possessive of *who:* "The committee, *whose* work was finished, adjourned."

Will. See **Shall.**

-wise. Avoid all confections like *mediawise, marketwise, customerwise, pricewise, gradewise, confectionwise*—except for humor. They are professional jargon, concocted on the pattern of established words like *clockwise, otherwise,* and *likewise.*

Would. For habitual acts, the simple past is more economical:

POOR	IMPROVED
The parliament *would meet* only when called by the king.	The parliament *met* only when called by the king.
Every hour, the watchman *would make* his round.	Every hour, the watchman *made* his round.

Would sometimes seeps into the premise of a supposition. Rule: Don't use *would* in an *if* clause.

WRONG	RIGHT
If he *would have* gone, he would have succeeded.	If he *had* gone, he would have succeeded.
	Had he gone, he would have succeeded [more economical].
I wish I *would have* learned it.	I wish I *had* learned it.

Would of. See **Could of, would of.**

You (I, we, one). See discussion, 9–11.

Index

83 84 85 86 87 9 8 7 6 5 4 3 2 1

CHECKLIST

1. Thesis stated in one sentence? (21–24)

2. Thesis at end of first paragraph? (22, 53–55)

3. Thesis clearly evident throughout paper? (25)

4. Each paragraph begun with topic sentence? (52, 56–60)

5. Each with transitional tag? (56–58, 60–62)

6. Paragraphs four or five sentences long? (51–52)

7. Your best point last? (33–34)

8. Conclusion an inverted funnel? (65–68)

9. Generalizations, and thesis, free from fallacies? (27–28, 109–10, 115–17, 124–25)

10. Sentences show some variety? (172–75)

11. Long sentences exhibit parallel construction? (164–71)

12. No passive, no *There is,*...no *It is...*? (179–81, 183)

13. Colons and semicolons properly used? (395–400)

14. Commas before every *and, but,* and *for* that needs them? (382–84)

15. A pair of commas around every inserted word, phrase, or clause? (384–87)

16. A comma before every *which*? Every *which* without comma changed to *that*? (184, 385, 484)

17. Every excess *of, which, that, -tion, to be,* and *the use of* dropped? (182–86)

18. Every noun-on-noun and *-type* revised? (186–88)

19. All excess wordage cut? (177–89)

20. No sentence that could be misread?

21. Have you said it as briefly and clearly as possible?

SET ANY OF THESE POINTS ASIDE—
IF YOU HAVE AN IRRESISTIBLE RHETORICAL REASON.